95

IN
WISDOM

The Religious, Philosophical and Ethical Doctrines of the Hindus

Dear Rajeev,
this has been
picked just for
you our "NETAJI."
enjoy
Neera
Deen

ॐ

INDIAN WISDOM

The Religious, Philosophical and Ethical Doctrines of the Hindus
with
A Brief History of the Sanskrit Literature

by

Monier Monier-Williams

INDIGO BOOKS

AN
INDIGO BOOK
PUBLISHED BY INDIGO BOOKS
Paperback division of
COSMO PUBLICATIONS,
24-B, Ansari Road, Darya Ganj,
New Delhi 110 002, India.

INDIGO BOOKS and
COSMO PUBLICATIONS
are wholly owned subsidiaries of
GENESIS PUBLISHING PVT. LTD.,
New Delhi, India

Indian Wisdom was first published in hardcover by Cosmo Publications in 1978, and reprinted in 2001. The INDIGO BOOKS edition is published by arrangement with Cosmo Publications.

First INDIGO Edition 2003

ISBN 81-292-0033-3

PRINTED AND BOUND IN INDIA

CONTENTS

CHAP.		PAGE
I.	THE HYMNS OF THE VEDA	1
II.	THE BRĀHMAṆAS AND UPANISHADS	24
III.	THE SYSTEMS OF PHILOSOPHY	46
IV.	THE NYĀYA	60
V.	THE SĀN·KHYA	79
VI.	THE PŪRVA-MĪMĀṈSĀ AND VEDĀNTA	98
VII.	IRREGULAR SYSTEMS AND ECLECTIC SCHOOL	118
VIII.	SMṚITI—THE VEDĀN·GAS	144
IX.	THE SMĀRTA SŪTRAS OR TRADITIONAL RULES	186
X.	THE DHARMA-ŚĀSTRAS OR LAW-BOOKS—MANU CONTINUED	213
XI.	THE LAW-BOOKS—MANU CONTINUED	278
XII.	THE ITIHĀSAS OR EPIC POEMS—THE RĀMĀYAṆA	306
XIII.	THE ITIHĀSAS OR EPIC POEMS—THE MAHĀ-BHĀRATA	370
XIV.	THE INDIAN EPICS COMPARED WITH EACH OTHER AND WITH THE HOMERIC POEMS	416
XV.	THE ARTIFICIAL POEMS. DRAMAS. PURĀṆAS. TANTRAS. NĪTI-ŚĀSTRAS	452
	INDEX	555

INDIAN WISDOM.

CHAPTER I.

In adopting the term 'Indian Wisdom' as the title of the present work, I wish at the outset to make it clear that, although my object is to draw attention to the best Indian writings, yet it by no means follows that every single extract from those writings will be put forth as an example of what is wise and just and true.

In point of fact, the following pages have a double object. They are designed as much to give a summary of the history of Sanskrit literature as to present the reader with examples of certain selected portions of that literature. In attempting this double task I am conscious of my inability to do justice in a single volume to the richness of the materials at my command. An adequate idea of the luxuriance and varied character of Sanskrit literature can with difficulty be conveyed to Occidental scholars. Naturally, too, the severe European critic will be slow to acquiesce in any tribute of praise bestowed on compositions too often marked by tedious repetitions, redundant epithets, and far-fetched conceits; just as the genuine Oriental, nurtured under glowing tropical skies, cannot easily be brought to appreciate the coldness and severe simplicity of an educated Englishman's style of writing. We might almost say that with Indian authors merit is apt to be measured by magnitude, quality by quantity, were it not for striking thoughts and noble sentiments which often reward the student who will take the trouble to release them from the surplusage of matter under which they lie concealed; were it not, also, that, with all this tendency to diffuseness, it is certainly a fact that nowhere do we find the art of condensation so successfully cultivated, as in some departments of Sanskrit literature.

Probably the very prolixity natural to Indian writers led to the opposite extreme of brevity, not merely by a law of reaction, but by the necessity for providing short summaries and epitomes as aids to the memory when oppressed by too great a burden.

However that may be, every student of Sanskrit will certainly note in its literary productions a singular inequality both as to quantity and quality; so that in studying Hindu literature continuously we are liable to be called upon to pass from the most exuberant verbosity to the most obscure brevity; from sound wisdom to little better than puerile unwisdom; from subtle reasoning to transparent sophistry; from high moral precepts—often expressed in language worthy of Christianity itself—to doctrines implying a social condition scarcely compatible with the lowest grades of culture and civilization.

In embarking, so to speak, on so vast an ocean of research, it will be necessary for me to start from that original source and fountain-head of all Indian religious thought, philosophy, and literature—the Veda.

Vedic literature, however, has been already so much written about, and so clearly and ably elucidated by other writers, that I shall be excused, if I pass very rapidly over this part of my subject.

In the first place, I think I may assume that most educated persons are aware that the Sanskrit word Veda means 'knowledge.' Some, however, may possibly need to be informed that the term Veda is properly only applied to divine *unwritten* knowledge, imagined to have issued like breath from the Self-existent (Brahman), and communicated to no single person, but to a whole class of men called Ṛishis or inspired sages. By them the divine knowledge thus apprehended was transmitted, not in writing, but through the ear, by constant oral repetition through a succession of teachers, who, as claiming to be its rightful recipients, were called Brāhmans. Manu (I. 3) declares that the Veda is itself the Self-existent Brăhmăn. Sāyana, on the other hand, affirms that the Veda is his breath (*aććhvasita*). There are, however, numerous inconsistencies in the accounts of the production of the Veda which seem not to have troubled the Brāhmans, or interfered with their faith in its divine origin. With reference to the statement that it issued from the Self-existent, like breath, one account makes it so issue by the power of A-ḍṛishṭa (see p. 74), without any deliberation or thought on his part; another makes the four Vedas issue from Brahman, like smoke from burning fuel; another educes them from the elements; another from the Gāyatrī. A hymn in the Atharva-veda (XIX. 54) educes them from Kāla or 'Time.' The Śatapatha-brāhmaṇa asserts that the Creator brooded over the three worlds, and thence produced three lights, fire, the air, and the sun, from which respectively were extracted the Ṛig, Yajur, and Sāma-veda. Manu (I. 23) affirms the same. In the Purusha-sūkta the three Vedas are derived from the mystical victim Purusha. Lastly, by the Mīmāṉsakas the Veda is declared to be itself an eternal sound, and to have existed absolutely from all eternity, quite independently of any utterer or revealer of its texts. Hence it is often called *śruta*, 'what is heard.' In opposition to all this we have the Ṛishis themselves frequently intimating that the Mantras were composed by themselves.

Here, then, we have a theory of inspiration higher even than that advanced by Muhammad and his followers, or by the most enthusiastic adherents of any other religion in the world. It is very true that this inspired knowledge, though its very essence was held to be mystically bound up with Śabda or 'articulate sound' (thought to be eternal), was ultimately written down, but the writing and reading of it were not encouraged. It was even prohibited by the Brāhmans, to whom alone all property in it belonged. Moreover, when at last, by its continued growth, it became too complex for mere oral transmission, then this Veda resolved itself, not into one single volume, like the Kurān, but into a whole series of compositions, which had in reality been composed by a number of different poets and writers at different times during several centuries.

There is this great difference, therefore, between the Kurān and the Veda, that whereas the reading of the former is regarded as a sacred duty, and constantly practised by all good Muslims, the Veda, even after it had been committed to writing, became absolutely a sealed book to the masses of Hindūs, and with the exception of some of the later Vedic works, called Upanishads, is to this day almost entirely unread, however much it may be still repeated in religious services, and its divine authority as an infallible guide nominally upheld.[1] In fact, the absolute and infallible authority of the Veda is held to be so manifest as to require no proof, and to be entirely beyond the province of reason or argument. Manu even extends this to Smṛiti (II. 10), where he says, 'By *śruti* is meant the Veda, and by *smṛiti* the books of tradition;

---

[1] The want of accuracy in repeating the Mantras of the Ṛig-veda is illustrated by the native editions of Manu. An edition (with the commentary of Kullūka) in my possession is a scholar-like production, but almost in every place where the Mantras of the Ṛig-veda are alluded to by Manu (as in VIII. 91, XI. 250, 252, 253, 254) errors disfigure the text and commentary.

the contents of both these must never be questioned by reason.'

Of what, then, does this Veda consist? To conduce to clearness we may regard it as separating itself into three quite distinct divisions, viz. :—

1. *Mantra*, or prayer and praise embodied in metrical hymns and texts.

2. *Brāhmaṇa*, or ritualistic precept and illustration written in prose.

3. *Upanishad*, 'mystical or esoteric doctrine' appended to the aforesaid Brāhmaṇa, in prose and occasional verse.

To begin, then, with the Mantra portion. By this is meant those prayers, invocations, and hymns which have been collected and handed down to us from a period after the Indian branch of the great Indo-European race had finally settled down in Northern India, but which were doubtless composed by a succession of poets at different times (perhaps between 1500 and 1000 years B.C.). These compositions, though very unequal in poetical merit, and containing many tedious repetitions and puerilities, are highly interesting and important, as embodying some of the earliest religious conceptions, as well as some of the earliest known forms, of the primitive language of that primeval Āryan race-stock from which Greeks, Romans, Kelts, Teutons, and the Slavonic races are all offshoots.

They are comprised in five principal collections of Mantras, called respectively Ṛik, Atharvan, Sāman, Taittirīya, and Vājasaneyin. Of these the Ṛig-veda—containing one thousand and seventeen hymns—is the oldest and most important, while the Atharva-veda is generally held to be the most recent, and is perhaps the most interesting. The Atharva-veda, in fact, seems in its present form to have been later than Manu. At least it does not appear to have been recognized as a fourth Veda in the time of Manu, though he mentions the revelation made to

Atharvan and An·giras (XI. 33). In book XI., verse 264, he declares that the Veda is only threefold, thus: *Ṛićo yajūṉshi ćānyāni sāmāni vividhāni ća, esha jñeyas trivṛid vedo yo vedainaṃ sa veda-vit.* The Atharvans were a class of priests descended from a man named Atharvan. They appear to have been the first to institute the worship of fire before the separation of the Indians and Iranians, for there were priests called Atharvans in both India and Persia.

As to the Sāma-veda and the two collections of the Yajur-veda (Taittirīya and Vājasaneyin, or Black and White), they all three borrow largely from the Ṛik, and are merely Brahmanical manuals, the necessity for which grew out of the complicated ritual gradually elaborated by the Hindū Āryans. A curious allusion to the Sāma-veda occurs in Manu IV. 123, &c., 'The Ṛig-veda has the gods for its deities, the Yajur-veda has men for its objects, the Sāma-veda has the Pitṛis, therefore its sound is impure.' Kullūka, however, in his commentary is careful to state that the Sāma-veda is not really impure, but only apparently so. This semblance of impurity may perhaps result from its association with deceased persons and its repetition at a time of A-śauća. The Sāma-veda is really a mere reproduction of parts of the Ṛik, transposed and scattered about piecemeal, only seventy-eight verses in the whole Sāma-veda being, it is said, untraceable to the present recension of the Ṛik. The greatest number of its verses are taken from the ninth Maṇḍala of the Ṛik, which is in praise of the Soma plant, the Sāma-veda being a collection of liturgical forms for the Soma ceremonies of the Udgātṛi priests, as the Yajus is for the sacrifices performed by the Adhvaryu priests. Hence we may affirm that the only two Vedic hymn-books worthy of being called separate original collections are the Rig-veda and Atharva-veda; and to these, therefore, we shall confine our examples.

To what deities, it will be asked, were the prayers and hymns of these collections addressed? This is an interesting inquiry, for these were probably the very deities worshipped under similar names by our Āryan progenitors in their primeval home somewhere on the table-land of Central Asia, or elsewhere, perhaps not far from the sources of the Oxus.[1] The answer is: They worshipped those physical forces before which all nations, if guided solely by the light of nature, have in the early period of their life instinctively bowed down, and before which even the more civilized and enlightened have always been compelled to bend in awe and reverence, if not in adoration.

To our Āryan forefathers in their primeval home God's power was exhibited in the forces of nature even more evidently than to ourselves. Lands, houses, flocks, herds, men, and animals were more frequently than in Western climates at the mercy of winds, fire, and water, and the sun's rays appeared to be endowed with a potency quite beyond the experience of any European country. We cannot be surprised, then, that these forces were regarded by our Eastern progenitors as actual manifestations, either of one deity in different moods or of separate rival deities contending for supremacy. Nor is it wonderful that these mighty agencies should have been at first poetically personified, and afterwards, when invested with forms, attributes, and individuality, worshipped as distinct gods. It was only natural, too, that a varying supremacy and varying honours should have been accorded to each deified force—to the air, the rain, the storm, the sun, or fire—according to the special atmospheric influences to which particular localities were exposed, or according to the

---

1 Professor Whitney and others doubt this usual assumption. Some even lean to the theory that somewhere in the North of Europe is the primeval home of the Aryans.

seasons of the year when the dominance of each was to be prayed for or deprecated.

This was the religion represented in the Vedas and the primitive creed of the Indo-Āryans about twelve or thirteen centuries before Christ. The first forces deified seem to have been those manifested in the sky and air. These were at first generalised under one rather vague personification, as was natural in the earliest attempts at giving shape to religious ideas. For it may be observed that all religious systems, even the most polytheistic, have generally grown out of some undefined original belief in a divine power or powers controlling and regulating the universe. And although innumerable gods and goddesses, gifted with a thousand shapes, now crowd the Hindū Pantheon, appealing to the instincts of the unthinking millions whose capacity for religious ideas is supposed to require the aid of external symbols, it is probable that there existed for the first Āryan worshippers a simpler theistic creed : even as the thoughtful Hindū of the present day looks through the maze of his mythology to the philosophical background of one eternal self-existent Being, one universal Spirit, into whose unity all visible symbols are gathered, and in whose essence all entities are comprehended.

In the Veda this unity soon diverged into various ramifications. Only a few of the hymns appear to contain the simple conception of one divine self-existent omnipresent Being, and even in these the idea of one God present in all nature is somewhat nebulous and undefined.

It is interesting to note how this idea, vaguely stated as it was in the Veda, gradually developed and became more clearly defined in the time of Manu. In the last verses of the twelfth book (123–125) we have the following : 'Him some adore as transcendently present in fire ; others in Manu, lord of creatures ; some as more distinctly present in Indra, others in pure air, others as the most high eternal Spirit. Thus the man who perceives in his own soul, the supreme soul present in all creatures, acquires equanimity towards them all, and shall be absorbed at last in the highest essence.

In the Purusha-sūkta of the Ṛig-veda (X. 90), which is one of the later hymns, probably not much earlier than the earliest Brāhmaṇa, the one Spirit is called Purusha. The more common name is Ātman or Paramātman, and in the later system *Brahman*, neut. (nom. *Brahmă*), derived from root *bṛih*, 'to expand,' and denoting the universally expanding essence or universally diffused substance of the universe. It was thus that the later creed became not so much monotheistic (by which I mean the belief in one god regarded as a personal Being external to the universe, though creating and governing it) as pantheistic; Brahman in the neuter being 'simple infinite being'—the only real eternal essence—which, when it passes into universal *manifested* existence, is called Brahmā, when it manifests itself on the earth, is called Vishṇu, and when it again dissolves itself into simple being, is called S'iva; all the other innumerable gods and demigods being also mere manifestations of the neuter Brahman, who alone is eternal. This, at any rate, appears to be the genuine pantheistic creed of India at the present day.

To return to the Vedic hymns—perhaps the most ancient and beautiful Vedic deification was that of Dyauś,[1] 'the sky,' as Dyaush-pitar, 'Heavenly Father' (the Zeus or Ju-piter of the Greeks and Romans). Then, closely connected with Dyaus, was a goddess A-diti, 'the Infinite Expanse,' conceived of subsequently as the mother of all

---

[1] From *dyu* or *dyo*, the same as the Old German Tiu or Ziu, who, according to Professor Max Müller, afterwards became a kind of Mars (whence Tues-day). For Dyaush-pitar see Ṛig-veda VI. 51. 5.

the gods. Next came a development of the same conception called Varuṇa, 'the Investing Sky,' said to answer to Ahura Mazda, the Ormazd of the ancient Persian (Zand) mythology, and to the Greek Οὐρανός—but a more spiritual conception, leading to a worship which rose to the nature of a belief in the great Πατὴρ ἡμῶν ὁ ἐν τοῖς οὐρανοῖς. This Varuṇa, again, was soon thought of in connection with another vague personification called Mitra (= the Persian *Mithra*), 'god of day.' After a time these impersonations of the celestial sphere were felt to be too vague to suit the growth of religious ideas in ordinary minds. Soon, therefore, the great investing firmament resolved itself into separate cosmical entities with separate powers and attributes. First, the watery atmosphere—personified under the name of Indra, ever seeking to dispense his dewy treasures (*indu*), though ever restrained by an opposing force or spirit of evil called Vṛitra; and, secondly, the wind—thought of either as a single personality named Vāyu, or as a whole assemblage of moving powers coming from every quarter of the compass, and impersonated as Maruts or 'Storm-gods.' At the same time in this process of decentralization—if I may use the term—the once purely celestial Varuṇa became relegated to a position among seven secondary deities of the heavenly sphere called Ādityas (afterwards increased to twelve, and regarded as diversified forms of the sun in the several months of the year), and subsequently to a dominion over the waters when they had left the air and rested on the earth.

Of these separately deified physical forces by far the most favourite object of adoration was the deity supposed to yield the dew and rain, longed for by Eastern cultivators of the soil with even greater cravings than by Northern agriculturists. Indra, therefore—the Jupiter Pluvius of early Indian mythology—is undoubtedly the principal divinity of Vedic worshippers, in so far at least as the greater number of their prayers and hymns are addressed to him.

What, however, could rain effect without the aid of heat? A force the intensity of which must have impressed an Indian mind with awe, and led him to invest the possessor of it with divine attributes. Hence the other great god of Vedic worshippers, and in some respects the most important in his connection with sacrificial rites, is Agni (Latin *Ignis*), 'the god of fire.' Even Sūrya, 'the sun' (Greek ἥλιος), who was probably at first adored as the original source of heat, came to be regarded as only another form of fire. He was merely a manifestation of the same divine energy removed to the heavens, and consequently less accessible. Another deity, Ushas, 'goddess of the dawn,'—the ἠώς of the Greeks,—was naturally connected with the sun, and regarded as daughter of the sky. Two other deities, the Aśvins, were fabled as connected with Ushas, as ever young and handsome, travelling in a golden car and precursors of the dawn. They are sometimes called Dasras, as divine physicians, 'destroyers of diseases'; sometimes Nāsatyas, as 'never untrue.' They appear to have been personifications of two luminous rays imagined to precede the break of day. These, with Yama, 'the god of departed spirits,' are the principal deities of the Mantra portion of the Veda.

We find, therefore, no trace in the Mantras of the Trimūrti or Triad of deities (Brahmā, Vishṇu, and S'iva) afterwards so popular. Nor does the doctrine of transmigration, afterwards an essential element of the Hindū religion, appear in the Mantra portion of the Veda; though there is a clear declaration of it in the Āraṇyaka of the Aitareya Brāhmaṇa. Nor is caste clearly alluded to, except in the later Purusha-sūkta (see p. 21).

But here it may be asked, if sky, air, water, fire, and the sun were thus worshipped as manifestations of the supreme universal God of the universe, was not the earth also an object of adoration with the early Hindūs? And unquestionably in the earlier system the earth under the name of Pṛithivī, 'the broad one,' *does* receive divine honours, being thought of as the mother of all beings. Moreover, various deities were regarded as the progeny resulting from the fancied union of earth with Dyaus, 'heaven.' This imaginary marriage of heaven and earth was indeed a most natural idea, and much of the later mythology may be explained by it. But it is remarkable that as religious worship became of a more selfish character, the earth, being more evidently under man's control, and not seeming to need propitiation so urgently as the more uncertain air, fire, and water, lost importance among the gods, and was rarely addressed in prayer or hymn.

In all probability the deified forces addressed in the hymns were not represented by images or idols in the Vedic period, though, doubtless, the early worshippers clothed their gods with human form in their own imaginations.[1]

I now begin my examples with a nearly literal translation of the well-known sixteenth hymn of the fourth book of the Atharva-veda, in praise of Varuṇa or 'the Investing Sky':[2]—

---

[1] See Dr Muir's Sanskṛit Texts, vol. v. p. 453.

[2] Ably translated by Dr. Muir (Sanskṛit Texts, vol. v. p. 63) and by Professor Max Müller. It may be thought that in giving additional translations of this and other hymns I am going over ground already well trodden; but it should be borne in mind that, as the design of the work is to illustrate *continuously* the development of Hindū knowledge and literature by a selection of good examples rendered into idiomatic English, I could not, in common justice to such a subject, exclude the best passages in each department of the literature merely because they have been translated by others. I here, however, once for all acknowledge with gratitude that, while making versions of my own, I have derived the greatest assistance from the translations of other scholars. It must be understood, too, that my examples are not put forth as

The mighty Varuṇa, who rules above, looks down
Upon these worlds, his kingdom, as if close at hand.
When men imagine they do ought by stealth, he knows it.
No one can stand or walk or softly glide along
Or hide in dark recess, or lurk in secret cell,
But Varuṇa detects him and his movements spies.
Two persons may devise some plot, together sitting
In private and alone; but he, the king, is there—
A third—and sees it all. This boundless earth is his,
His the vast sky, whose depth no mortal e'er can fathom.
Both oceans [1] find a place within his body, yet
In that small pool he lies contained. Whoe'er should flee
Far, far beyond the sky, would not escape the grasp
Of Varuṇa, the king. His messengers descend
Countless from his abode—for ever traversing
This world and scanning with a thousand eyes its inmates.
Whate'er exists within this earth, and all within the sky,
Yea all that is beyond, king Varuṇa perceives.
The winkings [2] of men's eyes, are numbered all by him.
He wields the universe, as gamesters handle dice.
May thy destroying snares cast sevenfold round the wicked,
Entangle liars, but the truthful spare, O king! [3]

I pass from the ancient Āryan deity Varuṇa to the more thoroughly Indian god Indra (see p. 10).

---

offering rival translations. They are generally intended to be as literal as possible consistently with the observance of English idiom, and on that account I have preferred blank verse; but occasionally they are paraphrases rather than translations, sentences and words being here and there omitted or transposed, or fragments joined together, so as to read like one continuous passage. In fact, it will be seen that my main design has been to offer English versions of the text for general readers, and for those students and educated men who, not being necessarily Sanskṛitists, are desirous of some insight into Hindū literature.

[1] That is, air and sea.

[2] The winking of the eye is an especial characteristic of humanity, distinguishing men from gods; *cf.* Nala V. 25, Māgha III. 42.

[3] Compare Manu VIII. 82: 'A witness who speaks falsely is fast bound by the snares of Varuṇa.' These snares are explained by Kullūka to be 'cords consisting of serpents' (*pāśaiḥ sarpa-rajjubhiḥ*).

The following metrical lines bring together various scattered texts relating to this Hindū Jupiter Pluvius:[1]—

Indra, twin brother of the god of fire,
When thou wast born, thy mother Aditi
Gave thee, her lusty child, the thrilling draught
Of mountain-growing Soma—source of life
And never-dying vigour to thy frame.
Then at the Thunderer's birth, appalled with fear,
Dreading the hundred-jointed thunderbolt—
Forged by the cunning Tvashṭṛi—mountains rocked,
Earth shook and heaven trembled. Thou wast born
Without a rival, king of gods and men—
The eye of living and terrestrial things.
Immortal Indra, unrelenting foe
Of drought and darkness, infinitely wise,
Terrific crusher of thy enemies,
Heroic, irresistible in might,
Wall of defence to us thy worshippers,
We sing thy praises, and our ardent hymns
Embrace thee, as a loving wife her lord.
Thou art our guardian, advocate, and friend,
A brother, father, mother, all combined.
Most fatherly of fathers, we are thine
And thou art ours; oh! let thy pitying soul
Turn to us in compassion, when we praise thee,
And slay us not for one sin or for many.
Deliver us to-day, to-morrow, every day.
Armed for the conflict, see! the demons come—
Ahi and Vritra, and a long array
Of darksome spirits. Quick, then, quaff the draught
That stimulates thy martial energy,
And dashing onward in thy golden car,
Drawn by thy ruddy, Ṛibhu-fashioned[2] steeds,
Speed to the charge, escorted by the Maruts.
Vainly the demons dare thy might; in vain

---

[1] The texts which furnish the basis of these and the succeeding verses will be found in the 5th volume of Dr. Muir's work, and there will also be found a complete poetical sketch of Indra (pp. 126–139).

[2] The Ṛibhus (Greek 'Ορφεύς) were the celestial artists of the Veda.

Strive to deprive us of thy watery treasures.
Earth quakes beneath the crashing of thy bolts.
Pierced, shattered, lies the foe—his cities crushed,
His armies overthrown, his fortresses
Shivered to fragments; then the pent-up waters,
Released from long imprisonment, descend
In torrents to the earth, and swollen rivers,
Foaming and rolling to their ocean home,
Proclaim the triumph of the Thunderer.

Let us proceed next to the all-important Vedic deity Agni, 'god of fire,' especially of sacrificial fire. I propose now to paraphrase a few of the texts which relate to him:—

Agni, thou art a sage, a priest, a king,
Protector, father of the sacrifice.
Commissioned by us men thou dost ascend
A messenger, conveying to the sky
Our hymns and offerings. Though thy origin
Be threefold, now from air and now from water,
Now from the mystic double Araṇi,[1]
Thou art thyself a mighty god, a lord,
Giver of life and immortality,
One in thy essence, but to mortals three;
Displaying thine eternal triple form,
As fire on earth, as lightning in the air,
As sun in heaven. Thou art a cherished guest
In every household—father, brother, son,
Friend, benefactor, guardian, all in one.
Bright, seven-rayed god! how manifold thy shapes
Revealed to us thy votaries! now we see thee,
With body all of gold, and radiant hair
Flaming from three terrific heads, and mouths
Whose burning jaws and teeth devour all things.
Now with a thousand glowing horns, and now
Flashing thy lustre from a thousand eyes,
Thou'rt borne towards us in a golden chariot,
Impelled by winds, and drawn by ruddy steeds,

---

[1] Two pieces of the wood of the *Ficus religiosa* used for kindling fire.

Marking thy car's destructive course, with blackness.
Deliver, mighty lord, thy worshippers.
Purge us from taint of sin, and when we die,
Deal mercifully with us on the pyre,
Burning our bodies with their load of guilt,
But bearing our eternal part on high
To luminous abodes and realms of bliss,
For ever there to dwell with righteous men.

The next deity is Sūrya, 'the Sun,'[1] who, with reference to the variety of his functions, has various names—such as Savitṛi, Aryaman, Mitra, Varuṇa, Pūshan, sometimes ranking as distinct deities of the celestial sphere. As already explained, he is associated in the minds of Vedic worshippers with Fire, and is frequently described as sitting in a chariot drawn by seven ruddy horses (representing the seven days of the week), preceded by the Dawn. Here is an example of a hymn (Ṛig-veda I. 50) addressed to this deity, translated almost literally:—

Behold the rays of Dawn, like heralds, lead on high
The Sun, that men may see the great all-knowing god.
The stars slink off like thieves, in company with Night,
Before the all-seeing eye, whose beams reveal his presence,
Gleaming like brilliant flames, to nation after nation.
With speed, beyond the ken of mortals, thou, O Sun,
Dost ever travel on, conspicuous to all.
Thou dost create the light, and with it dost illume
The universe entire; thou risest in the sight
Of all the race of men, and all the host of heaven.
Light-giving Varuṇa! thy piercing glance doth scan
In quick succession all this stirring, active world,
And penetrateth too the broad ethereal space,
Measuring our days and nights and spying out all creatures.
Sūrya with flaming locks, clear-sighted god of day,
Thy seven ruddy mares bear on thy rushing car.
With these thy self-yoked steeds, seven daughters of thy chariot,

[1] Yāska makes Indra, Agni, and Sūrya the Vedic Triad of gods.

Onward thou dost advance. To thy refulgent orb
Beyond this lower gloom and upward to the light
Would we ascend, O Sun, thou god among the gods.

As an accompaniment to this hymn may here be mentioned the celebrated Gāyatrī. It is a short prayer to the Sun in his character of Savitṛi or 'the Vivifier,' and is the most sacred of all Vedic texts. Though not always understood, it is to this very day used by every Brāhman throughout India in his daily devotions. It occurs in Ṛig-veda III. 62. 10,[1] and can be literally translated as follows:—

Let us meditate (or, we meditate) on that excellent glory of the divine Vivifier. May he enlighten (or stimulate) our understandings. [*Tat Savitur vareṇyam bhargo devasya dhīmahi, Dhiyo yo naḥ praćodayāt.*]

May we not conjecture, with Sir William Jones, that the great veneration in which this text has ever been held by the Hindūs from time immemorial, indicates that the more enlightened worshippers adored, under the type of the visible sun, that divine light which alone could illumine their intellects?

I may here also fitly offer a short paraphrase descriptive of the Vedic Ushas, the Greek Ἠώς, or 'Dawn:'—

Hail, ruddy Ushas, golden goddess, borne
Upon thy shining car, thou comest like
A lovely maiden by her mother decked,
Disclosing coyly all thy hidden graces
To our admiring eyes; or like a wife
Unveiling to her lord, with conscious pride,
Beauties which, as he gazes lovingly,
Seem fresher, fairer each succeeding morn.
Through years on years thou hast lived on, and yet
Thou'rt ever young. Thou art the breath and life

[1] Note that the Ṛishi or author was Viśvāmitra, a *Kshatriya.*

Of all that breathes and lives, awaking day by day
Myriads of prostrate sleepers, as from death,
Causing the birds to flutter from their nests,
And rousing men to ply with busy feet
Their daily duties and appointed tasks,
Toiling for wealth or pleasure or renown.

Before leaving the subject of the Vedic deities I add a few words about Yama, 'the god of departed spirits.' It appears tolerably certain that the doctrine of metempsychosis has no place in the Mantra portion of the Veda,[1] nor do the authors of the hymns evince any sympathy with the desire to get rid of all action and personal existence, which became so remarkable a feature of the theology and philosophy of the Brāhmans in later times. But there are many indirect references to the immortality of man's spirit and a future life, and these become more marked and decided towards the end of the Ṛig-veda. One of the hymns in the last Maṇḍala is addressed to the Pitṛis or fathers, that is to say, the spirits of departed ancestors who have attained to a state of heavenly bliss, and are supposed to occupy three different stages of blessedness,—the highest inhabiting the upper sky, the middle the intermediate air, and the lowest the regions of the atmosphere near the earth. Reverence and adoration are always to be offered them, and they are presided over by the god Yama, the ruler of all the spirits of the dead, whether good or bad. The earlier legends represent this god as a kind of first man (his twin sister being Yamī), and also as the first of men that died. Hence he is described as guiding the spirits of other men who die to the same world. In some passages, however, Death is said to be his messenger, he himself dwelling in celestial light,

---

[1] In Maṇḍala I. 164. 32, *bahu-prajāḥ* is explained by *bahu-janma-bhāk*, 'subject to many births,' but it may mean 'having abundant offspring.'

to which the departed are brought, and where they enjoy his society and that of the fathers. In the Veda he has nothing to do with judging or punishing the departed (as in the later mythology), but he has two terrific dogs, with four eyes, which guard the way to his abode. Here are a few thoughts about him from various hymns in the tenth Maṇḍala of the Ṛig-veda:—

To Yama, mighty king, be gifts and homage paid.
He was the first of men that died, the first to brave
Death's rapid rushing stream, the first to point the road
To heaven, and welcome others to that bright abode.
No power can rob us of the home thus won by thee.
O king, we come; the born must die, must tread the path
That thou hast trod—the path by which each race of men,
In long succession, and our fathers, too, have passed.
Soul of the dead! depart; fear not to take the road—
The ancient road—by which thy ancestors have gone;
Ascend to meet the god—to meet thy happy fathers,
Who dwell in bliss with him. Fear not to pass the guards—
The four-eyed brindled dogs—that watch for the departed.
Return unto thy home, O soul! Thy sin and shame
Leave thou behind on earth; assume a shining form—
Thy ancient shape—refined and from all taint set free.

Let me now endeavour, by slightly amplified translations, to convey some idea of two of the most remarkable hymns in the Ṛig-veda. The first (Maṇḍala X. 129), which may be compared with some parts of the 38th chap. of Job, attempts to describe the mystery of creation thus:—

In the beginning there was neither nought nor aught,
Then there was neither sky nor atmosphere above.
What then enshrouded all this teeming Universe?
In the receptacle of what was it contained?
Was it enveloped in the gulf profound of water?
Then was there neither death nor immortality,
Then was there neither day, nor night, nor light, nor darkness,
Only the Existent One breathed calmly, self contained.
Nought else than him there was—nought else above, beyond.

Then first came darkness hid in darkness, gloom in gloom.
Next all was water, all a chaos indiscreet,
In which the One lay void, shrouded in nothingness.
Then turning inwards he by self-developed force
Of inner fervour and intense abstraction, grew.
And now in him Desire, the primal germ of mind,
Arose, which learned men, profoundly searching, say
Is the first subtle bond, connecting Entity
With Nullity. This ray that kindled dormant life,
Where was it then ? before ? or was it found above ?
Were there parturient powers and latent qualities,
And fecund principles beneath, and active forces
That energized aloft ? Who knows ? Who can declare ?
How and from what has sprung this Universe ? the gods
Themselves are subsequent to its development.
Who, then, can penetrate the secret of its rise ?
Whether 'twas framed or not, made or not made ; he only
Who in the highest heaven sits, the omniscient lord,
Assuredly knows all, or haply knows he not.

The next example is from the first Maṇḍala of the Ṛig-veda (121). Like the preceding, it furnishes a good argument for those who maintain that the purer faith of the Hindūs is properly monotheistic :—

What god shall we adore with sacrifice ? [1]
Him let us praise, the golden child that rose
In the beginning, who was born the lord—
The one sole lord of all that is—who made
The earth, and formed the sky, who giveth life,
Who giveth strength, whose bidding gods revere,
Whose hiding-place is immortality,
Whose shadow, death ; who by his might is king
Of all the breathing, sleeping, waking world—
Who governs men and beasts, whose majesty
These snowy hills, this ocean with its rivers
Declare ; of whom these spreading regions form
The arms ; by whom the firmament is strong,

---

[1] In the text this question is repeated at the end of every verse. A literal translation will be found in Muir's Sanskṛit Texts, vol. iv. p. 16.

Earth firmly planted, and the highest heavens
Supported, and the clouds that fill the air
Distributed and measured out; to whom
Both earth and heaven, established by his will,
Look up with trembling mind; in whom revealed
The rising sun shines forth above the world.
Where'er let loose in space, the mighty waters
Have gone, depositing a fruitful seed
And generating fire, there *he* arose,
Who is the breath and life of all the gods,
Whose mighty glance looks round the vast expanse
Of watery vapour—source of energy,
Cause of the sacrifice—the only God
Above the gods. May he not injure us!
He the Creator of the earth—the righteous
Creator of the sky, Creator too
Of oceans bright, and far-extending waters.

Let me now give a few verses (not in regular order and not quite literally translated) from the celebrated Purusha-sūkta, one of the most recent of the hymns of the Ṛig-veda (Maṇḍala X. 90). It will serve to illustrate the gradual sliding of Hindū monotheism into pantheism, and the first foreshadowing of the institution of caste, which for so many centuries has held India in bondage:—

The embodied spirit [1] has a thousand heads,
A thousand eyes, a thousand feet, around
On every side enveloping the earth,
Yet filling space no larger than a span.[2]
He is himself this very universe,
He is whatever is, has been, and shall be.
He is the lord of immortality.
All creatures are one-fourth of him, three-fourths

[1] According to the Upanishads and the Tattva-samāsa the all-pervading self-existent spirit is called Purusha, *puri śayanāt*, from dwelling in the body.

[2] Dr. Muir translates (literally), 'He overpassed the earth by a space of ten fingers.' The Kaṭha Upanishad (II. 4. 12) says that Purusha, 'the soul,' is of the measure of a thumb (*angushṭha-mātraḥ*).

Are that which is immortal in the sky.
From him, called Purusha, was born Virāj,
And from Virāj was Purusha produced[1]
Whom gods and holy men made their oblation.
With Purusha as victim they performed
A sacrifice. When they divided him,
How did they cut him up? what was his mouth?
What were his arms? and what his thighs and feet?
The Brāhman was his mouth, the kingly soldier[2]
Was made his arms, the husbandman his thighs,
The servile S'ūdra issued from his feet.

I close my examples of the Mantras with slightly amplified versions of two hymns—one in praise of Time, personified as the source of all things, taken from the Atharva-veda; the other addressed to Night, from the Ṛig-veda.[3]

The following is the hymn to Time (Atharva-veda XIX. 53). A few verses at the end are omitted, one or two lines transposed, and a few inserted from the next hymn on the same subject:—

Time, like a brilliant steed with seven rays,
And with a thousand eyes, imperishable,
Full of fecundity, bears all things onward.
On him ascend the learned and the wise.
Time, like a seven-wheeled, seven-naved car, moves on.

---

[1] This is tantamount to saying that Purusha and Virāj are in substance the same. Virāj, as a kind of secondary creator, is sometimes regarded as male, sometimes as female. Manu (I. 11) says that Purusha, 'the first male,' was called Brahmā, and was produced from the supreme self-existent Spirit. In I. 32 he says that Brahmā (see Kullūka's commentary), having divided his own substance, became half male, half female, and that from the female was produced Virāj, and that from Virāj was born Manu—the secondary progenitor and producer of all beings.

[2] The second caste or Kshatriya is here called Rājanya. By 'husbandman' in the next line is of course meant the third or Vaiśya caste.

[3] Both literally translated into prose by Dr. Muir, Texts, vol. v. p. 408, vol. iv. p. 498.

His rolling wheels are all the worlds, his axle
Is immortality. He is the first of gods.
We see him like an overflowing jar;
We see him multiplied in various forms.
He draws forth and encompasses the worlds;
He is all future worlds; he is their father;
He is their son; there is no power like him.
The past and future issue out of Time,
All sacred knowledge and austerity.
From Time the earth and waters were produced;
From Time, the rising, setting, burning sun;
From Time, the wind; through Time the earth is vast;
Through Time the eye perceives; mind, breath, and name
In him are comprehended. All rejoice
When Time arrives—the monarch who has conquered
This world, the highest world, the holy worlds,
Yea, all the worlds—and ever marches on.

The hymn to Night is my last example. It is taken from the tenth Maṇḍala of the Ṛig-veda (127):—

The goddess Night arrives in all her glory,
Looking about her with her countless eyes.
She, the immortal goddess, throws her veil
Over low valley, rising ground, and hill,
But soon with bright effulgence dissipates
The darkness she produces; soon advancing
She calls her sister Morning to return,
And then each darksome shadow melts away.
Kind goddess, be propitious to thy servants
Who at thy coming straightway seek repose,
Like birds who nightly nestle in the trees.
Lo! men and cattle, flocks and wingëd creatures,
And e'en the ravenous hawks, have gone to rest.
Drive thou away from us, O Night, the wolf;
Drive thou away the thief, and bear us safely
Across thy borders. Then do thou, O Dawn,
Like one who clears away a debt, chase off
This black, yet palpable obscurity,
Which came to fold us in its close embrace.
Receive, O Night, dark daughter of the Day,
My hymn of praise, which I present to thee,
Like some rich offering to a conqueror.

CHAPTER II.

The Brāhmaṇas and Upanishads.

HAVING thus endeavoured to gain an insight into portions of the Vedic Mantras, turn we now to the second division of the Veda, called Brāhmaṇa, or ritualistic precept and illustration. This division stands to the Mantra portion in a relation somewhat resembling that of the Talmud to the Mosaic code, and of the Hadīs or Sunna to the Kurān. There is, however, a noteworthy difference; for the Mosaic code alone contains the true revelation of divine law for the Jew, and the Kurān for Muslims, whereas the Brāhmaṇas are as much Veda and Śruti—as much revelation, according to the Hindū idea of revelation—as the Mantras.

In fact, in their relation to caste and the dominance of the Brāhmans, these Brāhmaṇas are even more important than the Hymns. When, however, we are asked to explain the contents of the Brāhmaṇas, we find it difficult to define their nature accurately. It is usual to consider them as a body of ritualistic precepts distributed under two heads of *Vidhi* and *Artha-vāda*, that is, rules and explanatory remarks. They are really a series of rambling and unsystematic prose compositions (the oldest of which may have been written seven or eight centuries B.C.), intended to serve as ceremonial directories for the use of the priests in the exercise of their craft, prescribing rules for the employment of the Mantras at sacrifices, speculating as to the meaning and effect of certain verses and metres, and giving detailed explanations of the origin, import, and conduct of the sacrifices, with the occasional addition of controversial remarks (*nindā*) and illustrations in the shape of legends and old stories. The great diffuseness of these compositions made them practically useless as directories to the ritual, until they themselves were furnished with guides in the form of Sūtras or aphoristic rules, to be afterwards described.

Each of the collections of Mantras has its own Brāhmaṇas. Thus the Ṛig-veda has the Aitareya-brāmaṇa (perhaps the oldest) and the Kaushītaki- (or Śāṅkhāyana-) brāhmaṇa. The two collections of the Yajur-veda have the Taittirīya-brāhmaṇa and the Śatapatha-brāhmaṇa,[1] which last, belonging to the Vājasaneyi-saṃhitā, is perhaps one of the most complete and interesting of these productions. The Sāma-veda has eight Brāhmaṇas, of which the best known are the Prauḍha (Pańća-viṉśa, Tāṇḍya) and the Shaḍ-viṉśa. The Atharva-veda has also a Brāhmaṇa, called Go-patha.[2]

Though much of the matter contained in these treatises is little better than silly sacerdotalism, yet they furnish valuable materials to any one interested in tracing out the growth of Brāhmanism and many curious and interesting legends.

One of the most remarkable of these legends, as introducing the idea of human sacrifice, is called 'the Story of Śunaḥśepa' in the Aitareya-brāhmaṇa[3] (Haug's edition, VII. 13; cf. Ṛig-veda, I. 24, 12, &c., V. 2. 7). It has

---

1 Edited, with the Vājasaneyi-saṃhitā, by Professor A. Weber of Berlin.

2 This Brāhmaṇa must be less ancient than others, as, according to some, the Atharva-veda was not recognized as a part of S'ruti, 'revelation,' at the time of the composition of the more ancient Brāhmaṇas.

3 Professor H. H. Wilson conjectured that this Brāhmaṇa was written about six centuries B.C. It is sometimes called Āśvalāyana-brāhmaṇa.

been well translated by more than one scholar. I here give a metrical epitome of part of the story: —

King Hariśćandra had no son; he asked
Great Nārada, the sage, 'What benefit
Comes from a son?' then Nārada replied—
'A father by his son clears off a debt,[1]
In him a self is born from self. The pleasure
A father has in his own son exceeds
All other pleasures. Food is life, apparel
Is a protection, gold an ornament,
A loving wife the best of friends, a daughter
An object of compassion,[2] but a son
Is like a light sent from the highest heaven.
Go then to Varuṇa, the god, and say—
"Let but a son be born, O king, to me,
And I will sacrifice that son to thee."'
This Hariśćandra did, and thereupon
A son was born to him, called Rohita.
One day the father thus addressed his son—
'I have devoted thee, my son, to him
Who granted thee to me, prepare thyself
For sacrifice to him.' The son said, 'No,'
Then took his bow and left his father's home.

The story goes on to relate that Varuṇa, being disappointed of his promised victim, punished Hariśćandra by afflicting him with dropsy. Meanwhile

For six long years did Hariśćandra's son
Roam in the forest; there one day he met
A famished Brāhman hermit, Ajīgarta,
Half dead with hunger in the wilderness.
The hermit was attended by his wife
And three young sons; then Rohita addressed him—

---

[1] A man is in debt to his forefathers till he has a son, because the happiness of the dead depends on certain ceremonies (called S'rāddha) performed by sons.

[2] Those who have lived in the East will perhaps understand why the birth of a daughter is here described as a calamity.

'O Brāhman, I will give a hundred cows
For one of these thy sons.' The father answered—
Folding his arms around his eldest boy—
'I cannot part with him.' The mother then
Clung to her youngest child and weeping said—
'I cannot part with him.' Then S'unaḥśepa,
Their second son, said, 'Father, I will go.'[1]
So he was purchased for a hundred cows
By Rohita, who forthwith left the forest,
And taking him to Hariśćandra said—
'Father, this boy shall be my substitute.'
Then Hariśćandra went to Varuṇa
And prayed, 'Accept this ransom for my son.'
The god replied, 'Let him be sacrificed,
A Brāhman is more worthy than a Kshatriya.'

Upon that, the sacrifice with the intended victim was prepared. Four great Ṛishis officiated as priests, but they could not find any one willing to bind the boy to the sacrificial post. His father Ajīgarta, who had followed his son to the place of sacrifice, then came forward and said—

'Give me a hundred cows and I will bind him.'
They gave them to him, and he bound the boy.
But now no person would consent to kill him.
Then said the father, 'Give me yet again

---

[1] The Brāhmaṇa merely states that they agreed together upon selling the middle son. This idea of the voluntary offer of himself on the part of S'unaḥśepa may, however, be borrowed from the Rāmāyaṇa, where the story is thus related (I. 61, 62):—

Ambarīsha, king of Ayodhyā, performed a sacrifice, but the victim being stolen by Indra, he is told by the priest that either the victim itself must be recovered, or a human victim substituted in its place. Ambarīsha wanders over the earth in search of the real victim, and meets at last with a Brāhman named Rićīka, to whom he offers a hundred thousand cattle for one of his sons. Rićīka refuses to let his eldest son go, and his wife will not part with the youngest. Upon this the middle son, S'unaḥ-śepa, volunteers to go, and is accepted. When about to be offered up as a sacrifice he is saved by Viśvāmitra, who teaches him a prayer to Agni, and two hymns to Indra and Vishṇu.

Another hundred cows and I will slay him.'
Once more they gave a hundred, and the father
Whetted his knife to sacrifice his son.
Then said the child, 'Let me implore the gods,
Haply they will deliver me from death.'
So S'unaḥśepa prayed to all the gods
With verses from the Veda, and they heard him.
Thus was the boy released from sacrifice,
And Hariśćandra was restored to health.

As a sequel to the preceding legend I extract the following curious passages from the Aitareya-brāhmaṇa, Book II. (Haug, 1–8), not in order, and not quite literally :—

The gods killed a man for their victim. But from him thus killed the part which was fit for a sacrifice went out and entered a horse. Thence the horse became an animal fit for being sacrificed. The gods then killed the horse, but the part fit for being sacrificed went out of it and entered an ox. The gods then killed the ox, but the part fit for being sacrificed went out of it and entered a sheep. Thence it entered a goat. The sacrificial part remained for the longest time in the goat, thence it became pre-eminently fit for being sacrificed.[1]

---

[1] This is curious as indicating that human sacrifice, if it prevailed to any extent, was superseded by the sacrifice of animals, here enumerated in the regular order of their fitness for sacrifice according to some supposed inherent efficacy in each class. Such sacrifices were held to be propitiatory, though one object of a Hindū's oblations was to afford actual nourishment to the gods, food being a supposed necessity of their being. The Aśva-medha, or 'horse-sacrifice,' was a very ancient ceremony, hymns 162 and 163 in Maṇḍala I. of the Ṛig-veda being used at this rite. It was regarded as the chief of all animal sacrifices, and in later times its efficacy was so exaggerated that a hundred horse-sacrifices entitled the sacrificer to displace Indra from the dominion of heaven. Some think that the horse was not actually immolated, but merely bound to the post. Mr. Hardwick, in his valuable work, 'Christ and other Masters,' gives some interesting remarks on the five heads of Hindū sacrifices (vol. i. p. 324). The five heads are—1. *Agni-hotra*, burnt-offerings and libations of butter on fire every morning and evening (see p. 121); 2, *Darśapūrṇamāsa*, half-monthly sacrifices at new and full moon; 3. *Cāturmāsya*, sacrifices every four

The gods went up to heaven by means of sacrifice. They were afraid that men and sages, after having seen their sacrifice, might inquire how they could obtain some knowledge of sacrificial rites and follow them. They therefore debarred them by means of the Yūpa (or post to which the victim was fastened), turning its point downwards. Thereupon the men and sages dug the post out and turned its point upwards. Thus they became aware of the sacrifice and reached the heavenly world.

The following lines may serve to give an outline of another curious legend in the Aitareya-brāhmaṇa (Haug's edition, I. 23), written perhaps seven or eight centuries B.C.:—

The gods and demons were engaged in warfare.
The evil demons, like to mighty kings,
Made these worlds castles; then they formed the earth
Into an iron citadel, the air
Into a silver fortress, and the sky
Into a fort of gold. Whereat the gods
Said to each other, 'Frame we other worlds
In opposition to these fortresses.'
Then they constructed sacrificial places,
Where they performed a triple burnt oblation.
By the first sacrifice they drove the demons
Out of their earthly fortress, by the second
Out of the air, and by the third oblation
Out of the sky. Thus were the evil spirits
Chased by the gods in triumph from the worlds.

I next give a metrical version of part of a well-known legend in the Śatapatha-brāhmaṇa (Professor Weber's edition, I. 8. 1. 1), which represents the Indo-Āryan tradition of the flood as it existed in India many centuries before the Christian era, perhaps not much later than the time of David:

---

months; 4. *Aśva-medha* and *paśu-yajña*, sacrifices of animals; 5. *Soma-yajña*, offerings and libations of the juice of the Soma or moon-plant (to Indra especially). Goats are still offered to Kālī, but Buddhism tended to abolish animal sacrifice in India.

There lived in ancient time a holy man,
Called Manu,[1] who by penances and prayers
Had won the favour of the lord of heaven.
One day they brought him water for ablution;
Then, as he washed his hands, a little fish
Appeared and spoke in human accents thus—
'Take care of me and I will be thy saviour.'
'From what wilt thou preserve me?' Manu asked.
The fish replied, 'A flood will sweep away
All creatures, I will rescue thee from that.'
'But how shall I preserve thee?' Manu said.
The fish rejoined, 'So long as we are small
We are in constant danger of destruction;
For fish eats fish; so keep me in a jar;
When I outgrow the jar, then dig a trench
And place me there; when I outgrow the trench,
Then take me to the ocean, I shall then
Be out of reach of danger.' Having thus
Instructed Manu, straightway rapidly
The fish grew larger; then he spake again—
'In such and such a year the flood will come;
Therefore construct a ship and pay me homage.
When the flood rises, enter thou the ship,
And I will rescue thee.' So Manu did
As he was ordered, and preserved the fish,
Then carried it in safety to the ocean;
And in the very year the fish enjoined
He built a ship and paid the fish respect,
And there took refuge when the flood arose.
Soon near him swam the fish, and to its horn
Manu made fast the cable of his vessel.
Thus drawn along the waters Manu passed
Beyond the northern mountain. Then the fish,
Addressing Manu, said, 'I have preserved thee;
Quickly attach the ship to yonder tree.
But, lest the waters sink from under thee;

---

[1] According to the later mythology this Manu was not the first Manu, held to be the author of the well-known Code, but the seventh or Manu (Vaivasvata) of the present period, regarded as a progenitor of the human race, and represented as conciliating the favour of the Supreme Being by his piety in an age of universal depravity.

As fast as they subside, so fast shalt thou
Descend the mountain gently after them.'
Thus he descended from the northern mountain.
The flood had swept away all living creatures;
Manu alone was left. Wishing for offspring,
He earnestly performed a sacrifice.
In a year's time a female was produced.
She came to Manu, then he said to her,
'Who art thou?' She replied, 'I am thy daughter.'
He said, 'How, lovely lady, can that be?'
'I came forth,' she rejoined, 'from thine oblations
Cast on the waters; thou wilt find in me
A blessing, use me in the sacrifice.'
With her he worshipped and with toilsome zeal
Performed religious rites, hoping for offspring.
Thus were created men, called sons of Manu.
Whatever benediction he implored
With her, was thus vouchsafed in full abundance.

We shall see hereafter that the fish which figures in this story is declared, in the Mahābhārata, to be an incarnation of Brahmā, the creator, who assumed this form to preserve the pious Manu from perishing in the waters.

The Brāhmaṇas express belief in a future life more positively than the Mantras. They also assert that a recompense awaits all beings in the next world according to their conduct in this. But the doctrine of transmigration, which became afterwards an essential element of the Hindū religion, is not developed.[1] There is a remarkable passage in the Śatapatha-brāhmaṇa (X. 4. 3. 9), some idea of which may be gained from the following lines:—

The gods lived constantly in dread of death—
The mighty Ender—so with toilsome rites
They worshipped and performed religious acts
Till they became immortal. Then the Ender
Said to the gods, 'As ye have made yourselves

[1] See the third of Professor Weber's Indische Streifen, and compare note 2, p. 56.

Imperishable, so will men endeavour
To free themselves from me; what portion then
Shall I possess in man?' The gods replied,
'Henceforth no being shall become immortal
In his own body; this his mortal frame
Shalt thou still seize; this shall remain thy own.
He who through knowledge or religious works
Henceforth attains to immortality
Shall first present his body, Death, to thee.'

I add one other passage extracted from the Aitareya-brāhmaṇa (Dr. Haug's edition, III. 44):—

The sun never sets nor rises. When people think to themselves the sun is setting, he only changes about (*viparyasyate*) after reaching the end of the day, and makes night below and day to what is on the other side. Then when people think he rises in the morning, he only shifts himself about after reaching the end of the night, and makes day below and night to what is on the other side. In fact, he never does set at all. Whoever knows this, that the sun never sets, enjoys union and sameness of nature with him and abides in the same sphere. [*Atha yad enam prātar udetīti manyante rātrer eva tad antam itvā atha ātmānaṃ viparyasyate, ahar eva avastāt kurute rātrīm parastāt. Sa vai esha na kadāćana nimroćati. Na ha vai kadāćana nimroćaty etasya ha sāyujyaṃ sarūpatāṃ salokatām aśnute ya evaṃ veda.*]

We may close the subject of the Brāhmaṇas by paying a tribute of respect to the acuteness of the Hindū mind, which seems to have made some shrewd astronomical guesses more than 2000 years before the birth of Copernicus.

The Upanishads.

I come now to the third division of the Veda, called Upanishad, or mystical doctrine (*rahasya*). The title Upanishad (derived from the root *sad* with the prepositions *upa* and *ni*[1]) may imply either something mystical that

[1] According to some authorities, *upa-ni-shad* means 'to set ignorance at rest by revealing the knowledge of the supreme spirit;' according to others, it means 'to sit down at the feet of a teacher so as to learn from him his most secret doctrines.'

underlies the surface, or the esoteric doctrine taught to a pupil *who sits near* his master. Whatever may be the true meaning of the word, these Upanishads do in fact lie at the root of what may be called the philosophical side of Hindūism. Not only are they as much *śruti*, or revelation, as the Mantra and Brāhmaṇa, but they are practically the only Veda of all thoughtful Hindūs in the present day.

There appear, in real truth, to be two sides to almost every religious system. Perhaps the one religion of the world that offers the same doctrines both to the learned and unlearned is Christianity. Its deeper truths may be mysteries, but they are not restricted to any single class of men; they are open to the reception of all, and offered equally to the apprehension of all. The case is different with other religions. We know that the Greeks and Romans had their so-called mysteries reserved only for the initiated. We have all heard of Esoteric Buddhism, Occultism, and Theosophy. Even the Kurān is held to possess an exoteric or evident meaning called *ẓahr*, and an esoteric, deeper significance called *baṭn*; and in later times a mystical system of pantheistic philosophy called Sūfī-ism was developed in Persia out of this esoteric teaching.

Very similar too is the Hindū idea of Veda or sacred knowledge. It is said to possess two quite distinct branches. The first is called Karma-kāṇḍa, which, embracing both Mantra and Brāhmaṇa, is for that vast majority of persons who are unable to conceive of religion except as a process of laying up merit by external rites. For these the one God, although really without form, assumes various forms with the sole object of lowering himself to the level of human understandings. The second branch of the Veda, on the other hand, is called Jñāna-kāṇḍa, and is reserved for that select few who are capable of the true knowledge.[1]

---

[1] The one implies action, the other cessation from all action. This division of the Veda is recognised by Manu, see XII. 88.

What then, it will be asked, is this true knowledge? The answer is, that the creed of the man who is said to possess the true Veda is singularly simple. He believes in the unity of all being. In other words, that there is but one real Being in the universe, which Being also constitutes the universe. This, it will be said, is simple pantheism, but it is at least a pantheism of a very spiritual kind; for this one Being is thought of as the great universal Spirit, the only really existing Soul, with which all seemingly existing material substances are identified, and into which the separate souls of men, falsely regarded as emanations from it, must be ultimately merged.

This, then, is the pantheistic doctrine everywhere traceable in some of the more ancient Upanishads, though often wrapped up in mystic language and fantastic allegory. A list of about 150 of these treatises has been given, but the absence of all trustworthy historical records in India makes it impossible to fix the date of any of them with certainty. Some of the more ancient, however, may be as old as 500 years before Christ. These are appended to the Āraṇyakas—certain chapters of the Brāhmaṇas so awe-inspiring and obscure that they were required to be read in the solitude of forests. Properly each Brāhmaṇa had its Āraṇyakas, but the mystical doctrines they contained were so mixed up with extraneous subjects that the chapters called Upanishads appear to have been added with the object of investigating more definitely such abstruse problems as the origin of the universe, the nature of deity, the nature of the soul, and the reciprocal connection of spirit and matter.

It is interesting to trace the rudiments of the later philosophy amid the labyrinth of mystic language, fanciful etymologies, far-fetched analogies, and puerile conceits which bewilder the reader of the Upanishads. Moreover, it is instructive to mark the connection of these treatises with the Brāhmaṇas, manifested by the frequent introduction of legendary matter and allusions to sacrificial rites. The language of both, though occasionally archaic, is less so than that of the Mantras, and differs little from classical Sanskṛit.

The following are some of the most important Upanishads:—the Aitareya Upanishad and Kaushītaki-brāhmaṇa Upanishad[1] of the Ṛig-veda; the Taittiriya belonging to the Taittiriya, or Black Yajur-veda; the Bṛihad-āraṇyaka attached to the Śatapatha-brāhmaṇa of the Vājasaneyin, or White Yajur-veda, and the Īśā or Īśāvāsya forming an actual part (the 40th chapter) of the Vājasaneyin (this being the only instance of an Upanishad attached to the Mantra rather than to the Brāhmaṇa portion of a Veda); the Ćhāndogya and Kena[2] belonging to the Sāma-veda; the Praśna, Muṇḍaka, Māṇḍukya, and Kaṭha belonging to the Atharva-veda. In some of these works (written generally in prose in the form of dialogues, with occasional variations in verse) striking thoughts, original ideas, and lofty sentiments may be found scattered here and there, as I hope now to show. I commence my examples with a nearly literal translation of about half of a very short Upanishad—the Īśā:[3]—

Whate'er exists within this universe
Is all to be regarded as enveloped
By the great Lord (*Īśā* from *Īś*), as if wrapped in a vesture.
Renounce, O man, the world, and covet not
Another's wealth, so shalt thou save thy soul.
Perform religious works, so may'st thou wish
To live a hundred years; in this way only

---

[1] Edited and translated for the Bibliotheca Indica by Professor Cowell.

[2] Also called Talava-kāra, and also assigned to the Atharva-veda.

[3] This has been well edited and translated into prose by Dr. Röer. Sir W. Jones translated the Īśā, but by no means literally.

May'st thou engage in worldly acts, untainted.
To worlds immersed in darkness, tenanted
By evil spirits, shall they go at death,
Who in this life are killers of their souls.
There is one only Being who exists
Unmoved, yet moving swifter than the mind;
Who far outstrips the senses, though as gods
They strive to reach him; who himself at rest
Transcends the fleetest flight of other beings;
Who, like the air, supports all vital action.
He moves, yet moves not; he is far, yet near;
He is within this universe, and yet
Outside this universe; whoe'er beholds
All living creatures as in him, and him—
The universal Spirit—as in all,
Henceforth regards no creature with contempt.
The man who understands that every creature
Exists in God alone, and thus perceives
The unity of being, has no grief
And no illusion. He, the all-pervading,
Is brilliant, without body, sinewless,
Invulnerable, pure, and undefiled
By taint of sin. He also is all-wise,
The Ruler of the mind, above all beings,
The Self-existent. He created all things
Just as they are from all eternity.

Next we may pass to a few passages selected from different portions of the Bṛihad-āraṇyaka Upanishad—a long and tedious but important work:—

In this universe there was not anything at first distinguishable. But indeed it was enveloped by Death, and Death is Voracity—that is to say, the desire to devour (I. 2. 1).

As the web issues from the spider, as little sparks proceed from fire, so from the one Soul proceed all breathing animals, all worlds, all the gods, and all beings (II. 1, 20).

Being in this world we may know the Supreme Spirit; if there be ignorance of him, then complete death ensues; those who know him become immortal (IV. 4. 14).

When a person regards his own soul as truly God, as the lord of what was and is to be, then he does not wish to conceal himself from that Soul (IV. 4. 15).

That Soul the gods adore as the light of lights (*jyotishāṃ jyotiḥ*), and as the immortal life (IV. 4. 16).

Those who know him as the life of life, the eye of the eye, the ear of the ear, and the mind of the mind, have comprehended the eternal pre-existing Spirit (IV. 4. 18).

By the mind is he to be perceived, in him there is no variation. Whoever sees variation in him obtains death after death (IV. 4. 19).

Infinitely full (or pervasive) is that Spirit (regarded as independent of all relation); infinite too is this Spirit (in his relations and attributes). From the infinite is drawn out the infinite. On taking the infinite from the infinite, there remains the infinite (V. 1).

'I am Brahma.' Whoever knows this, 'I am Brahma,' knows all. Even the gods are unable to prevent his becoming Brahma (I. 4. 10).

Man indeed is like a lofty tree, the lord of the forest. His hair is like the leaves, his skin the external bark. From his skin flows blood as sap from the bark; it issues from his wounded body like sap from a stricken tree. If a tree be cut down, it springs up anew from the root. From what root does mortal man grow again when hewn down by death? [Cf. Job xiv. 7–10.] The root is Brahma, who is knowledge and bliss (III. 9. 28).

The Ćhāndogya Upanishad of the Sāma-veda has some interesting passages. In the seventh chapter occurs a dialogue between Nārada and Sanat-kumāra, in which the latter, in explaining the nature of God, asserts that a knowledge of the four Vedas, Itihāsas, Purāṇas, and such works, is useless without the knowledge of Brahma, the universal Spirit (VII. 1. 4):—

The knowledge of these works is a mere name. Speech is greater than this name, Mind than Speech, Will than Mind, Sensation (or the capacity of feeling) is greater than Mind, Reflection is higher than Sensation, Knowledge than Reflection, Power than Knowledge, and highest of all stands Prāṇa or Life. As the spokes of a wheel are attached to the nave, so are all things attached to Life.[1]

This Life ought to be approached with faith and reverence, and viewed as an Immensity which abides in its own glory. That immensity extends from above and from below, from behind and from before, from the south and from the north. It is the Soul of the universe. It is God himself. The man who is conscious of this divinity incurs neither disease, nor pain, nor death.

But lest the deity might from this description be confounded with space, it is afterwards stated that he is inconceivably minute, dwelling in a minute chamber of the heart; and lest this should lead to the notion of his being finite, he is afterwards declared to be the Envelope of all creation.

In another part of the work (VI. 10) human souls are compared to rivers:—

These rivers proceed from the East towards the West, thence from the ocean they rise in the form of vapour, and dropping again they flow towards the South and merge into the ocean.

Again (VIII. 4), the supreme Soul is compared to a bridge which cannot be crossed by disease, death, grief, virtue, or vice:—

Crossing this bridge, the blind cease to be blind, the wounded to be wounded, the afflicted to be afflicted, and on crossing this bridge nights become days; for ever-refulgent is the region of the universal Spirit.

Here is a portion of a passage in the Chāndogya Upanishad (VI. 2) which has some celebrity as containing the well-known Vedāntist formula *ekam evādvitīyam*:—

In the beginning there was the mere state of being (τὸ ὄν)—one only without a second. Some, however, say that in the beginning there was

---

[1] Cf. the hymn to Prāṇa, Atharva-veda, XI. 4 (Muir's Texts, vol. v. p. 394). It begins thus, 'Reverence to Prāṇa, to whom this universe is subject, who has become the lord of all, on whom all is supported.' The text of this Veda has been edited in a masterly manner by Professors W. D. Whitney and R. Roth.

the state of non-being (τὸ μὴ ὄν)—one only without a second. Hence out of a state of non-being would proceed a state of being. But, of a truth, how can this be? How can being (τὸ ὄν) proceed out of non-being? In the beginning, then, there was the mere state of being—one only without a second. It willed,[1] 'I shall multiply and be born.' It created heat. That heat willed, 'I shall multiply and be born.' It created water. The water willed, 'I shall multiply and be born.' It created aliment. Therefore, wherever rain falls much aliment is produced. That deity willed, 'Entering these three divinities in a living form, I shall develop name and form.'

In the Muṇḍaka Upanishad[2] there are some interesting passages. The following is from the second section of the second Muṇḍaka (5):—

Know him, the Spirit, to be one alone. Give up all words contrary to this. He is the bridge of immortality.

The following remarkable passage from the third Muṇḍaka (1. 1–3) is quoted by the Sāṅkhyas in support of their doctrine of a duality of principle, but is also appealed to by Vedāntists. It rests on a Mantra of the Ṛig-veda (I. 164. 20), explained by Sāyaṇa in a Vedantic sense:[3]—

---

[1] I follow Dr. Röer. Subjoined are divided Sanskṛit words of the fragment taken from the original text:—*Sad eva idam agre āsīd, ekam eva advitīyam. Tad ha eke āhur asad eva idam agre āsīd, ekam eva advitīyam, tasmād asataḥ saj jāyeta. Kutas tu khalu syād iti, katham asataḥ saj jāyeta iti. Sat tv eva idam agre āsīd ekam eva advitīyam. Tad aikshata bahu syām prajāyeya iti, tat tejo asṛijata. Tat teja aikshata bahu syām prajāyeya iti, tad apo asṛijata. Tā āpa aikshanta bahvaḥ syāma prajāyemahi iti tā annam asṛijanta. Tasmād yatra kva ća varshati tad eva bhūyishṭham annam bhavati. Sā iyaṃ devatā aikshata, aham imās tisro devatā jīvena ātmanā anupraviśya nāma-rūpe vyākaravāṇi iti.*

[2] The name Muṇḍaka is derived from Muṇḍ, 'to shave,' because he who understands the doctrine of this Upanishad is 'shorn' of all error.

[3] Subjoined is the Mantra:—*Dvā suparṇā sayujā sakhāyā samānaṃ vṛiksham parishasvajāte, Tayor anyaḥ pippalam svādv atty an-aśnann anyo abhićākaśīti,* 'two birds associated together as friends inhabit the same tree. The one of them tastes the sweet fig, the other looks on

Two birds (the Paramātman and Jīvātman or supreme and individual souls) always united, of the same name, occupy the same tree (abide in the same body). One of them (the Jīvātman) enjoys the sweet fruit of the fig (or fruit of acts), the other looks on as a witness. Dwelling on the same tree (with the supreme Soul), the deluded (individual) soul, immersed (in worldly relations), is grieved by the want of power; but when it perceives the Ruler, separate (from worldly relations) and his glory, then its grief ceases. When the beholder sees the golden-coloured maker (of the world), the lord, the soul, the source of Brahmā, then having become wise, shaking off virtue and vice, without taint of any kind, he obtains the highest identity (Röer's edition, p. 305).

Here are two or three other examples from the same Upanishad :—

As the spider casts out and draws in (its web), as from a living man the hairs of the head and body spring forth, so is produced the universe from the indestructible Spirit (I. 1. 7).

As from a blazing fire consubstantial sparks proceed in a thousand ways, so from the imperishable (Spirit) various living souls are produced, and they return to him too (II. 1. 1).

As flowing rivers are resolved into the sea, losing their names and forms, so the wise, freed from name and form, pass into the divine Spirit, which is greater than the great. He who knows that supreme Spirit becomes spirit (III. 2. 8, 9).

One of the most ancient and important Upanishads is the Kaṭha. It enjoys considerable reputation in India, and is also well known by Sanskṛit students in Europe. It opens with the story of Naćiketas.

---

without enjoying.' S'an-kara, commenting on the Upanishad, explains *sakhāyā* by *samāna-khyātau*, 'of the same name.' He also remarks that the Pippala or Aśvattha, 'holy fig-tree,' having roots above and branches bent downwards, is allegorical, and that each tree, springing from an unperceived root, is emblematic of the body, which really springs from and is one with Brahma. In the Kaṭha VI. 1 and Bhagavad-gītā XV. 1–3 the same tree is said to typify the universe. It is supposed to be the male of the Vaṭa or Banyan (*Ficus Indica*).

He was the pious son of a sage who had given all his property to the priests, and who, in a fit of irritation, devoted his son to Death.

Naćiketas is described as going to Death's abode, and there, having propitiated Yama, he is told to choose three boons. The youth chose, for the first boon, that he might be restored to life and see his reconciled father once more; for the second, that he might know the fire by which heaven is gained. When asked to name the third boon, he addresses the god of death thus,—

Some say the soul exists after death, others say it does not exist. I request, as my third boon, that I may be instructed by thee in the true answer to this question.

Death tries to put him off, entreating him to choose any other boon than this; but the youth persisting in his demand to be enlightened as to the mysteries of the next world, Yama at length gives way and enlarges upon the desired theme in the following manner (Vallī II.):—

The good, the pleasant, these are separate ends,
The one or other all mankind pursue;
But those who seek the good, alone are blest;
Who choose the pleasant miss man's highest aim.
The sage the truth discerns, not so the fool.
But thou, my son, with wisdom hast abandoned
The fatal road of wealth that leads to death.
Two other roads there are all wide apart,
Ending in widely different goals—the one
Called ignorance, the other knowledge—this,
O Naćiketas, thou dost well to choose.
The foolish follow ignorance, but think
They tread the road of wisdom, circling round
With erring steps, like blind men led by blind.
The careless youth, by lust of gain deceived,
Knows but one world, one life; to him the Now
Alone exists, the Future is a dream.
The highest aim of knowledge is the soul;
This is a miracle, beyond the ken

Of common mortals, thought of though it be,
And variously explained by skilful teachers.
Who gains this knowledge is a marvel too.
He lives above the cares—the griefs and joys
Of time and sense—seeking to penetrate
The fathomless unborn eternal essence.
The slayer thinks he slays, the slain
Believes himself destroyed, the thoughts of both
Are false, the soul survives, nor kills, nor dies;
'Tis subtler than the subtlest, greater than
The greatest, infinitely small, yet vast,
Asleep, yet restless, moving everywhere
Among the bodies—ever bodiless—
Think not to grasp it by the reasoning mind;
The wicked ne'er can know it; soul alone
Knows soul, to none but soul is soul revealed.

In the third Vallī (3, 4, &c.) of the same Upanishad the soul is compared to a rider in a chariot, the body being the chariot, the intellect the charioteer, the mind the reins, the passions or senses the horses, and the objects of sense the roads. The unwise man neglects to apply the reins; in consequence of which the passions, like unrestrained vicious horses, rush about hither and thither, carrying the charioteer wherever they please.[1]

In the fifth Vallī (11) the following sentiment occurs:—

As the sun, the eye of the whole world, is not sullied by the defects of the (human) eye or of external objects, so the inner soul of all beings is not sullied by the misery of the world.

---

[1] Compare Manu II. 88, 'In the restraint of the organs running wild among objects of sense, which hurry him away hither and thither, a wise man should make diligent effort, like a charioteer restraining restive steeds.' So Plato in the Phaedrus (54, 74) compares the soul to a charioteer (the reason) driving a pair of winged steeds, one of which (the will) is obedient to the rein, and tries to control its wild and vicious yoke-fellow (the appetite): Τριχῇ διειλόμην ψυχὴν ἑκάστην, ἱππομόρφω μὲ νδύο τινὲ εἴδη, ἡνιοχικὸν δὲ εἶδος τρίτον, κ. τ. λ.

I now add a few extracts from one of the most modern of these treatises, called Śvetāśvatara,[1] which may serve to show how epithets of the Supreme Being are heaped together by the writers of the Upanishads without much order and often with apparent contradiction :—

Him may we know, the ruler of all rulers,
The god of gods, the lord of lords, the greater
Than all the greatest, the resplendent being,
The world's protector, worthy of all homage.
Of him there is not cause nor yet effect.
He is the cause, lord of the lord of causes,
None is there like him, none superior to him,
His power is absolute, yet various,
Dependent on himself, acting with knowledge,
He the one god is hidden in all beings,
Pervades their inner souls and rules their actions,
Dwelling within their hearts, a witness, thinker,
The singly perfect, without qualities.
He is the Universe's maker, he
Its knower, soul and origin of all,
Maker of time, endowed with every virtue,
Omniscient, lord of all embodied beings,
Lord of the triple qualities, the cause
Of man's existence, bondage and release,
Eternal, omnipresent, without parts,
All-knowing, tranquil, spotless, without blame,
The light, the bridge of immortality,
Subtler than what is subtlest, many-shaped,
One penetrator of the universe,
All-blest, unborn, incomprehensible,
Above, below, between, invisible
To mortal eyes, the mover of all beings,
Whose name is Glory, matchless, infinite,
The perfect spirit, with a thousand heads,
A thousand eyes, a thousand feet, the ruler

---

1 Of the Yajur-veda, though sometimes found (according to Colebrooke) in Atharva-veda collections. See Weber's Indische Studien, I. 420–439.

Of all that is, that was, that is to be,
Diffused through endless space, yet of the measure
Of a man's thumb, abiding in the heart,
Known only by the heart, whoever knows him
Gains everlasting peace and deathlessness.[1]

I close these extracts from the Upanishads by a metrical version of part of the first chapter of a short Upanishad called Maitrāyaṇi or Maitrāyaṇīya, belonging to the Black Yajur-veda:[2]—

In this decaying body, made of bones,
Skin, tendons, membranes, muscles, blood, saliva,
Full of putrescence and impurity,
What relish can there be for true enjoyment?[3]
In this weak body, ever liable
To wrath, ambition, avarice, illusion,
To fear, grief, envy, hatred, separation
From those we hold most dear, association
With those we hate; continually exposed
To hunger, thirst, disease, decrepitude,
Emaciation, growth, decline, and death,
What relish can there be for true enjoyment?
The universe is tending to decay,
Grass, trees, and animals spring up and die.
But what are they? Earth's mighty men are gone,
Leaving their joys and glories; they have passed
Out of this world into the realm of spirits.
But what are they? Beings greater still than these,
Gods, demigods, and demons, all have gone.

---

[1] Most of these epithets will be found in the following sections of the Śvetāśvatara Upanishad VI. 7, 8, 11, 17, 19, IV. 14, 17, 19, &c. Compare the extract from the Purusha-sūkta given at p. 21.

[2] Also called Maitrāyaṇī, Maitrāyaṇa, Maitrī, and Maitri. Under the latter name it has been well edited and translated for the Bibliotheca Indica by Professor E. B. Cowell. It is in seven chapters, the first of which was translated into prose by Sir W. Jones, but without any name. My version is partly based on his, but I have consulted Professor Cowell's more accurate translation.

[3] Compare Manu VI. 77.

But what are they? for others greater still
Have passed away, vast oceans have been dried,
Mountains thrown down, the polar star displaced,
The cords that bind the planets rent asunder,
The whole earth deluged with a flood of water,
E'en highest angels driven from their stations.
In such a world what relish can there be
For true enjoyment? deign to rescue us;
Thou only art our refuge, holy lord.[1]

---

[1] The following sentiment occurs in the text before the concluding line: *Andhodapāna-stho bheka iva aham asmin saṃsāre* :—

Living in such a world I seem to be
A frog abiding in a dried-up well.

Compare some of the Stoical reflections of Marcus Aurelius, given by Archdeacon F. W. Farrar in his 'Seekers after God:'—

'Oil, sweat, dirt, filthy water, all things disgusting—so is every part of life.'

'Enough of this wretched life, and murmuring, and apish trifles.'

'All the present time is a point in eternity. All things are little, changeable, perishable.'

CHAPTER III.

The Systems of Philosophy.

I MUST now advert in a general way to the six systems of philosophy which grew out of the Upanishads. They are sometimes called the six Śāstras or bodies of teaching, sometimes the Shaḍ Darśanas or six Demonstrations. They are—

1. The Nyāya, founded by Gotama.
2. The Vaiśeshika, by Kaṇāda.
3. The Sāṅ·khya, by Kapila.
4. The Yoga, by Patañjali.
5. The Mīmāṉsā, by Jaimini.
6. The Vedānta, by Bādarāyaṇa or Vyāsa.

They are delivered in Sūtras or aphorisms, which are held to be the basis of all subsequent teaching under each head. These Sūtras are often so brief and obscure as to be absolutely unintelligible without a commentary. They are commonly called 'aphorisms, but really are mere memorial suggestions of the briefest possible kind, skilfully contrived for aiding the recollection of the teachers of each system. Probably the first to comment upon the Sūtras thus delivered was the author of them himself. He was followed by a vast number of other commentators in succeeding generations (generally a triple set), and by writers who often embodied in treatises or compendiums of their own the tenets of the particular school to which they were attached. The most celebrated of all commentators is the great Śaṅ·kara Āćārya, a native of Malabar, who lived probably between 650 and 740 A.D., and wrote almost countless works, including commentaries on the Upanishads, Vedānta-sūtras, and Bhagavad-gītā.

It is as impossible to settle the date of any of the Sūtras with certainty as it is to determine the period of the composition of any single work in Sanskṛit literature. Moreover, it is scarcely practicable to decide as to which of the six systems of philosophy preceded the other in point of time, though probably the Sāṅkhya was the most ancient. All we can say is, that about 500 years before the commencement of the Christian era a great stir seems to have taken place in Indo-Āryan, as in Grecian minds, and indeed in thinking minds everywhere throughout the then civilized world. Thus when Buddha arose in India, Greece had her thinkers in the disciples of Pythagoras, Persia in those of Zoroaster,[1] and China in those of Confucius. Men began to ask themselves earnestly such questions as—What am I? whence have I come? whither am I going? How can I explain my consciousness of personal existence? What is the relationship between my material and immaterial nature? What is this world in which I find myself? Did a wise, good, and all-powerful Being create it out of nothing? or did it evolve itself out of an eternal germ? or did it come together by the combination of eternal atoms? If created by a Being of infinite wisdom, how can I account for the inequalities of condition in it—good and evil, happiness and misery? Has the Creator form, or is he formless? Has he any qualities or none?

Certainly in India no satisfactory solution of questions such as these was likely to be obtained from the prayers and hymns of the ancient Indo-Āryan poets, which, though

---

[1] Zoroaster himself, however, seems to have lived many centuries before. Pythagoras and Confucius were probably contemporaries of Buddha.

called Veda or 'knowledge' by the Brāhmans, did not even profess to furnish any real knowledge on these points, but merely gave expression to the first gropings of the human mind, searching for truth by the uncertain light of natural phenomena.[1]

Nor did the ritualistic Brāhmaṇas contribute anything to the elucidation of such topics. They merely encouraged the growth of a superstitious belief in the efficacy of sacrifices and fostered the increasing dependence of the multitude on a mediatorial caste of priests, supposed to be qualified to stand between them and an angry god. Still these momentous questions pressed for solution, and the minds of men finding no rest in mere traditional revelation, and no satisfaction in mere external rites, turned inwards, each thinker endeavouring to think out the great problems of life for himself by the aid of his own reason. Hence were composed those vague mystical rationalistic speculations called Upanishads, of which examples have been already given. Be it remembered that these treatises were not regarded as antagonistic to revelation, but rather as completory of it. They were held to be an integral portion of the Veda or true knowledge; and, even more —they so rose in the estimation of thoughtful persons that they ended by taking rank as its most important portion, its grandest and noblest utterance, the apex to which all previous revelation tended. Probably the simple fact was, that as it was found impossible to stem the progress of free inquiry, the Brāhmans with true wisdom determined on making rationalistic speculation their own, and dignifying its first development in the Upanishads with the title of Veda. Probably, too, some

---

[1] The second aphorism of the Sān-khya-kārikā states distinctly that Ānuśravika, or knowledge derived from S'ruti—the revelation contained in the Veda—is ineffectual to deliver from the bondage of existence.

of their number (like Jāvāli) became themselves infected with the spirit of scepticism, and were not to be restrained from prosecuting free philosophical investigations for themselves.

There are not wanting, however, evident indications that the Kshatriyas or second caste were the first introducers into India of rationalistic speculation. The great Buddha was a Kshatriya, and the Ćhāndogya Upanishad (V. 3) has a remarkable passage which, as bearing upon this point, I here abridge (Röer's edition, p. 315) :—

A youth called S'vetaketu (the son of a Brāhman named Gautama) repaired to the court of the king of Pańćāla, Pravāhaṇa, who said to him, 'Boy, has thy father instructed thee ?' 'Yes, sir,' replied he. 'Knowest thou where men ascend when they quit this world ?' 'No, sir,' replied he. 'Knowest thou how they return ?' 'No, sir,' replied he. 'Knowest thou why the region to which they ascend is not filled up ?' 'No, sir,' replied he. 'Why then saidst thou that thou hadst been instructed ?' The boy returned sorrowful to his father's house and said, 'The king asked me certain questions which I could not answer.' His father said, 'I know not the answers.' Then he, Gautama, the father of the boy, went to the king's house. When he arrived, the king received him hospitably and said, 'O Gautama, choose as a boon the best of all worldly possessions.' He replied, 'O king, thine be all worldly possessions; tell me the answers to the questions you asked my son.' The king became distressed in mind (knowing that a Brāhman could not be refused a request), and begged him to tarry for a time. Then he said, 'Since you have sought this information from me, and since this knowledge has never been imparted to any other Brāhman before thee, therefore the right of imparting it has remained with the Kshatriyas among all the people of the world.'

This story certainly appears to favour the supposition that men of the caste next in rank to that of Brāhmans were the first to venture upon free philosophical speculation. However that may be, it was not long before Brāhmanism and rationalism advanced hand in hand, making only one compact, that however inconsistent with each other, neither should declare the other to be a false guide. A Brāhman might be a rationalist, or both rationalist and Brāhman might live together in harmony, provided both gave a nominal assent to the Veda, maintained the inviolability of caste, and the ascendency and trustworthiness of the Brāhmans, as teachers both of religion and philosophy.[1]

And no doubt some common philosophical creed must have prevailed among such teachers long before the crystallisation of rationalistic speculation into separate systems. If not distinctly developed in the Upanishads, it is clearly traceable throughout Manu;[2] and as it is not only the faith of every Indian philosopher at the present day, but also of the greater number of thinking Brāhmans, whether disciples of any particular philosophical school or not, and indeed of the greater number of educated Hindūs, whether nominal adherents of Vishṇu or Śiva, or to whatever caste they may belong—its principal features may be advantageously stated before pointing out the chief differences between the six systems.

1. In the first place, then, rationalistic Brāhmanism—as I propose to call this common faith—holds the eternity of soul, both retrospectively and prospectively.[3] It looks upon soul as of two kinds: *α.* the supreme Spirit or

---

[1] The summary of Buddhism given here in the previous edition of 'Indian Wisdom' has been omitted, because the reader who wishes for an account of Buddhism can refer to my recent volume called 'Buddhism,' published by John Murray, of Albemarle Street, London.

[2] See Manu XII. 12, 15–18.

[3] Plato appears to have held the same: *Ψυχὴ πᾶσα ἀθάνατος, τὸ γαρ ἀεικίνητον ἀθάνατον*, Phaed. 51. And again: *'Επειδὴ δὲ ἀγένητόν ἐστι, καὶ ἀδιάφθορον αὐτὸ ἀνάγκη εἶναι*, Phaed. 52. And again: *Τοῦτο δὲ οὔτ' ἀπόλλυσθαι οὔτε γίγνεσθαι δυνατόν.* Cicero expresses it thus: *Id autem nec nasci potest nec mori*, Tusc. Quaest. I. 23. Plato, however, seems to have given no eternity to individual souls, except as emanations from the divine; and in Timaeus 44 he distinguishes two parts of the soul, one immortal, the other mortal.

Self (called variously *Atman, Paramātman, Brahman, Purusha,* &c.); *b.* the personal individuated spirit of living beings (*jīvātman*);[1] and it maintains that if any entity is eternal it cannot have had a beginning, or else it must have an end. Hence the personal spirit of every human being, just as the supreme Spirit, has existed everlastingly and will never cease to exist.[2]

2. In the second place, this creed asserts the eternity of the visible universe, or of that substance out of which the universe has been evolved; in other words, of its substantial or material cause.[3] But, according to one system (the

---

[1] All the systems, as we shall see, are not equally clear about the existence of a supreme Spirit. One at least practically ignores it. I use the word 'spirit' (in preference to 'soul') as the best translation of Ātman, Brahman, and Purusha, because 'soul' may convey the idea of thinking and feeling, whereas pure spirit, according to Hindū philosophy, neither thinks nor feels, because that would imply the existence of some object of thought and feeling. The translation 'self' seems scarcely more suitable than 'soul.'

[2] The Muslims have two words for eternity: 1. ازل *azl*, 'that eternity which has no beginning' (whence God is called *Azalī*, 'having no beginning'); and 2. ابد *abd*, 'that eternity which has no end.'

[3] The term for substantial or material cause is *samavāyi-kāraṇa*, literally, 'inseparable inherent cause;' in the Vedānta *upādāna-kāraṇa* is used. Though the Greek philosophers are not very definite in their views as to the eternity of matter or its nature, yet they seem to have acquiesced generally in the independent existence of some sort of primordial substance. Plato appears to have held that the elements before the creation were shapeless and soulless, but were moulded and arranged by the Creator (Timaeus 27) out of some invisible and formless essence (*ἀνόρατον εἶδός τι καὶ ἄμορφον*, Timaeus 24). Aristotle in one passage describes the views of older philosophers who held that primeval substance was affected and made to undergo changes by some sort of affections like the Sānkhya Guṇas, whence all the universe was developed: *Τῆς μὲν οὐσίας ὑπομενούσης τοῖς δὲ πάθεσι μεταβαλλούσης, τοῦτο στοιχεῖον καὶ ταύτην τὴν ἀρχὴν φασιν εἶναι τῶν ὄντων*, Metaph. I. 3. (See Wilson's Sāṅkhya-kārikā, p. 53.) Aristotle adds his own opinion, 'It is necessary there should be a certain nature (*φύσις*)—either one or more—out of which other entities are produced.'

Sāṅkhya), the external world is evolved out of an eternally existing productive germ united to eternally existing individual spirits. According to another (the Vedānta), this external world is evolved out of the eternal Illusion (Māyā), which overspreads the one eternal Spirit and is one with it, though having no real existence. In truth, a Hindū philosopher's belief in the eternity of the world's substance, whether that substance has a real material existence or is simply illusory, arises from that fixed article of his creed, '*Ex nihilo nihil fit*,' *nāvastuno vastu-siddhiḥ*. In other words, *A-sataḥ saj jāyeta kutas*, 'How can an entity be produced out of a nonentity?'[1]

3. In the third place, the spirit, though itself sheer thought and knowledge, can only exercise thought, con-

---

[1] Οὐδὲν γίνεται ἐκ τοῦ μὴ ὄντος, 'Nothing is produced out of nothing.' All the ancient philosophers of Greece and Rome seem also to have agreed upon this point, as Aristotle affirms (περὶ γὰρ ταύτης ὁμογνωμόνουσι τῆς δόξης ἅπαντες οἱ περὶ φύσεως). Lucretius (I. 150) starts with laying down the same principle:—'Principium hinc nobis exordia sumet Nullam rem e nihilo gigni divinitus unquam.' Aristotle, in the third chapter of the first book of his Metaphysics, informs us that Thales made the primitive substance out of which the universe originated water, Anaximenes and Diogenes made it air, Heracleitus made it fire, Empedocles combined earth, air, fire, and water. Anaximander, on the other hand, regarded the primordial germ as an indeterminate but infinite or boundless principle (τὸ ἄπειρον). Other philosophers affirmed something similar in referring everything back to a confused chaos. Parmenides made Desire his first principle, and Hesiod, quoted by Aristotle, says poetically,—

'First indeed of all was chaos; then afterwards
Earth with her broad breast (cf. Sanskṛit *pṛithivī*);
Then Desire (ἔρος), who is pre-eminent among all the Immortals.'

Lastly, the Eleatics, like the Indian Vedāntists, were thoroughly pantheistic, and held that the universe was God and God the universe; in other words, that God was τὸ ἕν, or the only one existing thing. With all these accounts compare the Ṛig-veda hymn on the creation, translated on p. 19.

sciousness, sensation, and cognition, and indeed can only act and will when connected with external and objective objects of sensation,[1] invested with some bodily form[2] and joined to mind (*manas*), which last (viz., mind) is an internal organ of sense (*antaḥ-karaṇa*)[3]—a sort of inlet of

---

[1] It is difficult to find any suitable word to express what the Hindūs mean by material objects. There seems, in real truth, to be no proper Sanskṛit word equivalent to 'matter' in its usual English sense. *Vastu*, as applied to the 'one reality,' is the term for the Vedāntist's universal Spirit; *dravya* stands for soul, mind, time, and space, as well as the five elements; *mūrtti* is anything which has definite limits, and therefore includes mind and the four elements, but not *ākāśa*, 'ether;' *pradhāna* is the original producer of the Sāṅkhya system; *padārtha* is used for the seven categories of the Vaiśeshika. What is here meant is not necessarily a collection of material atoms, nor, again, that imperceptible substance propounded by some as lying underneath and supporting all visible phenomena (disbelieved in by Berkeley), and holding together the attributes or qualities of everything, but rather what is seen, heard, felt, tasted, and touched, which is perhaps best denoted by the Sanskṛit word *vishaya*, the terms *samavāyi-kāraṇa* and *upādāna-kāraṇa* being generally used for the substantial or the material cause of the universe.

[2] All the systems assign to each person two bodies: *a.* an exterior or gross body (*sthūla-śarīra*); *b.* an interior or subtle body (*sūkshma-śarīra* or *liṅga-śarīra*). The last is necessary as a vehicle for the spirit when the gross body is dissolved, accompanying it through all its transmigrations and sojournings in heaven or hell, and never becoming separated from it till its emancipation is effected. The Vedānta affirms the existence of a third body, called *kāraṇa-śarīra* or causal body, described as a kind of inner rudiment or latent embryo of the body existing with the spirit, and by some regarded as Ignorance united with the spirit in dreamless sleep. The Platonists and other Greek and Roman philosophers seem to have held a similar doctrine as to a subtle material envelope investing the soul after death, serving as its ὄχημα or vehicle. See Plato, Timaeus 17. This is like the idea of a deceased person's ghost or shade (εἴδωλον, umbra, imago, simulacrum). Cf. Virgil, Aeneid, VI. 390, 701.

[3] *Manas* is often taken as the general term applicable to all the mental powers, but *Manas* is properly a subdivision of *antaḥ-karaṇa*, which is divided into *Buddhi*, 'perception or intellection;' *Ahankāra*,

thought to the spirit—belonging only to the body, only existing with it, and quite as distinct from the spirit as any of the external organs of the body.[1] The supreme Spirit has thus connected itself in successive ages with objects and forms, becoming manifest either as Brahmā the creator, or in the form of other gods, as Vishṇu and Śiva, or again in the form of men.

4. Fourthly, this union of the spirit with the body is productive of bondage, and in the case of human spirits, of misery, for when once so united the spirit begins to apprehend objects through the senses, receiving therefrom painful and pleasurable impressions. It also becomes conscious of personal existence and individuality; then it commences acting; but all action, whether good or bad, leads to bondage, because every act inevitably entails a consequence, according to the maxim, *Avaśyam eva bhoktavyaṃ kṛitaṃ karma śubhāśubham*, 'The fruit of every action good or bad must of necessity be eaten.' Hence, if an act be good it must be rewarded, and if bad it must be punished.[2]

5. Fifthly, in order to accomplish the entire working

'self-consciousness;' and *Manas*, 'volition or determination;' to which the Vedānta adds a fourth division, *Ćitta*, 'the thinking or reasoning organ.'

[1] This idea of the mind agrees to a great extent with the doctrine of Lucretius, stated in III. 94, &c. :—

'Primum animum dico (mentem quem saepe vocamus)
In quo consilium vitae regimenque locatum est,
Esse hominis partem nihilo minus ac manus et pes
Atque oculi partes animantis totius extant.'

The remainder of his description of the mind is very interesting in connection with the Hindū theory.

[2] In the Pańća-tantra (II. 135, 136) we read: 'An evil act follows a man, passing through a hundred thousand transmigrations; in like manner the act of a high-minded man. As shade and sunlight are ever closely joined together, so an act and the agent stick close to each other.'

out of these consequences or 'ripenings of acts,' as they are called (*karma-vipākāḥ*),[1] it is not enough that the personal spirit goes to heaven or to hell. For all the systems contend that even in heaven or hell merit or demerit, resulting from the inexorable retributive efficacy of former acts, continues clinging to the spirit as grease does to a pot after it has been emptied. The necessity for removal to a place of reward or punishment is indeed admitted;[2] but this is not effectual or final. In order that the consequences of acts may be entirely worked out, the spirit must leave heaven or hell and return to corporeal existence. Thus it has to pass through innumerable bodies, migrating into higher, intermediate, or lower forms, from a god[3] to a demon, man, animal, or plant, or even

---

[1] Bad consequences are called *Dur-vipāka*. Some of these, in the shape of diseases, &c., are detailed by Manu (XI. 48–52). Thus any one who has stolen gold in a former life will suffer from whitlows on his nails, a drinker of spirits will have black teeth, and the killer of a Brahman, consumption. In the S'abda-kalpa-druma, under the head of *Karma-vipāka*, will be found a long catalogue of the various diseases with which men are born as the fruit of evil deeds committed in former states of existence, and a declaration as to the number of births through which each disease will be protracted, unless expiations (*prāyaśćitta*) be performed in the present life, as described in the eleventh book of Manu.

[2] The twenty-one hells (*Narakas*) are enumerated in Manu IV. 88–90. One is a place of terrific darkness; another a pit of red-hot charcoal; another a forest whose leaves are swords; another is filled with fetid mud; another is paved with iron spikes. These are not to be confounded with the seven places under the earth, of which Pātāla is one, the abode of a kind of serpent demon. The Buddhists have one hundred and thirty-six hells, with regular gradations of suffering. Hindūs and Buddhists have also numerous heavens. The former make six regions rising above earth, the seventh; viz., *bhūr* (earth), *bhuvar*, *svar*, *mahar*, *janar*, *tapaḥ*, *satya*.

[3] The gods themselves are only finite beings. They are nothing but portions of the existing system of a perishing universe. In fact, they are represented as actually feeding on the oblations offered to them (see Bhagavad-gītā III. 11); they go through penances (see Manu XI. 221); they are liable to passions and affections like men and animals, and are

a stone, according to its various shades of merit or demerit.[1]

6. Sixthly, this transmigration of the spirit through a constant succession of bodies is to be regarded as the root of all evil.[2] Moreover, by it all the misery, in-

---

subject, as regards their corporeal part, to the same law of dissolution, while their souls obey the same necessity of ultimate absorption into the supreme soul. The following occurs in the Sān-khya-kārikā (p. 3 of Wilson):—'Many thousands of Indras and other gods have, through time, passed away in every mundane age, for time cannot be overcome.' Muir's Texts, vol. v. p. 16.

[1] According to Manu XII. 3, *Śubhāśubha-phalaṃ karma mano-vāg-deha-sambhavaṃ karma-jā gatayo nṛīṇām uttamādhama-madhyamāḥ*, 'An act either mental, verbal, or corporeal bears good or evil fruit; the various transmigrations of men through the highest, middle, and lowest stages are produced by acts.' This triple order of transmigration is afterwards (XII. 40, &c.) explained to be the passage of the soul through deities, men, and beasts and plants, according to the dominance of one or other of the three Guṇas, goodness, passion, or darkness. And each of these three degrees of transmigration has three sub-degrees. The highest of the first degree is Brahmā himself, the lowest of the lowest is any *sthāvara* or 'stationary substance,' which is explained to mean either a vegetable or a mineral; other lowest forms of the lowest degree are in an upward order worms, insects, fish, reptiles, snakes, tortoises, &c. Again, in VI. 61, 63, we read: Let the man who has renounced the world reflect on the transmigrations of men caused by the fault of their acts (*karma-dosha*); on their downfall into hell and their torments in the abode of Yama; on their formation again in the womb and the glidings of the soul through ten millions of other wombs. Again, in XII. 54, 55, &c.: Those who have committed great crimes, having passed through terrible hells for many series of years, at the end of that time pass through various bodies. A Brahman-killer enters the body of a dog, boar, ass, camel, bull, goat, sheep, stag, bird, &c. The violator of the bed of a Guru migrates a hundred times into the forms of grasses, shrubs, plants, &c. In I. 49, XI. 143–146, it is clearly implied that trees and vegetables of all kinds have internal consciousness (*antaḥ-sañjñā*), and are susceptible of pleasure and pain.

[2] The doctrine of metempsychosis, however, does not appear to have taken hold of the Hindū mind when the Mantras were composed. There seems at least to be no allusion to it in the Ṛig-veda (see note, p. 18). It

equality of fortune, and diversity of character in the world is to be explained.[1] For even great genius, aptitude for special work, and innate excellence are not natural gifts,

---

begins to appear, though not clearly defined, in the Brāhmaṇas, and is fully developed in the Upanishads, Darśanas, and Manu. A passage in the Śatapatha-brāhmaṇa (XI. 6. 1. 1.), quoted by Professor Weber and Dr. Muir, describes animals and plants as revenging in a future state of existence injuries and death inflicted on them by men in this life.

In Greece and Rome the doctrine of transmigration seems never to have impressed itself deeply on the popular mind. It was confined to philosophers and their disciples, and was first plainly taught by Pythagoras, who is said to have asserted that he remembered his own previous existences. He was followed by Plato, who is supposed by some to have been indebted to Hindū writers for his views on this subject. In the Timaeus (72, 73) he affirms his opinion that those who have lived unrighteously and effeminately will, at their next birth, be changed to women; those who have lived innocently but frivolously will become birds; those who have lived without knowledge of the truths of philosophy will become beasts; and those whose lives have been marked by the extreme of ignorance and folly will become fishes, oysters, &c. He sums up thus: *Κατὰ ταῦτα δὴ πάντα τότε καὶ νῦν διαμείβεται τὰ ζῶα εἰς ἄλληλα, νοῦ καὶ ἀνοίας ἀποβολῇ καὶ κτήσει μεταβαλλόμενα.* Virgil, in the sixth book of the Aeneid (680–751), describes the condition of certain souls, which, after going through a sort of purgatory for a thousand years in the lower regions, again ascend to earth and occupy new bodies.

The Jews seem to have known something of the doctrine, if we may judge by the question proposed to our Lord: 'Who did sin, this man (*i.e.*, in a former life) or his parents, that he was born blind?' (John ix. 2).

[1] Among Greek philosophers, Aristotle, in the eleventh book of his Metaphysics (ch. 10), goes into the origin of evil, and his view may therefore be compared with that of Hindū philosophers. He recognizes good as a paramount principle in the world, but admits the power of evil, and considers matter (ὕλη) as its prime and only source, much in the same way as the Gnostics and other early Christian philosophical sects, who, like Indian philosophers, denied the possibility of anything being produced out of nothing, and repudiated the doctrine that God could in any way be connected with evil. They, therefore, supposed the eternal existence of a sluggish, inert substance, out of which the world was formed by God, but which contained in itself the principle of evil.

but the result of habits formed and powers developed through perhaps millions of previous existences. So, again, sufferings of all kinds—weaknesses, sicknesses, and moral depravity—are simply the consequences of acts done by each spirit, of its own free will, in former bodies, which acts exert upon that spirit an irresistible power called very significantly *Adṛishṭa,* because felt and *not seen.*

Thus the spirit has to bear the consequences of *its own acts only.* It is tossed hither and thither at the mercy of a force set in motion by itself alone, but which can never be guarded against, because its operation depends on past actions wholly beyond control and even unremembered. Nor does the absence of all recollections of acts done in former states of existence seem to strike Hindū philosophers as an objection to their theory of transmigration. They say that we do not remember our state of infancy and childhood up to the age of three or four years, and yet we do not doubt that the individuality of old people is different from their earliest individuality.[1] Most of the

---

[1] The Garbha Upanishad (4) attributes the loss of memory to the pain and pressure suffered by the soul in the act of leaving the womb. Cases are recorded of men who were gifted with the power of recollecting former existences. Gautama Buddha, we know, is said to have possessed the power. In the Phaedo of Plato (47) Cebes is described as saying to Socrates, 'According to that doctrine which you are frequently in the habit of advancing, if it is true, that all knowledge is nothing else than reminiscence (ὅτι ἡμῖν ἡ μάθησις οὐκ ἄλλο τι ἢ ἀνάμνησις τυγχάνει οὖσα), it is surely necessary that we must at some former time have learned what we now remember. But this is impossible, unless our soul existed somewhere before it came into this human form.' Cicero, in Tusc. Quaest. I. 24, says, speaking of the soul, 'Habet primam memoriam, et eam infinitam rerum innumerabilium, quam quidem Plato recordationem esse vult superioris vitae.' Cf. S'akuntalā, Act V. 104, 'Can it be that the dim memory of events long past, or friendships formed in other states of being, flits like a passing shadow o'er the spirit?' Virgil (Aeneid VI. 714) wisely

systems evade the difficulty by maintaining that at each death the soul is divested of mind, understanding, consciousness, and brain-memory.

7. Seventhly and lastly, from a consideration of these essential articles of Hindū Rationalism it is plain that the great aim of philosophy is to teach a man to abstain from every kind of action; from liking or disliking, from loving or hating, and even from being indifferent to anything.

The living personal spirit must shake off the fetters of action, and getting rid of body, mind, and all sense of separate personality, return to the condition of simple spirit.

This constitutes *Pramā* or *Jṅāna*, the true measure of all existing difficulties—the right apprehension of truth—which, if once acquired by the spirit, confers upon it final emancipation, whether called *Mukti*, *Moksha*, *Niḥśreyasa*, *Apavarga*, or *Nirvāṇa*. This, in short, is the *summum bonum* of philosophical Brāhmanism; this is the only real bliss,—the loss of all personality and separate identity by absorption into the supreme and only really existing Being—mere life with nothing to live for, mere joy with nothing to rejoice about, and mere thought with nothing upon which thought is to be exercised.[1]

Having thus attempted to set forth the common tenets of Indian philosophy, I must next indicate the principal points in which the systems differ from each other.

---

makes the souls who are to occupy new bodies upon earth throng the banks of Lethe that they may drink a deep draught of oblivion from its waters.

[1] Mr. Hardwick has well shown that the great boon conferred by the Gospel, in contradistinction to these false systems, is the recognition of man's responsible free agency and the permanence of his personality. 'Not to be' is the melancholy result of the religion and philosophy of the Hindūs. See 'Christ and other Masters,' vol. i. p. 355. Christianity satisfies the deepest want of man's religious life, viz., to know and love God as a person. See Canon Liddon's 'Elements of Religion,' p. 36.

CHAPTER IV.

The Nyāya.

We begin with the Nyāya of Gotama or Gautama, with its important supplement, the Vaiśeshika, not because this is first in order of time (see p. 46), but because it is generally the first studied, and much of its terminology is adopted by the other systems.[1]

The word Nyāya signifies 'going into a subject,' that is, investigating it analytically. In this sense of 'analysis,' Nyāya is exactly opposed to the word San·khyā, 'synthesis.' It is common to suppose that the Nyāya is chiefly concerned with logic; but this is merely one part of a single topic. The fact rather is that this system was intended to furnish a correct method of philosophical inquiry into *all the objects and subjects* of human knowledge, including, *amongst others*, the process of reasoning and laws of thought. The Nyāya proper differs from its later development, the Vaiśeshika, by propounding sixteen topics in its first Sūtra. The first topic of these sixteen is *Pramāṇa*,

---

[1] The Nyāya Sūtras, consisting of five books, with the commentary, were printed at Calcutta in 1828, under the title of Nyāya-sūtra-vṛitti. Four of the five books were edited and translated by the late Dr. Ballantyne. He also published the Nyāya compendium, called Tarka-san·graha. A favourite text-book of this system is the Bhāshā-paricćheda, with its commentary, called Siddhānta-muktāvalī. This has been edited and translated by Dr. Röer. The Vaiśeshika Sūtras, consisting of ten books, have been edited and translated by Mr. A. E. Gough. Professor E. B. Cowell's edition of the Kusumāñjali, a Nyāya treatise proving the existence of a God, is a most interesting work.

that is, the means or instruments by which *Pramā* or the right measure of any subject is to be obtained. Under this head are enunciated the different processes by which the mind arrives at true and accurate knowledge.

These processes are declared in the third Sūtra of the first book to be four, viz.:—

a. *Pratyaksha*, 'perception by the senses.' b. *Anumāna*, 'inference.' c. *Upamāna*, 'comparison' or 'analogy.' d. *Sabda*, 'verbal authority' or 'trustworthy testimony,' including Vedic revelation.

The treatment of the second of these, viz., inference, possesses more interest for Europeans, as indicating that the Hindūs have not, like other nations, borrowed their logic and metaphysics from the Greeks.

Inference is divided in Sūtra I. 32 into five Avayavas or 'members.'

1. The *pratijñā* or proposition (stated hypothetically).
2. The *hetu* or reason.
3. The *udāharaṇa* (sometimes called *nidarśana*) or example (equivalent to the major premiss).
4. The *upanaya* or application of the reason (equivalent to the minor premiss).
5. The *nigamana* or conclusion. (*i.e.*, the *pratijñā* or 'proposition' re-stated as proved).

This method of splitting an inference or argument into five divisions is familiarly illustrated by native commentators thus:—

1. The hill is fiery; 2. for it smokes; 3. whatever smokes is fiery, as a kitchen-hearth (or, inversely, not as a lake, which is invariably without fire); 4. this hill smokes; 5. therefore this hill is fiery.

Here we have a combination of enthymeme and syllogism, which seems clumsy by the side of Aristotle's more concise method; the fourth and fifth members being repetitions of the second and first, which, therefore, appear superfluous. But it possesses some advantages when regarded, not as a syllogism, but as a full and complete rhetorical statement of an argument.

Perhaps the most noticeable peculiarity in the Indian method, stamping it as an original and independent analysis of the laws of thought, is the use of the curious terms, *Vyāpti*, 'invariable pervasion' or 'concomitance'; *Vyāpaka*, 'pervader' or 'invariably pervading attribute'; and *Vyāpya*, 'invariably pervaded.' These terms are employed in making a universal affirmation or in affirming universal distribution; as, for example, 'Wherever there is smoke there is fire.' 'Wherever there is humanity there is mortality.' In such cases an Indian logician always expresses himself by saying that there is an invariably pervading concomitance of fire with smoke and of mortality with humanity.

Similarly, fire and mortality are called the pervaders (*Vyāpaka*), smoke and humanity the pervaded (*Vyāpya*). The first argument would therefore be thus briefly stated by a *Naiyāyika*: 'The mountain has invariably fire-pervaded smoke, therefore it has fire.'

To show the importance attached to a right understanding of this technical expression *Vyāpti*, and to serve as a specimen of a Naiyāyika writer's style, I now make an abridged extract from San-kara-miśra's comment on the fourteenth Sūtra of the first daily lesson of the third book of the Vaiśeshika Sūtras (Gough, p. 86):—

It may be asked, What is this invariable concomitance? (*Nanu keyaṃ vyāptiḥ*). It is not merely a relation of co-extension. Nor is it the relation of totality. For if you say that invariable concomitance is the connection of the middle term with the whole of the major term (*kṛitsnasya sādhyasya sādhana-sambandhaḥ*), such connection does not exist in the case of smoke, &c. [for although fire exists wherever smoke exists, smoke does not always exist where fire exists, not being found in red-hot iron]. Nor is it natural conjunction; for the nature of a thing is the thing's proper mode of being. Nor is it invariable co-inherence of the major, which is absent only when there is absolute non-existence of that of which the middle is predicated; for volcanic fire must always be non-existent in a kitchen-hearth, though smoky. Nor is it the not being a subject of incompatibility with the predicate. Nor is it the possession of a form determined by the same connection as something else; as, for instance, the being fiery is not determined by connection with smoke, for the being fiery is more extensive. We proceed, then, to state that invariable concomitance is a connection requiring no qualifying term or limitation (*an-aupādhikaḥ sambandhaḥ*).[1] It is an extensiveness co-extensive with the predicate (*sādhya-vyāpaka-vyāpakatvam*). In other words, invariable concomitance is invariable co-inherence of the predicate.[2]

The second head or topic of the Nyāya is *Prameya*, by which is meant all the objects or subjects of *Pramā*—those points, in short, about which correct knowledge is to be obtained. This topic includes all the most important subjects investigated by Indian philosophy. The Prameyas are twelve, as given in the ninth Sūtra; thus:—

1. Soul (*ātman*). 2. Body (*śarīra*). 3. Senses (*indriya*). 4. Objects of sense (*artha*). 5. Understanding or intellection (*buddhi*). 6. Mind (*manas*). 7. Activity (*pravṛitti*). 8. Faults (*dosha*). 9. Transmigration (*pretya-bhāva*). 10. Consequences or fruits (*phala*). 11. Pain (*duḥkha*). 12. Emancipation (*apavarga*).

In his first topic Gautama provides for hearing opposing disputants who desire to discuss fairly any of these Prameyas which form his second topic.

With regard to his fourteen other topics, they seem to

---

[1] Hence, 'the mountain is smoky because it has fire' is not *vyāpti*, but *ati-vyāpti*, because the *upādhi* or qualification *ārdrendana-jāta*, 'produced by wet wood,' must be added to make the argument correct. When the middle term (fire) and the major (smoke) are made co-extensive then the fault of *ati-vyāpti* is removed.

[2] It would be difficult to convey to a general reader any idea of the terseness with which the use of long compounds enables all this to be expressed in the original Sanskṛit. Of course the obscurity of the style is proportionably great, and the difficulty of translation enhanced. Mr. Gough, however, is not responsible for every word of the above.

be not so much philosophical categories as an enumeration of the regular stages through which a controversy is likely to pass. In India argument slides into wrangling disputation even more easily than in Europe, and these remaining topics certainly illustrate very curiously the captious propensities of a Hindū disputant, leading him to be quick in repartee and ready with specious objections in opposition to the most conclusive logic.

There is, first, the state of *Saṃśaya*, or 'doubt about the point to be discussed.' Next, there must be a *Prayojana*, or 'motive for discussing it.' Next, a *Dṛishṭānta*, or 'familiar example,' must be adduced in order that a *Siddhānta*, or 'established conclusion,' may be arrived at. Then comes an objector with his *Avayava*, or 'argument' split up, as we have seen, into five members. Next follows the *Tarka*, or 'refutation (*reductio ad absurdum*) of his objection,' and the *Nirṇaya*, or 'ascertainment of the true state of the case.' But this is not enough to satisfy a Hindū's passion for disputation. Every side of a question must be examined—every possible objection stated—and so a further *Vāda*, or 'controversy,' takes place, which of course leads to *Jalpa*, 'mere wrangling,' followed by *Vitaṇḍa*, 'cavilling'; *Hetv-ābhāsa*, 'fallacious reasoning';[1] *Ćhala*, 'quibbling artifices'; *Jāti*, 'futile replies'; and *Nigraha-ṣthāna*, 'the putting an end to all discussion' by a demonstration of the objector's incapacity for argument.

The above are Gotama's sixteen topics. After enumerating them he proceeds to state how deliverance from the misery of repeated births is to be attained; thus,—

---

[1] As an example of fallacious argument may be taken the sixteenth Aphorism of the third book of the Vaiśeshika Sūtras, *yasmād vishāṇī tasmād aśvaḥ*, 'because this has horns, therefore it is a horse;' or the next Sūtra, *yasmād vishāṇī tasmād gauḥ*, 'because it has horns, therefore it is a cow,' which last is the fallacy of 'undistributed middle.'

Misery, birth, activity, fault, false notions; on the removal of these in turn (beginning with the last), there is the removal also of that which precedes it; then ensues final emancipation.

That is to say, from false notions comes the fault of liking, disliking, or being indifferent to anything; from that fault proceeds activity; from this mistaken activity proceed actions involving either merit or demerit, which merit or demerit forces a man *nolens volens* to pass through repeated births for the sake of its reward or punishment. From these births proceed misery, and it is the aim of philosophy to correct the false notions at the root of this misery.

A Naiyāyika commentator, Vātsyāyana, thus comments on the foregoing statement (Banerjea, p. 185):—

From false notion proceed partiality and prejudice; thence come the faults of detraction, envy, delusion, intoxication, pride, avarice. Acting with a body, a person commits injury, theft, and unlawful sensualities,—becomes false, harsh, and slanderous. This vicious activity produces demerit. But to do acts of charity, benevolence, and service with the body; to be truthful, useful, agreeable in speech, or given to repetition of the Veda; to be kind, disinterested, and reverential—these produce merit (*dharma*). Hence merit and demerit are fostered by activity. This activity is the cause of vile as well as honourable births. Attendant on birth is pain. That comprises the feeling of distress, trouble, disease, and sorrow. Emancipation is the cessation of all these. What intelligent person will not desire emancipation from all pain? For, it is said, food mixed with honey and poison is to be rejected. Pleasure joined with pain is to be avoided.

I pass at once to the most important part of the Nyāya system, its supplement:—

The Vaiśeshika.

We now come to the *Vaiśeshika* development of the Nyāya, attributed to an author Kaṇāda.[1] This is not

[1] This was probably a mere nickname, meaning 'Feeder on Atoms.' He is also called Ulūka. Gautama, the author of the Nyāya proper,

so much a branch of this system as a supplement to it, extending the Nyāya to physical inquiries, which it does very imperfectly, it is true, and often with strange fancies and blunders; but, nevertheless, with occasional exactness and not unfrequently with singular sagacity. It is certainly the most interesting of all the systems, both from its more practical character and from the parallels it offers to European philosophical ideas. It begins by arranging its inquiries under seven *Padārthas*, which, as they are more properly categories (*i.e.*, an enumeration of certain general properties or attributes that may be predicated or affirmed of existing things[1]), are now the generally received categories of *Naiyāyikas*. They are as follow: 1. Substance (*dravya*). 2. Quality or property (*guṇa*). 3. Act or action (*karman*). 4. Generality or community of properties (*sāmānya*). 5. Particularity or individuality (*viśesha*). 6. Co-inherence or perpetual intimate relation (*samavāya*). 7. Non-existence or negation of existence (*abhāva*).[2]

---

had also a nickname, *Aksha-pāda*, 'eye-footed,' having his eyes always fixed in abstraction on his feet, or supernaturally gifted with eyes in his feet, because too absent to see with those in his head.

[1] Thus man is a substance, so also is a chair and a stone; whiteness, blackness, breadth, and length, though very different things, are yet all qualities, &c.

[2] It is interesting to compare the ten Aristotelian categories. They are: 1. Οὐσία, 'Substance.' 2. Ποσόν, 'How much?' 'Quantity.' 3. Ποιόν, 'Of what kind?' 'Quality.' 4. Πρός τι, 'In relation to what?' 'Relation.' 5. Ποιεῖν, 'Action.' 6. Πάσχειν, 'Passiveness' or 'Passivity.' 7. Ποῦ, 'Where?' 'Position in space.' 8. Πότε, 'When?' 'Position in time.' 9. Κεῖσθαι, 'Local situation.' 10. Ἔχειν, 'Possession.' Mr. J. S. Mill, in his Logic, declares that this enumeration is both redundant and defective. Some objects are admitted and others repeated under different heads. 'It is like,' he says, 'a division of animals into men, quadrupeds, horses, asses, and ponies.' Action, passivity, and local situation ought not to be excluded from the category of relation, and the distinction between position in space and

Kaṇāda, however, the author of the Sūtras, enumerated only six categories. The seventh was added by later writers. This is stated in the fourth Sūtra of Book I.; thus (Gough's translation, p. 4):—

The highest good results from knowledge of the truth which springs from particular merit, and is obtained by means of the similarity and dissimilarity of the categories, substance, attribute, action, generality, particularity, co-inherence.

The commentator adds:—

In this place there is mention of six categories, but in reality non-existence is also implied by the sage as another category.

The seven categories are all subdivided.

Let us begin with the first category of *Dravya* or 'substance.' The fifth Sūtra makes the following enumeration of nine Dravyas:—

Earth (*pṛithivī*), water (*āpas*), light (*tejas*), air (*vāyu*), ether (*ākāśa*), time (*kāla*), space (*diś*), soul (*ātman*), the internal organ, mind (*manas*) are the substances.

The commentator adds:—

If it be objected, there is a tenth substance, darkness (*tamas*), why is it not enumerated? for it is recognised by perception, and substantially belongs to it, because it is possessed of colour and action; and because devoid of odour, it is not earth; and because it possesses dark colour,

---

local situation is merely verbal. His own enumeration of all existing or describable things is as follows:—1. 'Feelings or states of consciousness.' Even the external world is only known as conceived by the mind. 2. 'The minds' which experience those feelings. 3. 'The bodies,' supposed to excite feelings or sensations. 4. 'The successions and co-existences, the likenesses and unlikenesses' between these feelings. Further, he shows that all possible propositions affirm or deny one or other of the following properties or facts:—1. Existence, the most general attribute. 2. Co-existence. 3. Sequence or Succession 4. Causation. 5. Resemblance. See Chambers's Encyclopaedia, under the article 'Categories.'

it is not water, &c.: we reply that it is not so, because it is illogical to imagine another substance, when it is necessarily produced by non-existence of light.

It should be stated that of these substances the first four (earth, water, light, and air) and the last (mind) are held to be atomic, and that the first four are both eternal and non-eternal—non-eternal in their various compounds, eternal in their ultimate atoms, to which they must be traced back.[1]

Next follows the second category of 'quality.' The sixth Sūtra enumerates seventeen qualities or properties which belong to or are inherent in the nine substances:—

Colour (*rūpa*), savour (*rasa*), odour (*gandha*), tangibility (*sparśa*), numbers (*san-khyāḥ*), extensions (*parimāṇāni*), individuality (*prithaktva*), conjunction (*saṃyoga*), disjunction (*vibhāga*), priority (*paratva*), posteriority (*aparatva*), intellections (*buddhayaḥ*), pleasure (*sukha*), pain (*duḥkha*), desire (*iććha*), aversion (*dvesha*), volitions (*prayatnāḥ*), are (the seventeen) qualities.

The commentator Śan-kara-miśra adds seven others,

---

[1] According to the Platonic school, substances (οὐσίαι) are ranged under two heads—*a.* νοηταὶ καὶ ἀκίνητοι; *b.* αἰσθηταὶ καὶ ἐν κίνησει: *a.* perceptible by the mind and immovable; *b.* perceptible by the senses and in motion. Aristotle, in his Metaphysics (XI. 1), seems to divide substances into three classes—*a.* Those that are cognizable by the mind, immovable, unchangeable, and eternal; *b.* Those cognizable by the senses and eternal; *c.* Those cognizable by the senses and subject to decay, as plants and animals. Οὐσίαι δὲ τρεῖς· μία μεν, αἰσθητή· ἧς ἡ μὲν ἀΐδιος, ἡ δὲ φθαρτὴ, ἣν πάντες ὁμολογοῦσιν, οἷον τὰ φυτὰ καὶ τὰ ζῶα· ἡ δ' ἀΐδιος. Ἄλλη δὲ ἀκίνητος. In another place (VII. 8) he defines substance as the essence or very nature of a thing (τό τι ἦν εἶναι). Again, in illustration (IV. 8), he says that whatever may be the cause of being is a substance, as soul in an animal (ἡ ψυχὴ τῷ ζώῳ); and again, as many inherent parts in anything as define and indicate *what it is*, e.g., superficies, a line, number, and that essence of which the formal cause (ὁ λόγος) is the definition; and, thirdly, he says that earth, fire, water, &c., and all bodies and all animals consisting of these, are substances. See the Rev. J. H. M'Mahon's useful translation, published by Bohn.

which, he says, are implied, though not mentioned, making twenty-four in all. They are :—

Gravity (*gurutva*), fluidity (*dravatva*), viscidity (*sneha*), self-reproduction (*sa<u>n</u>skāra*, implying—*a.* impetus as the cause of activity; *b.* elasticity; *c.* the faculty of memory), merit, demerit, and sound.

In point of fact the Nyāya goes more philosophically and more correctly than the other systems into the qualities of all substances. The twenty-four which it enumerates may be regarded as separating into two classes, according as they are the sixteen qualities of material substances or the eight properties of soul. These eight are intellection, volition, desire, aversion, pleasure, pain, merit, and demerit.

The third category, *Karman*, 'act' or 'action,' is thus divided in Sūtra I. 1. 7 :—

Elevation (literally throwing upwards), depression (throwing downwards), contraction, dilatation, and going (or motion in general) are the (five kinds of) acts. [*Utkshepaṇam avakshepaṇam ākuñcanam prasāranaṃ gamanam iti karmāṇi.*]

The fourth category, *Sāmānya*, 'generality,' is said to be twofold, viz., higher (*para*) and lower (*apara*); the first being 'simple existence,' applicable to genus; the second being 'substantiality,' applicable to species.

The fifth category, *Viśesha*, 'particularity,' belongs to the nine eternal substances of the first category, viz., soul, time, place, ether, and the five atoms of earth, water, light, air, and mind, all of which have an eternal ultimate difference, distinguishing each from the other.

The sixth category, *Samavāya*, 'co-inherence' or 'intimate relation,' is of only one kind. This relation appears to be that which exists between a substance and its qualities, between atoms and what is formed out of them, or between any object and the general idea connected with it, and is thought to be a real entity, very much in accordance with the Platonic realism of the Middle Ages. It is the relation between a jar and the earth which composes it, between a cloth and its threads, between the idea of round and any round thing, between a whole and its parts, between a genus or species and its individuals, between an act and its agent, between individuality and eternal substance.

In connection with this sixth category may be mentioned the Nyāya theory of causation. Sūtra I. 2. 1, 2 states :—

From non-existence of cause (*kāraṇa*) is non-existence of effect (*kārya*), but there is not from non-existence of effect non-existence of cause.

In the Tarka-saṅgraha a cause is declared to be 'that which invariably precedes an effect which otherwise could not be,' and three kinds of causes are enumerated, viz. :—

a. Co-inherence cause, or that resulting from intimate and constant relation—perhaps best rendered by 'substantial cause' (*samavāyi-kāraṇa*), as threads are the substantial cause of cloth. This corresponds to the material cause of Aristotle. *b.* Non-substantial cause (*a-samavāyi-kāraṇa*), as the putting together of the threads is of cloth. This corresponds to the formal cause. *c.* Instrumental cause (*nimitta-kāraṇa*), as the weaver's tools, the loom, or the skill of the weaver himself, &c., are of cloth. This corresponds to the efficient cause.[1]

---

[1] Aristotle's four causes are :—1. Material cause, *i.e.*, the matter (ὕλη) from which anything is made, as marble of a statue, silver of a goblet. 2. Formal cause, *i.e.*, the specific form or pattern according to which anything is made, as a drawing or plan is the formal cause of the building of a house. 3. Efficient cause, *i.e.*, the origin of the principle of motion (ὅθεν ἡ ἀρχὴ τῆς κινήσεως), as the energy of a workman is the prime mover in producing any work. 4. Final cause, *i.e.*, the purpose for which anything is made, the motive for its production, or the end served by its existence. According to Dr. Ballantyne (Lecture on the Nyāya, p. 23), Aristotle's final cause has a counterpart in the Naiyāyika's *prayojana*, i.e., motive, purpose, or use. The writer in Chambers's Encyclopaedia, under the head of 'Cause,' shows that these causes of Aristotle and the Nyāya should rather be called the aggregate of *conditions* necessary to the production of any work of man.

As to the seventh category of non-existence or negation, four kinds are specified, viz.:—

a. Antecedent (or the non-existence of anything before it began to exist, as a jar not yet made). *b.* Cessation of existence (as of a jar when it is smashed to pieces). *c.* Mutual non-existence (as of a jar in cloth). *d.* Absolute non-existence (as of fire in a lake).

Without dwelling longer on the seven categories, we must briefly indicate how the views of the *Nyāya* and *Vaiśeshika,* as to the external world and the nature of soul, differ from those of the other systems. First, then, as to the formation of the world. This is supposed to be effected by the aggregation of *Aṇus* or 'atoms.' These are innumerable and eternal, and are eternally aggregated, disintegrated, and redintegrated by the power of Adṛishṭa. According to Kaṇāda's Sūtras (IV. 1) an atom is 'something existing, having no cause, eternal' (*sad akāraṇavan nityam*). They are, moreover, described as less than the least, invisible, intangible, indivisible, imperceptible, by the senses; and—what is most noteworthy in distinguishing the Vaiśeshika system from others—as having each of them a *Viśesha* or eternal essence of its own. The combination of these atoms is first into an aggregate of two, called *Dvy-aṇuka.* Three of them, again, are supposed to combine into a *Trasa-reṇu,* which, like a mote in a sunbeam, has just sufficient magnitude to be perceptible.[1]

According to Colebrooke's statement of the Vaiśeshika theory, the following process is supposed to take place in

---

1 The binary compound only differs from the single atom by number, and not by measure, size, or perceptibility. Both are infinitesimal, and, being joined, can only produce an infinitesimal result (like multiplied fractions). It is the tertiary compound which first introduces magnitude and causes measure, just as a jar's measure is caused by that of its two halves. See Professor Cowell's translation of the Kusumāñjali, p. 66.

the aggregation of atoms to form earth, water, light, and air :—

Two earthly atoms concurring by an unseen peculiar virtue (*a-dṛishṭa*), or by the will of God, or by time, or by other competent cause, constitute a double atom of earth; and by concourse of three binary atoms a tertiary atom is produced, and by concourse of four triple atoms a quaternary atom, and so on to a gross, grosser, or grossest mass of earth; thus great earth is produced; and in like manner great water from aqueous atoms, great light from luminous, and great air from aerial.[1]

From the Tarka-saṅgraha we may continue the account thus :—

a. Earth possesses the property of odour, which is its distinguishing quality. It is of two kinds, eternal and non-eternal—eternal in the form of atoms (*paramāṇu-rūpā*), non-eternal in the form of products (*kārya-rūpā*). The non-eternal character of aggregated earth is shown by the

---

[1] As these Lectures were delivered before classical scholars, I thought it superfluous, at the time of their delivery, to indicate all the obvious points of comparison between Indian and European systems. Reference might here, however, be made to the doctrines of Epicurus, especially as expounded by Lucretius, who begins his description of the coalescing of atoms or primordial seeds to form the world and various material objects thus :—

> 'Nunc age, quo motu genitalia materialia
> Corpora res varias gignant, genitasque resolvant
> Et qua vi facere id cogantur, quaeve sit ollis
> Reddita mobilitas magnum per inane meandi
> Expediam.' (II. 61–64.)

Nearly the whole of the second book of Lucretius might be quoted. It is full of interest in connection with the Vaiśeshika system. Cicero's criticisms on the Epicurean theory are also interesting in relation to this subject. In his De Natura Deorum (II. 37) he says, 'If a concourse of atoms could produce a world (*quod si mundum efficere potest concursus atomorum*), why not also a portico, a temple, a house, a city, which are much less difficult to form?' We might even be tempted to contrast some of the discoveries of modern chemists and physicists with the crude but shrewd ideas of Indian philosophers prosecuting their investigations more than 2000 years ago without the aids and appliances now at every one's command.

want of permanence in a jar when crushed to powder. When aggregated it is of three kinds, organized body (*śarīra*), organ of sense (*indriya*), and unorganic mass (*vishaya*). The organ connected with it is the nose or sense of smell (*ghrāṇa*), which is the recipient of odour. *b.* Water possesses the property of being cool to the touch. It is also of two kinds, eternal and non-eternal, as before. Its organ is the tongue or taste (*rasana*), the recipient of savour, which is one of the qualities of water. *c.* Light is distinguished by being hot to the feel.[1] It is similarly of two kinds, and its organ is the eye (*ćakshus*), the recipient of colour or form, which is its principal quality. *d.* Air is distinguished by being sensible to the touch. It is similarly of two kinds, and is colourless. Its organ is the skin (*tvać*), the percipient of tangibility. *e.* Ether is the substratum of the quality of sound. It is eternal, one, and all-pervading. Its organ is the ear (*śrotra*), the recipient of sound.[2]

The great commentator Śaṅ-karāćārya (quoted by Professor Banerjea, p. 62) states the process thus :—

'At the time of creation action is produced in aerial atoms, which is dependent on A-dṛishṭa. That action joins its own atom with another. Then from binaries, by gradual steps, is produced the air. The same is the case with fire. The same with water. The same with earth. The same with organized bodies.[3] Thus is the whole universe produced from atoms.'[4]

---

[1] Light and heat are regarded by Naiyāyikas as one and the same substance. Curiously enough, gold is described as mineral (*ākara-ja*) light.

[2] Professor H. H. Wilson has observed (Sāṅ-khya-kārikā, p. 122) that something like the Hindū notion of the senses and the elements partaking of a common nature is expressed in the dictum of Empedocles :—

Γαίῃ μὲν γὰρ γαῖαν ὀπώπαμεν, ὕδατι δ' ὕδωρ,
Αἰθέρι δ' αἰθέρα δῖαν, ἀτὰρ πυρὶ πῦρ ἀΐδηλον.

'By the earthly element we perceive earth; by the watery, water; by the aerial element, the air of heaven; and by the element of fire, devouring fire.' Plato, Repub. VI. 18, has the following :—'Αλλ' ἡλιοειδέστατόν γε οἶμαι τῶν περὶ τὰς αἰσθήσεις ὀργάνων, 'I regard it (the eye) as of all the organs of sense possessing most likeness to the sun.' See Muir's Texts, V. 298.

[3] In Manu (I. 75–78) and the Sāṅ-khya and the Vedānta the order of the elements is ether, air, light or fire, water, and earth. See p. 83.

[4] Compare Cicero, De Natura Deorum II. 33, 'Since there are four

With regard to the question whether God or the supreme Soul is to be regarded as having taken part in the bringing together and arranging of these atoms, it should be noted that although the name of *Īśvara* is introduced once into Gotama's Sūtras,[1] it is not found in Kaṇāda's.[2] Probably the belief of both was that the formation of the world was simply the result of *Adṛishṭa*, or 'the unseen force, which is derived from the works or acts of a previous world,' and which becomes in Hindū philosophy a kind of god, if not the only god (see p. 58). Later Naiyāyika writers, however, affirm the existence of a supreme Soul, *Paramātman*, distinct from the *Jīvātman*, or 'human soul;' and this supreme Soul is described as eternal, immutable, omniscient, without form, all-pervading, all-powerful, and, moreover, as the framer of the universe.

Thus the Tarka-saṅgraha states (Ballantyne, p. 12):—

The seat of knowledge is the soul (*ātman*). It is twofold, the living soul (*jīvātman*) and the supreme soul (*paramātman*). The supreme soul

---

sorts of elements, the continuance of the world is caused by their reciprocal action and changes (*vicissitudine*). For from the earth comes water; from water arises air; from air, ether; and then conversely in regular order backwards, from ether, air; from air, water; from water, earth, the lowest element.

[1] The Sūtra is IV. 5. 19, and is as follows. Some one suggests, 'God is the (sole) cause, because we see that the acts of men are occasionally unattended by their fruits' (*īśvaraḥ kāraṇam purusha-karmāphalya-darśanāt*). The next Aphorism is an answer to this suggestion, and seems to assert that God was *not* the cause of the universe; thus, 'Not so, because in the absence of men's acts the fruit is not produced.' The next Aphorism runs thus: 'It (man's agency?) is not the (sole) cause, because that is caused by that.' The word 'sole,' however, is introduced by the commentator, and all three Aphorisms seem designedly obscure.

[2] According to Banerjea, p. 62; but the commentators say it is implied in the third Sūtra.

is lord, omniscient, one only, subject to neither pleasure nor pain, infinite and eternal.

Indeed the Nyāya is held by some to be the stronghold of Theism.

As to the living individual souls of corporeal beings, the Nyāya view is that they are eternal, manifold,[1] eternally separate from each other and distinct from the body, senses, and mind, yet capable of apprehension, volition (or effort), desire, aversion, pleasure, pain, merit, and demerit.

In the Vaiśeshika Aphorisms (III. 2. 4) other characteristic signs (*lingāni*) of the living soul are given, such as the opening and shutting of the eyes, the motions of the mind and especially life.[2] The commentator, in commenting upon this, describes the soul as the 'governor or superintendent over the body.' Here is the passage (Gough, p. 110) :—

Vitality is a mark of the existence of the soul; for by the word 'life' the effects of vitality, such as growth, the healing of wounds and bruises, are implied. For as the owner of a house builds up the broken edifice or enlarges a building which is too small, so the ruler of the body effects by food, &c., the increase and enlargement of the body, which is to him in the stead of a habitation, and with medicine and the like causes what is wounded to grow again and mutilated hands or feet to heal. Thus a superintendent of the body (*dehasya adhishṭhātā*) is proved like a master of a house.

It should be added that souls are held to be infinite, ubiquitous, and *diffused everywhere throughout space*, so

[1] According to the Vaiśeshika-sūtra III. 2. 20, *Vyavasthāto nānā*, 'because of its circumstances (or conditions), soul is manifold.' The commentator adds, 'Circumstances are the several conditions; as, one is rich, another mean; one is happy, another unhappy; one is of high, another of low birth; one is learned, another reads badly. These circumstances evince a diversity and plurality of souls.'

[2] Plato (Phaedrus 52) defines soul as τὸ αὐτὸ αὑτὸ κινοῦν, quoted by Cicero, Tusc. Quaest. I. 23.

that a man's soul is as much in England as in Calcutta, though it can only apprehend and feel and act where the body happens to be.

The Nyāya idea of the mind or internal organ (*Manas*) is that it, like the soul, is a Dravya or 'eternal substance.' Instead, however, of being diffused everywhere like the soul, it is atomic, like earth, water, fire, and air. Indeed, if it were infinite, like the soul, it might be united with all subjects at once, and all apprehensions might be contemporaneous, which is impossible. It is therefore regarded as a mere atom or atomic inlet to the soul, not allowing the latter to receive more than one thought or conception at a time. So in Nyāya-sūtra I. 3. 16, and in Vaiśeshika VIII. 1. 22, 23, it is affirmed as follows:—

'The characteristic of the mind is that it does not give rise to more than one notion simultaneously.' 'Ether, in consequence of its universal pervasion, is infinitely great, and so likewise is soul. In consequence of non-existence of that universal pervasion, the internal organ (mind) is an atom.'[1]

In regard to the authority to be accorded to the Veda, the views of the Nyāya appear by no means unorthodox. Gautama, in his Aphorisms (II. 58–60, 68), declares plainly that the Veda is not false, that it is not chargeable either with self-contradiction or tautology, and that it is an instrument of true knowledge. Similarly, the third Aphorism of Kaṇāda may be regarded as a kind of confession of faith in the Veda, intended apparently, like that of Gautama, to counteract imputations of heterodoxy.

In further proof of the Theism claimed for the Nyāya

---

[1] The theory propounded by Lucretius was that the mind is composed of exceedingly subtle atoms; he says (III. 180) of it, 'Esse aio persubtilem atque minutis Perquam corporibus factum constare.' As to ether, see note 4, p. 105.

I here give a short passage from the Kusumāñjali, a Naiyāyika treatise by Udayana Āćārya, which will serve as a specimen of the sort of arguments employed to prove the existence of a personal God (Īśvara) in opposition to atheistical objectors. This work has been ably edited and translated by Professor E. B. Cowell.[1] The following is merely the opening of the fifth chapter, with a portion of Hari-dāsa's comment:—

An omniscient and indestructible Being is to be proved from the existence of effects, from the combination of atoms, from the support of the earth in the sky, from traditional arts, from belief in revelation, from the Veda, from its sentences, and from particular numbers.

Comment: The earth must have had a maker, because it is an effect like a jar. Combination is an action, and therefore the action which produced the conjunction of two atoms at the beginning of a creation must have been accompanied by the volition of an intelligent being. Again, the world depends upon some being who wills to hinder it from falling, like a stick supported by a bird in the air. Again, the traditional arts (*pada*) now current, as that of making cloth, &c., must have proceeded from an independent being. Again, the knowledge derived from the Veda is derived from a virtue residing in its cause, because it is true knowledge[2] (this virtue consisting in the Veda's being uttered by a fit person, and therefore necessarily implying a personal inspirer).

From this brief statement of the distinctive features of the Nyāya school, it is clear that this system, at least in its Vaiśeshika cosmogony, is dualistic in the sense of assuming the existence of gross material *eternal atoms*,

---

[1] I have referred to his edition and to Dr. Muir's extracts in the appendix to the third volume of his Texts.

[2] Those who wish to pursue the argument should consult Professor Cowell's translation. It is interesting to compare Cicero, De Natura Deorum (II. 34): 'But if all the parts of the universe are so constituted that they could not be better for use or more beautiful in appearance, let us consider whether they could have been put together by chance or whether their condition is such that they could not even cohere unless divine wisdom and providence had directed them (*nisi sensu moderante divinâque providentiâ*).'

side by side either with *eternal souls* or with the supreme Soul of the universe. It sets itself against any theory which would make an impure and evil world spring from a pure and perfect spirit. Nor does it undertake to decide positively what it cannot prove dialectically,—the precise relation between soul and matter.

CHAPTER V.

The Sān·khya.

THE Sān·khya[1] philosophy, though possibly prior in date, is generally studied next to the Nyāya, and is more peremptorily and categorically dualistic (*dvaitavādin*). It utterly repudiates the notion that impure matter can originate from pure spirit, and, of course, denies that anything can be produced out of nothing.

The following are Aphorisms, I. 78, 114–117, propounding its doctrine of evolution, which may not be altogether unworthy of the attention of Darwinians:—

There cannot be the production of something out of nothing (*nāvastuno vastu-siddhiḥ*); that which is not cannot be developed into that

---

[1] Kapila, the reputed founder of this school (sometimes fabled as a son of Brahmā, sometimes as an incarnation of Vishṇu and identified with the sage described in the Rāmāyaṇa as the destroyer of the sixty thousand sons of Sagara, who in their search for their father's horse disturbed his devotions), was probably a Brāhman, though nothing is known about him. See Mahā-bhārata XII. 13703. The word *Kapila* means 'of a tawny brown colour,' and may possibly have been applied as a nickname, like Aksha-pāda and Kaṇāda. He is the supposed author of two works, viz., *a.* the original Sān·khya Sūtras, sometimes called *Sān·khya-pravaćana*, comprising 526 aphorisms in six books; *b.* a short work called the Tattvasamāsa or 'Compendium of Principles' (translated by Dr. Ballantyne). The original Sūtras are of course accompanied with abundant commentaries, of which one of the best known is the Sān·khya-pravaćana-bhāshya, by Vijñāna-bhikshu, edited with an able and interesting preface by Dr. Fitz-Edward Hall. A very useful and popular compendium of the doctrines of this system, called the Sān·khya-kārikā, was edited and translated by Professor H. H. Wilson.

which is. The production of what does not already exist (potentially) is impossible, like a horn on a man (*nāsad-utpādo nṛi-śṛingavat*); because there must of necessity be a material out of which a product is developed; and because everything cannot occur everywhere at all times (*sarvatra sarvadā sarvāsambhavāt*); and because anything possible must be produced from something competent to produce it.[1]

'Thus,' remarks a commentator, 'curds come from milk, not water. A potter produces a jar from clay, not from cloth. Production is only manifestation of what previously existed.' Aphorism 121 adds, 'Destruction is a resolution of anything into its cause.'

In the Sāṅkhya, therefore, instead of an analytical inquiry into the universe as actually existing, arranged under topics and categories, we have a synthetical system propounded, starting from an original primordial *tattva* or 'eternally existing essence,'[2] called *Prakṛiti* (a word meaning 'that which evolves or produces everything else').

---

[1] See the note on the dogma *Ex nihilo nihil fit*, p. 52. We are also here reminded of Lucretius I. 160, &c.:—

Nam si de Nihilo fierent ex omnibu' rebus
Omne genus nasci posset; nil semine egeret;
E mare primum homines, e terrâ posset oriri
Squammigerum genus et volucres; erumpere caelo
Armenta, atque aliae pecudes; genus omne ferarum
Incerto partu culta ac deserta teneret:
Nec fructus iidem arboribus constare solerent,
Sed mutarentur: ferre omnes omnia possent.

'If things proceed from nothing, everything might spring from everything, and nothing would require a seed. Men might arise first from the sea, and fish and birds from the earth, and flocks and herds break into being from the sky; every kind of beast might be produced at random in cultivated places or deserts. The same fruits would not grow on the same trees, but would be changed. All things would be able to produce all things.'

[2] It is usual to translate *tat-tva*, 'that-ness,' by 'principle;' but such words as 'essence,' 'entity,' and in some cases even 'substance,' seem to convey a more definite idea of its meaning. It corresponds to the barbarous term 'quiddity' (from *quid est?*), discarded by Locke and modern English philosophers. Certainly 'nature' is anything but a

It is described by Kapila in his sixty-seventh Aphorism as 'a rootless root,'[1] *amūlam mūlam*, thus :—

From the absence of a root in the root, the root (of all things) is rootless.

Then he continues in his sixty-eighth Aphorism :—

Even if there be a succession of causes (one before the other) there must be a halt at some one point; and so Prakṛiti is only a name for the primal source (of all productions).

---

good equivalent for *Prakṛiti*, which denotes something very different from matter or even the germ of mere material substances. It is an intensely subtle original essence wholly distinct from soul, yet capable of evolving out of itself consciousness and mind as well as the whole visible world. *Praka-roti iti prakṛiti* is given as its derivation in the Sarva-darśana-san·graha, p. 147, where *pra* seems to stand for 'forth,' not 'before.' The commentator on the Sān·khya-kārikā (p. 4) uses the word *padārtha* as applicable to all the twenty-five Tattvas. A Vedāntist would not regard *tat-tva* as an abstract noun from *tat*, 'that,' but would say it meant 'truth,' and in its etymology contained the essence of truth, viz., *tat tvam*, 'that art thou.'

[1] In a passage in the Timaeus (34) Plato propounds a theory of creation in allegorical and not very intelligible language, which the reader can compare with the Sān·khyan view: Ἐν δ' οὖν νῷ παρόντι χρὴ γένη διανοηθῆναι τριττά, τὸ μὲν γιγνόμενον, τὸ δ' ἐν ᾧ γίγνεται τὸ δ' ὅθεν ἀφομοιούμενον φύεται τὸ γιγνόμενον, καὶ δὴ καὶ προσεικάσαι πρέπει τὸ μὲν δεχόμενον μητρί, τὸ δ' ὅθεν πατρί, τὴν δὲ μεταξὺ τούτων φύσιν ἐκγόνῳ, διὸ δὴ τὴν τοῦ γεγονότος ὁρατοῦ καὶ πάντως αἰσθητοῦ μητέρα καί ὑποδοχὴν μήτε γῆν μήτε ἀέρα μήτε πῦρ μήτε ὕδωρ λέγωμεν, μήτε ὅσα ἐκ τούτων μήτε ἐξ ὧν ταῦτα γέγονεν· ἀλλ' ἀνόρατον εἶδός τι καὶ ἄμορφον, πανδεχές. 'For the present, therefore, we ought to consider three things, that which is produced, that in which it is produced, and that from which a thing is produced, having a natural resemblance. And especially it is proper to compare that which receives to the mother, that from which it receives to the father, and the nature which is between these to the child. Then, as to this mother and receptacle of things created which are visible and altogether perceptible, we cannot term it either earth, air, fire, or water, nor any one of their compounds, nor any of the elements from which they were produced, but a certain invisible and shapeless essence, which receives all things,' &c. Compare note 3, p. 51.

Beginning, then, with this original eternal germ or element, the Sān·khya reckons up synthetically, whence its name of 'Synthetic enumeration,'[1] twenty-three other Tattvas or 'entities,' which are all productions of the first, evolving themselves out of it as naturally and spontaneously as cream out of milk or milk out of a cow.

The twenty-fifth entity is *Purusha*, 'the soul,' which is neither producer nor produced, but eternal, like Prakṛiti. It is quite distinct from the producing or produced elements and creations of the phenomenal world, though liable to be brought into connection with them. In fact, the object of the Sān·khya system is to effect the liberation of the soul from the fetters in which it is involved by union with Prakṛiti. It does this by conveying the Pramā or 'correct knowledge' of the twenty-four constituent principles of creation, and rightly discriminating the soul from them; its *Pramāṇas*, or 'means of obtaining the correct measure of existing things,' being reduced from four (see p. 61) to three, viz., *Dṛishṭa*, *Anumāna*, and *Āpta-vaćana*, 'perception by the senses, inference, and credible assertion or trustworthy testimony.'

The third Aphorism of the Sān·khya-kārikā thus reckons up the catalogue of all existing entities :—

The root and substance of all things (except soul) is Prakṛiti. It is no production. Seven things produced by it are also producers. Thence come sixteen productions. Soul, the twenty-fifth essence, is neither a production nor producer.

Hence it appears that from an original *Prakṛiti* (variously called *Mūla-prakṛiti*, 'root-principle;' *Amūlam mūlam*, 'rootless root;' *Pradhāna*, 'chief one;' *A-vyakta*,

---

[1] Hence Sir W. Jones called the Sān·khya the Numeral philosophy. It has been compared partly with the metaphysics of Pythagoras, partly (in its Yoga) with the system of Zeno; also with that of Berkeley.

'unevolved evolver;' *Brahman*, 'supreme;' *Māyā*, 'power of illusion'[1]), seven other producers are evolved, and as so evolved are regarded as Vikāras or 'productions.' The first production of the original producer is *Buddhi*, commonly called 'intellect or intellectual perception' (and variously termed *Mahat*, from its being the *Great* source of the two other internal faculties, Ahan-kāra and Manas or 'self-consciousness and mind'). Third in order comes this *Ahan-kāra*, the 'I-making' faculty, that is, self-consciousness or the sense of individuality (sometimes conveniently termed 'Ego-ism'), which produces the next five principles, called *Tanmātras* or 'subtle elementary particles,' out of which the grosser elements (*Mahā-bhūta*) are evolved.[2] These eight constitute the producers.

Then follow the sixteen that are productions (*Vikāra*) only; and first in order, as produced by the *Tanmātras*, come the five grosser elements already mentioned, viz.:—

a. *Ākāśa*,[3] 'ether,' with the distinguishing property of sound, or, in other words, the substratum of sound (which sound is the *vishaya* or object for a corresponding organ of sense, the ear). b. *Vāyu*, 'air,'

---

1 According to Gauḍapāda's commentary on Sān-khya-kārikā, 22.

2 These Tanmātras appear nearly to correspond to the πρῶτα στοιχεῖα of Plato (Theaet. 139), or rather to the στοιχεῖα στοιχείων, 'elements of elements' (Theaet. 142), and to the ῥιζώματα of Empedocles.

3 Ākāśa, as shown elsewhere (see p. 105, note 4), must not be exactly identified with the modern 'ether,' though this word is usually taken as its nearest possible equivalent. In some of its properties and functions it more corresponds with the *inane*, 'vacant space,' of Lucretius. *Quapropter locus est intactus Inane, vacansque* (I. 335). At any rate, one synonym of *ākāśa* is *śūnya*. Cicero, De Nat. Deorum II. 40, seems to identify *ether* with sky or space, which stretches to the remotest point and surrounds all things. The Rāmāyaṇa, II. 110. 5, makes Brahmā spring from ether, but the Epic and Purānic accounts of ākāśa are very inconsistent. Some say that it was created and is perishable, others that it was not created and is eternal. See Muir's Texts, IV. 119, Mahā-bhārata XII. 6132.

with the property of tangibility (which is the *vishaya* for the skin). c. *Tejas* or *jyotis*, 'fire or light,' with the property of form or colour (which is the *vishaya* for the eye). d. *Apas*, 'water,' with the property of savour or taste (which is the *vishaya* for the tongue). e. *Pṛithivī* or *bhūmi*, 'earth,' with the property of odour or smell (which is the *vishaya* for the nose).

Each of these elements after the first has also the property or properties of the preceding besides its own.

Next follow the eleven organs produced, like the Tanmātras, by the third producer, Ahan·kara, viz., the five organs of sense, the five organs of action,[1] and an eleventh organ standing between these two sets, called *Manas*, 'the mind,' which is an internal organ of perception, volition, and action.

The eight producers, then, with the five grosser elements, ether, air, fire, water, earth, and with the eleven organs, constitute the true elements and constituent substances of the phenomenal world. As, however, the most important of the producers, after the mere unintelligent original germ, is the third, called *Ahan·kāra*, 'self-consciousness or individuality,' it is scarcely too much to maintain that, according to the Sān·khya view, the whole world of sense is practically created by the individual Ego,[2] who is, nevertheless, quite distinct from the soul, as this soul is supposed to possess in itself no real consciousness of separate individuality, though deluded by it.

It should also be noted that, according to the Sān·khya theory, Prakṛiti, though a subtle elementary essence, is

---

[1] The five organs of sense or perception (*buddhīndriyāṇi*) are, ear, skin, eye, nose, tongue; those of action (*karmendriyāṇi*) are, larynx, hand, foot, and the excretory and generative organs.

[2] This idea of personal individual creation is what chiefly distinguishes the Sān·khya from the pantheism of the Vedānta, which denies all real personal individuality. It has also led to the Sān·khya system being compared to the theory of Berkeley.

yet to be regarded as consisting of three ingredients or constituent principles in equipoise, called Guṇas. These are *Sattva*, *Rajas*, and *Tamas*, 'goodness or purity, passion or activity, and darkness or ignorance.'

Thus Kapila (Aphorism 61) affirms as follows:—

Prakṛiti is the state of equipoise (*Sāmyāvasthā*) of goodness, passion, and darkness.

Evidently, then, these three constituents of the primal elementary germ are really themselves elementary substances, and not qualities, although they are called Guṇas, and although such expressions as goodness, purity, &c., convey more the notion of a quality than of any actual substance. According to the Sāṅkhya-pravaćana-bhāshya,—

These Guṇas are not like the 'qualities' of the Vaiśeshika. They are substances possessing themselves qualities or properties, such as conjunction, disjunction, lightness, motion, weight, &c. The word Guṇa, therefore, is employed because these three substances form the triple cord by which the soul, like an animal (*purusha-paśu*), is bound.[1]

It is plain, indeed, that as one meaning of the word Guṇa is 'rope' or 'cord,' the Sāṅkhya three Guṇas may be supposed to act like a triple-stranded rope, binding and confining souls in different degrees.[2] In point of fact, goodness, passion, and darkness are imagined to be the actual substances of which Prakṛiti is constituted, just as trees are the constituents of a forest. Moreover, as they are the ingredients of Prakṛiti, so they make up the whole

---

[1] Aristotle (Metaph. I. 3) describes primordial substance as undergoing changes through different affections, something after the manner of the Sāṅkhya Guṇas. See note 3, p. 51.

[2] Manu states the doctrine of the three Guṇas very similarly (XII. 24, 25, &c.): 'One should know that the three Guṇas (bonds or fetters) of the soul are goodness, passion, and darkness (bound); by one or more of these, it continues incessantly attached to forms of existence. Whenever any one of the three Guṇas predominates wholly in a body, it makes the embodied spirit abound in that Guṇa.'

world of sense evolved out of Prakṛiti. Except, however, in the case of the original producer, they are not conjoined in equal quantities. They form component parts of everything evolved, but in varying proportions, one or other being in excess. In other words, they affect everything in creation unequally; and as they affect man, make him divine and noble, thoroughly human and selfish, or bestial and ignorant, according to the predominance of goodness, passion, or darkness respectively. The soul, on the other hand, though bound by the Guṇas, is itself wholly and entirely free from such constituent ingredients (*nirguṇa*). It stands twenty-fifth in the catalogue of Tattvas, and is to be wholly distinguished from the creations evolved by the three evolvers, *Prakṛiti, Buddhi*, and *Ahankāra*. It has, in short, nothing whatever in common with the world-evolver, Prakṛiti, except eternal existence.

But although *Prakṛiti* is the sole originator of creation, yet, according to the pure Sān-khya, it does not create for itself, but rather for each individual soul which comes into connection or juxtaposition with it, like a crystal vase with a flower. Souls, indeed, exist eternally separate from each other and from the world-evolver Prakṛiti; and with whatever form of body they may be joined, they are held to be all intrinsically equal, and each retains its individuality, remaining one and unchanged through all transmigrations.[1] But each separate soul is a witness of the act of creation without participating in the act. It is a looker-

---

[1] This *separate* eternal existence of innumerable individual souls is the great feature distinguishing the Nyāya and Sān-khya from the Vedānta, which holds the oneness of all soul. And yet it would seem that each soul must be regarded as universally diffused both in Sān-khya and Nyāya (see p. 75); for unless the soul is all-pervading it cannot be eternal. All Hindūs hold that nothing can be eternal that is divisible into parts; and all things have parts except the infinite (soul) and the infinitesimal (atoms).

on, uniting itself with unintelligent *Prakṛiti*, as a lame man mounted on a blind man's shoulders, for the sake of observing and contemplating the phenomena of creation, which *Prakṛiti* herself is unable to observe. In the Sān·khya-kārikā (19) we read :—

> The soul is witness, solitary, bystander, spectator, and passive. For its contemplation of *Prakṛiti* the union of both takes place, as of the halt and blind ; by that union a creation is formed.

It appears, too, that all Prakṛiti's performances are solely for the benefit of soul, who receives her favours ungratefully. Thus, in the Sān·khya-kārikā 59, 60, we have the following :—

> As a female dancer, having exhibited herself to a spectator, desists from the dance, so does Prakṛiti desist, having manifested herself to soul. By various means Prakṛiti, endowed with qualities (*guṇavat*), acting as a benefactress, accomplishes without profit to herself the purpose of soul, who is devoid of qualities (*aguṇa*) and makes no return of benefit.

In fact, Prakṛiti is sometimes reproached with boldness in exposing herself to the gaze of soul, who takes no interest whatever in the sight. There is something to a European mind very unreal, cloudy, and unpractical in all this. Certainly no one can doubt that the Sān·khya view of the soul is inferior to that of the Nyāya, which ascribes to it, when joined to mind, activity, volition, thought, and feeling (see p. 76). Obviously, too, its view of all existing things is even more atheistical than that of the earliest Naiyāyikas. For if the creation produced by the Evolver, Prakṛiti, has an existence of its own independent of all connection with the particular Purusha to which it is joined, there can be no need for an intelligent Creator of the world or even of any superintending power.[1]

[1] I presume this is the reason why in a catalogue of MSS. edited by Rājendralāl Mitra the Sān·khya is styled the Hylotheistic philosophy.

Here are two or three of Kapila's Aphorisms bearing upon the charge of atheism brought against him. An objection is made that some of his definitions are inconsistent with the supposed existence of a supreme Lord (*Īśvara*). To this he replies in the ninety-second and following Aphorisms, thus:—

(They are not inconsistent) because the existence of a supreme Lord is unproved (*Īśvarāsiddheḥ*). Since he could not be either free (from desires and anxieties) or bound by troubles of any kind, there can be no proof of his existence. Either way he could not be effective of any creation. (That is, if he were free from anxieties he could have no wish to create; and if he were bound by desires of any kind, he would then be under bondage, and therefore deficient in power.)

The commentary of Gauḍa-pāda on Sān·khya-kārikā 61 ought, however, to be here quoted:—

The Sān·khya teachers say, 'How can beings composed of the three Guṇas proceed from Īśvara (God), who is devoid of Guṇas? Or how can they proceed from soul, equally devoid of qualities? Therefore they must proceed from Prakṛiti. Thus from white threads white cloth is produced; from black threads, black cloth;' and so from Prakṛiti, composed of the three Guṇas, the three worlds composed of the three Guṇas are produced. God (Īśvara) is free from Guṇas. The production of the three worlds composed of the Guṇas from him would be an inconsistency.

Again, with reference to the soul, we have the following in Kapila's ninety-sixth Aphorism:—

'There is a ruling influence of the soul (over Prakṛiti) caused by their proximity, just as the loadstone (draws iron to itself).' That is, the proximity of soul to Prakṛiti impels the latter to go through the steps of production. This sort of attraction between the two leads to creation, but in no other sense is soul an agent or concerned in creation at all.[1]

---

[1] It is stated in Kapila's fifty-eighth Aphorism, quoted by Dr. Ballantyne, that the bondage of the soul caused by its union with Prakṛiti is after all merely nominal, and not real, because it resides in the mind, and not in the soul itself (*vān·mātram na tu tattvaṃ ćitta-sthiteḥ*). See Mullens' Essay, p. 183.

Notwithstanding these atheistical tendencies, the Sān-khya evades the charge of unorthodoxy by a confession of faith in the Veda. Hence in Aphorism 98 we have:—

The declaration of the meaning of the texts of the Veda is an authority, since the author of them knew the established truth.

And it should be noted that some adherents of the Sān·khya maintain the existence of a supreme Soul,[1] called Hiraṇya-garbha, and of a general ideal phenomenal universe with which that supreme Soul is connected and into which all the subcreations of inferior souls are by him gathered. Nor can it be affirmed that the Sān·khya proper commits itself to a positive denial of the existence of a supreme Being, so much as to an ignoring of what the founder of the school believed to be incapable of dialectic demonstration. As, however, the original World-evolver only evolves the world for the sake of the spectator, soul, this is practically an admission that there can be no realization of creation without the union of Prakṛiti with Purusha, the personal soul. In all probability Kapila's own idea was that every Purusha, though he did not himself create, had his own creation and his own created universe comprehended in his own person.[2] It may easily be supposed that this union of Purusha and Prakṛiti began soon to be compared to that of male and female; and it may be conjectured that the idea of the production of the universe by the male and female principles associating together, which was symbolized by the Ardha-nārī form of Śiva, and which lies at the root of the whole later

---

[1] Or, according to Professor E. B. Cowell, 'personified Sum of existence.' Elphinstone's India, p. 126, note.

[2] Something after the manner of Berkeley, who held that the 'without' was all within, though he believed in the real existence of external objects produced by other minds and wills.

mythology of India, was derived mainly from the Sān-khya philosophy.

It was not indeed to be expected that the uneducated masses could make anything of a metaphysical mysticism which could not be explained to them in intelligible language. How could they form any notion of a primordial eternal energy evolving out of itself twenty-three other elements or substances to form a visible world for the soul, described as apathetic, inactive, devoid of all qualities, and a mere indifferent spectator, though in close contact with the individual Evolver and deluded by its self-consciousness? But they could well understand the idea of a universe proceeding from Prakṛiti and Purusha as from mother and father. Indeed the idea of a union between the female principle, regarded as an energy, and the male principle, is of great antiquity in Hindū systems of cosmogony. In the Ṛig-veda and Brāhmaṇas there are various allusions, as we have already seen, to a supposed union of Earth and Heaven, who together produce men, gods, and all creatures.[1]

Buddhism, moreover, which represented many of the more popular philosophical ideas of the Hindūs perhaps as early as the fifth century B.C., has more in common with Sān-khya doctrines than with any of the other systems.

Even the cosmogony of Manu, although a compound of various theories, presents a process of evolution very similar, as we shall see hereafter, to that of the Sān-khya.

Again, the antiquity and prevalence of Sān-khyan ideas is proved by the frequent allusions to them in the great Indian epic poem, called Mahā-bhārata;[2] and the per-

---

[1] See Muir's Texts, vol. v. pp. 22, 23.

[2] In the Sabhā-parvan (Muir, vol. iv. p. 173) Kṛishṇa is described as undeveloped Prakṛiti, the eternal creator (*esha prakṛitir a-vyaktā kartā ćaiva sanātanaḥ*). On the other hand, in the Vana-parvan (1622, &c.,

manence of their popularity till at least the first century of our era is indicated by the fact that the celebrated philosophical poem called Bhagavad-gītā attempts to reconcile the Sān·khya with Vedāntist views.[1]

Perhaps, however, the extensive prevalence of Sān·khyan ideas in India is best shown by the later cosmogony and mythology. In those repositories of the popular Hindū creed, the Purāṇas and Tantras, Prakriti becomes a real Mother of the universe. It is true that in some of the Purāṇas there is occasional confusion and perversion of Sān·khyan doctrines. Thus, for example, in the Vishṇu-purāṇa I. 2. 22, we have the following :—

'There was neither day nor night, neither sky nor earth ; there was neither darkness nor light nor anything else. There was then the One, Brahma, the Male, possessing the character of Pradhāna (*prādhānika*).'[2] And farther on : 'The principles or elements, commencing with Mahat, presided over by Purusha and under the influence of Pradhāna, generated an egg, which became the receptacle of Vishṇu in the form of Brahmā.'

But generally in the later mythology, especially as represented by the Tantras, the Sān·khya principle of Prakṛiti takes the form of female personifications, who are thought of as the wives or creative female energies of the principal male deities, to whom, on the other hand, the name Purusha, in the sense of the supreme Soul or the supreme Male, is sometimes applied.[3] This is especially the case with the Śakti or female energy of Śiva, worshipped by a vast number of persons as the true *Jagad-ambā*, or 'Mother of the universe.'

Muir, vol. iv. p. 195) the god S'iva is declared to be the cause of the causes of the world (*loka-kāraṇa-kāraṇam*), and therefore superior and antecedent to Pradhāna and Purusha. Again, in S'ānti-parvan 12725, 12737, 13041, &c., the sons of Brahmā are called Prakṛitayaḥ.

1 See Chapter VII. on the Eclectic School and Bhagavad-gītā.

2 Compare the Ṛig-veda hymn, translated at p. 19 of this book.

3 Vishṇu or Kṛishṇa is called Purushottama, and the name Purusha is equally given to Brahmā and S'iva.

These proofs of the ancient popularity of the Sāṅkhya and its influence on the later mythology may help us to understand that, although in modern times there are comparatively few students of the Sāṅkhya among the Paṇḍits of India, there is still a common saying current everywhere (which will be found in Mahā-bhārata, Śānti-parvan, 11676), *Nāsti Sāṅkhya-samaṃ jñānaṃ nāsti Yoga-samam balam*, 'There is no knowledge equal to the Sāṅkhya and no power equal to the Yoga.'

The Yoga.

The Yoga,[1] commonly regarded as a branch of the Sāṅkhya, is scarcely worthy of the name of a system of philosophy, though it has undoubted charms for the naturally contemplative and ascetical Hindū, and lays claim to greater orthodoxy than the Sāṅkhya proper, by directly acknowledging the existence of Īśvara or a supreme Being.[2] In fact, the aim of the Yoga is to teach the means by which the human soul may attain complete union with the supreme Soul. This fusion (*laya*) or union of individual with universal spirit may be effected even in the body. According to Patañjali, the author of the system, the very word *Yoga* is interpreted to mean the act of 'fixing or concentrating the mind in abstract meditation,' and this is said to be effected by preventing

---

[1] I have given a later account of the Yoga and its connection with Buddhism in my recent work on Buddhism (John Murray, Albemarle Street, London), p. 223.

[2] The Yoga was propounded by Patañjali (of whom nothing is known, except that he was probably not the same person as the author of the Mahā-bhāshya) in Aphorisms called the Yoga-sūtra, a work in four books or chapters, two of which, with some of the commentary of Bhoja-rājā or Bhoja-deva, were translated by Dr. Ballantyne. Other commentators were Vāćaspati-miśra, Vijñāna-bhikshu, and Nāgoji-bhaṭṭa.

the modifications of *Ćitta* or the thinking principle [which modifications arise through the three Pramāṇas, perception, inference, and verbal testimony, as well as through incorrect ascertainment, fancy, sleep, and recollection], by the constant habit (*abhyāsa*) of keeping the mind in its unmodified state—a state clear as crystal when uncoloured by contact with other substances—and by the practice of *Vairāgya*—that is, complete suppression of the passions. This *Vairāgya* is only to be obtained by *Īśvara-praṇidhāna* or the contemplation of the supreme Being, who is defined to be a particular Purusha or Spirit unaffected by works, afflictions, &c., and having the appellation *Praṇava* or *Om*. The repetition of this monosyllable is supposed to be attended with marvellous results, and the muttering of it with reflection on its meaning[1] is said to be conducive to a knowledge of the Supreme and to a prevention of all the obstacles to Yoga. The eight means of mental concentration are—1. *Yama*, 'forbearance,' 'restraint.' 2. *Niyama*, 'religious observances.' 3. *Āsana*, 'postures.'[2] 4. *Prāṇāyāma*, 'suppression of the breath' or 'breathing in a peculiar way.' 5. *Pratyāhāra*, 'restraint of the senses.' 6. *Dhāraṇa*, 'steadying of the mind.' 7. *Dhyāna*, 'contemplation.' 8. *Samādhi*, 'profound meditation,' or rather a state of religious trance, which, according to the Bhagavad-gītā (VI. 13), is most effectually attained by such practices as fixing the eyes intently and incessantly on the tip of the nose, &c.[3] The

[1] *Om* is supposed to be composed of the three letters A, U, M, which form a most sacred monosyllable (*ekākshara*), significant of the supreme Being as developing himself in the Triad of gods, Brahmā, Vishṇu, and S'iva. See Bhagavad-gītā VIII. 13, and especially Manu II. 83, 84.

[2] One of these postures is called *paryan-ka-bandhana* or *paryan-ka-granthi*, 'bed-binding' or 'bed-knot,' and is performed by sitting on the hams with a cloth fastened round the knees and back. See line 1 of the Mṛić-ćhakaṭikā.

[3] See the account of the Bhagavad-gītā, p. 130 of this volume.

system of Yoga appears, in fact, to be a mere contrivance for getting rid of all thought, or at least for concentrating the mind with the utmost intensity upon nothing in particular. It is a strange compound of mental and bodily exercises, consisting in unnatural restraint, forced and painful postures, twistings and contortions of the limbs, suppressions of the breath, and utter absence of mind. But although the Yoga of Patañjali professes to effect union with the universal Spirit by means such as these, it should be observed that far more severe austerities and self-imposed physical mortifications are popularly connected with the Yoga system. All Hindū devotees and ascetics, especially those who, as forming a division of the Śaiva sect, identify the terrific god Śiva with the supreme Being, are commonly called Yogins or Yogīs, and indeed properly so called, in so far as the professed object of their austerities is union with the Deity.[1]

The variety and intensity of the forms of austerity practised by such Yogīs in India would appear to surpass all credibility were they not sufficiently attested by trustworthy evidence. A few illustrations may not be out of place here, or at least may be instructive, especially as bearing upon an interesting field of inquiry, viz., first, how is it that faith in a false system can operate with sufficient force upon a Hindū to impel him to submit voluntarily to almost incredible restraints, mortifications of the flesh, and physical tortures? and secondly, how is it that an amount of physical endurance may be exhibited by an apparently weakly and emaciated Asiatic, which would be impossible in a European, the climate and diet in the one case tending to debilitate, in the other to invigorate?

---

[1] The name Fakīr or Faqīr, sometimes given to Hindū devotees, ought to be restricted to Muslims. It is an Arabic word, meaning 'poor,' 'indigent.'

In the Śakuntalā (Act VII. verse 175) there is a description of an ascetic engaged in Yoga, whose condition of fixed trance and immovable impassiveness had lasted so long that ants had thrown up a mound as high as his waist without being disturbed, and birds had built their nests in the long clotted tresses of his tangled hair. This may be thought a mere flight of poetical fancy, but a Mohammedan traveller, whose narrative is quoted by Mr. Mill (British India, I. 355), once actually saw a man in India standing motionless with his face turned towards the sun. The same traveller, having occasion to revisit the same spot sixteen years afterwards, found the very same man in the very same attitude. Such men have been known to fix their gaze on the sun's disk till sight has been extinguished. This is paralleled by a particular form of austerity described in Manu VI. 23, where mention is made of the *Pańća-tapās*, a Yogī who, during the three hottest months (April, May, and June), sits between four blazing fires placed towards the four quarters, with the burning sun above his head to form a fifth. In fact, a Yogī was actually seen not long ago (Mill's India, I. 353) seated between four such fires on a quadrangular stage. He stood on one leg gazing at the sun while these fires were lighted at the four corners. Then placing himself upright on his head, with his feet elevated in the air, he remained for three hours in that position. He then seated himself cross-legged and continued bearing the raging heat of the sun above his head and the fires which surrounded him till the end of the day, occasionally adding combustibles with his own hands to increase the flames.

Again, in the Asiatic Monthly Journal for March 1829, an account is given of a Brāhman who, with no other apparatus than a low stool, a hollow bamboo, and a kind of crutch, poised himself apparently in the air, about four feet from the ground, for forty minutes. This actually took place before the governor of Madras. Nor does there appear to be any limit to the various forms of austerity practised by Hindū devotees. We read of some who acquire the power of remaining under water for a space of time quite incredible; of others who bury themselves up to the neck in the ground, or even below it, leaving only a little hole through which to breathe; of others who keep their fists clenched for years till the nails grow through the back of their hands; of others who hold one or both arms aloft till they become immovably fixed in that position and withered to the bone; of others who roll their bodies for thousands of miles to some place of pilgrimage; of others who sleep on beds of iron spikes. One man was seen at Benares (described in the Asiatic Researches, vol. v. p. 49) who was alleged to have used such a bed for thirty-five years. Others have been known to chain themselves for life to trees; others, again, to pass their lives, heavily chained, in iron cages. Lastly, the extent to which some Indian ascetics will carry fasting far exceeds anything ever heard of in Europe, as may be understood by a reference to the rules of the lunar penance given by Manu (XI. 20, XI. 216–220). This penance is a kind of fast which consists in diminishing the consumption of food every day by one mouthful for the waning half of the lunar month, beginning with fifteen mouthfuls at the full moon until the quantity is reduced to 0 at the new moon, and then increasing it in like manner during the fortnight of the moon's increase.

Of course all these mortifications are explicable by their connection with the fancied attainment of extraordinary sanctity and supernatural powers.

As a conclusion to the subject of Yoga, I quote a remarkable passage from Professor Banerjea (Dialogues, pp. 69, 70):—

The Yogī may not see or hear what passes around,—he may be insensible to external impressions, but he has intuition of things which his neighbours cannot see or hear. He becomes so buoyant, or rather so sublimated by his Yoga, that gravitation, or, as Bhāskarāćārya calls it, the attractive power of the earth, has no influence on him. He can walk and ascend in the sky, as if he were suspended under a balloon. He can by this intuitive process inform himself of the mysteries of astronomy and anatomy, of all things, in fact, that may be found in any of the different worlds. He may call to recollection the events of a previous life. He may understand the language of the brute creation. He may obtain an insight into the past and future. He may discern the thoughts of others. He may himself vanish at pleasure, and, if he choose to do so, enter into his neighbour's body and take possession of his living skin.

By these and other doctrines of Hindū philosophy we are often reminded that the human mind repeats itself according to the sentiment expressed in Ecclesiastes i. 9, 'The thing that hath been, it is that which shall be; and that which is done is that which shall be done: and there is no new thing under the sun.' Certainly almost all extravagant ideas now current seem to have their counterpart, if not their source, in the East. The practisers of self-imposed superstitious restraints and mortifications, not to speak of the votaries of animal magnetism, clairvoyance, and so-called spiritualism, will find most of their theories represented or rather far outdone by corresponding notions existing in this Yoga system invented by the Hindūs considerably more than 2000 years ago, and more or less earnestly believed in and sedulously practised up to the present day.

CHAPTER VI.

The Pūrva-mīmāṉsā and Vedānta.

OUR next subject is the Mīmāṉsā of Jaimini,[1] which is sometimes connected with the Vedānta, this latter being called the *Uttara-mīmāṉsā* or *Brahma-mīmāṉsā*—as founded on the Upanishads or latter part of the Vedas—while Jaimini's system is styled the *Pūrva-mīmāṉsā* or *Karma-mīmāṉsā*, as concerned with the Mantras and Brāhmaṇas only. It is more usual, however, to indicate the opposition of the two systems to each other by calling the one Mīmāṉsā and the other Vedānta. In fact, Jaimini's system, like the Yoga, cannot suitably be called a subdivision of any other system, for it is in real truth not a system of philosophy, but rather of *ritualism*. It does not concern itself, like the other systems, with investigations into the nature of soul, mind, and matter, but with a correct interpretation of the ritual of the Veda and the solutions of doubts and discrepancies in regard to Vedic texts caused by the discordant explanations of opposite

---

[1] Jaimini, as usual, enunciated his doctrines in aphorisms. His work called the Mīmāṉsā-sūtra or Jaimini-sūtra is in twelve books. It has been partly edited and translated by Dr. Ballantyne. A commentary on it was written by Śabara-svāmin, which is being published in the Bibliotheca Indica, and this again was commented on by the celebrated Mīmāṉsā authority, Kumārila (also styled Kumārila-bhaṭṭa, Kumārila-svāmin), whose work was again followed by numerous other commentaries and treatises. A compendious explanation of the system, called *Jaiminīya-nyāya-mālā-vistara*, was written by Mādhavācārya. Jaimini must have been a learned Brāhman, but nothing is known as to the date of his life.

schools. Its only claim to the title of a philosophy consists in its *mode* of interpretation, the topics being arranged according to particular categories (such as authoritativeness, indirect precept, &c.), and treated according to a kind of *logical method*, commencing with the proposition to be discussed, the doubt arising about it, the *Pūrva-paksha* or primâ facie and wrong view of the question, the *Uttara-paksha* or refutation of the wrong view, and the conclusion. The main design of the whole system appears to be to make a god of ritualism. Hence it consists chiefly of a critical commentary on the Brāhmaṇa or ritual portion of the Veda in its connection with the Mantras, the interpretation given being an exposition of the obvious literal sense and not of any supposed occult meaning underlying the text, as in the Upanishads and Vedānta. Jaimini was, in point of fact, the opponent of both rationalism and theism. Not that he denied a God, but the real tendency of his teaching was to allow no voice or authority to either reason or God. The Veda was to be everything. A supreme Being might exist, but was not necessary to the system. The Veda, said Jaimini, is itself authority and has no need of an Authorizer. His first Aphorism states the whole aim and object of his system, viz., a desire to know duty (*dharma-jijṅāsā*). When amplified, it may be thus stated :—

Understand, O student, that, after studying the Veda with a preceptor, a desire to know *Dharma* or duty is to be entertained by thee.

The fifth Aphorism asserts the strange doctrine of an original and perpetual connection between a word and its sense. It is thus paraphrased :—

The connection of a word with its sense is contemporaneous with the origin of both. In consequence of this connection, the words of the Veda convey unerring instruction in the knowledge of duty.

But it is to be understood that *Dharma* or duty consists in the performance of the ritual acts prescribed by the Veda because they are so prescribed, without reference to the will or approval of any personal god, for Dharma is itself the bestower of reward. Some recent Mīmāṉsakas, however, maintain that Dharma ought to be performed as an offering to a supreme Being, and that it is to be so performed as a means of emancipation. Even a verse of the Bhagavad-gītā is quoted in support of this view. Kṛishṇa, regarded by his worshippers as a manifestation of the supreme lord of the universe, says to Arjuna,—

Whatever thou doest, whatever thou eatest, whatever thou sacrificest, whatever thou givest away, whatever austerity thou practisest, do that as an offering to me (IX. 27). (See Lecture VII. on the Eclectic School and Bhagavad-gītā, p. 131 of this volume.)

Some singular speculations occur in Jaimini's system. As he maintains the inherent authority of the Veda, without any dependence on an eternal Authorizer or Revealer, so he asserts its own absolute eternity, and declares that only eternally pre-existing objects are mentioned in it. This theory is supported by affirming that sound is eternal, or rather that an eternal sound underlies all temporary sound. From Aphorism 18 we gather the following :—

Sound must be eternal, because its utterance [exhibition] is intended to convey a meaning to others. If it were not eternal it would not continue till the hearer had learned its sense, and thus he would not learn the sense, because the cause had ceased to exist.

If, on the other hand (says a commentator), it continues to exist for any period, however short, after ceasing to be perceived, it is impossible to assign any other instant at which there is any evidence of the discontinuance of its existence, whence its eternity is inferred.[1]

---

[1] See Muir's Texts, vol. iii. pp. 53, 57; Dr. Ballantyne's Mīmāṉsā-sūtra, p. 23.

This eternity of sound is further pretended to be established by the two following short passages, one from the Ṛig-veda (VIII. 64. 6) and one from Smṛiti, with which I close this brief notice of the Mīmāṉsā :—

'Send forth praises, O Virūpa, with an eternal voice.'

'An eternal voice, without beginning or end, was uttered by the self-existent.'[1]

Let me conclude these remarks on the singular theory of the eternity of sound by observing that the Chinese are said to have a saying, 'The echoes of a word once uttered vibrate in space to all eternity.'

The Vedānta.

Of orthodox systems there only remains the Vedānta of Vyāsa or Bādarāyaṇa;[2] but this is in some respects the

---

[1] The whole text of the Ṛig-veda (VIII. 64 or 75. 6) is *Tasmai nūnam abhidyave vāćā Virūpa nityayā, vṛishṇe ćodasva sushṭutim*, 'send forth praises to this heaven-aspiring and prolific Agni, O Virūpa, with an eternal voice.' Nitya, though taken by the Mīmāṉsakas in the sense of 'eternal,' probably means only 'unceasing.' Dr. Muir's Texts, vol. iii. p. 51. The text from Smṛiti has only as yet been found in Mahābhārata, Sānti-parvan 8. 533, *An-ādi-nidhanā nityā vāg utsṛishṭā svayam-bhuvā.*

[2] The reputed author of this system, Bādarāyaṇa, is very loosely identified with the legendary person named Vyāsa, who is supposed to have arranged the Vedas and written the Mahā-bhārata, Purāṇas, and a particular Dharma-śāstra or law-book. No doubt the name Vyāsa, 'arranger,' was applied as a kind of title to various great writers or compilers, and in this sense it seems to have been given to the founder of the Vedānta system. He propounded his views, as usual, in Sūtras, but Bādarāyaṇa's Aphorisms are generally called Brahma-sūtra, or sometimes Sārīraka-sūtra, and the system itself is variously styled Brahma-mīmāṉsā and Sārīraka-mīmāṉsā (investigation into the supreme Soul or embodied Spirit). The text of the Sūtras and the celebrated commentary by San-karāćārya have been edited in the Bibliotheca

most important of all the six, both from its closer conformity to the pantheistic doctrines propounded in the Upanishads, on which treatises as forming the end of the Veda it professes to be founded, and from its greater adaptation to the habits of thought common among thinking and educated Hindūs, as much in present as in former periods. The pantheism pervading the Upanishads and leading directly to the Vedānta system has already been illustrated by a selection of examples.

The following simple confession of a Vedāntist's faith can be added from the Ćhāndogya Upanishad (III. 14):—

All this universe (τὸ πᾶν) indeed is Brahma; from him does it proceed; into him it is dissolved; in him it breathes.[1] So let every one adore him calmly.

Here, then, we have presented to us a different view of the origin of the world. In the Nyāya it was supposed to proceed from a concurrence of innumerable eternal atoms; in the Sān·khya from one original eternal element called Prakṛiti; both operating independently, though associated with eternal spirits, and, according to one view, presided over by a supreme Spirit. But in the Vedānta there is no real material world at all, as distinct from the universal Spirit. Hence the doctrine of this school is called *A-dvaita*, 'non-dualism.' The universe exists but merely as an illusory form of the one eternal essence (τὸ ἕν). He is the all-pervading Spirit, the only really existing substance

---

Indica by Dr. Röer, and a portion translated by Professor Banerjea. Dr. Ballantyne also edited and translated a portion of the Sūtras and commentary and a popular compendium called the Vedānta-sāra. A vast number of other commentaries and treatises on the Vedānta exist.

[1] This is expressed in the text by one compound, *taj-jalān*, interpreted as equivalent to *taj-ja*, *tal-la*, *tad-ana*. The whole text is *sarvaṃ khalv idam brahma taj-jalān iti śānta upāsīta*. The philosophy of the Sūfīs, alleged to be developed out of the Kurān (see p. 33), appears to be a kind of pantheism very similar to that of the Vedānta.

(*vastu*). Even as early as the Ṛig-veda the outlines of this pantheistic creed, which became more definite in the Upanishads and Vedānta, may be traced. The germ of the Vedānta is observable in the Purusha-sūkta, as we have already shown by the example given at p. 21. The early Vedāntic creed has the merit of being exceedingly simple. It is comprised in these three words, occurring in the Ćhāndogya Upanishad (see p. 38), *Ekam evādvitīyam*, 'one only Essence without a second;' or in the following line of nine short words, *Brahma satyaṃ jagan mithyā jīvo brahmaiva nāparaḥ*, 'Brahma is true, the world is false, the spirit is only Brahma and no other.'

As the Nyāya has much in common with the practical philosophy of Aristotle, which gave to things and individuals, rather than to ideas, a real existence, so the Vedānta offers many parallels to the idealism of Plato.[1]

[1] Plato does not always state his theory of ideas very intelligibly, and probably modified them in his later works. He seems, however, to have insisted on the doctrine that mind preceded and gave rise to matter, or, in other words, that the whole material world proceeded from or was actually produced by the Creator according to the idea or pattern of a world existing eternally and for ever the same in his own mind. In the Timaeus (10) he says: 'To discover the Maker and Father of this universe (τοῦ παντός) is difficult, and, when he has been discovered, it is impossible to describe him to the multitude. According to which of two patterns (πρὸς πότερον τῶν παραδειγμάτων) did he frame the world? According to one subsisting for ever the same? Or according to one which was produced? Since, then, this universe is beautiful and its Artificer good, he evidently looked in modelling it to an eternal (ἀΐδιον) pattern.' Similarly, Plato seems to have held that the human mind has existing within it certain abstract ideas or ideal forms which precede and are visibly manifested in the actual concrete forms around us. For example, the abstract ideas of goodness and beauty are found pre-existing in the mind, and, as it were, give rise to the various good and beautiful objects manifested before our eyes. In the same manner all circular things must have been preceded by some ideal circular form existing as an eternal reality. For, according to

Bādarāyaṇa's very first Aphorism states the object of the whole system in one compound word, viz., *Brahma-jijñāsā*, 'Brahma-inquisitiveness,' *i.e.*, the desire of knowing Brahman (neut.), or the only really existing being.

Here we may quote a portion of Śan·karāćārya's commentary (Röer's edition, pp. 29 and 43):—

The knower of Brahma attains the supreme good and supreme object of man (*param purushārtham* = τὸ ἀγαθόν, τὸ ἄριστον, summum bonum).

A really existing substance (*vastu*) cannot alternately be thus and not thus, cannot (optionally) be and not be. The knowledge of a substance just as it is in reality (*i.e.*, true knowledge) is not dependent on a man's own personal notions (*na purusha-buddhy-apeksham*).[1] It depends on the substance itself. To say of one and the same post that it is either a post or a man or something else is not true knowledge (*tattva-jñānam*). It is a false notion (*mithyā-jñānam*).[2] That it is a post is alone the truth, because it is dependent on the substance itself (*vastu-tantratvāt*). Thus the proving of an existing substance is dependent on the substance itself. Thus the knowledge of Brahma is dependent on the substance itself (not on the notion a man may form of Brahma), because it relates to a really existing substance (*bhūta-vastu-vishayatvāt*).

Plato, these abstract ideas had a real, eternal, unchanging existence of their own, quite separate from and independent of the ever-varying concrete objects and appearances connected with them.

[1] S'an·kara appears here to argue against a doctrine like that ascribed to Protagoras, πάντων μέτρον ἄνθρωπος, 'the individual man is the stan dard of all things.'

[2] One of Plato's causes of mistaken notion is that when two persons or things have been seen and their forms impressed on the mind, they are yet, owing to imperfect observation, mistaken the one for the other: 'It remains that I may form a false notion in this case, when knowing you and Theodorus and having the impression of both of you on that waxen tablet of the mind (ἐν ἐκείνῳ τῷ κηρίνῳ) made by a seal ring as it were, seeing you both from a distance and not sufficiently distinguishing you, I fit the aspect of each to the impression of the other, changing them like those that put their shoes on the wrong feet: τότε δὴ συμβαίνει ἡ ἑτεροδοξία καὶ τὸ ψευδῆ δοξάζειν,' Theaet. 122. Compare Banerjea's translation of the Brahma-sūtra, p. 2.

In the second Aphorism Brahma[1] is defined to mean 'that from which the production of this universe results.'

Śan·kara adds a fuller definition, thus (Röer's edition, p. 38):—

Brahma is that all-knowing, all-powerful Cause from which arises the production, continuance, and dissolution of the universe, which (universe) is modified by name and form, contains many agents and patients (*kartṛi-bhoktṛi-saṃyukta*), is the repository (*āśraya*) of actions and effects, and in the form of its arrangement cannot be conceived even by the mind.

The Aphorisms which follow, as far as the 28th, proceed to define and describe the character of God as the supreme Soul of the universe. I here give a summary[2] of the most interesting of them, with portions of the commentary:—

That the supreme Being is omniscient follows from the fact that he is the source of the Veda (*śāstra-yonitvāt*). As from that Being every soul is evolved, so to that same Being does every soul return. How can souls be merged into Prakṛiti?[3] for then the intelligent would be absorbed in the unintelligent. He, the supreme Being, consists of joy. This is clear from the Veda, which describes him as the cause of joy; for as those who enrich others must be themselves rich, so there must be abundant joy with him who causes others to rejoice. Again, he, the one God, is the light (*jyotis*). He is within the sun and within the eye. He is the ethereal element (*ākāśa*).[4] He is the

---

[1] The name *Brahman* is, in fact, derived from the root *bṛih* or *vṛih*, 'to grow and expand,' and therefore means literally the one essence which grows or expands. *Vṛiksha*, 'a tree,' is from the same root.

[2] See Dr. Ballantyne's translation, and that of Professor Banerjea.

[3] The Prakṛiti or Pradhāna of the Sān·khya system.

[4] Professor Banerjea considers that the word 'ether' is not a good rendering for *ākāśa*, which pervades everything. There is ākāśa in our cups and within our bodies, which are surely not ethereal. One of the synonyms of ākāśa is *śūnya*, and this may be compared in some respects to the 'inane' or space of Lucretius (I. 330):—

Nec tamen undique corporeâ stipata tenentur
Omnia naturâ; namque est in rebus inane.

'And yet all things are not on all sides held and jammed together in close and solid parts; there is a space (or void) in things.'

life and the breath of life (*prāṇa*). He is the life with which Indra identified himself when he said to Pratardana, 'I am the life, consisting of perfect knowledge. Worship me as the life immortal.'[1]

From other portions of the Aphorisms it appears that the τὸ ἕν, or one universal essence called Brahma, is to the external world what yarn is to cloth, what milk to curds, what earth to a jar, and gold to a bracelet. He is both creator and creation,[2] actor and act. He is also Existence, Knowledge, and Joy (*Sać-ćid-ānanda*), but is at the same time without parts, unbound by qualities (*nir-guṇa*, see p. 85), without action, without emotion, having no consciousness such as is denoted by 'I' and 'Thou,'[3] apprehending no person or thing, nor apprehended by any, having neither beginning nor end, immutable, the only real entity.

This is surely almost tantamount to asserting that pure Being is identical with pure Nothing, so that the two extremes of Buddhistic Nihilism and Vedāntic Pantheism, far as they profess to be apart, appear in the end to meet.

---

[1] This is from the Kaushītaki-brāhmaṇa Upanishad, chapter 3. See Professor E. B. Cowell's translation.

[2] A true Vedāntic spirit is observable in the Orphic hymns when they identify Zeus with the universe; thus, 'Zeus is the ether; Zeus is the earth; Zeus is the heaven; Zeus is all things.' Orphic. Fragm. IV. 363, VI. 366. Compare also Virgil, Aeneid VI. 724, &c.:—

'Principio caelum ac terras, camposque liquentes
Lucentemque globum Lunae, Titaniaque astra,
Spiritus intus alit, totamque infusa per artus
Mens agitat molem et magno se corpore miscet.'

[3] As shown by Professor Banerjea, S'an-kara compares the second person *Thou* with darkness, because there cannot be a real Thou. So S'an-kara affirms that 'Thou' and 'I' are as opposed as darkness and light. Plato speaks similarly of darkness and light in connection with nonentity and real entity. Sophist. 254.

I add two or three extracts from Śan·karāćārya's comment on Sūtra II. 1. 34:[1]—

It may be objected that God is proved not to be the cause of the universe. Why? From the visible instances of injustice (*vaishamya*) and cruelty (*nairghṛiṇya*). Some he makes very happy, as the gods, &c.; some very miserable, as the brutes, &c.; and some in a middling condition, as men, &c. Being the author of such an unjust creation, he is proved to be subject to passions like other persons—that is to say, to partiality and prejudice—and therefore his nature is found wanting in spotlessness. And by dispensing pain and ruin, he is chargeable with malicious cruelty, deemed culpable even among the wicked. Hence, because of the instances of injustice and cruelty, God cannot be the cause of the universe. To this we reply: Injustice and cruelty cannot be charged upon God. Why? Because he did not act independently (*sāpekshatvāt*). God being dependent (*sāpekshaḥ*) creates this world of inequalities. If you ask on what he is dependent, we reply, on merit and demerit (*dharmādharmau*). That there should be an unequal creation dependent on the merit and demerit of the souls created, is no fault of God. As the rain is the common cause of the production of rice and wheat, but the causes of their specific distinctions as rice and wheat are the varying powers of their respective seeds; so is God the common cause in the creation of gods, men, and others; but of the distinctions between gods, men, and others, the causes are the varying works inherent in their respective souls.

In commenting on the next Aphorism (35), he answers the objection, 'How could there be previous works at the original creation?' The objection and reply are thus stated:[2]—

The supreme Being existed at the beginning, one without a second (see p. 103). Hence, before the creation there could be no works in dependence on which inequalities might be created. God may be dependent on works after distinctions are made. But before the

---

[1] Quoted by Professor Banerjea and Mr. Mullens, and translated by them. Dialogues, p. 120, &c. Essay on Hindū Philosophy, p. 190. The Aphorism is, *Vaishamya-nairghṛiṇye na sāpekshatvāt tathāhi darśayati.*

[2] The original Sūtra is, *Na karmāvibhāgād iti ćen nānāditvāt.*

creation there could be no works caused by varying instruments, and therefore we ought to find a uniform creation (*tulyā srishṭiḥ*). We reply: This does not vitiate our doctrine, because *the world is without beginning* (*anāditvāt saṃsārasya*). The world being without beginning, nothing can prevent works and unequal creations from continuing in the states of cause and effect, like the seed and its plant (*vījān-kura-vat*).

Other objections to the Vedānta theory are thus treated by Śan-kara:—

How can this universe, which is manifold, void of life, impure, and irrational, proceed from him who is one, living, pure, and rational? We reply: The lifeless world can proceed from Brahma, just as lifeless hair can spring from a living man. But in the universe we find him who enjoys and him who is enjoyed; how can he be both? We reply: Such are the changes of the sea. Foam, waves, billows, bubbles, are not different from the sea. There is no difference between the universe and Brahma. The effect is not different from its cause. He is the soul; the soul is he. The same earth produces diamonds, rock-crystal, and vermilion. The same sun produces many kinds of plants. The same nourishment is converted into hair, nails, &c. As milk is changed into curds, and water into ice, so is Brahma variously transformed without external aids. So the spider spins its web from its own substance. So spirits assume various shapes.

Such a creed really implies (though some Vedāntists deny this) that the world is all Māyā, 'a mere illusion.' In point of fact, a true Vedāntist, though he affirms that Brahma alone is real, allows a *vyāvahārika*, 'practical existence,' to souls, the world, and Īśvara, as distinguished from *pāramārthika*, 'real,' and *prātibhāsika*, 'apparent or illusory existence.' How, indeed, can it be denied that external things exist, when we see them before our eyes and feel them at every instant? But how, on the other hand, can it be maintained that an impure world is the manifestation of a pure spiritual essence? To avoid this difficulty, the supreme Spirit is represented as ignoring himself by a sort of self-imposed ignorance, in order to draw out from himself for his own amusement the separate individuated spirits and various appearances, which, although really parts of his own essence, constitute the apparent phenomena of the universe. Hence the external world, the living spirits of individual men, and even Īśvara, the personal God, are all described as created by a power which the Vedāntist is obliged, for want of a better solution of his difficulty, to call Māyā, 'Illusion,' or A-vidyā,[1] 'Ignorance,' that is, 'False knowledge' or 'False notion.'

Of this power there are two distinct forms of operation, viz., 1. that of envelopment (*āvaraṇa*), which, enveloping the soul, causes it to imagine that it is liable to mundane vicissitudes—that it is an agent or a patient; that it rejoices or grieves, &c.—as if a person under a delusion were to mistake a rope for a snake: 2. that of projection (*vikshepa*), which, affecting the soul in its state of pure intelligence, raises upon it the appearance of a world, producing first the five subtile elements and drawing out from them seventeen subtile bodies (also called *linga-śarīra*, comprising the five organs of sense, the five organs of action, the five vital airs, with *buddhi* and *manas*, and the five gross elements in the same order as in the Sāṅkhya (see p. 83). Hence the soul mistakes itself for a mere mortal, as it mistook the rope for a snake.[2]

By reason of Māyā or A-vidyā, then, the Jīvātman, or 'personal spirit of every individual,' mistakes the world, as well as its own body and mind, for realities, just as a rope in a dark night might be mistaken for a snake. The moment the personal soul is set free from this self-imposed Delusion or Ignorance by a proper understanding of the

---

[1] Something like the Ἀγνοία of Plato. See Banerjea's translation of the Sūtras, p. 3.

[2] See Ballantyne's Lecture on the Vedānta-sāra, p. 25. Reference may also be made to the Vedānta-paribhāshā, a text-book of the most modern Vedāntic school.

truth, through the Vedānta philosophy, all the illusion vanishes and the identity of the Jīvātman and of the whole phenomenal universe with the Paramātman, or 'one only really existing spirit,' is re-established.[1]

Let me here introduce a version of part of a short Vedāntic tract in verse, called *Ātma-bodha*, 'knowledge of soul,' attributed to the great Śan·karāćārya. It is highly esteemed as an exposition of Vedāntic doctrines, and has therefore been inserted by Dr. Häberlin in his anthology of shorter poems.[2] The following metrical lines may serve as a specimen of some of the ideas contained in this well-known epitome of Hindū pantheistic philosophy:—

Knowledge alone effects emancipation.
As fire is indispensable to cooking,
So knowledge is essential to deliverance (2).
Knowledge alone disperses ignorance,
As sunlight scatters darkness—not so acts;
For ignorance originates in works (3).
The world and all the course of mundane things
Are like the vain creation of a dream,[3]
In which Ambition, Hatred, Pride, and Passion
Appear like phantoms mixing in confusion.
While the dream lasts the universe seems real,
But when 'tis past the world exists no longer (6).
Like the deceptive silver of a shell,[4]
So at first sight the world deludes the man
Who takes mere semblance for reality (7).
As golden bracelets are in substance one
With gold, so are all visible appearances
And each distinct existence one with Brahma (8).

---

1 See the passage from the Muṇḍaka Upanishad, quoted p. 39.

2 There is also a Tamil version and commentary translated by the Rev. I. F. Kearns, Madras, 1867. I have consulted the Tamil commentary as given by Mr. Kearns.

3 Cf. Shakspeare's 'We are such stuff As dreams are made on, and our little life Is rounded with a sleep.' Tempest, Act iv. Scene 1.

4 That is, the mother-of-pearl oyster (*śukti*).

By action of the fivefold elements[1]
Through acts performed in former states of being,
Are formed corporeal bodies, which become
The dwelling-place of pleasure and of pain (11).
The soul inwrapped in five investing sheaths[2]
Seems formed of these, and all its purity
Darkened, like crystal laid on coloured cloth (14).
As winnowed rice is purified from husk,
So is the soul disburdened of its sheaths
By force of meditation,[3] as by threshing (15).
The soul is like a king whose ministers
Are body, senses, mind, and understanding.[4]
The soul is wholly separate from these,
Yet witnesses and overlooks their actions (18).
The foolish think the Spirit acts, whereas
The senses are the actors, so the moon
Is thought to move when clouds are passing o'er it (19).
When intellect and mind are present, then
Affections, inclinations, pleasures, pains
Are active; in profound and dreamless sleep
When intellect is non-existent, these
Exist not; therefore they belong to mind (22).
As brightness is inherent in the sun,
Coolness in water, warmness in the fire,
E'en so existence, knowledge, perfect bliss,[5]

---

1 This is called *Pañći-kṛita* or *Pañći-karaṇa*, the production of the body, and indeed of the whole world, by the action of the five elements (see p. 83), being a dogma of the Vedānta.

2 See the remarks, p. 113.

3 *Yukti* seems here to be equivalent to *yoga*. It may also mean 'argument,' 'reasoning.'

4 The soul is supposed by Vedāntists to have three conditions besides the conditions of pure intelligence, viz., waking, dreaming, and profound or dreamless sleep (*su-shupti*). While awake, the soul, associated with the body, is active and has to do with a real creation. While dreaming, it has to do with an unreal or illusory world. When profoundly and dreamlessly asleep, it is supposed to have retired by the channel of some of the pericardial arteries into the perfect repose of union with the supreme Soul. See Vedānta-sūtra III. 2. 1–10.

5 Hence the Vedāntist's name for the one universal Spirit, *Saććid-ānanda*.

And perfect purity inhere in soul (23).
The understanding cannot recognize
The soul, nor does the soul need other knowledge
To know itself,[1] e'en as a shining light
Requires no light to make itself perceived (27, 28).
The soul declares its own condition thus—
'I am distinct from body, I am free
From birth, old age, infirmity, and death.
I have no senses; I have no connection
With sound or sight or objects of sensation.
I am distinct from mind, and so exempt
From passion, pride, aversion, fear, and pain.
I have no qualities,[2] I am without
Activity, and destitute of option,[3]
Changeless, eternal, formless, without taint,
For ever free, for ever without stain.
I, like the boundless ether, permeate
The universe within, without, abiding
Always, for ever similar in all,
Perfect, immovable, without affection,
Existence, knowledge, undivided bliss,
Without a second, One, supreme am I' (31–35).
The perfect consciousness that 'I am Brahma'
Removes the false appearances projected
By Ignorance,[4] just as elixir, sickness (36).
The universal Soul knows no distinction
Of knower, knowledge, object to be known.
Rather is it enlightened through itself
And its own essence, which is simple knowledge (40).
When contemplation rubs the Araṇi[5]

---

[1] The celebrated Hindū maxim, *Atmānam ātmanā paśya*, 'know (see) thyself by thyself,' or 'know the soul by the soul,' has, therefore, a deeper philosophical meaning than the still more celebrated Greek precept γνῶθι σεαυτόν, attributed to Thales.

[2] The epithet *nir-guṇa*, 'quality-less,' so commonly applied to the supreme Being in India, will be better understood by a reference to p. 85.

[3] *Nir-vikalpa* may perhaps be translated, 'destitute of all reflection,' or perhaps, 'free from all will.'

[4] *Avidyā-vikshepān*, 'the projections of ignorance.' See p. 109.

[5] See note, p. 15.

Of soul, the flame of knowledge blazing up
Quickly consumes the fuel ignorance (41).
The saint [1] who has attained to full perfection
Of contemplation, sees the universe
Existing in himself, and with the eye
Of knowledge sees the All as the One Soul (46).
When bodily disguises [2] are dissolved,
The perfect saint becomes completely blended
With the one Soul, as water blends with water,
As air unites with air, as fire with fire (52).
That gain than which there is no greater gain,
That joy than which there is no greater joy,
That lore than which there is no greater lore,
Is the one Brahma—this is certain truth (53).
That which is through, above, below, complete,
Existence, wisdom, bliss,[3] without a second,[4]
Endless, eternal, one—know that as Brahma (55).
That which is neither coarse nor yet minute,
That which is neither short nor long, unborn,
Imperishable, without form, unbound
By qualities, without distinctive marks,
Without a name—know that indeed as Brahma (59).
Nothing exists but Brahma, when aught else
Appears to be, 'tis, like the mirage, false [5] (62).

With regard to the five sheaths (*pańća-kośa*) alluded to in the fourteenth verse of the Ātma-bodha, it must be noted that in the Vedānta the individuated soul, when separated off from the supreme Soul, is regarded as enclosed in a succession of cases (*kośa*) which envelop it and, as it were, fold one over the other, 'like the coats of an onion.' [6] The first or innermost sheath is called the *Vijńāna-maya-kośa* or 'sheath composed of mere intellection,' associated with

[1] Yogin, see p. 92.
[2] *Upādhi*, a term for the illusive disguises assumed by Brahma.
[3] *Saé-éid-ānandam.* [4] *A-dvayam.*
[5] *Mithyā yathā maru marīéikā.*
[6] As remarked by Dr. Ballantyne, Lecture on the Vedānta-sara, p. 29.

the organs of perception. This gives the personal soul its first conception of individuality. The second case is called the *Mano-maya* or 'sheath composed of mind,' associated with the organs of action. This gives the individual soul its powers of thought and judgment. The third envelope is called the *Prāṇa-maya* or 'breathing sheath,' *i.e.*, the sheath composed of breath and the other vital airs associated with the organs of action. The fourth case is called the *Anna-maya* or 'covering supported by food,' *i.e.*, the corporeal form or gross body; the three preceding sheaths, when combined together, constituting the subtile body. A fifth case, called *Ānanda-maya* or 'that composed of supreme bliss,' is also named, although not admitted by all. It must be regarded as the innermost of all, and ought therefore, when five are enumerated, to be placed before the Vijñāna-maya. Moreover, a collective totality of subtile bodies is supposed to exist, and the soul, which is imagined to pass through these subtile bodies like a thread, is called the *Sūtrātman*, 'thread soul' (occasionally styled the *Prāṇātman*), and sometimes identified with Hiraṇya-garbha.

Of course the Vedānta theory, if pushed to its ultimate consequences, must lead to the neglect of all duties, religious and moral, of all activity, physical or intellectual, and of all self-culture. If everything (τὸ πᾶν) be God, then you and he and I must be one. Why should any efforts be made for the advancement of self or for the good of others? Everything we have must be common property. According to the Bṛihad-āraṇyaka Upanishad (IV. 5):—

Where there is anything like duality there one sees another, one smells another, one tastes another, one speaks to another, one hears another, one minds another, one regards another, one knows another; but where the whole of this (τὸ πᾶν) is one spirit, then whom and by what can one see? whom and by what can one smell? whom and by what can one taste? to whom and by what can one speak? whom and by what can one hear? whom and by what can one mind? whom and by what can one regard? whom and by what can one know?

This Indian pantheism is paralleled by some phases of modern German thought, as described by Dean Mansel in the following extract from one of his Essays lately published :—

With German philosophers the root of all mischief is the number two—Self and Not-self, Ego and Non-ego. The pantheist tells me that I have not a real distinct existence and unity of my own, but that I am merely a phenomenal manifestation, or an aggregate of many manifestations of the one infinite Being. If [then] we shrink from Nihilism, there remains the alternative of Pantheism. The instincts of our nature plead against annihilation and maintain, in spite of philosophy, that there must really exist something somewhere. Granting that something exists, why is that something to be called Ego? What qualities can it possess which shall make it *I* rather than *Thou*, or any one being rather than any other being? I am directly conscious of the existence of a self. But this consciousness is a delusion. This self is but the phenomenal shadow of a further self, of which I am not conscious. Why may not this also be a shadow of something further still? Why may there not be a yet more remote reality, which is itself neither self or not-self, but the root and foundation, and at the same time the indifference of both? This ultimate existence, the one and sole reality, is then set up as the deity of philosophy, and the result is pure pantheism.

Perhaps it may not be out of place here to contrast with Indian ideas Aristotle's grand conception of the nature of God as propounded in the eleventh book of his Metaphysics.[1] In chapter vii. of that book Aristotle says (not, however, quite in the order here given) :—

The principle of life is in God; for energy of mind constitutes life, and God is this energy. He, the first mover, imparts motion and pursues the work of creation as something that is loved (κινεῖ δὲ ὡς ἐρώμενον). His course of life (διαγωγή) must be similar to what is most excellent in our own short career. But he exists for ever in this excellence, whereas this is impossible for us. His pleasure consists in the exercise of his essential energy, and on this account vigilance, wakefulness, and percep-

---

[1] This work has been well translated by the Rev. J. H. M'Mahon.

tion are most agreeable to him. Again, the more we examine God's nature the more wonderful does it appear to us. He is an eternal (ἀΐδιον) and most excellent (ἄριστον) Being. He is indivisible (ἀδιαίρετος), devoid of parts (ἀμερής), and having no magnitude (μέγεθος), for God imparts motion through infinite time, and nothing finite, as magnitude is, can have an infinite capacity. He is a being devoid of passions and unalterable (ἀπαθὲς καὶ ἀναλλοίωτον).[1]

Before quitting the subject of the Vedānta philosophy it should be stated that in many points the Vedānta agrees with the Sāṅkhya. The order of creation in both is nearly the same, though the 'Originant' in one case is *Prakṛiti*, in the other *A-vidyā*, 'ignorance' (or 'false knowledge'). But even here an attempt is made by some to establish a community of ideas by identifying both *Prakṛiti* and *A-vidyā* with *Māyā* or 'illusion.' In both systems the gross elements proceed from subtile principles, imperceptible to sense, in the same order (see the Sāṅkhyan account of the elements, p. 83). In both there is a subtile as well as a gross body.[2] The nature of the soul in being incapable of cognition without the help of the mind or internal organ (*antaḥ-karaṇa*) is described in nearly similar language by both. Again, this internal

---

[1] Hence, according to the translator, Aristotle's idea of God is that he is a Being whose essence is love, manifested in eternal energy, the final cause of this energy being the happiness of his creatures, in which he himself participates for ever. Aristotle, again, warns his disciples against regarding God's nature through the medium of their own subjectivity. There is a celebrated passage in book XI. chap. viii., in which he says that traditions have been handed down representing the heavens as gods, and the divine essence (τὸ θεῖον) as embracing the whole of nature; and these traditions, he affirms, are kept up to win over the multitude and secure obedience to the laws and for the sake of general expediency. On that account gods are described as existing in the form of man (ἀνθρωποειδεῖς), or even as taking the shape of animals.

[2] The gross body is sometimes called the nine-gated city of Brahma (*Brahma-pura*), from its being the abode of the soul and from its having nine openings.

organ (*antaḥ-karaṇa*) is held by both to stand between the organs of perception and those of action, as an eleventh organ partaking of the nature of each (see p. 84). But while the Sāṅ-khya divides the internal organ into *Buddhi*, 'intellectual perception,' *Ahankāra*, 'self-consciousness,' and *Manas*, 'the reasoning mind,' the first being the great source of the others (see p. 83), the Vedānta propounds a fourth division, viz., *Ćitta* or 'the faculty of thought.' On the other hand, the Vedānta adds two Pramāṇas or 'instruments of true knowledge' (*An-upalabdhi*, 'non-perception' or 'negative proof,' and *Arthāpatti*, 'inference from circumstances') to the four admitted by the Nyāya (see p. 61), while the Sāṅ-khya rejects the Nyāya *Upamāna*, and retains as its only three Pramāṇas, *Pratyaksha*, *Anumāna*, and *Śabda*.

CHAPTER VII.

Irregular Systems and Eclectic School.

BEFORE passing to the Eclectic School I may mention that a celebrated work by Mādhava, called Sarva-darśana-san-graha, gives a concise description of various Hindū systems and sects, religious and philosophical, orthodox and heterodox, even including the science of applying quicksilver (*raseśvara*, regarded as a form of Śiva) or its preparations to various chemical and alchemical operations, and embracing also Pāṇini's theory of grammar.

Mādhava lived in the fourteenth century. He was elder brother of Sāyaṇa, and associated with him in the commentary on the Ṛig-veda. (By Mr. Burnell, however, in his preface to the Vaṉśa-brāhmaṇa, he is *identified* with Sāyaṇa.) He was also prime minister in the court of Bukka I. at Vijaya-nagara. He wrote many works (*e.g.*, an introduction to the Mīmāṉsā philosophy, called Nyāya-mālā-vistara, a commentary on Parāśara's law-book, the Kāla-nirṇāya, &c.), besides the Sarva-darśana-san-graha. This latter treats of fifteen systems as follow: 1. Ćārvāka-darśana; 2. Bauddha-d°; 3. Ārhata-d°; 4. Rāmānuja-d°; 5. Pūrṇa-prajña-d°; 6. Nakulīśa-pāśupata-d°; 7. Śaiva-d°; 8. Pratyabhijñā-d°; 9. Raseśvara-d°; 10. Aulūkya-d°; 11. Akshapāda-d°; 12. Jaimini-d°; 13. Pāṇini-d°; 14. Sān-khya-d°; 15. Pātañjala-d°. The Vedānta is not here included. The third in the list is the system of the Jainas or Jains, whom Mādhava calls Ārhata.[1] Rāmānuja, the

---

[1] In the previous edition of Indian Wisdom a short account was here given of the Jainas. This has been superseded by my summary of

founder of the fourth, was a Vaishṇava Reformer, who, according to H. H. Wilson, lived about the middle of the twelfth century. The fifth is the doctrine of Ānandatīrtha, surnamed Madhvāćārya, and also called Madhyamandira, his epithet *Pūrṇa-prajña* merely meaning 'one whose knowledge is complete. The sixth is the system of a branch of the Māheśvaras, as shown by Professor E. B. Cowell (Colebrooke's Essays, I. pp. 431, 434). He conjectures that Śiva himself, called Nakulīśa, may have been the supposed founder of this sect, and points out that the Pāśupatas are worshippers of Śiva as *Paśu-pati*, 'master of all inferior creatures' (explained by some to mean 'lord of *paśu* or the soul entangled in the bonds of matter'). The eighth is like the sixth and that of the Māheśvaras, a form of Śaiva doctrine, but more pantheistic, the Śaivas maintaining that God is in creating, *Karmādi-sāpeksha*, 'dependent on the acts, &c., of individual souls,' while this eighth asserts that God's will is the only cause of creation; for it is said, 'He being independent (*nir-apekshaḥ*) and regarding no face but his own, threw all existences as a reflection on the mirror of himself.' Hence *pratyabhijñā* is defined as *pratimābhimu-khyena jñānam*, 'recognition as of a visible object or image.' The tenth is the Vaiśeshika. (See note, p. 65.) I propose here to speak of the first only.

The Ćārvākas.

Nothing is known about Ćārvāka, the Pyrrho and Epicurus of India and founder of the materialistic school. His system is the worst form of all heresies, and therefore honoured with the first place in Mādhavāćārya's Sarva-

---

the Jaina system, and of the particular points which distinguish it from Buddhism, in my recent volume on Buddhism (p. 529), published by Mr. Murray, Albemarle Street.

darśana-san·graha. In the Śānti-parvan of the Mahā-bhārata (1410, &c.) there is a story of a Rākshasa named Cārvāka, who, in the disguise of a mendicant Brāhman, reviled Yudhishṭhira, during his triumphant entry into Hastināpura, and uttered profane and heretical doctrines. He was, however, soon detected, and the real Brāhmans, filled with fury, killed him on the spot. This legend may possibly rest on some basis of fact.

The creed of the Ćārvākas, who are sometimes called Lokāyatas or Lokāyatikas,[1] is said to have been derived from the Vārhaspatya Sūtras (Aphorisms of Vṛihaspati). They reject all the Pramāṇas, or 'sources of true knowledge,' except Pratyaksha, 'perception by the senses' (see p. 61); they admit only four Tattvas or 'eternal principles, viz., earth, air, fire, and water, and from these intelligence (*ćaitanya*) is alleged to be produced; they affirm that the soul is not different from the body; and, lastly, they assert that all the phenomena of the world are spontaneously produced, without even the help of Adṛishṭa (see p. 58). I sum up their views with a version of a passage in the Sarva-darśana-san·graha (Īśvara-ćandra Vidyāsāgara's edition, p. 6), setting forth the opinions of the Ćārvāka materialists according to the supposed teaching of Vṛihaspati.[2] The sentiments, it will be perceived, are worthy of the most sceptical, materialistic, and epicurean of European writers:—

---

[1] By some this name is given to a subdivision of the Ćārvākas. The name Ćārvāka is applied to any adherent of the materialistic school; see Vedānta-sāra, 82–85.

[2] I have consulted Professor E. B. Cowell's appendix to Colebrooke's Essay, and Dr. Muir's prose translation as given by him in his article on 'Indian Materialists' (Royal Asiatic Society's Journal, vol. xix., art. xi.). He compares a passage in the Vishṇu-purāṇa III. 18, which contains similar sentiments. Cf. also the speech of the rationalistic Brāhman Jāvāli, addressed to Rāma in the Rāmāyaṇa.

No heaven exists, no final liberation,
No soul, no other world, no rites of caste,
No recompense for acts; the Agnihotra,[1]
The triple Veda, triple self-command,[2]
And all the dust and ashes of repentance—
These yield a means of livelihood for men,
Devoid of intellect and manliness.
If victims slaughtered at a sacrifice
Are raised to heavenly mansions,[3] why should not
The sacrificer immolate his father?
If offerings of food can satisfy[4]
Hungry departed spirits, why supply
The man who goes a journey with provisions?
His friends at home can feed him with oblations.
If those abiding in celestial spheres
Are filled with food presented upon earth,
Why should not those who live in upper stories
Be nourished by a meal spread out below?
While life endures let life be spent in ease
And merriment;[5] let a man borrow money
From all his friends and feast on melted butter.
How can this body when reduced to dust
Revisit earth? and if a ghost can pass
To other worlds, why does not strong affection
For those he leaves behind attract him back?
The costly rites enjoined for those who die

---

[1] See note, p. 28.

[2] *Tri-daṇḍa*, 'control over thoughts, words, and actions,' denoted by the three Daṇḍas or staves carried by ascetics. See Manu XII. 10, 11.

[3] This, as Dr. Muir points out, refers to Manu V. 42, where it is stated that animals duly sacrificed are conveyed to mansions of supreme felicity. Cf. Mahā-bhārata, Āśvamedhika-parvan 793, &c.

[4] This is a hit at the S'rāddha, one of the most important of all Hindū religious acts, when oblations of cakes and libations of water are made to the spirits of deceased fathers, grandfathers, and progenitors. The strict observance of these ceremonies at regular intervals is at least an evidence of the strength of filial feeling among Hindūs. Respect for parents and their memory has all the sanction of religion, and is even more insisted on as a religious duty than in Europe.

[5] 'Let us eat and drink, for to-morrow we die' (1 Cor. xv. 32). See Dr. Muir's note. Compare such Horatian precepts as Epod. XIII. 3, &c.

Are a mere means of livelihood devised
By sacerdotal cunning—nothing more.
The three composers of the triple Veda
Were rogues, or evil spirits, or buffoons.
The recitation of mysterious words
And jabber [1] of the priests is simple nonsense.

Eclectic School of the Bhagavad-gītā.

As a fitting conclusion to the subject of Indian philosophy let me endeavour to give some idea of one of the most interesting and popular works in the whole range of Sanskṛit literature, called Bhagavad-gītā, the Song of Bhavagat—that is, the mystical doctrines (*Upanishadaḥ* [2]) sung by 'the adorable one'—a name applied to Kṛishṇa when identified with the supreme Being. This poem, abounding in sentiments borrowed from the Upanishads, and commented on by the great Vedāntic teacher Śankarāćārya, may be taken to represent the Eclectic school of Indian philosophy. As the regular systems or Darśanas were more or less developments of the Upanishads, so the Eclectic school is connected with those mystical treatises through the Śvetāśvatara Upanishad [3] of the Black Yajur-

---

[1] Two curious Vedic words, *jarbharī* and *turpharī*, are given in the text as specimens of what I suppose modern scoffers might call 'Vedic slang.' They occur, as Dr. Muir points out, in Ṛig-veda X. 106. 6, and Nirukta XIII. 5. For their explanation see Böhtlingk and Roth and my Sanskṛit-English Dictionary.

[2] At the end of each chapter the name of the chapter is given in the plural; thus, *Iti śrī-bhagavad-gītāsu upanishatsu*, &c. See note 4, p. 125.

[3] The name of this Upanishad is derived from a sage, S'vetāśvatara, who, at the end of the work (VI. 21), is said to have taught the doctrine of Brahma to the most excellent of the four orders. It has been translated by Dr. Röer into English, and nearly all by Professor Weber into German (Indische Studien I. 422–429). The author must have been a S'aiva (not a Vaishṇava, like the author of the Bhagavad-gītā), as he identifies Rudra with the supreme Being. According to Wilson,

veda (see p. 43). This latter is doubtless a comparatively modern work, but whether composed before or after the Bhagavad-gītā, certain it is that the design of both appears to be the same. They both aim at reconciling the conflicting views of different systems, and both do so by attempting to engraft the Sāṅkhya and Yoga upon Vedānta doctrines.[1] Although, therefore, the order of creation and much of the cosmogony and other Sāṅkhya views are retained in both, the paramount sovereignty of the supreme Soul of the universe (Brahma) as the source and ultimate end of all created things, and yet wholly independent of all such creations, is asserted by both.

Some extracts from the Śvetāśvatara, describing the character and attributes of this supreme Being, who is everything and in everything, have already been given at p. 43. The following are additional extracts from the first and third chapters (Röer, pp. 50, 55, 58) :—

This (absolute Brahma) should be meditated on as eternal and as abiding in one's own soul; for beside him there is nothing to be known (*nātaḥ paraṃ veditavyaṃ hi kiñcit*). As oil in seeds (*tileshu*), butter in cream, water in a river, and fire in wood, so is that absolute Soul perceived within himself by a person who beholds him by means of truth and by austerity.

He is the eye of all, the face of all, the arm of all, the foot of all.

Thou art the black bee (*nīlaḥ pataṅgaḥ*), the green bird with red-coloured eye, the cloud in whose womb sleeps the lightning, the seasons, the seas. Without beginning thou pervadest all things by thy almighty power; for by thee are all the worlds created.

The following, again, is an example of a passage occur-

Śveta, 'white,' *Śvetāśva*, 'white-horsed,' *Śveta-śikha*, 'white-haired,' and *Śveta-lohita*, 'white-blooded,' were names of four disciples of S'iva. Weber suspects here a mission of Syrian Christians, and thinks that both the Upanishad and the Gītā, the latter especially, may have borrowed ideas from Christianity.

[1] See Dr. Röer's introduction for a full explanation of this.

ring in the fourth chapter (5), which is decidedly Sān-khyan in its tone:—

The one unborn (individual soul), for the sake of enjoyment, lies close to the One unborn (*Prakṛiti*), which is of a white, red, and black colour [answering evidently to the three Sān-khyan Guṇas], which is of one and the same form, and produces a manifold offspring. Then the other unborn (or eternal soul) abandons her (*Prakṛiti*) whose enjoyment he has enjoyed.

Let us now turn to the Bhagavad-gītā. The real author of this work is unknown. It was at an early date dignified by a place in the Mahā-bhārata, in which poem it lies imbedded, or rather inlaid like a pearl,[1] contributing with other numerous episodes to the mosaic-like character of that immense epic. The Bhagavad-gītā, however, is quite independent of the great epic; and it cannot be questioned that its proper place in any arrangement of Sanskṛit literature framed with regard to the continuous development and progress of Hindū thought and knowledge should be at the close of the subject of philosophy. The author was probably a Brāhman and nominally a Vaishṇava, but really a philosopher whose mind was cast in a broad and comprehensive mould. He is supposed to have lived in India during the first or second century

---

[1] It has been interpolated into the Bhīshma-parvan of the Mahābhārata, and is divided into eighteen chapters or into three sections, each containing six lectures, commencing at line 830 of the twenty-fifth chapter of the Parva, and ending at line 1532. Such is the estimation in which the work is held both in Asia and Europe, that it has been translated into Hindī, Telugu, Kanarese, and other Eastern languages, and is also well known by European translations, of which that of Sir C. Wilkins, published in London in 1785, was the first. Mr. J. C. Thomson's edition and translation, published, with an elaborate introduction, by Stephen Austin in 1855, is, on the whole, a very meritorious production, and I am glad to acknowledge my obligations to it.

of our era.[1] Finding no rest for his spirit in any one system of philosophy, as commonly taught in his own time, much less in the corrupt Brāhmanism which surrounded him, he was led to make a selection from the various schools of rationalistic and dogmatic thought, so as to construct a composite theory of his own. This he did with great perspicuity and beauty of language, interweaving various opinions into one system by taking, so to speak, threads from the Sān-khya, Yoga, and Vedānta, as well as from the later theory of Bhakti or 'faith in a supreme Being.'[2] With these threads he weaves, as it were, a woof of many-coloured hues of thought, which are shot across a stiff warp of stern uncompromising pantheistic doctrines, worthy of the most decided adherent of the Vedānta school.[3] Of these cross threads the most conspicuous are those of the Sān-khya system, for which the author of the Gītā has an evident predilection. The whole composition is skilfully thrown into the form of a dramatic poem or dialogue, something after the manner of the book of Job or a dialogue of Plato.[4] The speakers

---

[1] Some consider that he lived as late as the third century, and some place him even later, but with these I cannot agree.

[2] The Aphorisms of Śāndilya, the editing of which was commenced by Dr. Ballantyne and continued by Professor Griffith, his successor at Benares, deny that knowledge is the one thing needful, and insist on the subjection of knowledge to the higher principle of *Bhakti*, 'faith in God.' The first Aphorism introduces the inquiry into the nature of faith, thus, *Athāto bhakti-jijñāsā.* Professor Weber and others think that the introduction of πίστις and ἀγάπη into the Hindū system is due to the influence of Christianity.

[3] The predominance of pantheistic doctrines, notwithstanding the attempt to interweave them with portions of the Sān-khya and Yoga systems, is denoted by the fact that the Vedāntists claim this poem as an exponent of their own opinions.

[4] It is, however, styled an Upanishad, or rather a series of Upanishads, because, like the Upanishads, it reveals secret and mystical

are the two most important personages in the Mahā-bhārata, Arjuna, and Kṛishṇa. Arjuna is perhaps the real hero of that epic. He is the bravest, and yet the most tender-hearted of the five sons of Pāṇḍu. The god Kṛishṇa, who is identified with Vishṇu,[1] and in this philosophical dialogue is held to be an incarnation of the supreme Being himself, had taken human form as the son of Devakī and Vasudeva, who was brother of Kuntī, wife of Pāṇḍu. Hence the god was cousin of the sons of Pāṇḍu, brother of Dhṛitarāshṭra, the sons of these brothers being of course related as cousins to each other. In the great war which arose between the two families, each contending for the kingdom of Hastināpura,[2] Kṛishṇa refused to take up arms on either side, but consented to act as the charioteer of Arjuna and to aid him with his advice. At the commencement of the Bhagavad-gītā the two contending

---

doctrines. For instance, at the close of the dialogue (XVIII. 63), Kṛishṇa says, 'I have thus communicated to you knowledge more secret than secret itself' (*iti me jñānam ākhyātaṃ guhyād guhyataraṃ mayā*).

[1] Professor Weber (Indische Studien I. 400) thinks that Brāhmans may have crossed the sea to Asia Minor at the beginning of the Christian era, and on their return made use of Christian narratives to fabricate the story of their deified hero, Kṛishṇa, whose very name would remind them of Christ. The legends of the birth of Kṛishṇa and his persecution by Kaṇsa remind us, says Weber, too strikingly of the corresponding Christian narratives to leave room for the supposition that the similarity is quite accidental. According to Lassen, the passages of the Mahābhārata in which Kṛishṇa receives divine honours are later interpolations, and the real worship of Kṛishṇa is not found before the fifth or sixth century. Dr. Lorinser, as we shall presently see, thinks he can trace the influence of Christianity throughout the Bhagavad-gītā. The legend of S'veta-dvīpa in the Mahā-bhārata (XII. 12703) certainly favours the idea of some intercourse with Europe at an early date. The legends relating to Kṛishṇa are found detailed at full in the tenth book of the Bhāgavata-purāṇa and its Hindī paraphrase, the Prem Sāgar.

[2] See the epitome of this great epic in a subsequent Chapter.

armies are supposed to be drawn up in battle array, when Arjuna, struck with sudden compunction at the idea of fighting his way to a kingdom through the blood of his kindred, makes a sudden resolution to retire from the combat, confiding his thoughts to Kṛishṇa thus (I. 28–33):—

Beholding these my relatives arrayed
Before my eyes in serried line of battle,
Preparing for the deadly fray, my limbs
Are all relaxed, my blood dries up, a tremor
Palsies my frame, the hairs upon my skin
Bristle with horror, all my body burns
As if with fever, and my mind whirls round,
So that I cannot stand upright, nor hold
The bow Gāṇḍīva slipping from my hand.
I cannot—will not fight—O mighty Kṛishṇa.
I seek not victory, I seek no kingdom.
What shall we do with regal pomp and power,
What with enjoyments or with life itself,
When we have slaughtered all our kindred here?

Kṛishṇa's reply to this speech is made the occasion of the long philosophical and theological dialogue which, in fact, constitutes the Bhagavad-gītā, the main design of which undoubtedly is to exalt the duties of caste above all other obligations, including the ties of friendship and affection, but at the same time to show that the practice of these duties is compatible with all the self-mortification and concentration of thought enjoined by the Yoga philosophy, as well as with the deepest devotion to the supreme Being, with whom Kṛishṇa claims to be identified.[1] As Arjuna belongs to the military caste, he is exhorted to

[1] There is a sect among the Hindūs called Gāṇapatyas, who identify Gaṇapati or Gaṇeśa with the supreme Being. Their doctrines are embodied in the Gaṇeśa-purāṇa, but they have a poem called the Gaṇeśa-gītā, which is identical in substance with the Bhagavad-gītā, the name of Gaṇeśa being substituted for that of Kṛishṇa.

perform his duties as a soldier. Again and again is he urged to fight, without the least thought about consequences, and without the slightest question as to the propriety of slaughtering his relations, if only he acts in the path of duty. Hence we have the following sentiments repeated more than once (III. 35, XVIII. 47, 48):—

Better to do the duty of one's caste,[1]
Though bad and ill-performed and fraught with evil,
Than undertake the business of another,
However good it be. For better far
Abandon life at once than not fulfil
One's own appointed work; another's duty
Brings danger to the man who meddles with it.
Perfection is alone attained by him
Who swerves not from the business of his caste.

Remembering the sacred character attributed to this poem and the veneration in which it has always been held throughout India, we may well understand that such words as these must have exerted a powerful influence for the last 1800 years; tending, as they must have done, to rivet the fetters of caste-institutions which, for several centuries preceding the Christian era, notwithstanding the efforts of the great liberator Buddha, increased year by year their hold upon the various classes of Hindū society, impeding mutual intercourse, preventing healthy interchange of ideas, and making national union almost impossible.

Before proceeding to offer further examples, we may remark that as the Bhagavad-gītā is divided into three sections, each containing six chapters, so the philosophical teaching is somewhat distinct in each section.

---

[1] Compare S'akuntalā, verse 133, 'Verily the occupation in which a man is born, though it be in bad repute, must not be abandoned.' The words used (*saha-jaṃ-karma*) are the same as those in the Bhagavad-gītā.

The first section dwells chiefly on the benefits of the Yoga system, pointing out, however, as we have already observed, that the asceticism of the Yoga ought to be joined with action and the performance of regular caste duties, and winding up with a declaration that the grand end and aim of all asceticism is to attain that most desirable pantheistic state which enables a man to see God in everything and everything in God. Arjuna is exhorted as a member of the soldier-caste to dismiss all doubt about the propriety of fighting and killing his relations, by an argument drawn from the eternal existence of the soul, which is nobly expressed thus (II. 11, &c.):[1] —

The wise grieve not for the departed, nor for those who yet survive.
Ne'er was the time when I was not, nor thou, nor yonder chiefs, and ne'er
Shall be the time when all of us shall be not; as the embodied soul
In this corporeal frame moves swiftly on through boyhood, youth, and age,
So will it pass through other forms hereafter—be not grieved thereat.
The man whom pain and pleasure, heat and cold affect not, he is fit
For immortality; whatever is not cannot be, whatever is
Can never cease to be. Know this — the Being that spread this universe
Is indestructible. Who can destroy the Indestructible?
These bodies that inclose the everlasting soul, inscrutable,
Immortal, have an end; but he who thinks the soul can be destroyed,
And he who deems it a destroyer, are alike mistaken; it
Kills not, and is not killed; it is not born, nor doth it ever die;
It has no past nor future—unproduced, unchanging, infinite; he
Who knows it fixed, unborn, imperishable, indissoluble,
How can that man destroy another, or extinguish aught below?
As men abandon old and threadbare clothes to put on others new,
So casts the embodied soul its worn-out frame to enter other forms.
No dart can pierce it; flame cannot consume it, water wet it not,
Nor scorching breezes dry it—indestructible, incapable

[1] I have endeavoured to give a more literal version than the well-known one of Dean Milman, though I have followed him in some expressions.

Of heat or moisture or aridity, eternal, all-pervading,
Steadfast, immovable, perpetual, yet imperceptible,
Incomprehensible, unfading, deathless, unimaginable.[1]

The duty of Yoga or 'intense concentration of the mind on one subject' (viz., the supreme Being, here identified with Kṛishṇa), till at last the great end of freedom from all thought, perfect calm, and absorption in the Deity are obtained, is enjoined with much force of language in the second and sixth books, from which I extract the following examples, translated nearly literally, but not quite according to the order of the text:—

That holy man who stands immovable,
As if erect upon a pinnacle,[2]
His appetites and organs all subdued,
Sated with knowledge secular and sacred,
To whom a lump of earth, a stone, or gold,[3]
To whom friends, relatives, acquaintances,
Neutrals and enemies, the good and bad,
Are all alike, is called 'one yoked with God.'
The man who aims at that supreme condition
Of perfect yoking[4] with the Deity
Must first of all be moderate in all things,
In food, in sleep, in vigilance, in action,
In exercise and recreation. Then
Let him, if seeking God by deep abstraction,
Abandon his possessions and his hopes,
Betake himself to some secluded spot,[5]
And fix his heart and thoughts on God alone.
There let him choose a seat, not high nor low,

---

[1] Compare the passage from the Kaṭha Upanishad, translated, p. 41.

[2] *Kūṭa-sthaḥ* (VI. 8) may mean 'standing erect like a peak.'

[3] Tersely expressed in Sanskrit by *sama-loshṭāśma-kāñćanaḥ* VI. 8.

[4] I use these expressions as kindred words to the Sanskṛit *yukta* and *yoga*. 'Joined' and 'junction' are also cognate expressions.

[5] Cf. Matt. vi. 6, 'But thou, when thou prayest, enter into thy closet, and when thou hast shut thy door, pray to thy Father which is in secret.'

And with a cloth or skin to cover him,
And Kuśa grass beneath him, let him sit
Firm and erect, his body, head, and neck
Straight and immovable, his eyes directed
Towards a single point,[1] not looking round,
Devoid of passion, free from anxious thought,
His heart restrained, and deep in meditation.
E'en as a tortoise draws its head and feet
Within its shell, so must he keep his organs
Withdrawn from sensual objects. He whose senses
Are well controlled attains to sacred knowledge,
And thence obtains tranquillity of thought.
Without quiescence there can be no bliss.
E'en as a storm-tossed ship upon the waves,
So is the man whose heart obeys his passions,
Which, like the winds, will hurry him away.
Quiescence is the state of the Supreme.
He who, intent on meditation, joins
His soul with the Supreme, is like a flame
That flickers not when sheltered from the wind.

I pass now to the second division of this poem, in which the pantheistic doctrines of the Vedānta are more directly inculcated than in the other sections. Kṛishṇa here in the plainest language claims adoration as one with the great universal Spirit, pervading and constituting the universe. I extract portions from different parts of this section without observing the order of the text, which contains much tautology, as well as repetitions of similar ideas in different language :—

Whate'er thou dost perform, whate'er thou eatest,
Whate'er thou givest to the poor, whate'er
Thou offerest in sacrifice, whatever
Thou doest as an act of holy penance,
Do all as if to me, O Arjuna (IX. 27).[2]

---

[1] The text (VI. 13) says, 'fixing his eyes on the tip of his nose' (*samprekshya-nāsikāgram*). See p. 93.

[2] Compare 1 Cor. x. 31, 'Whether therefore ye eat, or drink, or whatsoever ye do, do all to the glory of God.' Dr. Lorinser, expand-

I am the ancient sage,[1] without beginning,
I am the Ruler and the All-sustainer,[2]
I am incomprehensible in form,
More subtle and minute than subtlest atoms;[3]
I am the cause of the whole universe;
Through me it is created and dissolved;
On me all things within it hang suspended,

---

ing the views of Professor Weber and others concerning the influence of Christianity on the legends of Kṛishṇa, thinks that many of the sentiments of the Bhagavad-gītā have been directly borrowed from the New Testament, copies of which, he thinks, found their way into India about the third century, when he believes the poem to have been written. He even adopts the theory of a parallel in the names of Christ and Kṛishṇa. He seems, however, to forget that fragments of truth are to be found in all religious systems, however false, and that the Bible, though a true revelation, is still in regard to the human mind, through which the thoughts are transfused, a thoroughly Oriental book, cast in an Oriental mould, and full of Oriental ideas and expressions. Some of his comparisons seem mere coincidences of language, which might occur quite naturally and independently. In other cases, where he draws attention to coincidences of ideas—as, for example, the division of the sphere of self-control into thought, word, and deed in chap. XVII. 14–16, &c., and of good works into prayer, fasting, and almsgiving—how could these be borrowed from Christianity, when they are also found in Manu, which few will place later than the fifth century B.C.? Thus a *Tri-daṇḍin* (Manu XII. 10) is explained to mean 'a triple commander,' who commands his thoughts, words, and actions (see note 2, p. 121); the same division is found in Manu II. 192, 236. Professor Cowell has pointed out that it occurs still earlier than Manu, in the Black Yajur-veda VI. 1. 7, and its Āraṇyaka X. 1. 10, and in the Aitareya-brāhmaṇa III. 28. Plato also has the same in his Protagoras (p. 348), and it is found in the Zand Avastā (Gāthā Ahunavaiti III. 3). Nevertheless, something may be said for Dr. Lorinser's theory. His German translation (1869) is rich in notes, pointing out parallels. See also the 'Indian Antiquary' for October 1873.

[1] *Kaviḥ purāṇaḥ* VIII. 9. 'Kavi' in Vedic Sanskṛit means 'wise,' and is an epithet applied to most of the gods, especially to Agni. The meaning 'poet' belongs to later Sanskṛit.

[2] *Sarvasya dhātā* VIII. 9.

[3] *Aṇor aṇīyān* VIII. 9. Compare p. 71 of this volume.

Like pearls upon a string.[1] I am the light
In sun and moon, far, far beyond the darkness;[2]
I am the brilliancy in flame, the radiance
In all that's radiant, and the light of lights,[3]
The sound in ether, fragrance in the earth,
The seed eternal of existing things,[4]
The life in all, the father, mother, husband,
Forefather, and sustainer of the world,
Its friend and lord. I am its way[5] and refuge,
Its habitation and receptacle,
I am its witness. I am Victory
And Energy; I watch the universe
With eyes and face in all directions turned.[6]
I dwell, as Wisdom, in the heart of all.[7]
I am the Goodness of the good, I am
Beginning, Middle, End, eternal Time,
The Birth, the Death of all.[8] I am the symbol A
Among the characters.[9] I have created all

---

1 VII. 7. Dr. Lorinser compares Rom. xi. 36, 'Of him, and through him, and unto him, are all things.' John i. 3, 'All things were made by him; and without him was not anything made that was made.'

2 *Prabhāsmi śaśi-sūryayoḥ* VII. 8.. *Tamasaḥ parastāt* VIII. 9. Cf. 1 John i. 5, 'God is light, and in him is no darkness at all.' See Ṛig-veda I. 50. 10.

3 *Jyotishāṃ jyotiḥ* XIII. 17. Cf. Bṛihad-āraṇyaka Upanishad, quoted p. 37 of this volume.

4 *Sarva-bhūtānāṃ vījam* VII. 10, X. 39. Cf. John i. 3, 'All things were made by him.'

5 *Gati* IX. 18. Cf. John xiv. 6, 'I am the way.'

6 *Viśvato-mukha*, 'facing in all directions,' IX. 15.

7 *Jñānaṃ hṛidi sarvasya nishṭhitam* XIII. 17. Cf. 2 Cor. iv. 6.

8 Compare Rev. i. 17, 18, 'I am the first and the last; and have the keys of hell and of death.' Mr. Mullens draws attention to parallel descriptions of the supreme Ruler in the Greek Orphic hymns: 'Zeus was the first and Zeus the last; Zeus is the head; Zeus, the centre; from Zeus have all things been made; Zeus is the breath of all things; Zeus is the sun and moon,' &c. See his Essay, p. 193, and cf. note 2, p. 102. Cf. also an inscription said to exist in a temple of Athene, 'Εγὼ εἰμὶ πᾶν τὸ γεγονὸς καὶ ὂν καὶ ἐσόμενον.

9 *Aksharāṇām a-kāro 'smi* X. 33. Compare Rev. i. 8, 'I am Alpha and Omega.'

Out of one portion of myself. E'en those
Who are of low and unpretending birth,[1]
May find the path to highest happiness,
If they depend on me; how much more those
Who are by rank and penance holy Brāhmans
And saintly soldier-princes like thyself.
Then be not sorrowful; from all thy sins
I will deliver thee.[2] Think thou on me,
Have faith in me, adore and worship me,[3]
And join thyself in meditation to me;
Thus shalt thou come to me, O Arjuna;
Thus shalt thou rise to my supreme abode,
Where neither sun nor moon have need to shine,
For know that all the lustre they possess is mine.[4]

---

[1] *Pāpa-yonayaḥ*, 'base-born,' IX. 32. The text states who these are, viz., Women, Vaiśyas, and Śūdras. This is significant in regard to the Hindū estimate of the female sex. A woman's religion is thought to consist in obedience first to her father and then to her husband, with attention to domestic duties. See Manu II. 67. But the joining of Vaiśyas with Śūdras is curious (cf. p. 149. 6). Brāhmans, Kshatriyas, and Rājarshis, *i.e.*, holy personages—half princes, half saints—are by birth and rank fitted for religious exercises, and more likely to reach heaven.

[2] *Ahaṃ tvāṃ sarva-pāpebhyo moćayishyāmi mā śućaḥ.* Cf. Matt. ix. 2, 'Be of good cheer; thy sins be forgiven thee.' A sense of original corruption seems to be felt by all classes of Hindūs, as indicated by the following prayer used after the Gāyatrī by many religious persons:—

Pāpo 'ham pāpa-karmāham pāpātmā pāpa-sambhavaḥ,
Trāhi mām, puṇḍarīkāksha sarva-pāpa-hara Hare,

'I am sinful, I commit sin, my nature is sinful, I am conceived in sin,
Save me, O thou lotus-eyed Hari, the remover of sin.'

[3] The original is, *Man-manā bhava mad-bhakto mad-yājī māṃ namaskuru* IX. 34. Cf. Prov. xxiii. 26, 'My son, give me thine heart.'

[4] *Na tad bhāsayate sūryo na Śaśāṅkaḥ* XV. 6. *Yad āditya-gataṃ tejo yać ćandramasi tat tejo viddhi māmakam* XV. 12. Cf. Rev. xxi. 23, 'The city had no need of the sun, neither of the moon, to shine in it: for the glory of God did lighten it.' Cf. also Mahā-bhārata III. 1745, &c., *Na tatra sūryāḥ somo vā dyotate na ća pāvakaḥ, Svayaiva prabhayā tatra dyotante puṇya-labdhayā*, 'there (in Indra's heaven) the sun shines not, nor the moon nor fire; there they (righteous men) shine by their own glory acquired by their own merit.'

I come now to chapter XI., called 'the Vision (or Revelation) of the Universal Form' (*viśva-rūpa-darśanam*). Arjuna, filled with awe at the discovery of the true nature of Kṛishṇa, acting as his charioteer, addresses him thus :—

Most mighty Lord supreme, this revelation
Of thy mysterious essence and thy oneness
With the eternal Spirit, clears away
The mists of my illusions. Show me then
Thy form celestial, most divine of men,[1]
If haply I may dare to look upon it.

To this Kṛishṇa replies :—

Thou canst not bear to gaze upon my shape
With these thy human eyes, O son of Pāṇḍu,
But now I gift thee with celestial vision;
Behold me in a hundred thousand forms,
In phases, colours, fashions infinite.

Here follows the description of Kṛishṇa's supernatural transformation :[2]—

Thus having said, the mighty Lord of all
Displayed to Arjuna his form supreme,
Endowed with countless mouths and countless eyes,
With countless faces turned to every quarter,
With countless marvellous appearances,
With ornaments and wreaths and robes divine,
With heavenly fragrance and celestial weapons.
It was as if the firmament were filled,
All in an instant, with a thousand suns,
Blazing with dazzling lustre, so beheld he
The glories of the universe collected
In the one person of the God of gods.[3]

---

[1] *Purushottama*, 'most excellent of men,' a common name for Kṛishṇa.

[2] The idea of this, Dr. Lorinser considers borrowed from the Gospel narrative of the transfiguration. It is certainly very instructive to contrast the simplicity of the Gospel scene: 'His face did shine as the sun, and his raiment was white as the light,' Matt. xvii. 2, Mark ix. 3.

[3] In the Udyoga-parva of the Mahā-bhārata (4419–4430) Kṛishṇa

Arjuna, with every hair on his body bristling with awe, bows his head at this vision, and folding his hands in reverence, gives utterance to a passionate outburst of enthusiastic adoration, which I here abridge :—

I see thee, mighty Lord of all, revealed
In forms of infinite diversity.
I see thee like a mass of purest light,
Flashing thy lustre everywhere around.
I see thee crowned with splendour like the sun,
Pervading earth and sky, immeasurable,
Boundless, without beginning, middle, end,
Preserver of imperishable law,
The everlasting Man ;[1] the triple world
Is awe-struck at this vision of thy form,
Stupendous, indescribable in glory.
Have mercy, God of gods ; the universe
Is fitly dazzled by thy majesty,
Fitly to thee alone devotes its homage.
At thy approach the evil demons flee,
Scattered in terror to the winds of heaven.
The multitude of holy saints[2] adore thee—
Thee, first Creator,[3] lord of all the gods,
The ancient One,[4] supreme Receptacle
Of all that is and is not, knowing all,
And to be known by all. Immensely vast,

---

reveals his form in the same way to the assembled princes, who are obliged to close their eyes at the awful sight, while the blind Dhṛitarāshṭra is gifted with divine vision that he may behold the glorious spectacle (4437).

[1] *Sanātanaḥ purushaḥ* (XI. 18) may be translated 'the eternal Spirit.'

[2] *Maharshis*, great saints and Siddhas, XI. 21. Cf. parts of the Te Deum. The Siddhas are semi-divine beings supposed to possess great purity, called Sādhyas in the earlier mythology (Manu I. 22). Siddhas and Sādhyas are sometimes confused, though mentioned separately in the text.

[3] Cf. John viii. 58, 'Before Abraham was, I am.'

[4] *Purushaḥ purāṇaḥ*, 'the most ancient person,' XI. 38. Cf. Daniel vii. 9, 'The Ancient of days did sit.'

Thou comprehendest all, thou art the All (XI. 40).
To thee earth's greatest heroes must return,
Blending once more with thy resplendent essence,
Like mighty rivers rushing to the ocean (XI. 28).
To thee be sung a thousand hymns of praise
By every creature and from every quarter,
Before, above, behind. Hail! Hail! thou All!
Again and yet again I worship thee.
Have mercy, I implore thee, and forgive,
That I, in ignorance of this thy glory,
Presumed to call thee Friend; and pardon too
Whate'er I have too negligently uttered,
Addressing thee in too familiar tones.
Unrivalled God of gods, I fall before thee
Prostrate in adoration, thou the Father
Of all that lives and lives not; have compassion,
Bear with me, as a father with a son,
Or as a lover with a cherished one.
Now that I see thee as thou really art,
I thrill with terror! Mercy! Lord of lords,
Once more display to me thy human form,
Thou habitation of the universe.[1]

Many other remarkable passages might be adduced in connection with the first two divisions of the subject-matter of the Bhagavad-gītā. I note the following:—

He who has brought his members under subjection, but sits with foolish mind thinking in his heart of sensual things, is called a hypocrite (*mithyācāra*). (III. 6. Cf. Matt. v. 28.)

Many are my births that are past; many are thine too, O Arjuna. I know them all, but thou knowest them not. (IV. 5. Cf. John viii. 14.)

For the establishment of righteousness am I born from time to time. (IV. 8. Cf. John xviii. 37, 1 John iii. 3.)

---

[1] XI. 45, 46. Dr. Lorinser compares the awe of our Lord's disciples, Matt. xvii. 6, 'They fell on their face, and were sore afraid.' Also of Simon Peter, Luke v. 8, 'When Simon Peter saw it, he fell down at Jesus' knees, saying, Depart from me; for I am a sinful man, O Lord.'

I am dearer to the wise than all possessions, and he is dear to me. (VI. 17. Cf. Luke xiv. 33, John xiv. 21.)

The ignorant, the unbeliever, and he of a doubting mind perish utterly. (IV. 40. Cf. Mark xvi. 16.)

In him are all beings, by him this universe was spread out. (VIII. 22. Cf. Acts xvii. 28.)

Deluded men despise me when I have taken human form. (IX. 11. Cf. John i. 10.)

In all the Vedas I am to be known. (XV. 15. Cf. John v. 39.)

As many uses as there are in a reservoir filled with waters coming from all parts (for bathing, washing, or drinking), so many does a knowing Brāhman find in all the Vedas. (II. 46. Mr. Thomson compares the various uses made of texts from our own sacred Scriptures.)

The next is suggestive of the doctrine that the condition of the soul for a future state is determined before death :—

Whatever a man's state of mind be at the moment when he leaves the body to that condition does he always go, being made to conform to that. (VIII. 6. Cf. Eccles. xi. 3. This is the dying Sanskāra which delays the passage to heaven.)

A similar passage occurs in the Ćhāndogya Upanishad :—

Man is a creature of intelligence (*kratu-maya*) ; whatever ideas he forms in this life, he becomes so when he departs to another, therefore he should reflect (on God, III. 14. 1).

The next is a paraphrase of XVI. 12–16. It may be compared with Luke xii. 17–20 :—

Entangled in a hundred worldly snares,
Self-seeking men, by ignorance deluded,
Strive by unrighteous means to pile up riches.
Then, in their self-complacency, they say,
'This acqusition I have made to-day,
That I will gain to-morrow ; so much pelf
Is hoarded up already, so much more
Remains that I have yet to treasure up
This enemy I have destroyed, him also

And others in their turn I will despatch.
I am a lord; I will enjoy myself;
I'm wealthy, noble, strong, successful, happy:
I'm absolutely perfect; no one else
In all the world can be compared to me.
Now I will offer up a sacrifice,
Give gifts with lavish hand and be triumphant.'
Such men, befooled by endless, vain conceits,
Caught in the meshes of the world's illusion,
Immersed in sensuality, descend
Down to the foulest hell of unclean spirits.

I add a few lines from chapter III., in which Kṛishṇa exhorts Arjuna to energetic action by an argument drawn from the example set by himself in his own everlasting exertions for the good of the world (cf. John v. 17). The order of the text is not observed in the following version, and the sentiment in lines 6, 7, is from chapter II. 47:—

Perform all necessary acts, for action
Is better than inaction, none can live
By sitting still and doing nought; it is
By action only that a man attains
Immunity from action. Yet in working
Ne'er work for recompense; let the act's motive
Be in the act itself. Know that work
Proceeds from the Supreme. I am the pattern
For man to follow; know that I have done
All acts already, nought remains for me
To gain by action, yet I work for ever
Unweariedly, and this whole universe
Would perish if I did not work my work (III. 19).

The third division of the poem, comprising the six last chapters, aims particularly at interweaving Sāṅkhya doctrines with the Vedānta, though this is done more or less throughout the whole work. It accepts the doctrine of a supreme presiding Spirit (called *Param Brahma* or *Adhyātmam*, XIII. 12, VIII. 1), as the first source of the universe, but asserts the eternal existence of Prakṛiti and

Purusha—that is, of an original eternal element and soul—both emanating from the supreme Being (then regarded as *Parā Prakṛiti*, 'supreme Prakṛiti'). It maintains the individuality and personality of souls, and affirms that the body (*kshetra*) and all the world of sense is evolved out of Prakṛiti by the regular Sān-khyan process, through Buddhi, Ahān-kāra, the five subtile elements, the five grosser elements, and the eleven organs, including mind. Thus, in XIII. 19 and in VII. 4–6, we read :—

Learn that *Prakṛiti* and *Purusha* also are both of them without beginning. And know that the Vikāras, or 'productions,' and the Guṇas (see p. 85) are sprung from Prakṛiti.

Earth, water, fire, air, ether, mind, intellect, and egoism, into these eight is my Prakṛiti divided. This Prakṛiti is the inferior one, but learn my superior Prakṛiti to be other than this. Understand that all things are produced from this other Prakṛiti.

Again, in VII. 12–14, Kṛishṇa, speaking of the three Guṇas, says :—

Know that all the three Guṇas, whether Sattva, Rajas, or Tamas (cf. p. 85), proceed only from me. I am not in them, but they in me.

All this universe, deluded by these three conditions consisting of the Guṇas, does not recognise me, the imperishable Being, superior to them all.

For this divine illusion (*Māyā*, i.e., 'illusory creation'), consisting of the three Guṇas, caused by me, is difficult to be passed over. Those only are delivered from it who have recourse to me.

The eclecticism of the Bhagavad-gītā will be sufficiently apparent from these examples. I close my brief survey of this celebrated poem by three or four passages (taken from chapter III. 27, chapter XIII. 29, 31), which form a fit conclusion to the subject, as they contain the gist of the whole argument, viz., that it is Arjuna's duty as a soldier to act like a soldier and to do the work of his caste, regardless of consequences; and that this may be done consistently with adhesion to the Vedāntic dogma of the soul's real inactivity and state of passionless repose :—

All actions are incessantly performed
By operation of the qualities
Of Prakṛiti ; deluded by the thought
Of individuality, the soul
Vainly believes itself to be the doer.
The soul existing from eternity,
Devoid of qualities, imperishable,
Abiding in the body, yet supreme,
Acts not, nor is by any act polluted.
He who perceives that actions are performed
By Prakṛiti alone, and that the soul
Is not an actor, sees the truth aright.

Kṛishṇa's last advice may be thus summed up :—

Act then and do thine own appointed task,
In every action my assistance ask,
Do all with heart and soul absorbed in me,
So shalt thou gain thine end and be from trouble free.

Arjuna's conclusion may be thus paraphrased :—

Eternal One ! thy glory just beheld
Has all illusion from my soul dispelled ;
Now by thy favour is my conscience clear,
I will thy bidding do and fight without a fear.

To any one who has followed me in tracing the outline of this remarkable philosophical dialogue, and has noted the numerous parallels it offers to passages in our sacred Scriptures, it may seem strange that I hesitate to concur in any theory which explains these coincidences by supposing that the author had access to the New Testament or that he derived some of his ideas from the first propagators of Christianity. Surely it will be conceded that the probability of contact and interaction between Gentile systems and the Christian religion in the first two centuries of our era must have been greater in Italy than in

India. Yet, if we take the writings and recorded sayings of three great Roman philosophers, Seneca, Epictetus, and Marcus Aurelius, we shall find them full of resemblances to passages in our Scriptures, while there appears to be no ground whatever for supposing that these eminent Pagan writers and thinkers derived any of their ideas from either Jewish or Christian sources. In fact, the Rev. F. W. Farrar, in his interesting and valuable work, 'Seekers after God,' has clearly shown that 'to say that Pagan morality kindled its faded taper at the Gospel light whether furtively or unconsciously, that it dissembled the obligation and made a boast of the splendour, as if it were originally her own, is to make an assertion wholly untenable.' He points out that the attempts of the Christian Fathers to make out Pythagoras a debtor to Hebraic wisdom, Plato an 'Atticizing Moses, Aristotle a picker up of ethics from a Jew, Seneca a correspondent of St. Paul, were due 'in some cases to ignorance, and in some to a want of perfect honesty in controversial dealing.'

His arguments would be even more conclusive if applied to the Bhagavad-gītā, the author of which was probably contemporaneous with Seneca. It must, indeed, be admitted that the flashes of true light which emerge from the mists of pantheism in the writings of Indian philosophers, must spring from the same source of light as the Gospel itself; but it may reasonably be questioned whether there could have been any actual contact of the Hindū systems with Christianity without a more satisfactory result in the modification of pantheistic and anti-Christian ideas. In order that the resemblances to Scripture in the writings of Roman philosophers may be compared with those just noted, I subjoin a few instances from 'Seekers after God' and Dr. Ramage's 'Beautiful Thoughts:'—

1. Seneca. 'God comes to men: nay, what is nearer, comes into men.' 'A sacred spirit dwells within us, the observer and guardian of

all our evil and our good.' Cf. 1 Cor. iii. 16. 'Let him who hath conferred a favour hold his tongue.' 'In conferring a favour nothing should be more avoided than pride.' Cf. Matt. vi. 3. 'If you wish to be loved, love.' 'Expect from another what you do to another.' 'We are all wicked; therefore whatever we blame in another we shall find in our own bosom.' 'A good man is God's disciple and imitator and His true offspring, whom that magnificent Father doth, after the manner of severe parents, educate hardly.' 'God is nigh to thee, He is with thee, He is in thee.' 'Temples are not to be built for God with stones piled on high; He is to be consecrated in the breast of each.' 'What a foolish thing it is to promise ourselves a long life, who are not masters of even to-morrow!' 'Live with men as if God saw you.' 'Other men's sins are before our eyes; our own behind our back.' 'The greater part of mankind are angry with the sinner and not with the sin.' 'The severest punishment a man can receive who has injured another, is to have committed the injury.'

2. Epictetus. 'If you always remember that in all you do in soul or body God stands by as a witness, in all your prayers and your actions you will not err; and you shall have God dwelling with you.' 'How should a man grieve his enemy? By preparing himself to act in the noblest manner.' Cf. Rom. xii. 20.

3. Marcus Aurelius. 'The best way of avenging thyself is not to become like the wrong-doer.' 'Men exist for the sake of one another. Teach them or bear with them.' Cf. 2 Thess. iv. 15, Col. iii. 13. 'In the morning when thou risest unwillingly let these thoughts be present, "I am rising to the work of a human being. Why, then, am I dissatisfied if I am going to do the things for which I exist and for which I was brought into the world?" Dost thou exist, then, to take thy pleasure, and not for action or exertion? Dost thou not see the little birds, the ants, the spiders, the bees working together to put in order their several parts of the universe?' Cf. Prov. vi. 6.

CHAPTER VIII.

Smṛiti—The Vedāngas.

HITHERTO we have been engaged in describing briefly and illustrating by selected examples the three divisions of the Veda, viz., Mantra, Brāhmaṇa, and Upanishad, and the six Darśanas or systems of philosophy developed out of the third of these divisions. All three portions of the Veda come under the head of *Śruti*, 'audition,' or *Śruta*,—that which is directly heard or revealed—the eternal voice of divine knowledge heard[1] by certain holy men called Ṛishis, and by them orally transmitted; or if committed to writing, then written down exactly as heard, without any intervention of human authorship. We now pass from Śruti and the six Darśanas to the second great head of Sanskrit literature, called *Smṛiti*, 'recollection,' or that which is remembered and handed down by tradition (as distinguished from 'audition'). This is believed to be founded on Śruti, 'direct revelation,' as its primary basis, and only possesses authority in so far as it is in harmony with such revealed truth.[2] The very essence of Smṛiti, however, is considered to be that it was delivered *memoriter* by human authors and put into the form of human composition. In its

---

[1] The expression generally used is that the Ṛishis *saw* the hymns, *ṛishi* being fancifully connected with *dṛishi*, as if from root *dṛiś*; but the terms *Śruti* and *Śruta*, taken in connection with the theory of the eternity of sound, indicate that the ear was the channel of communication.

[2] If *Veda-vāhya*, it is declared to be *nishphala*. Manu XII. 95.

widest acceptation, Smṛiti may be said to include six principal subjects or departments, viz., I. *six Vedāngas*, 'limbs for supporting the Veda,' or, in other words, helps to aid the student in reading, understanding and applying it to sacrificial rites (and hence called *Pravaćana*, Manu III. 184): they are—1. Kalpa, 'ceremonial directory,' comprising rules relating to the Vedic ritual and the whole complicated process of sacrifices, which rules are called Śrauta-sūtra, because they are *Vedic*, and relate directly to the application of the Mantra and Brāhmaṇa portion of Śruti, being especially guides to the Brāhmaṇas; 2. Śikshā, 'the science of pronunciation;' 3. Ćhandas, 'metre;' 4. Nirukta, 'exposition of difficult Vedic words;' 5. Vyākaraṇa, 'grammar;' 6. Jyotisha, 'astronomy,' including arithmetic and mathematics, especially in connection with astrology. Of these Vedān-gas, 1. and 6. are for employing the Veda at sacrifices, 2. and 3. are for reading, 4. and 5. for understanding it. II. The *Smārta-sūtra*, a comprehensive term for such rules as do not relate to *Śrauta* or *Vedic* ceremonies, which were usually on a grand scale and public in their character, but rather to religious acts of a private and personal kind, falling naturally under two divisions, viz., *a.* family or domestic rites (*gṛihya*) performed at stated periods; *b.* conventional usages and every-day practices (*samayāćāra*); on which account these Smārta Sūtras must be separated into two classes, *a.* Gṛihya-sūtra, *b.* Sāmayāćārika-sūtra. III. The *Dharma-śāstras* or 'Law-books, and especially the *Laws of Manu*, and other so-called inspired law-givers—supposed to have grown out of the Smārta Sūtras. IV. The *Itihāsas* or 'legendary poems,' under which head I place as portions of Smṛiti the two great epic poems called Rāmāyaṇa and Mahā-bhārata, and then, for convenience, as following and depending on these, but not as properly Smṛiti, the artificial poems (Kāvyas) and erotic poems and the dramas, almost all of which in their subject-matter are closely connected with the two great epics. V. The *eighteen Purāṇas* or ancient legendary histories and traditions, with their train of eighteen inferior Purāṇas (*Upa-purāṇa*) and subsequent Tantras. VI. The *Nīti-śāstras* or ethical and didactic writings of all kinds, including collections of fables and moral precepts.

I propose now to take these six divisions of post-Vedic literature in order, beginning with I. the Vedān-gas.

I. *The Vedān-gas.*

They are six in number. Let us consider them (not quite according to the Hindū order) in the following sequence: 1. *Kalpa*; 2. *Śikshā*; 3. *Ćhandas*; 4. *Nirukta*; 5. *Vyākaraṇa*; 6. *Jyotisha.*

The Vedān-gas—Kalpa, 'ceremonial directory.'

In the first place, then, as regards *Kalpa*; this denotes, as we have seen, a kind of ceremonial directory or rubric put forth in the form of short aphoristic Sūtras or rules, called *Śrauta*, because serving as guides for the application of the Mantra and Brāhmaṇa portion of Śruti to the conduct of sacrificial rites. There are Śrauta Sūtras for each of the five Saṃhitās of the Veda. Thus, for the Ṛig-veda there are the *Āśvalāyana*, *Śāṅkhāyana*, and *Śaunaka* Śrauta Sūtras; for the Sāma-veda, the *Maśaka*, *Lāṭyāyana*, and *Drāhyāyaṇa*; for the Taittirīya or Black Yajur-veda, the *Āpastamba*, *Baudhāyana*, *Satyāshāḍha Hiraṇya-keśin. Mānava*, *Bhāradvāja*, *Vādhūna*, *Vai-khānasa*, *Laugākshi*, *Maitra*, *Kaṭha*, and *Vārāha*; for the Vājasaneyi or White Yajur-veda there is only the *Kātyāyana*;[1] for the Atharva-veda only the *Kauśika*.

---

[1] Edited by Professor Weber to complete the series of his great edition of the White Yajur-veda with its Brāhmaṇa (the S'atapatha).

I should remark here that the word *Sūtra* (derived from the root *Siv*, 'to sew') means properly 'string,' and that this name was applied to any series[1] of rules or aphorisms, either because they were, figuratively, strung together, or because they were written on leaves held together by strings.[2] It is perhaps essential to the true nature of a Brāhmanical Sūtra that it should be a rule or dogma expressed as briefly as possible. In the grammatical Sūtras not a single letter is allowed which can by any contrivance be dispensed with, and moreover in these Sūtras letters and syllables are often used symbolically, like algebraic signs, to indicate ideas which would otherwise require a whole sentence or more to express them at full. In the philosophical Sūtras, as we have already seen, great brevity and a rigid economy of words is also practised, the aim being to furnish the shortest possible suggestive memorial sentences as an aid to the memory of both teachers and learners in an age when books were scarce and paper and printing unknown (see p. 46). This extreme conciseness is not always maintained, especially in later Sūtra works, but it generally holds good that the older the Sūtra the greater its curtness and elliptical obscurity, so that without a commentary or a key to their interpretation these ancient aphorisms are quite unintelligible. In later times, as books became more common, the necessity for elaborate and overstrained conciseness was gradually removed,[3] and rules and aphorisms, though still strung together in Sūtra style, were more fully and explicitly and even sometimes metrically stated.[4] In fact, these later Sūtra works may be regarded as simple

---

1 *Sūtra* in the singular may denote a whole collection of rules.

2 This last is the theory of the late Professor Goldstücker.

3 This relaxation led at last to the very opposite extreme of prolixity, as in the Buddhist Sūtras.

4 In some Sūtra works there is an occasional admixture of S'lokas.

collections of formulated precepts or dogmas adapted to serve as convenient manuals to particular systems of teaching, whether in ritual, philosophy, law, or grammar. If Sanskṛit scholars are asked to state the age of the oldest Sūtra works, they are again obliged to confess their inability to fix any precise date. The most ancient are probably not older than the fifth or sixth century B.C., and the time of the compilation of the most recent is perhaps not far removed from the commencement of the Christian era. I have placed the Kalpa Sūtras first because they are probably oldest, being closely connected with the Brāhmaṇa or ritual portion of Śruti, and thence called Śrauta.

The following translation of the first ten Sūtras of Kātyāyana's Śrauta-sūtra, which belong to the Śatapatha-brāhmaṇa and White Yajur-veda (see Weber's edition), will give some idea of the nature of these rules. To make each aphorism intelligible, additional matter has to be introduced from the commentary of Yājñika-deva. This I have done parenthetically in the examples here given. I have also given the original text of the Sūtras in italics :—

1. Now, therefore, the right (of engaging in sacrificial acts is about to be laid down in the following rules). [*Athāto 'dhikāraḥ.*]

2. (Sacrificial) acts (like the Agni-hotra, &c.) are attended with recompense (such as the attainment of heaven, of wealth, of a son, &c.) [*Phala-yuktāni karmāṇi.*]

3. (According to the *primâ facie* view of the matter there must be a right) of all (creatures, *e.g.* of men, even though blind, dumb, lame, or deaf, of gods, of Ṛishis, and of animals, but not of plants, to engage in sacrificial acts), without distinction (because all such creatures are capable of desiring recompense). [*Sarveshām aviśeshāt.*]

4. But (according to the orthodox view, the right belongs) to human beings (only), because (they only, as the Veda declares, have) the power of undertaking (sacrificial acts, and not to gods, Ṛishis, and animals). [*Manushyāṇāṃ vārambha-sāmarthyāt.*]

5. Cripples, those ignorant of the Veda, eunuchs, and S'ūdras (are to be) excepted. [*Aṅga-hīnāśrotriya-shaṇḍha-śūdra-varjam.*]

6. (The right belongs) to Brāhmans, Kshatriyas,[1] and Vaiśyas (but not to S'ūdras), according to the Vedic precept. [*Brāhmaṇa-rājanya-vaiśyānāṃ śruteḥ.*]

7. A woman also (has the right), since there is no difference (between her and her husband in regard to the desire for heaven). [*Strī ćāviśeshāt.*]

8. And since it is so seen (in the Veda). [*Darśanāć-ća.*]

9. (According to one view, the right belongs) to a man of the Rathakāra[2] ('chariot-maker') caste, (so far as regards the rite) of placing the sacred fire (on the sacrificial ground, on the score of this caste being reckoned among the first three classes). [*Rathakārasyādhāne.*]

10. (But according to the orthodox view) it is settled (that the Rathakāra is not to be reckoned among the first three classes). [*Niyataṃ ća.*]

The Vedāngas—Śikshā, 'phonetic directory.'

The next Vedān·ga in our list is *Śikshā* or the science of proper pronunciation, especially as teaching the laws of euphony peculiar to the Veda. This comprises the knowledge of letters, accents, quantity, the right use of the organs of articulation, and phonetics generally. One short comparatively modern treatise on phonetics, consisting in one recension of thirty-five and in another of fifty-nine verses (ascribed to Pāṇini), and a chapter of the Taittirīyāraṇyaka are regarded as the representatives of this subject; but the Vedic Prātiśākhyas and other works on Vedic phonetics may be included under it,[3] and it will be

[1] The word *Rājanya* is used here and in the Purusha-sūkta for Kshatriya, see p. 21.

[2] This mixed caste, held to be the offspring of a Māhishya by a Karaṇī, is also called Saudhanvana. It appears to have enjoyed some religious privileges, perhaps because the Ṛibhus were Ratha-kāras, see note, p. 14. Cf. Ṛig-veda III. 60. 4.

[3] A number of works bearing the name of *Śikshā*, and dealing with phonetics and other kindred subjects, have been recently brought to notice. See Haug on *the Vedic Accent* (Munich, 1874).

convenient so to regard them. These Prātiśākhyas are grammatical, or rather phonetic, treatises written in the Sūtra style (some of them perhaps of a more recent date than Pāṇini),[1] regulating the euphonic combination of letters and their peculiar pronunciation according to the practice of the different Śākhās, 'branches,' of the Vedas, in those traditional versions of the Vedic texts handed down by different families. The Prātiśākhyas do not undo words in the same way as the Vyākaraṇa, but take actually formed words as they occur in the hymns, and teach the phonetic changes they undergo, the mode of pronouncing the accents, &c. In fact, they show how the Pada text is converted by a process of euphonic combination into the Saṃhitā.

Since the chief virtue of the Vedic texts was in their oral repetition, and since so much importance was attached to the proper pronunciation and accentuation of every syllable, it may be easily supposed that these phonetic manuals were of great value to persons who had to repeat Mantras every day as an essential part of their religious exercises. They probably served as guides and aids to the memory, both for teachers in instructing their pupils and for pupils in learning to recite the Veda. Four Prātiśākhyas are extant, viz. : 1. one to the Śākala-śākhā of the Ṛig-veda, ascribed to Śaunaka;[2] 2. another to a Śākhā of the Taittirīya or Black Yajur-veda;[3] 3. another to a Śākhā of the Mādhyandinas, of the family of the Vājasaneyins or 'followers of the White Yajur-veda,' whence

---

[1] The late Professor Goldstücker, in his work on Pāṇini, decides that all the Prātiśākhyas must have been posterior to Pāṇini, but this opinion is shared by few other scholars.

[2] Edited and translated into French by M. Adolphe Regnier, and into German by Professor Max Müller.

[3] Edited, with its commentary, and translated by Professor William D. Whitney.

this is called the Vājasaneyi-prātiśākhya;[1] it is ascribed to an author, Kātyāyana, probably identical with the writer of the Vārttikas or 'supplementary rules' to Pāṇini; 4. an Atharva-veda-prātiśākhya, called Śaunakīyā Ćaturādhyāyikā,[2] 'Śaunaka's treatise in four chapters.' No Prātiśākhya has yet been found to the Sāma-veda.

The relative age of the Prātiśākhyas in their present form is an open question. That to the Ṛig-veda has been by some confidently declared the oldest, though written in Ślokas with occasional admixture of other metres.

I here translate the fifth and sixth Sūtras of this Prātiśākhya, as they contain a statement of some of the points which form the subject of the work :—

Heaviness (*i.e.*, prosodial length), lightness (*i.e.*, prosodial shortness), equality, shortness, longness, and prolation (of vowels), elision, augmentation, and change, original form, non-change of Visarga into a sibilant, regular order, the mixed tone, high tone, low tone, breath and sound,[3] and both (combined),—all this must be accurately understood by one who reads (or repeats) the words of the Veda.

[*Gurutvaṃ laghutā sāmyaṃ hrasva-dīrgha-plutāni ća* ।
Lopāgama-vikārāś-ća prakṛitir vikramaḥ kramaḥ ‖
Svaritodātta-nīćatvaṃ śvāso nādas tathobhayam ।
Etat sarvaṃ ća vijñeyaṃ ćhando-bhāshām adhīyatā ‖]

The first Atharva-veda-prātiśākhya states the subject of the treatise (Whitney, p. 9), and gives a fourfold division of all the parts of speech in its first Sūtra, thus :—

The two qualities of the four kinds of words—noun (*nāma*), verb (*ākhyāta*), preposition (*upasarga*), and particle (*nipāta*)—as euphonically joined and as separate words, are here the subject (*prātijñam*).

---

1 Edited and translated by Professor Weber in the 'Indische Studien.'

2 Also edited, with a most valuable English translation and notes, by Professor William D. Whitney.

3 We learn from the Atharva-veda-prātiśākhya I. 12, 13, that in the surd consonants there is mere breath, and in the sonant, sound.

That is to say, the design of the Prātiśākhya is to form a Saṃhitā out of a Pada text. In fact, it supposes all the words of the Veda to be separated from each other (as they are in the Pada), and then teaches how they are to be euphonically connected, as they must be in the Saṃhitā.[1]

The second chapter introduces a number of rules of Sandhi, which will be familiar to the students of Pāṇini's Grammar. The first Sūtra consists of one word, which must be amplified thus (Whitney's edition, p. 72):—

(The following rules are to be understood as of force when the separate words of the disjointed text are put together) in the Saṃhitā [Saṃhitāyām].

Then follow the rules, of which I subjoin three or four examples (II. 10, 11, 18, 19, III. 20):—

Before *ś*, *n* becomes *ṅ* [*na-kārasya śa-kāre ṅakāraḥ*].
Also before a sonant palatal (as before *j*) [*ća-vargīye ghoshavati*].
After the preposition *ud*, there is elision of the letter *s* of the roots *sthā* and *stambh* [*lopa udaḥ sthā-stambhoḥ sa-kārasya*].
There is elision of *R* before *r* [*rephasya rephe*].
When *r* is elided (the preceding vowel is lengthened) [*ra-lope*].

The Vājasaneyi-prātiśākhya (I. 27) gives a still more complete enumeration of the parts of speech, thus :—

Words are made up of inflected verbal bases [*i.e.*, bases having the personal endings, technically called *tiṅ*], nouns derived from verbs by Kṛit affixes, nouns derived from nouns by Taddhita affixes and four kinds of compounds (Avyayī-bhāva, Tatpurusha, Dvandva, Bahu-vrīhi). [*Tiṅ-kṛit-taddhita-ćatushṭaya-samāsāḥ śabda-mayam.* See Professor Max Müller's Ancient Sanskṛit Literature, p. 164.]

---

[1] In the *Krama* text the 1st word is recited with the 2nd, that is repeated with the third, that with the 4th, &c. In the *Jaṭā*, the 1st word and 2nd, 2nd and 1st, and 1st and 2nd again; next the 2nd and 3rd, 3rd and 2nd, and 2nd and 3rd, and so on. In the *Ghana*, the 1st and 2nd, 2nd and 1st, 1st and 2nd again, 3rd; then 3rd, 2nd, 1st, 1st, 2nd, 3rd; then the 2nd begins a new Ghana.

The Vedāngas—Ćhandas, 'metre.'

This Vedān·ga is imperfectly represented by the *Ćhandaḥ-śāstra* ascribed to Pin·gala or Pin·gala-nāga, which may be as old as the second century B.C., and treats of Prākṛit as well as Sanskṛit metres, including only a few Vedic. Other works on metres are the Nidāna-sūtra in ten Prapāṭhakas and the Śruta-bodha. In truth, prosody, like every other subject in Sanskṛit literature, affords field for almost endless investigation. It is a complete study in itself, and its importance in the estimation of the Hindūs is shown by the excessive cultivation and elaboration bestowed upon their whole metrical system. A knowledge of the metre of each hymn of the Veda was considered essential to the right use and proper recitation of the Mantras. Hence we find Sāyaṇa, in his introduction to the first hymn of the Ṛig-veda, quoting the following precept:—

> He who shall cause any one to repeat (*adhyāpayet*) or shall himself repeat (any hymn of the Veda) without having acquainted himself with the name of the Ṛishi to whom it was revealed, the metre (*ćhandas*) in which it was written, the deity to whom it was addressed, and its right application (*yoga*), is the worst of sinners (*pāpīyān*).

Again, immediately afterwards, he adds:—

> Any one who makes use of (a hymn) without knowing the Ṛishi, the metre, the deity, the right interpretation according to the Brāhmaṇas (*brāhmaṇārtha*), and the accents is called 'a Mantra-thorn' (*mantra-kaṇṭaka*, as destroying or obstructing its efficacy).

In the ninth verse of the Purusha-sūkta of the Ṛig-veda (see p. 21) the metres are said to have sprung from Purusha himself, thus:—

> From that universal sacrifice sprang the Ṛić and Sāman verses, the metres, and the Yajus (*ćhandāṉsi jajñire tasmād yajus tasmād ajāyata*).

The Taittirīya-saṃhitā VII. 1. 1. 4, &c., describes the

creation of several metres by Prajāpati (Muir, vol. i. p. 15):—

Prajāpati desired 'may I be propagated.' He formed the Trivṛit from his mouth. After it were produced the deity Agni, the metre Gāyatrī, &c.

In Manu IV. 99, 100, we have the following:—

Let not a man repeat the Veda without clear pronunciation (of the letters, accents, &c., *svara varṇādi*, Kullūka). Let him always be careful to recite it as composed in metre (*ćhandas-kṛitam*).

It is remarkable that in Pāṇini's Grammar the usual name for the Veda is Ćhandas (see p. 169).

From the importance thus assigned to the metrical structure of the hymns we shall be prepared to find frequent allusions to the subject of metres in the Brāhmaṇas. In fact, these treatises attach a kind of mystical efficacy to their right use, and whole chapters of the Upanishads enlarge on the same fanciful theme. The Gāyatrī is held in especial veneration, the most sacred text of the Ṛig-veda being in this metre. (See p. 17.)

The following passage is from the Śatapatha-brāhmaṇa I. 2, 5, 6, &c. (Muir's Texts, vol. iv. p. 123):—

The gods having placed Vishṇu to the east surrounded him with metres (*ćhandobhir abhitaḥ paryagṛihṇan*); saying, 'On the south side I surround thee with the Gāyatrī metre; on the west I surround thee with the Trishṭubh metre; on the north I surround thee with the Jagatī.' Having thus surrounded him with metres, they placed Agni on the east, and thus they went on worshipping and toiling. By this means they acquired this whole earth (*tena imāṃ sarvām pṛithivīṃ samavindanta*).

Again, in the fourteenth Brāhmaṇa of the Bṛihad-āraṇyaka Upanishad we read (Röer, p. 254):—

The *Ṛićaḥ*, *Yajūṇshi*, and *Sāmāni* are eight syllables (*ashṭāv aksharāṇi*); the second Pāda (*padam*) of the Gāyatrī consists of eight syllables (*ashṭākṣharam*). This Pāda of the Gāyatrī represents that nature of the three Vedas. Whoever knows this Pāda of the Gāyatrī conquers all that is conquerable by the knowledge of the three Vedas.

Hence we cannot be surprised that some of the most sacred metres, especially the Gāyatrī, were in the end personified and invested with divine functions. Our present purpose and limits do not admit of our giving schemes of even the commonest forms of Sanskṛit metre, whether Vedic or Post-vedic. They will be found enumerated in the third edition of my Sanskṛit Grammar, pp. 388–392.[1] Let me merely observe that great licence is allowed in Vedic prosody, so that in the Gāyatrī, which may be regarded as consisting either of three divisions of eight syllables each (whence it is called *tri-padā*) or of six feet of four syllables each, the quantity of each syllable is very irregular, although the second, fourth, and sixth feet generally contain two iambics.

Of Post-vedic metres we have so great a variety that it becomes necessary to arrange them under classes and orders, genera and species. In truth, the elaboration of every kind of complicated metre is carried to an extent quite beyond the ordinary practice of poetical composition in other languages. 'A Hindū poet,' says Dr. Yates, 'may proceed to any length he pleases, within the limits of *a thousand syllables to the half-line*,' or quarter-stanza. The Daṇḍaka metre (of which a specimen occurs in the drama called Mālatī-mādhava, Act V.)[2] offers more than any other an almost incredible capability of expansion. It will admit, indeed, of the stanza extending 27 × 4 to 999 × 4 syllables. But the commonest form of metre, chiefly found in epic poetry—the Anushṭubh or Śloka—is short and easy. It consists of four half-lines of eight syllables each or two lines of sixteen syllables each,

---

[1] See also Colebrooke's Essay on Sanskṛit and Prākṛit metres and Professor Weber's articles in the 'Indische Studien.'

[2] Beginning *Praćalita-kari-kṛitti*, &c. It has fifty-four syllables to the quarter-verse. This specimen is translated in the Asiatic Researches, vol. x. p. 456.

the last two feet of each line being iambics (see my Sanskṛit Grammar, p. 288). The Indra-vajrā (with its Upendra-vajrā variety) is also a common metre, and one of the most rhythmical. It nearly corresponds to one occurring in Horace's fourth Ode :—

Vūlcānŭs ārdēns ūrĭt ōffĭcīnās,
Trăhūntquĕ sīccās māchĭnaē cărīnās.

But to make the Latin agree with the Sanskṛit metre we must suppose the first syllable of *machinae* and of *urit* to be short. It might be represented in an English line thus, 'Dówn cōmes thĕ rāin, ānd wĭth ĭt cōmes thĕ thūndēr,' an emphasis being placed on the first syllable.

The Vedāṅgas—Nirukta, 'exposition.'

The object of this Vedāṅga is etymological explanation or interpretation of difficult Vedic words. Doubtless, numerous works devoted to this object once existed, but all have perished except one, which is now the typical representative of the whole class.[1] This is a compilation, accompanied with an exposition, by an author named Yāska, who, according to the best authorities, lived before Pāṇini,[2] probably about 400 years B.C., or about 1800 years before Sāyaṇa. His work consists first of three bare lists or catalogues of words in five chapters : viz., *a.* The *Naighaṇṭuka* in three chapters of synonyms or rather of collections of words said to have the same meaning as some one word of known signification given at the end, one such collection being called a Nighaṇṭu. The

[1] No less than seventeen Nairuktikas or 'interpreters of the Veda' are mentioned by name as having preceded Yāska. See Dr. Muir's article on the interpretation of the Veda, p. 321.

[2] Pāṇini himself implies (IV. I. 112) that the name Yāska means a descendant of Yaska.

synonyms in each collection vary from two (III. 22) to one hundred and twenty-two (II. 14), and can scarcely be called synonyms in the strict sense. For example, when it is said that *vartate*, 'he turns;' *loṭate*, 'he rolls;' *sarpati*, 'he creeps;' *sravati*, 'he flows;' *sraṉsate*, 'he drops;' *plavate*, 'he swims;' *ḍīyate*, 'he flies;' *patati*, 'he falls,' and 122 other words are all synonyms of *gamati*, 'he goes,' or *gati*, 'going,' this must be understood very widely as intending to include all forms and varieties of motion. Again, in I. 12, we have a collection of 101 words, which are all said to be synonyms of water (*udaka*), but it is obvious that the only attribute most of these have in common is, that they are varieties of fluids, including, for example, nectar (*amṛita*) and clarified butter (*havis*). Seeing, therefore, that many of the words brought together are old Vedic words of doubtful meaning, quite unknown to classical Sanskṛit, and seeing that a complete explanation of the gradations and modifications of sense under each head of synonyms is wanting, the practical utility of these lists is of course very small indeed. *b.* The *Naigama*, a collection of 278 separate words (*padāni*) occurring in the Veda (*nigama*), all in one chapter of three sections. *c.* The *Daivata* or 151 words relating to deities and religious or sacrificial acts, in one chapter of six short sections. Whether these collections were drawn up by Yāska himself or by some previous compiler is not certain, but there is no doubt that the second and most important part of the work, viz., the Nirukta or 'explanation' of the words in these lists, is his own composition. Although, therefore, the term Nirukta is sometimes applied to the lists of words, it more properly belongs to Yāska's explanation of them, which occupies twelve chapters. The first of the twelve is a kind of introduction, which contains some interesting discussions of philological questions and a sort of summary or sketch of grammar;

the following two chapters are an imperfect exposition of the Naighaṇṭuka or 'lists of synonymous words,' the deficiency of which has been to a certain extent supplied by Durga, a commentator on Yāska; the next three chapters explain the Naigama or 'single Vedic words,' and the last six the Daivata or 'deities addressed in the hymns.' Thus the three collections with their explanations occupy seventeen chapters. The value of the work[1] consists in its being the oldest extant commentary on the Veda. When words are explained, Vedic passages are quoted in illustration, and the author often enters into curious etymological investigations, which possess great interest from their universally admitted antiquity, but are difficult to understand from the extreme brevity and obscurity of their style.

I here abridge some valuable remarks from Dr. John Muir's article on the 'Interpretation of the Veda,' in the Royal Asiatic Society's Journal (vol. ii. new series, p. 320):—

The Nirukta makes frequent reference to the Brāhmaṇas, and alludes to various schools of Vedic interpretation which existed anterior to its author, such as the Nairuktas or 'etymologists,' the Aitihāsikas or 'legendary writers,' and the Yājṅikas or 'ritualists.' Yāska supplies specimens of the mode of explaining the hymns adopted by different schools of interpreters. Thus we are told (Nirukta XI. 29, 31) that the Nairuktas understood Anumati, Rākā, Sinīvālī, and Kuhū to be goddesses, while the Yājṅikas took them for the new and full moons. The gods called Aśvins were a great enigma. The Nirukta (XII. 1) gives the following answers to the question who they were: 'Heaven and Earth,' say some; 'Day and Night,' say others; 'the Sun and Moon,' say others; 'two Kings, performers of holy acts,' say the Aitihāsikas. Again, Nirukta (VI. 13) tells us that Aurṇabhāva understood Nāsatyau (an epithet of the Aśvins) as 'true, not false.' Agrāyaṇa took it to mean 'leaders of truth' (*satyasya praṇetārau*); while Yāska himself suggests that it may mean 'nose-born' (*nāsikā-prabhavau*). Again, we

[1] It has been ably edited by Professor Roth.

are informed (Nirukta III. 8) that some understood the five peoples (*pañća-janāḥ*) mentioned in Ṛig-veda X. 53. 4 to be the Gandharvas, Pitṛis, gods, Asuras, and Rakshases; whilst Aupamanyava took them for the four castes and the Nishādas. So, again, Kātthakya understood Narāśaṇsa to designate 'sacrifice,' but S'ākapūṇi took it for a name of Agni (Nir. VIII. 4. 5). In like manner, Yāska's predecessors were not agreed as to what was meant by Vishṇu's three steps in Ṛig-veda I. 22. 17; S'ākapūṇi maintaining that they were planted on the earth, the atmosphere, and the sky respectively; and Aurṇabhāva that the hill over which the sun rises, the meridian, and the hill where he sets, were the localities referred to. One of these predecessors (Kautsa) had the audacity to assert that Vedic exposition was useless, as the hymns were obscure, unmeaning, or mutually contradictory. As instances of obscurity he cites the texts in which the words *amyak* (Ṛig-veda I. 169. 3), *yādṛiśmin* (V. 44. 8), *jārayāyi* (VI. 12. 4), and *kāṇukā* (VIII. 66. 4) occur. In regard to this charge, Yāska replies that it is not the fault of the post that the blind man does not see it. In the Nirukta-pariśishṭa the 'four defined grades or stages of speech' referred to in Ṛig-veda I. 164. 45, are said to be explained by the Ṛishis as meaning the four mystic words, *om*, *bhūh*, *hhuvaḥ*, *svar*; by the grammarians, as denoting nouns, verbs, prepositions, and particles; by the ritualists, as the hymns, liturgical precepts, Brāhmaṇas, and ordinary language; by the etymologists, as the Ṛig, Yajush, Sāman, and the current language; by others, as the speech of serpents, birds, reptiles, and the vernacular; by the spiritualists, as that of beasts, musical instruments, wild animals, and soul.

It is evident from the above remarks that great difference of opinion existed among expositors of the Veda even in Yāska's time, considerably more than 2000 years ago, and that the objections of sceptics and rationalists had to be met and answered by orthodox theologians like himself. He commences his own exposition thus (I. 1):—

The traditional collection of words has been thus traditionally repeated. That must now be explained. They call this traditional collection the Nighaṇṭus. [*Samāmnāyaḥ samāmnātaḥ sa vyākhyātavyas tam imaṃ samāmnāyaṃ nighaṇṭava ity āćakshate.*]

Perhaps as good an example of Yāska's condensed style as can be offered is a passage quoted and explained by Professor Goldstücker from Roth's edition, I. 3. It is interesting as showing that, for the better interpretation of the Veda, Yāska aimed at giving some sort of exposition of grammar and grammatical science as then understood:—

(The ancient grammarian) S'ākaṭāyana says that prepositions when not attached (to nouns or verbs) do not express meanings; but Gārgya says that they illustrate (or modify) the action which is expressed by a noun or verb, and that their senses are various (even when detached). Now they express that sense which inheres in them; that is, that which modifies the sense of a noun or verb. The preposition *ā* is in the sense of limit; *pra* and *parā* express the reverse of that; *abhi*, direction towards; *prati*, the reverse of that; *ati* and *su*, superiority; *nir* and *dur*, the reverse of these two; *ni* and *ava*, the act of taking down; *ud*, the reverse of these two; *sam*, combining together; *vi* and *apa*, the reverse of that; *anu*, similarity or being after; *api*, conjunction; *upa*, the being appended; *pari*, being all around; *adhi*, being above or supremacy: thus they express various meanings, and these must be taken into consideration. [*Na nirbaddhā upasargā arthān nir-āhur iti Śākaṭāyano, nāmākhyātayos tu karmopasaṃyoga-dyotakā bhavanty uććāvaćāḥ padārthā bhavantīti Gārgyas, tad ya eshu padārthaḥ prāhur ime taṃ nāmākhyātayor artha-vikaraṇam; ā ity arvāg-arthe, pra parety etasya prātilomyam; abhīty ābhimukhyam, pratīty etasya prātilomyam; ati su ity abhipūjitārthe, nir dur ity etayoḥ prātilomyaṃ; ny aveti vinigrahārthīyā, ud ity etayoḥ prātilomyaṃ; sam ity ekībhāvaṃ, vy apety etasya prātilomyam; anv iti sādṛiśyāparabhāvam; apīti saṃsargaṃ; upety upajanam; parīti sarvato-bhāvam; adhīty uparibhāvam aiśvaryaṃ vaivam uććāvaćān arthān prāhus ta upekshitavyāḥ.*]

There is a still more interesting passage on the subject of derivation a little further on in the same chapter (I. 12):—

So these four kinds of words have been enumerated, nouns (*nāman*), verbs (*ākhyāta*), prepositions (*upasarga*), and particles (*nipāta*). S'ākaṭāyana affirms that nouns are derived from verbs, and on this point there is an agreement of the etymologists (*nairukta-samayaḥ*). But Gārgya and some of the grammarians say that not all (nouns are derived from verbs). For if all nouns came from verbs, then whatever performs the same action ought to have the same name. Thus, if *aśva*, 'a horse,' were derived from the root *aś*, 'to pass through,' then every one who passes along a road ought to be called *aśva*; and if *tṛiṇa*, 'a blade of grass,' were derived from the root *tṛid*, 'to pierce,' then everything that pierces ought to be called *triṇa*. Again, if all nouns were derived from verbs, then everything would have as many names as there are states with which it could be connected. Thus, *sthūṇā*, 'a post,' might be called *dara-śayā*, 'hole-sleeper,' because resting in a hole, or *saṅ-janī*, 'joiner together, because things are joined by being attached to it. [Yāska ends by taking the side of S'ākaṭāyana. See Professor Max Müller's Ancient Sanskṛit Literature, p. 165.]

The thirteenth and fourteenth chapters, commonly called the Nirukta-pariśishṭa, are thought to be the work of a more recent author than Yāska. There are numerous classical glossaries by later lexicographers, *e.g.*:—

The Amara-kosha (sometimes called Tri-kāṇḍa, 'having three chapters'), by the Bauddha Amara-siṉha, probably not later than A.D. 500; the Abhidhāna-ratna-mālā, by Halāyudha; the Abhidhāna-ćintāmaṇi, by the Jaina Hema-ćandra; the Viśva-prakāśa, by Maheśvara; the Dharaṇi; the Medinī; the Hārāvalī, &c.

The Vedān·gas—Vyākaraṇa, 'grammar.'

This word *Vy-ā-karaṇa* means literally 'undoing,' and is applied first to linguistic analysis, and then generally to grammar, but especially to Pāṇini's grammar.[1] It is the opposite to *Saṉskaraṇa*, 'putting together,' whence the formed language is called *Saṉskṛita*, 'constructed.' Strictly, the great Vyākaraṇa of Pāṇini can scarcely be regarded as a Vedān·ga, seeing that it only treats of the Vedic idiom exceptionally. The grammatical Sūtras which preceded his time, and which have nearly all perished, must have constituted the Vyākaraṇa division of works ancillary to the study of the Veda.[2] Nevertheless, the grammar of

---

[1] No Paṇḍit would use Vyākaraṇa except for Sanskṛit grammar, and a man's Sanskṛit scholarship is often summed up by describing him as knowing 'the Vyākaran.'

[2] Pāṇini himself mentions several grammarians as having preceded him, such as Āpiśali, Kāśyapa, Gārgya, Gālava, Ćakravarmaṇa, Bhāradvāja, S'ākaṭāyana, S'ākalya, Senaka, and Sphoṭāyana. The Uṇādi-sūtras

Pāṇini, which is the great standard of correct Sanskṛit, is usually taken to represent this Vedāṅ-ga, and as it is one of the most remarkable literary works that the world has ever seen, and as no other country can produce any grammatical system at all comparable to it, either for originality of plan or for analytical subtlety, a brief description of its characteristic features may be introduced here.

Little or nothing is known of Pāṇini, the author of the grammar. He is described as a descendant of Paṇin and grandchild of an inspired legislator named Devala. His mother's name was Dākshī (whence he is called Dāksheya), and Śalātura in the Gandhāra country (Kandahar), north-west of Attock on the Indus, is said to have been his birth-place (whence his name Śālāturīya). He belonged, therefore, to the North-Western or Western school. As, however, in later times he became more and more an object of reverence, he was at last actually canonized by his admirers, that is to say, exalted to the rank of a Ṛishi or inspired Muni. Hence he is fabled to have *seen* rather than composed his grammar, which was declared to have been supernaturally revealed to him, the first fourteen Sūtras especially having been communicated, according to the legend, by the god Śiva. It is, of course, quite impossible to fix with certainty at what period Pāṇini lived. The late Professor Goldstücker thought he had good grounds for deciding that the great grammarian preceded Buddha. This would place him in the sixth century B.C.

(commented on by Ujjvala-datta), giving the affixes, commencing with *uṇ*, for the formation of words whose meaning has deviated from accordance with their etymology, and whose root is not always clear, are thought by some to be anterior to Pāṇini. Possibly he may have made a list of them himself. At any rate, he mentions the *affixes* in III. 3. 1, III. 4. 75. Śāntanava's Phiṭ-sūtras on accent are probably later than Pāṇini. They have been well edited by Professor Kielhorn. I believe Dr. Bülher has found part of a work which claims to be Śākaṭāyana's grammar.

Other scholars, whose opinions are entitled to respect, consider that an earlier date cannot be assigned to him than the middle of the fourth century B.C.

His work—perhaps the most original of all productions of the Hindū mind—is sometimes called the Ashṭādhyāyī, sometimes Ashṭakam Pāṇinīyam, because it consists of eight lectures (Adhyāyas), each of which is again subdivided into four chapters (Pādas). In these eight Adhyāyas are contained 3996 Sūtras or Aphorisms.[1] The first Adhyāya explains the technical terms used in the grammar and the rules for their interpretation and application.[2] A root is called Dhātu, and a crude base Prātipadika, but a root never appears without some appendage (*anubandha*) in the shape of indicatory syllables or letters (technically called *it*) which do not really form part of the root, but merely denote certain peculiarities in its inflection, conjugation, &c. Similar indicatory letters and syllables (*it*) are attached either at the beginning or end of all affixes, augments, &c.[3] The case affixes are called *sup*, and the personal endings or terminations of verbs *tiṅ*.

---

1 Three or four of these are supposed to be later additions. In the excellent edition of Professor Böhtlingk there are 3997, including the fourteen S'iva Sūtras. Pāṇini is also the supposed author of the oldest Dhātu-pāṭha or dictionary of roots with their Anubandhas.

2 A rule giving the key to Pāṇini's Sūtras and their application is called a Paribhāshā; one which explains the technical terms is a Sañjñā.

3 For example, the root *nid* is called *nidi* to show that a nasal is inserted in conjugation, thus, *nindāmi*, *nindasi*, &c. The affix *maya* is called *mayaṭ* to show that its feminine is *mayī*. Sometimes these *Its* or *Anubandhas* serve to distinguish two roots or affixes, which, although similar in sound, have different senses; for example, the root *dā*, 'to give,' is called *ḍudāñ*, while *dā*, 'to divide,' is called *dāp*; the affix *vat*, meaning 'like,' is called *vati*, while the affix *vat*, meaning 'possessed of,' is called *vatup*. Sometimes the only use of these Anubandhas is to enable Pratyāhāras to be formed; thus the case-ending of the accusative dual is called *auṭ* merely for the sake of forming the Pratyāhāra *suṭ*.

Between the latter and the root a conjugational syllable is inserted, called *vikaraṇa.* The third chapter of the first Adhyāya treats of the proper use of the active voice (*Parasmai-pada*) and middle or reflexive voice (*Ātmane-pada*). The second Adhyāya explains compound words. The third, fourth, and fifth Adhyāyas enumerate the various affixes and their meanings. Those belonging to verbs occupy the third Adhyāya; those affixed to nouns, the fourth and fifth. The sixth, seventh, and eighth Adhyāyas treat of the changes which roots and affixes undergo by augments and substitutions of various kinds. For brevity and economy of words nothing can be more successful than the system in which all this immense and intricate subject is explained. The Sūtras of Pāṇini are indeed a perfect miracle of condensation, their main design apparently being to aid the memory of teachers rather than learners by the briefest possible suggestions. When a single letter can be saved every other consideration is sacrificed to this paramount object; and to attain a greater amount of abridgment than could be effected by the use of ordinary words an arbitrary symbolical language is coined, the key to which must be acquired before the rules themselves can be rendered intelligible.[1] Perhaps the closing Sūtra of the whole work may be taken as the best instance of the consummate brevity attained. It consists of two letters, as follows: *a a.* This is said to mean:—

> Let short *a* be held to have its organ of utterance contracted, now that we have reached the end of the work in which it was necessary to regard it as otherwise.

Here is one from the sixth Adhyāya (1. 77): *Iko yaṇ aći.* This, of course, is not Sanskṛit, but a kind of gram-

---

[1] For example, *śyan* stands for the characteristic of roots of the fourth class, *yak* for the passive, *ṇić* for the causal, *san* for the desiderative, *yan* for the intensive.

matical algebra. *Ik* is a symbol standing for the four vowels *i*, *u*, *ṛi*, *lṛi*, and gifted with an imaginary genitive case *ikaḥ* (here changed to *iko*). *Yaṇ* is a symbol for the letters *y*, *v*, *r*, *l*; and *ać* (supposed to possess a locative case *aći*) represents all the vowels. The rule at full is :—

The letters *y*, *v*, *r*, *l*, take the place of *i*, *u*, *ṛi*, *lṛi*, short or long, respectively, when followed by any dissimilar vowel.

Moreover, an aphorism which stands at the head of a series, and is hence called an *Adhikāra* or 'governing rule,' is never repeated, but must be supplied after the whole series till the influence (*anuvṛitti*) of this governing Sūtra is supposed to cease, such cessation being called *nivṛitti*. Thus the seventy-fourth Sūtra of the third chapter of Adhyāya I. is *ṇićaś-ća*, which must be interpreted thus :—

And after a verbal base ending in the causal affix (*ṇić*) the Ātmane-pada must come when the result of the action returns to the agent.

Of course nearly all the matter necessary to make this rule intelligible has to be supplied from other rules, and especially from the Adhikāra rule 12, which is separated by sixty-two intervening Sūtras.

In short, a careful examination of Pāṇini's grammar will dispose the student to appreciate Colebrooke's remark that 'the endless pursuit of exceptions and limitations so disjoins the general precepts, that the reader cannot keep in view their intended connection and mutual relation. He wanders in an intricate maze, and the clue of the labyrinth is continually slipping from his hand.'

In point of fact, however, this grammar ought not to be examined from a European point of view at all. We must not forget that an Indian Paṇḍit's ideas of grammar are very different from our own. Europeans are apt to look on a grammar of any kind as a necessary evil, only to be tolerated because indispensable to the attainment of a desired end beyond. With us the grammar of a language is in most cases a mere passage to its literature, a dreary region to be traversed as soon as possible. A Paṇḍit, on the other hand, regards grammar as we should regard the natural sciences. It is with him a something to be studied and elaborated for its own sake. According to the late Professor Goldstücker, 'Pāṇini's work is indeed a kind of natural history of the Sanskṛit language.'[1] It gives an account of the linguistic facts and phenomena as it finds them, tracing them out as they occur without regard to any scientific or methodical arrangement of materials. Thus the prolongation of vowels is dealt with as a fact, and is followed out through a whole chapter in order to trace all the instances in which such a lengthening takes place, whether in declension or conjugation or the composition of words. Hence the rules of declension and conjugation do not follow each other in their usual order according to the European system, but are scattered about in a disjointed and often very perplexing manner, so that it becomes necessary to search for and put together Aphorisms in widely separated parts of the work to enable the statement of some grammatical law or process to be completed.

Pāṇini's grammar was criticized and its deficiencies supplied by the celebrated Kātyāyana, who is called Vārttika-kāra, as author of the Vārttikas or 'supplementary rules and annotations.' He must have lived some time after Pāṇini, perhaps in the century following. Some, however, believe the two grammarians to have been contemporaneous. Kātyāyana, again, was criticized by his rival Patañjali, who generally supports Pāṇini against the composer of the supplementary rules. To Patañjali we owe one of the most wonderful grammatical

[1] See Chambers's Encyclopaedia, article Pāṇini.

works that the genius of any country has ever produced, viz., the Mahābhāshya or 'great commentary,'[1] written not so much to explain Pāṇini as to defend such of his Aphorisms as had been criticized by Kātyāyana. He was probably not the same person as the author of the Yoga philosophy. According to some, his mother's name was Goṇikā; he was born at Gonarda in the east of India, and he lived for some time in Kashmīr, where his work was well known. According to Professor Goldstücker, he wrote between 140 and 120 B.C.;[2] but Professor Weber places him about twenty-five years after Christ. These three men, Pāṇini, Kātyāyana, and Patañjali, compose the great Indian triumvirate of grammarians, from whose authority there is no appeal in anything which relates to Vyākaraṇa. About one hundred and fifty grammarians and commen-

---

1 The whole of this great work has been lately edited by two Paṇḍits at Benares. See the able article on it by Professor Weber in the last volume of the 'Indische Studien.' A copy has been kindly sent to me by Professor A. E. Gough. Patañjali's additions to the Vārttikas are called *Ishṭis* or Desiderata. He is also the author of many Kārikās or memorial verses on grammar. A compendium of such verses was also made by Bhartṛi-hari.

2 See the 'Indian Antiquary' for February 1873. See also an article on Patañjali in Chambers's Encyclopaedia, where it is well said that Patañjali's method is analogous to that of other classical commentaries; it establishes, usually by repetition, the correct reading of the text in explaining every important or doubtful word, in showing the connection of the principal parts of the sentence, and in adding such observations as may be required. Frequently Patañjali attaches his own critical remarks to the emendations of Kātyāyana, often in support of the views of the latter, but not seldom, too, in order to refute his criticisms and to defend Pāṇini; while, again, at other times, he completes the statement of one of them by his own additional rules. Rāmkṛishṇa Gopal Bhāṇḍārkar, writing in the 'Indian Antiquary' for October 1872, states his opinion that Patañjali lived when Pushpamitra was reigning at Pāṭali-putra, and 'that he probably wrote the third chapter of his Bhāshya between 144 B.C. and 142 B.C.' Professor Weber, however, controverts this conclusion.

tators followed in their footsteps, each criticizing or commenting on his predecessors. Among these may be mentioned Kaiyaṭa or Kaiyyaṭa, who commented on Patañjali in a work called the Bhāshya-pradīpa, and was himself commented on by Nāgojī-bhaṭṭa in the Bhāshya-pradīpoddyota.[1] One of the best of the more modern commentaries on Pāṇini is Vāmana's Kāśikā Vṛitti, so called because composed at Kāśī or Benares. A grammarian named Bhaṭṭoji-dīkshita attempted to arrange the Aphorisms on a plan more in accordance with modern ideas. His useful work is called the Siddhānta-kaumudī.[2] A second and greater simplification of Pāṇini is the Madhyama-kaumudī, and a still greater is the Laghu-kaumudī of Varada-rāja,[3] which is in fact a kind of abridgment of the Siddhānta-kaumudī, current in the north-west of India.

Vopadeva, a grammarian who is said to have flourished about the latter half of the thirteenth century at the court of Hemādri, king of Deva-giri (Dowlatābād), wrote a grammar for beginners on a system of his own, called the Mugdha-bodha,[4] which is much valued as an authority in Bengal, and referred to by many native commentators, such, for example, as Bharata-mallika or Bharata-sena, who therefore called his commentary on the Bhaṭṭi-kāvya, Mugdha-bodhinī.

Vopadeva's arrangement and many of his technical terms and symbolical expressions (including the technical forms of his affixes) differ from those of Pāṇini, and the only allusion to Vedic peculiarities is in the last Sūtra of the work (XXVI. 220), which is as follows :—

---

[1] This Nāgojī-bhaṭṭa was also the author of a grammatical work called Paribhāshendu-śekhara, lately edited at Bombay, with a translation, by Professor F. Kielhorn.

[2] A new edition of this was published not long ago in India.

[3] This was edited and translated by Dr. Ballantyne.

[4] It has been edited, like Pāṇini, by Professor Böhtlingk.

Manifold forms and irregularities are allowed in the Veda. [*Bahulam brahmaṇi*, which corresponds to Pāṇini's often-repeated *bahulam̱ ćhandasi*, II. 4. 39, II. 4. 73, &c. Cf. also Pāṇini's *vyatyayo bahulam*, 'opposition to the usual rule is frequent in the Veda,' III. 1. 85.]

In fact, Vopadeva[1] does not aim at the completeness of Pāṇini. He omits all notice of the accents, and his treatment of the laws of euphonic combination is by no means exhaustive. In his explanation of declension and conjugation he is more satisfactory, and he gives numerous useful examples and paradigms, but usually contents himself with general rules, and does not, like Pāṇini, trouble himself to trace out minute particulars or examine into every corner of an intricate subject with a view to a careful search for all possible exceptions. Professor Böhtlingk has given an analysis of the Mugdha-bodha in the preface to his excellent edition of the work. Vopadeva's first chapter explains technical terms; the second treats of euphonic laws; the third, of declension; the fourth, of the formation of feminines; the fifth, of the use of the cases; the sixth, of compound words; the seventh, of Taddhita affixes; the eighth, of technical terms applicable

---

[1] It is very necessary to know the commonest of Vopadeva's technical expressions, as they are not only occasionally used by some native commentators, but are also employed in some instances by European expounders of Sanskṛit grammar. They often deviate from Pāṇini's system. For example, the memorial terminations usually given for verbs are those of Vopadeva (VIII. 1); *dhu* stands for dhātu, 'a root;' *vri* for vṛiddhi; *kva* for the terminations of the singular; *vva* for bahuvaćana, those of the plural; *li* for lin̄ga, a nominal base; *lidhu* for nominal verbs; *śup* and *up* for the characteristic *u* of the eighth class of roots; *tum* and *ćatum* instead of Pāṇini's *tumun*, for the Kṛit affix *tum* forming the infinitive; *śāna* (not *śānać*) for the termination of the present participle Ātmane; *śri* for the pronominals (called Sarvanāman by Pāṇini); *samāhāra* for Pāṇini's *pratyāhāra* (see my Sanskṛit-English Dictionary). Nevertheless, Vopadeva adopts a great number of Pāṇini's technical terms.

to verbs and of roots of the first class; the ninth and tenth, of roots of the second and third classes; the eleventh to the seventeenth, of roots of the fourth to the tenth classes, one chapter being devoted to each class; the eighteenth, of causal verbs; the nineteenth, of desideratives; the twentieth, of intensives; the twenty-first, of nominals; the twenty-second, of the use of the Parasmai-pada; the twenty-third, of the use of the Ātmane-pada; the twenty-fourth, of passives, impersonals, and reflexive verbs; the twenty-fifth, of the use of the tenses and moods; the twenty-sixth, of Kṛit affixes and of affixes added to roots to form participles, &c.

I conclude by observing that a popular grammar called the *Kātantra* (or *Kalāpa*) is being well edited for the Bibliotheca Indica by Professor J. Eggeling.

The Vedāṅgas—Jyotisha, 'astronomy.'

This Vedāṅ-ga should rather be called 'the astronomical or astrological calendar.' Strictly speaking, it is represented by a short tract, consisting of thirty-six verses, in a comparatively modern style, to which scholars cannot assign a date earlier than 300 years B.C. According to the best authorities, no genuine Sūtras on astronomy have as yet been discovered. The object of the Jyotisha Vedāṅ-ga is to fix the most auspicious days and seasons for commencing sacrifices. This treatise, brief and unsatisfactory as it is, nevertheless deserves attention as embodying some of the most ancient astronomical ideas, among which may be mentioned the measure of a day by thirty Muhūrtas or hours of forty-eight minutes, the division of the zodiac into twenty-seven parts or lunar asterisms (the first of which is Kṛittikā), and the traditional place of the solstitial points, from which the attempt has been repeatedly made (by Jones, Davis,

Colebrooke, Pratt, and others) to deduce a date for the treatise itself, as well as for the whole Vedic literature.

The following is Colebrooke's translation of verses seven and eight of the Jyotisha tract,[1] which verses have been the subject of much controversy in relation to their bearing on the determination of dates from a comparison of the present position of the solstitial points:—

The sun and moon turn towards the north at the beginning of S'ravishṭhā (= Dhanishṭhā), but the sun turns towards the south in the middle of the constellation over which the serpents preside; and this (turn towards the south and towards the north) always happens in the months of Māgha and S'rāvaṇa. [*Prapadyete Śravishṭhādau sūrya-ćandramasāv udak, Sārpārdhe dākshiṇārkas tu, māgha-śrāvaṇayoḥ sadā.*] In the northern passage an increase of day and decrease of night take place amounting to a Prastha (or thirty-two Palas) of water; in the southern, both are reversed (*i.e.*, the days decrease and the nights increase), and the difference amounts, by the journey, to six Muhūrtas. [*Gharma-vṛiddhir apām prasthaḥ kshapā-hrāsa udag-gatau, Dakshiṇe tau viparyastau shaṇ-muhūrty ayanena tu.*]

Whatever may be the value of these verses in an astronomical point of view, it is clear that a superstitious belief in the importance of choosing auspicious days and lucky moments for the performance of rites and ceremonies, whether public or domestic, began to show itself very early in India, and that it grew and strengthened simultaneously with the growth of priestcraft and the

---

1 See Professor E. B. Cowell's new edition of Colebrooke's Essays, republished by his son, Sir T. E. Colebrooke, p. 98; and see especially Professor Whitney's valuable notes on this point (p. 126). The latter shows that the date derivable from the statement made in the Jyotisha has a necessary uncertainty of about four centuries (from the 14th to the 10th B.C.), and he claims that the actual uncertainty is still greater—that, in fact, the statement is worth nothing as yielding any definite date at all. Weber had before pointed out that the difference of six Muhūrtas between the longest and shortest day or night is accurate only in the extreme north-western corner of India.

elaboration of a complex ritual. The influence of the sun upon the atmosphere and soil made itself so manifest that it was only natural to infer that similar influences belonged to the moon, planets, and stars; and the personification and deification of all the most conspicuous luminaries which resulted from the supposed power inherent in their rays, of course intensified the superstitious feeling of dependence upon their favourable aspects for the success, not only of religious acts, but of all the affairs of life. Pernicious as such superstitious ideas were in their effect on the mind and all mental progress, they were nevertheless productive of good in impelling the acute Hindū to study the movements of the heavenly bodies, and stimulating him to undertake arithmetical and mathematical investigations. In all probability, astronomical and mathematical science had an independent origin in India. It is at least certain that they were cultivated with some success at a very early epoch, though of course very roughly in the absence of all optical and mechanical appliances. We have already given an example from the Aitareya-brāhmaṇa, which contains certain shrewd guesses at scientific truth in regard to the sun (see p. 32).

In some of the earliest hymns of the Veda the Nakshatras or lunar mansions[1] are mentioned in connection with the moon (see Ṛig-veda I. 50. 2). Moreover, some of the phases of the moon, such as *Anumati*, 'the moon one digit less than full;' *Rākā*, 'the full moon;' *Kuhū* (or

[1] For the twenty-seven Vedic Nakshatras see my Sanskṛit-English Dictionary (also Appendix). The word *Nakshatra* at first meant a star or asterism in general; then it was applied to the selected series of asterisms through or near which the moon passes; and finally it was loosely used for the part of the moon's path, the 27th or 28th of the zodiac, marked by each asterism. In the later mythology the lunar mansions were fabled as the twenty-seven daughters of Daksha and wives of the moon.

Gungu), 'the new moon;' and *Sinīvālī*, 'the first thin crescent preceding or following new moon,' are personified (see Ṛig-veda II. 32. 8), so that we are justified in inferring that the movements of the moon in the zodiac and its use as the time-measurer and month-maker (*māsa-kṛit*) [1] were studied and noted by the Hindūs perhaps as early as 1400 years B.C. The twenty-seven lunar mansions implied a lunar division of the zodiac into twenty-seven equal parts of 13° 20′ to each part. Such a division (into twenty-seven or twenty-eight parts) is shared by other Asiatic peoples, as the Arabs and Chinese, and the question where it originated has provoked much discussion, without leading to any definite and certain results.[2] The names of the Indian months have certainly been taken from the asterisms in which the moon was supposed to be full at different times of the year, and, what is still more significant, the names of some of these lunar asterisms have clearly been derived from ancient Vedic deities, like the Aśvins,[3] &c. In the Yajur-veda and

---

[1] This is a Vedic name of the moon. A root *mā*, 'to measure,' meaning also 'the measurer,' is first applied to the moon in Sanskṛit, and then to a lunation or period measured by one revolution of the moon. Something similar has happened in the cognate Āryan languages. At least we know that the words for 'month' are generally derived from the moon, our word 'month' being nothing but *moonth*. In Ṛig-veda X. 85. 2 occurs the following: *Atho nakshatrāṇām eshām upasthe Soma āhitaḥ*, 'Soma is deposited in the lap of these Nakshatras.'

[2] The various opinions and the arguments by which they have been supported have been lately reviewed by Professor Whitney in his 'Oriental and Linguistic Studies,' vol. ii. pp. 341–421. He regards the matter as still unsettled. The solar signs of the zodiac and much of the later astronomy, with many astronomical terms (such as *horā* = ὥρα; *kendra* = κέντρον; *dṛikāna*, the third of a zodiacal sign = δέκανος; *liptā*, the minute of a degree, = λεπτός), were borrowed from the Greeks.

[3] The names of the months are Māgha (from the Nakshatra *Maghā*), Phālguna (from *Phalgunī*), Ćaitra (from *Ćitrā*), Vaiśākha (from *Viśākhā*), Jyaishṭha (from *Jyeshṭhā*), Āshāḍha (from *Ashāḍhā*), Śrāvaṇa (from

Brāhmaṇas occur the expressions Nakshatra-darśa and Gaṇaka, applied to observers of the heavens, either as astronomers or astrologers;[1] and the adjustment of the lunar to the solar year by the insertion of a thirteenth or intercalary month (*mala-māsa*, *malimluća*, *adhimāsa*, sometimes called *Purushottama*) is probably alluded to in an ancient hymn (Ṛig-veda I. 25. 8), and frequently in more recent parts of the Veda. (Vājasaneyi-saṃhitā 22. 30, Atharva-veda V. 6. 4, &c.)

Whatever conclusions we may arrive at as to the original source of the first astronomical ideas current in the world, it is probable that to the Hindūs is due the invention of algebra[2] and its application to astronomy and geometry. From them also the Arabs received not only their first conceptions of algebraic analysis, but also those invaluable numerical symbols and decimal notation now current everywhere in Europe, which have rendered untold service to the progress of arithmetical science. It will not,

---

Śravaṇa), Bhādrapada or Bhādra (from *Bhadra-padā*), Āśvina (from *Aśvinī*), Kārttika (from *Kṛittikā*), Mārgaśīrsha, commonly called Agrahāyaṇa (from *Mṛiga-śiras*), Pausha (from *Pushya*). I have arranged these names so as to correspond as nearly as possible with our months, *Māgha* representing January—February, and the others continuing in regular order; but practically the Hindū calendar generally begins with Vaiśākha, this being considered the first month in the year.

[1] Of course astronomy and astrology were mixed up together, and the progress of the former was impeded in India by its subservience to the latter.

[2] The name Algebra (from the Arabic *al jabr*, 'the reduction of parts to a whole or of fractions to integers') shows that Europe received algebra like the ten numerical symbols from the Hindūs through the *Arabs*. The Sanskrit word for algebra, *Vija-gaṇita*, means 'calculation of seeds,' 'calculation of original or primary elements,' *i.e.*, analysis. If the Greeks did not receive their first ideas of algebra from the Hindūs, it may at least be taken as proved (from all that Colebrooke has so ably written on the subject) that the Hindūs were certainly not indebted to the Greeks, but invented their system independently.

therefore, be irrelevant if I introduce here a short account of the chief Hindū astronomical and mathematical works, with a few illustrative extracts.

By some authorities nine principal astronomical treatises, called Siddhāntas, are named, viz., the *Brahma-siddhānta*, *Sūrya-s°*, *Soma-s°*, *Vṛihaspati-s°*, *Garga-s°*, *Nārada-s°*, *Parāśara-s°*, *Pulastya-s°*, *Vasishṭha-s°*; by others five, viz., the *Pauliśa-s°*, *Romaka-s°*,[1] *Vāsishṭha-s°*, *Saura-s°*, and *Brāhma-s°* or *Paitāmaha-s°*, and these five, sometimes called collectively the Pańća-siddhāntikā, are said to be the original Siddhāntas. Whether the Sūrya-s° is the same as the Saura-s° appears somewhat doubtful, but this treatise, fabled to have been revealed by Sūrya 'the Sun' himself, is perhaps the best known of all Hindū astronomical works both in India and Europe.[2]

The earliest Hindū astronomer whose name has come down to us is Ārya-bhaṭa, who lived, according to Colebrooke, about the fifth century of our era. Others place him, or another astronomer of his name, in the third century. Ārya-bhaṭa is the author of three works, the Āryabhaṭīya, Daśa-gītikā, and Āryāshṭa-śata, and is said to have asserted a diurnal revolution of the earth on its axis, to have known the true theory of the causes of lunar and solar eclipses, and noticed the motion of the solstitial and equinoctial points.[3] Professor Kern has just published an edition of the *Āryabhaṭīya*.

After Ārya-bhaṭa came the astronomer Varāha-mihira, who lived about the sixth century of our era, and was

---

1 This title Romaka-s° points to an exchange of ideas on astronomical subjects between India, Greece, and Rome.

2 It has been well edited by Dr. Fitz-Edward Hall, and there are two translations of it, one published in America with notes (by Professor Whitney), and another by Bāpudeva Śāstrī.

3 According to Brahma-gupta, as quoted by the writer of the article Sanskṛit Literature in Chambers's Encyclopaedia, which I have consulted.

born at Ujjayinī. He wrote a work on nativities called Vṛihaj-jātaka, another well-known astrological work called Bṛihat-saṃhitā (recently translated by Professor Kern,[1] an extract from which is given p. 179), and a summary of the five original Siddhāntas called Pañća-siddhāntikā.

Next to Ārya-bhaṭa and Varāha-mihira lived Brahmagupta (probably towards the end of the sixth century), who wrote the Brahma-siddhānta, containing the chapters on arithmetic (*gaṇita*) and algebra (*kuṭṭaka*[2]) in Colebrooke's Indian Algebra.

Fourth and last of celebrated astronomers and mathematicians came Bhāskara or Bhāskarāćārya, who is supposed to have lived in the twelfth century and composed a well-known book called the Siddhānta-śiromaṇi, containing the treatises on algebra (*Vīja-gaṇita*) and arithmetic (*Līlāvati*[3]), translated by Colebrooke.

I proceed now to select specimens of the contents of the above works. The first extract gives the Indian division of time taken from the Sūrya-siddhānta (I. 11–13), Bhāskara's Siddhānta-śiromaṇi (I. 19, 20), and other works with their commentaries (Burgess, pp. 5, 6). It illustrates very curiously the natural taste of the Hindūs for hyperbole, leading them to attempt almost infinite calculations of inconceivable periods in the one direction, and infinitesimal subdivisions of the most minute quantities in the other. Without any reliable chronology in regard to the precise dates of any great events in their own history, they yet delight in a kind of chronology or 'science of

---

[1] For the Journal of the Royal Asiatic Society.

[2] *Kuṭṭaka* properly means a 'pulverizer' or multiplier.'

[3] *Līlāvatī*, 'delightful by its elegance,' is merely the name of the chapter on arithmetic (*pāṭī-gaṇita*, divided into *vyakta-gaṇita*, 'distinct computation,' and *avyakta-g°*, 'indistinct.' The name is also applied to a supposed 'charming woman,' to whom instruction in arithmetic is given.

time,' making time past, present, and future a subject of the most elaborate and minute computations. Hence we find them heaping billions upon millions and trillions upon billions of years, and reckoning up ages upon ages, Aeons upon Aeons, with even more audacity than modern geologists and astronomers. In short, an astronomical Hindū ventures on arithmetical conceptions quite beyond the mental dimensions of any one who feels himself incompetent to attempt the task of measuring infinity. Here is the time-table enumerating the subdivisions of what is called *real* and *unreal* time :—

'That which begins with respirations (*prāṇa*) is called real (*mūrta*) time ; that which begins with atoms (*truṭi*) is called unreal (*amūrta*) time. Ten long syllables (*gurv-akshara*) make one respiration (*prāṇa, asu*) ; six respirations make one Vināḍī (also called *pala* or *vighaṭikā* of twenty-four seconds) ; sixty Vināḍīs = one Nāḍī or Nāḍikā (also called *daṇḍa, ghaṭī, ghaṭikā* of twenty-four minutes) ; sixty Nāḍīs = one day (a sidereal day and night) ; thirty sidereal days = one civil (*sāvana*) month ; a civil month consists of thirty sunrises ; a lunar month of thirty lunar days (*tithi*) ; a solar (*saura*) month is determined by the entrance of the sun into a sign of the zodiac.' And now with regard to unreal time : 'One hundred atoms (*truṭi*) = one speck (*tatpara*); thirty specks = one twinkling (*nimesha*) ; eighteen twinklings = one bit (*kāshṭhā*) ; thirty bits = one minute (*kalā*) ; thirty minutes = one half-hour (*ghaṭikā*) ; two half-hours = one hour (*kshaṇa*) ; thirty hours = one day.' This makes the atom $\frac{1}{33750}$ of a second.

Considerable variations occur in Manu and the Purāṇas. According to Manu (I. 64) thirty Kalās = one Muhūrta or hour of forty-eight minutes. The Vishṇu-purāṇa (Wilson, p. 22) makes the atom = $\frac{1}{2110}$ of a second, and goes back beyond an atom to a Paramāṇu or infinitesimal atom, which it makes = $\frac{1}{38000}$ of a second. All, however, agree in dividing the day into thirty hours, just as the month is divided into thirty Tithis or lunar days, and the year into three hundred and sixty days, an intercalary month being inserted once in five years, which is thought to be the most ancient Hindū method of computing time.[1] The Sūrya-siddhānta then proceeds, like Manu (I. 68. 71), to reckon up vast periods of time through ages[2] (*yuga*) and great ages (*mahā-yuga*), till it arrives at an Aeon (*kalpa*), the total duration of which is said to be 4,320,000,000 years. In verse 24 we read (Burgess, p. 12):—

One hundred times four hundred and seventy-four divine years passed while the All-wise was employed in creating the animate and inanimate creation, plants, stars, gods, demons, and the rest.

Further on, we have the division of a circle, which corresponds with our own:—

Sixty seconds (*vikalā*) make a minute (*kalā*), sixty minutes make a degree (*bhāga*), thirty degrees make a sign (*rāśi*), twelve signs make a revolution (*bhagaṇa*).

The following is the measurement of the earth:—

Twice 800 *yojanas* are the diameter of the earth; the square root of ten times the square of that is the earth's circumference.

According to Bhāskara the earth's diameter is 1581 *yojanas*, so that if the *yojana* is reckoned at about four and a half English miles (which is given as one estimate of its length, though its value varies), the calculation in both cases is not very far from accurate.

At the commencement of Sūrya-siddhānta, Chapter II., we have a strange theory of planetary motion (p. 47):—

---

[1] Almanacs and horoscopes (*Janma-patra*) are called *Pañćāṅga*, as treating of five things, viz., solar days (commonly called Vāras, from the days of the week, Āditya-v°, Soma-v°, Maṅgala-v°, Budha-v°, Guru-v°, Śukra-v°, Śani-v°), lunar days (Tithis), the twenty-seven Nakshatras, the twenty-seven Yogas, the eleven Karaṇas.

[2] There are properly four Yugas or ages in every Mahāyuga, viz., *Kṛita*, *Tretā*, *Dvāpara*, and *Kali*, named from the marks on dice, the Kṛita being the best throw of four points, and the Kali the worst of one point.

Forms of time (*kālasya mūrtayaḥ*) of invisible shape (*adṛiśya-rūpāḥ*) stationed in the zodiac (*bhagaṇāśritāḥ*), called conjunction (*śīghroćća*), upper apsis (*mandoćća*), and node (*pāta*), are causes of the motion of the planets. The planets attached to these Beings by cords of air are drawn away by them with the right and left hand, forward or backward, according to nearness, toward their own place. A wind, moreover, called *Pravaha*, impels them towards their own apices (*ućća*); being drawn away forward and backward, they proceed by a varying motion.

In the previous Chapter (29, 34) the following statement occurs:—

In an age (*yuga*) the revolutions of the sun, Mercury (*Budha*), and Venus (*Śukra*), and of the conjunctions of Mars (*Man-gala*, *Bhauma*), Saturn (*Śani*), and Jupiter (*Vṛihaspati*), moving eastward, are four million, three hundred and twenty thousand. Of the asterisms, one billion, five hundred and eighty-two million, two hundred and thirty-seven thousand, eight hundred and twenty-eight.

I next give a portion of a remarkable passage from Varāha-mihira's *Bṛihat-saṃhitā* or 'complete system of natural astrology' (see Dr. Kern's translation, p. 433, of vol. iv. of the Royal Asiatic Society's Journal):—

An astrologer ought to be of good family, friendly in his appearance, and fashionable in his dress; veracious and not malignant. He must have well-proportioned, compact, and full limbs, no bodily defect, and be a fine man, with nice hands, feet, nails, eyes, chin, teeth, ears, brows, and head, and with a deep and clear voice; for generally one's good and bad moral qualities are in unison with one's personal appearance. As to mathematical astronomy, he must know the divisions of the heaven and of time, in ages, years, half-years, seasons, months, half-months, days, watches, hours, half-hours, minutes, respirations, moments, subdivisions of a moment, &c., as taught in the five Siddhāntas (see p. 175). He must know the reason why there are four kinds of months—the solar (*saura*), natural (*sāvana*), stellar (*nākshatra*), and lunar (*ćāndra*) months—and how it happens that there are intercalary months and subtractive days. He must know the beginning and end of the Jovian cycle of sixty years, of the lustrums, years, days, hours, and their respective lords. He must foretell the moment of commencement and separation, the direction, measure, duration, amount of obscuration, colour and place of the eclipses of sun and moon; also the future conjunctions and hostile encounters of the nine planets.[1] He must be skilful in ascertaining the distance of each planet from the earth, expressed in *yojanas;* further, the dimensions of their orbits and the distance of the places on earth, in *yojanas.* He ought to be clever in geometrical operations and in the calculation of time. If, moreover, he knows how to speak pithily, because he thoroughly understands all sorts of captious questions; if the science he expounds, by being put to the test by his own exertion and unceasing study, has become more refined—like gold is rendered purer by being put on the touchstone, by purification in fire, and by careful workmanship—then he may be said to be a scientific man. It has been said: 'How can one who solves no difficulty, nor answers any question, nor teaches his pupils, be styled a scientific man?' And thus it has been said by the great seer Garga: 'The king who does not honour a scholar accomplished in horoscopy and astronomy comes to grief.' 'As the night without a light, as the sky without the sun, so is the king without an astrologer; like a blind man he erreth on the road.' 'No one who wishes for well-being should live in a country where there is no astrologer.' 'No one that has studied astrology can go to the infernal regions.' 'A person who, without knowing the science, exercises the profession of an astrologer is a wicked man and a disgrace to society. Consider him to be a mere star-gazer. But such a one as properly knows horoscopy, astronomy, and natural astrology, him ought the king to honour and his service he ought to secure.'

With regard to Colebrooke's translation of Bhāskara's work on algebra (*Vīja-gaṇita*), the following extract is taken from the translator's introduction (p. xxii.):—

The motions of the moon and sun were carefully observed by the Hindūs, and with such success that their determination of the moon's synodical revolution is a much more correct one than the Greeks ever achieved. They had a division of the ecliptic into twenty-seven and twenty-eight parts, suggested evidently by the moon's period in days, and seemingly their own. It was certainly borrowed by the Arabs.[2]

[1] The nine planets are the Sun and Moon, Mercury, Venus, Mars, Jupiter, Saturn, with Rāhu and Ketu or the ascending and descending nodes.

[2] The Arabs, however, appear to have adopted the division of the zodiac into twenty-eight segments. Professor Whitney thinks that

They were particularly conversant with the most splendid of the primary planets; the period of Jupiter being introduced by them, in conjunction with those of the sun and moon, into the regulation of their calendar in the form of the cycle of sixty years, common to them and the Chaldeans.

We may add that from certain expressions in Bhāskara's work (see p. 106; Banerjea's Dialogues, p. 69[1]) it is inferred that some idea of the laws of gravitation was formed by Hindū astronomers as early as the twelfth century of our era. The precession of the equinoctial points (*vishuvat*, *krānti-pāta*) was well known to Bhāskara, and the effect of the moon in causing tides seems to have been suspected much earlier (cf. Raghu-vaṉśa V. 61).

The points in which Hindū algebra appears particularly distinguished from the Greek are (Colebrooke, p. xvi.):—

In addition to a better and more comprehensive algorithm (or notation): 1st. The management of equations involving more than one unknown term. 2nd. The resolution of equations of a higher order, in which, if they achieved little, they had at least the merit of the attempt and anticipated a modern discovery in the solution of biquadratics. 3rd. General methods for the solution of indeterminate problems of first and second degrees, in which they went far, indeed, beyond Diophantus, and anticipated discoveries of modern algebraists. 4th. Application of algebra to astronomical investigation and geometrical demonstration, in which they hit on some matters re-invented in later times. One of their anticipations of modern discoveries is the demonstration of the noted proposition of Pythagoras concerning the square of the base of a rectangular triangle being equal to the squares of the two legs containing the right angle.

As to the notation or algorithm of algebra, Colebrooke remarks (p. x.):—

The Hindū algebraists use abbreviations and initials for symbols. They distinguish negative quantities by a dot, but have not any mark,

---

the Arabs did not borrow their lunar zodiac from the Hindūs. See p. 173 and the authorities there referred to.

[1] See also the 'Indian Antiquary' for July 1872, p. 224.

besides the absence of the negative sign, to discriminate a positive quantity. No marks or symbols indicating operations of addition or multiplication, &c., are employed; nor any announcing equality or relative magnitude (greater or less).[1] But a factum is denoted by the initial syllable of a word of that import, subjoined to the terms which compose it, between which a dot is sometimes interposed. A fraction is indicated by placing the divisor under the dividend, but without a line of separation. The symbols of unknown quantity are not confined to a single one, but extend to ever so great a variety of denominations, and the characters used are initial syllables of the names of colours, excepting the first, which is the initial of *yāvat-tāvat* (applied to the *first* unknown quantity, *i.e.*, 'so much' of the unknown as this coefficient number). Colour, therefore, means unknown quantity or the symbol of it. Letters are likewise employed as symbols, either taken from the alphabet or else initial syllables of words signifying the subjects of the problem. Initials of the terms for square and solid respectively denote those powers. An initial syllable is in like manner used to mark a surd root (see the next extract and succeeding examples).

The following is from the Vīja-gaṇita (Chap. VI.):—

This is analysis by equation comprising several colours. In this the unknown quantities are numerous, two and three or more, for which *yāvat-tāvat* and the several colours are to be put to represent the values. They have been settled by the ancient teachers of the science, viz., black (*kāla*), blue (*nīla*), yellow (*pīta*), red (*lohita*), green (*haritaka*), white (*śveta*), variegated (*ćitra*), tawny (*kapila*), tan-coloured (*pin·gala*), grey (*dhūmra*), pink (*pāṭala*), mottled (*śavala*), blackish (*śyāmala*), another kind of black (*mećaka*), &c. Or letters (that is, *k*, &c.) are to be employed as names of the unknown. [In practice the initial syllables of the above words are used thus, *yā*, *kā*, *nī*, *pī*, *lo.*]

I here give some of the Sanskṛit equivalents for terms in arithmetic and algebra:—

An absolute quantity which has specific form is *rūpa* (applied in the singular to a unit, in the plural to an integer number, and often expressed by the first syllable *rū*). A surd or irrational number is

---

[1] The sign of equality was first used by Robert Recorde (because, he said, 'No two things can be more equal than a pair of parallels'), and those of relative magnitude by Harriot.—Colebrooke.

karaṇī (often denoted by the first syllable *ka*). A nought or cipher is *śūnya, ća;* a fraction which has a cipher for its denominator *ća-hara;* minus *ṛina, kshaya* (negative quantity); plus *dhana, sva* (positive quantity). A result or product is *bhāvita* (often expressed by the first syllable *bhā;* hence the product of two unknown quantities is expressed by *yā, kā bhā*, or *kā, nī bhā;* so also the square of the first unknown quantity multiplied by the cube of the second is thus abbreviated, *yā va, kā gha, bhā*).

It may be interesting to note the system of numeration increasing in decuple proportion given in Chapter II. of the Līlāvatī. This method, with the invention of the nine numerical figures (*an·ka*) and of the nought (*śūnya*) and of the decuple value assigned to each according to its position in the series, is thought to be of divine origin :—

Unit (*eka*), ten (*daśa*), hundred (*śata*), thousand (*sahasra*), ten thousand (*ayuta*), a hundred thousand (*laksha*, commonly called 'a lac'), million (*prayuta*), ten millions (*koṭi*, commonly called 'a krore'), a hundred millions (*arbuda*), a thousand millions (*abja* or *padma*), ten thousand millions (*kharva*), a hundred thousand millions (*nikharva*), a billion or million of millions (*mahā-padma*), ten billions (*śan·ku*), a hundred billions, (*jaladhi* or *samudra*), a thousand billions (*antya*), ten thousand billions (*madhya*), a hundred thousand billions (*parārdha*).

I add four specimens of problems from the Līlāvatī and Vīja-gaṇita (Colebrooke, pp. 24, 124, 191, 269, 272) :—

1. Out of a swarm of bees, one-fifth part settled on a Kadamba blossom; one-third on a S'ilīndhra flower; three times the difference of those numbers flew to the bloom of a Kuṭaja. One bee, which remained, hovered about in the air. Tell me, charming woman, the number of bees.

2. How many are the variations of form of the (ten-armed) god S'ambhu (S'iva) by the exchange of his ten attributes held reciprocally in his several hands, viz., the rope (*pāśa*), the hook for guiding an elephant (*an·kuśa*), the serpent, the hour-glass-shaped drum (*ḍamaru*), the human skull, the trident (*triśūla*), the club shaped like the foot of a bedstead (*khaṭvān·ga*), the dagger, the arrow, the bow? And those of the (four-armed) Hari (Vishṇu) by the exchange of the mace, the discus (*ćakra*), the lotus, and the conch (*śan·kha*)? Answer, 3,628,800; 24.

3. Eight rubies, ten emeralds, and a hundred pearls, which are in thy ear-ring, my beloved, were purchased by me for thee at an equal amount; and the sum of the rates of the three sorts of gems was three less than half a hundred: tell me the rate of each, auspicious woman.

4. What four numbers are such that the product of them all is equal to twenty times their sum? The answer to this last is: Here let the first number be *yā* 1; and the rest be arbitrarily put 5, 4, and 2. Their sum is *yā* 1, *rū* 11, and multiplied by 20, *yā* 20, *rū* 220. Product of all the quantities, *yā* 40. Statement for equation, $\begin{matrix} yā\ 40, & rū\ 0 \\ ya\ 20, & rū\ 220 \end{matrix}$. Hence by the first analysis, the value of *yā* is found 11, and the numbers are 11, 5, 4, 2.

I should mention here that attached to each Veda there are certain works called *Pariśishṭa* or 'Supplements' intended to supply directions omitted in the Śrauta Sūtras, &c. There are also the *Anukramaṇī* or 'Indices' giving the first words of every hymn, the metre, the names of the authors and of the deities addressed, the number of verses, &c.

There are also Upa-vedas or 'secondary Vedas,' which, however, have really little or no connection with either the Veda or Smṛiti. They are, 1. *Āyur-veda*, 'the science of life' or medicine (regarded as belonging to the Atharva-veda, and by some to the Ṛig-veda); 2. *Gandharva-veda*, 'the science of music' (as a branch of the Sāma-veda); 3. *Dhanur-veda*, 'the science of archery' or military art (connected with the Yajur-veda); *Sthāpatya-veda*, 'the science of architecture,' including the Śilpa-śāstra:—

As to 1, Two great medical writers are *Ćaraka* and *Su-śruta*, whose works treat of anatomy, physiology, materia medica, pharmacy, surgery (*śalya*), toxicology (*visha*), omens, and the evil influence of planets and demons (*bhūta*) in causing diseases. (See Wilson's Essays, vol. i. pp. 269–276, 380–393.) Su-śruta's work, in six books, has been well edited at Calcutta by Srī Madhusūdana Gupta. As to 2, Works on music treat of notes, scales, melodies, singing, musical instruments, and sometimes of dancing. Six primary modes or modifications of melody, called Rāgas, are enumerated, which are personified, and each of them married to five or sometimes six Rāgiṇīs. The chief musical works are the *Saṅgīta-ratnākara*, by Śārṅ-ga-deva; the *Saṅgīta-darpaṇa*, by Dāmodara; and the *San·gīta-dāmodara*, by S'ubhan·kara. As to 3, This science is by some ascribed to Viśvāmitra, by others to Bhṛigu. As to 4, Some assert that there are sixty-four treatises on the sixty-four S'ilpas or 'mechanical arts,' such as architecture, sculpture, carpentry, jewellery, farriery, &c. The principal work on architecture is the *Māna-sāra*, 'essence of measurement,' in fifty-eight chapters, giving rules for the construction of buildings, temples, ornamental arches (*toraṇa*), &c. Other works, by celebrated Sthapatis or 'architects,' describe the soil suited for building and rites in honour of the *Vāstu-purusha*, 'spirit presiding over sites.'

CHAPTER IX.

II. *The Smārta Sūtras or Traditional Rules.*

In our classification of Smṛiti or Post-Vedic literature, at the commencement of the last chapter, we placed the Smārta Sūtras under the second head, and pointed out that they were to a great extent the source of the subsequent law-books which form, in our arrangement, the third head of Smṛiti. We also observed that the term *Smārta-sūtra* is a general expression for collections of aphoristic rules which are distinguished from the Śrauta-sūtra of the Kalpa Vedāṅga, because they do not relate to Śrauta or Vedic ceremonies, but rather to *Gṛihya* or 'domestic rites' and *Samayāćāra* or 'conventional every-day practices.' Hence the Smārta Sūtras are commonly subdivided into, a. *Gṛihya Sūtras*, and b. *Sāmayāćārika Sūtras.* It will be desirable, therefore, before commencing our survey of Manu's celebrated Law-book, to advert briefly to these sources from which some of its materials were derived, and especially to the Gṛihya Sūtras.[1] Of these there are collections of different schools attached to each Veda. Thus to the Ṛig-veda belong the *Āśvalāyana*[2] and *Śaṅkhāyana* Gṛihya Sūtras; to the Sāma-veda those of *Gobhila;*[2] to the Vājasaneyi-saṃhitā

---

[1] Probably, however, Manu owes more to the Sāmayāćārika than to the Gṛihya Sūtras, although these latter are now best known to us by printed editions. We find that the authors of Gṛihya Sūtras have often the same name as the authors of law-books.

[2] There are also, as we have seen, Āśvalāyana S'rauta-sūtra under the head of 'Kalpa,' and probably each school had all three sets of Sūtras complete, though they are seldom all preserved. The Āśvalāyana

or White Yajur-veda those of *Pāraskara*; to the Taittirīya or Black Yajur-veda those of *Kāṭhaka*, *Baudhāyana*, *Bhāradvāja*, *Āpastamba*,[1] the *Maitrāyaṇīya*, *Mānava* (which last have perished, though some of their Kalpa-sūtras have been preserved, see p. 205), &c.

In fact, every Brāhmanical family or school (*ćaraṇa*[2]) had probably its own traditional recension (*śākha*, p. 150) of the Mantra and Brāhmaṇa portion of the Vedas, as well as its own Kalpa, Gṛihya, and Sāmayāćārika Sūtras; and even at the present day the domestic rites of particular families of Brāhmans are performed in accordance with the Sūtras of the Veda of which they happen to be adherents.

Since these Gṛihya and Sāmayāćārika Sūtras are older than Manu, they are probably as old as the sixth century B.C., but possibly the works we possess represent comparatively recent collections of the original texts.

It has been already pointed out that the Śrauta Sūtras are a kind of rubric for the more public solemn sacrifices (Jyotishṭoma, Agnishṭoma, Aśva-medha, &c.) enjoined by the Veda. The subject of the Gṛihya is rather that indicated by Manu when he says (III. 67):—

> Let the householder observe domestic rites with the sacred fire kindled at his marriage (called *Gārhapatya*) according to rule, and perform the five devotional acts and the daily domestic oblations.

Gṛihya Sūtras and part of the Pāraskara have been edited and translated into German by Professor Stenzler (Leipzig, 1864, 1865), and the former have also been edited by Paṇḍits for the Bibliotheca Indica (Calcutta, 1869). The Gobhilīya Gṛihya Sūtras are being edited for the Bibliotheca Indica.

[1] The Āpastambas appear to have preserved all three sets of Sūtras complete, for there are also Āpastamba S'rauta-sūtra and Sāmayāćārika-sūtra. According to Professor Bhaṇḍārkar there are numbers of Brāhmans in the south of India who are adherents of the Black Yajur-veda, and who receive *dakshiṇā* or 'fees' from rich men for repeating it with the Āpastamba Sūtras.

[2] A work called the *Ćaraṇa-vyūha* gives catalogues of these schools.

[*Vaivāhike 'gnau kurvīta gṛihyaṃ karma yathā-vidhi Pañća-yajña-vidhānaṃ ća paktiṃ* (= *pākam ćānvāhikīṃ gṛihī.*)]

Indeed the word Gṛihya means 'household,' and these Sūtras do in fact give rules for the five diurnal acts of domestic devotion called *Mahā-yajña* (or *Pañća-yajña*, four of them being also *Pāka-yajña*, Manu II. 86), as well as for the domestic ceremonies named *Sanskāras*, common to all the three higher classes, and not restricted to Brāhmans. The twelve Sanskāras are described at p. 239. They are generally performed at the one domestic hearth, instead of with all the three fires (called collectively *Tretā*), of the *Vitānas* or 'hearths used at public sacrifices.'

I proceed to give a brief account of Āśvalāyana's Gṛihya Sūtras of the Ṛig-veda, making one prefatory remark that the Hindū race affords perhaps the only example of a nation who, although apparently quite indifferent to the registering of any of the great facts of their political life, or even to the recording of any of the most remarkable events of their history—as, for example, the invasion of the Greeks under Alexander the Great—nevertheless, at a very early period, regulated their domestic rites and customs according to definite prescribed rules, which were not only written down, but preserved with religious care, and are many of them still in force. Moreover, as this race belongs to the same original race-stock as ourselves, the antiquity of their customs must of necessity invest them with great interest in our eyes.

The domestic oblations called Pāka-yajña (Manu II. 86, 143) are distinguished from the Vaitānika[1] in the first two Sūtras, thus (Stenzler's edition, I. 1, 2):—

---

[1] Kullūka, on Manu V. 84, derives *vitāna* from *vitan*, 'to spread out,' and explains *Vaitānika* to be those S'rauta oblations which are performed when the Gārhapatya fire is spread over both the Āhavanīya and Dakshiṇa hearths (*vaitānaṃ śrauto homaḥ gārhapatya-kuṇḍa-sthān agnīn āhavanī-*

The Vaitānika oblations (performed with all the three sacred fires[1]) have been explained (in the S'rauta-sūtra), we will now describe those (performed with the) domestic (fire only). There are three kinds of Pāka-yajña, viz., those that are offered in fire (such as oblations of butter, &c.); those that are presented without being offered in fire; those that are offered to the supreme Being (*Brahmaṇi*) in the feeding of Brāhmans (*Brāhmaṇa-bhojane*).

Book I. ii. enumerates the gods to whom oblations are to be offered, such as Agni, Indra, Soma, Heaven and Earth, Yama, Varuṇa, the Viśve Devāḥ (cf. Manu III. 90, 121), Brahman, &c. These, it will be observed, are generally Vedic deities. The third prescribes the mode of preparing the place where oblations are to be made.

The fourth commences with the following Sūtra:—

The ceremonies of tonsure (*ćaula* = *ćūḍā-karman*), investiture with the sacred cord (*upanayana*), shaving the beard (*go-dāna*), and marriage must be performed during the northern course of the sun (*udag-ayane*) in the light half of the month (*āpūryamāṇe pakshe*), and under an auspicious constellation (*kalyāṇe-nakshatre*).

These Sanskāra ceremonies are then described (beginning with marriage), and whenever Mantras or texts of the

---

yādi-kuṇḍeshu vitatya kriyate). See also Manu VI. 9. There is much difference of opinion as to the exact meaning of *pāka-yajña*. Stenzler translates it by 'Koch-opfer,' and thinks it means an oblation offered on the domestic fire when the daily food is cooked. Some of the commentators, on the other hand, interpret *pāka* by 'small,' 'simple,' and some by 'good.' In Manu II. 86 four Pāka-yajñas or 'domestic oblations' are mentioned (which Kullūka explains by *Vaiśvadeva-homa*, *bali*, *nitya-śrāddha*, and *atithi-bhojana*), thus identifying them with four of the Mahā-yajñas, see p. 194. Seven different kinds of Pāka-yajña will be found enumerated in my Sanskṛit-English Dictionary.

[1] In Manu III. 100, 185, five sacred fires are mentioned, and a Brāhman who keeps them all burning, called a *Pañćāgni* (= *Agnihotrin*), is regarded as peculiarly pious. They are, 1. *Dakshiṇa* (*Anvāhārya-paćana* in the Brāhmaṇas); 2. *Gārhapatya*; 3. *Āhavanīya*; 4. *Sabhya*; 5. *Āvasathya*. The three first fires are the most important, and are collectively called *Tretā*. Agnihotrīs are still met with in India.

Veda have to be repeated during the performance of each rite, the first word or words of the several texts are cited. Thus before the marriage ceremony an oblation of clarified butter is to be offered with repetition of the text: *Tvam Aryamā bhavasi yat kanīnām*, &c., 'Thou art Aryaman in relation to maidens' (Ṛig-veda V. 3. 2).

The fifth chapter prescribes the due selection of a wife after proper inquiry as to family and condition. Sūtra 3 says:—

A man ought to marry a woman who is possessed of intelligence, beauty, good character, and auspicious marks, and who is free from disease. (Compare the directions Manu III. 4–10.)

The sixth chapter specifies and describes the eight forms of marriage, called, *Brāhma*, *Daiva*, *Prājāpatya*, *Ārsha*, *Gāndharva*, *Āsura*, *Paiśāća*, and *Rākshasa*. They are also enumerated by Manu (III. 21), but not quite in the same order, and by Yājñavalkya (I. 58, 61). Manu (III. 27–34) describes them more fully than Āśvalāyana.

Book I. vii. prescribes a common marriage ceremony:—

West of the (sacred) fire a stone (for grinding corn and condiments, such as is used by women in all households) is placed, and north-east a water-jar. The bridegroom offers an oblation, standing, looking towards the west, and taking hold of the bride's hands while she sits and looks towards the east. If he wishes only for sons, he clasps her thumbs and says, 'I clasp thy hands for the sake of good fortune;' the fingers alone, if he wishes for daughters; the hairy side of the hand along with the thumbs, if he wishes for both (sons and daughters). Then, whilst he leads her towards the right three times round the fire and round the water-jar, he says in a low tone, 'I am he, thou art she; thou art she, I am he; I am the heaven, thou art the earth; I am the Sāman, thou art the Ṛić. Come; let us marry, let us possess offspring; united in affection, illustrious, well disposed towards each other (*sumanasyamānau*), let us live for a hundred years.' Every time he leads her round he makes her ascend the mill-stone, and says, 'Ascend thou this stone, be thou firm as a stone' (*aśmeva tvaṃ sthirā bhava*). Then the bride's brother, after spreading melted butter on the joined palms of her hands, scatters parched grains of rice on them twice. Then, after pouring the oblation of butter on the fire, some Vedic texts are recited. Then the bridegroom unlooses the two braided tresses of hair, one on each side of the top of the bride's head, repeating the Vedic text, 'I loose thee from the fetters of Varuṇa with which the very auspicious Savitṛi has bound thee' (Ṛig-veda X. 85. 24[1]). Then he causes her to step seven steps towards the north-east quarter, saying to her, 'Take thou one step (*ekapadī bhava*) for the acquirement of sap-like energy (*ishe*); take thou two steps for strength (*ūrje dvipadī bhava*); take thou three steps for the increase of wealth (*rāyas-poshāya*); take thou four steps for well-being (*māyo-bhavyāya*); take thou five steps for offspring (*prajābhyaḥ*); take thou six steps for the seasons (*ṛitubhyaḥ*); take thou seven steps as a friend (*sakhā saptapadī bhava*[2]); be faithfully devoted to me; may we obtain many sons! may they attain to a good old age!' Then bringing both their heads into close juxtaposition, some one sprinkles them with water from the jar. He should then remain for that night in the abode of an old Brāhman woman whose husband and children are alive. When the bride sees the polar star and Arundhatī and the seven Ṛishis, let her break silence and say, 'May my husband live and may I obtain children.'

In Book I. viii. 12, 13, 14, we have the following:—

When he (the bridegroom) has completed the marriage ceremonial he should give the bride's dress to one who knows the Sūryā-sūkta (Ṛig-veda X. 85), and food to the Brāhmans; then he should make them pronounce a blessing on him. [*Ćarita-vrataḥ sūryā-vide vadhū-vastraṃ dadyāt | annam brāhmaṇebhyaḥ | atha svasty-ayanaṃ vāćayīta.*]

Book I. ix. directs that after the marriage (*pāṇi-grahaṅa*) the first duty of the bridegroom is to attend to the kindling and maintaining of the household fire. The tenth chapter prescribes the performance of the rite called *Sthālī-pāka*, which appears to have been an oblation of

---

[1] The text in the original is *Pra tvā munćāmi Varuṇasya pāśād yena tvābadhnāt Savitā suśevaḥ.* It is from the well-known Sūryā-sūkta (X. 85), describing the marriage ceremony of Sūryā, the youthful daughter of the Sun, united to Soma, the Moon.

[2] Sakhā is Vedic for Sakhī. See Scholiast on Pāṇini IV. 1. 62.

rice, &c., cooked in a kind of caldron. The eleventh gives the rules for the ritual of animal sacrifice (*paśu-kalpa*), and the twelfth for the *Ćaitya-yajña*, which seems to have been a ceremonial performed at monuments, accompanied with offerings, perhaps to the memory of deceased persons. The thirteenth, fourteenth, fifteenth, sixteenth, and seventeenth chapters prescribe certain domestic ceremonies connected with the birth and treatment of children, which are included under the Sanskāras enjoined in the second Book of Manu. They are as follows :—

Garbha-lambhana, a rite performed on the first signs of conception, and *Puṉsavana*, one that takes place on the first indication of the conception of a living male (cf. Manu II. 27).

Sīmantonnayana, 'arranging the parting of the mother's hair,' observed in the fourth, sixth, or eighth month of pregnancy.

Hiraṇya-madhu-sarpishām prāśanam, 'feeding an infant with honey and clarified butter from a golden spoon' before cutting the navel-string at birth = *jāta-karman* (Manu II. 29).

Anna-prāśana, 'feeding an infant with rice' between the fifth and eighth month (Manu II. 34).

Ćaula (= *ćūḍā-karman*), 'tonsure' or shaving the hair except one lock on the crown, performed in the third year (cf. Manu II. 35).

In Book I. xix. we have precise directions in regard to investiture (*upanayana*) with the sacred thread (*yajño-pavīta*),—a ceremony of great importance, supposed to confer on the recipients (like the Christian rite of baptism) a second spiritual birth. This is enjoined for a Brāhman in his eighth year, for a Kshatriya in his eleventh, and for a Vaiśya in his twelfth, though the time may be extended in each case. These are therefore the three twice-born (*dvi-ja*) classes. (Cf. Manu II. 36–38). The twenty-second gives rules for the guidance of the young Brāhman as a Brahma-ćārin or 'student of the Veda' in the house of his preceptor after investiture by him. It begins thus :—

'Thou art now a Brahma-ćārī, take care to wash out thy mouth daily with water (=*upa-spṛiś*, *ā-ćam* in Manu II. 51, 53), do thy appointed work (*karma kuru*), sleep not in the day-time (*divā mā svāpsīḥ*, cf. *divā-svapna*, Manu VII. 47), obey thy preceptor, study the Veda (*Vedam adhīshva*); every morning and evening go out to beg for alms; every evening and morning collect fuel for the fire.' The period of studentship is to last for twelve years or until the student has acquired a knowledge of the Vedas (*grahaṇāntam*; cf. Manu III. 1; II. 53–60).

The fourth and fifth chapters of the second Book prescribe the Ashṭakā and Anvashṭakya Śrāddha ceremonies.

The subject of Book II. vii. viii. is Vāstu-parīkshā, 'examination of soil and situation' before fixing on a site, or laying the foundation of a house, thus:—

A piece of ground (should be chosen) which does not contain saline soil, and the title to which is not likely to involve legal disputes, and which is well stocked with plants and trees, and where there is plenty of Kuśa grass and Vīraṇa (fragrant grass). All thorny shrubs and plants with milky sap should be rooted out. A hole should be dug knee-deep and filled again with the excavated earth. If the earth when restored to the hole appears more than enough to fill it, the soil is excellent; if just enough, it is fairly good; if too little, it is bad. [*Adhike praśastaṃ same vārttaṃ nyūne garhitam*, VIII. 3.] At sunset the hole should be filled with water and allowed to stand all night. If in the morning it is still full of water, the soil is excellent; if it is moist, the soil is fairly good; if dry, bad. White, sweet-tasting, sandy soil is good for Brāhmans, red for Kshatriyas, yellow for Vaiśyas.

Book II. x. prescribes a solemn entrance into the new house (*gṛiha-prapadana*), after having stored it with seed-grain. The owner is then to cause the adjacent land belonging to him to be ploughed up and sown at the right season, and, standing at a particular spot with his back to the wind, he is to offer oblations, repeating a hymn of the Ṛig-veda (IV. 57), part of which I here translate freely:—

May the land's Lord be present as our friend!
So shall we prosper.[1] May the god accord us

[1] Lit. 'with the Lord of land as our friend,' &c. [*Kshetrasya patinā vayaṃ hiteneva jayāmasi*.]

Cattle and horses, nourishment and food!
By gifts like these he manifests his favour.
God of the land! bestow on us sweet water.
To us may every herb be sweet as honey!
To us may sky and atmosphere and rain
Be kind! and may the god who owns the soil
Be gracious! may we fearlessly approach him!
For us may oxen plough auspiciously![1]
May peasants labour happily! may ploughshares
Draw every furrow smoothly! may the ploughmen[2]
Follow the oxen joyfully! May he,
The rain-god, water happily the earth
With sweetest showers! may the god of air
And sun[3] bestow on us prosperity!

The first chapter of the third Book prescribes the five solemn offerings or devotional acts which every twice-born man is required to perform every day. These correspond to the five *Mahā-yajñāḥ* of Manu III. 69–71, sometimes called the five Sacraments. They are acts of homage directed—1. to the gods; 2. to all beings; 3. to departed ancestors; 4. to the Ṛishis or authors of the Veda; 5. to men (1. *deva-yajña*, 2. *bhūta-y°*, 3. *pitṛi-y°*, 4. *brahma-y°*, 5. *manushya-y°*). The first is performed by an oblation (*homa*) to the gods offered on the domestic fire; the second by an offering (*bali*) to animals and all creatures; the third by pouring out water to the spirits of the departed; the fourth by repetition of the Veda; the fifth by gifts to men and hospitality to guests (cf. Manu III. 81, &c., where, however, they are not given in the same order).

The second and third chapters treat of the fourth diurnal act of devotion (*brahma-yajña*), and direct the twice-born man how he is to conduct his private devotions, and how and what he is to repeat to himself (*svādhyāya-vidhi*):—

---

[1] *Śunam = sukham.*

[2] *Kīnāśāḥ.*

[3] This is the native interpretation of Śunā-sīrā. See Wilson.

He is to go in an easterly or northerly direction outside his place of abode, wearing his sacrificial cord (*yajňopavīta*) over his shoulder; he is first to bathe, and, having sipped water (*ăćamya*), to sit down on Kuśa grass placed so that the points are directed towards the east (Manu II. 75), and to repeat the sacred syllable *om*, the three Vyāhṛitis (*bhūr*, *bhuvaḥ*, *svar*), and the Sāvitrī (or *Gāyatrī*, see p. 17; cf. Manu II. 75–77, 79). Then he is to repeat, for as long a time as he may think proper, portions of some of the Ṛić, Yajus, Sāman, Atharvān-giras, Brāhmaṇas, Kalpas, Gāthās, Nārāśaṇsīs, Itihāsas, and Purāṇas[1] (see note 2, p. 245).

With regard to this subject, see p. 245 of this volume. Book III. vii. declares that if a twice-born man, being in good health, allows himself to fall asleep while the sun is setting, he is to pass the remainder of the night in an upright position, without uttering a word, and at sunrise to repeat five verses, from the fourth to the eighth inclusive, of Ṛig-veda X. 37, beginning, 'With whatever light, O sun, thou dispellest the darkness.' [*Yena sūrya jyotishā bādhase tamo*, &c.] Again, if the sun should rise while he is asleep, he is to continue standing and silent during the day, and to repeat the last four verses of the same hymn (cf. Manu II. 219–222). The eighth, ninth, and tenth chapters prescribe the ceremonies to be performed by a twice-born man whose period of studentship with his preceptor is completed, and who is about to return (*samāvartamāna*) home, and become a householder:—

He is to procure various articles for himself and his preceptor (at any rate for the latter), such as a necklace, two ear-rings, a suit of clothes, a parasol, a pair of shoes, a staff, a turban, perfumes, &c. (cf. Manu II. 245, 246). Having completed his studies and received permission from his preceptor to depart, and having inquired what fee (*artha*) he is to pay, he must perform an ablution (*snāna*). He is then to make certain vows of purity, after which he becomes elevated to the condition of

---

[1] The modern Brahma-yajňa of pious Brāhmans is based on this Sūtra.

a Snātaka (cf. Manu III. 4) or Brāhman who, after purification, has passed from the first stage of life—that of a student—to the second stage or that of a householder (*griha-stha*).

The fourth Book is perhaps the most interesting. In the first four chapters it prescribes the funeral rites to be performed at the burning of dead bodies,[1] and gives some directions as to the subsequent Śrāddha ceremonies :—

When a man dies, a piece of ground is to be excavated in a *Śmaśāna* or 'burning-ground' south-east or south-west of his abode. His relations are to carry the fires and the sacrificial implements (*yajña-pātrāṇi*) to the excavated place. Those of them who are most advanced in years (*pravayasaḥ*) are to walk behind in single file—the men separated from the women—bearing the corpse, the hair and nails of which have all been cut off or clipped, and leading the sacrificial animal, either a cow or a black she-goat. The remaining relations and connexions are to follow with their garments and sacrificial cords hanging down (*adho-nivītāḥ*), and their hair dishevelled—the elder in front, the younger behind. When they reach the prepared ground, the performer of the ceremony is to sprinkle water on it with a branch of the Śamī tree, repeating Ṛig-veda X. 14. 9 :—

'Depart (ye evil spirits), slink away from here; the Fathers (his departed ancestors) have made for him this place of rest, distinguished (*vyaktam*) by days (*ahobhir*), waters (*adbhir*), and bright lights (*aktubhiḥ*).'[2]

Then he is to deposit the fires around the margin of the excavated place—the Āhavanīya fire to the south-east, the Gārhapatya to the north-west, and the Dakshiṇa to the south-west (see note, p. 189). Then some one who understands what is required, is to collect a heap of fire-wood and pile it up inside the sacrificial ground (*antar-vedi*). Next, a layer of Kuśa grass is to be spread over the heap along with

---

[1] See the article 'Über Todtenbestattung,' by Professor Max Müller in vol. ix. of the Zeitschrift der Deutschen Morgenländischen Gesellschaft, in which a portion of this division of the Āśvalāyana Gṛihya Sūtras is translated into German. With regard to the importance of the following extracts as bearing upon Satī (*Suttee*), see p. 251 of this volume.

[2] The meaning of this is not very clear. I understand it as denoting that the ground is open and well exposed to daylight and well sprinkled with water and surrounded with the fires.

the black skin of the goat and the clipped hair, and the dead body is to be placed upon it with the feet towards the Gārhapatya fire and the head towards the Āhavanīya. North of the body his wife is to be made to lie down (on the funeral pile), along with the bow of the dead man if he was a soldier (*Kshatriya*). Then either her husband's brother (*devaraḥ*), who is in the place of a husband to her (*patisthānīyaḥ*), or a pupil, or an old servant causes her to rise up, repeating the words of Ṛig-veda X. 18. 8:—

'Rise up, O woman (*udīrshva nāri*), come back to the world of life; thou art lying by a dead man; come back. Thou hast sufficiently fulfilled the duty of a wife and mother (*janitvam*) to the husband who wooed thee (*didhishos*) and took thee by the hand.' (See note 2, p. 252.)

Next, the brother-in-law is to take back the bow, repeating Ṛig-veda X. 18. 9:—

'I take the bow out of the hand of the dead man for our own protection, for our glory, and for our strength; remain thou there, we will remain here as heroes, (so that) in all battles we may conquer our foes.'

Then he is to place the various sacrificial implements and portions of the sacrificial animal in the two hands and on different parts of the body of the corpse. This being done, he is to order the three fires to be kindled (*agnīn prajvālayati*). If the Āhavanīya fire reaches the dead man first, then his spirit is borne to heaven; if the Gārhapatya, then his spirit is taken to the middle region (*antariksha-loka*); if the Dakshiṇa, then it remains in the world of mortals (*manushya-loka*). When all three reach him together, this is the most auspicious sign of all. While the body is burning, portions of hymns of the Ṛig-veda (such as X. 14. 7, 8, 10, 11; X. 16. 1–4; X. 17. 3–6; X. 18. 11; X. 154. 1–5) are to be repeated.

The following are examples of some of the verses:—

Open thy arms, O earth, receive the dead
With gentle pressure and with loving welcome.
Enshroud him tenderly, e'en as a mother
Folds her soft vestment round the child she loves (X. 18. 11).
Soul of the dead! depart; take thou the path—
The ancient path—by which our ancestors
Have gone before thee; thou shalt look upon
The two kings, mighty Varuṇa and Yama,
Delighting in oblations; thou shalt meet

The Fathers and receive the recompense
Of all thy stored-up offerings above.
Leave thou thy sin and imperfection here;
Return unto thy home once more; assume
A glorious form. By an auspicious path
Hasten to pass the four-eyed brindled dogs—
The two road-guarding sons of Saramā;
Advance to meet the Fathers who, with hearts
Kindly disposed towards thee, dwell in bliss
With Yama; and do thou, O mighty god,
Intrust him to thy guards [1] to bring him to thee,
And grant him health and happiness eternal (X. 14. 7–11).[2]

When a dead body is burnt by one who knows and can repeat these verses properly, then it is certain that the soul (invested with a kind of subtile body [3]) rises along with the smoke to heaven (*sahaiva dhūmena svargaṃ lokam eti ha vijñāyate*).

Then the performer of the ceremony is to repeat the verse (Rig-veda X. 18. 3):—

We living men, survivors, now return
And leave the dead; may our oblations please
The gods and bring us blessings! now we go
To dance and jest and hope for longer life.

After this they are to move to a spot where there is a pool of still water, dip themselves once, cast a handful of water into the air, pronouncing the name of the dead man and that of his family (*e.g.*, 'O Devadatta Kāśyapa, this water is for thee'); then coming out of the water, they are to put on other clothes and to sit down till the stars appear or else till the sun is quite invisible, when they are to proceed homewards, the younger ones walking first, the elder behind. Before

---

1 These are the four-eyed watch-dogs mentioned before.

2 Part of this has been freely rendered in a version given p. 19.

3 The eighth Sūtra of Chapter IV. states that a hole ought to be dug north-eastward of the Āhavanīya fire and strewn with the plants Avakā and Śīpāla; and the commentator adds that the soul of the dead man, invested with its vehicular subtile body (called *ātivāhika* and sometimes *adhishṭhāna* and distinct from the *liṅga* or *sūkshma*, being *angushṭhamātra*, 'of the size of a thumb'), waits in this hole until the gross body is burnt, and then emerging, is carried with the smoke to heaven.

entering the house they are (for purification) to touch a stone, fire, cow-dung, grains of barley, oil, and water. During one night they are not to cook any food, but to eat only what is already prepared, and for three nights they are not to touch anything containing salt.

Book IV. v. prescribes the gathering together the bones and ashes of the deceased (*sañćayana*, Manu V. 59):—

This is to take place after the tenth day of the dark half of the month, on an odd day (*i.e*, the eleventh, thirteenth, fifteenth, &c.), and under a single Nakshatra (*i.e.*, not under one like Ashāḍhā, which is both *pūrvā* and *Puttarā*).

The bones and ashes of a man are to be placed in an undecorated funeral vase or long vessel (*alakshaṇe kumbhe*), and those of a woman in a female vase (of a fuller shape, supposed to resemble the female figure). A hole is to be excavated and the bones thus collected in a vessel are to be placed in it, while Ṛig-veda X. 18. 10 is repeated:—

'Go to thy mother Earth, the Widely-extended (*uru-vyaćasam*), the Broad, the Auspicious; may she be to thee like a young maiden, soft as wool (*ūrṇa-mradā*), to a pious person! may she protect thee from the embrace of the goddess of corruption!' (*Nirṛiter upasthāt.*)

Then earth is to be scattered over the excavation, and Ṛig-veda X. 18. 11, 12 are to be repeated (see p. 197 for verse 11). Lastly, a cover or lid is to be placed over the vase or long vessel and the hole is to be filled up with earth, so that the vessel is quite hidden from view, while Ṛig-veda X. 18. 13 is repeated:—

'I raise up the earth around thee for a support, placing this cover on thee without causing injury. May the Fathers guard this funereal monument for thee! May Yama establish a habitation for thee there!'

This being accomplished, the relations are to return home, without looking about, and after they have performed an ablution they are to offer the first S'rāddha to the deceased person separately (*ekoddishṭa*).

Book IV. vii. prescribes four kinds of *Śrāddha*, *i.e.*, offerings to deceased persons and Pitṛis or ancestors generally: 1. *Pārvaṇa*, 'monthly,' to ancestors for three generations on the days of conjunction or new moon (cf. Manu III. 282; those to ancestors generally being called *Nitya*, 'constant,' 'daily,' and others *Ashṭakā*, as performed on the eighth day of certain months); 2. *Kāmya*, 'voluntary,' performed for some object of desire (as the obtaining of a son); 3. *Ābhyudayika*, performed as thank-offerings on occasions of family rejoicing (as at the Sanskāras) or for increase of prosperity, &c. (*Vṛiddhi-pūrta*); 4. *Ekoddishṭa*, 'special,' having reference to one person recently deceased, and not to ancestors generally. It is repeated annually on the anniversary of his death. (Those which are occasional are sometimes called *Naimittika*.) To these funeral ceremonies Brāhmans are to be invited. They are to be feasted, and gifts presented to them. The guests are to be made to sit down with their faces towards the North, and water is to be poured into their hands with Kuśa grass and Sesamum seed (*tila*, cf. Manu III. 223). Cakes of rice (*piṇḍa*) and libations of water are to be offered with the auspicious exclamation Svadhā. There is also another Śrāddha called *Daiva*, in honour of the Viśve Devāḥ, 'deities collectively,' or of a particular troop of deities, ten in number. Hence some distinguish eight kinds of Śrāddha (see p. 247); and the Nirṇaya-sindhu, twelve.

A fuller description of these solemn Śrāddhas is given by Manu III. 123-286, and in verse 202 the meaning of the term Śrāddha is explained as follows:—

Mere water (*vāry api*) offered with faith (*śraddhayā*) to the Pitṛis in silver or plated (*rājatānvitaiḥ*) vessels procures imperishable bliss (*akshayāyopakalpate*).

I close my account of the Āśvalāyana Gṛihya Sūtras by remarking that the rules relating to funeral ceremonies in the fourth Book, of which an abstract has just been given, possess great interest in their connexion with the eighteenth hymn of the tenth Maṇḍala of the Ṛig-veda. Although the Sūtras direct that the texts of this hymn are to be used, yet the rite must have undergone considerable modifications since the period when the hymn was composed.

It may be gathered from a study of the text of the hymn, that at the early period when the Āryan race first settled on the plains of Hindūstān, there was not the same prolonged and elaborate observance of funeral rites, which in later times was converted into an excuse for the ostentatious and costly feasting of priests and guests (see p. 249). But there was no less solemnity in the conduct of the ceremonial, no less exhibition of grief for the dead in the tender treatment of his remains, and no less affectionate respect for his memory,—a feeling cherished as a religious duty, more tenaciously in India than in Europe.

We notice, too, even at that early epoch an evident belief in the soul's eternal existence and the permanence of its personality hereafter, which notably contrasts with the later ideas of transmigration, absorption into the divine essence, and pantheistic identification with the supreme Soul of the universe.

We learn also from this same hymn that the body in ancient times was not burnt but buried; nor can we discover the slightest allusion to the later practice of Satī or cremation of the widow with her husband.

The corpse of the deceased person was deposited close to a grave dug ready for its reception, and by its side his widow, if he happened to be a married man, seated herself, while his children, relatives, and friends ranged themselves in a circle round her. The priest stood near at an altar, on which the sacred fire was kindled, and having invoked Death, called upon him to withdraw from the path of the living, and not to molest the young and healthy survivors, who were assembled to perform pious rites for the dead, without giving up the expectation of a long life themselves. He then placed a stone between the dead body and the living relations, to mark off the boundary-line of Death's domain, and offered up a prayer that none of those present might be removed to another world before attaining to old age, and that none of the younger might be taken before the elder. Then the widow's married female friends walked up to the altar and offered oblations in the fire; after which the widow herself withdrew from the inner circle assigned to the dead, and joined the survivors outside the boundary-line, while the officiating priest took the bow out of the hand of the deceased, in order to show that the manly strength which he possessed during life, did not perish with him, but remained with his family. The body was then tenderly laid in the grave with repetition of the words of the hymn already translated, 'Open thy arms, O Earth, receive the dead,' &c. (see p. 197). The ceremony was concluded by the careful closing of the tomb with a stone slab. Finally a mound of earth was raised to mark and consecrate the spot.[1]

With regard to the Sāmayāćārika Sūtras little remains to add to what has already been stated. Not many collections of this third class of Sūtras (as distinguished from the Śrauta and Gṛihya) have been preserved. Were they better known to us, we should probably find that they furnished materials for Manu's compilation, even more than the Gṛihya Sūtras appear to have done. It is for this reason that, as introductory to the Dharmaśāstras or Law-books, they are sometimes called Dharmaśūtras. Since 'conventional, every-day practices' constitute the proper subject of these Sūtras, and it is clear that conventional usages may often come under the head of Gṛihya or 'domestic rites,' it may easily be understood that the Sāmayāćārika not unfrequently go over the same ground as the Gṛihya Sūtras. For instance, we find them both giving rules for the Sanskāras &c. (see p. 239).

---

[1] A fuller account of the whole rite will be found in Professor Stenzler's 'Rede über die Sitte,' which I have consulted throughout.

Perhaps the best known Sāmayāćārika Sūtras are those of Āpastamba belonging to the Black Yajur-veda (see note 1, p. 187). An account of these will be found in Professor Max Müller's 'Ancient Sanskṛit Literature' (p. 100, &c.), and in No. 732 of Rājendralāla Mitra's MSS. They commence as follows:—

1. Therefore let us now explain the Sāmayāćārika duties. [*Athātaḥ sāmayāćārikān dharmān vyākhyāsyāmaḥ.*]

2. These agreements which were made by men who knew the law are an authority. [*Dharma-jña-samayaḥ pramāṇam.*]

3. And the Vedas (are an authority). [*Vedāś-ća.*]

III. *The Dharma-śāstras or Law-books—Manu.*

At least forty-seven independent Law-books[1] are enumerated, and of these at least twenty are still extant and are mentioned by Yājñavalkya (I. 3–5), as follows:—

1. That of Manu. 2. Yājñavalkya (second in importance to Manu). 3. Atri. 4. Vishṇu. 5. Hārītā. 6. Uśanas. 7. An-giras. 8. Yama. 9. Āpastamba. 10. Saṃvarta. 11. Kātyāyana. 12. Vṛihaspati. 13. Parāśara. 14. Vyāsa. 15. S'an-kha. 16. Likhita. 17. Daksha. 18. Gotama or Gautama. 19. S'ātātapa. 20. Vasishṭha. There is also a Law-book, the joint production of S'an-kha and Likhita; and others ascribed to Nāradā, Bhṛigu, &c. (see the end of Chapter X.); and Kullūka, the commentator on Manu, mentions the names of Baudhāyana, Medhātithi, Govinda-rāja, &c.

Let us first endeavour to gain some idea of the character of the most celebrated and ancient of these books commonly called 'the Code of Manu.'

This well-known collection of laws and precepts is perhaps the oldest and most sacred Sanskṛit work after

[1] Professor Stenzler enumerates forty-six, Dr. Röer forty-seven. The names of the authors of some of these law-books are the same as those of some of the Gṛihya Sūtras, *e.g.*, Āpastamba, Pāraskara, and Baudhāyana. The same men may have been authors of both Sūtras and Dharma-śāstras.

the Veda and its Sūtras. Although standing in a manner at the head of Post-vedic literature, it is connected with the Veda through these Sūtras, as the philosophical Darśanas are through the Upanishads. Even if not the oldest of Post-vedic writings (see note, p. 207), it is certainly the most interesting, both as presenting a picture of the institutions, usages, manners, and intellectual condition of an important part of the Hindū race at a remote period, and as revealing the exaggerated nature of the rules by which the Brāhmans sought to secure their own ascendency, and to perpetuate an organized caste-system in subordination to themselves. At the same time it is in other respects perhaps one of the most remarkable books that the literature of the whole world can offer, and some of its moral precepts are worthy of Christianity itself.

Probably the compilation we now possess is an irregular compendium of rules and maxims by different authors, which existed unwritten for a long period of time, and were handed down orally. An original collection is alluded to by commentators under the titles Vṛiddha and Vṛihat, which is said to have contained 100,000 couplets, arranged under twenty-four heads in one thousand chapters; whereas the existing Code contains only 2685 verses. Possibly abbreviated versions of old collections were made at successive periods, and additional matter inserted, the present text merely representing the latest compilation.

At any rate we must guard against a supposition that the expression 'Code,' often applied to this collection, is intended to denote a systematic arrangement of precepts which existed as actual laws in force throughout one country. It is probable that the whole of India was never under one government. Some few powerful monarchs are known to have acquired sovereignty over very extensive territories, and were then called Ćakra-vartins, but we must beware of imagining that Manu's Law-book is a record of national ordinances and institutions prevalent over the whole of such territories. No doubt ultimately it worked its way to acceptance with the entire Hindū community; and certainly in the end it not only secured for itself a high place in popular estimation and a degree of reverence only second to that accorded to the Veda, but it became, moreover, the chief authority as a basis of Hindū jurisprudence. Originally, however, its position must have been different. It merely represented certain rules and precepts (perhaps by different authors) current among a particular tribe, or rather school of Brāhmans called Mānavas, who probably lived in the North-western region between the rivers Sarasvatī and Dṛishadvatī (see p. 208), not far from Delhi and the scene of the great social conflict described in the Mahābhārata.[1] This tribe seems to have belonged to the Taittirīyakas, 'adherents of the Black Yajur-veda;' and their Mantras, Brāhmaṇa, and Śrauta Sūtras are still extant,[2] but their Gṛihya and Sāmayāćārika Sūtras appear to have perished. In all probability, too, many of the rules, as we have them presented to us, were simply theoretical,—inserted to complete an ideal of what ought to constitute a perfect system of religious, ceremonial, moral, political, and social duties. Who the real compiler and promulgator of the Institutes was, is not known. He was probably a learned Brāhman of the Mānava school.

We must, of course, make a due allowance for the

---

[1] The inference deducible from II. 17, 18, that the Mānavas lived in the region of the earliest Āryan settlements, must have weight in determining the antiquity of the Code and its value as representing the ancient social life of the Hindūs before their advance into the Dekhan.

[2] A counterpart of a MS. of a commentary on part of the Mānava-kalpa-sūtra has been edited by the late Professor Goldstücker.

mythical element in the Code, as, for instance, when a divine sage named Manu[1] (or Svāyambhuva—'sprung from the great self-existent Being') is made to say (I. 58–60) as follows :—

The god (Brahmā) having framed this system of laws himself, taught it fully to me in the beginning. I then taught it to Marīći and the nine other sages, my offspring (of whom Bhṛigu is one, cf. I. 35). Of these (my sons) Bhṛigu is deputed by me to declare the Code to you (Ṛishis) from beginning to end, for he has learned from me to recite the whole of it. Then the great sage, Bhṛigu, having been thus appointed by Manu to promulgate his laws, addressed all the Ṛishis with a pleased mind, saying, 'Listen!'

Manu, therefore, is supposed to speak in his own person as far as I. 60. After that, Bhṛigu is the speaker, and the closing verse of the whole Code (XII. 126) describes it as *Mānavaṃ Śāstram Bhṛigu-proktam*, 'enunciated by Bhṛigu; while in XI. 243 Prajāpati or Brahmā himself

---

[1] This name of the supposed divine progenitor of all beings is derived from the root *man*, which means 'to think,' or 'reason' (and especially according to the Hindū theory, 'to think upon and understand the Veda,' whence the desiderative form *Mīmāṉsā* from the same root, signifying 'investigation of the meaning of the Veda'). Bhṛigu states (I. 61) that Manu sprang from Svayambhū, and that six other Manus descended from him; whereas Manu himself (I. 33–36) declares that he was created by Virāj, the male power produced by Brahmā, and that being so created he produced the ten Maharshis or Prajāpatis, who again produced seven Manus. The name, however, is generic. In every Kalpa or interval from creation to creation there exist fourteen successive Manus, whence each whole period is called a *Manvantara*, described as innumerable in I. 80. In the present creation there have been as yet seven Manus: 1. Manu *Svāyambhuva*, the supposed author of the Code, who produced the ten Prajāpatis or 'patriarchs' for peopling the universe; 2. *Svāroćisha*; 3. *Auttami*; 4. *Tāmasa*; 5. *Raivata*; 6. *Ćākshusha*; 7. *Vaivasvata*, son of the Sun, the Manu of the present period, regarded as a kind of Indian Adam or Noah (see note, p. 30). According to some, this last Manu was the author of the Code, and therefore, as progenitor of the Solar line of kings, a Kshatriya.

is declared to have created it by the power of austerity (*tapasā*).

We need hardly, however, explain that these are merely ideal personages, introduced dramatically like Kṛishṇa in the Bhagavad-gītā; or rather perhaps are later additions, designed to give an air of antiquity and divine authority to the teaching of the Code.

The work in its present form can scarcely, I think, be assigned to a date earlier or later than the fifth century B.C.[1] Strictly speaking, or at least according to European notions, it is, as I have already hinted, no orderly codification of national statutes and customs, but rather an unsystematic compilation from previous sources,[2] which,

---

[1] Sir W. Jones held that Manu's book was drawn up in about the year 1280 B.C. Mr. Elphinstone placed it 900 years B.C. Possibly some parts of it may represent laws and precepts which were current among the Mānavas at the latter date, but no one would now assign so early a date to the actual compilation of the Code. Nor can it, I think, reasonably be placed later than the fifth century B.C. The gods mentioned are chiefly Vedic, and the fourfold caste system is that of the Purusha-sūkta (see p. 21). There is no direct allusion to Buddhism, though many of Manu's precepts are decidedly Buddhistic, having frequent parallels in the Dhamma-pada, which indicate that Buddhistic ideas were gaining ground in the locality represented by the Code. Nor is there any allusion to Satī, nor to the worship of Vishṇu and S'iva, which, from a statement of Megasthenes, may be inferred to have prevailed in India soon after Alexander's invasion. Nor is there any mention of the stories of the Mahābhārata and Rāmāyaṇa. At the same time the former Epic often contains verses identical with those of Manu. These are probably either taken from Manu or derived from a common source. Possibly, however, portions of the Mahābhārata may be older than Manu. Certainly in III. 232 occur the words *Dharma-śāstra*, *Ākhyāna*, *Itihāsa*, *Purāṇa*, and *Khila*, as titles of sacred works, and Kullūka explains *Itihāsa* by *Mahā-bhārata*, but these words may refer to the older works, which were the sources of the present compilations.

[2] An evidence in favour of the supposition that more than one person may have had a hand in the Code is deducible from the emphasis laid

by blending civil and criminal law with religious, moral, and ceremonial precepts, philosophical doctrines, and metaphysical theories, confounds the ordinances of government with the obligations of religion, domestic life, and private morals. It is in twelve Chapters or Books.

In verse 6 of Book II. we have a statement as to the 'root' or basis of all law (*dharma-mūlam*). This is declared to be (1.) the whole Veda (*Vedo 'khilaḥ*), (2.) the traditional law (*Smṛiti*), (3.) morality (*Śīlam*) of those who know the Veda, and (4.) the practices and customs (*āćāraḥ*), established from time immemorial, of good men. In matters indifferent a man is free to follow his own inclination (*ātma-tushṭi*).

Again, in verses 107, 108 of Book I. it is said:—

In this (Code) appears the whole system of law, with definitions of good and bad actions, and the traditional practices (*āćāra*) of the four classes, which usages are held to be eternal (*śāśvataḥ*, since they reach back to a period beyond the memory of man). Traditional practice (*āćāra*) is equivalent to supreme law (*paramo dharmaḥ*), since it is so pronounced by the Veda and by Smṛiti (*Smārta*).

This Law-book, therefore, is a metrical compendium of rules of Smṛiti, Śīla, and Āćāra, most of which had been previously collected and propounded under the name of Gṛihya and Sāmayāćārika Sūtras. At the end of Book I. a summary of subjects is given, but we may more conveniently examine the contents of the twelve books under six principal heads, viz., 1. Veda, 'sacred knowledge' and religion; 2. Vedānta or Ātma-Vidyā, as terms for philosophy in general; 3. Āćāra; 4. Vyavahāra; 5. Prāyaś-ćitta; 6. Karma-phala.

It will be found that after eliminating the purely reli-

---

upon certain maxims which are especially ascribed to Manu himself, such, for example, as V. 41, 131; VI. 54; VIII. 124, 168, 279, 339; IX. 158, 182, 239; X. 63, 78, all of which introduce some phrase like *Manur abravīt*.

gious and philosophical precepts the greater number of rules propounded fall under the third head of *Āćāra*, 'established practices,' which are described (II. 17, 18) as *Sad-āćāra*, 'approved practices,' sanctioned by the Veda and Smṛiti, if they are those which prevailed between the two sacred rivers, Sarasvatī and Dṛishadvatī, in the region called Brahmāvarta. The word Āćāra is, in truth, a very wide term, including under it all the observances of caste, regarded as constituting the highest law and highest religion—such observances, for instance, as the division of a Brāhman's life into four periods, the conduct of a student in the house of his preceptor, investiture with the sacred cord, the five diurnal devotional acts, the domestic ceremonies of marriage, funeral rites, the various modes of gaining subsistence (*vṛitti*), the rules of diet, the laws concerning women, and, in short, all the observances of private morality and social economy.[1]

The fourth head, *Vyavahāra*, 'practices of law and kingly government,' embraces the procedure of legal tribunals and all the rules of judicature and civil and criminal law.

The fifth head of *Prāyaś-ćitta*, 'penitential exercises,' comprehends all the rules of penance and expiation.

The sixth head, *Karma-phala*, 'recompenses or consequences of acts,' is concerned not so much with rules of conduct as with the doctrine of transmigration; the unavoidable effect of acts of all kinds being to entail repeated births through numberless existences until the attainment of final beatitude.

All these rules apply especially to the highest class, viz., Brāhmans, whose ascendency in the social scale is in fact the first Āćāra, which must be accepted as *paramo dharmaḥ*, 'the highest law and highest religion.'

[1] In Book V. 4 there is a curious passage which attributes Death's power over Brāhmans to four causes, viz., 1. omitting to repeat the Veda, 2. neglect of Āćāra, 3. idleness, 4. sins of diet.

It is only natural that, since the precepts included under these six heads were framed by Brāhmans, they should have been framed with especial reference to the life of Brāhmans, the regulations for which engross six Books, and are besides introduced everywhere throughout the other six. But as the Brāhman could not be supported in his priority of rank without the strong arm of the Kshatriya or military class, a large portion of the work is devoted to the definition of the Kshatriya's duties and an exaggerated delineation of the kingly character and office, while the Vaiśyas and Śūdras, though essential to Manu's Ćāturvarṇya or fourfold social system,[1] and the mixed classes are little noticed. (See p. 226, &c.)

[1] 'Caste' is quite a modern word, and is supposed to be a corruption of the Portuguese *casta*, 'a race.' Manu's word for the four classes is *varṇa*, 'colour,' which suggests some original distinction of colour as marking the dominant races. The later term for caste is *jāti*, 'birth,' corrupted into *jāt*. Of Manu's four castes the Brāhmans alone remain, though the Rājputs claim to be descendants of the ancient Kshatriyas. The mixed castes of the present day are almost innumerable, each separate trade forming a separate one. In Bengal there are the Rajaks, 'washermen,' the Tāntīs, 'weavers,' the Kaṇsāris, 'braziers,' the Jāliyās, 'fishermen,' the Surīs, 'spirit sellers;' besides low and servile castes, such as the Bāgdis, Bediyās, Ḍoms, Hāḍis. Moreover, we find castes within castes, so that even the Brāhmans are broken up and divided into numerous races, which again are subdivided into numerous tribes, families, or sub-castes. There are the Kānyakubja Brāhmans, the Sārasvata, the Gauḍa or Gauṛ (Gor), the Maithila, the Utkala, the Drāviḍa, the Karṇāṭa, the Mahārāshṭra, the Gurjara, &c., all of which races are subdivided into a greater or less number of tribes and families, forming, as it were, sub-castes, which do not intermarry. It is said that in Bengal religion was once at so low an ebb that a king, named Ādiśūra (*Ādīśvara*), sent to the Rājā of Kanyākubja or Kanouj for some high-caste Brāhmans to revive it. These were accordingly sent, and, having settled in Bengal, became divided into one hundred and fifty-six tribes, of which one hundred were called Vārendra and fifty-six Rāḍha or Rāṛh, as belonging to the district of Rāḍhā in the West of Bengal. Of the former eight, and of the latter six, are regarded

Hence, after an account of the creation of the world in the first Book, the four stages of a Brāhman's life are the first and only subjects treated of in regular order in the second, third, fourth, fifth, and sixth Books; the sixth being devoted to the duties of the last two stages of anchorite (*vāna-prastha*) and religious mendicant (*bhikshu*). The fifth Book contains, moreover, rules and regulations about food, the killing of animals, purification after defilement, the duties of wives and the position of women generally. The seventh and eighth Books propound the rules of government and judicature, principally, of course, for the guidance of the second great class or Kshatriyas, from which the king was chosen. The ninth Book contains further precepts on the subject of women, husband and wife, their offspring, and the law of inheritance and

---

as Kulīna or 'noble.' Kullūka, the commentator on Manu, was a Vārendra Brāhman. The six Kulīna Rāṛh tribes are called Banerjea, (Bandyopādhyāya), Mukhurjea (Mukhopādhyāya), Ćaturjea (Ćaṭṭopādhyāya), Gānguli, Goshāla, Kanjalāla. The caste which in Bengal now comes next in rank to the Brāhman is the Vaidya or Baidya, 'medical' (= Ambashṭha, Manu X. 8); and the Kanouj Brāhmans, when they settled in Bengal, brought with them a number of Kāyasthas or 'writers,' from whom sprang the present numerous Kāyastha or 'writer-caste,' subdivided into various tribes, such as Gos (Ghosha), Bose (Vasu), Mitra, De, Datta, Pālita, Dāsa, Sena, &c. After them come the Nava Śāk or 'nine divisions,' viz., Gopa, Mālī Tailī, Tantrī, Modaka, Varajī ('betel-grower'), Kulāla, Karmakāra, Nāpita. See Professor Cowell's Colebrooke's Essays, II. 169. The power of caste and the effect of contact with Europeans in weakening it, are illustrated by the following extract from Dr. Hunter's valuable work on Orissa: 'Elderly Uriyas have more than once deplored to me the hopeless degeneracy of their grown-up sons, many of whom have actually no objection to wearing English shoes. In 1870 a Uriya Brāhman held the post of sub-inspector of police in Purī itself, within the shadow of Jagan-nāth, although a leather belt formed part of his uniform. Five years ago a Brāhman who accidentally touched leather would have had to choose between public expiation or degradation and expulsion from caste.' Vol. ii. p. 147.

division of property. At the end (221, &c.) there are additional rules of government for kings and a few precepts which have direct reference to the two remaining principal castes—the Vaiśyas and Śūdras—the former comprising agriculturists and merchants; the latter, slaves and servants. The tenth Book treats of the mixed classes, arising out of intermarriage between the four original principal castes. It also describes the employments to which the several classes are restricted, and states the occupations permitted to Brāhmans, Kshatriyas, Vaiśyas, and Śūdras in times of great exigency and distress. There are some verses at the end (122–129) which are interesting as treating directly of the duties and position of Śūdras. The eleventh Book gives rules for expiation and penance (*prāyaś-ćitta*), both for sins committed in this life—especially sins against caste—and for the effects of offences perpetrated in previous bodies, as shown in congenital diseases, &c. (XI. 48, 49). The twelfth continues the subject of the recompenses or consequences of acts (*karma-phala*), good or bad, as leading to reward in heaven or punishment in various hells (XII. 75, 76), and to triple degrees of transmigration (see p. 275). It closes with directions as to the best means of obtaining final beatitude and absorption into the universal Essence.

From this outline of the contents of the so-called Code of Manu, we may perceive that the most diversified topics are introduced, some of which are quite out of the province of a mere code of laws or even of a collection of social and moral precepts. In the next chapter I propose examining the contents more in detail.

CHAPTER X.

The Dharma-śāstras or Law-books—Manu continued.

THE Code of the Mānavas, which we have assigned in its present form to about the fifth century B.C. (see p. 207), and which for convenience we may call 'Manu's Law-book,' is a metrical version of the traditions (*smṛiti*) of the Mānavas, probably before embodied in their Gṛihya and Sāmayāćārika Sūtras (p. 205), the metre being Anushṭubh or that of the common Śloka[1] (p. 155). My aim in the present chapter will be to analyze and arrange in a connected manner the contents of the Code,[2] offering prose translations of selected passages and pointing out in a general way the characteristic features of (1) its sacred knowledge and religion, (2) its philosophy, (3) its *Āćāra* or 'social rules and caste organization,' (4) its *Vyavahāra* or 'criminal and civil laws and rules of government,' (5) its system of *Prāyaś-ćitta* or 'penance,' (6) its system of *Karma-phala* or 'future recompenses of acts done in this life.' In the next chapter I propose to give specimens of

---

[1] The use of the common Epic S'loka throughout the *whole* work is one reason for regarding it as Post-vedic, but we must not forget that the Anushṭubh metre is found even in the Veda (see X. 85; X. 90, &c.)

[2] I have used the Calcutta edition, which has the excellent commentary of Kullūka-bhaṭṭa. I have always consulted Sir W. Jones' translation, and I owe much to Dr. Johaentgen's tract, *Über das Gesetzbuch des Manu.* When Kullūka lived is not known, but he describes himself in his modest preface (written in the S'ārdūla-vikrīḍita metre) as a Brāhman, the son of Bhaṭṭa-divākara, of the Vārendra tribe of Gauḍa (Gauṛ) or Bengal, and as having fixed his abode at Benares. I did not read Mr. Talboys Wheeler's analysis till my own was completed.

the most striking passages, under the last four heads, in a metrical English version.

I. First, then, as to its religious teaching. We may notice that this generally agrees with the later Vedic period, especially that represented by the Purusha-sūkta and some of the Brāhmaṇas.

'Divinely revealed knowledge' in general is called *Veda* (IV. 125, &c.); sometimes *Trayī vidyā* (IV. 125); sometimes *Brahman* (nom. neut. *brahma*, I. 23; II. 81; VI. 83, in which last passage this title is also applied to the Vedānta or Upanishads); sometimes *Śruti* (as distinguished from Smṛiti, II. 10); sometimes *Ćhandāṉsi* (when the metrical Mantras are especially intended, IV. 95–97; III. 188); once *Ārsha* (neut., XII. 106), and even *Vāć*, 'word,' described as a Brāhman's weapon (XI. 33).

The three Vedas are mentioned by name in I. 23, IV. 123, 124; XI. 264, and their Saṃhitā in XI. 77, 200, 258, 262. In I. 23 we read that Brahmā milked out the triple Veda (*trayam brahma*), Ṛik, Yajus, and Sāman from Fire, Air, and the Sun, for the complete performance of sacrifice; and in II. 77 he is said to have milked out the sacred text called Sāvitrī (= Gāyatrī, p. 17) from the three Vedas.[1] The Brāhmaṇa portion of the Veda does not seem to be directly mentioned, except under the name of Brahma, as distinguished from the Mantra portion, called Ćhandas (IV. 100). The eternity and infallible authority of the Veda and the duty and expiatory efficacy

[1] See p. 5. In XI. 265 the three Vedas are said to be included in the triliteral Om. In IV. 125, Om, the Vyāhṛitis (viz., Bhūḥ, Bhuvaḥ, Svar), and the Sāvitrī text are described as extracted from the three Vedas. In III. 185, a Brāhman who understands the application of some portion of the Yajur-veda is called *Tri-ṇāćiketa*, and one skilled in some part of the Ṛig-veda a *Tri-suparṇa*, though it is clear from Kullūka's remarks that the exact meaning of these words was not known in his time.

of a complete knowledge of all three Vedas (XI. 262) are insisted on in the strongest language. In illustration, I here give a version of a passage in Book XII. 94, &c. :—

The Veda is of patriarchs and men,
And e'en of gods, a very eye eternal,
Giving unerring light ; it is beyond
All finite faculties, nor can be proved
By force of human argument—this is
A positive conclusion. Codes of laws
Depending on the memory of men—
Not grounded on the Veda—heresies
And false opinions, all are held to be
Barren and worthless and involved in darkness.
Whatever doctrine rests not on the Veda
Must pass away as recent, false, and fruitless.
The triple world and quadruple distinction
Of classes and of Āśramas,[1] with all
That has been, is, and ever will be, all
Are through the Veda settled and established.
By this eternal Veda are sustained
All creatures ; hence we hold it as supreme—
Chief instrument of happiness to man.
Command of armies, regal dignity,
Conduct of justice and the world's dominion
He merits who completely knows the Veda.
As with augmented energy the fire
Consumes e'en humid trees, so he who knows
This book divine burns out the taint of sin
Inherent in his soul through former works.
For he who apprehends the Veda's truth,
Whatever be his Order, is prepared
For blending with the great primeval Spirit,
E'en while abiding in this lower world.

The inferior relationship of the Sāma-veda to the two others is remarkable. The Ṛig-veda is said to be most concerned with the gods, the Yajur-veda with the religious

[1] That is, the four orders or stages of life (of student, householder, anchorite, and mendicant) into which a Brāhman's life is divided.

rites of men, and the Sāma-veda with those of the Pitṛis (IV. 124). Hence the sound of the latter is described as impure (*a-śući*, see p. 6).

In unison with this, an order of precedence is prescribed in III. 145. The preference at a Śrāddha is directed to be given to a priest called Bahv-ṛića (elsewhere Hotṛi), who has made the Ṛig-veda his special study; then to one who has studied all the branches (*Śākhānta-ga*) and especially the Yajur-veda, and who is called Adhvaryu; and lastly to a Sāma-veda priest, who is styled Ćhando-ga (= Udgātṛi).

It is clear that when the Code was compiled the Atharva-veda had not yet been generally accepted as a fourth Veda, though it must have existed, as there is express allusion (XI. 33) to the revelation[1] made to *Atharvan* and *Angiras*.

I annex three other remarkable examples of the estimation in which the Veda was held :—

A Brāhman by retaining the Ṛig-veda in his memory incurs no guilt, though he should destroy the three worlds (XI. 261).

This Veda is the refuge (*śaraṇa*) of those who do not understand it (*ajñānām*) as well as those who do (*vijānatām*), of those who seek heaven and of those who seek immortality (*ānantyam*, VI. 84).

When there is (apparent) contradiction of two precepts in the Veda (*śruti-dvaidham*) both are declared to be law; both have been justly promulgated (*samyag-uktau*) by ancient sages as valid law. Thus, there is a Vedic precept (enjoining the sacrifice to be performed) when the sun has risen, and before it has risen, and when neither sun nor stars are visible (*samayādhyushite*). Wherefore the oblation to fire (*yajñaḥ* = *agni-hotra-homaḥ*) may be made at all times (II. 14, 15).

The doctrine of the Upanishads is directly mentioned in VI. 29 and alluded to elsewhere, thus :—

He should study the Upanishad portion of the Veda (*aupanishadīḥ śrutīḥ*) for the sake of attaining union with the universal Spirit.

Let the whole Veda be studied (or repeated) by a twice-born man

[1] Described by Kullūka as consisting of charms and incantations.

along with the Upanishads. [*Vedaḥ kṛitsno 'ahigantavyaḥ sa-rahasyo dvijanmanā*, II. 165; cf. also II. 140, XI. 262.]

He should continually repeat (*japet*) that part of the Veda (*brahma*) which is on the subject of sacrifice (*adhiyajñam*), and that relating to the deities (*adhidaivikam*), and that relating to soul (*ādhyātmikam*), and that declared in the Upanishads (*Vedāntābhihitam*, VI. 83).

The Kalpa Sūtras are probably referred to in II. 140.

A knower of Nirukta (see p. 156) is reckoned among the Brāhmans who compose a Parishad in XII. 111, but no reference is made to Yāska, nor is it likely that his work then existed (see p. 156).

In I. 11. 50 the name Brahman is applied to the supreme Being (=*Brahmā*, Kullūka); in XII. 50 the Creator of the universe is called Brahmā (see p. 9); in XI. 243, XII. 121, Prajāpati. In I. 6 the supreme Spirit is termed Svayambhū, 'the Self-existent;' in I. 10, Nārāyaṇa. In XII. 121 the names Vishṇu and Hara occur; but generally the gods named belong more to the Vedic than to the Epic and Purānic period. For instance, in Book IX. 303 we have the following list of deities:—

Of Indra, Sūrya, Vāyu (or Māruta), Yama, Varuṇa, Ćandra, Agni, and Pṛithivī, let the king emulate the power and conduct.

There is no allusion to the Post-vedic Tri-mūrti or popular worship of Brahmā, Vishṇu, and Śiva, nor to the still more recent worship of the Śakti—that is to say, 'the energy' represented by the wives of the deities, especially by Durgā, wife of Śiva. Nor, again, is there any recognition of that principle of *bhakti* or 'faith' in Kṛishṇa, as supreme Lord of the universe, which was a subsequent development of Hindū religious thought (p. 125).

The doctrine of transmigration is, however, fully stated, and, as a consequence of this, the hells described in the Code (IV. 88–90; XII. 75, 77), though places of terrible torture, resolve themselves into merely temporary purgatories, while the heavens (IV. 182, 260; VI. 32; II. 244) become only steps on the road to union with Brahma.

The three worlds (*trailokya, loka-traya*) alluded to in XI. 236, 261, are probably the heavens, atmosphere, and earth.

What must strike every one as singular in regard to the religion of the Code is the total absence of allusion to public and congregational services or teaching in temples. Public sacrifices are certainly mentioned, but the chief rites of religion were evidently of a domestic kind, and the priests, whatever their ancient functions may have been, were at the time of the composition of the Code more like domestic chaplains (see p. 230). Little, too, is said about idols[1]—certainly nothing to countenance the adoration of them or to encourage Brāhmans to undertake the care of idol-temples, nor are there directions as to offering rice, flowers, and perfumes at idol-shrines, which oblations (*naivedya*) are commonly presented before images in temples at the present day.

II. In the second place, as to the philosophy of Manu's Law-book. It is plain, from a passage already quoted, that a love for rationalistic speculations (*hetu-śāstra*) and a spirit of free scepticism were beginning to show themselves in India at the time the Code

---

[1] It is very doubtful whether idolatry was at all commonly practised at the time of the compilation of the Code. We have already seen that there is no satisfactory proof of the existence of idols in the Vedic period. See p. 12 of this volume. In Manu III. 152 a Devalaka, 'attendant on an idol' (= *pratimā-paričāraka*), is directed to be shunned. Certainly in II. 176 the Brāhman student is enjoined to perform *devatābhyarčanam*, 'worship of the deities,' and this is interpreted by Kullūka to mean *pratimādishu hari-harādi-deva-pūjanam*, 'doing homage to Vishṇu and S'iva before images,' &c., but whether Manu really intended to denote *pratimā* by *devatā* is questionable. In IX. 285, however, the accidental breaker of images (*pratimānām bhedakaḥ*) is directed to repair them and pay a fine.

was compiled; and it is possible that Buddha's adherents, though not mentioned by name, were pointed at with reprobation under the designation *Nāstikāḥ*, 'atheists' (= *Ćārvāka*, Kullūka II. 11), and *Pāshaṇḍinaḥ*, 'heretics' (= *Śākya-bhikshu-kshapaṇakādi*, Kullūka IV. 30; I. 118). The Code itself may have been an attempt to stem the current of opinion which was setting in the direction of Buddhism and rationalistic Brāhmanism. The compiler, however, thought it necessary to adopt some of the current philosophical theories, and accordingly we find them interspersed throughout the work, though more directly stated at the beginning and end. They are of that vague and misty kind which probably prevailed at the period preceding the crystallization of the various systems into distinct schools. The words Sāṅkhya, Yoga, Nyāya, Vaiśeshika, and Mīmāṉsā do not occur as designations of philosophical systems. We notice indeed a strong leaning towards the Sāṅkhyan line of thought, though we find only a confused statement of some leading ideas of that system, without any mention of its twenty-five Tattvas. The growth of pantheistic ideas, as foreshadowed in the Purusha-sūkta of the Ṛig-veda (see p. 21), is also traceable. All existing things are said to emanate from Brahma, the one self-existent Spirit, to whom all things must also return. Ātma-vidyā, equivalent to Brahma-vidyā and to the Vedānta doctrine, is directed to be studied in VII. 43, and Vedāntic ideas pervade the whole twelfth Book, which, however, may possibly be due to later additions. Still more remarkable is the attention directed to be given to the study of Ānvīkshikī, 'logic' (VII. 43 = *tarka-vidyā*); and although the Nyāya and Mīmāṉsā had evidently not become schools, we find from XII. 111 that a Parishad or 'assembly of twelve Brāhmans,' competent to decide on disputed points of law, includes a Haituka

(= *nyāya-jña*) and a Tarkin (= *mīmāṉsaka*, Kullūka). Moreover, in XII. 106, it is declared that he only understands the Veda who investigates it by the rules of Tarka (= *mīmāṉsādi-nyāya*), agreeably to Vedic doctrine—all of which precepts are, of course, inconsistent with the reprobation of Haitukas in II. 11, IV. 30; as well as with a precept in II. 10, where Śruti and Smṛiti are affirmed to be *a-mīmāṉsye*, 'not to be reasoned about.'

The cosmogony adopted presents us with a compound of both the Sān·khya and Vedānta theories of creation before they had diverged into distinct systems. There is, however, in Book I. a synthetical scheme advanced which, though a confusion of two separate statements, one made by Manu himself (I. 14, &c.), the other by Bhṛigu (I. 74, &c.), certainly more accords with the Sān·khyan doctrine than with any other (see p. 90). I here abridge the account, commencing I. 5 :—

This universe first existed only in darkness (*tamo-bhūtam*), imperceptible, undefinable, as if immersed in sleep (*prasuptam*). Then the Self-existent (*Svayam-bhū*, described by the same epithet as the Sān·khyan *Prakṛiti*, viz., *A-vyakta*, 'undiscerned' or 'undeveloped'), having willed to produce various beings from his own substance, first with a thought created the waters, and placed on them a productive seed or egg (*vīja* or *aṇḍa*). Then he himself was born in that egg in the form of Brahmā. Next he caused the egg to divide itself, and out of its two divisions framed the heaven above and the earth beneath. Afterwards, having divided his own substance, he became half male, half female (I. 32), and from that female produced Virāj (see note 1, p. 22), from whom was created Manu, the secondary progenitor of all beings. Then he (Brahmā, according to Kullūka on I. 14) from the supreme Soul (*Ātman*) drew forth *Manas* (= *Mahat* or *Buddhi*, 'Intellect,' as explained by Kullūka on I. 74, 75,[1] in which passage *Manas* is the principle of thought and stands for both Buddhi and Ahan·kāra).

---

[1] But according to I. 14 (Kullūka) *Manas* must be distinguished from *Buddhi*, and regarded as a product of Ahan·kāra, as in the Sān·khya system.

Next to that came Ahan-kāra, and, after that, the Tan-mātras or 'subtile principles of the elements.' From these seven active principles (called 'the seven Purushas,' I. 19)—viz., Mahat or Buddhi (called *Manas* in I. 14, 74, 75), Ahan-kāra, and the five subtile elements—were evolved the five gross or material elements (*mahā-bhūta*), the organs of sense, and the whole world of sense. (Compare the Sān-khyan doctrine at pp. 83, 84.)

It is curious to compare Strabo XV. 59 (see p. 276).

All this confusion and obscurity in the account of the creation is symptomatic of diversity of authorship. Of the two narratives, that of Bhṛigu is the simplest. But both (I. 14 and I. 74) make 'the principle of thought' the first product—that which is and is not (*sad-asad-ātmakam*)—to which belongs a real existence, and yet not eternity, because it is a product (see Sān-khya-pravaćana V. 56). I now abridge what follows according to Bhṛigu's statement:—

The first Manu Svāyambhuva produced six other Manus, and these seven Manus (see note, p. 206), each in his own period, were the creators of all things (I. 61–63).

In order to show the duration of a Manv-antara or Manu-period, the divisions of time from a moment to a day of Brahmā (12,000,000 years) are specified (I. 64–73):—

A Manu-period consists of seventy-one times the 12,000 years, which constitute an age of the gods (I. 79). Each Mahā-yuga or great age of the world is subdivided into four Yugas or ages, viz., 1. Kṛita, 2. Tretā, 3. Dvāpara, and 4. Kali, each decreasing in excellence; and the life of man lasts for 400 years in the first, 300 years in the second, 200 years in the third, and 100 years in the present or Kali age.[1]

In I. 87–101 the account of the creation is concluded by a description of the origin of the four castes from the mouth, arm, thigh, and foot of Brahmā, and the pre-eminence assigned to Brāhmans (see extracts, pp. 233, 234).

---

1 We find it constantly implied in Hindū writings that the natural term of human life in the present age is 100 years.

In the twelfth Book the leaning towards a Sān·khyan line of thought is again conspicuous. In 24–38 we have a description of the three Guṇas of the Sān·khya, viz., Sattva, Rajas, and Tamas, all three of which are said to pervade, and one or other of which predominate in every mortal frame (see note 2, p. 85). In XII. 24 it is asserted that these three form the constituent substances of *ātman* (self or soul), and that the first developed principle—Mahat or Buddhi—is also pervaded by them. Again, the triple degrees of transmigration, highest, middle, and lowest, through gods, men, and beasts, are supposed to result from acts done under the dominance of these three Guṇas (see note 1, p. 56). We have also the three Pramāṇas of the Sān·khya philosophy clearly laid down in XII. 105:—

Three means of attaining true knowledge or three standards of truth, viz., perception by the senses (*pratyaksha*), inference (*anumāna*), and the Veda (*Śabda*) or various books founded on it—these three must be known thoroughly by one wishing for a clear idea of duty (see pp. 61, 82 of this volume).

Although, however, the germ of the Sān·khya is clearly traceable, there is an evident commingling of pantheistic ideas, tending towards the Vedānta, in the frequent declaration that all existing things emanate from, and will ultimately be absorbed into Brahma, 'the universal Spirit.' The distinction between the Jīvātman and Paramātman (see p. 51) is recognised in VIII. 91, which verse Kullūka explains by a reference to the Vedic allegory of the two birds (quoted p. 40 of this volume). Nevertheless, we miss in Manu what we find in the later philosophical schools, a clear definition of the subtile body, as composed of the subtile elements, and a plain statement of its relationship to the individual soul and of its accompanying the soul through all its transmigrations. The survival of this soul over the dissolution of the gross body is indeed plainly implied; but Manu's doctrine is that if a man has been wicked the soul clothed in a kind of body, composed of coarse and impure elements, undergoes along with it torment in hell for a time (XII. 21); whereas, if a man has been virtuous, the soul invested in a kind of ethereal and shining body (*kha-śarīrin*), composed of pure elementary particles of air, wind, and fire, enjoys bliss in heaven with it for a certain period (IV. 243, III. 93, II. 82, XII. 20); after which both the wicked and the virtuous are born again.

Nor do we find any precise definition of Brahman (neut.) as pure absolute Spirit,—the only really existing entity,—according to the Vedānta doctrine. Brahma seems rather to be regarded as a kind of shining ethereal essence, out of which the universe was evolved and into which it becomes absorbed (cf. II. 28; IV. 232; VI. 79, 81, 85; XII. 123–125).

III. Thirdly, as to the Āćāra, 'rules and precepts of conduct,' and social legislation of the Mānavas.

The organization of classes in I. 87–91 is so simple that this simplicity, if it be not merely theoretical, bears witness to the antiquity of a considerable portion of the Code. According to Book X. 3, 4, there are only four pure classes (*varṇāḥ*, p. 210), as follows:—

The Brāhman (or priestly class), the Kshatriya (or military class), and the Vaiśya (or agricultural class) constitute the three twice-born (*dvi-jāti* or *dvi-ja*) classes (as obtaining a second spiritual birth through investiture with the sacred thread, see p. 239); the Śūdra (or servile class) is once-born (*eka-jāti*), and constitutes the fourth class; there is no fifth class.

From priority of birth, from superiority of origin (in being sprung from the mouth of the Creator), from possession of the Veda (*niyamasya* [= *vedasya*] *dhāraṇāt*, i.e., from the right of studying, teaching, and expounding it), and from a distinction in the reception of the sacrificial thread (as the most important of the twelve Sanskāras or 'purificatory rites,' specified in II. 27, &c.), the Brāhman is the lord (*prabhu*) of all the classes (X. 3. See p. 233).

The only allusion in the Veda to this fourfold division is in the Purusha-sūkta (Ṛig-veda X. 90. 12), which, as we have seen (p. 21), is one of its most recent hymns.

A similar division into classes or professions is found to have prevailed in almost all countries.[1]

In the same tenth Book of Manu, however, we have a more developed social system depicted, and a number of mixed castes (*varṇa-san·karaḥ, san·kara-jātīyāḥ*, X. 12) are described as resulting from the intermarriage of the pure classes:[2]—

---

[1] Megasthenes (according to Strabo's India, 39), the Greek ambassador of Seleukos Nikator (Alexander's successor between the Euphrates and Indus, B.C. 312) at the court of Sandrokottos (Ćandragupta) in Pāṭaliputra (Παλίβοθρα), divided the Hindū people into seven classes, viz., philosophers, husbandmen, shepherds, tradesmen or artificers, soldiers, spies or overseers (ἔφοροι), and councillors of state (see note 2, p. 237); perhaps because Herodotus divided the inhabitants of Egypt into seven, viz., priests, soldiers, cowherds, swineherds, tradesmen, interpreters, and pilots; but Diodorus and Plato made only five divisions, and Strabo only three. From Plato's Timaeus (6) it appears that a similar division of professions existed among the Athenians. *Πρῶτον μὲν τὸ τῶν ἱερέων γένος, ἀπὸ τῶν ἄλλων χωρὶς ἀφωρισμένον, μετὰ δὲ τοῦτο τὸ τῶν δημιουργῶν, ὅτι καθ' αὑτὸ ἕκαστον ἄλλῳ δὲ οὐκ ἐπιμιγνύμενον δημιουργεῖ, τότε τῶν νομέων καὶ τὸ τῶν θηρευτῶν, τότε τῶν γεωργῶν· καὶ δὴ καὶ τὸ μάχιμον γένος ᾔσθησαί που τῇδε ἀπὸ πάντων τῶν γενῶν κεχωρισμένον, οἷς οὐδὲν ἄλλο πλὴν τὰ περὶ τὸν πόλεμον ὑπὸ τοῦ νόμου προσετάχθη μέλειν.* Again, from a passage in Herodotus (I. 101), it is inferred that a similar distinction existed among the Medes. In Malcolm's History of Persia (I. 205) the Persian monarch Jamshīd is said to have divided the Persians into four classes. Mr. Mill also points out an instructive passage in Plato's Republic (II. 11), in which, describing the simplest form of a political association, he makes it to consist of four or five classes of men: *Εἴη δ' ἂν ἥ γε ἀναγκαιοτάτη πόλις ἐκ τεττάρων ἢ πέντε ἀνδρῶν.* Finally, we read in Millar's Historical View of the English Government (I. 11) that the Anglo-Saxons were originally divided into four great classes—artificers and tradesmen, husbandmen, soldiers, and clergy.

[2] Mr. W. F. Sinclair gives some interesting information (in the February and March numbers of the 'Indian Antiquary') in regard to

By unlawful intermarriage of the classes (*vyabhićāreṇa varṇānām*), by their marrying women who ought not to be married, and by neglect of their own duties, mixed classes are produced (X. 24).

These have a great variety of names, such as Mūrdhāvasikta, Māhishya, Karaṇa or Kāya-stha, Ambashṭha or Vaidya, Āyogava, Dhigvaṇa, Pukkasa, Ćaṇḍāla (see p. 229), and are restricted to particular occupations. Still

---

the various subdivisions or sub-castes of Brāhmans, and adds a list of forty mixed castes now found in the Dekhan. With regard to the Brāhmans, he places at the head the *Chitpāvan* ('race of the corpse' or 'race of the burning-ground') or *Konkanasth* (= *Kon·kaṇa-stha*) Brāhmans, to whom the notorious Nāna Sāhib of Bithūr belonged. Then come the *Deśasth* (= *Deśa-stha*) or *Ṛigvedī* Brāhmans, who claim for themselves descent from the Ṛishis, and therefore the highest rank; then the *Yajur-vedī*, who are chiefly engaged in trade; and then the *Devrukh* (?), who are mostly agricultural. There are also in the Dekhan *Telangī* (*i.e.*, *Telingī*, from Sanskṛit *tri-lin·ga*) Brāhmans, from the Karṇāṭak, chiefly engaged in trade; Kanouj Brāhmans (from Hindūstān), who are often Sipāhīs in native regiments or *employés* upon the railway, and some other tribes. With regard to the forty mixed castes enumerated by Mr. Sinclair, I here subjoin some of them as given by him, with a few notes of my own—*Prabhūs* (Sanskṛit *prabhu*), who are the highest, and divided into *Kāyasth* and *Pathare*; *Sonārs* (= *Suvarṇa-kāra*) or goldsmiths, a subdivision of whom are the *Ratha-kāra* Sonārs, who claim to be of Brāhman race (cf. note 2, p. 149); *Vāṇīs* (Banias, Banians = Baniyās, Sanskṛit *baṇik*), who are grocers and grain-dealers, and are distinguished by great reverence for animal life; *Bhāṭiyās* or cloth and cotton merchants; *Khattrīs*, who claim Rājput (= *Kshatriya*) descent, but are dealers in cloth, gold and silver lace, &c.; *Vaiśyas*, who claim to be a remnant of the original Vaiśyas, and are traders; *Mārvāḍī*, merchants, from *Mārvāḍ* or *Marwār*; *Simpīs* or tailors; *Sūtars* (= *Sūtra-dhāra*) or carpenters; *Sikalgars* (*Saiqal-gar*), turners and weapon-sharpeners; *Lohārs* (= *Loha-kāra*) or smiths; *Telīs* (= *Tailī*, from *Tailin*) or oilmen; *Koshṭīs* and *Sālīs* or weavers; *Kumbhārs* (= *Kumbha-kāra*) or potters; *Kolīs*, who are Bhistīs or water-bearers; *Parīts* or washermen; *Loṇārīs* (= *Lavaṇa-kārin*) or preparers of salt and lime and charcoal; *Rangārīs* (= *Ran·ga-kārin*) or dyers; *Chambhārs* (= *Ćarma-kārin*) or leather-cutters and shoemakers, &c.

the superiority of the Brāhmans in the Hindū lawyer's scheme is the hinge on which the whole social system turns. In fact, the state of society depicted is that of pure and unmitigated Brāhmanism,—a state of things which, if it really admitted of the amount of Brāhmanical arrogance described as existing, would more than account for the Buddhist reaction. The Brāhmans are made to constitute the great central body around which all other classes and orders of beings revolve like satellites. Not only are they invested with the highest dignity and importance, but they are bound together, and their position secured by the most stringent rules; while the other three classes of soldiers, agriculturists, and servants are made powerless for combined resistance by equally stringent regulations, one class being separated from the other by insurmountable lines of demarcation.

We must, however, guard against supposing that a Brāhman claimed to take the lead merely in the character of a priest. To understand more clearly the nature of Brāhmanical ascendency we must ask ourselves the question, What physical and moral forces led to the first movements which ended in the crystallization of social distinctions into the caste-system?

It seems probable, then, that the formation of hard lines of separation between the classes was more the result of gradual and natural adjustment than of preconcerted plan. There can be little doubt that when the Āryan Hindūs came into India as immigrants and conquerors, they were without any systematic arrangement of classes. Their first seat was in the Pañjāb, around the five chief affluents of the Indus and in the neighbourhood of Delhi. This was a productive plain watered by rivers.[1] Hence it

[1] By degrees they spread themselves over the whole region called by Manu (II. 21, 22) Āryāvarta, 'the abode of Āryas,' *i.e.*, the great central

happened that, although in their primeval abode, somewhere in Central Asia, they were probably half nomad, half agricultural, they became, when fairly settled in Hindūstān, a nation of agriculturists.[1] The soil, too, being fertile, yielded more than enough to supply the necessities of the cultivators. Hence the surplus produce enabled a large non-agricultural population to spring up. Some of these applied themselves to trade and the improvement of mechanical arts; others were enabled to devote themselves to one of three occupations: 1. mental and religious culture; 2. military exercises; 3. domestic service.[2] It was, indeed, absolutely necessary that the cultivators who were called Vaiśyas, because they 'settled down' on the soil and gradually acquired an hereditary right to its occupation,[3] should have a class of military men above

---

plains (Madhya-deśa), extending from the western to the eastern sea, and bounded on the north and south by the Himālaya and Vindhya mountains. Only in this region were the three first classes allowed to dwell, but Śūdras might sojourn wherever they liked. (See Manu II. 21–24.)

1 The very name Ārya is, as every one now knows, connected with the root 4 *ṛi = ar*, whence *aratrum*, 'a plough' (cf. Sanskṛit *aritra*). It is curious to note how Brāhmans, after their segregation as the dominant class, sought to depreciate agriculture. Manu (X. 84) says, 'Some think that agriculture (*kṛishi*) is an excellent thing, but it is a mode of existence blamed by the good, because the iron-mouthed ploughshare wounds the earth and the creatures living in it.' Mr. W. F. Sinclair informs us in the 'Indian Antiquary,' that in the Dekhan the cultivators of the soil are by the modern races of Brāhmans considered pure Śūdras.

2 The same happened in the fertile plains of Egypt and Mesopotamia.

3 In modern times they are called Ryots, from the Arabic رعية *ra''īyat*, 'protected people' (root رعي 'to pasture, guard'). The Hindū term Vaiśya is more expressive of their original condition. It is derived from the root *viś*, 'to enter into,' 'sit down on,' 'settle down on,' 'occupy' (whence *veśa*, 'an abode'), cognate with *vicus*, 'a village,' and *οἶκος*, 'an abode,' and our affix 'wick' at the end of names of towns, denoting originally a settlement or station of cultivators. Hence the root *viś*, when used as a substantive, means 'a man of the people.' The Vaiśyas

them, with leisure either to cultivate arms, and so defend the land thus occupied from the attacks of other invaders, or to undertake the cares of government, and so protect property from the dangers incident to anarchy. These ultimately received the name *Kshatriya.* But in the earliest times, as represented by the Vedic hymns, they were called *Rājanya,* 'the kingly class.' (See the Purusha-sūkta, translated p. 21, and see p. 22, note 2.) Doubtless, when this class first arose they must have constituted the most powerful order of society; and so, indeed, practically they must have always remained, notwithstanding the intellectual superiority of the Brāhmanical class.[1] That the close interdependence of the two higher classes was recognized by the Brāhmans themselves is shown by the following:—

---

were allowed to become merchants if they preferred trading to agriculture; but the only provision for classes of artisans and mechanics, is from the mixed classes. This indicates that Manu's division belongs to an early period, before the industrial and mechanical arts had acquired much importance, though they must have been considerably advanced even in Vedic times (as shown by Dr. Muir, Texts V. 450–472). The Hindū village system of the present day seems to have been developed out of that represented in Manu's Code. Almost everywhere are found bodies of agriculturists who have settled on the soil from time immemorial, and formed themselves into little republics presided over by a half-elective, half-hereditary headman, and a number of village officials (properly twelve, *e.g.*, watchman, accountant, priest, schoolmaster, doctor, barber, astrologer, &c.), the lands around the village forming a sort of jurisdiction, and disputes being settled by gatherings of the villagers under trees, while various low-caste menials who have no interest in the soil are attached to the community.

[1] The name Kshatriya comes from *kshatra,* 'dominion,' which is probably from root 1 *kshi* = κτάομαι, 'to possess, rule.' It is fancifully derived from *kshatāt tra,* 'preserving from injury,' in Raghu-vaṉśa II. 53. Manu X. 119 says, 'While defending the Vaiśyas by his arms (*śastreṇa vaiśyān rakshitvā*) he may raise from them the rightful revenue (*dharmyam āhārayed balim*),' which was really taken from the soil in kind.

A Kshatriya cannot thrive without a Brāhman, nor a Brāhman without a Kshatriya. The Brāhman and the Kshatriya when associated together prosper in this world and the next (IX. 322).

It was also necessary that there should be a class willing to perform personal domestic service. These were called Śūdras; and this class was probably made up to some extent of the remnants of the Turanian tribes, who were conquered by the Āryan Hindūs, and who were mostly driven southwards.[1] But, although servants, they were neither slaves nor serfs. They merely occupied the lowest step in the social organization. It is true that in theory (X. 129) they were debarred from any superfluous accumulation of wealth, yet, in point of fact, they sometimes rose to affluence, and even became kings:[2]—

[1] It may be questioned whether S'ūdra (though found in the Purusha-sūkta, Ṛig-veda X. 90. 12) is a genuine Sanskṛit word. At least no satisfactory etymology is given for it, and this favours the idea of its denoting some pre-Āryan race. The fanciful derivation from *Śuć*, 'to grieve,' and *dru*, 'to run,' is hardly worth noticing. Besides the Turanian races who partially blended with the Āryans there were doubtless other aboriginal tribes who occupied the hills and outlying districts and who were called Mleććhas, as constituting those more barbarous and uncultivated communities who stood aloof and would not amalgamate with the Āryans. *Mleććha-deśa* is defined to be a country where the four classes do not dwell. In Manu X. 44 a number of degraded tribes are mentioned, such as Pauṇḍrakas, Oḍras, Draviḍas, Kāmbojas, Yavanas, S'akas, Pāradas, Ćīnas, Kirātas, &c. As these were probably powerful warlike tribes, they are declared by Manu to be outcaste Kshatriyas. It is clear that the mountaineer Kirātas were a martial race; nor could they have been greatly despised, for Arjuna lived among them and adopted their style of life in order to learn archery from S'iva, regarded as their god. See my account of the Kirātārjunīya and the 'Indian Antiquary' for June, 1874, p. 178. The most degraded outcastes were men called Ćāṇḍālas or Ćaṇḍālas (children of a S'ūdra man and a Brāhmaṇī); they were expelled from towns, where they could not even walk except by day; they wore only dead men's clothes, rusty iron ornaments, &c. (X. 51–56).

[2] Professor Cowell, in a note to Elphinstone's India, p. 18, well

As a Śūdra, without censuring others, performs lawful acts, so, without being censured, he obtains exaltation in this world and the next (X. 128).

Again, the gradual assumption of superiority over the Kshatriyas, Vaiśyas, and Śūdras, by a class of men who called themselves Brāhmans,[1] seems to have been due to the operation of a law of intellectual development, such as has been common among all nations in their progress towards civilization, in all periods of the world's history. Those who were intellectually superior took advantage of that growth of religious cravings which generally accompanies political growth, and formed themselves into a fraternity of religious teachers, who afterwards became priests. Religion, or a sense of dependence upon God and a desire to propitiate Him, has always formed a marked feature of the Hindū character. Hence in India, the fraternity of priests multiplied with unusual rapidity; so that a considerable number of the sacerdotal class were

---

shows that the condition of a Śūdra was very superior to that of the helot, slave, and serf of the Greek, Roman, and feudal system. The Purāṇas record dynasties of Śūdra kings, and even Manu notices these. In II. 238 it is said, 'A believer in Scripture may receive pure knowledge even from a Śūdra.' In modern times cultivators of the soil are in some places regarded as Śūdras. There are occasional passages in the Mahābhārata depreciating caste and even Vedic knowledge in comparison with moral character; cf. the Rāja-dharma of the Śānti-parvan 2955.

[1] According to some scholars the original meaning of *brahman* was 'prayer,' or rather 'devotional spirit pervading and filling the soul' (root *bṛih* or *vṛih*). Hence it came afterwards to mean Veda, 'sacred knowledge,' in which sense it is often used by Manu. Similarly, *brahman* and *brāhmaṇa* meant originally 'a prayer-offerer,' and afterwards 'religious teacher,' the signification 'priest' not having been attached to these words till sacrificial ideas had fully developed themselves in the Hindū mind. It is a mistake to suppose that Brāhmaṇa and priest are convertible terms. Brāhmans are rather 'men of the first class.'

thrown out of employment and forced to engage in secular occupations. In this manner it came to pass that although all priests were properly Brāhmans, all Brāhmans were by no means necessarily priests. Nor was it likely that with the partial secularization of the Brāhmans the complicated Vedic ceremonial could be long maintained. Some public sacrifices, such as the Agnishṭoma, were still performed, but the more intricate rites enjoined by the Brāhmaṇas and occasionally practised in ancient times, lasting for long periods, and requiring for their efficacious performance a staff of sixteen different orders of priests,[1] fell into partial if not entire desuetude. It was found, however, indispensable to the retention of power over the other classes that some sacerdotal offices should be maintained. In proportion, indeed, to the neglect of high ceremonial observances was there an increased strictness in exacting a knowledge of the Veda, and the discharge of domestic rites for which a priest's teaching and superintendence were required.

In II. 84, 85, it is declared that all Vedic rites, oblations to fire, and solemn sacrifices gradually pass away (*ksharanti*), but that the act of repeating the Veda, especially the repetition of the Gāyatrī with the four mystic syllables, is ten times better than the appointed sacrifice (see pp. 245, 246).

Manu is careful to assign distinct functions and titles to the priests qualified for these duties; thus we read :—

Some Brāhmans are intent on knowledge (of the supreme Spirit), others are intent on acts of austerity (*tapo-nishṭhāḥ*), others on acts of austerity and repetition of the Veda combined, and others on sacrificial rites (III. 134).

He who is selected for the office of preparing the sacred fire, for con-

---

[1] See their names all given in my Sanskrit-English Dictionary under Ṛitv-ij, p. 181, col. 1.

ducting the Pāka-yajña (see note, p. 188) and performing the Agnishṭoma [1] and other sacrifices, is called the *Ṛitv-ij* of his employer (II. 143).

He who having invested his pupil with the sacred thread afterwards instructs him in the whole Veda, with the rules of ceremonial (*sakalpam* [2]) and the Upanishads, is called an *Ācārya* (II. 140).

He who, for the sake of a livelihood, gives instruction in one part only of the Veda or in the Vedān-gas (such as grammar, &c.) is called an *Upādhyāya* or sub-teacher (II. 141).

The Brāhman who performs the Sanskāra ceremonies on conception, &c., according to rule, and who feeds the child with rice (*i.e.*, performs the *anna-prāśanam* in the sixth month, see II. 34 and p. 192 of this volume), is called a *Guru* [3] (II. 142).

Manu, however, found it necessary to conciliate the Kshatriya class. The most exalted eulogies were lavished on kings; but Brāhmans were to act as their advisers and to have much of the judicial authority and interpretation of the laws in their own hands, and were always theoretically superior in rank—a circumstance which led in the end to jealousies, feuds, and even internecine warfare between the first two classes. Certain privileges also naturally fell to the Vaiśyas, and both they and the Kshatriyas were equally with the Brāhmans entitled to the appellation *Dvi-ja*, 'twice-born.' Their whole status, however, depended upon various domestic rites, to the

---

[1] The Agnishṭoma is a protracted sacrifice of five days' duration, performed by one who is desirous of obtaining heaven. It is either a part or a modification of the Jyotishṭoma, and in ancient times required sixteen priests.

[2] That is, probably, 'the Kalpa Sūtras.'

[3] The title Guru, however, appears to have been applied in a general way to all spiritual preceptors, cf. p. 238. It is sometimes used alone as a distinctive epithet of Prabhā-kara, a teacher of the Mīmānsā, often named in conjunction with Kumārila, to denote whom the title Bhaṭṭa is generally employed in the same way. According to Yājñavalkya I. 34, a Guru is one who imparts the Veda, while an Ācārya is one who invests with the Yajñopavīta or 'sacred thread.' Similarly in the Panjāb the teachers of the Grantha (Granthīs) are called Gurus.

due conduct of which the superintendence of Brāhmans was indispensable. Yet, in spite of the importance and dignity thus attached to the priestly office, a Brāhman, according to Manu's Code, was by *birth* and *divine right* —not by profession or self-elevation—at the head of all creatures. He was born a Brāhman and did not become one. He not only inherited superiority as his birthright, but was created a leader of mankind—a sort of deity in human shape—by the fiat of the great Creator himself.

He is declared, in Book I. 87, to have proceeded from the mouth of Brahmā, as the Kshatriya did from his arm, the Vaiśya from his thigh, and the Śūdra from his foot. Manu's theory, in short, was that the distinction of caste and the inherent superiority of one class over the three others was as much a law of nature and a matter of divine appointment, as the creation of separate classes of animals, with insurmountable differences of physical constitution, such as elephants, lions, horses, and dogs.

That the Brāhmans assumed a pre-eminence nothing short of divine, is clear from numerous passages. I select the following :—

Since the Brāhman sprang from the most excellent part, since he has the priority arising from primogeniture (*jyaishṭhyāt*), and since he possesses the Veda, he is by right the lord (*prabhu*) of this whole creation (I. 93. See also p. 223 of this volume).

A Brāhman, whether learned or unlearned, is a mighty divinity (*daivatam mahat*), just as fire is a mighty divinity, whether consecrated (*praṇīta*) or unconsecrated (IX. 317).

Even when Brāhmans employ themselves in all sorts of inferior occupations (*an-ishṭeshu*), they must under all circumstances be honoured, for they are to be regarded as supreme divinities (*paramaṃ daivatam*, IX. 319).

From his high birth alone (*sambhavenaiva*) a Brāhman is regarded as a divinity even by the gods (*devānām api*). His teaching must be accepted by the rest of the world as an infallible authority (*pramāṇam*), for the Veda (*brahma*) itself is the cause (of its being so accepted, XI. 84).

Consistently with the divine nature thus ascribed to the Brāhman, he is declared to possess powers of the most tremendous and awe-inspiring character:—

Let not a king, although fallen into the greatest distress (through a deficiency of revenue), provoke Brāhmans to anger (by taking revenue from them), for they, if once enraged, could instantly (by pronouncing curses and mystical texts) destroy him with all his army and retinue.

Who, without bringing destruction on himself, can provoke those men, by whose imprecation (*abhiśāpena*, Kullūka) all-devouring fire was created, and by whom the undrinkable ocean was swallowed,[1] and the wasted moon restored to its full size[2] (*āpyāyitaḥ* = *paścāt pūritaḥ*, IX. 313, 314)?

What king would gain increase of revenue by oppressing those who, if angry, could create other worlds and guardians of worlds (*loka-pālān*), and could create new gods and mortals (IX. 315)?

A Brāhman well skilled in the law, need not make any representation to the king (if he has received an injury), for, by his own power (*svavīryeṇa*), he may punish (*śishyāt*) those who injure him. His own power is stronger than the power of the king, therefore by his own might may a Brāhman chastise (*nigrihṇīyāt*) his foes. He may, with-

---

[1] This seems to refer to the legend of Agastya, who is said to have swallowed the ocean and was afterwards raised to be regent of the star Canopus. Much, however, of the detail of this legend must be later.

[2] This refers to the legend of Ćandra, 'the Moon,' afflicted with consumption for fifteen days by his father-in-law, Daksha, because of his (the Moon's) partiality for Rohiṇī, one of Daksha's daughters, some of whom had become his wives. On the Moon's repentance, his wasted strength and size were restored. Manu IX. 129 states that Daksha gave ten of his daughters to Dharma, thirteen to Kaśyapa, and twenty-seven to Soma, the Moon. The legend of Daksha's daughters is found (like many other of Manu's allusions) in the Taittirīya-saṃhitā, ii. 3, 5: 'Prajāpati had thirty-three daughters—he gave them to king Soma; among them he only went to Rohiṇī. The others jealous returned [to their father]: he went after them, he sought them again; but he [the father] did not give them again to him. He said to him, "Take an oath that you will go to them alike, then I will give them to you again." He took an oath; he gave them back to him. He only out of them went to Rohiṇī. Him, the king [Soma], consumption attacked. This is the origin of the Rāja-yakshma.'

out hesitation, make use of (as magical formularies) the sacred texts (*śrutīḥ*) revealed to Atharvan and An-giras (*Atharvān-girasīḥ*, see p. 6); for the uttering of texts (*vāk = abhićāra-mantroććāraṇam*) is the weapon (*śastram*) of a Brāhman; with that he may destroy his foes (XI. 31–33).

The crime of striking and killing a Brāhman involves, of course, terrible consequences, thus :—

He who merely assails a Brāhman with intent to kill him will continue in hell (*narakam*) for a hundred years, and he who actually strikes him, a thousand years (XI. 206. Compare also IV. 165, where it is said that the hell to which he will be consigned, and where he will be made to wander about incessantly, is called *Tāmisra*, 'profound darkness').

As many particles of dust (*pāṇśūn*) as the blood of a Brāhman absorbs from the soil, so many thousands of years must the shedder of that blood abide in hell (XI. 207).

The above may be thought an exaggeration of the powers and status claimed by the highest order of Hindū society, and doubtless the compiler of the Code often draws an ideal picture of a condition of things which never actually existed, and was never likely to exist; much in the same manner as we in England maintain that our king can do no wrong. Yet in the matter of the Brāhman we are compelled to accept the colouring as, in the main, truthful. Some time ago there appeared in a leading journal a report of a sermon preached by a converted Brāhman, in which the preacher asserted that the Brāhmans of the present day pretend to 'dethrone the Creator and put themselves in his place. Moreover, that he himself (the preacher) had claimed and received divine honours, and had seen believers (among his own fellow-countrymen) greedily drink the water in which his feet had been washed.'[1]

[1] The Rev. Nārāyan S'eshādri (a Marāṭhī name derived from the serpent-like folds of the serpent S'esha, Vishṇu's seat), who preached on Easter Sunday, April 5, 1874 (in a Presbyterian Church in Kensington

It may be asked how did the Brāhman, laden with all this weight of dignity and theoretically debarred from all other occupations, except studying and teaching the Veda, and performing religious rites, contrive to support himself? The answer is that he took care to provide for his own material comforts [1] by making the efficacy of all repetitions of the Veda and all sacrificial rites depend upon the gifts (*dakshiṇāḥ*) with which they were accompanied:—

A sacrifice performed with trifling presents (*alpa-dakshiṇaḥ*) destroys the organs of sense, fame, heaven, life, reputation, offspring, cattle; therefore let no man undertake a sacrifice who has not plenty of money to make liberal gifts (XI. 40).

Park Road), a sermon, the report of which appeared in the next day's *Daily News*. He embraced the Christian faith on September 13, 1843. He had to give up father, mother, three brothers, and three sisters. Such is the condition of Brāhmanical society that a man must renounce all former associations when converted. I subjoin a further portion of the matter reported as preached. 'He had been emptied of Hindooism. This creed dealt largely in the marvellous; for instance, it is said that one great saint drank up all the ocean in three sips, and was afterwards seated among the constellations on account of this feat. But there was a philosophic as well as a popular form of Hindooism. There were atheistical and theistical forms, the latter having as many advocates in India as it had in this country, in Germany, and in the United States. He dwelt at length on the pantheistic notion of Brahm, which ignored man's responsibility. Man's sins, in fact, became God's sins; and gradually the preacher had become convinced that this was blasphemy.'

[1] This appears to hold good even in the present day; for Professor Rāmkṛishṇa Bhāṇḍārkar, writing in the 'Indian Antiquary' for May 1874, remarks that repetition of the Veda for *dakshiṇā* still prevails in Gujarāt, and to a much greater extent in the Marāṭhī country and Tailangana. 'Numbers of Brāhmans go about to all parts of the country in search of *dakshiṇā*, and all well-to-do natives patronise them according to their means, by getting them to repeat portions of their Veda, which is mostly the Black Yajush, with Āpastamba for their Sūtra. Hardly a week passes here in Bombay in which no Tailanga Brāhman comes to ask me for *dakshiṇā*.'

Let a man, according to his ability, give wealth to Brāhmans who know the Vedas and keep apart from the world. By so doing he obtains heaven when he dies (XI. 6).

A king, even though dying (from want), must not receive taxes from a Brāhman learned in the Vedas, nor must he allow such a Brāhman dwelling in his country to pine away with hunger. Of that king in whose territory a Brāhman learned in the Vedas wastes with hunger, the whole kingdom will in a short time be wasted with famine (VII. 133, 144).

All that exists in this universe is the Brāhmans' property (I. 100).

Moreover, when the increase of the Brāhmanical class compelled the secularization of many of its members, they were allowed to engage in the occupations of the other classes. This was at first only permitted under circumstances of exigency and distress. Some verses in XII. 71, X. 75, 76, 80–82, lay down the law on this point:—

A Brāhman who swerves from his own peculiar duty is, on departing this life, born again as a vomit-eating demon called Ulkā-mukha (XII. 71).

Repetition (or study) of the Veda (*adhyayanam*), expounding it (or literally, teaching others to repeat it, *adhyāpanam*), sacrificing (*yajanam*) and assisting others to sacrifice (*yājanam*), giving (*dānam*) and receiving gifts (*pratigrahaḥ*) are the six legitimate acts[1] (*shaṭ-karmāṇi*) of a Brāhman. Of these six acts, three are the means of his subsistence, viz., assisting at sacrifices, teaching the Veda, and receiving presents from a pious giver (*viśuddhāt*). These three privileges (*dharmāḥ*) are limited to Brāhmans, and do not extend to Kshatriyas (X. 75–77). Hence a Brāhman is called *Tri-karman*, 'one who engages in three acts.'

The most proper occupation for the Brāhman is teaching and expounding the Veda (*vedābhyāsaḥ*); for a Kshatriya, defending the people; for a Vaiśya, agriculture, keeping cattle, and trade (*vārtā-karma*[2]). Yet a Brāhman, unable to subsist by his proper employment, may live by the duty of a soldier, for that is the next in dignity. If it be asked, how is

---

[1] Called the 'six privileges.' A particular tribe of Konkan Brāhmans is said to be excluded from these privileges because its members eat fish.

[2] This word *vārtā-karman*, as may be gathered from Kullūka's commentary on these three verses, includes *krishi*, *go-raksha*, and *bāṇijya*. The caste-division of Megasthenes (note 1, p. 224) separates these three.

he to live if unable to subsist by either of these occupations? the answer is that he may adopt the mode of life of a Vaiśya (X. 80–82. See also X. 101. 102. Cf. note 3, p. 227).

Here are some of the rules by which the whole existence of a Brāhman from the cradle to the grave was regulated :—

Every Brāhman was supposed to pass through four Āśramas or 'Orders,'—that is to say, his life was divided into four stages or periods according as he became successively, 1. Religious student (*brahma-ćārin*); 2. Householder (*gṛiha-stha*); 3. Anchorite or hermit (*vānaprastha*); 4. Religious mendicant (*bhikshu* or *parivrājaka* or *sannyāsin*). For the regulation of his life in the first two of these periods the most minute instructions are spread over the 2nd, 3rd, 4th, and 5th Books with much wearisome detail and repetition.[1]

To begin with the religious student. The young Brāhman is to reside with his preceptor (*guru*) until he has gained a thorough knowledge of the three Vedas. This residence may continue for thirty-six years, or for half that time, or for a quarter of it, according to his capacity for acquiring the requisite instruction (cf. Gṛihya Sūtras, p. 193). He may even be a student for life (*naishṭhika*, III. 1, II. 243).

He is of course to go through all the twelve Sanskāras or 'purificatory rites' (II. 27, &c.). They are supposed to purify a man from the taint of sin derived from his parents (*gārbhikam enas*), and are enjoined, with certain variations, on all the three first classes alike; some being performed

---

[1] It is interesting to find that Megasthenes (Strabo XV. 1, 59), three centuries B.C., had noted that Brāhmans, even from the time of conception (ἤδη δ' εὐθὺς καὶ κυομένους), were under the care of learned men, and lived for thirty-seven years as philosophers before becoming householders.

before the birth of a male child, and some during the first year after birth. I here enumerate them :—

1. *Garbhādhāna* or *Garbha-lambhana*, 'the ceremony on conception' (p. 192); 2. *Puṉsavana* (p. 192); 3. *Sīmantonnayana* (p. 192); 4. *Jāta-karman* (p. 192); 5. *Nāma-karman* or *Nāma-karaṇa*, 'the ceremony of giving a name' on the tenth or twelfth day after birth (Manu II. 30); 6. *Nish-kramaṇa*, 'taking out the child' in the fourth month to see the sun (II. 34); 7. *Anna-prāśana* (p. 192); 8. *Ćūḍā-karman* or *Ćaula* (p. 192); 9. *Upanayana* (p. 192); 10. *Keśānta*, 'cutting off the hair,' performed on a Brāhman in his sixteenth year, on a Kshatriya in his twenty-second, on a Vaiśya in his twenty-fourth (Manu II. 65); 11. *Samāvartana*, performed on the student's return home after completing his studies with his preceptor (pp. 195, 242); 12. *Vivāha*, 'marriage.' This last is the principal purificatory rite for women; but they are allowed some of the others, provided there is an omission of the Mantras or Vedic texts, with which all the Saṉskāras were accompanied (II. 66, 67).

It is noteworthy that marriage is the twelfth Saṉskāra, and hence a religious duty incumbent upon all, completing the purification and regeneration of the twice-born :—

Of the above twelve rites, 1, 2, 3, and 10 are little observed. The other eight are more worthy of attention; 8 and 9 are of considerable legal importance even in the present day, and 7 is still practised. 7 and 12 are said to be the only rites allowed to S'ūdras. Other Saṉskāras, practised in some parts of India, are mentioned, such as *Karṇa-vedha*, 'boring the ears;' and occasionally the imparting of the Sāvitrī or 'sacred Vedic text' (= Gāyatrī, p. 17), which ought to be performed at Upanayana, is reserved for a separate ceremony four days later.

But the most important of the above Saṉskāras is *Upanayana*, 'investiture with the sacred cord,' already described in the Gṛihya Sūtras (p. 192). This cord, which is a thin coil of three threads, commonly called the *Yajñopavīta* or 'sacrificial thread,' is worn over the left shoulder and allowed to hang down diagonally across the body to the right hip, and the wearing of it by the three twice-born classes was the mark of their second birth.[1] A third birth is mentioned for Brāhmans (II. 169):—

The first birth is from the natural mother; the second from the binding on of the girdle (*mauñji-bandhane*); the third is at initiation into sacrificial rites (as the *jyotishṭoma*, &c.), according to a precept of the Veda.

There was some difference in the kind of thread worn, according to the class of the wearer. In II. 44 we read:—

The sacred cord of a Brāhman must be of cotton (*kārpāsa*) so as to be put on over his head in a coil of three threads (*tri-vṛit*); that of a Kshatriya of flax or hemp (*śaṇa*); that of a Vaiśya of wool (*āvika*).

[In the previous two verses Manu intimates that a Brāhman must also have a girdle (*mekhalā*) either of Muñja grass or of Kuśa grass. From II. 169, 170, it might be inferred that the girdle and sacrificial thread are equivalent, but II. 174 clearly distinguishes them. The leather mantle, thread, girdle, staff, and underclothing are, all five, prescribed at the time of Upanayana, and the binding on of the girdle seems to complete the rite.]

The ceremony of investiture begins by the youth's standing opposite the sun and walking thrice round the fire. Then girt with the thread, he asks alms from the assembled company. This begging for alms still constitutes part of the rite, and indicates that the youth undertakes to provide himself and his preceptor (*guru, āćārya*), with food (p. 193). The Guru then initiates him into the daily use of the Sāvitrī or holy prayer in the three measured Gāyatrī (pp. 17, 154), preceded by three suppressions of breath (*tribhiḥ prāṇāyāmaiḥ*), the triliteral syllable *Om*, and three Vyāhṛitis or mystical words, *Bhūr Bhuvaḥ Svar*,[2] and admits him to the privilege of repeating the

---

[1] It is still worn, but the word *Yajñopavīta* for 'the sacred thread' has been corrupted into Jane-o. In Bengālī it is called *Poitā* for *Pavitra*.

[2] The utterance of these three mystical words, meaning 'earth, the middle region, and heaven' (note 2, p. 55), together with the awful

three Vedas, and of performing other religious rites, none of which are allowed before investiture (II. 171, 173). The Guru or Āćārya is thus his spiritual father.

Purifications, ablutions, and libations (called Savanas) are enjoined on Vānaprasthas or 'hermits' (p. 254) at all the three Sandhyās,[1] that is, at the three divisions of the day—sunrise, noon, and sunset—but on Brahma-ćārins and Gṛiha-sthas at the two Sandhyās of sunrise and sunset only, when the Gāyatrī (p. 17) is by all means to be repeated. Thus in II. 222, we have :—

Let him constantly observe the two Sandhyās according to rule, sipping water, with all his organs controlled and with fixed attention, repeating the Gāyatrī prayer (*japyam*, which ought to be repeated).

The young Brāhman is also every day to bathe; to offer oblations of water (*tarpaṇa*) to the gods, holy sages (*Ṛishis*) generally, and departed ancestors (*Pitṛis*); to reverence the deities [according to Kullūka, *Devatā* = *pratimā* the images of the deities]; and to offer an oblation of fuel to the sacred fire (II. 176). But in V. 88 he is forbidden to perform the regular offerings of water to deceased persons, till his studentship is completed. He is to abstain from meat, perfumes, unguents, sensuality, wrath covetousness, dancing, music, gambling, detraction

---

syllable *Om* (pp. 93, 214), is supposed to be attended with marvellous and mysterious effects (see II. 76, 79, 83, 84). Note the sacredness attached to the number three.

[1] See Book VI. 22, 24, and compare Kullūka, *savaneshu snāyāt, prātar-nadhyandina-sāyaṃ savaneshu trishu devarshi-pitṛi-tarpaṇaṃ kurvan.* Sandhyā often means 'twilight,' but is applied to morning and evening twilight and to the change from midday to afternoon. With reference to the Hindū and Mohammedan custom of performing religious rites three times a day, we may compare a passage in Daniel, who 'kneeled upon his knees three times a day, and prayed, and gave thanks before his God,' Dan. vi. 10. And David says, 'Evening, and morning and at noon, will I pray, and cry aloud,' Ps. lv. 17.

of others, falsehood, impurity of all kinds, and is never to injure any being (II. 177–179).

Every day, too, both morning and evening, he is to go round the neighbouring villages begging for food for himself and his preceptor, and collecting fuel for the maintenance of the sacred fire (II. 187).

He is always to pay the most profound respect to his religious teacher (*guru*), as well as to his parents and to all persons older than himself:—

By reverencing his mother he gains this terrestrial world; by reverencing his father, the middle world; by constant attention to his spiritual master (*guru*), the celestial world of Brahmā (II. 233).

A youth who habitually salutes and constantly reveres the aged prospers in four things, life, knowledge, fame, and strength (II. 121).

In short, even Christians may learn from Hindūs, as indeed from Oriental nations generally,[1] 'to love, honour, and succour their father and mother, to submit themselves to all their governors, teachers, spiritual pastors and masters, and to order themselves lowly and reverently to all their betters; and, moreover, to extend the duty of 'hurting nobody by word or deed' to animals and the whole inferior creation.[2]

On completing his studies the young Brāhman is to give some valuable present to his preceptor. He is then to perform the proper Saṉskāra ceremony of ablution (*snāna*) on the occasion of his solemn return to his own home (*samāvartana*), as already described (see pp. 195, 239):—

Let not a student who knows his duty make a present to his spiritual master before the ceremony on his return; but when, being permitted by his preceptor, he is about to perform the requisite ablution (*snāsyan*),

---

[1] Notably from the Chinese as well as from the Hindūs.

[2] I am told, however, that, notwithstanding the strict rules of *a-hiṉsā*, the 'Society for Prevention of Cruelty to Animals' might find work to do in some parts of India.

let him offer him some valuable article (*gurv-artham*, such as a field, gold, a jewel, cow, horse, &c.) as a gift to the best of his ability (II. 245, 246).

The young Brāhman's return to his own house is made an occasion of festivity; he is decked with flowers and receives a present of a cow (III. 3). He is then to select a wife of the same class with himself, endowed with auspicious marks (*lakshaṇa*), and thereupon he enters the second Āśrama, and becomes a householder (*gṛiha-stha*). Some curious directions for his guidance in choosing a wife are given (III. 8–10):—

Let him not marry a girl with reddish hair, nor one with a superfluity of limbs (as, for instance, one with six fingers), nor one who is sickly, nor one with either too little or too much hair, nor one who talks too much, nor one who is red-eyed, nor one named after a constellation, a tree, or a river, nor one with a barbarous name (*antya* = *mleććha*), or the name of a mountain, a bird, a snake, a slave, or any frightful object. But let him marry a woman without defective or deformed limbs, having an agreeable name, whose gait is like that of a flamingo (*haṉsa*) or elephant,[1] whose hair and teeth are moderate in quantity, and whose whole body is soft.

We have seen that marriage is a Saṉskāra. Hence it is a religious duty and a purificatory rite (p. 239).

It is clear from III. 12–15, IX. 45, 101, that, as a general rule, a twice-born man is expected to have one wife only; but polygamy is not illegal, and he might take other wives of classes different from his own, being careful to settle their precedence according to the order of these classes (IX. 85). A Brāhman might thus have four wives, one from his own class and one from each of the three classes below him; a Kshatriya three; and a Vaiśya two. But the sons of inferior wives are degraded and called

[1] That is, having a kind of rolling gait, corresponding to Homer's εἰλίπους.

Apasadaḥ (X. 10). Nevertheless, if there be four wives of a Brāhman in the order of the classes, and sons are born to all four wives, there is a rule for dividing the inheritance between them (IX. 149).

Manu's eight forms of marriage are specified in the Gṛihya Sūtras (see p. 190). Of these the first four, viz., that of Brahmā (which is described as 'the gift of a daughter to a man learned in the Veda'), the Devas (*daiva*), Ṛishis (*ārsha*), and Prajāpatis (*prājāpatya*), are the most approved for a Brāhman. The Gāndharva marriage ('from affection without any nuptial rite') and Rākshasa ('marrying a girl carried off as a prize in war') were allowable for Kshatriyas; the Āsura and Paiśāća were prohibited.

A description has been given of one of the oldest marriage rites (p. 190), as well as of the ceremony on commencing residence in a new house (p. 193). The householder is to fulfil every day all his domestic religious duties (*gṛihyaṃ karma*), some of which, such as the morning and evening oblation (*agnihotra, sāyam-prātar-homa*), are to be performed with the fire of the nuptial ceremony maintained ever afterwards (*vaivāhike' gnau*, III. 67, see p. 28).

He is especially to perform the five *Mahā-yajñāḥ*, great devotional acts[1] (III. 70, &c.): viz., 1. towards the divine

[1] The Musalmans have also five principal devotional acts, but these are not all diurnal. They are—1. Prayer (*namāz*) five times a day, practically reduced to three times, morning, midday, and evening. 2. Alms-giving (*zakāt*). 3. Fasting (*roza*), especially keeping the great fast during the ninth month, Ramazān (رمضان), once a year. 4. Pilgrimage to Mecca (*haj*) once in a lifetime. 5. Confession of faith (*shahādat*), *i.e.*, repeating the *tawḥīd* or 'declaration of faith in the unity of God:' 'there is no god but God, and Muhammad is the apostle of God.' A Hājjī is a pilgrim who has performed the Haj. There is no duty of pilgrimage among the five necessary devotional acts prescribed by Manu, but the Hindū system has, nevertheless, it

Ṛishis, by repetition and teaching of the Veda (*Brahma-yajña*); 2. towards departed fathers (*Pitṛi-y°*), by the Srāddha ceremonies; 3. towards the gods (*Deva-y°*), by oblations (*homa*[1]) to Fire, Prajāpati, Heaven and Earth, Indra, Soma, &c. (85–89); 4. towards all creatures (*Bhūta-y°*), including good and evil spirits supposed to people the air, by the *bali* or offering of rice-grains, &c., generally scattered on the house-top or outside the door for animals to devour (91); 5. towards men, by hospitality (*Manushya-y°*). A description of all five has already been given (p. 194). The last four are sometimes called Pāka-yajñas (II. 86). Of these five, the first, viz., repetition of the Veda (*Brahma-yajña, japa-y,° svādhyāya,*[2] III. 81, II. 85, 86), and espe-

---

Haj. Purī, in Orissa (the abode of Jagan-nāth), is described by Mr. Hunter as the Jerusalem of India. It is really only one of the Indian Meccas. Other great places of pilgrimage (*Tīrthas*) are Haridvār, in the Himālaya (one of the most celebrated), where the Ganges is supposed to have descended from the head of S'iva on to the earth; Ćitrakūṭ, in Bundelkhand, Rāma's first abode after his banishment; Jvālā-mukhī, in the Pañjāb, where Satī, wife of S'iva, burned herself, and her presence is thought to be denoted by gas flaming from the ground.

[1] The *homa* or 'oblation of butter' was the peculiar offering to the god of fire, as the Soma juice was to Indra, the rain-god. See note, p. 28.

[2] It seems to me that Sir W. Jones' usual translation of this and similar words by '*reading* and *studying* the Veda,' conveys a somewhat wrong idea. The words generally used to denote the performance of the Brahma-yajña rather imply 'going over inaudibly to one's self,' 'repeating or muttering texts in a low tone of voice.' It is doubtful whether the Veda was ever read or studied as we should read a book in the present day. Neither the word Veda nor any of the words connected with it imply truth written down like our word 'Scripture;' and for a long period the writing of it was discouraged, if not prohibited. The very object of the long residence with a Guru (see p. 238) was to learn to repeat the sacred texts by heart, not to study them. Indeed, very little mention of writing is made in Manu. Even written evidence is not alluded to as it is in Yājñavalkya. In connection with the repetition of the Veda at the present day I here give the substance of an interesting article by Professor Bhāṇḍārkar in the 'Indian Antiquary'

cially of the Gāyatrī text, is regarded as the most efficacious; and a peculiar virtue is attributed to its being repeated in a low tone or even mentally:—

The Japa-yajña or 'repetition of the Veda' is declared to be ten times superior to the Vidhi-yajña (or appointed oblations at the changes of the moon, called *Darśa* and *Paurṇamāsa*, see note, p. 28); a hundred times superior, if it is muttered in a low voice (*upāṇśu*); and a thousand times superior, if it is only mentally repeated (*mānasaḥ*, II. 85).

The four Pāka-yajñas, even when accompanied with the Vidhi-yajña, are not together worth a sixteenth part of the Japa-yajña (II. 86).

A Brāhman becomes fit for beatitude by simple repetition of the Veda, whether he perform other rites or not; of this there is no doubt (II. 87).

Let him habitually repeat (*abhyaset = japet*) the Veda at the right season without weariness, for that is called his highest duty (*paro dharmaḥ*); every other duty is called subordinate (*upa-dharmaḥ*, IV. 147).

The filial piety of the Hindūs is notably manifested

---

for May 1874. Every Brāhmanic family is devoted to the study of a particular Veda or S'ākhā of a Veda, and its family domestic rites are performed in accordance with the Sūtra of that Veda. In Northern India the favourite Veda is the White Yajur-veda in its Mādhyandina S'ākhā, but the study has almost died out except at Benares. (According to Mr. Burnell the Black Yajur-veda is the favourite in the Telugu country.) Brāhmans of each Veda are divided into two classes—Gṛihasthas, who are devoted to worldly avocations, and Bhikshukas, who study the sacred texts and perform religious rites. Both classes have to repeat the Sandhyā-vandana or 'morning and evening prayers' (see p. 241), which principally consist of the Gāyatrī (see p. 17), recited five, ten, twenty-eight, or a hundred and eight times. Besides these prayers, many perform daily the Brahma-yajña, incumbent on all alike on certain occasions. This for Ṛig-vedī Brāhmans consists of—1. Part of Ṛig-veda I. 1. 2. Aitareya-brāhmaṇa I. 1. 3. Portions of the Aitareya-āraṇyaka (1–5). 4. The opening text or a portion of the White Yajur-veda. 5. Of the Sāma-veda. 6. Of the Atharva-veda. 7. Of the Āśvalāyana Kalpa-sūtra. 8. Of the Nighaṇṭu. 9. Of the Nirukta. 10. Of the Ćhandas. 11. Of the Jyotisha. 12. Of the S'ikshā. 13. Of Pāṇini. 14. Of Yājñavalkya's Smṛiti. 15. Of the

in the importance attached to the *Śrāddhas*, sometimes reckoned as twelve in number (the three principal being *Nitya*, 'daily;' *Pārvaṇa*, 'monthly;' *Ekoddishṭa*, 'special,' p. 199), consisting of an offering of water (*udaka-dāna*, *tarpaṇa*) and cakes of rice-meal, &c. (*piṇḍa*) to a deceased father, grandfather, and great-grandfather, and to fore-fathers and progenitors (*Pitṛis*) collectively, on which offerings they are supposed really to feed (III. 237). The custom was probably very ancient, as the Pitṛis are addressed with the utmost reverence in the Ṛig-veda (VI. 52. 4, VII. 35. 12, X. 14. 7, 8, &c. See p. 18 of this volume).

The actual funeral, when the bodies of all deceased persons (except those of infants up to two years old, cf. p. 299) are burnt, is described at p. 196. The offering to deceased fathers at the Śrāddha is the key to the Hindū law of inheritance. It furnishes the principal evidence of kin-

---

Mahābhārata. 16. Of Kaṇāda's Sūtra. 17. Of Jaimini's Mīmāṇsā. 18. Of Bādarāyaṇa's Vedānta-sūtra. This course of Svādhyāya is based on Āśvalāyana's Sūtra III. 23 (given at p. 195 of this volume). No. 1 corresponds to his Ṛić; 4, 5, 6 to his Yajur, Sāman, and Atharvāṅgiras; 2, 3 to his Brāhmaṇas, &c. Those Bhikshukas who have studied the whole Veda follow Āśvalāyana's precept *yāvan manyeta tāvad adhītya*. Some of them are also Yājñikas, skilled in the performance of sacred rites, and some are Vaidikas, whose sole occupation in life is to learn the Vedas by heart in the Saṃhitā, Pada, Krama, Jaṭā, and Ghana arrangement of the texts (see p. 152) without making a single mistake in the Sandhi changes or even in the accents. The Ṛig-vedīs pronounce the accents differently from the Taittirīyas, while the Mādhyandinas indicate the accents by movements of the right hand. In addition to the Mantra portion of the Veda, the Ṛig-vedīs learn to recite the Brāhmaṇa portion and the Vedāṅgas, including the Kalpa and Gṛihya Sūtras. At a public recitation the first place is given to Ṛig-vedīs, the second to Yajur-vedīs, and the third to Sāma-vedīs (cf. p. 215). As the Black and White Yajur-vedīs are liable to quarrel about precedence, they are not generally invited to recital-meetings (*Mantra jāgaras*) together.

ship, on which the title to participate in the patrimony is founded, no power of making wills being recognized in Manu or any other authoritative code of Hindū jurisprudence (see p. 265). The *Gotra* or family is in fact a corporate body bound together by what may be called *Sapiṇḍa*ship (*Sapiṇḍatā*) and *Samānodaka*ship (*Samānodaka-bhāva*, Manu V. 60). All who offer the funeral cake (*piṇḍa*) and water (*udaka*) together are Sapiṇḍas and Samānodakas to each other, and a kind of intercommunion and interdependence is thus continually maintained between the dead and living members of a family—between past, present, and future generations. Practically, however, the closeness of the interconnection extends only to three generations on each side, so that if we imagine a clasp connecting two short chains of three links each, this will represent the householder uniting father, grandfather, and great-grandfather, on the one side, with son, grandson, and great-grandson on the other—in all seven persons connected by the Piṇḍa (Manu V. 60). The first three are supposed to be dependent on the living paterfamilias for their happiness, and even for their support, through the constant offering of the sacred cakes and water; and he himself, the moment he dies, becomes similarly dependent on the three succeeding generations.

The connection of *Samānodaka*ship lasts longer, and ends only when the family names are no longer known (V. 60).

The object of such Śrāddhas is twofold, viz., first, the re-embodying of the soul of the deceased in some kind of form after cremation of the corpse, or simply the release of the subtile body which is to convey the soul away (see p. 197). Secondly, the raising him from the regions of the atmosphere, where he would have otherwise to roam for an indefinite period among demons and evil spirits to a particular heaven or region of bliss.

There he is eventually half deified among the shades of departed kinsmen. Manu, however, is not clear as to the precise effect of the Śrāddha. He merely states that its performance by a son or the nearest male kinsman is necessary to deliver a father from a kind of hell called *Put*,[1] and that the spirits of the departed (Pitṛis) feed on the offered food (III. 237).

Special Śrāddhas such as these (p. 199), which form to this very day the most important religious rite among the Hindūs, are accompanied with much feasting and costly gifts to the Brāhmans invited to assist at their celebration[2] (III. 145). The performance of the first Śrāddha is more particularly marked by largesses of all kinds, and sometimes, it is said, costs a rich man a sum equivalent to several thousand pounds.[3] It should take place the day after mourning expires, and then at intervals during twelve successive months, this monthly ceremony being called by Manu *Anvāhārya* (III. 123). Afterwards it should be performed on all anniversaries of a father's death. Other Śrāddhas are described at p. 199.

It is curious to learn from III. 150–168 Manu's idea of the persons to be excluded from these ceremonies (viz., thieves, spirit-drinkers, atheists, men with diseased nails or teeth, dancers, physicians, &c., see note, p. 270).

At some Śrāddhas the old Dharma-śāstras Ākhyānas, Itihāsas, and Purāṇas were recited (III. 232, note, p. 206).

---

[1] See Manu IX. 138. Whence a son who performs the rite is called *Put-tra*, 'the rescuer from Put.' This explains the desire of every Hindū for the birth of a son rather than a daughter; but it seems inconsistent that the Śrāddha should have an effect irrespective of deeds done during life.

[2] In Book III. 145 we have *yatnena bhojayeć ćhrāddhe bahv-ṛićam veda-pāragam*, see p. 201. Manu, however, discouraged too much feasting (*vistara*), and limited the number of guests, see III. 125, 126.

[3] That of the Bengālī millionaire, Ramdoolal Dey, cost £50,000, according to Mr. Wheeler.

With reference to the subject of diet, it is clear from V. 15. 5, &c., that as a general rule the eating of flesh (*māṉsa*) and of fish (*matsya*) by twice-born men was prohibited; that the drinking of spirituous liquor was included among the five great sins (see p. 270); and that many other kinds of food, such as garlic, onions, leeks (*laśuna, gṛiñjana, palāṇḍu*), mushrooms (*kavaka, ćhatrāka*), and carnivorous birds (*kravyādāḥ pakshiṇaḥ*, V. 11), were forbidden. But it is an argument for the antiquity of Manu's Law-book that it directs flesh-meat (*āmisha*) to be eaten at some of these Śrāddhas (III. 123, IV. 131). I annex a few interesting passages which bear upon the killing of animals for sacrifice and the eating of flesh-meat under certain circumstances:—

Never let a Brāhman eat the flesh of cattle unconsecrated with Mantras, but let him eat it only when hallowed with texts of the Veda (IV. 36).

On a solemn offering to a guest (*madhu-parka*) at a sacrifice, and in holy rites to departed ancestors or to the gods—on these occasions and no other may cattle be slain (V. 41).

As many hairs as grow on any animal, so many similar deaths shall one who slays it unnecessarily (*vṛithā*) endure hereafter from birth to birth. By the Self-existent himself were animals created for sacrifice, which was ordained for the welfare (*bhūtyai*) of all this universe; therefore slaughter of animals for sacrifice is no slaughter (V. 38, 39).[1]

In eating meat (*māṉsa-bhakshaṇe*) and in drinking wine (*madye*) there is no crime (provided it be on a lawful occasion, V. 56).

Hospitality is enjoined on the householder, in the strongest language, as a religious duty (see also p. 282):—

No guest (*atithi*) who arrives in the evening, brought by the setting sun (*sūryoḍhaḥ*), must be dismissed. Whether he arrives in season or out of season, let him be allowed to sojourn in the house and be well entertained.

---

[1] This is another indication of the priority of at least part of Manu's Code to the general spread of Buddhism, which reformation led to the almost total abolition of animal sacrifice in India.

A Brāhman sojourning in a house and not honoured takes to himself all the merit of the householder's good deeds (III. 100).

Let the householder not eat anything himself till he has made his guest eat. The honouring of a guest confers wealth, reputation, life, and heaven (III. 105, 106. Compare also IV. 29).

An oblation (of food) in the fire of a Brāhman's mouth delivers (the offerer) from great guilt (III. 98).

With regard to the householder's wife and the condition of women as depicted by Manu, we may observe that their position is one of entire subordination, amounting, in theory, to a complete abnegation of what in these days would be called 'women's rights.' But although it is certain that the inferiority of women is a fixed Oriental dogma which no contact with Europeans is likely entirely to eradicate, yet it must be borne in mind that the practice does not always conform to the theory. The influence of Hindū mothers in their own families, and the respect paid to them by their children, have always been great; and it is one indication of the antiquity of Manu's Code that, although some of its precepts pronounce women unfit for independence, and debarred from the study of the Veda, others concede to them an amount of freedom to which they became strangers in times subsequent to the influx of Mohammedan customs.[1] In some cases a girl, if unmarried for three years, is even allowed to choose her own husband,[2] when she is called Svayaṃ-varā (IX. 90, 92). It is very true that Manu distinctly directs (V. 162, IX. 47, 65) that no second husband is to be allowed to widows, but he nowhere alludes to that exaggerated devotion which induced the Satī or 'devoted wife' to burn herself with her husband's body—a custom which from

1 The seclusion of Hindū women is chiefly due to the introduction of Muslim customs when the Mohammedans invaded India.

2 Girls of the Kshatriya class sometimes chose their own husbands, as we know from the story of Nala and other episodes of the Mahābhārata.

about the time of Alexander's invasion,[1] more than 300 years B.C., till the year 1829, has led to the sacrifice of innumerable lives, and has left a blot on the annals of our own administration.[2]

---

[1] It is clear from Strabo XV. 30 and 62 that Satī prevailed in India about the time of Alexander. Strabo says that the Kathaei (= Kanyā-kubja or perhaps Kshatriya), a tribe in the Pañjāb, in order to prevent wives poisoning their husbands, made a law that they should be burnt with them when they died (συγκατακαίεσθαι τεθνεῶσι τοῖς ἀνδράσι τὰς γυναῖκας), and that some wives burnt themselves voluntarily (ἀσμένας). Compare also Diodorus Siculus (XIX. 33), who describes how, after the battle between Antiochus and Eumenes, one of the wives of the Indian general Κητεὺς (= Ketu or Khatrī?) burnt herself, after contending with the other for the honour. But Arrian makes no mention of any Satī. He only describes (VII. 2, 3) how Κάλανος (perhaps = Sanskṛit Kalyāṇa), one of a sect of Indian wise men who went naked, burnt himself upon a pile. The description is like that of the self-cremation of the ascetic S'arabhan-ga in Rāmāyaṇa III. 9. Cf. Cicero Tusc. Disp. II. 22 and de Divin. I. 23. The following is a portion of the latter passage: 'Est profecto quiddam etiam in barbaris gentibus praesentiens, atque divinans: siquidem ad mortem proficiscens Calanus Indus, cum adscenderet in rogum ardentem, O praeclarum discessum, inquiet, e vitâ!' The idea of Satī seems to have been borrowed by the Hindūs from the Scythians (Herod. IV. 71). A similar custom prevailed among the Thracians (Herod. V. 5). Cf. also Propertius III. 13, 'Ardent victrices, et flammae pectora praebent, Imponuntque suis ora perusta viris.' Mādrī, wife of Pāṇḍu, became a Satī (Mahā-bhārata, Ādi-parva 4896). Compare Dr. Rost's edition of Wilson's Works, vol. ii. pp. 270–309).

[2] The practice of Satī was for a long time thought to be so intimately connected with the religious belief of the Hindūs, that our Government did not venture to put a stop to it. It was known to be enjoined in the Brahma-purāṇa and Codes of Vyāsa, An-giras, &c.; and such authorities as Colebrooke (see his life by his son, p. 287) and H. H. Wilson (in 1828) gave their opinion against interference, although it was ascertained that neither the Veda nor Manu directed or even hinted at concremation of the living wife with the dead husband. To Raghunandana (according to Dr. F. Hall) is due the alteration of the last word of a Ṛig-veda text (X. 18, 7, see p. 201) on which the authority for Satī was made to rest: *Anaśravo 'namīvāḥ su-ratnā ā rohantu janayo yonim agre*, 'without tears, without sorrow, bedecked with jewels, let the wives

Indeed, the marriage of widows is even spoken of as practised, though reprehended (IX. 66–68); and a damsel given away in marriage may be re-betrothed, if her husband die before she is actually married (69).

The following passages will be sufficient to fill up the picture of Hindū domestic life (see also p. 284):—

Day and night must women be made to feel their dependence on their husbands. But if they are fond of worldly amusements (*vishayeshu sajjantyaḥ*), let them be allowed to follow their own inclinations (IX. 2).

Even if confined at home by faithful guardians they are not (really) guarded; but those women who guard themselves by their own will (*ātmānam ātmanā yās tu raksheyuḥ*) are well guarded (IX. 12).

Let not (a husband) eat with his wife, nor look at her eating (IV. 43).

Women have no business to repeat texts of the Veda (*nāsti strīṇāṃ kriyā mantrair*), thus is the law established (IX. 18).

Domestic rites are to be performed in common with a wife (*sādhāraṇo dharmaḥ patnyā saha*), so it is ordained in the Veda (IX. 96).

No sacrifice is permitted to women separately (from their husbands), no religious observance (*vratam*), no fasting (*uposhitam*). As far as a wife obeys her husband so far is she exalted in heaven (V. 155).

A husband must continually be revered (*upaćaryaḥ*) as a god (*devavat*) by a virtuous wife (V. 154).

A virtuous wife who remains unmarried after the death of her husband goes to heaven, even though she have no son (V. 160).

We have already indicated that in the third and fourth periods of his life a Brāhman, according to Manu, is to

---

go up to the altar first,' where *agneḥ*, 'of fire,' was substituted for *agre*, 'first.' (Compare pp. 197, 201, 202). It is true that our Government adopted a middle course, and prohibited the burning of the widow, except under strict regulations, and except with her own full consent, and officials were to be present to see the rules enforced; but I have been informed by a distinguished friend (Mr. Seton-Karr) who held high offices in India, that, in consequence of our half-sanction, the number of widows actually returned as burnt, rose in one year to 800, while in other years (between 1815 and 1828) it varied from 300 to 600. Lord William Bentinck passed a law in 1829 (Reg. xvii.) which suppressed the practice with entire success and without difficulty.

become first an anchorite (*vānaprastha*) and then a religious mendicant (*bhikshu* or *parivrājaka*). It is indeed wholly improbable that all Brāhmans conformed to this rule, but the second verse of the sixth Book prescribes that when the father of a family perceives his hair to be turning grey, or as soon as his first grandchild is born, and after he has paid his three debts,[1] he is to retire to a forest and there as a hermit to practise austerities:—

Having taken up his sacred fire (*agni-hotram*) and all the domestic utensils for making oblations to it, and having gone forth from the town to the forest, let him dwell there with all his organs of sense well restrained (VI. 4).

With many kinds of pure food let him perform the five Mahā-yajñas or 'devotional rites' (VI. 5).

Let him also offer the Vaitānika oblations with the (three sacred) fires according to rule (see p. 188, note 1, p. 189).

Let him roll backwards and forwards on the ground, or stand all day on tiptoe (*prapadaiḥ*), let him move about by alternately standing up and sitting down, going to the waters to bathe at the three Savanas (sunrise, sunset, and midday, VI. 22. See p. 241).

Let him practise the rules of the lunar penance (VI. 20. See p. 96).

In the hot weather let him be a Pañća-tapās (VI. 23. See p. 95).

Let him offer libations (*tarpayet*) to the gods and Pitṛis, performing ablutions at the three Savanas (VI. 24).

Having consigned the three sacred fires (*vaitānān*) to his own person (by swallowing the ashes) according to prescribed rules, let him remain without fire, without habitation, feeding on roots and fruits, practising the vow of a Muni (*i.e.*, the *Mauna-vrata* of perpetual silence, VI. 25).

Book VI. 33 directs him for the fourth period of his life to wander about as a Bhikshu or Parivrājaka, 'religious mendicant' (*ćaturtham āyusho bhāgam parivrajet*). Here are a few rules for the regulation of this final stage of his existence, when he is sometimes called a *Sannyāsin*,

---

[1] These three debts (*trīṇi ṛiṇāni*) are, 1. to the gods, 2. to the Pitṛis, 3. to the Ṛishis. The 1st is liquidated by sacrifices, the 2nd by begetting a son for performance of the S'rāddha, the 3rd by repetition of the Veda.

'one who has given up the world;' sometimes a *Yati*, 'one who has suppressed his passions:[1]'—

Let him remain without fire, without habitation (*a-niketaḥ*); let him resort once a day to the town for food, regardless of hardships, resolute, keeping a vow of silence (*muni*), fixing his mind in meditation (VI. 43).

With hair, nails, and beard well clipped, carrying a bowl (*pātrī*), a staff (*daṇḍī*), and a pitcher (*kusumbhavān*), let him wander about continually, intent on meditation and avoiding injury to any being (VI. 52).

In this manner, having little by little (*śanaiḥ śanaiḥ*) abandoned all worldly attachments (*san-gān*), and freed himself from all concern about pairs of opposites[2] (*dvandva*), he obtains absorption into the universal Spirit (*brahmaṇy avatishṭhate*, VI. 81).

IV. Let us now note, in the fourth place, the chief characteristics of Manu's ordinances of government and judicature (*vyavahāra*), and a few of the most remarkable

---

[1] I find that some of M. Barth's remarks in the 'Revue Critique' for June 13, 1874, bear on what I have stated with regard to Manu's ordinances in the preceding pages: 'Si nous remontons plus haut, aux livres védiques, aux plus anciens comme aux plus modernes, nous trouvons la nation Indienne divisée en un grand nombre de petites principautés, où domine le principe ethnique de la peuplade et du clan. Cette organisation qui n'avait certainement pas beaucoup changé à l'époque du Buddha, s'accorde encore moins avec le système de Manu, qui suppose une certaine uniformité et l'existence de grands états. La plupart de ces peuplades avaient sans doute un état social analogue: de temps immémorial elles étaient divisées en 4 classes. . . . Mais il est difficile de préciser le degré de rigueur de cette division. Encore à une époque relativement récente (Ćhāndog. Up. iv. 4. 2) la plus jalouse, et la plus fermée de ces classes, celle des Brâhmanes, ne paraît pas très scrupuleuse quant à la pureté du sang. Je ne puis donc voir autre chose dans la théorie officielle de la caste qu'une sorte de thème convenu dont il faut faire usage avec la plus grande prudence, thème dont la donnée fondamentale a dû, parce qu'elle était consacrée par une tradition sainte, se prêter successivement, et d'une façon plus ou moins artificielle à l'explication d'états de société bien différents.'

[2] Such as honour and dishonour (*mānāpamāna*), joy and sorrow, &c.

civil and penal laws and rules of evidence.[1] The treatment of these subjects, which ought to constitute the most important department of a code of laws, is only commenced by Manu in the second half of his work, and is chiefly comprised in one quarter of it, viz., the seventh, eighth, and ninth Books. As the state of society depicted in the first six Books is of a simple and primitive character, recognizing only four principal divisions of the people, so the only form of government prescribed in the seventh Book is of a paternal and patriarchal description. The king is to rule by divine right, and, though a despot, to act like a father[2] towards his subjects (*varteta pitṛi-van nṛishu*, VII. 80). That he was treated as a kind of divinity is evident :—

The Creator created a king for the protection of the whole world by drawing forth eternal particles (*mātrāḥ śāśvatīḥ*) from the essence of Indra, Anila (Wind), Yama (god of justice), Sūrya (Sun), Agni (Fire), Varuṇa, Ćandra (Moon), and Kuvera (god of wealth, VII. 3, 4).

A king, even though a child, must not be treated with contempt, as if he were a mortal ; he is a great divinity in human shape (VII. 8).

He is directed to appoint seven or eight ministers (VII. 54) and to consult them first apart, and then collectively, as a kind of council. His prime minister (VII. 58) is to be a Brāhman,[3] and in him he is to place implicit confidence (59). He is to have a standing army (VII. 102, 103), commander-in-chief (VII. 65), and an ambassador (*dūtaḥ*) of great knowledge and abilities (VII. 63). The following is very significant :—

---

[1] I have here consulted Elphinstone's and Mill's India.

[2] Compare S'akuntalā, Act V. : *Tvayi parisamāptam bandhu-kṛityam prajānām*, 'in thee (the king) is comprehended the whole duty of a kinsman towards thy subjects.' Δεσπότης is said to be = Sanskṛit *dāsa-pati*, 'lord of conquered races.'

[3] This rule was followed by Sivajī in the constitution of the Marāṭhī empire, and the Peshwa or chief of the eight Pradhānas, 'principal ministers,' ultimately superseded S'ivajī's weak successors and usurped the supremacy.

Determination not to retreat in battle (*san-grāmeshu anivartitvam*), protection of the people, and obedience (*śuśrūshā*) to Brāhmans is the highest duty of kings, and secures their felicity in heaven (VII. 88).

The king's mode of life and the distribution of his time are carefully regulated (VII. 145, &c.) He is to rise in the last watch of the night, then to hold a court, then to assemble his council and deliberate on the affairs of his kingdom and all the eightfold business of kings (VII. 154); after that, to engage in manly exercises, then to dine, taking care that his food is not poisoned (VII. 218), and then to regulate his family; after that, he is allowed some relaxation; then he is to review his troops; then to perform religious exercises; and lastly, being himself well armed, to receive the report of his spies (*ćāra*), informers and secret emissaries (*praṇidhi*), who are regarded as of great importance.[1] He is to conclude the day by a frugal meal and musical recreations, and to go to bed early (VII. 225).[2] The rules for diplomacy and war show that India

---

[1] In IX. 256 a king is called *ćāra-ćakshuḥ*, 'spy-eyed.'

[2] The royal office was no sinecure. This is evident from the Mahabhārata and Daśa-kumāra-ćarita as well as from Manu. It appears that the day and night were each divided into eight portions of one hour and a half each, reckoned from sunrise, and thus distributed. Day—1. the king being dressed is to audit accounts; 2. he is to pronounce judgments in appeals; 3. he is to breakfast; 4. he is to receive and make presents; 5. he is to discuss political questions with his ministers; 6. he is to amuse himself; 7. he is to review his troops; 8. he is to hold a military council. Night—1. he is to receive the reports of his spies and envoys; 2. he is to dine; 3. he is to retire to rest after the perusal of some sacred work; 4. and 5. he is to sleep; 6. he is to rise and purify himself; 7. he is to hold a private consultation with his ministers and instruct his officers; 8. he is to attend upon the Purohita or 'family priest' for the performance of religious ceremonies (Wilson's Hindū Theatre, i. 209). Megasthenes (Strabo XV. 1, 55) says that the Indian king may not sleep in the daytime, but continues the whole day judging causes. Compare Macaulay's account of the daily life of Frederic the Great (Essays, p. 805).

was divided into a number of unequal states. Intrigues are to be carried on with the leaders of the enemy, and negotiation is declared to be better than force (VII. 197, 198). In battle the king is to set an example of personal bravery (VII. 87). The chief weapon is the bow (VII. 74). Elephants, chariots, cavalry, and infantry form the *Ćatur-an·ga* or 'fourfold army,'[1] and minute directions are given for its marching (VII. 187, &c.).

With regard to internal administration, it is clear from the Code that the country was partitioned into divisions governed by vicegerents, to whom the king delegated his own despotic powers, and whose authority was again delegated to other subordinate governors, who again divided their power by committing it to other rulers of townships in a regular chain, the highest governor ruling over a thousand towns, the next over a hundred, the next over twenty, the next over ten (cf. Luke xix. 17), and the lowest ruling over one town:—

Let the lord of one town (*grāmikaḥ*) notify of his own accord, and in due order, to the lord of ten towns (*grāma-daśeśāya*) any crimes which have taken place in his own district, and the lord of ten to the lord of twenty; let the lord of twenty notify everything to the lord of a hundred, and the lord of a hundred to the lord of a thousand (VII. 116, 117).

Another important subject is revenue, which the monarch is to obtain from the following sources:—1. Taxes on the produce of land, which was probably held in common by village communities, though occasional grants may have been made to individuals, the king being theoretically the only absolute proprietor of the soil (*bhūmer adhipatiḥ*), VIII. 39).[2] 2. Taxes on the produce of labour.

---

[1] In VII. 185 a sixfold (*shaḍ-vidha*) army is spoken of, the two other component parts being officers and attendants.

[2] In later times a sort of middle-man, to whom the name *Zamīndār*

3. Taxes on certain metals and commodities added to capital stock. 4. Taxes on purchases and sales. 5. A kind of poll-tax. 6. Another kind paid in labour.

With regard to 1, the usual proportion of produce taken by the king was a sixth part, but in times of necessity (as of war or invasion), he might even take a fourth of the crops. But, even though dying for want of money, he is never to receive a tax from a Brāhman conversant with the Veda (VII. 133).[1] The following passages illustrate the above six heads of taxation :—

1. A sixth, an eighth, or a twelfth part of grain may be taken by the king (according to the goodness or badness of the soil, VII. 130).

The king who, without giving protection, takes a sixth part of the grain as tax (*bali*) is declared to draw upon himself all the sins of all his subjects (VIII. 308).

A military king (*kshatriyaḥ*) who takes even a fourth part in a time of necessity (*āpadi*) while protecting his subjects to the utmost of his ability is freed from all culpability (X. 118).

2. Moreover, he may take a sixth part of the annual increase of trees (*dru*), meat, honey, clarified butter, perfumes, medicinal herbs, liquids, flowers, roots, and fruits, of leaves (*patra*), pot-herbs (*śāka*), grass, wicker-work (*vaidala*), hides, earthenware vessels, and all articles made of stone (VII. 131, 132).

3. Of cattle and gold and silver (*hiraṇyayoḥ*) added to the capital stock (*mūlād adhikayoḥ*), a fiftieth part may be taken by the king (VII. 130).

Of old treasures and precious metals in the earth the king may take

---

(introduced by the Muhammadans) is applied, acquired an ownership nearly absolute in the soil; or, at any rate, intervened between the Ryot or 'cultivator' and the king, receiving a share of the produce from the former and paying a stipulated proportion to the sovereign.

[1] In S'akuntalā, Act II., Māṭhavya says to the king, 'Say you have come for the sixth part of their grain which they owe you for tribute.' The Mahā-bhārata allows secularized Brāhmans to be taxed. Strabo (XV. 1, 40) says, 'The whole land belongs to the king, but the Indians work it on condition of receiving the fourth part of the crops (ἐπὶ τετάρταις).'

one half, because he protects his subjects and is the paramount lord of the soil (VIII. 39).

4. Having well considered the rates of purchase and sale, the length of transit (*adhvānam*), with cost of food, &c., on the journey (*saparivyayam*), the profit gained, and expense of insurance (*yoga-kshemam*), let him make merchants pay taxes on their commodities (VII. 127).

5. The king should cause the lower classes (*prithag-janam = nikrishṭa-janam*, Kullūka) in his kingdom, who live by petty trading, to pay some small sum (per head) in the name of the annual tax (VII. 137).

6. The king should cause inferior artisans and artificers (such as blacksmiths, &c.) and men of the servile class (*śūdrān*), who support themselves by their own labour, to work for one day in every month (VII. 138).

As regards the administration of justice, this is also to be performed by the king in person, aided by Brāhmans or else by a Brāhman acting as his deputy, assisted by three others (VIII. 9, 10). In Book VII. 14 we read :—

For the use of the king the great Creator (*Īśvaraḥ*) created in the beginning his own son Justice, composed of particles of his own divine essence, to act as the protector of all creatures (by wielding) the rod of punishment.

The terrible consequences of neglecting to wield this rod are described in VII. 20, &c. (see p. 285). The king is not to encourage litigation (*notpādayet kāryam*, VIII. 43). Nevertheless, he is to be ready every day to decide causes in the court (*sabhā*) when brought before him. The mode of conducting a trial is simple and patriarchal. In VIII. 23 we read :—

Let the king, having seated himself on the judgment-seat, with his body suitably attired and his mind collected (*samāhitaḥ*), and having offered homage (*praṇamya*) to the gods who are guardians of the world, commence the trial of causes (*kārya-darśana*). (Cf. Strabo XV. 1, 55.)

The litigant parties are to be heard in person, and the plaintiff's accusation is to be made *vivâ voce*. The witnesses are to be examined by the judge, who is to observe their countenances carefully (VIII. 25, 26). In his decision the judge is to attend to local usage, established practice (*āćāra*), the decisions of former judges (VIII. 45, 46), and written codes of law (*śāstra*, VIII. 3).

Let me pass on to notice the broad features of the civil and criminal code. It is, of course, very desirable that the distinction between civil and criminal laws should be clearly marked out. They are, however, mixed together very confusedly in the eighteen heads or divisions of law given by Manu (Book VII. 4–7) as follows :—

The eighteen titles or branches of law are : 1. recovery of debts (*riṇādānam*) ; 2. deposits (*nikshepaḥ*) ; 3. sale of property by one who is not the rightful owner (*asvāmi-vikrayaḥ*) ; 4. engaging in business after joining partnership, association in trade (*sambhūya samutthānam*) ; 5. non-delivery of what has been given (*dattasyānapakarma*) ; 6. non-payment of wages (*vetanasya adānam*) ; 7. breach of contract (*saṃvido vyatikramaḥ*) ; 8. annulling of purchase or sale (*kraya-vikrayānuśayaḥ*) ; 9. disputes between the owner and tender of cattle or between master and servant (*vivādaḥ svāmipālayoḥ*) ; 10. the law respecting disputes about boundaries (*sīmā-vivāda-dharmaḥ*) ; 11, 12. the two kinds of assault, viz., blows and abuse, or assault with blows and assault with slander (*pārushye-daṇḍa-vāćike*) ; 13. theft and larceny (*steyam*) ; 14. robbery with violence (*sāhasam*) ; 15. adultery (*strī-san-grahaṇam*) ; 16. the law regulating (the duties of) husband and wife (*strī-pun-dharmaḥ*) ; 17. partition of patrimony or inheritance (*vibhāgaḥ*) ; 18. gambling with dice and betting on animals, such as fighting-cocks (*dyūtam āhvayaś ća*).

The first nine of the above titles and the sixteenth and seventeenth belong to civil law ; those from the eleventh to the fifteenth, and the eighteenth relate to criminal law ; the tenth belongs partly to civil, partly to criminal. With reference to the whole arrangement of the subject, Mr. James Mill's History of India (vol. i. p. 195, &c.) has some valuable remarks, the substance of which I here give :—

Though no arrangement would appear more natural than the division of laws into *civil* and *penal*, we find them here mixed together. Another obvious ground of division—the distinction between the laws about *persons* and the laws about *things*—which prevailed in Roman law and was transferred, rude as it was, to English, seems never to have occurred to Hindū lawyers in the time of Manu. The first nine of the heads in Manu's arrangement relate to contracts, but the division is rude and imperfect. It begins with 'Loans,' one of the most refined of contracts. The subject of 'purchase and sale' is divided into two parts, but one occupies the third place in the list, the other the eighth, and a number of heterogeneous subjects intervene. 'Partnership' occupies a middle place between two subjects, to neither of which it has any relation. 'Non-payment of wages' stands immediately before 'Breach of contract,' as a separate title, though it ought to be included under that head. In fact, this seventh head is so general that it comprehends the whole subject of contracts. When the subject of contracts is ended, the principal branches of criminal law are introduced. After these and some other topics follows the great subject of inheritance.[1]

Under the head of *Civil Law* the most interesting of Manu's ordinances are on the important subject of *property*, whether acquired by possession or occupancy (*lābha, bhukti, bhoga*), by purchase (*kraya*), by contract (*saṃvid, vyavahāra*), by labour (*karma-yoga*), by donation (*pratigraha*), by inheritance (*dāya*). I note the following:—

He who has acquired any property through the sale of it (*vikrayāt*) in the presence of a number (of buyers and sellers) justly obtains the right to that property by reason of having paid the purchase money (VIII. 201).

The property of infants who are heirs let the king hold in trust until the owner has completed his term of studentship or till he is of age (at sixteen, VIII. 27).

Let the king fix the rate of sale and purchase of all marketable commodities (*sarva-paṇyānām*), after having considered the distance (from which they have been imported), the remoteness of the place to which they are sent, the time they are kept, and the gain or loss upon them. Once in every five nights or once a fortnight he should fix the proper rate in the presence of those (who understand it, VIII. 401, 402).

---

[1] In consulting Mr. James Mill I have found that some of his statements must be taken with considerable qualification, prejudiced as he appears to have been against everything Hindū.

A lost article, when found, should be guarded by trusty men. Any thieves convicted of stealing it should be condemned to be trampled to death by the royal elephant (VIII. 34).

It is evidence of a somewhat rude state of society that in certain cases a man is allowed to repent of a bargain and to have a contract annulled, thus :—

When a man has bought or sold anything (not perishable, such as land or copper), and may afterwards repent, he may restore it or take it back within ten days (*antar-daśāhāt*, VIII. 222).

Marriage is regarded as a contract, but the same liberty of annulling is in this case not allowed :—

If a man shall give away in marriage a girl who has any defects (*doshavatīm*) without notifying these defects, the king must fine him ninety-six Paṇas (*kuryād daṇḍam shaṇṇavatim paṇān*, VIII. 224).

The repetition of the nuptial texts (*pāṇigrahaṇikā mantrāḥ*) are the settled mark (*niyataṃ lakshaṇam*) of a marriage contract. Of those texts (the one) repeated on (making) the seventh step (viz., *sakhā saptapadī bhava*, see p. 191) is decided by the wise to be (the sign of) the completion (*nishṭhā*) of the contract (VIII. 227).

Throughout Eastern countries, especially in ancient times, the insecurity of property has led to two practices little resorted to by the peoples of modern Europe, viz., concealment of valuable articles and the habit of entrusting them for safety to the keeping of others. We can understand, therefore, the importance assigned in Manu's Law-book (Book VIII. 179, &c.) to the subject of 'deposits' or, according to legal phraseology, 'bailments.' This branch of law opens thus :—

A wise man should make a deposit (*nikshepaṃ nikshipet*) with a person of good family, of good conduct, acquainted with law, a speaker of truth, possessing numerous relations, wealthy and honourable (VIII. 179).

If a bailee (*nyāsa-dhārin*) fail to restore a deposit, and there are no witnesses, the judge is to cause secret agents (*praṇidhi*) to deposit gold with him, and should he fail to redeliver it, he is to be made to pay (*dāpyaḥ*) the equivalent of both deposits (VIII. 181–184).

Another proof of a primitive state of society may be found in the rules respecting interest and the premium paid for the use of borrowed property. This is sometimes allowed to be paid in kind;[1] as, for instance, when grain, fruit, wool, animals, &c., have been borrowed, showing that coined money was still uncommon as a general circulating medium. (Compare the mention of *nāṇaka*, 'coin,' in the later Code of Yājñavalkya II. 241.)

Interest on money (*kusīda-vṛiddhiḥ*) received all at once (and not by the month, &c.) must not exceed the double (of the sum lent);[2] on grain (*dhānye*), fruit (*sade*), wool (*lave*), and beasts of burden (*vāhye*) it must not exceed five times the value (*pañćatā*, VIII. 151).

The rate of interest (*vṛiddhi*) is not only high, but varies according to the class of the man to whom anything is lent; but compound interest (*ćakra-vṛiddhi*) is not approved (VIII. 153):—

A money-lender (*vārdhushikaḥ*) may take two per cent. (*dvikaṃ śatam*) as interest per month from a Brāhman, three (*trikam*) from a Kshatriya, four (*ćatushkam*) from a Vaiśya, and five (*pañćakam*) from a Śūdra, in the order of the classes (VIII. 142).

In VIII. 156, 157, there is a law bottomry, which is interesting as showing that sea-voyages were undertaken in Manu's time.

The recovery of debts is enforced by stringent laws, and the debtor is not only made to pay what he owes, but an additional fine to the king, thus:[3]—

---

[1] Compare Deut. xxiii. 19, 20, 'Thou shalt not lend upon usury to thy brother; usury of money, usury of victuals, usury of anything that is lent upon usury: unto a stranger thou mayest lend upon usury,' &c.

[2] Principal doubled by accumulated interest is called in Marāṭhī *Dāmdupaṭ*. Even now a village Mahājan will take from 50 to 75 per cent.

[3] No sanction, however, is given by Manu to the later practice of *Dharnā* or 'sitting at the door of a house to compel payment of a debt.'

When a debt has to be paid (*riṇe deye*) which is admitted to be just, the debtor owes a fine of five per cent. (*pañćakaṃ śatam*) in addition, and ten per cent. if it be repudiated (though it be just, VIII. 139).

The laws respecting herdsmen (*paśu-pāla*) and their employers (*svāmin*) are carefully laid down (VIII. 229, &c.). I note one instance (VIII. 232):—

The herdsman himself must restore an animal that has been lost (*nashṭa*), or destroyed by vermin (*kṛimibhiḥ*), or killed by dogs, or has perished by falling into a hole (*vishame*) through want of his having exerted himself to save it (*hīnam purusha-kāreṇa*).

We may also observe that the hire of some kinds of agricultural labourers is directed to be paid in kind:[1]—

That hired herdsman whose hire is paid with milk must be allowed by the owner of the cattle to milk the best cow out of ten (*daśato-varām*), unless he be paid with some other kind of food (VIII. 231).

The most important subject connected with property is the law of inheritance (*dāya*) treated of in the ninth Book of Manu's Code. And here we cannot fail to be struck with the remarkable circumstance that Hindū law does not allow the owner of property any testamentary power.[2] Indeed, a proper word for 'will' or 'testament' does not exist in the Sanskṛit language. It must be borne in mind that in a patriarchal state of society all family property

---

The person so sitting refuses to eat, and as long as he does so the debtor must abstain from food too, and if the suitor perishes the crime of his death falls on the debtor. Originally the person sitting in Dharnā, either on his own behalf or that of another, was a Brāhman. See H. H. Wilson's Glossary of Indian Terms.

[1] Payments in kind in aid of money wages are not unusual even in the present day. Even quite recently in British territory the land-tax was sometimes paid in kind, and is still so paid in some native states.

[2] Our Government made this legal by the Hindū Wills Act (xxi. of 1870). Certain peculiar documents, however, resembling wills, but bearing other titles, were previously recognized by our courts.

was supposed to be held in common by a sort of joint ownership, the father or principal person in a household being regarded as a head partner.

In India, where customs become stereotyped for centuries, this primitive idea of a common title to the family property has continued to prevail up to recent times. The family is, as we have seen, a corporate society, whose bond of union is the sacred oblation offered in common by its living to its deceased members. On the death of a father the sons or nearest relatives succeed to the inheritance by simple right of *Sa-piṇḍa*ship, that is, by a right obtained through the common offering of rice-cakes (*piṇḍa*) and of water, &c., to a deceased father, grandfather, and great-grandfather at the Śrāddha ceremonies (see p. 248). It must be noted, however, that although the whole family has a joint-interest in the property, the estate cannot be divided during the lifetime of the parents, and even at their death the eldest son is allowed to take the father's place as chief manager of the family partnership, thus :—

The eldest brother may take the paternal property (*pitryaṃ dhanam*) entirely (into his own hands). The rest of the family (*śeshāḥ*) may live under him (*tam upajīveyuḥ*) exactly as they lived under the father (IX. 105).

An eldest brother conducting himself as he ought (towards his younger brothers) is to be regarded by them as a mother and father (IX. 110).

Nevertheless, the brothers are allowed, if they like, to separate, and full directions are given in Book IX. 112, &c., for the partition of the family estate; a distinction being made according to merit as well as age, and some being, very unjustly according to our ideas, disqualified :—

After the death of the father and mother, the brothers having assembled together may make a partition of the paternal property, but they have no power to do so during the lifetime of their parents (IX. 104).

Either let them live together (*sahavaseyuḥ*) or separately, from religious motives; since the number of religious rites (such as the five *Mahā-yajñāḥ*, see p. 244) are increased by separation of households, therefore separation is legal (IX. 111).

The portion taken out (of the estate) by the eldest son is a twentieth, along with the best of all the chattels; by the middle son, a fortieth; and by the youngest, an eightieth (IX. 112).

A deduction (*uddhāra*) being thus made, the remainder should be allotted among the brothers in equal shares; if no deduction is made they should share in the following manner:—Let the eldest take a double share and the next born a share and a half (if they excel in learning and merit), and let the younger sons have a share each (IX. 116, 117).

Those brothers who are addicted to vicious habits (such as gambling, licentiousness, &c.) forfeit a right (*nārhanti*) to any share in the inheritance (IX. 214).

Impotent persons (*klīva*), those who have lost caste (*patita*), those who are blind, deaf, insane, paralyzed (*jaḍa*), dumb, defective in limb or sense, are also debarred from sharing (IX. 201).

But a wise heir will in common justice supply all such persons with food and raiment (*grāsāććhādanam*) to the best of his ability. Otherwise he is guilty of a great crime (IX. 202).

It must be observed that women are generally excluded from a direct title to share in the division of property:—

Three persons are declared to have no property of their own (*a-dhanāḥ*), a wife, a son, and a slave. Whatever money they earn is his to whom they belong (VIII. 416).

Nevertheless, some marriage portions (*śulka*) or gifts received by a married woman at and after the nuptial ceremony, are regarded as her own peculiar property. These constitute what is still called *Strī-dhana*,[1] 'a

---

[1] Commonly written Stridhun. Mr. Herbert Cowell, in his Tagore Law Lectures for 1871 (p. 28), says, that although this property is supposed to belong exclusively to a wife, the husband has a concurrent power over it, so that he may use it in any exigency, without being held accountable for it. Strī-dhana is now, however, acquired 'by gift, by earnings, and by inheritance,' and the Dāyabhāga lays down that

woman's (separate) wealth or dower,' which, according to Manu, is sixfold :—

Whatever was given over the nuptial fire (*adhy-agni*), whatever she receives while being led in procession from her father's to her husband's house (*adhyāvāhanikam*), a gift (from her husband) in token of affection (*prīti*), and a similar gift received from her brother, from her mother, from her father, all these are declared to be a woman's own property (IX. 194).

Those young girls, too, who are unmarried (*kanyāḥ*) at a father's death are directed (IX. 118) to receive an allotment out of the shares accruing to their brothers. The following also (IX. 130) is noteworthy :—

A man's own son is even as himself, and a daughter is like a son. How, then (if he have no son), ought any one else than a daughter, who is part of his own person (*ātmani tishṭhantī*), to inherit his own property?

I pass on to a brief notice of Manu's *Criminal Code*. The three most conspicuous features of his penal laws are exactly those which mark the earliest forms of criminal legislation, viz., severity, inconsistency, and a belief in the supposed justice of the *lex talionis*, the latter leading to punishments which in later times would be considered unjustifiably disproportionate to the offences committed, and sometimes barbarously cruel.[1] Thus :—

---

the husband has power over the wife's earnings and 'any presents she may receive from any other but kindred.'

[1] Mr. Mill on this point quotes Sir W. Jones, who is not, like himself, disposed to view everything Hindū in an unfavourable light. 'The cruel mutilations practised by the native powers are shocking to humanity.' We know what was said by our Lord about 'an eye for an eye and a tooth for a tooth,' Matt. v. 38. See Lev. xxiv. 20; Deut. xix. 21. Compare the laws of Draco and of the ancient Egyptians. Strabo (XV. 1. 54) says of the Hindūs, 'He who has given false testimony suffers mutilation of the extremities (ἀκρωτηριάζεται), and he who maims a limb is condemned to suffer maiming.'

With whatever member of the body a low-born man may injure a superior, that very member of his must be mutilated (VIII. 279).

A once-born man insulting (*kshipan*) twice-born men with abusive language (*vāćā dāruṇayā*) must have his tongue cut (VIII. 270).

Should he mention their name and caste with insulting expressions (as, 'Hallo! there, Yajńadatta, vilest of Brāhmans'), a red-hot iron spike ten fingers long is to be thrust into his mouth (VIII. 271).

Should he, through arrogance, attempt to instruct a Brāhman in his duty (saying, 'You ought to do so and so'), the king is to have boiling oil poured into his mouth and ears (VIII. 272).

Thieves are to have their hands cut off, and then to be impaled on a sharp stake (IX. 276).

A goldsmith detected in committing frauds is to have his body cut to pieces with razors (IX. 292).

Perhaps the most objectionable feature in the penal code is not the cruel retaliation, which was probably more a matter of theory than actual practice, but the leniency with which Brāhmans are directed to be treated. It will be observed that a graduated scale is prescribed according to the rank of the offender and the class to which he belongs, thus:—

A king must never kill a Brāhman, though he may be found guilty of all possible crimes (*sarva-pāpeshv api sthitam*); let him expel him from the kingdom unharmed in body and intact in all his property. There is no greater injustice on earth than the killing of a Brāhman. The king, therefore, must not harbour a thought about putting him to death (VIII. 380, 381).

A Kshatriya insulting a Brāhman must be fined a hundred Paṇas (*śatam daṇḍam arhati*); a Vaiśya doing the same must pay one hundred and fifty or two hundred Paṇas; a Śūdra doing the same must receive corporal punishment[1] (*badham arhati*, VIII. 267).

Five great crimes (*mahā-pātakāni*) are enumerated in Book XI. 54, which are described as entailing the highest degree of guilt, though certainly from a European point of view they cannot all be regarded as equally heinous:—

---

[1] *Badha* might be rendered 'capital punishment,' but Kullūka explains it by 'the lash.'

1. Killing a Brāhman (*brahma-hatyā*); 2. drinking intoxicating liquor (*surā-pāna*); 3. stealing gold from a Brāhman (*steya*); 4. adultery with the wife of a Guru or spiritual teacher (*gurv-anganāgamaḥ*); and 5. associating with any one guilty of such sins.

Severe penances voluntarily performed, rather than legal penalties judicially inflicted, are enjoined for some of these crimes (see p. 274); and they are declared in XI. 49 to involve rather singular consequences (*phala*) in future states of existence. Thus for 1. a man will suffer from consumption (*kshaya-rogitvam*) in a future life (see also XI. 73); for 2. he will have discoloured teeth; for 3. diseased nails (*kaunakhyam*).[1]

Moreover, in XII. 54–57, much more awful results are alleged to follow hereafter; inasmuch as those who are guilty of these great crimes are condemned to dwell for a vast number of years in terrible hells (*ghorān narakān*) before entering on new states of being. After protracted torture in one or other of these hells (see p. 217) a Brāhman-slayer (*brahma-hā*) must enter the body of a dog, boar, ass, camel, bull, goat, sheep, stag, bird, or outcaste Ćaṇḍāla, according to the degree of his guilt; a spirit-drinker will become a worm, insect, moth, &c.; a gold-stealer will pass a thousand times into the bodies of spiders, snakes, noxious demons, &c. (Compare p. 276.)

Some crimes in the second degree are the following:—

Falsely asserting oneself to be of too high a caste, falsely accusing a Guru, forgetting texts of the Veda through neglect of repeating them (*brahmojjhatā*), giving false testimony (*kauṭa-sākshyam*), eating impure food, stealing deposits, incest, intercourse with women of the lowest class.

A long list of crimes in the third degree (*upapātaka*) is given in XI. 59–66. Some of them are:—

---

[1] For this reason it is directed in Book III. 153, 154, that consumptive persons and persons with diseased nails (*ku-nakhin*) and discoloured teeth (*śyāva-dantaka*) ought to be excluded from S'rāddhas.

Killing a cow (*go-badhaḥ*); neglect of repetition of the Veda (*i.e.*, of the daily Brahma-yajña); neglect of the sacred fire; usury (*vārdhushyam*); selling a tank or garden or wife or child; neglecting investiture (*vrātyatā*); superintendence over mines of any kind (*sarvākareshv adhikāraḥ*); cutting down green trees for fuel; performing religious rites for selfish motives (*ātmārtham*); reading infidel books (*asac-ćhāstrādhigamanam*); addiction to music and dancing (*kauśīlavyasya kriyā*); atheism (*nāstikyam*).

For many of these crimes also voluntary penances constitute the only punishment. Thus the killer of a cow must undergo great hardships and make atonement by attending upon a herd, guarding them from injury, following them day and night in all weathers for three months, swallowing the dust raised by their hoofs, &c. (XI. 108–115).

Trial by ordeal (*divya*) is recognized by Manu, though the ten different forms of it are not all specified as in later works:[1]—

Let him cause a man (whose veracity is doubted) to take hold of fire or dive under water (*apsu nimajjayet*), or touch the heads of his wife and sons one by one. The man whom flaming fire burns not and water forces not up (*āpo nonmajjayanti*), and who suffers no harm, must be instantly held innocent of perjury (VIII. 114, 115).

It remains to notice a few of the laws of evidence. Fearful denunciations are pronounced against those who deliver false testimony in a court of justice (VIII. 82). The strictest rules are also to be observed in selecting witnesses competent to give trustworthy evidence (see

---

[1] These ten forms (some of which are given by Yājñavalkya, see p. 297) are—1. *Tulā*, 'the balance;' 2. *Agni*, 'fire;' 3. *Jala*, 'water;' 4. *Visha*, 'poison;' 5. *Kośa*, 'drinking water in which an idol has been washed;' 6. *Taṇḍula*, 'ejecting chewed rice-grains;' 7. *Tapta-māsha*, 'taking a Māsha weight of gold out of heated oil;' 8. *Phāla*, 'holding a hot ploughshare;' 9. *Dharmādharma*, 'drawing concealed images of virtue and vice out of a vessel filled with earth;' 10. *Tulasī*, 'holding the leaves of holy basil.' This holy basil is said to be sacred to Vishṇu.

p. 287). At least three witnesses are required to establish a fact in dispute :—

If a man is summoned (*kṛitāvasthaḥ*) by a creditor for a debt and denies it when questioned, he is to be proved guilty by three witnesses at least (*try-avaraiḥ sākshibhiḥ*) in the presence of a Brāhman appointed by the king [1] (VIII. 60).

Witnesses are to deliver their testimony *vivâ voce,* and no directions are given about written documents, which makes it probable that this kind of evidence, though fully recognized by Yājñavalkya (see p. 297), was not received, or at least not usual, at the early epoch when Manu's Law-book was composed. If the testimony is contradictory, the judge is to decide by the majority of credible witnesses. If the number of witnesses is equal, he is to be guided by the testimony of those who are most distinguished for virtuous qualities (VIII. 73). A similar rule is propounded by Yājñavalkya (see p. 298). It is a noteworthy point that women are, as a rule, debarred from giving evidence, except for women (VIII. 68). Moreover, the distinctions between the credibility of witnesses must strike a European mind as somewhat extraordinary and whimsical. A man who has male offspring is thought more worthy of credence than a man who has female (VIII. 62), perhaps because he is supposed to have a greater stake in the common weal. A hungry or thirsty and tired person is excluded from all right of bearing testimony (VIII. 67). The reason for the following is not very clear :—

In cases of robbery with violence (*sāhaseshu*), theft, and adultery (*steya-san-grahaṇeshu*), calumny and assault (*vāg-daṇḍayoḥ pārushye*), a judge must not examine (the competence of) witnesses too strictly (*na parīksheta sākshiṇaḥ*, VIII. 72).

---

[1] Compare Yājñavalkya's rules about witnesses, which are a development of those of Manu. See p. 298.

The following precept is calculated, I fear, to diminish the favourable impression which the laws of the Mānavas, taken together and regarded relatively to circumstances, must produce on a candid mind :—

In certain cases a man stating a fact falsely from a pious motive (*dharmataḥ*), even though he knows the truth, is not excluded from heaven ; such a statement they call divine speech.

Whenever the death of a Brāhman, Kshatriya, Vaiśya, or S'ūdra may result from speaking the truth, then an untruth may be told, for falsehood is in this case preferable to truth (VIII. 103, 104).

A similar precept occurs in Yājṅavalkya's Code, but an expiation is there prescribed. (See the examples, p. 298.)

V. I now turn to some of the Prāyaś-ćitta or 'penances' enjoined in the eleventh Book of Manu :—

A twice-born man performing the *Prājāpatya* penance (*i.e.*, that called after Prajāpati) must for three days eat only once in the morning, for three days only once in the evening, for three days food unsolicited (but given as alms), and for three days more nothing at all (XI. 211).

A twice-born man performing the penance called *Ati-kṛiććhra* ('very severe') must eat, as before (*i.e.*, as described in the last), a single mouthful (*grāsam*) for three times three days, and for the last three days must fast entirely (XI. 213).

A Brāhman performing the penance called *Tapta-kṛiććhra* ('hot and severe') must swallow hot water, hot milk, hot clarified butter, and hot air, each of them for three days successively, after bathing and keeping his organs of sense all restrained (XI. 214).

The act of fasting for twelve days, performed by one whose heart is restrained, and whose mind is attentive, is called the *Parāka* penance, which removes all guilt (XI. 215).

Eating for one day the excrement and urine of a cow mixed with milk, curds, clarified butter and water boiled with Kuśa grass, and fasting entirely for a day and night is the penance called *Sāntapana* (XI. 212).

This last penance is to be performed by any one who does any voluntary act causing loss of caste (*jāti-bhraṇśa-karaṃ karma*) ; if the act be involuntary, the Prājāpatya is to be performed. (See XI. 124.)

The *Pańćagavya* penance consists in swallowing the

five products of a cow mentioned above under the Sāntapana penance. This is declared to be a sufficient atonement for having stolen food, a carriage, bed, chair, roots, flowers, or fruit (XI. 165). A variety of other curious penances and expiations are enumerated :—

A twice-born man having, through infatuation, drunk intoxicating liquor, may (as an expiation) drink the same liquor when boiling hot (*agni-varṇām*). If his body is completely scalded by this process he is absolved from guilt (XI. 90).

When the divine knowledge (*brahma*) which is in his body (*kāya-gatam*) is once immersed in spirituous liquor, his Brāhmanical rank departs and he descends to the condition of a Śūdra (XI. 97).

He who says 'hush' (*hūm*) to a Brāhman, or 'thou' to one who is his superior (in knowledge) must perform an ablution, eat nothing for the rest of the day, and appease the Brāhman's anger by prostrating himself at his feet (XI. 204).

If a Brāhman who has drunk the Soma-juice (at a Soma-sacrifice, see p. 6) smells the breath of a man who has been drinking spirituous liquor, he is absolved from the taint by thrice suppressing his breath under water and swallowing clarified butter (XI. 149).

One of the most severe penances is called *Ćāndrāyaṇa* or 'the lunar penance,' described in VI. 20, XI. 216–221. We have already given a short account of this (see p. 96), and have only here to note, as peculiar, some of the offences for which it is required to be performed :—

The Ćāndrāyaṇa is declared to be an expiation for carrying off a man or woman, for seizing a field or house, and for taking without permission the water of a well or reservoir (XI. 163). It is also to be performed for acts which cause mixture of caste and exclusion from society (XI. 125).

The following will show that the greatest atoning efficacy is attached to a repetition of the Veda :—

Having repeated (*japitvā*) the Sāvitrī (or Gāyatrī, see p. 17) three thousand times with a collected mind, and having drunk milk for one month in a cow-house, a Brāhman is delivered from the guilt of receiving gifts from wicked persons (*asat-pratigrahāt*, XI. 194).

Desiring to obtain absolution (*ćikīrshan apanodanam*) for all his sins great and small, he should repeat once a day for a year the text beginning *Ava* and that beginning *Yatkiṃ ćedam* (Ṛig-veda VII. 89. 5).

Having accepted a prohibited gift or eaten improper food, he is absolved by repeating for three days the texts (Ṛig-veda IX. 58) beginning *Tarat sa mandī dhāvati* (XI. 252, 253).

Although he be guilty of many crimes (*bahv-enāḥ*) he is absolved (*śudhyate*) by repeating (*abhyasya*) for a month the text beginning *Somārudrā* (Ṛig-veda VI. 74. 1, Atharva-veda VII. 42. 1, and the three texts beginning *Aryamaṇam varuṇam mitram*, &c. (Ṛig-veda IV. 2. 4), while performing ablution in a running stream (XI. 254).

By intently (*samāhitaḥ*) repeating three times the whole Samhitā (and Brāhmaṇa *Kullūka*) of the Ṛig, Yajur, and Sāma-veda with their Upanishads (*sa-rahasya*), he is absolved from all his sins (XI. 262).

VI. The sixth and last head is that of *karma-phala*, 'acts-recompenses.' I select a few passages illustrative of the most characteristic of all Hindū doctrines—that of the soul's transmigration through three stages of being, until a complete recompense of its acts is effected.

Book XII. 3, 9, 11, 39, 40, declares that the triple order of transmigration through the highest, middle, and lowest stages, results from good or bad acts, words, and thoughts produced by the influence of the three Guṇas, Sattva, Rajas, and Tamas (see note 1, p. 56); and that for sins of act, a man takes a vegetable or mineral form (*sthāvaratām*); for sins of word, the form of a bird or beast; for sins of thought, that of a man of the lowest caste; but that a triple self-command (p. 132, note 1, p. 288) leads to emancipation from all births and final beatitude:—

Those who are endowed with the Sattva Guṇa ('purity') take the form of gods (*devatvam*), those who are filled with Rajas ('passion') become men, and those who are overwhelmed with Tamas ('darkness and ignorance') become beasts (XII. 40).

But in XII. 41, 50 each of the three orders of transmigration is described as divided into a threefold scale of being, the gradations and subdivisions of which proceed on principles which are not very consistent or intelligible:—

1. *a.* Highest highest—Brahmā, the creator, Marīći, &c. *b.* Highest middle—Sacrificers (*yajvānaḥ*), Ṛishis, incarnate deities (*devāḥ* = *devatāḥ vigrahavatyaḥ*), regents of the stars, Pitṛis, Sādhyas, &c. *c.* Highest lowest—Ascetics, religious mendicants, Brāhmans, demigods borne in heavenly cars (*vaimānikāḥ*), those that preside over the lunar mansions, Daityas, &c. (XII. 48–50).

2. *a.* Middle highest—Gandharvas, Guhyakas, Yakshas, Apsarases, &c. *b.* Middle middle—Kings, Kshatriyas, the chaplains of kings (*purohitāḥ*), &c. *c.* Middle lowest—Club-fighters (*jhallāḥ*), prize-fighters (*mallāḥ*), actors, those who live by the use of weapons, gamblers, and drinkers (XII. 45–47).

3. *a.* Lowest highest—Dancers, birds (*suparṇāḥ* = *pakshiṇaḥ*), deceitful men, Rākshasas, Piśāćas, &c. *b.* Lowest middle—Elephants, horses, S'ūdras, despicable Mlećchas, lions, tigers, boars. *c.* Lowest lowest—Vegetables and minerals (*sthāvarāḥ* = *vṛikshādayaḥ*), worms, insects, fish, reptiles, tortoises, cattle, animals of various kinds (XII. 42–44).

It is curious to note the effect of apparently slight sins of commission and omission in degrading a man to lower conditions of being, or in exposing him to diseases :—

Through speaking ill (*parīvādāt*) of his preceptor, a man will be born an ass; if he reviles him, a dog; if he uses his property without leave, a worm; if he envies him, an insect (II. 201).

If a man steal grain he shall be born a mouse; if brass, a gander; if water, a water-duck; if honey, a gad-fly; if milk, a crow; if syrup, a dog; if ghee, a weasel (XII. 62).

A Brāhman neglecting his own appointed caste duty (*dharmāt svakāt*) will be born as a vomit-eating demon; a Kshatriya, as a demon feeding on excrement and dead bodies; a Vaiśya, as a demon feeding on putrid carrion (*Ulkā-mukha*, *Kaṭa-pūtana*, and *Maitrāksha-jyotika*, XII. 71, 72).

A stealer of grain will be afflicted with dyspepsia (in a future existence); a stealer of the words (of the Veda, by repeating it without authority), with dumbness; a stealer of cloth, with leprosy; a horse-stealer with lameness (XI. 51). Compare p. 270.[1]

[1] It may be interesting to annex to this Chapter a few of the statements of Megasthenes (300 years B.C.) about the Brāhmans (Strabo XV. 1, 59): 'They practise the greatest austerities to prepare for death (ἀσκήσει πλείστῃ χρῆσθαι πρὸς τὸ ἑτοιμοθάνατον), which they hold to be birth to a real and happy life (γένεσιν εἰς τὸν ὄντως βίον καὶ τὸν εὐδαίμονα); they maintain

that nothing of what happens to men is good or bad; that the world was created and is perishable; that it is spheroidal; that the God who made and rules it pervades every part of it; that water was the first element created; that besides the four elements there is a fifth (πρὸς τοῖς τέτταρσι στοιχείοις πέμπτη τίς ἐστι φύσις); and that the earth is in the centre of the universe. Besides, like Plato, they weave many fables (μύθους) about the immortality of the soul and punishments in hell. As to the Hindūs generally—they are ignorant of writing, have no written laws, and arrange everything from memory (XV. 53, 66). They do not employ slaves (54). They worship Jupiter Pluvius (τὸν ὄμβριον Δία), the river Ganges, and the gods of the country; those who live in the mountains worship Dionysos (= S'iva); those in the plains, Herakles (= Vishṇu, XV. 58, 69); they never drink wine except at sacrifices (53). It is not permitted to any one to marry a person of another caste, nor to change from one business or trade to another, nor to engage in many pursuits, unless he belong to the caste of philosophers (XV. 49). These philosophers are of two kinds, Brachmanes and Garmanes (Βραχμᾶνες, Γαρμᾶνες = Brāhmans and S'ramaṇas or Buddhist ascetics, 59). Both practise endurance (καρτερίαν), and will remain a whole day in one posture without moving (60. Cf. also XV. 61, 63).'

CHAPTER XI.

The Law-books—Manu continued.

I NOW endeavour to give, as literally as possible, a metrical version of some of Manu's most noteworthy precepts, selected from different parts of the Code, under the four heads of *Āćāra*, 'rules of conduct;' *Vyavahāra*, 'rules of government and judicature;' *Prāyaś-ćitta*, 'penance;' *Karma-phala*, 'rewards and punishments of acts.'

Āćāra, 'rules of conduct.'

A Brāhman from exalted birth is called
A god among the gods, and is a measure
Of truth for all the world, so says the Veda (XI. 84).

Knowledge,[1] descending from her home divine,
Said to a holy Brāhman, I am come
To be thy cherished treasure, trust me not
To scorners, but to careful guardians,
Pure, self-restrained, and pious; so in them
I shall be gifted with resistless power (II. 114, 115).

The man with hoary head is not revered
As aged by the gods, but only he
Who has true knowledge;[2] he, though young, is old (II. 156).

A wooden elephant, an antelope
Of leather, and a Brāhman without knowledge—
These are three things that only bear a name (II. 157).

---

[1] In II. 117 knowledge is divided into three parts—1. *Laukika*, 'secular;' 2. *Vaidika*, 'Vedic;' 3. *Ādhyātmika*, 'spiritual' or that which relates to soul.

[2] Strabo XV. 1, 54, says of the Hindūs, Οὐδὲ τῇ ἡλικίᾳ τῶν γερόντων προνομίαν διδόασιν ἂν μὴ καὶ τῷ φρονεῖν πλεονεκτῶσι.

As with laborious toil the husbandman,
Digging with spade beneath the ground, arrives
At springs of living water, so the man
Who searches eagerly for truth will find
The knowledge hidden in his teacher's mind (II. 118).

With pain the mother to her child gives birth,
With pain the father rears him; as he grows
He heaps up cares and troubles for them both;
Incurring thus a debt he ne'er can pay,
Though he should strive through centuries of time (II. 227).

Think constantly, O son, how thou mayest please
Thy father, mother, teacher—these obey.
By deep devotion seek thy debt to pay.
This is thy highest duty and religion (II. 228).

Who finds around him only wicked sons,
When called by fate to pass the gloom of death,
Is like a man who seeks to cross a flood
Borne on a raft composed of rotten wood (IX. 161).

Even though wronged, treat not with disrespect
Thy father, mother, teacher, elder brother (II. 226).

From poison thou mayest take the food of life,
The purest gold from lumps of impure earth,
Examples of good conduct from a foe,
Sweet speech and gentleness from e'en a child,
Something from all; from men of low degree
Lessons of wisdom, if thou humble be (II. 238, 239).

Wound not another, though by him provoked,
Do no one injury by thought or deed,
Utter no word to pain thy fellow-creatures (II. 161).

Say what is true, speak not agreeable falsehood (IV. 138).

Treat no one with disdain,[1] with patience bear
Reviling language; with an angry man
Be never angry; blessings give for curses (VI. 47, 48).

---

[1] In IV. 135 the householder is especially warned against treating with contempt a Brāhman well versed in the Veda, a Kshatriya, and a serpent, because (says Kullūka) the first has the power of destroying

E'en as a driver checks his restive steeds,
Do thou, if thou art wise, restrain thy passions,
Which, running wild, will hurry thee away (II. 88).

When asked, give something, though a very trifle,
Ungrudgingly and with a cheerful heart,
According to thy substance; only see
That he to whom thou givest worthy be (IV. 227, 228).

Pride not thyself on thy religious works,
Give to the poor, but talk not of thy gifts.
By pride religious merit melts away,
The merit of thy alms by ostentation (IV. 236, 237).

None sees us, say the sinful in their hearts;
Yes, the gods see them, and the omniscient Spirit
Within their breasts. Thou thinkest, O good friend,
'I am alone,' but there resides within thee
A Being who inspects thy every act,
Knows all thy goodness and thy wickedness (VIII. 85, 91).

The soul is its own witness; yea, the soul
Itself is its own refuge; grieve thou not,
O man, thy soul, the great internal Witness (VIII. 84).

The Firmament, the Earth, the Sea, the Moon,
The Sun, the Fire, the Wind, the Night, and both
The sacred Twilights,[1] and the Judge of souls,[2]
The god of Justice, and the Heart itself—
All constantly survey the acts of men (VIII. 86).

When thou hast sinned, think not to hide thy guilt
Under a cloak of penance and austerity (IV. 198).

No study of the Veda nor oblation,
No gift of alms, nor round of strict observance
Can lead the inwardly depraved to heaven (II. 97).

---

him by his unseen power of magical texts and spells, the other two by their seen power (*dṛishṭa-śaktyā*). Cf. the passages relative to the power of the Brāhmans, translated p. 234.

[1] See the account of the Sandhyās, p. 241.

[2] Yama, see p. 19.

If with the great Divinity who dwells
Within thy breast thou hast no controversy,
Go not to Ganges' water to be cleansed,
Nor make a pilgrimage to Kuru's fields (VIII. 92).[1]

Iniquity once practised, like a seed,
Fails not to yield its fruit to him who wrought it,
If not to him, yet to his sons and grandsons (IV. 173).

Contentment is the root of happiness,
And discontent the root of misery.
Wouldst thou be happy, be thou moderate (IV. 12).

Honour thy food, receive it thankfully,
Eat it contentedly and joyfully,
Ne'er hold it in contempt; avoid excess,
For gluttony is hateful, injures health,
May lead to death, and surely bars the road,
To holy merit and celestial bliss (II. 54, 57).

Desire is not extinguished by enjoyment,
Fire is not quenched by offerings of oil,
But blazes with increased intensity (II. 94).

Shrink thou from worldly honour as from poison,
Seek rather scorn; the scorn'd may sleep in peace,
In peace awake; the scorner perishes (II. 162, 163).

Daily perform thy own appointed work
Unweariedly; and to obtain a friend—
A sure companion to the future world—
Collect a store of virtue like the ants
Who garner up their treasures into heaps;
For neither father, mother, wife, nor son,
Nor kinsman, will remain beside thee then,
When thou art passing to that other home—
Thy virtue will thy only comrade be (IV. 238, 239).

Single is every living creature born,
Single he passes to another world,
Single he eats the fruit of evil deeds,
Single, the fruit of good; and when he leaves

[1] See note, p. 244.

His body like a log or heap of clay
Upon the ground, his kinsmen walk away;
Virtue alone stays by him at the tomb
And bears him through the dreary trackless gloom (IV. 240–242).[1]

Thou canst not gather what thou dost not sow;
As thou dost plant the tree so will it grow (IX. 40).

Depend not on another, rather lean
Upon thyself; trust to thine own exertions.
Subjection to another's will gives pain;
True happiness consists in self-reliance (IV. 160).

Strive to complete the task thou hast commenced;
Wearied, renew thy efforts once again;
Again fatigued, once more the work begin,
So shalt thou earn success and fortune win (IX. 300).

Never despise thyself, nor yet contemn
Thy own first efforts, though they end in failure;
Seek Fortune with persistency till death,
Nor ever deem her hard to be obtained (IV. 137).

Success in every enterprise depends
On Destiny[2] and man combined, the acts
Of Destiny are out of man's control;
Think not on Destiny, but act thyself (VII. 205).

Be courteous to thy guest who visits thee;
Offer a seat, bed, water, food enough,
According to thy substance, hospitably;
Naught taking for thyself till he be served;
Homage to guests brings wealth, fame, life, and heaven (III. 106, IV. 29).

He who possessed of ample means bestows
His gifts on strangers while his kindred starve,
Thinks to enjoy the honey of applause,
But only eating poison dies despised—
Such charity is cruelty disguised (XI. 9).

---

[1] Dr. Muir has pointed out that the expression *tamas tarati dustaram*, 'he crosses the gloom difficult to be passed,' may be taken from Atharva-veda IX. 5. 1, *tīrtvā tamāṉsi bahudhā mahānti*.

[2] *Daiva* is here the Adṛishṭa described p. 58.

III. The third Book gives various rules for *Prāyaś-ćitta*, 'penance, expiation, and purification.' Many of the laws are like those of Manu. It will suffice to note a few examples which have reference to funeral ceremonies :—

A child under two years old must be buried, and no offering of water should be made to him. (The corpse of) any other deceased person should be accompanied by (a procession of) relations to the burning-place (*ā-śmaśānāt*, III. 1. See p. 196. Cf. Manu V. 68, 69, 103).

It is then to be burnt with common fire (*laukikāgninā*) while they repeat the hymn to Yama (*yama-sūktam*) and the sacred chant (*gāthām*, III. 2).

It is usual (for the relatives) to pour out a libation of water once (to the deceased), uttering his name and family, (and then) remaining silent (see p. 198).

But religious students and outcastes are not allowed to offer the oblations of water (III. 5. Cf. Manu V. 88).

The funeral oblation is not allowed for heretics (*pāshaṇḍin*), persons without any fixed station (*an-āśritāḥ*), thieves, women who have killed their husbands, or who have lived an independent life (*kāma-gāḥ*), or have been drunkards, or have committed suicide (*ātma-tyāginyaḥ*, III. 6. Cf. Manu V. 89, 90).

When the relatives have poured out water, have completed their ablutions, and have seated themselves on a spot covered with soft grass, (the elder ones) may repeat to the others some verses from the ancient Itihāsas, such as the following (III. 7) :—

Does it not argue folly to expect
Stability in man, who is as transient
As a mere bubble and fragile as a stalk ?
Why should we utter wailings if a frame,
Composed of five material elements,
Is decomposed by force of its own acts,
And once again resolved into its parts ?
The earth, the ocean, and the gods themselves
Must perish, how should not the world
Of mortals, light as froth, obey the law
Of universal death and perish too (III. 8–11) ?

After hearing verses of this kind they should return home, the younger ones leading the way, stopping solemnly outside the door of the house to chew leaves of the Nimb tree (*Nimba-patrāṇi*, III. 12).

After they have rinsed out their mouths and touched fire, water, cow-dung, white mustard-seed, and placed their feet on a stone, they should enter the house slowly (III. 13. Cf. the account of the funeral procession in the Gṛihya-sūtras, pp. 196–199).

Impurity caused by the ceremonies connected with touching a corpse (*śīvam āśaućam*) lasts for either three nights or ten nights (III. 18. Cf. Manu V. 59, 64).

Those who preserve this Law-book diligently in their memories shall obtain reputation in this world and shall go to heaven (III. 330).

He who repeats only three verses out of this Law-book at a Śrāddha causes perpetual satisfaction to his departed ancestors; of this there is no doubt. A Brāhman may obtain merit, a Kshatriya may become victorious, and a Vaiśya may become rich in corn and money by preserving this book in his memory (III. 332, 333).

The eighteen principal Codes posterior to Manu and Yājṅavalkya.

A list of eighteen of the most important of these has been given at p. 203. They are all extant in some form or other, as described by Colebrooke.[1] Little or nothing is known about the authorship of any one of them. They have arisen from the necessity of framing new laws or modifying old ones to suit particular localities and particular periods. In order to invest them with antiquity and authority, they are all eighteen ascribed, like the Codes of Manu and Yājṅavalkya, to various mythical inspired sages. The fact is, that although Manu and Yājṅavalkya still form the basis of Hindū jurisprudence, many of their laws are regarded by more recent Hindū legislators as only intended for the first three ages of the world, and therefore as having no force, or superseded by others, in the present fourth and more degenerate Kali-

---

[1] See Professor E. B. Cowell's edition of his Essays, vol. i. pp. 468–470. The works or their abridgments, ascribed to these eighteen inspired law-givers, have been all printed at Calcutta.

yuga (see note 2, p. 178). Thus the author of the work ascribed to Nārada[1] says:—

Marriage with the widow of a deceased brother, the slaughter of cattle in entertaining guests, flesh-meat at funeral obsequies, and the entrance into the third order (or that of a Vānaprastha, 'hermit') are forbidden in the fourth age.

The following acts, allowed under certain circumstances by ancient law, are also forbidden in the fourth age:—

Drinking any spirituous liquor, even at a religious ceremony;[2] the gift of a young married woman to another bridegroom if her husband should die while she is still a virgin; the marriage of twice-born men with women not of the same class; any intercourse with a twice-born man who has passed the sea in a ship; the slaughter of a bull at a sacrifice, &c.

And the author of Parāśara's Code[3] affirms:—

The laws of various ages are different. Manu's Law-book belongs to the Kṛita age, Gautama's to the Tretā, that of S'an·kha and Likhita to the Dvāpara, and Parāśara's Code to the Kali age.

Many modern lawyers, however, regard the whole of Smṛiti, beginning with Manu, as one, and assert that the inconsistencies and contradictions it contains are all capable of explanation.

I here annex a few particulars relative to the eighteen principal Codes posterior to Manu and Yājṇavalkya:—

1. That attributed to *Atri*, one of Manu's ten Prajāpatis (I. 35), is in verse, and written in a perspicuous style. 2. That of *Vishṇu* is also in verse, and is regarded as an excellent treatise, an abridgment of which is also extant. 3. That of *Hārīta*, on the contrary, is in prose, but has been abridged in a metrical form. 4. That of *Uśanas* or S'ukra is in verse, and an abridgment is extant. 5. A short treatise of about seventy verses is ascribed to *An·giras*, one of Manu's Prajāpatis and Maharshis (I. 35). 6. A tract consisting of one hundred verses, commented on by Kullūka-bhaṭṭa, is mythically attributed to *Yama* (brother of Manu

[1] Quoted by Sir W. Jones, vol. viii. p. 153.

[2] As, for example, the Sautrāmaṇī.

[3] Quoted by Professor Stenzler in his preface to Yājṅavalkya.

Vaivasvata), ruler of the world of spirits. 7. That of *Āpastamba* is in prose, but an abridgment in verse also exists. 8. *Saṃvarta's* Code has also a metrical abridgment. 9. *Kātyāyana's* law-treatise is full and perspicuous. 10. *Vṛihaspati's* has been abridged, and it is doubtful whether we possess the abridgment or the Code itself. 11. *Parāśara's* treatise is regarded by some as the highest authority for the Kali or fourth age of the world. It has been commented on by Mādhavāćārya. 12. A law-treatise is ascribed to the celebrated *Vyāsa*, son of Parāśara. 13, 14. Two separate tracts in verse by *Śaṅkha* and *Likhita* exist, but their joint treatise in prose is the one usually cited by Kullūka and others. It is supposed to be adapted to the Dvāpara age. 15. A Code in verse of no special interest is attributed to *Daksha*, one of Manu's ten Prajāpatis (I. 35). 16. A prose treatise written in a clear style bears the name of *Gautama*. It is held to have been written for the Tretā age. 17. Śātātapa's Code is chiefly on penance and expiation. There is an abridgment of it in verse. 18. The treatise attributed to Vaśishṭha, another of Manu's Prajāpatis (I. 35), is a mixture of prose and verse.

Of other codes ascribed to various mythical lawgivers in the Padma-purāṇa, &c., it will be sufficient to mention those of Marīći, Pulastya, Bhṛigu, Nārada (Manu I. 35), Kaśyapa, Viśvāmitra, Gārgya, Baudhāyana, Paiṭhīnasi, Sumantu, Lokākshi, Kuthumi or Kuṭhumi, and Dhaumya.

Besides, there are a vast number of legal treatises and commentaries based on ancient codes by modern lawyers, whose works are current and more or less esteemed as authorities in different parts of India. They form five schools, of which I here give a brief account.

The Five Schools of Hindū Law.

These are the schools of—1. Bengal, 2. Benares, 3. Mithilā (North Behār and Tirhut), 4. Madras (*Drāviḍa*), and 5. Bombay (*Mahā-rāshṭra*).[1] There are certain

---

[1] I have here consulted Mr. Herbert Cowell's Tagore Law Lectures, copies of which have always been kindly given to me by the Senate of the Calcutta University.

books regarded as special authorities in each of these principal schools.

1. In Bengal both Manu and Yājñavalkya are of course held in great reverence as original sources of law. We have already noted that the best commentary on Manu is one called Manv-artha-muktāvalī, by Kullūka-bhaṭṭa (see note 2, p. 213). There is also a commentary by Medhātithi (partially lost, and completed by another author); another by Govinda-rāja; another by Dharaṇī-dhara, Bhāguri, and others. To Yājñavalkya belong at least four other commentaries besides the Mitāksharā, viz., that of Aparārka (which is the oldest of all); of Śūla-pāṇi (called the Dīpa-kalikā); of Deva-bodha, and of Viśva-rūpa. Śūla-pāṇi is also the author of a work on penance and expiation. The Mitāksharā of Vijñāneśvara[1] is, however, the principal commentary on Yājñavalkya (as before noticed). It is much studied in Bengal, but the chief authority in the Bengal school is a well-known work, somewhat different in character and principles, called the Dāya-bhāga or 'treatise on inheritance,' ascribed to Jīmūta-vāhana,[2] by some thought to have been a prince of the house of Silāra, who either composed this work himself or caused it to be compiled rather earlier than the beginning of the sixteenth century. It should be stated that both the Mitāksharā and Dāya-bhāga are developments of, rather than commentaries on, Manu and Yājñavalkya. Although they profess to be based on these ancient books, they sometimes modify the laws there propounded to suit a more advanced social system. In other

---

1 Vijñāneśvara belonged to a sect of Sannyāsins founded by Śaṅkarāćārya, and his commentary may have been written as early as the ninth century of our era.

2 Translated by Colebrooke. Jīmūta-vāhana's work seems to have been called Dharma-ratna, and only the chapter on inheritance is preserved.

cases they discuss doubtful points and supply omissions; while they, in their turn, have been commented on by succeeding lawyers, whose works introduce still further modifications on various important points,[1] thus:—

Three principal commentaries on the Mitāksharā are named, viz., the Subodhinī of Viśveśvara-bhaṭṭa (thought by Colebrooke to be as old as the fourteenth century); a later work by Bālam-bhaṭṭa; and a third (called the Pratītāksharā) by Nanda-paṇḍita, who was also the author of the work on adoption called Dattaka-mīmāṅsā and of the Vaijayantī (see next page). The commentaries on the Dāya-bhāga are numerous. Some of these (published under the patronage of Prasanna Kumār Thākur) are, that of S'rīkṛishṇa-tarkālan·kāra, which, with a treatise by the same author called Dāya-krama-san·graha, is highly esteemed in Bengal; that of S'rī-nāthāćārya-ćūḍāmaṇi; that of Aćyuta-ćakravartin; and that of Maheśvara. Before any of these ought to be placed the works of a celebrated Brāhman (who lived at the beginning of the sixteenth century), named Raghu-nandana, in about twenty-seven books, on rites and customs and the times of their observance. His treatises, intended to comment on and support Jīmūta-vāhana, are called Smṛiti-tattva, Tithi-tattva, &c., the former including the Vyavahāra-tattva and Dāya-tattva.[2]

2. As regards the school of Benares and Middle India it should be noted that the Mitākshara of Vijnāneśvara is acknowledged as an authority, and studied by the adherents of this school, as it is to a certain extent by all five schools. But in the Benares school certain popular commentaries on the Mitākshara, such as the Vīra-mitrodaya of Mitra-miśra and the Vivāda-tāṇḍava of Kamalākara, have great weight.

3. In the Maithila school or that of Mithilā (North Behār

[1] The certainty we feel as to the accuracy of the texts of all important Sanskrit works is due to the practice of writing commentaries, which always quote the words of the original, and so prevent changes. Again, the accuracy and genuineness of the best commentaries are secured by other commentaries on them.

[2] Printed at Calcutta in 1828. Raghu-nandana is often called Smārta-bhaṭṭāćārya.

and Tirhut), besides the Code of Yājñavalkya with the Mitāksharā, the Vivāda-ćintāmaṇi and Vyavahāra-ćintāmaṇi of Vāćaspati Miśra[1] are much studied; also the Vivāda-ratnākara of Caṇḍeśvara (who lived about 1314) and the Vivāda-ćandra, composed by a learned female named Lakhimā-devī, who is said to have set the name of her kinsman, Misarū-miśra, to her own works.

4. In the Drāviḍian or South-Indian school, besides the Mitāksharā, as before, there is the Smṛiti-ćandrikā and Dattaka-ćandrikā of Devana-bhaṭṭa; Mādhavāćārya's commentary on Parāśara's Code (called Parāśara-smṛiti-vyākhyā); and Nanda-paṇḍita's commentary on Vishṇu's Code (called Vaijayantī), and on Parāśara's Code, and his treatise on the law of adoption called Dattaka-ćandrikā.

5. In the Western school (of Bombay and Mahā-rāshṭra), besides the Mitāksharā, certain treatises by Nīlakaṇṭha-bhaṭṭa, particularly one called Vyavahāra-mayūkha,[2] have the most weight.

---

[1] Often called Miśra. His work has been translated by Prasanna Kumār Thākur, and printed at Calcutta in 1863. A copy was kindly sent to me by the translator.

[2] A translation of this by Mr. H. Borrodaile of the Bombay Civil Service was published at Surat at the Mission Press in 1827.

CHAPTER XII.

IV. *The Itihāsas or Epic Poems—The Rāmāyaṇa.*[1]

In India, literature, like the whole face of nature, is on a gigantic scale. Poetry, born amid the majestic scenery of the Himālayas, and fostered in a climate which inflamed the imaginative powers, developed itself with Oriental luxuriance, if not always with true sublimity. Although the Hindūs, like the Greeks, have only two great epic poems[2]—the Rāmāyaṇa and Mahā-bhārata—yet to compare these vast compositions with the Iliad and the Odyssey, is to compare the Indus and the Ganges, rising in the snows of the world's most colossal ranges, swollen by numerous tributaries, spreading into vast shallows or branching into deep divergent channels, with the streams of Attica or the mountain-torrents of Thessaly. There is, in fact, an immensity of bulk about this, as about every other department of Sanskṛit literature, which to a European mind, accustomed to a more limited horizon, is absolutely bewildering.

---

[1] A portion of the matter of this chapter and of that on the Mahā-bhārata was delivered by me as a public Lecture before the University of Oxford, on the 9th of May 1862, and was afterwards published in a little work called 'Indian Epic Poetry,' which is now out of print.

[2] I am here speaking of that form of epic poetry which may be called natural and spontaneous as distinguished from artificial. Whether the Indian Epics (Itihāsas) or even the Iliad can be strictly said to answer Aristotle's definition of Epos, is another question. Artificial epic poems (Kāvyas) are not wanting in later Sanskṛit, and specimens will be given in a subsequent chapter.

Nevertheless, a sketch, however imperfect, of the two Indian Epics can scarcely fail to interest Occidental scholars; for all true poetry, whether European or Asiatic, must have features of resemblance; and no poems could have achieved celebrity in the East as these have done, had they not addressed themselves to feelings and affections common to human nature, and belonging alike to Englishmen and Hindūs.

I propose, therefore, in the next three chapters, to give a brief general idea of the character and contents of the Rāmāyaṇa and Mahā-bhārata,[1] comparing them in some important particulars with each other, and pointing out the most obvious features of similarity or difference, which must strike every classical scholar who contrasts them with the Iliad and the Odyssey.

It is, of course, a principal characteristic of epic poetry, as distinguished from lyrical, that it should concern itself more with external action than internal feelings. It is this which makes Epos the natural expression of early national life. When centuries of trial have turned the mind of nations inwards, and men begin to speculate, to reason, to elaborate language and cultivate science, there may be no lack of refined poetry, but the spontaneous production of epic song is, at that stage of national existence, as impossible as for an octogenarian to delight in the giants and giant-killers of his childhood. The Rāmāyaṇa and Mahā-bhārata then, as reflecting the Hindū character in ancient times, may be expected to abound in stirring incidents of exaggerated heroic action.

Songs in celebration of great heroes were probably current in India quite as early as the Homeric poems in

---

[1] A more complete analysis of the Rāmāyaṇa and Mahā-bhārata was given by me at the end of the little work called 'Indian Epic Poetry,' and will probably be reprinted with additions hereafter.

Greece. No mention, indeed, is made of Rāma, Arjuna, and Yudhi-shṭhira in the hymns of the Ṛig-veda, but the deeds of Indra and other gods and heroes, who were supposed to protect the more civilized Āryas from the barbarous An-āryas, are there narrated and lauded, and it is in the songs composed in their praise that we may trace the foreshadowings of Indian epic poetry. Again, we know that Itihāsas, or legendary narratives, were recited orally at the period when the Gṛihya Sūtras and Manu were composed (see p. 195; note 1, p. 207; and p. 249). Such narratives doubtless recounted the adventures of the popular heroes of the period, with all the warmth of colouring natural to writers whose imaginations were stimulated by an Eastern climate and environments; but it is scarcely credible that they could have achieved much popularity had they not rested on a basis of historical truth.

It is certainly likely that at some early date, not long after the first settlement of the Āryan races in the country of the five rivers, rival tribes of immigrants, called Kurus, advancing from that region towards the plains of Hindūstān, contended for supremacy. It is, moreover, probable that soon after their final occupation of the Gangetic districts, a body of invaders headed by a bold leader, and aided by the warlike but uncivilized hill-tribes, forced their way southwards into the peninsula of India as far as Ceylon. The heroic exploits of the chieftains in both cases would naturally become the theme of epic poetry, and the wild Aborigines of the Vindhya and neighbouring hills would be poetically converted into monkeys,[1] while

---

[1] Strabo (XV. 29) relates that on a particular occasion a large number of monkeys came out of a wood and stood opposite the Macedonian troops, who seeing them apparently stationed in military array, mistook them for a real army and prepared to attack them as enemies.

the powerful pre-Āryan races of the south would be represented as many-headed ogres and bloodthirsty demons.[1]

---

[1] We must be careful not to confound the great Drāviḍian races occupying the Madras Presidency and speaking Tamil, Telugu, Kanarese, and Malayālam, with the uncivilized aboriginal tribes found on the hills and in the jungles of India. The Drāviḍian races (probably symbolized by the Rāvaṇas and Vibhīshaṇas of epic poetry) were the precursors of the Sanskṛit-speaking Āryans, and possibly had their origin in the same districts of Central Asia, whence they immigrated by the same mountain-passes into the Pañjāb and Northern India. They may have partially amalgamated with the advancing Āryans, but were mostly driven southwards. There they attained a considerable independent civilization. Their languages, although eventually more or less intermingled with Sanskṛit words, are agglutinating (commonly called Turanian) in structure, and possess an extensive and important literature of their own. On the other hand, the hill-tribes and others (such as were symbolized by the monkey-armies of Hanumat)—the Goṇḍs of Central India, the Bhīls of the hills to the west of the Goṇḍs, the Khoṇḍs or Kus of the eastern districts of Goṇḍvāna and the ranges south of Orissa, the Santhāls and Kols of the hills to the west of Bengal, the Khāsias and Gāros of the eastern border—are the present representatives of numerous wild Tartar tribes who swarmed into India at various epochs, some of them probably coming from Chinese Tartary and Tibet, and taking the course of the Brahma-putra into Bengal. These speak an infinite number of different dialects and are almost all mutually unintelligible. If the term Turanian is to embrace races so widely separated by language and customs as the Drāviḍians and various hill-tribes of India, the sooner it is expelled from the vocabulary of philologists and ethnologists the better. At any rate, there must be two great classes of Turanian languages, the North and the South; the former comprising the three sisters Tungusic (or Mantchu), Mongol, and Turkish, besides Samoyedic and Finnish, while the latter takes in Tibetan, Siamese, Burmese, and the Drāviḍian languages; the monosyllabic Chinese standing, as it were, between the two. Perhaps the dialects of the Himālayan tribes have, of all hill-dialects, the best title to be ranked among the South Turanian class. Dr. Caldwell, in his valuable Comparative Grammar of the South-Indian Languages, has discussed the affiliation of the Drāviḍian family with great ability. He considers that the Drāviḍians were the first inhabitants of India, and that they were driven southwards by other invaders, who were afterwards subdued by the Āryans. The rude dialects

These races, who are called *An-ārya*, 'ignoble,' in opposition to *Ārya*, 'noble,' had been gradually driven southwards or towards the hills by the Āryan settlers. They probably made great resistance in the North at the time the Ṛig-veda was composed. They are there called Dasyus, Yātudhānas, &c., and described as monstrous in form, godless, inhuman, haters of Brāhmans, disturbers of sacred rites, eaters of human and horse flesh (Ṛig-veda X. 87, 16; Muir's Texts II. 435). In the epic poems they are generally called Rākshasas or evil demons, the relentless enemies of gods and good men and of all sacred rites.[1]

---

of the more southern hill-tribes are partially connected with the Drāviḍian, especially the Tuḍa, Koṭa (two dialects of the Nīl-giri hills), Goṇḍ, and Khoṇḍ (Ku). The Ramūsies and most of the Korawars speak a patois of Telugu. The Male-arasars ('hill-kings') of the Southern Ghāts speak partly corrupt Malayālam and corrupt Tamil. The Lāmbādies, or gipsies, speak a dialect of Hindūstānī. Among the barbarous tribes of the South are included the Vedārs of the forests of Ceylon.

[1] In one place (Rāmāyaṇa III. i. 15) they are described as black, with woolly hair and thick lips. The following is from III. i. 22, &c.: 'Men-devouring Rākshasas of various shapes and wild beasts dwell in this vast forest. They harass the devotees in the settlements. These shapeless and ill-looking monsters testify their abominable character by various cruel and terrific displays of it. These base-born wretches (*an-ārya*) perpetrate the greatest outrages. Changing their shapes and hiding in the thickets they delight in terrifying devotees. They cast away the sacrificial ladles and vessels (*śrug-bhāṇḍam*), pollute the cooked oblations, and defile the offerings with blood. They utter frightful sounds in the ears of the faithful.' Virādha, a Rākshasa, is said (Rāmāyaṇa III. vii. 5; Muir II. 427) to be 'like a mountain-peak, with long legs, a huge body, a crooked nose, hideous eyes, a long face, pendent belly, &c., like Death with an open mouth.' The Nishādas of the Purāṇas, though described as dwarfish, have similar features, and are no doubt intended for the same race. In the same way, in describing races unknown to the Greeks, such as the Cyclopes, Laestrygones, Centauri, &c., Homer and other Grecian writers are given to exaggeration, and relate the most absurd fables.

It is to the subjugation of these non-Āryan races by heroic Āryan leaders who were Kshatriyas, as well as to the rivalry between different tribes of the settlers themselves, that we owe the circumstances out of which the two great Epics arose. Whether the celebrated Āryan warriors of the Rāmāyaṇa and Mahā-bhārata were identical with those of the Itihāsas of which mention is made in the Gṛihya Sūtras and in Manu (III. 232) cannot be proved; but this much is clear, that the exploits of the three Rāmas, Arjuna, &c., became, soon after Manu's time, the theme of song, and that these heroes were in the first instance represented as merely men of great strength and prowess, whose powers, however extraordinary, were not more than human. The oral descriptions of their deeds and adventures by public reciters formed the original basis of the two great Epics, and were naturally the peculiar property of the Kshatriya and conquering class. Probably these narratives were in the first instance delivered in prose, which became gradually interspersed with the simplest forms of metre, such as that called Anushṭubh or Śloka.[1]

It is easy indeed for the most cursory reader of the Rāmāyaṇa and Mahā-bhārata to trace a substratum or basis (*mūla*) of simple heroic narration underlying the mass of more recent accretions. But to what date is this first framework of the poems to be referred? And again—When occurred that first process of brāhmanizing which obscured and transformed its original character? And lastly—When was the structure completed and the

[1] The oldest part of the Mahā-bhārata has a section entirely in prose (see note 1, p. 371). The invention of the Śloka is attributed to Vālmīki, the reputed author of the Rāmāyaṇa, with the object doubtless of establishing his claims to be regarded as one of the earliest and most ancient of Indian poets. This metre is found in the Veda.

whole work moulded into a form similar to that we now possess?

With regard to the first of these questions, I have now to submit five reasons in support of the view that the earliest or pre-brāhmanical composition of both Epics took place at a period not later than the fifth century B.C., as follows:—

1. The Rāmāyaṇa records no case of Satī. In the Mahā-bhārata, Mādrī, wife of Pāṇḍu, is made to immolate herself with her husband,[1] and the four wives of Vasu-deva and some of Kṛishṇa's wives do the same;[2] but it is remarkable that none of the numerous widows of the slain heroes are represented as burning themselves in the same manner. This shows that the practice of Satī was beginning to be introduced in the North-west of India near the Pañjāb (where we know it prevailed about 300 years B.C.), but that it had not at the time of the earliest composition of the Rāmāyaṇa reached the more eastern districts. But if one Epic records no Satī, and the other only rare cases—notwithstanding the numerous opportunities for referring to the practice afforded by the circumstances of the plot—it follows that we ought to place the laying down of the first lines of both compositions before the third century B.C., when we know from Megasthenes that it prevailed generally even as far east as Magadha.

2. The first construction, or, so to speak, 'first casting' of the stories of Rāma and of the Pāṇḍavas as poems with definite plots, seems to have been pre-buddhistic quite as clearly as it was pre-brāhmanical—by which I mean, that it took place anterior to the actual establishment of Buddhism as a rival system. Only one direct mention of Buddha and Buddhism occurs in the Rāmāyaṇa, and the verses in which it occurs (II. cviii. 30–38), and in which Buddha is compared to a thief, are admitted to be an interpolation and not part of the original poem. Nor can it be proved that any such direct reference occurs in the original Mahā-bhārata. Nevertheless, there are numerous allusions (not bearing the stamp of later additions) in both Epics, especially the latter, to that development of rationalistic inquiry and Buddhistic scepticism, which we know commenced about 500 years B.C.[3]

---

[1] Ādi-parvan 4896. See also 3030.

[2] Mausala-parvan 194, 249.

[3] Note particularly the infidel doctrines expressed by the Brāhman Jāvāli (see p. 351), and Book I. 12. of the Bengālī recension of the

3. It is evident from the Aśoka inscriptions that the language of the mass of the people in Hindūstān in the third century B.C. was not pure Sanskṛit. It consisted rather of a variety of provincial Sanskritic dialects, to which the general name of Prākṛit is applied. If, then, the first redaction of these popular poems had taken place as late as the third century, is it likely that some forms of Prākṛit would not have been introduced into the dialogues and allowed to remain there, as we find has been done in the dramas, the oldest of which—the Mṛićcha-kaṭikā—can scarcely be much later than the second century B.C.? It is true that the language of the original story of both Epics, as traceable in the present texts, is generally simple Sanskṛit, and by no means elaborate or artificial; but this is just what might have been understood by the majority of the people about five centuries B.C., before the language of the people had become generally prakriticized.

4. When the story of the poems was first put together in a continuous form, it is clear that the Dekhan and more westerly and southerly regions of India had not been occupied by the Āryans. But we know from the Aśoka inscriptions that the empire of the kings of Magadha and Pālibothra in the third century radiated in all directions, as inscriptions are found in the Pañjāb, at Delhi, in Kuttack, and as far west as Gujarāt.

5. The Greek writer, Dion Chrysostomos, who was born about the middle of the first century, and was especially honoured by the emperor Trajan, mentions (Or. LIII. 555) that records existed in his time of epic poems, recited by the Hindūs, which had been copied or translated from Homer. These statements, as Professor Lassen has shown (Ind. Alt. III. 346), must have been taken from the accounts of Megasthenes, who lived at the court of Ćandra-gupta (see note 1, p. 224). They indicate that poems resembling the Iliad were current in India at least as early as the third or fourth century B.C., though it by no means follows that the Hindū poets borrowed a single idea from Homer.[1]

Rāmāyaṇa, where S'ramaṇas, or Buddhist mendicants, are mentioned (see also p. 121).

[1] The passage in Dion Chrysostomos is as follows: Ὁπότε καὶ παρ' Ἰνδοῖς ᾄδεσθαι φασὶ τὴν Ὁμήρου ποίησιν, μεταβαλόντων αὐτὴν εἰς τὴν σφετέραν διάλεκτόν τε καὶ φωνήν (Reiske's Edit., p. 253). There seems too great a disposition among European scholars to regard the Hindūs as destitute of all originality. I cannot but agree with Professor Lassen that Megasthenes was mistaken, though obviously the story of the great war between the rival tribes, and that of the carrying off of Sītā by a South-Indian chief, have, of course, points of resemblance to the Iliad, which may have

These points seem to merit consideration in fixing 500 B.C. as an approximate date for the first or pre-brāhmanical and pre-buddhistic versions of the two poems. The names of the authors of these original versions appear to have perished, unless it be held (which seems highly improbable) that the story of Rāma must be assigned to Vālmīki from its very first existence as a Kāvya.

We come next to the second stage of their construction. We have suggested the fifth century B.C. as the probable date of the rise of Brāhmanism, as depicted in Manu (see p. 207), and with it of Buddhistic scepticism. The ambitious Brāhmans, who aimed at religious and intellectual supremacy, gradually saw the policy of converting the great national Epics, which they could not suppress, into instruments for moulding the popular mind in accordance with their own pattern. Possibly, too, they may have hoped to turn them into important engines for arresting the progress of Buddhistic rationalism. Accordingly, I conjecture that in the fourth century B.C. they commenced reconstructing and remodelling the two great Epics. They proceeded, in short, to brāhmanize what was before the property of the Kshatriya or warrior caste. This process was of course committed to poets who were Brāhmans, and was not completed all at once. Those songs which described too plainly the independence of the military caste, were modified, obscured by allegory, and rendered improbable by monstrous fable and mytho-

suggested the idea of plagiarism. The sufferings of king Dhṛita-rāshṭra are like those of Priam, and the lamentations of the wives of the slain heroes after the battles between the Pāṇḍavas and Kauravas are like those of Hecuba and Andromache, while the martial deeds of Arjuna and Duryodhana resemble those of Achilles and Hector. According to Professor Weber the passage in Dion contains the earliest notice by other writers of the Indian epic poems. He is, moreover, of opinion that the Indian poets really took ideas from Homer.

logical embellishments. Any circumstance which appeared opposed to the Brāhmanical system, was speciously explained away, glossed over, or mystified.[1] If unbelievers, like Jāvāli, were brought on the scene, it was only that their arguments might be refuted, and their characters reprobated (see p. 351). The great Kshatriya dynasties were made to trace back their origin to Brāhmanical sages (see p. 344). Kings were allowed to undertake nothing except under the direction of Brāhman ministers;[2] while the great heroes themselves were not really Kshatriyas, or even human beings, but emanations of the Deity.

In the case of the Rāmāyaṇa, the unity of the story was never broken by calling in the aid of more than one author, whose name was Vālmīki, and who must have completed the task single-handed. Hence it never lost its character of a Kāvya, or poem, with a clear and coherent plot. On the other hand, the brāhmanizing of the story of the great war between the Pāṇḍavas and Kauravas seems to have attracted a succession of poets, who interwove their own compositions into the original

---

[1] Thus when Dasaratha kills a boy while hunting (see p. 349), the dying youth is made to explain that, although a hermit's son, he is no Brāhman, thereby relieving the king from the guilt of Brāhmanicide, which, according to Manu, was unpardonable either in this world or the next (Manu VIII. 381, XII. 55). Again, the account of the victory of the Kshatriya Rāma-ćandra over the Brāhman Paraśu-rāma—the mythical champion of the sacerdotal caste—is surrounded with a haze of mysticism (see p. 329, note 2; p. 347); while the episode which relates at full Viśvāmitra's quarrel with the great saint Vaśishṭha, and the success of the former, though a Kshatriya, in elevating himself to a Brāhman's rank, introduces the wildest hyperbole, with the manifest object of investing the position of a Brāhman with unapproachable grandeur, and deterring others from attempts in the same direction (see p. 361).

[2] King Daśaratha in the Rāmāyaṇa is described as surrounded by Brāhman ministers (see p. 340).

texture of the work, so that its individuality, and even the name of its first author, disappeared under the constant accession of new matter. Hence we must suppose, in the case of the Mahā-bhārata, more than one Brāhmanical redaction and amplification, which need not be assumed for the completion of the Rāmāyaṇa. Moreover, the great mass of ever-increasing materials under which the original story of the Pāṇḍavas became almost lost to view, and under which the title to the name Kāvya merged in that of a rambling Itihāsa, had to be adjusted and arranged by an imaginary compiler, called Vyāsa.

The first orderly completion, then, of the two poems in their brāhmanized form, may have taken place, I think, in the case of the Rāmāyaṇa about the beginning of the third century B.C., and in the case of the Mahā-bhārata (the original story of which is possibly more ancient than that of the Rāmāyaṇa) still later,—perhaps as late as the second century B.C. The posteriority of the brāhmanized Mahā-bhārata may be supported by the more frequent allusions it contains to the progress of Buddhistic opinions, and to intercourse with the Yavanas or Greeks, who had no considerable dealings with the Hindūs till two or three centuries after Alexander's invasion.[1]

---

[1] A candid study of Professor Weber's writings, and especially of the reproduction of his views lately put forth in the 'Indian Antiquary,' has led me to modify to a certain extent the statements in my Lecture on 'Indian Epic Poetry,' delivered May 9, 1862; but I cannot agree in thinking that the work of Vālmīki is to be referred to as late a date as the beginning of the Christian era. Nor can I concur in the opinion that the Rāmāyaṇa is later than, and to a certain extent a copy of the Buddhist story of Rāma, called Daśaratha-jātaka, in which Rāma is represented as the brother of Sītā, and in which there are certain verses almost identical with verses in the present text of the Rāmāyaṇa. Nor do I think that the great Indian Epic has been developed out of germs furnished by this or any other Buddhistic legends. Still less can I give in my adhesion to the theory that the

It is, however, necessary to refer the final construction of both poems in their present form to a third and still later epoch, and even to assign portions of them to the early centuries of our own era, if we are to accept as integral parts of the two Epics such a supplement to the Rāmāyaṇa as the Uttara-kāṇḍa, and such additions to the Mahā-bhārata as the Bhagavad-gītā and Hari-vaṇśa, as well as those later episodes which identify Rāma and Kṛishṇa with the Supreme Being. And here again in this final construction of both poems, we must bear in mind, that the deification of Rāma represents an earlier stage of Vishṇu-worship than that of Kṛishṇa; and that the Rāmāyaṇa, as now presented to us, contains far fewer recent additions than the Mahā-bhārata.

My reasons, therefore, for placing the first Brāhmanical construction of the two Indian Epics in the third and second century B.C. respectively, and for commencing an account of epic poetry with the story of Rāma, rather than with that of Pāṇḍavas, will be clear. It must be remembered, however, that the priority of one poem over the other cannot be made to rest on any certain chronological basis. Indeed, the Mahā-bhārata describes a conflict between rude colonists in a district nearer to the earliest settlements of the Āryans, while the Rāmāyaṇa is concerned with a more established kingdom (Kośala), and a more civilized and luxurious capital city (Ayodhyā).

Before commencing our summary of either story it will be desirable to note more particularly when and how the doctrine of divine incarnation was imported into both poems, imparting to them that religious and sacred

---

Hindū Epics took ideas from the Homeric poems; or to the suggestion of Mr. Talboys Wheeler, that the story of the Rāmāyaṇa was invented to give expression to the hostile feeling and contention between the Brāhmans and Buddhists of Ceylon, alleged to be represented by the Rākshasas.

character which they have ever since retained, and which is a distinguishing feature in comparing them with the epic poetry of other nations. We know from the statements of Megasthenes, preserved in Strabo and Diodorus, that the worship of Vishṇu in his heroic incarnations prevailed in Hindūstān about 300 years before Christ (see note, p. 276). The deification of great men probably began with the desire of the Brāhmans to incorporate the most eminent Kshatriya heroes into their system. It proceeded, however, from necessity rather than from any wish to do honour to the warrior caste. The Buddhistic movement in India had broken down the Brāhmanical monopoly and introduced a rival principle. Some counteracting and equally popular expansion of religious creed seemed essential to the very existence of Brāhmanism, and it became absolutely necessary to present the people with deities of their own as a counter-attraction to Buddhism. Hence the previously human heroes Rāma and Kṛishṇa were exalted by the Brāhmans to divine rank, and even Buddha himself was, in the end, adopted into their system and represented as one of the ten incarnations of the god Vishṇu.[1]

But the idea of divine incarnation had taken possession of the Hindū mind still earlier. It is probable that in that primeval country, where the ancestors of Greeks and Hindūs had their common home, men satisfied their first religious instincts by idealizing and worshipping, under no defined form and without precise ritual, the principal forces and energies of nature—the air, the rain, the wind,

---

[1] Heroism, undaunted bravery, and personal strength will always find worshippers in India. It is recorded that a number of Pañjābī Hindūs commenced worshipping the late John Nicholson, one of the bravest and noblest of men, under the name Nikkil Seyn. He endeavoured to put a stop to the absurdity, but they persisted in their worship notwithstanding.

the storm, the fire, the sun—the elements on which, as an agricultural and pastoral race, their welfare depended. This was the earliest religion of nature which the Āryan family carried with them when they first left their home, and which they cherished in their wanderings; and in this we may trace the germ of their subsequent religious systems. When they had settled down in new resting-places, their religious cravings naturally found utterance in prayers, hymns, and a simple form of ritual. Religion, or a sense of dependence on a higher Power, and a desire to realize his presence, grew with their growth and strengthened with their strength. But in all ages and countries the religion of the mass of mankind rapidly assumes an anthropomorphic character. A richly peopled mythology arose in India and Greece as naturally as poetry itself. The one was the offspring of the other, and was in fact the poetical expression of those high aspirations which marked the Āryan character. Soon the Hindū, like the Greek, unguided by direct revelation, personified and deified not only the powers of external nature, but all the internal feelings, passions, moral and intellectual qualities and faculties of the mind. Soon he began to regard every grand and useful object as a visible manifestation of the supreme Intelligence presiding over the universe, and every departed hero or benefactor as a mere reflection of the same all-wise and omnipresent Ruler. Hence, to give expression to the varied attributes and functions of this great Being, thus visibly manifested to the world, both Hindū and Greek peopled their pantheons with numerous divine and semi-divine creations, clothing them with male and female forms, and inventing in connection with them various fanciful and often monstrous myths, fables, and allegories, which the undiscriminating multitude accepted as realities, without at all understanding the ideas they symbolized. In India we are able to trace back the development of these anthropomorphic ideas to their source in the Ṛig-veda, and thence follow them step by step through Manu, the epic poems, and Purāṇas. In the Ṛig-veda a god Vishṇu is often named as a manifestation of the Solar energy, or rather as a form of the Sun; and the point which distinguishes him from the others is his striding over the heavens in three paces, supposed to symbolize the three stages of the Sun's daily course in his rising, culminating, and setting (see note 1, p. 329). Subsequently he takes a foremost place among the twelve Ādityas, or twelve distinct forms of the Sun in the twelve months of the year. In the Brāhmaṇas he is identified with sacrifice (*Yajña*), and once described as a dwarf (*Vāmana;* Śatapatha-brāhmaṇa XIV. 1, 1, 6, I. 2, 5, 5). In Manu, Brahman, the universal Soul, is represented as evolving his essence in the form of Brahmā, the Creator of all things, and various other visible manifestations of the Deity are recognized, as in the Veda. In Book XII. 121, Vishṇu and Hara (= Śiva) are mentioned as present in the human body, the former imparting movement to its muscles, the latter bestowing strength.

In all this, however, there was not enough to satisfy the cravings of the human heart for a religion of faith in a personal god—a god sympathizing with humanity, and even with the lower forms of animal life, loving all his creatures, interested in their affairs, and ever at hand to assist them in their difficulties. Nor, on the other hand, was there sufficient to meet the demands of other constituent parts of man's complex nature for a religion of activity and good works; of austerity and subjugation of the passions; of contemplation and higher spiritual knowledge. Soon, therefore, the great Spirit of the universe began to be viewed still more anthropomorphically, through the medium of man's increasing subjectivity, as a Being who not only created man but condescended to human sympathies, and placed himself in the closest connection with all his creatures, whether gods, men, or animals.

But first arose the inquiry why and how this great Being willed to create at all? To account for this it was conceived that when the universal and infinite Being Brahma (*nom. case of the neut. Brahman*)—the only really existing entity, wholly without form and unbound and unaffected by the three Guṇas or by qualities of any kind (pp. 85, 107)—wished to create for his own entertainment the phenomena of the universe, he assumed the quality of activity (*rajas*) and became a male person as Brahmā (*nom. case masc.*) the Creator. Next, in the progress of still further self-evolution, he willed to invest himself with the second quality of goodness (*sattva*) as Vishṇu the Preserver, and with the third quality of darkness (*tamas*)[1] as Śiva the Destroyer. This development of the doctrine of triple manifestation (*tri-mūrti*), which appears first in the brāhmanized version of the Indian Epics, had already been adumbrated in the Veda in the triple form of fire (see p. 15), and in the triad of gods, Agni, Sūrya, and Indra (see note, p. 16); and in other ways.[2]

In fact the Veda, rather than Manu, was the source of the later incarnations (see notes, pp. 326–329). It was the Vedic Vishṇu (connected with Sūrya, 'the Sun') who

---

1 In the Kumāra-sambhava II. 4, we have the following:—*Namas trimūrtaye tubhyam prāk-sṛishṭeḥ kevalātmane Guṇa-traya-vibhāgāya paśćād bhedam upeyushe*, 'Hail to thee of triple form, who before creation wast simple Soul, and afterwards underwent partition for the distribution of the three Guṇas.'

2 The thirty-three gods (3 multiplied by 11) of the Ṛig-veda (*tribhir ekādaśdir devebhir yātam*, I. 34, 11, I. 45, 2) point to the same idea of triple manifestation.

became Vishṇu the world-preserver, while Rudra (connected with Indra and the Maruts), the god of tempests, became the world-dissolver Śiva. Under the latter form, the Supreme Being is supposed to pass from the operation of creation and preservation to that of destruction, these three separate acts being assigned to separate deities who are themselves finite, and obey the universal law of dissolution at the end of a Kalpa (see note 3, p. 330), when they again become merged in simple Soul (*kevalātman*). But as it was essential that even the god of dissolution should connect himself with humanity, and as, according to a fundamental dogma of Hindūism, all death leads to new life, all destruction to reproduction, it was natural that the latter operation should be chosen as the link of connection, rather than the former. His function of destroyer is, therefore, interchanged with that of creator (note 3, p. 323); he himself is called Śiva, 'the Auspicious,' and his character is oftener typified by the reproductive Lin-ga (without necessary implication of sensual ideas) than by any symbol of destruction. Under this image, in fact, he is generally worshipped in India.[1] Nevertheless, he is also represented in human form, living in the Himālaya mountains along with his wife Pārvatī,[2] sometimes in the act

---

[1] Twelve celebrated Lin-gas were set up, about the tenth century, in twelve great shrines, in twelve chief cities of India, of which Somnath was one. The representation of the generative organ is not offensive to delicacy even when surrounded by the Yoni, or female symbol. Quite enough, however, is implied to account for the degeneration of Śiva-worship in modern times, as expressed in the works called Tantras and in the practices of the Śāktas. The representation of Śiva as Ardhanārī, half male, half female, symbolizes the unity of the generative principle. Some think the god Śiva with the Lin-ga (Phallus) was adopted by the Āryans from the aborigines. The word Śiva means 'auspicious,' and being first applied euphemistically to the god of tempests (Rudra) afterwards passed into the name of the god of destruction.

[2] The *śakti* or active energy of a deity is personified as his wife, and

of trampling on and destroying demons, wearing round his black neck (*nīla-kaṇṭha*) a serpent and a necklace of skulls, and furnished with a whole apparatus of external emblems (such as a white bull on which he rides, a crescent, a trident,[1] tiger's skin, elephant's skin, rattle, noose, &c.), the exaggeration of which imparts a childish and grotesque character to Hindū symbolism when regarded from a European point of view. Again, Mahādeva, or the great deity Śiva, is sometimes connected with humanity in one other personification very different from that just noted, viz., that of an austere naked ascetic, with matted hair[2] (*Dig-ambara, Dhūrjaṭi*), living in a forest apart from his consort, abiding in one spot fixed and immovable (*Sthāṇu*)—teaching men by his own example, first, the power to be acquired by penance (*tapas*), mortification of the body,[3] and suppression of the passions; and, secondly, the great virtue of abstract meditation (*samādhi*), as leading to the loftiest spiritual knowledge (*jñāna*) and ultimately to union (*yoga*) or actual

---

those who worship the female principle are called Śāktas. Pārvatī, daughter of the mountain, and worshipped under the name Durgā in Bengal, is the chief object of the adoration of Śāktas and Tāntrikas.

1 This three-pronged symbol may denote creation, destruction, and regeneration. He has also three eyes (one of which is in his forehead), in allusion to either the three Vedas or time past, present, and future (whence he is called *Try-ambaka*), and five faces (whence his name *Pañćānana*); the crescent moon also symbolizing his power over the measurement of time. He is sometimes said to manifest himself under eight forms—ether, air, fire, water, earth, sun, moon, the sacrificing priest (whence his name *Ashṭa-mūrti*). His black throat was caused by the deadly poison churned out of the ocean, which would have destroyed the universe had he not swallowed it.

2 The hair is so worn by Śiva-worshipping Yogīs (see p. 95).

3 In Mahā-bhārata, Sauptika-parvan 769, Brahmā, the Creator, is represented as calling on Śiva to create living creatures; and the latter, to qualify himself for the task, undergoes a severe penance under water.

identification with the great Spirit of the universe (*Paramātman*).[1]

These three manifestations of Brahmā, Vishṇu, and Śiva, whose functions are sometimes interchanged,[2] exhibit the three sides of Hindūism as developed in the epic poems, and still more unfolded in the subsequent Purānas. The first is the religion of activity and works, the second that of faith and love, the third that of austerity, contemplation, and spiritual knowledge. This last is regarded as the highest, because it aims at entire cessation of action and total effacement of all personal entity and identity by absorption into simple Soul.

In medieval times bitter rivalries and disputes sprung up between the upholders of these three doctrines ex-

---

[1] In the character of 'lord of abstract meditation,' S'iva is called *Yogeśa, Yogin.* Indeed, in some of the Purāṇas the origin of the Yoga (see p. 94) is ascribed to S'iva. In Book I. 55 and III. 45–50 of the Kumāra-sambhava, and in the opening invocation or Nāndī of the Mṛićchakaṭikā, there is a description of S'iva's posture and whole appearance while engaged in profound meditation. He is seated on his hams in the posture called *paryan-ka-bandha* (p. 93, note 2), with his breath suppressed and his vision fixed on his nose. While in this situation the god of love attempted to inspire him with affection for Pārvatī, daughter of Himālaya, in order that a son might be born to S'iva for the destruction of the Daitya Tāraka, who had extorted, by his penances, so many boons from Brahmā, that the whole universe had become subject to him. S'iva, indignant at the interruption of his austerities, reduced Kāma (Love) to ashes by a flash from his eye. Pārvatī then herself followed S'iva's example, and commenced a course of penance whereby she conciliated S'iva and became his wife. A son, Kārttikeya, 'god of war,' was then born, who killed Tāraka. This is the subject of the Kumāra-sambhava. The use of ashes rubbed upon the body and of Rudrāksha berries, to form rosaries, is of great importance in S'iva-worship.

[2] Thus, Vishṇu-worship (like S'iva-worship) is connected with the highest spiritual knowledge in the Bhagavad-gītā. See also note 3, p. 323. In some parts of India a saint *Dattātreya* is revered as combining the Hindū Triad in himself.

pressed by the worship of Brahmā, Vishṇu, and Śiva[1] respectively. Each sect was jealous of the superiority of his own system, and particular Purāṇas were devoted to

---

[1] Brahmā, 'the Creator,' however, is supposed to have done his work. Hence the worship of this manifestation fell into desuetude, and only in one place do traces of it continue, viz., Pushkara in Ājmīr (Rājputāna). Even the worship of the other two manifestations began in time to languish, until that of S'iva was revived by the great teacher and reformer S'an-karāćārya (sometimes described as an incarnation of S'iva) in the eighth century; and that of Vishṇu or Kṛishṇa by Rāmānuja in the twelfth, and by Vallabhāćārya at the end of the fifteenth. S'iva is now the favourite manifestation with Brāhmans and the better classes, as Kṛishṇa is with the others. Benares is a stronghold of S'iva-worship (whence his name Kāśī-nātha), but even there Kṛishṇa is the popular god of the lower orders. The chiefs of many monasteries in the south of India are to this day called S'an-karāćāryas. A popular festival, or rather fast (*upavāsa, vrata*), called S'iva-rātri, in honour of the god S'iva (under the form of the Lin-ga), is kept for a whole day and night, on the 14th of the dark half of the month Māgha (January—February). The spring festival (*utsava*), commonly called Hūlī or Holī, celebrated a few days before the full moon of Phālguna (February—March), and still more popular than the last, is said to be in honour of Kṛishṇa and the Gopīs dancing round fires. Their frolics are commemorated in a variety of sports and jokes. In some parts of India the Holī corresponds to the Dola-yātrā or 'swinging festival,' when figures of Kṛishṇa and his favourite wife Rādhā are swung in an ornamented swing. The Dīvālī (*dīpālī*) or 'festival of lights,' at the end of Aśvin and beginning of Kārtik (October—November), is in honour of Vishṇu's wife Lakshmī. Those who worship Durgā or Pārvatī, wife of S'iva, are called S'āktas (see note 2, p. 322). Besides the three principal sects of *Śaivas, Vaishṇavas,* and *Śāktas,* three other inferior ones are often named, viz., the *Gāṇapatyas* or worshippers of Gaṇa-pati or Gaṇeśa, the *Sauryas* or *Sauras,* worshippers of Sūrya, 'the sun,' and the *Bhāgavatas,* who are supposed to worship Bhagavat, 'the Supreme Being.' There are also the Sikhs of the Pañjāb, disciples of Guru Nānak Shah—born near Lahore—who in the reign of Baber, at the end of the fifteenth century, attempted to combine Hindūism with Islām, and promulgated about the time of our Reformation a book called the Ādi Grantha, 'first Book' (prohibiting idol-worship and teaching the unity of the Godhead pantheistically), as a kind of new

the exaltation of the one god or the other. But in the present day the strife of sects has generally given way to universal toleration, and a liberal school of theology has arisen in India. Most thinking men among the educated classes, whatever may be the form of religion to which they nominally incline, regard the names Brahmā, Rāma, Kṛishṇa, and Śiva as mere convenient symbols for different manifestations of the one Supreme Being, who may be worshipped under different external forms and by separate methods, according to the disposition, circumstances, and preference (*ishṭi*) of his worshippers. They hold, in short, that there are three ways or means of salvation, 1. the way of works (*karman*), 2. that of faith (*bhakti*), 3. that of spiritual knowledge (*jñāna*); and heaven, they assert, may be reached by any one of these three roads or by a combination of all. The second, however, represents the popular side of the Indian creed, as of all religions, false or true.

It is as Vishṇu, then, that the Supreme Being, according to the Hindūs, exhibited his sympathy with human trials, his love for the human race, his respect for all forms of life, and his condescension towards even the inferior animals as integral parts of his creation. Portions of his essence, they assert, became incarnate in the lower animals, as well as in men, to rescue the world in great emergencies. Nine principal occasions have already occurred in which the god has thus interposed for the salvation of his creatures. A tenth

---

Veda. He was succeeded by nine other Gurus, each of whom was in some way remarkable. The tenth, Govind, added another 'Book' to the first, and, meeting with persecution under Aurangzīb, converted the Sikhs from peaceable disciples of a peculiar teacher into a military nation and enemies of the Mogul empire. The Sikh chiefs formed themselves into confederacies called Misals, over whom Runjit Siṅh eventually became supreme.

has still to take place. These incarnations are briefly as follows:[1]—

1. *Matsya*, the fish. In this Vishṇu became a fish to save the seventh Manu, the progenitor of the human race, from the universal deluge.[2] (See the story told p. 393.)

2. *Kūrma*,[3] the tortoise. In this he descended to aid in recovering certain valuable articles lost in the deluge. For this purpose he stationed himself as a tortoise at the bottom of the ocean, that his back might serve as a pivot for the mountain Mandara, around which the gods and demons twisted the great serpent Vāsuki. They then stood opposite to each other, and using the snake as a rope and the mountain as a churning-stick, churned the ocean[4] for the recovery of the Amṛita or 'nectar,' the goddess Lakshmī,[5] and twelve other sacred things which had been lost in the depths.

3. *Varāha*, the boar. In this he descended to deliver the world from the power of a demon called Hiraṇyāksha, who had seized the earth and carried it down into the

---

[1] It should be mentioned that the Bhāgavata-purāṇa gives twenty-two incarnations of Vishṇu. Muir's Texts IV. 156.

[2] The oldest version of this legend, which furnished the germ of the subsequent incarnation, is found in the S'atapatha-brāhmaṇa, as given pp. 30–31 of this volume. The legend is also told in Mahā-bhārata Vana-parvan 12747, &c., where the fish is represented as an incarnation of Brahmā; and in the Bhāgavata-purāṇa VIII. 24, 7, where it is identified with Vishṇu. Muir's Texts I. 208, &c.

[3] In S'atapatha-brāhmaṇa VII. 4, 3, 5, Prajāpati (or Brahmā) is said to have assumed the form of the tortoise: 'Having assumed the form of a tortoise, Prajāpati created offspring. That which he created he made (*akarot*); hence the word *kūrma*.' Muir's Texts IV. 27.

[4] In this there appears to be an allegory, and the lesson that may be supposed to be taught is, that nothing valuable can be produced or recovered by man without great labour—without, as it were, stirring the lowest depths of his whole nature.

[5] Goddess of beauty, and wife of Vishṇu, a kind of Hindū Venus, Aphrodite (ἀφροδίτη, 'foam-born').

lowest depths of the sea. Vishṇu, as a boar, dived into the abyss, and after a contest of a thousand years, slew the monster and raised the earth.[1] In the earlier legends the universe is represented as a mass of water, and the earth being submerged, was upheaved by the tusks of the divine boar. According to some, the object of this incarnation was to recover the lost Vedas. It is noticeable that the first three incarnations are all connected with the tradition of a universal deluge.

4. *Nara-siṉha*, the man-lion. In this he assumed the shape of a creature, half man, half lion, to deliver the world from the tyranny of a demon called Hiraṇya-kaśipu, who had obtained a boon from Brahmā that he should not be slain by either god or man or animal. Hence he became so powerful that he usurped the dominion of the three worlds, and appropriated the sacrifices made to the gods. When his pious son Prahlāda praised Vishṇu, the demon tried to destroy the boy, but Vishṇu appeared out of a pillar in the form Nara-siṉha and tore Hiraṇya-kaśipu to pieces.

These first four incarnations are said to have taken place in the Satya or first age of the world.

5. *Vāmana*, the dwarf. In the second or Tretā age Vishṇu descended as a dwarf, to deprive the demon Bali (who resembles Rāvaṇa and Kaṉsa in the stories of

---

[1] The germs of the fable in the earlier literature are very simple. In Taittirīya-brāhmaṇa I. 1, 3, 5, we read: 'This universe was formerly water. Prajāpati, as a boar, plunged beneath. He found the earth below. Breaking off a portion of her he rose to the surface.' In Śatapatha-brāhmaṇa XIV. 1, 2, 11, occurs the following: 'The earth was formerly so large—*Emūsha*, a boar, raised her up' (Muir's Texts IV. 27). In the Rāmāyaṇa II. 110, Brahmā, not Vishṇu, is represented as taking the form of the boar: 'All was water only in which the earth was formed. Thence arose Brahmā. He, becoming a boar, raised up the earth,' &c. See Muir's Texts I. 53, IV. 36, &c.

Rāma and Kṛishṇa) of the dominion of the three worlds. Vishṇu presented himself before him as a diminutive man, and solicited as much land as he could step in three paces. When his request was granted he strided in two steps over heaven and earth, but out of compassion left the lower world or Pātāla in the demon's possession.[1]

6. *Paraśu-rāma*, Rāma with the axe. In this Vishṇu was born as the son of the Brāhman Jamad-agni and descendant of Bhṛigu, in the second age, to restrain the Kshatriyas from arrogating dominion over the Brāhmanical caste. Paraśu-rāma is said to have cleared the earth twenty-one times of the Kshatriya class[2] (see p. 347).

---

[1] The germ of this incarnation in the Ṛig-veda. I quote one passage: 'Vishṇu strode over this (universe); in three places he planted his step' (I. 22, 17). Hence Vishṇu is called *Tri-vikrama*. See also p. 320 of this volume and Muir's Texts, vol. iv. p. 63. An account of the Dwarf incarnation is given in Rāmāyaṇa (Schlegel) I. 31, 2, and (Bombay ed.) I. 29, 2, &c. (Gorresio I. 32, 2). It is noticed in the Mahā-bhārata, S'ānti-parvan 12943, &c., Vana-parvan 484, &c.

[2] Though now regarded as the mythical type of Brāhmanism, arrayed in opposition to the military caste, he was probably, in the first instance, the hero of a quarrel caused by a Kshatriya stealing a cow from a Brāhman named Jamad-agni. In revenge, his son Paraśu-rāma slew the Kshatriya, upon which the other Kshatriyas murdered Jamad-agni, and a fierce contest ensued between his son and the murderers. All this points to the historical fact of constant struggles between the two leading classes, and it may be inferred from the circumstance that Paraśu-rāma is described as fighting with (and conquered by) Rāma-ćandra, as well as with Bhīshma in the Mahā-bhārata, that the Kshatriyas held their own if they did not gain the upper hand. The story of Paraśu-rāma is told in the Vana-parvan 11071, &c., and in the S'ānti-parvan 1707, &c.; also in the ninth book of the Bhāgavata and in the Padma and Agni Purāṇas. In the Vana-parvan 8679, Paraśu-rāma is described as struck senseless by Rāma-ćandra. The Udyoga-parvan 7142, &c., relates the long single combat between Paraśu-rāma and Bhīshma. They both repeatedly strike each other senseless. Ultimately they are persuaded by some Munis to leave off fighting. In Ādi-parvan 272–280, the destruction of the Kshatriyas

7. *Rāma* (commonly called Rāma-ćandra,[1] 'the mild or moon-like Rāma'), the hero of the Rāmāyaṇa, son of king Daśaratha of the Solar race, and therefore a Kshatriya. Vishṇu took this form at the close of the second or Tretā age, to destroy the demon Rāvaṇa (see p. 343).

8. *Kṛishṇa*, 'the dark god'—the most popular of all the later deities of India.[2] This incarnation of Vishṇu, at the end of the Dvāpara or third age of the world,[3]

---

by Paraśu-rāma is said to have taken place between the Tretā and Dvāpara ages. Muir's Texts I. 447. Tradition ascribes the formation of the Malabar coast to Paraśu-rāma, who is said to have compelled the ocean to retire and to have caused fissures in the western Ghāts by blows of his axe.

[1] The addition of Ćandra, to distinguish this Rāma from the other two, is only found in the later literature (see note, p. 360).

[2] Especially in Bengal. In the upper provinces (except at Mathurā or Muttra, Kṛishṇa's own city), Oude, Behār, and the greater part of Hindūstān Proper, the seventh incarnation, Rāma-ćandra, is principally worshipped. That Kṛishṇa-worship is comparatively modern is shown by the fact that in the old Buddhist Sūtras the gods reverenced at the time Buddhism arose are named, viz., Brahmā, Nārāyaṇa, S'iva, Indra, &c., but not Kṛishṇa.

[3] The Kali-yuga or fourth age of the world was supposed to commence at the death of Kṛishṇa. Hence the events of the Mahā-bhārata must have taken place during the third or Dvāpara age, and those of the Rāmāyaṇa at the end of the second or Tretā age. From the gambling scene in the Second Act of the Mṛiććhakaṭikā, it is probable that the names of the four ages are connected with throws of dice; Kṛita being the best throw; Tretā, the throw of three or the second best throw; and Dvāpara, the throw of two or a worse throw; the worst of all being Kali. The Hindū notion appears to have been that gambling prevailed especially in the Dvāpara and Kali Yugas. In the episode of Nala, the personified Dvāpara enters into the dice, and the personified Kali into Nali himself, who is then seized with the fatal passion for play. The Hindū idea of a succession of four Yugas or ages, in which a gradual deterioration of the human race takes place, has its counterpart among the Romans in the Golden, Silver, Brazen, and Iron ages, as described in Ovid's Metamorphoses (I. 89, &c.). But the Hindū system of mundane periods is more elaborately

as the eighth son of Vasu-deva and Devakī of the Lunar race, was for the destruction of the tyrant Kaṉsa, the representative of the principle of evil, corresponding to Rāvaṇa in the previous incarnation.

The details of the later life of Kṛishṇa have been interwoven with the later portions of the Mahā-bhārata, but they do not belong to the plot, and they might be omitted without imparing its unity. He is certainly not the hero of the great Epic. He appears as a great chief who takes the part of the real heroes—the Pāṇḍavas [1]—and his claims to deification are often disputed. His earlier days and juvenile feats, though not found in the oldest parts of the Mahā-bhārata, may be gathered from the Hari-vaṉśa and Purāṇas, especially the tenth book of the Bhāgavata-purāṇa, from which we learn as follows :—

---

extended, and perhaps agrees better with modern scientific theories (see p. 178, note 2). A Mahā-yuga or period of four ages comprises 12,000 years of the gods, which (according to the Vishṇu-purāṇa) are equal to 12,000 × 360 (the assumed number of days in an ordinary year), and therefore to 4,320,000 years of mortals, when another cycle of four ages is commenced. One thousand of these periods of four ages constitute a Kalpa or day of Brahmā = 4,320,000,000 human years (comprising under it fourteen Manv-antaras or periods presided over by fourteen successive Manus), after which there is a universal collapse (*pratisaňćara, mahā-pralaya*) of all creation—including Brahmā, Vishṇu, S'iva, gods, demons, men, animals—into Brahman or simple being. In the present Kalpa or Aeon, six Manus have passed away, of whom the first was Svāyambhuva, the present or seventh being Vaivasvata. Manu's account is confused, and some think the periods of his four Yugas are no more than 4800, 3600, 2400, and 1200 ordinary years respectively (Manu I. 69–71). There is no allusion to mundane periods in the Ṛig-veda, but there is in the Aitareya-brāhmaṇa (VII. 15). The present Kali-yuga is reckoned to have begun February 18th, 3102 B.C. at midnight, on the meridian of Ujjayinī. Whitney's 2nd Series of Oriental Studies, p. 366; Muir's Texts I. 43; Weber's Indische Studien I. 286, 460.

[1] Later additions to the Mahā-bhārata make the Pāṇḍavas also incarnations of certain deities.

Vasu-deva (a descendant of the Yadu who with Puru, as sons of Yayāti, formed the two branches of the lunar dynasty) had two wives, Rohiṇī and Devakī. The latter had eight sons, of whom the eighth was Kṛishṇa. It was predicted that one of these would kill Kaṉsa, king of Mathurā and cousin of Devakī. He therefore imprisoned Vasu-deva and his wife, and slew their first six children. The seventh, Bala-rāma, was abstracted from Devakī's womb, transferred to that of Rohiṇī, and thus saved. The eighth was Kṛishṇa, born with black skin and the mark called *Śrī-vatsa* on his breast.[1] His father, Vasu-deva, escaped from Mathurā with the child, and, favoured by the gods, found a herdsman named Nanda—of the race of the Yādavas—whose wife, Yaśodā, had just had a son, whom Vasu-deva conveyed to Devakī, after substituting his own son in its place. Nanda took the infant Kṛishṇa and settled first in Gokula or Vraja, and afterwards in Vṛindāvana, where Kṛishṇa and Bala-rāma grew up together, roaming in the woods, and joining in the sports of the herdsmen's sons. While still a boy, Kṛishṇa destroyed the serpent Kāliya, and lifted up the mountain Govardhana on his finger to shelter the Gopīs from the wrath of Indra, who, enraged by their love for Kṛishṇa, tried to destroy them by a deluge. He is described as sporting constantly with these Gopīs or shepherdesses, of whom a thousand became his wives, though only eight are specified, Rādhā being the favourite. Kṛishṇa built Dvārakā in Gujarāt, and thither transported the inhabitants of Mathurā after killing Kaṉsa.

According to some, Kṛishṇa is not an incarnation of Vishṇu, but Vishṇu himself; in which case, *Bala-rāma*, 'the strong Rāma,'[2] born at the end of the Dvāpara or third age of the world, as son of Vasu-deva and Devakī, and

[1] The anniversary of the birthday of Kṛishṇa, called Janmāshṭamī, because his birth is said to have occurred on the eighth day of the month Bhādra (August—September), is celebrated as a great festival. Professor Weber has lately published some valuable information on this subject.

[2] This third Rāma, usually held to be the seventh son of Vasu-deva, and sometimes called *Halāyudha*, 'armed with a plough-shaped weapon,' sometimes *Musalin*, 'club-armed,' is the Hindū Hercules. In Mahā-bhārata I. 7308 (as well as in the Vishṇu-purāṇa), he is said to have been produced from a white hair of Vishṇu, as Kṛishṇa was from a black. Elsewhere he is said to be an incarnation of the great serpent S'esha, and in Anuśāsana-parvan 6163 he is regarded as a

elder brother of Kṛishṇa, is sometimes substituted for Kṛishṇa as the eighth incarnation of Vishṇu.

9. *Buddha.* According to the Brāhmans, Vishṇu assumed the form of the great sceptical philosopher, in the fourth age of the world, to delude the Daityas or demons into neglecting the worship of the gods, and thus exposing them to destruction.

10. *Kalki* or *Kalkin*, who is yet to appear at the close of the fourth or Kali age, when the world has become wholly depraved, for the final destruction of the wicked, for the re-establishment of righteousness upon the earth, and the renovation of all creation with a return to a new age of purity (*satya-yuga*). According to some, he will be revealed in the sky, seated on a white horse, with a drawn sword in his hand, blazing like a comet.[1]

Looking more closely at these ten incarnations, we may observe that in the first three Vishṇu is supposed to be present in the body of animals, and in the fourth to take the form of a being half animal, half human. This last may be regarded as a kind of intermediate link, the object

---

Nāga, or semi-divine being, half man, half serpent; and at his death (recorded in Mausala-parvan 117), a large Nāga is described as coming out of his mouth and entering the ocean. Diodorus Siculus, in his account of the Indians (II. 39), has the following:—'It is said that Hercules also (as well as Διονύσος, worshipped by the inhabitants of the mountains) lived amongst them; and, like the Greeks, they represent him with a club and lion's skin; and that in strength of body and bravery, he excelled all mortals, and purged the earth and sea from monsters (θηρίων). And that since he had numerous sons from his many wives, but only one daughter, when they were grown up, he divided the whole of India into equal parts, so that each of his sons should have a kingdom of his own, and his one daughter he made queen. And that he founded many cities, and among them the largest and most celebrated was Palibothra (Παλίβοθρα); and that after his death, he obtained divine honours.'

[1] According to Vishṇu-purāṇa IV. 24, he is to be born as Kalki in the family of Vishṇu-yaśas, an ancient Brāhman of Śambhala.

of which is to prevent too great abruptness in connecting the Deity with the higher forms of worldly existence. From the mixed manifestation of half a lion, half a man, the transition is natural to that of a complete man. The divine essence passing into human forms commences with the smallest type of humanity, represented by a dwarf. Thence it rises to mighty heroes, who deliver the world from the oppression of evil demons and tyrants whose power increases with the deterioration of mankind during the four ages. In the tenth and final manifestation, which remains to be revealed, evil and wickedness are to be entirely rooted out. We see in all this the working of the Hindū idea of transmigration. Even in Manu's time it was an accepted dogma that the souls of men, popularly regarded as emanations from the Deity, might descend into the bodies of animals, or rise to those of higher beings. It was therefore an easy expansion of such a doctrine to imagine the divine Soul itself as passing through various stages of incarnation for the delivery of the world from the effects of evil and sin, and for the maintenance of order in the whole cycle of creation.

Let me introduce here a curious legend from the Bhāgavata-purāṇa X. lxxxix.—also told in the Prem Sāgar. I translate it (with a little amplification) as well illustrating the distinctive characters of the three gods, Brahmā, Vishṇu, and Śiva. (The Sanskrit text is given at p. 516.)

The great sage Bhṛigu, one of the ten Maharshis or primeval patriarchs created by the first Manu (I. 35), was asked which god was the greatest. He said he would endeavour to ascertain, and first went to Brahmā; on approaching whom, he purposely omitted an obeisance. Upon this, the god reprehended him very severely, but was pacified by seasonable apologies. Next he entered the abode of Śiva, in Kailāsa, and omitted to return the god's salutation. The vindictive deity was enraged, and would have destroyed the sage, but was conciliated by his wife Pārvatī. Lastly, he repaired to Vaikuṇṭha, the heaven of Vishṇu, whom he found asleep with his head on Lakshmī's lap. To make a trial of his forbearance, he boldly gave the god a kick on his breast, which awoke him. Instead of showing anger, however, the god arose, and on seeing Bhṛigu, inquired tenderly whether his foot was hurt, and then proceeded to rub it gently. 'This,' said Bhṛigu, 'is the mightiest god; he overpowers by the most potent of all weapons—sympathy and generosity.'

The Rāmāyaṇa.

I proceed now to give a brief account of Vālmīki's[1] poem, the Rāmāyaṇa (*Rāma-ayana*, 'the goings or doings of Rāma'), which in its present form consists of about 24,000 stanzas, mostly in the common heroic Anushṭubh metre.[2]

It should be noted in the first place that the purity of

---

[1] Vālmīki is thought to have been born in that part of India which corresponds to Kośala, the chief town of which was Ayodhyā (reigned over by Daśaratha, Rāma's father), and which was close to the region of Videha, whose king, Janaka, was the father of Sītā, and whose connection with Yājñavalkya is described in the Brāhmaṇa of the White Yajur-veda, and in some of the Mahā-bhārata legends. Vālmīki himself is believed to have been an adherent of the Black Yajur-veda, and it is certain that the story of Rāma was carefully preserved among the Taittirīyakas, and that Vālmīki interweaves their legends into his narrative. According to Mr. Cust (Calcutta Review XLV.) Vālmīki resided on the banks of the Jumnā, near its confluence with the Ganges at Allahabad; and tradition has marked a hill in the district of Banda, in Bundelkund, as his abode. Some actually assert that he began life as a highway robber, but repenting of his misdeeds, betook himself to a hermitage on this hill, where he eventually received Sītā, the wife of Rāma, when banished by her over-sensitive husband. There were born her two sons, Kuśa and Lava (sometimes combined into one compound, thus—*Kuśī-lavau*), who were taught to sing the poem descriptive of their unknown father's actions, and from whom are traced the proudest Rajput castes. The reviewer thinks it not unlikely that Vālmīki may have been contemporaneous with the heroes whom he describes.

[2] The metre in which the greater part of the Rāmāyaṇa and Mahābhārata is written is the common S'loka (see my Sanskṛit Grammar,

its text has been exposed to risks, which the longer Epic has escaped. Its story was more popular and attractive. It was shorter, and far less burdened with digressions; it had more unity of plot; its language was simpler and presented fewer difficulties. As a result of these circumstances it was more easily committed to memory. Hence it happened that, even after the final settlement of its text, it became orally current over a great part of India. We know from the fourth chapter of the first book that it had its minstrels and reciters like the Greek ῥαψῳδοί, and variations in the wording of the narratives became almost unavoidable. In process of time, as written copies of the poem multiplied, the unfettered flow of the common heroic metre facilitated slight alterations and interpolations by transcribers who sometimes aimed at being poets themselves. Hence we have at least three versions of the text of the poem: one belonging to Benares and the North-west; another, which is generally, though not always, more diffuse and open to suspicion of interpolations, peculiar to Calcutta and Bengal Proper; and a third, to Western India (Bombay). These principal recensions, as well as all the known MSS., whatever may be their occasional variations,[1] divide the poem into seven books, as follows:—

---

935), in which only five syllables out of sixteen in each line are really fixed. The others may be either long or short. The Indra-vajrā variety of Trishṭubh is, however, frequently used in the Mahā-bhārata; and in the Rāmāyaṇa, at the end of the chapters, we have often the Jagatī (Gram. 937, 941). The former of these has eleven syllables to the half-line, the latter twelve; and the quantity of every syllable being fixed, there is less simplicity and freedom of style.

[1] Professor Weber shows that the variations now discovered in MSS. of the Rāmāyaṇa in different parts of India are so great, that it is no longer possible to talk of three recensions only. With regard to the Bengal (Gauḍa) recension, it may be observed that in that part of India, where there is less demand for MSS., learned men have been

1. *Bāla-kāṇḍa*, the section relating to the boyhood of Rāma. 2. *Ayodhyā-k°*, descriptive of the transactions in Ayodhyā and the banishment of Rāma by his father, king Daśaratha. 3. *Araṇya-k°*, narrating events in the forest-abode of Rāma after his banishment, including the carrying off of Sītā by Rāvaṇa. 4. *Kishkindhyā-k°*, detailing the occurrences at Kishkindhyā, the capital city of Rāma's ally Sugrīva. 5. *Sundara-k°*, 'the beautiful section,' giving an account of the miracles by which the passage of the straits and the arrival of the invading armies in Lan-kā (Ceylon) were effected. 6. *Yuddha-k°*, describing the actual war with Rāvaṇa in Lan-kā, the victory over his armies and his destruction by Rāma, the recovery of Sītā, the return to Ayodhyā, the reunion of the four brothers, and final coronation of Rāma. 7. *Uttara-k°*, narrating the concluding events of the history of Rāma after his coronation on returning to Ayodhyā—his sensitiveness to the gossip and scandal of the citizens, his consequent banishment of Sītā to the hermitage of Vālmīki, notwithstanding the absolute certainty of her blameless conduct during her captivity in Rāvaṇa's palace, the birth of his twin sons, Kuśa and Lava, in the hermitage, his final reunion with her, and translation to heaven. All this supplement to the story has been dramatized by Bhava-bhūti in his Uttara-rāma-ćaritra, and the whole previous history in his Mahā-vīra-ćaritra.

We have already noted that the seventh Book, as well

---

their own scribes, and have always tampered more freely with original texts than the unlearned copyists of the North. In 1806 and 1810 Carey and Marshman published the text and translation of two books out of the seven which complete this recension; but here and there they have followed the northern. Twenty years afterwards Augustus William Schlegel published the text of two books of the northern version, with a Latin translation of the first; and after another interval of twenty years Signor Gorresio, a learned Italian scholar, published, at the expense of king Charles Albert, a very beautiful and accurate edition of the Bengal recension, with an Italian translation, which I have generally followed in my summary of the narrative. The remainder of that particular recension, the editing of which was commenced by Schlegel, was left unprinted. More than ten years have elapsed since editions of the more reliable recension, with commentary, were put forth at Calcutta and Bombay. That of Calcutta is dated Saṃvat, 1917. Mr. R. Griffith's poetical translation of the Rāmāyaṇa, which has appeared since, deserves, and has received, the greatest commendation.

as the introductory chapters of the first, giving a summary of the plot, and the passages identifying Rāma with Vishṇu or the Supreme Being (such as VI. cii. 12, Gorresio), are in all probability comparatively modern appendages.

No suspicion, however, of interpolations and variations avails to impair the sacred character of the poem in the eyes of the natives.[1] Some idea of the veneration in which it is held may be formed from the verses at the end of the introductory chapter, which declare—

He who reads and repeats this holy life-giving Rāmāyaṇa is liberated from all his sins and exalted with all his posterity to the highest heaven.

Brahmā also, in I. 2, 40, is made to utter the following prophecy in the presence of the poet Vālmīki :—

As long as the mountains and rivers shall continue on the surface of the earth, so long shall the story of the Rāmāyaṇa be current in the world. [*Yāvat sthāsyanti girayaḥ saritaś-ća mahītale Tāvad Rāmāyaṇa-kathā lokeshu praćarishyati.*]

The main story of the poem,[2] although often interrupted by long episodes which have little bearing on the plot, flows in a far more continuous and traceable course than that of the Mahā-bhārata. It may be divided into four principal parts or periods, corresponding to the chief epochs in the life of Rāma. I. The account of his youth-

---

[1] Weber has noted that in the Sarva-darśana-saṅgraha (p. 72, l. 15) a passage is quoted from the Skanda-purāṇa which places the Mūla-rāmāyaṇa, 'original Rāmāyaṇa,' as a Śāstra after the four Vedas, the Bhārata, and the Panća-rātraka. Some of the Sargas in the Uttara-kāṇḍa have no comment as being *prakshipta*.

[2] While writing my account of the Rāmāyaṇa, I have consulted an able article on this poem in the Calcutta Review (XLV.), to which I am under great obligations. The author of the article is my friend Mr. R. N. Cust, a late distinguished member of the Bengal Civil Service.

ful days; his education and residence at the court of his father Daśaratha, king of Ayodhyā; his happy marriage to Sītā; and his inauguration as heir-apparent or crown-prince. II. The circumstances that led to his banishment; the description of his exile and residence in the forests of Central India. III. His war with the giants or demons of the South for the recovery of his wife Sītā, carried off by their chief Rāvaṇa; his conquest and destruction of Rāvaṇa, and reunion with Sītā. IV. His return with Sītā to Ayodhyā; his restoration to the throne of his father; and his subsequent banishment of Sītā.[1]

The poem opens with a description of Ayodhyā,[2] and an eulogium on Daśaratha and his ministers, of whom the most eminent were the two prime ministers Vasishṭha and Vāmadeva. Besides these, there were eight other

---

[1] According to Professor Lassen the development of the story of Ramā may be divided into four stages. The first construction of the poem did not carry the narrative beyond the banishment of Rāma to the Himālaya and the circumstances which caused his wife Sītā and his brother Lakshmaṇa to follow him into exile. The second changed the place of banishment to the Godāvarī, and described the protection afforded to the hermits against the attacks of the aborigines. The third embraced the account of the first attempts to subdue the inhabitants of the Dekhan. The fourth amplification, which resulted from the knowledge gained by the Hindūs of the island of Ceylon, included the description of Rāma's expedition against Lan·kā. See Ind. Alt. II. p. 5c5.

[2] Although Ayodhyā is the base of operations in the Rāmāyaṇa, yet the poet carries us through a vast extent of country, conducting us now beyond the Sutlej into the Pañjāb, now across the Vindhya mountains into the Dekhan, and now across the Narmadā and Godāvarī to the most southern parts of India, even to the island of Ceylon. The geography of the poem, however, though far more interesting, and extending to wider points in every direction, than that of the Mahābhārata, is not always to be trusted. The river Sarayū is now called the Gogra.

councillors (*amātyāḥ*), agreeably to the precept laid down by Manu (see p. 256, with note 2). These are of course all Brāhmans, and direct the affairs of the government. King Daśaratha has no son (VIII. 1)—a serious calamity in India, where a son is needed for the due performance of the Śrāddha (see p. 249, with note 1). The usual remedy for this misfortune was a great sacrifice, purposely cumbered with a most tedious and intricate ceremonial, not to be performed except by Brāhmans, who received in return enormous gifts. The Rākshasas were, of course, eagerly on the watch for any flaw, defect, or mistake. If any occurred, the whole ceremony was seriously obstructed, and its efficacy destroyed.

Ṛishyaśṛin-ga, therefore, a celebrated sage, is married to Daśaratha's daughter Śāntā, and induced to assist at the celebration of a great Aśva-medha or horse-sacrifice.

The episode in which the story of this sage is told is very curious:—

It so happened, that in the neighbouring kingdom of An-ga, now known as Bhagulpore, in Bengal, there had been a great dearth, and the king, Lomapāda, had been assured that the only chance of obtaining rain was to entice the ascetic Ṛishyaśṛin-ga from his retirement, and induce him to marry the king's daughter, or rather the adopted child of Lomapāda, and real daughter of Daśaratha. This ascetic was the son of Vibhāṇḍaka, a sainted mortal of frightful power, who had produced him apparently without a mother, and had brought him up alone in the wilderness, where he had never seen or even heard of the fascinations of women. The plan was to send a party of young females, disguised as ascetics, and inveigle the great saint from his retreat. The description of the surprise and unsettlement of mind, the interruption of devotion, and heart's unrest, that befell the unhappy saint when he received his strange guests, is very singular. In the end, the ascetic is seduced from his hermitage, put on board a vessel on the Ganges, married to the king's daughter, and brought to Ayodhyā, to conduct the sacrifice.[1]

[1] I have consulted here Mr. Cust's article in the Calcutta Review (XLV.). He there remarks that 'we might laugh at the conceit of

The horse-sacrifice,[1] therefore, was successfully performed. We are told that no oblation was neglected, nor any mistake committed; all was in exact conformity to the Veda (I. xiii. 10). The queen Kauśalyā, mother of Rāma, and the other two queens, Sumitrā and Kaikeyī,[2] remain with the slaughtered horse for one whole

---

such a case being possible had not a modern traveller in the Levant, Mr. Curzon, assured us of the existence of a similar case in one of the convents of Mount Athos in the nineteenth century. He there found a monk in middle life who had never set eyes on women, nor had any notion of them beyond what could be formed from a black and hideous altar-picture of the Virgin Mary. The cruel traveller, by an accurate description of the many charms of the fair sisterhood, entirely destroyed the poor monk's peace of mind for the future.'

[1] The horse chosen for this purpose was let loose and allowed to roam about for a year. If no one was able to seize it during this period, it was deemed fit for sacrifice; but the seizure was sometimes effected by the god Indra, whose tenure of heaven was imperilled by the great power acquired by those who completed many Aśva-medhas. Another year was consumed in preparations for the sacrifice. The description of the ceremony in I. xiii., is curious. Twenty-one Yūpas or sacrificial posts were erected, to which were tied various animals, and the horse. Near the latter the queens of Daśaratha watched for a whole night. The marrow (*vapā*) of the horse [*patatrin* = horse; according to the commentator, *purā aśvānām pakshāḥ santīti*] was then taken out and dressed, and the horse itself cut up and offered in the fire, and the king, smelling the smoke of the burning flesh, became absolved from his sins. Various other sacrifices seem to have accompanied the Aśva-medha, such as the Ćatushṭoma, Jyotishṭoma, Atirātra, Abhijit, &c. The *Pravargya* and *Upasad* are described in Aitareya-brāhmaṇa I. 18, 1, 23–25. Compare the Aśva-medha hymns of the Ṛig-veda (I. 162, 163) and the rules for this sacrifice given in S'atapatha-brāhmaṇa XIII. and Kātyāyana's Sūtras XX. 6, 78. An important part of the proceedings was the feasting and the largesses. King Daśaratha is described as giving to the priests a million cows, a hundred million pieces of gold, and four times as many pieces of silver.

[2] Of Daśaratha's three wives, the chief, Kauśalyā, is said to have been of his own race and country (probably so called from Kośala, the country of Daśaratha); the second, Kaikeyī, was the daughter of Aśva-

night (I. xiii. 36, 37). The gods, Brahmā, Vishṇu, and Śiva, along with Indra and his troop of Maruts, assemble to receive their shares of the sacrificial oblations, and being satisfied, promise four sons to Daśaratha (I. xiv. 9). The scene then changes to the abode of the gods, where a deputation of the deities waits on Brahmā, and represents to him that the universe is in danger of being destroyed by the chief of the Rākshasas or evil demons, called Rāvaṇa, who from his island-throne in Ceylon menaces earth and heaven with destruction. His power is described as so great that—

Where he is, there the sun does not give out its heat; the winds through fear of him do not blow; the fire ceases to burn; and the ocean, crowned with rolling billows, becomes motionless (I. xiv. 17).

The secret of this power lay in a long course of austerity,[1] which, according to the Hindū doctrine, gained for

pati, king of Kekaya, supposed to be in the Pañjāb (whence the king himself is sometimes called Kekaya); and the third, Sumitrā, was probably from Magadha or Behār. The father of the last is said to have been a Vaiśya. It is noticeable that Aśva-pati, king of Kekaya, is mentioned in the Brāhmaṇa of the White Yajur-veda as nearly contemporary with Janaka, father of Sītā.

[1] According to the Hindū theory, the performance of *tapas* or austerities of various kinds was like making deposits in the bank of heaven. By degrees an enormous credit was accumulated, which enabled the depositor to draw to the amount of his savings, without fear of his drafts being refused payment. The merit and power thus gained by weak mortals was so enormous, that gods as well as men were equally at the mercy of these all but omnipotent ascetics. Hence both Ṛishis and Rākshasas and even gods, especially Śiva (p. 323), are described as engaging in self-inflicted austerities, in order to set mere human beings an example, or perhaps not to be supplanted by them, or else not to be outdone in aiming at re-absorption into Brahma. In these cases it is incorrect (as remarked by Professor Banerjea) to translate *tapas* by 'penance,' if expiation for sin is thereby implied. It is simply self-inflicted pain and suffering, with a view to the acquisition of superhuman powers, or of final emancipation. The

him who persevered sufficiently, however evil his designs, superiority to the gods themselves, and enabled Rāvaṇa to extort from the god Brahmā this remarkable boon—that neither gods, genii, demons, nor giants should be able to vanquish him. As, however, in his pride, he scorned to ask security from man also, he remained vulnerable from this one quarter, if any mortal could be found capable of coping with him. While the discussion of the matter is carried on in heaven, Vishṇu joins the conclave, and at the request of the other gods, promises to take the form of man that he may kill Rāvaṇa, and consents to become incarnate for this purpose, in the family of Daśaratha, king of Ayodhyā (Oude), of the Solar dynasty.

It should be stated here that, according to the legendary history of India, two lines of rulers were originally dominant in the north of India, called Solar and Lunar, under whom numerous petty princes held authority and to whom they acknowledged fealty. Under the Solar dynasty the Brāhmanical system gained ascendency more rapidly and completely than under the Lunar kings in the more northern districts, where fresh arrivals of martial tribes preserved an independent spirit among the population already settled in that district.

This Solar line, though practically commencing with Ikshvāku, is fabled to have derived its origin from the Sun, and even from an earlier source—the god Brahmā himself. Perhaps the object of the Brāhman poet or later constructor of the poem might have been to connect Rāma in his then acknowledged character of an incar-

root *tap* signifies first 'to burn' and then 'to torment.' It is connected with Lat. *tepeo*. Also with Greek τέφρα, root ταφ, θάπτω, which last originally signified 'to burn,' not 'to bury,' dead bodies. As, however, 'penance' is derived from *poena*, 'pain,' it is perhaps a suitable equivalent for the Sanskṛit *tapas*.

nation of Vishṇu, with the solar Vishṇu of the Veda (see p. 320). However this may have been, nothing shows more clearly than the legendary pedigree of Rāma how the whole poem was subjected to a brāhmanizing process. We see from it that the most powerful line of Kshatriya kings is thus made to owe its origin to Brāhmanical sages of the greatest sanctity I here abridge the genealogy :—

Ikshvāku was the son of Manu Vaivasvata (*i.e.*, the seventh Manu, or Manu of the present period). The latter was a son of Vivasvat or the Sun (commonly called Sūrya). The Sun again was a son of the Muni Kaśyapa, who was the son of the Ṛishi Marīći, who was the son of Brahmā. From Ikshvāku sprang the two branches of the Solar dynasty, viz., that of Ayodhyā or Oude, which may be said to have commenced in Kakutstha, the grandson of Ikshvāku (as the latter's son Vikukshi, father of Kakutstha, did not reign), and that of Mithilā, or Videha (North Behār and Tirhut), which commenced in another of Ikshvāku's sons, Nimi. Thirty-fifth in descent from Kakutstha came Sagara; fourth from him Bhagīratha; third from him Ambarīsha; and fifteenth from him Raghu, who was father of Aja, who was father of Daśaratha. Hence we have the following order of names: Brahmā, Marīći, Kaśyapa, Vivasvat or Sūrya, Vaivasvata, Ikshvāku [Vikukshi], Kakutstha [. . . . .], Sagara [. .], Dilīpa, Bhagīratha [. .], Ambarīsha [. . .], Nala [. . . . .], Raghu, Aja, Daśaratha, Rāma.

This explains why Rāma is variously called Kākutstha, Rāghava, Dāśaratha, Dāśarathi, &c.[1]

We are thus brought to the real commencement of the story—the birth of Rāma.[2] Four sons are born from the

---

[1] This list agrees with the usual one as exhibited in Prinsep's table; but there is considerable variation in the genealogy, as given in Rāmāyaṇa II. cx. and in the Raghu-vaṇśa. For instance, the son of Ikshvāku is said to be Kukshi, and his son Vikukshi; the son of Dilīpa is Bhagīratha, and his son is Kakutstha, and his son is Raghu. In the Raghu-vaṇśa, Raghu, father of Aja (V. 36), is said to be the son of Dilīpa (III. 13).

[2] In Schlegel's and the Bombay Rāmāyaṇa, the horoscope of Rāma's

three wives of Daśaratha; the eldest, Rāma, possessing half the nature of Vishṇu, from Kauśalyā; the second, Bharata, possessing a fourth part, from Kaikeyī; and the other two, Lakshmaṇa and Śatru-ghna, sharing the remaining quarter between them, from Sumitrā. The brothers are all deeply attached to each other; but Lakshmaṇa (often called Saumitri) is especially the companion of Rāma, and Śatru-ghna of Bharata.[1]

While yet striplings, Rāma and his brothers are taken by Viśvāmitra (see p. 361) to the court of Janaka, king of Mithilā or Videha.[2] He had a wonderful bow, once the property of Śiva, and had given out, that the man who

birth is given. His birthday is called *Rāma-navamī* (see p. 365, note 1), because he is said (I. xix. 1, 2, II. xv. 3) to have been born on the 9th Tithi of Caitra, about the vernal equinox, Jupiter being in Cancer (*Karkaṭa*). Weber thinks that the mention of the Zodiacal sign and the planet Jupiter is a proof of the late date to be assigned to the composition of the Rāmāyaṇa, or at least of this passage, seeing that the Hindūs obtained their knowledge of the signs and planets from the Greeks, and these latter only completed their Zodiac in the first century B.C. Weber, however, remarks that in the Rāmāyaṇa Ceylon is never called Tāmraparṇī or Siṇhala (by which name alone it was known to the Greeks), but always *Lan-kā*.

[1] Although in xix. the birth of Bharata is narrated after that of Rāma, he is supposed to have been born after the twins; and we read in I. xv. that the divine nectar containing the essence of the god Vishṇu was drunk by Sumitrā next to Kauśalyā. According to Schlegel, Bharata was eleven months junior to Rāma, and the twins only three months. Probably the mother of Bharata was higher in rank than Sumitrā, which would give him the precedence. Lakshmaṇa was to Rāma like another self (*Rāmasya Lakshmaṇo vahiḥprāṇa ivāparaḥ, na ća tena vinā nidrāṃ labhate, na taṃ vinā mishṭam annam upānītam aśnāti*, I. xix. 20–22).

[2] It is evident that Mithilā (North Behār and Tirhut), situated quite towards the east, was an Āryan country at this time, for Janaka is described (Rām. I. 12) as conversant with all the Śāstras and Vedas. He is a frequent interlocutor in the Bṛihad-āraṇyaka.

could bend it should win his beautiful daughter Sītā.[1] On the arrival of Rāma and his brothers the bow is brought on an eight-wheeled platform, drawn by no less than 5000 men. Rāma not only bends the bow, but snaps it asunder with a concussion so terrible that the whole assembly is thrown to the ground, and the earth quivers as if a mountain were rent in twain.

Sītā thus becomes the wife of Rāma, and she remained his one wife—the type of wife-like devotion. Rāma also remained her faithful lord—the type of all that a husband ought to be in loving tenderness and fidelity.[2]

On their way back to Ayodhyā, Daśaratha and his sons are met by Paraśu-rāma, and here we have introduced the curious episode of the conflict between the second Rāma and the previous incarnation of Vishṇu—who suddenly appears on the scene (though not till various strange omens and awful portents had given notice of his approach) to challenge the young son of Daśaratha. The object of this digression, which is clearly not part of the original story, seems to be, that the ex-incarnation of

[1] Called Sītā because not born from a woman, but from a furrow (*sītā*) while Janaka was ploughing (I. lxvi. 14). This has given rise to a theory that the story of Rāma allegorizes the introduction of agriculture into the south of India. The name Sītā occurs in Taittirīya-brāhmaṇa II. 3, 10, 1–3, as applied to the daughter of Savitṛi, or Prajāpati, and as in love with the Moon, who on his part loves another daughter, Śraddhā, but in the end is brought to love Sītā. (See also Ṛig-veda IV. 57, 6, 7; Atharva-veda XI. 3, 12.) This is a variation of the older legend which represents Savitṛi as giving his daughter Sūryā in marriage to the Moon. This may account for the name *Rāma-ćandra*, 'moon-like Rāma,' which was ultimately given to the hero of the Rāmāyaṇa.

[2] In this respect he contrasts very remarkably with the five Pāṇḍavas—the heroes of the Mahā-bhārata—who had one wife between them as common property, besides others on their own private account.

Vishṇu, as a Brāhman, may, by acknowledging himself justly superseded by the Kshatriya incarnation, give a Brāhmanical sanction to the deification of the second Rāma; but much mythological mysticism is mixed up with the narrative, with the apparent design of obscuring the actual facts of the Kshatriya hero's victory, which could not, if stated in plain language, be otherwise than mortifying to Brāhmanical pride. I here abridge the story as told in Rāmāyaṇa I. lxxiv., &c. (Schlegel; Muir's Texts, vol. iv. pp. 176, 177):—

When the king and his son Rāma were returning home after the marriage of the latter to Sītā, he was alarmed by the ill-omened sounds uttered by certain birds, which, however, were counteracted, as the sage Vasishṭha assured the king, by the auspicious sign of his being perambulated by the wild animals of the forest. Then a hurricane shook the earth, uprooting the trees, and thick darkness veiled the sun. Finally, Paraśu-rāma appeared, fearful to behold, brilliant as fire, with his axe in his hand, and a bow on his shoulder. He was angry at the breaking of the bow of S'iva, of whom he was a disciple. Being reverently received, he proceeded to tell Rāma, Daśaratha's son, that he had heard of his success in breaking S'iva's bow, and had brought another bow, once the property of Vishṇu (I. lxxv. 13), which he asked Rāma to bend, and fit an arrow on the string, adding, that if he succeeded in bending it, he (Paraśu-rāma) would challenge him to single combat. Rāma replies that though his powers were slighted by his rival, he would give him a proof of his strength. Whereupon, he angrily snatches the bow from Paraśu-rāma, bends it, fits an arrow on the string, and tells his challenger that he will spare his life because he is a Brāhman, but will either destroy his supernatural power of movement, or deprive him of the abode in bliss he had acquired by his austerities. The gods now arrive to be witnesses of the scene. Paraśu-rāma becomes disheartened, loses his strength, and entreats not to be deprived of his faculty of moving in the air (lest he should be unable to fulfil his promise, made to Kaśyapa, to leave the earth every night). He then continues to say that by the bending of the bow he recognizes Rāma's divinity, and that he regards defeat by the lord of the three worlds as no disgrace. The second Rāma then shoots the arrow, and thereby in some mysterious manner destroys Paraśu-rāma's abode in the celestial world.

Daśaratha and his party now return to the capital, and

preparations are made for the inauguration of Rāma as successor to the throne, when Kaikeyī, mother of his brother Bharata, jealous of the preference shown to the son of Kauśalyā, demands of the king the fulfilment of a promise, made to her in former years, that he would grant her any two boons she asked. A promise of this kind in Eastern countries is quite inviolable; and the king being required to banish his favourite son Rāma for fourteen years to the forest of Daṇḍaka, and to instal Bharata, is forced to comply.

Rāma, therefore, with his wife Sītā and his brother Lakshmaṇa, is banished. They establish themselves in the forest near the river Godāvarī.[1] Meanwhile the heart-broken king pines away in inconsolable anguish. Here occurs a touching episode (II. lxiii.). The king, in the midst of his despondency, confesses that his present bereavement is a punishment for a deed of blood committed by himself accidentally in his youthful days. Thus it happened: (I translate as nearly as I can word for word, in a metre resembling the sixteen-syllable heroic verse of the original, omitting portions here and there):—

One day when rains refreshed the earth, and caused my heart to swell with joy,
When, after scorching with his rays the parchëd ground, the summer sun
Had passed towards the south; when cooling breezes chased away the heat,
And grateful clouds arose; when frogs and pea-fowl sported, and the deer
Seemed drunk with glee, and all the winged creation, dripping as if drowned,
Plumed their dank feathers on the tops of wind-rocked trees, and falling showers
Covered the mountains till they looked like watery heaps, and torrents poured
Down from their sides, filled with loose stones and red as dawn with mineral earth,
Winding like serpents in their course; then at that charming season I,
Longing to breathe the air, went forth, with bow and arrow in my hand,
To seek for game, if haply by the river-side a buffalo,
Or elephant or other animal might cross, at eve, my path,
Coming to drink. Then in the dusk I heard the sound of gurgling water:

---

[1] The Daṇḍaka forest is described as beginning south of the Jumnā, and extending to the Godāvarī. The whole of that country was a wilderness, inhabited by savage tribes (Rākshasas), and infested by wild beasts.

Quickly I took my bow, and aiming toward the sound, shot off the dart.
A cry of mortal agony came from the spot,—a human voice
Was heard, and a poor hermit's son fell pierced and bleeding in the stream.
'Ah! wherefore then,' he cried, 'am I a harmless hermit's son struck down?
Hither to this lone brook I came at eve to fill my water-jar.
By whom have I been smitten? whom have I offended? Oh! I grieve
Not for myself or my own fate, but for my parents, old and blind,
Who perish in my death! Ah! what will be the end of that loved pair,
Long guided and supported by my hand? this barbëd dart has pierced
Both me and them.' Hearing that piteous voice, I Daśaratha,
Who meant no harm to any human creature, young or old, became
Palsied with fear; my bow and arrows dropped from my senseless hands;
And I approached the place in horror; there with dismay I saw,
Stretched on the bank, an innocent hermit-boy, writhing in pain and smeared
With dust and blood, his knotted hair dishevelled, and a broken jar
Lying beside him. I stood petrified and speechless. He on me
Fixed full his eyes, and then, as if to burn my inmost soul, he said,
'How have I wronged thee, monarch? that thy cruel hand has smitten me—
Me, a poor hermit's son, born in the forest: father, mother, child
Hast thou transfixed with this one arrow: they, my parents, sit at home
Expecting my return, and long will cherish hope—a prey to thirst
And agonizing fears. Go to my father—tell him of my fate,
Lest his dread curse consume thee, as the flame devours the withered wood.
But first in pity draw thou forth the shaft that pierces to my heart,
And checks the gushing life-blood, as the bank obstructs the bounding stream.'[1]
He ceased, and as he rolled his eyes in agony, and quivering writhed
Upon the ground, I slowly drew the arrow from the poor boy's side.
Then with a piteous look, his features set in terror, he expired.
Distracted at the grievous crime, wrought by my hand unwittingly;
Sadly I thought within myself, how best I might repair the wrong,
Then took the way he had directed me towards the hermitage.
There I beheld his parents, old and blind; like two clipped wingless birds
Sitting forlorn, without their guide, awaiting his arrival anxiously,
And, to beguile their weariness, conversing of him tenderly.
Quickly they caught the sound of footsteps, and I heard the old man say,
With chiding voice, 'Why hast thou lingered, child? Quick give us both to drink
A little water. Long forgetful of us, in the cooling stream
Hast thou disported; come in—for thy mother yearneth for her son.
If she or I in ought have caused thee pain, or spoken hasty words,
Think on thy hermit's duty of forgiveness; bear them not in mind.
Thou art the refuge of us refugeless—the eyes of thy blind sire.
Why art thou silent? Speak! Bound up in thee are both thy parents' lives.'
He ceased, and I stood paralyzed—till by an effort resolutely

---

[1] I have omitted the youth's statement that he is not a Brahman, but begotten by a Vaiśya on a Śūdrā woman (II. lxiii. 48, &c.).

Collecting all my powers of utterance, with faltering voice I said,
'Pious and noble hermit; I am not thy son; I am the king:
Wandering with bow and arrow by a stream, seeking for game, I pierced
Unknowingly thy child. The rest I need not tell. Be gracious to me.'
Hearing my pitiless words, announcing his bereavement, he remained
Senseless awhile; then drawing a deep sigh, his face all bathed in tears,
He spake to me as I approached him suppliantly, and slowly said,
'Hadst thou not come thyself, to tell the awful tale, its load of guilt
Had crushed thy head into ten thousand fragments. This ill-fated deed
Was wrought by thee unwittingly, O king, else hadst thou not been spared,
And all the race of Rāghavas had perished. Lead us to the place:
All bloody though he be, and lifeless, we must look upon [1] our son
For the last time, and clasp him in our arms.' Then weeping bitterly
The pair, led by my hand, came to the spot and fell upon their son.
Thrilled by the touch, the father cried, 'My child, hast thou no greeting for us?
No word of recognition: wherefore liest thou here upon the ground?
Art thou offended? or am I no longer loved by thee, my son?
See here thy mother. Thou wert ever dutiful towards us both.
Why wilt thou not embrace me? speak one tender word. Whom shall I hear
Reading again the sacred S'āstra in the early morning hours?
Who now will bring me roots and fruits to feed me like a cherished guest?
How, weak and blind, can I support thy aged mother, pining for her son?
Stay! Go not yet to Death's abode—stay with thy parents yet one day,
To-morrow we will both go with thee on the dreary way. Forlorn
And sad, deserted by our child, without protector in the wood,
Soon shall we both depart toward the mansions of the King of death.'
Thus bitterly lamenting, he performed the funeral rites; then turning
Towards me thus addressed me, standing reverently near—'I had
But this one child, and thou hast made me childless. Now strike down
The father: I shall feel no pain in death. But thy requital be
That sorrow for a child shall one day bring thee also to the grave.'

After narrating this affecting incident of his early life, king Daśaratha, struck with remorse, sickens and dies.[2]

Soon afterwards the ministers assemble, and decide that Bharata shall assume the government (II. lxxix.), but he declines to deprive his elder brother Rāma of his rightful inheritance, and declares his intention of setting out for

---

[1] This is literally translated. It is well known that blind people commonly talk of themselves as if able to see.

[2] His body is burnt with much pomp. We have already noted, as a proof of the antiquity of the poem, that his widows are not burnt with him (see p. 312).

the forest with a complete army (*ćatur-anga*) to bring Rāma back, and his determination to undergo in his place the appointed term of fourteen years' exile in the forest (II. lxxix. 8, 9).

After some trouble he discovers Rāma's retreat at Ćitrakūṭa.[1] There and then he breaks the sad news of his father's death, and entreats him to return to Ayodhyā and assume the sovereignty (cii.).

Next ensues a generous contest between the brothers; Bharata imploring Rāma to accept the throne, and Rāma insisting on the duty of fulfilling his father's vow (cvi., cvii.).

Here occurs the episode in which the Brāhman Jāvāli, who is a sort of impersonation of scepticism, tries in a brief address (II. cviii.) to instil atheistic and irreligious sentiments into Rāma, hoping to shake his resolution and induce him to accept the kingdom. His speech, which is full of interest as indicating the prevalence of infidel and materialistic doctrines at the time when the brahmanized version of the Rāmāyaṇa was completed, may be thus abridged:—

You ought not by abandoning your paternal kingdom to enter upon a wrong road, beset with difficulties and troubles. Permit yourself to be enthroned in Ayodhyā. Daśaratha (your father) is dead and is now nothing to you, nor you to him. Any one who feels attachment for any other person is insane, since no one is anything to any other. I

---

[1] The isolated hill Ćitra-kūṭa is the holiest spot of the worshippers of Rāma, and is crowded with temples and shrines of Rāma and Lakshmaṇa. Every cavern is connected with their names; the heights swarm with monkeys, and some of the wild-fruits are still called Sītā-phal. It is situated on a river called the Piśunī, described as the Mandākinī (II. xcv.), fifty miles south-east of the town of Bandah in Bundelkund, lat. 25. 12, long. 80. 47. The river is lined with ghats and flights of stairs suitable for religious ablutions. It is worthy of note that at some holy places all distinctions of caste are laid aside by the Hindūs.

grieve for those who swerve not from virtue and justice; such persons suffer affliction here, and when they die incur annihilation. Men are careful to offer oblations to their progenitors, but what can a dead man eat? If an oblation eaten here by one person, passes into the body of another, then let a S'rāddha be offered to a man who is travelling abroad; he need not eat upon his journey (cf. the doctrine of the Ćārvākas, p. 120). The books composed by theologians (in which men are enjoined to) worship, give gifts, offer sacrifice, practise austerities, abandon the world, are mere artifices to draw forth gifts (*dāna-saṃvananā*). Make up your mind (*kuru buddhim*) that no one exists hereafter. Have regard only to what is visible and perceptible by the senses (*pratyaksham*). Cast everything beyond this behind your back (*prishṭhataḥ kuru*). (See Dr. Muir's article on Indian Materialists, Journal of the Asiatic Society, vol. xix. p. 303.)

Rāma's reply, in which he indignantly rebukes Jāvāli, is a noble vindication of religion and faith, but his reference to Buddhism and his designation of Buddha himself as a *Ćora* or thief (II. cviii. 33) must be regarded as interpolations.[1]

In the end Bharata desists from pressing his brother to accept the throne, but only consents to take charge of the kingdom as a deposit. He bears away Rāma's shoes on his head in token of this (cxiii. 1), and takes up his abode outside Ayodhyā, at Nandi-grāma, until the return of the rightful king, never transacting any business without first laying it before the shoes (cxv.). Before dismissing him, the forgiving Rāma entreats him not to indulge angry feelings towards his mother for having caused the family calamities, in these words:—

Cherish thy mother Kaikeyī, show no resentment towards her (II. cxii. 27).

After Bharata's departure ten years of Rāma's banishment pass in moving from one hermitage to another. In

---

[1] Other allusions to rationalistic doctrines will be found scattered throughout the Rāmāyaṇa.

the description of the quiet life of the exiles we find that their morning and evening devotions are never omitted, and that Sītā dutifully waits on her husband and brother-in-law, never eating till they have finished.[1] When they travel, Rāma walks first, Sītā in the middle, and Lakshmaṇa behind (III. xv. 1). At length they move westward to visit the hermitage of the sage Agastya, near the Vindhya mountains. He advises Rāma to live for the remainder of his exile in the neighbourhood of Janasthāna at Pañćavatī on the Godāvarī[2] (xix.). This district is infested by Rākshasas, and, amongst others, by Rāvaṇa's sister, Śūrpa-ṇakhā, who becomes smitten with love for Rāma. He of course repels her, telling her that he is already married (xxiv. 1); but this only rouses the jealousy of Śūrpa-ṇakhā, who makes an attack on Sītā, and so infuriates the fiery Lakshmaṇa that he thoughtlessly cuts off her ears and nose[3] (xxiv. 22). Śūrpa-ṇakhā, smarting with pain and bent on revenge, repairs to her brother Rāvaṇa, the demon-monarch of Ceylon.

The description of Rāvaṇa (III. xxxvi.; Bombay ed. xxxii.) is as follows:—

This mighty demon had ten faces, twenty arms, copper-coloured eyes, a huge chest, and bright teeth like the young moon. His form was as a thick cloud, or a mountain, or the god of death with open mouth. He had all the marks of royalty; but his body bore the impress of wounds inflicted by all the divine arms in his warfare with the gods. It was scarred by the thunderbolt of Indra, by the tusks of (Indra's) elephant Airāvata, and by the discus of Vishṇu. His strength was so great that he could agitate the seas and split the tops of mountains. He was a breaker of all laws, and a ravisher of other men's wives. He once penetrated into Bhogavatī (the serpent-capital of Pātāla),

---

[1] This custom remains unaltered to the present day. Compare Manu IV. 43: 'Let him not eat with his wife, nor look at her eating.'

[2] A spot now known as Nāsik, in the Bombay Presidency.

[3] It was from this circumstance that Pañćavatī is now called Nāsik (*nāsikā*, 'the nose').

conquered the great serpent Vāsuki, and carried off the beloved wife of Takshaka. He defeated Vaiśravaṇa (*i.e.*, his own brother Kuvera, the god of wealth), and carried off his self-moving chariot called Pushpaka. He devastated the divine groves of Ćitra-ratha, and the gardens of the gods. Tall as a mountain peak, he stopped with his arms the sun and moon in their course, and prevented their rising. The sun, when it passed over his residence, drew in its beams in terror. He underwent severe austerities in the forest of Gokarṇa for ten thousand years, standing in the midst of five fires (see p. 95) with his feet in the air; whence he was released by Brahmā, and obtained from him (among other boons, see p. 343) the power of taking what shape he pleased.[1]

The better to secure the mighty Rāvaṇa's co-operation, Śūrpa-ṇakhā succeeds in inspiring him with a passion for Sītā (III. xxxviii. 17), whom he determines to carry off. Having with difficulty secured the aid of another demon, Mārīća—who was the son of the Tāḍakā (I. xxvii. 8) formerly killed by Rāma—Rāvaṇa transports himself and his accomplice in the aërial car Pushpaka to the forest near Rāma's dwelling. Mārīća then assumes the form of a beautiful golden deer, which so captivates Sītā (III. xlviii. 11) that Rāma is induced to leave her with Lakshmaṇa, that he may catch the deer for her, or kill it. Mortally wounded by his arrow, the deer utters cries for help, feigning Rāma's voice, which so alarms Sītā that

[1] One cannot help comparing part of this description with Milton's portrait of Satan. The majestic imagery of the English poet stands out in striking contrast to the wild hyperbole of Vālmīki. It appears from III. liii. (Gorresio) that Rāvaṇa was the son of Viśravas, who was the son of the sage Pulastya, who was the son of Brahmā. Hence Rāvaṇa was the brother of the god Kuvera (though by a different mother), and in verse 30 he calls himself his brother and enemy. Both he and Kuvera are sometimes called Paulastya. Vibhīshaṇa and Kumbha-karṇa were also brothers of Rāvaṇa, and, like him, propitiated Brahmā by their penances, and, like him, obtained boons, but the boon chosen by Vibhīshaṇa was that he should never swerve from virtue, and by Kumbha-karṇa (whose size was gigantic and appetite voracious) that he should enjoy deep sleep for long periods of time. (See Mahābhārata III. 15916.)

she persuades Lakshmaṇa against his will to leave her alone and go to the assistance of his brother. Meanwhile Rāvaṇa approaches in the guise of a religious mendicant. All nature seems petrified with terror as he advances (III. iii. 10, 11); and when Sītā's eyes fall on the stranger, she starts, but is lulled to confidence by his mendicant's dress, and offers him food and water. Suddenly Rāvaṇa declares himself. Then throwing off his disguise he avows his intention to make her his queen. Sītā's indignation bursts forth, but her wrath is powerless against the fierce Rāvaṇa, who takes her up in his arms, places her in his self-moving car, and bears her through the sky to his capital. As Sītā is carried along, she invokes heaven and earth, mountains and streams (lv. 43). The gods and saints come to look on, and are struck with horror, but they stand in awe of the ravisher, and know that this is part of the plan for his destruction. All nature shudders, the sun's disc pales, darkness overspreads the heavens (lviii. 16–43). It is the short-lived triumph of evil over good. Even the great Creator Brahmā rouses himself, and exclaims, 'Sin is consummated' (III. lviii. 17).

Arrived in the demon-city, Rāvaṇa forces Sītā to inspect all the wonders and beauties of his capital (III. lxi.), and then promises to make them hers, if she will consent to become his queen. Indignantly rejected, he is enraged, and delivers her over to the guardianship of a troop of Rākshasīs or female furies, who are described as horrible in appearance, and cannibal in their propensities (III. lxii. 29–38). Tormented by them, she seems likely to die of despair, but Brahmā in compassion sends Indra to her with the god of sleep,[1] and a vessel containing celestial food (lxiii. 7, 8) to support her strength.

---

[1] Similarly in the Odyssey (IV. 795) Minerva sends a dream to console and animate Penelope.

Terrible is the wrath of the usually gentle Rāma when on his return he finds that Sītā is carried off by Rāvaṇa (lxix.). He and Lakshmaṇa at once set off on a long search, determined to effect her rescue. After many adventures, in the course of which they have a battle with a headless fiend called Kabandha, who opposes their progress, but is killed, and then restored to life by them (III. lxxiv.), they make an alliance with Sugrīva, king of the monkeys (foresters), and assisted by Hanumat, one of the monkey-generals, and by Rāvaṇa's brother Vibhīshaṇa, invade Lan-kā, the capital of Rāvaṇa, in Ceylon (IV. lxiii.).

To transport the army across the channel, a bridge is constructed under the direction of the monkey-general Nala, son of Viśva-karman:—

Thousands of monkey bridge-builders, flying through the sky in every direction, tear up rocks and trees, and throw them into the water. In bringing huge crags from the Himālayas, some are accidentally dropped, and remain to this day monuments of the exploit. At length a pier[1] is formed twenty Yojanas long and ten wide (V. xcv. 11–15), by which the whole army crosses, Vibhīshaṇa taking the lead. The gods, Ṛishis, Pitṛis, &c., look on, and utter the celebrated prophecy—

'*As long as the sea shall remain, so long shall this pier* (setu) *endure, and the fame of Rāma be proclaimed.*'[2]

---

[1] The god of the ocean at first objected to a regular embankment (V. xciv. 8), though a pier (described as a *setu*) was afterwards constructed: the line of rocks in the channel is certainly known in India as Rāma-setu. In maps it is called 'Adam's bridge.' Everywhere in India are scattered isolated blocks, attributed by the natives to Rāma's bridge-builders. More than this, the hill Govardhana, near Muttra, and the whole Kymar range in Central India are firmly believed to have arisen from the same cause.

[2] 'In the midst of the arm of the sea is the island Ramesurum (Rāmeśvara), or the pillar of Rāma, of as great repute and renown as the pillars of the western Hercules. There to this day stands a temple of massive Cyclopean workmanship, said to have been built by the hero, the idol of which is washed daily with water from the Ganges.

After various engagements, described with much wearisome exaggeration, the great battle between Rāma and Rāvaṇa takes place :—

The gods assemble to take the side of the former, and all the demons and evil spirits back their own champion (VI. lxxxvii. 8). Rāvaṇa is mounted on a magic car, drawn by horses having human faces (*manushyavadanair hayaiḥ*); and, in order that the two champions may fight on an equality, Indra sends his own car, driven by his charioteer Mātali, for the use of Rāma. Both armies cease fighting, that they may look on (xci. 2); but the gods and demons in the sky, taking the part of either warrior, renew their ancient strife.[1] The heroes now overwhelm each other with arrows. Rāma cuts off a hundred heads from Rāvaṇa successively; but no sooner is one cut off than another appears in its place[2] (xcii. 24), and the battle, which has already lasted seven days and seven nights without interruption, seems likely to be endlessly protracted, until Mātali informs Rāma that Rāvaṇa is not vulnerable in the head. Thereupon Rāma shoots off the terrible arrow of Brahmā,[3] given to him by the sage Agastya, and the demon-king falls dead (xcii. 58).

From the highest point is a commanding view of the ocean, and the interminable black line of rocks stretching across the gulf of Manaar. Thither, from all parts of India, wander the pilgrims, who are smitten with the wondrous love of travel to sacred shrines. From Chuteerkote (*Ćitra-kūṭa*), near the Jumnā, it is roughly calculated to be one hundred stages. We have conversed with some who have accomplished the great feat: but many never return; they either die by the way, or their courage and strength evaporate in some roadside hermitage. Whatever may be its origin, there is the reefy barrier, compelling every vessel from or to the mouths of the Ganges, to circumnavigate the island of Ceylon.' Calcutta Review, XLV.

[1] This is just what takes place in the Iliad before the great battle between Achilles and Hector, the gods taking their respective places on either side (Il. XX.). It is interesting to compare the simple Homeric narrative with the wild improbabilities of the Indian poem.

[2] This reminds one of Hercules and the Hydra.

[3] Here called *paitāmaham astram*, and described as having the wind for its feathers, the fire and the sun for its point, the air for its body, and the mountains Meru and Mandara for its weight (VI. xcii. 45). It had the very convenient property of returning to its owner's quiver

Great portents and prodigies precede the fall of Rāvaṇa, and when the victory is consummated a perfect deluge of flowers covers the conqueror. The generous Rāma causes magnificent obsequies to be performed over the body of his enemy, which is duly consumed by fire,[1] and then places Vibhīshaṇa on the throne of Laṅkā (VI. xcvii. 15). Rāma then sends Hanumat with a message to Sītā, and Vibhīshaṇa brings her into his presence in a litter (*śivikā*); but Rāma allows her to come before him on foot, that she may be seen by all the army.

The monkeys crowd round her, admiring her incomparable beauty, the cause of so much toil, danger, and suffering to themselves.[2] On seeing her, Rāma is deeply moved. Three feelings distract him—joy, grief, and anger (xcix. 19)—and he does not address his wife. Sītā, conscious of her purity, is hurt by his cold reception of her, and bursts into tears, uttering only the words, *hā āryaputra*, 'alas! my husband!' Rāma then haughtily informs her, that having satisfied his honour by the destruction of the demon who had wronged his wife, he can do no more. He cannot take her back, contaminated as she must certainly be (VI. c.). Sītā asserts her innocence in the most dignified and touching language, and directs Lakshmaṇa to prepare a pyre, that she may prove her purity. She enters the flames, invoking Agni (ci.); upon which all the gods with the old king Daśaratha appear, and reveal to Rāma his divine nature,[3] telling him that he is Nārāyaṇa, and that Sītā is Lakshmī (cii.). Agni, the god of fire, then presents himself, holding Sītā, whom he places in Rāma's arms unhurt.[4] Thereupon

---

after doing its work. There appear to have been various forms of this unerring weapon.

[1] Contrast this with Achilles' treatment of the fallen Hector.

[2] The whole scene is very similar to that in Iliad III. 121, &c., where Helen shows herself on the rampart, and calls forth much the same kind of admiration.

[3] He never appears to be conscious of it, until the gods enlighten him. (See VI. cii. 10, cxix.) This is not the case with Kṛishṇa in the Mahā-bhārata. It is probable, as we have seen, that all these passages are later additions.

[4] The whole description of Sītā's repudiation by Rāma is certainly one of the finest scenes in the Rāmāyaṇa.

Rāma is overjoyed, and declares that he only consented to the ordeal that he might establish his wife's innocence in the eyes of the world (ciii.). Daśaratha then blesses his son, gives him good advice, and returns to heaven (civ.); while Indra, at the request of Rāma, restores to life all the monkeys killed during the war (cv.).

Rāma and Lakshmaṇa, along with Vibhīshaṇa, Sugrīva, and the allies, now mount the self-moving car Pushpaka, which is described as containing a whole palace within itself, and set out on their return to Ayodhyā; Rāma, to beguile the way as they travel through the sky, recounting to Sītā all the scenes of their late adventures lying beneath their feet[1] (cviii.). On their reaching the hermitage of Bharadvāja at Prayāga, the car is stopped; and the fourteen years of banishment having now expired (cix.), Hanumat is sent forward to announce their return to Bharata. Rāma and the three brothers are now once more reunited, and, accompanied by them and by Sītā and the monkeys, who assume human forms (cxii. 28), he makes a magnificent entry into Ayodhyā. He is then solemnly crowned, associates Lakshmaṇa in the empire, and, before dismissing his allies, bestows on them splendid presents (cxii.). Hanumat, at his own request, receives as a reward the gift of perpetual life and youth (cxii. 101). Every one returns happy and loaded with gifts to his own home, and Rāma commences a glorious reign at Ayodhyā (cxiii.).

Such is a brief sketch of the Rāmāyaṇa, omitting the Uttara-kāṇḍa or supplementary chapters, which contain the concluding events in the life of Rāma (see p. 337).

---

[1] Kālidāsa devotes nearly the whole of the thirteenth chapter of his Raghu-vaṇśa to this subject, which he makes a convenient pretext for displaying his geographical and topographical knowledge, as in the Megha-dūta. Bhava-bhūti does the same in the seventh act of his drama, Mahā-vīra-ćaritra; and Murāri, the same in his play on the same subject.

Much of the story, exaggerated as its later details are, probably rests, as we have already pointed out, on a foundation of historical truth.

It is clear, too, that a moral lesson is intended to be conveyed by the whole narrative. Under the story of the conflict between the armies of the noble Rāma and the barbarous races of the South, figured by the Rākshasas, there appears to lie a typical representation of the great mystery of the struggle ever going on between the powers of good and evil. With regard, however, to any other allegorical and figurative ideas involved, as, for example, that Rāma is a mere impersonation of the Solar energy;[1] Sītā, of agriculture or of civilization introduced into the South of India by immigrants from the North; the Rākshasas, of night, darkness or winter—whatever ingenuity there may be in any or all of these theories, it seems very questionable whether any such conceptions ever entered into the mind of the author or authors of any part of the poem.

---

[1] Certainly Rāma belongs to the Solar race of kings, but this points to the connection of the Epic Vishṇu (of whom Rāma came to be regarded as an incarnation) with the Solar Vishṇu of the Veda. Professor Weber remarks that as Rāma is at a later period called Rāma-ćandra, and is even in one place called Ćandra alone, the mildness so conspicuous in his character might be explained by supposing that he was originally a kind of moon-genius, and that the legend in the Taittirīya-brāhmaṇa (see note 1, p. 346) representing the love of Sītā (the field-furrow) for the Moon might be regarded by some zealous mythologists as the first germ of the story of the Rāmāyaṇa; the beautifying ointment (*anga-rāga*) which Anasūyā, wife of Atri, poured over the limbs of Sītā (III. 2), representing the dew spread over the furrow in which the moonlight is reflected. Weber, however, thinks that as the name Rāma-ćandra was not given to the second Rāma till a late date (the first application of it occurring in Bhava-bhūti's Mahā-vīra-ćaritra III. 18), the converse is rather true, viz., that a poetical spirit among the Brāhmans connected Rāma with the Moon merely on account of the mildness of his character.

Time would fail, if we were to attempt even the briefest epitome of all the episodes in the Rāmāyaṇa. I note two others in addition to those already given. That of Viśvāmitra (I. 51–65), which is one of the most interesting, may be thus abridged:[1]—

Viśvāmitra, son of Gādhi, was a prince of the Lunar race, sovereign of Kanoj, and the district of Magadha. He had a tremendous conflict with the Brāhman Vaśishṭha for the possession of the cow of plenty (Kāmadhenu, also called S'avalā), which no doubt typified the earth (*go*) or India. At the command of Vaśishṭha, the cow created hordes of barbarians, such as Pahlavas (Persians), S'akas (Scythians), Yavanas (Greeks), Kambojas, &c., by whose aid Vaśishṭha conquered Viśvāmitra. Hence the latter, convinced of the superior power inherent in Brāhmanism, determined to raise himself to that dignity, and in order to effect this object, increased the rigour of his austerities for thousands of years. The gods, who always had a hard struggle to hold their own against resolute ascetics, did what they could to interrupt him, and partially succeeded. Viśvāmitra yielded for a time to the seductions of the nymph Menakā, sent by them to entice his thoughts towards sensual objects. A daughter (S'akuntalā) was the result of this temporary backsliding. However, in the end, the obstinate ascetic was too much for the whole troop of deities. He obtained complete power over his passions, and when the gods still refused to brāhmanize him, he began creating new heavens and new gods, and had already manufactured a few stars, when the celestial host thought it prudent to concede the point, and make him a veritable Brāhman.

Another curious episode is the story of the Ganges (I. 36–44):[2]—

Gan·gā, the personified Ganges, was the eldest daughter of Himavat, lord of mountains, her younger sister being Umā. Sagara, a king of Ayodhyā, of the Solar race, had 60,000 sons, who were directed by their father to look for a horse which had been stolen by Rākshasa at an Aśva-medha or horse-sacrifice. Having first searched the earth unsuccessfully, they proceeded to dig up the ground towards the lower regions.

---

[1] The episode of Viśvāmitra includes under it the story of Ambarīsha given at p. 27 of this volume.

[2] The story is also told in the Mahā-bhārata, Vana-parvan 9920, &c.

Meeting with the sage Kapila, they accused him of the theft, which enraged him to such a degree, that without more ado he reduced them all to ashes. Sagara's grandson some time afterwards found their remains, and commenced performing the funeral obsequies of his relatives, but was told that it was necessary for Gan·gā to water the ashes with her sacred stream. Neither Sagara, however, nor his grandson could devise any means for effecting the descent of the heavenly river It was reserved for his great-grandson, Bhagīratha, by his austerities to bring down the sacred stream from heaven. In her descent she fell first with great fury on the head of S'iva, who undertook to break her fall.

Mr. Ralph Griffith has translated the description of this descent with great skill and taste. I subjoin a portion of his version (vol. i. p. 194):—

On S'iva's head descending first
A rest the torrents found,
Then down in all their might they burst
And roared along the ground.
On countless glittering scales the beam
Of rosy morning flashed,
Where fish and dolphins through the stream
Fallen and falling dashed.
Then bards who chant celestial lays,
And nymphs of heavenly birth,
Flocked round upon that flood to gaze
That streamed from sky to earth.
The gods themselves from every sphere,
Incomparably bright,
Borne in their golden cars drew near
To see the wondrous sight.
The cloudless sky was all aflame
With the light of a hundred suns,
Where'er the shining chariots came
That bore those holy ones.
So flashed the air with crested snakes
And fish of every hue,
As when the lightning's glory breaks
Through fields of summer blue.
And white foam-clouds and silver spray
Were wildly tossed on high,
Like swans that urge their homeward way
Across the autumn sky.

Then, by further austerities, Bhagīratha forced the sacred river to flow over the earth, and to follow him thence to the ocean (therefore called Sāgara), and thence to the lower regions (Pātāla), where she watered the ashes of Sagara's sons, and became the means of conveying their souls to heaven. Hence a common name for the Ganges is Bhāgīrathī.

Another name for the river Ganges is Jāhnavī, because in its course it inundated the sacrificial ground of the sage Jahnu, who thereupon without any ceremony drank up its waters, but consented to discharge them again from his ears.

Notwithstanding the wilderness of exaggeration and hyperbole through which the reader of the Indian Epics has occasionally to wander, there are in the whole range of the world's literature few more charming poems than the Rāmāyaṇa. The classical purity, clearness, and simplicity of its style, the exquisite touches of true poetic feeling with which it abounds, its graphic descriptions of heroic incidents and nature's grandest scenes, the deep acquaintance it displays with the conflicting workings and most refined emotions of the human heart, all entitle it to rank among the most beautiful compositions that have appeared at any period or in any country. It is like a spacious and delightful garden; here and there allowed to run wild, but teeming with fruits and flowers, watered by perennial streams, and even its most tangled thickets intersected with delightful pathways. The character of Rāma is nobly pourtrayed. It is only too consistently unselfish to be human. We must, in fact, bear in mind that the poet is bent on raising his hero to the rank of a god. Yet though occasionally dazzled by flashes from his superhuman nature, we are not often blinded or bewildered by it. At least in the earlier portion of the poem he is not generally represented as more than a heroic, noble-minded, pious, and virtuous man—a model son, husband, brother—whose bravery, unselfish generosity, filial obedience, tender attachment to his wife, fraternal affection, and freedom from all resentful feelings, we cannot help admiring. When he falls a victim to the spite of his father's second wife, he cherishes no sense of wrong. When the sentence of banishment is pronounced, not a murmur escapes his lips. In noble language he expresses his resolution to sacrifice himself rather than allow his parent to break his pledged word; and he persists in this determination, notwithstanding the entreaties of his mother Kauśalyā, the taunting remarks of his fiery brother Lakshmaṇa, and his own anxious fear for the safety of his wife Sītā, who resolves to accompany him. Again, after the death of his father, when Bharata urges Rāma to accept the government, and when all the citizens add their entreaties, and the atheistical Jāvāli his sophistical arguments (see p. 351), Rāma replies:—

There is nothing greater than truth; and truth should be esteemed the most sacred of all things. The Vedas have their sole foundation in truth. Having promised obedience to my father's commands, I will neither, through covetousness nor forgetfulness nor blind ignorance, break down the barrier of truth (II. cix. 17).

As to Sītā, she is a paragon of wife-like virtues. Her pleadings for permission to accompany her husband into banishment breathe such noble devotion to her lord and master, that I close my examples with a few extracts:[1]—

A wife must share her husband's fate. My duty is to follow thee
Where'er thou goest. Apart from thee, I would not dwell in heaven itself.
Deserted by her lord, a wife is like a miserable corpse.
Close as thy shadow would I cleave to thee in this life and hereafter.
Thou art my king, my guide, my only refuge, my divinity.

---

[1] I have translated these nearly literally, but not consecutively, in the sixteen-syllable metre of the original. The substance of them will be found in the text of Gorresio's Rāmāyaṇa, vol. ii. p. 74, &c.

It is my fixed resolve to follow thee. If thou must wander forth
Through thorny trackless forests, I will go before thee, treading down
The prickly brambles to make smooth thy path. Walking before thee, I
Shall feel no weariness: the forest-thorns will seem like silken robes;
The bed of leaves, a couch of down. To me the shelter of thy presence
Is better far than stately palaces, and paradise itself.
Protected by thy arm, gods, demons, men shall have no power to harm me.
With thee I'll live contentedly on roots and fruits. Sweet or not sweet,
If given by thy hand, they will to me be like the food of life.
Roaming with thee in desert wastes, a thousand years will be a day;
Dwelling with thee, e'en hell itself would be to me a heaven of bliss.

As if in support of the prophecy recorded in the beginning of the work (see p. 338) the story of Rāma down to the death of Rāvaṇa and recovery of Sītā, is still regularly recited every year throughout a great part of India, at an annual festival in the beginning of October, called Rāma-līlā.[1] Moreover, Hindū writers never seem tired of working up the oft-repeated tale into various forms. Hence the history of the adventures of Rāma, or at least some reference to them, is found in almost every work of the subsequent literature. I conclude this chapter with instances:—

---

[1] On the day in the month Aśvin or beginning of October, when the Bengālīs consign their images of Durgā to the waters (*i.e.*, at the Durgāpūjā, of which the fourth day is called Daśahara, and during which for a whole fortnight all business is suspended, and even thieves and rogues allow themselves a vacation), Hindūs of other provinces perform the Rāma-līlā, a dramatic representation of the carrying off of Sīta, concluding with the death of Rāvaṇa, of which that day is the anniversary. Rāma's birth is celebrated on the 9th of the month Ćaitra (April), called Rāma-navamī. The sequel of the story of Rāma, as contained in the Uttara-kāṇḍa and Uttara-rāma-ćarita, is not so popularly known. See an article in the 'Indian Antiquary' for May 1872, by the Rev. K. M. Banerjea. It is noteworthy that the Rāma legends have always retained their purity, and, unlike those of Brahmā, Kṛishṇa, S'iva, and Durgā, have never been mixed up with indecencies and licentiousness. In fact, the worship of Rāma has never degenerated to the same extent as that of some of these other deities.

In the Mahā-bhārata (Vana-parvan 15872–16601) the Rāmopākhyāna is told very nearly as in the Rāmāyaṇa, but there is no mention of Vālmīki as its author, and no allusion to the existence of the great sister Epic. Mārkaṇḍeya is made to recount the narrative to Yudhishṭhira, after the recovery of Draupadī (who had been carried off by Jayad-ratha, as Sītā was by Rāvaṇa), in order to show that there were other examples in ancient times of virtuous people suffering violence at the hands of wicked men. It is probable (and even Professor Weber admits it to be possible) that the Mahā-bhārata episode was epitomized from the Rāmāyaṇa, and altered here and there to give it an appearance of originality. There are, however, remarkable differences. The story in the Mahā-bhārata, although generally treating Rāma as a great human hero only, begins with the circumstances which led to the incarnation of Vishṇu, and gives a detailed account of what is first mentioned in the Uttara-kāṇḍa of the Rāmāyaṇa—the early history of Rāvaṇa and his brother. The birth of Rāma, his youth, and his father's wish to inaugurate him as heir-apparent are then briefly recounted. Daśaratha's sacrifice, Rāma's education, his winning of Sītā, and other contents of the Bāla-kāṇḍa are omitted. The events of the Ayodhyā-kāṇḍa and much of the Araṇya-kāṇḍa are narrated in about forty verses. A more detailed narrative begins with the appearance before Rāvaṇa of the mutilated S'ūrpa-ṇakhā (see p. 353), but many variations occur; for instance, Kabandha is killed, but not restored to life (see p. 356); the story of S'avarī is omitted, and there is no mention of the dream sent by Brahmā to comfort Sītā (see p. 355).[1]

There are other references to, and brief epitomes of parts of the story of the Rāmāyaṇa in the Mahā-bhārata, *e.g.*, in Vana-parvan 11177–11219; in Droṇa-parvan 2224–2246; in S'ānti-parvan 944–955; in Hari-vaṇśa 2324–2359, 8672–8674, 16232.

The story of Rāma is also (as Professor Weber observes) referred to in the *Mṛicchakaṭikā* (Act I.); and although not mentioned in Kālidāsa's

[1] These and other differences have led Professor Weber to suggest the inquiry whether the Mahā-bhārata version may not be more primitive than that of the Rāmāyaṇa, and possibly even the original version, out of which the other was developed. 'Or ought we,' he asks, 'to assume only that the Mahā-bhārata contains the epitome of an earlier recension of our text of the Rāmāyaṇa; or should both texts, the Rāmopākhyāna and the Rāmāyaṇa, be regarded as resting alike upon a common groundwork, but each occupying an independent standpoint?'

dramas, it is alluded to in his *Megha-dūta* (verses 1, 99); and in his *Raghu-vanśa*—which is a kind of abridged Rāmāyaṇa—the poet Vālmīki is named (XV. 63, 64). Moreover, the Rāmāyaṇa forms the basis of a Prākṛit work called the *Setu-bandha* (ascribed to one Kālidāsa, and mentioned in Daṇḍin's *Kāvyādarśa* I. 34), as well as of the *Bhaṭṭi-kāvya*, or grammatical poem of Bhaṭṭi (written, according to Lassen, Ind. Alt. III. 512, in Valabhi-pura under king S'rīdhara-sena, between 530 and 545 of the Christian era), and of the two celebrated dramas of Bhava-bhūti, called *Mahā-vīra-ćaritra* and *Uttara-rāma-ćaritra* (whose date is fixed by Lassen between 695 and 733). The last of these dramas quotes verses from the Rāmāyaṇa in three places, one in the second and two in the sixth Act. Indeed, the dramatic literature which makes use of the adventures of Rāma for the subject-matter of the plots of its plays is extensive. Besides the two dramas of Bhava-bhūti, there is the *Hanuman-nāṭaka* or *Mahā-nāṭaka*, 'great drama,' in fourteen acts, fabled to have been composed by the monkey-chief Hanumat himself, who first wrote it on the rocks, and then to please Vālmīki (lest it should throw his Rāmāyaṇa into the shade), cast it into the sea, whence some portions were recovered in Bhoja's time and arranged by Miśra-dāmodara (probably about the tenth century). There is also the *Anargha-rāghava* or *Anarghya-rāghava* in seven acts by Murāri; the *Prasanna-rāghava* by Jaya-deva (probably not the author of the Gīta-govinda); the *Abhirāma-maṇi* in seven acts by Sundara-miśra; the *Ćampū rāmāyaṇa* by Vidarbha-rāja (or Bhoja) in five acts; the *Rāghavābhyudaya*; the *Bāla-rāmāyaṇa* by Rāja-śekhara; the *Udātta-rāghava*; the *Ćhalita-rāma*; (the last three quoted by the well-known work on the *Ars poetica* called *Sāhitya-darpaṇa*); the *Dūtāṅgada*, a short piece by Su-bhaṭa, and others.

Other works mentioned by Weber as noticing the Rāmāyaṇa are that of *Varāha-mihira*—written between 505 and 587 of our era—which takes for granted that Rāma was honoured as a demigod about that time; the *Śatruñjaya māhātmya* written in Valabhi under king S'īlāditya about A.D. 598; the *Vāsava-dattā* of Subandhu (about the beginning of the seventh century, Weber's Indische Streifen I. 373, 380), in which mention is made of the Sundara-kāṇḍa as a section of the Rāmāyaṇa; the *Kādambarī* of Bāṇa (written a little later, Indische Streifen I. 354), in which repeated reference is made to the great Epic (I. 36, 45, 81); the *Sapta-śataka* of Hāla (35, 316), on which Weber has written a treatise; the *Praćaṇḍa-pāṇḍava* of Rāja-śekhara (about the end of the tenth century); the *Daśa-rūpa* of Dhanañjaya (I. 61, about the same date); the *Sapta-śatī* of Govardhana (32, about the tenth century or later); the *Damayantī-kathā* of Trivikrama-bhaṭṭa (11);

the *Rāja-taran·giṇī* (I. 166); the *Sārn·gadhara-paddhati* (Böhtlingk, Ind. Spr. 1586), &c.

The eighteen Purāṇas (which are to a great extent drawn from the two great Epics) contain, of course, numerous allusions to the Rāmāyaṇa, and sometimes relate the whole story. The *Agni-purāṇa* has an epitome of the seven Books in seven chapters. The *Padma* and *Skanda* also devote several chapters to the same subject. The *Vishṇu-purāṇa* has also a section (IV. 4) about Rāma, and in III. 3 describes Vālmīki as the Vyāsa of the 24th Dvāpara. The *Brahmāṇḍa-purāṇa*—a confused medley of various subjects—has a *Rāmāyaṇa-māhātmya*, and in this Purāṇa is also contained the well-known Adhyātma-rāmāyaṇa, 'Spiritual Rāmāyaṇa,' divided into seven Books, bearing the same titles as those of Vālmīki's Rāmāyaṇa. Its object is to show that Rāma was a manifestation of the Supreme Spirit, and Sītā (identified with Lakshmī), a type of Nature.

This Adhyātma-rāmāyaṇa contains two chapters, held to be especially sacred: 1. The *Rāma-hṛidaya* or first chapter, in which the inner or hidden nature of Rāma is explained and his identification with Vishṇu, as the Supreme Spirit, is asserted; 2. the *Rāma-gītā* or fifth chapter of the seventh Book, in which the author, who is evidently a Vedāntist, sets forth the advantage of giving up all works in order to meditate upon and become united with the Supreme Spirit.

There is also a remarkable work called *Vāsishṭha-rāmāyaṇa* (or *Yoga-vāsishṭha* or *Vāsishṭham Mahā-rāmāyaṇam*) in the form of an exhortation with illustrative narratives addressed by Vasishṭha to his pupil, the youthful Rāma, on the best means of attaining true happiness, and considered to have been composed as an appendage to the Rāmāyaṇa by Vālmīki himself.

We ought also here to mention the celebrated Hindī Rāmāyaṇa by the poet Tulasī-dāsa (Tulsī-dās). This poem is so well known and so greatly esteemed in some parts of India, that it is sometimes affirmed that there are three epic poems called Rāmāyaṇa: 1. that of Vālmīki, 2. that attributed to Vyāsa called Adhyātma-rāmāyaṇa, 3. the Hindī Epic by Tulasī-dāsa.

I conclude the list by noting the following comparatively modern artificial poems on the same subject:—1. the *Rāghavapāṇḍavīya* by Kavi-rāja, a very singular production, much admired and imitated by later Indian writers, being nothing less than a poem worded with such dexterous 'double-entendre,' that it may serve as an epitome of either the Rāmāyaṇa or Mahā-bhārata; 2. the *Rāghava-vilāsa* by Viśva-nātha (author of the Sāhitya-darpaṇa); 3. the *Rāma-vilāsa* by Rāma-ćaraṇa; 4. another *Rāma-vilāsa* by Hari-nātha (in imitation of the Gīta-govinda); 5. the *Rāmaćandra-ćaritra-sāra* by Agni-veśa; 6. the *Raghu-nāthābhyu-daya* mentioned by Professor Weber.[1]

With regard to the composition called *Ćampū*, this is a kind of highly artificial style in alternations of prose and verse (*gadya* and *padya*).

---

[1] The story of the Rāmāyaṇa and Mahā-bhārata, as given in full by Mr. Talboys Wheeler in his History of India, is most interesting and instructive, although it does not profess to be an analysis made by himself from the original Sanskṛit.

CHAPTER XIII.

The Itihāsas or Epic Poems—The Mahā-bhārata.

I PASS on now to the Mahā-bhārata—probably by far the longest epic poem that the world has ever produced. Its main design is to describe the great contest between the descendants of king Bharata.[1] He was the most renowned monarch of the Lunar dynasty, and is alleged to have reigned in the neighbourhood of Hastinā-pur or ancient Delhi, and to have extended his authority over a great part of India, so that India to this day is called by the natives Bhārata-varsha. The great Epic, however, is not so much a poem with a single subject as a vast cyclopædia or thesaurus of Hindū mythology, legendary history, ethics, and philosophy. The work, as we now possess it, cannot possibly be regarded as representing the original form of the poem. Its compilation appears to have proceeded gradually for centuries. At any rate, as

---

[1] The title of the poem is *Mahā-bhāratam*, a compound word in the neuter gender, the first member of which, *mahā* (for *mahat*), means 'great,' and the second, *bhārata*, 'relating to Bharata.' The title of a book is often in the neuter gender, some word like *kāvyam*, 'a poem,' being understood. Here the word with which Mahā-bhāratam agrees may be either *ākhyānam*, 'a historical poem,' or *yuddham*, 'war.' It is curious that in the *San-graha-parva*, or introductory summary (l. 264), the word Mahā-bhārata is said to be derived from its large size and great weight, because the poem is described as outweighing all the four Vedas and mystical writings together. Here is the passage :—*Ekataś ćaturo Vedān Bhāratam̧ ćaitad ekataḩ Purā kila suraiḩ sarvaiḩ sametya tulayā dhr̥itam, Ćaturbhyaḩ sarahasyebhyo Vedebhyo hy adhikam̧ yadā, Tadā prabhr̥iti loke 'smin* [*mahattvād bhāravattvāć-ća*] *Mahā-bhāratam ućyate.*

we have already indicated (pp. 316, 317), it seems to have passed through several stages of construction and reconstruction, until finally arranged and reduced to orderly written shape by a Brāhman or Brāhmans, whose names have not been preserved.[1] The relationship which the original Brāhman compiler bore to the scattered legends and lays of India, many of them orally transmitted until transferred to the Mahā-bhārata, was similar to that borne by Pisistratus to the Homeric poems. But the Hindūs invest this personage, whoever he was, with a nimbus of mystical sanctity, and assert that he was also the arranger of various other celebrated religious works, such as the Vedas and Purāṇas. He is called Vyāsa, but this is, of course, a mere epithet derived from the Sanskṛit verb *vy-as*, meaning 'to dispose in regular sequence,' and therefore would be equally applicable to any compiler.[2]

---

1 Professor Lassen, in his 'Indische Alterthumskunde' (II. 499, new edition), considers that it may be proved from an examination of the Introduction to the Mahā-bhārata that there were three consecutive workings-up (*bearbeitung*) of that poem by different authors. The first or oldest version, called simply *Bhārata*, which contained only 24,000 verses, began with the history of Manu, the progenitor of the Kshatriya or military class (Ādi-parvan 3126), and a short section—describing the pedigree of Vyāsa, and how he appeared at the Snake-sacrifice, and how, at the request of Janamejaya, he commissioned Vaiśampāyana to relate the story of the strife between the Pāṇḍavas and Kauravas (I. 2208, &c.)—might have formed the introduction (*einleitung*) to this oldest Bhārata. The second reconstruction or re-casting of the poem—thought by Professor Lassen to be identical with the Itihāsa mentioned in Āśvalāyana's Gṛihya-sūtras, and recited at S'aunaka's Horse-sacrifice—took place about 400 B.C. It began with the history of king Vasu, whose daughter Satyavatī was mother of Vyāsa; and the section called *Paushya* (I. 661), the antiquity of which is indicated by its being almost entirely in prose, might have served as its introduction. The section called *Pauloma* (I. 851) probably formed the commencement of the third reconstruction of the great Epic, which he considers must have preceded the era of Aśoka.

2 *Vivyāsa Vedān yasmāt sa tasmād Vyāsa iti smṛitaḥ* (I. 2417).

Many of the legends are Vedic, and of great antiquity; while others, as we have already pointed out, are comparatively modern—probably interpolated during the first centuries of the Christian era. In fact, the entire work, which consists of about 220,000 lines in eighteen Parvans or sections, nearly every one of which would form a large volume, may be compared to a confused congeries of geological strata. The principal story, which occupies little more than a fifth of the whole, forms the lowest layer; but this has been so completely overlaid by successive incrustations, and the mass so compacted together,

---

Similarly the name Homerus (Ὅμηρος) is thought by some to come from ὁμοῦ and ἄρω. It may seem strange that the compilation of wholly different works composed at very different epochs, such as the Vedas, Mahā-bhārata, and Purāṇas undoubtedly were, should be attributed to the same person; but the close relationship supposed by learned natives to subsist between these productions, will account for a desire to call in the aid of the same great sage in their construction. The following passage from the Vedārtha-prakāśa of Mādhava Āćārya (who lived in the fourteenth century) commenting on the Taittirīya Yajur-veda (p. 1), translated by Dr. Muir in his Sanskṛit Texts, vol. iii. p. 47, attributes the actual composition of the Mahā-bhārata to the sage Vyāsa, and gives a remarkable reason for his having written it:—'It may be said that all persons whatever, including women and S'ūdras, must be competent students of the Veda, since the aspiration after good (*ishṭam me syād iti*) and the deprecation of evil are common to all mankind. But it is not so. For though the expedient exists, and women and S'ūdras are desirous to know it, they are debarred by another cause from being competent students of the Veda. The scripture (*śāstra*) which declares that those persons only who have been invested with the sacrificial cord are competent to read the Veda, intimates thereby that the same study would be a cause of unhappiness to women and S'ūdras (who are not so invested). How then are those two classes of persons to discover the means of future happiness? We answer, from the Purāṇas and other such works. Hence it has been said: Since the triple Veda may not be heard by women, S'ūdras, and degraded twice-born men, the Mahābhārata (*Bhāratam ākhyānam*) was, in his benevolence, composed (*kṛitam*) by the Muni.'

that the original substratum is not always clearly traceable. If the successive layers can ever be critically analysed and separated, the more ancient from the later additions, and the historical element from the purely fabulous, it may be expected that light will be thrown on the early history of India, religious, social, and political —a subject still veiled in much obscurity, notwithstanding the valuable researches of Professor Lassen and others.

I now give the names of the eighteen sections or Books which constitute the poem, with a brief statement of their contents :—

1. *Ādi-parvan*, 'introductory Book,' describes how the two brothers, Dhṛita-rāshṭra and Pāṇḍu, are brought up by their uncle Bhīshma; and how Dhṛita-rāshṭra, who is blind, has one hundred sons—commonly called the Kuru princes—by his wife Gāndhārī; and how the two wives of Pāṇḍu—Pṛithā (Kuntī) and Mādrī—have five sons, called the Pāṇḍavas or Pāṇḍu princes.

2. *Sabhā-parvan* describes the great *Sabhā* or 'assembly of princes' at Hastinā-pura, when Yudhi-shṭhira, the eldest of the five Pāṇḍavas, is persuaded to play at dice with S'akuni and loses his kingdom. The five Pāṇḍavas and Draupadī, their wife, are required to live for twelve years in the woods.

3. *Vana-parvan* narrates the life of the Pāṇḍavas in the Kāmyaka forest. This is one of the longest books, and full of episodes such as the story of Nala and that of the Kirātārjunīya.

4. *Virāṭa-parvan* describes the thirteenth year of exile and the adventures of the Pāṇḍavas while living disguised in the service of king Virāṭa.

5. *Udyoga-parvan.* In this the preparations for war on the side of both Pāṇḍavas and Kauravas are described.

6. *Bhīshma-parvan.* In this both armies join battle on Kuru-kshetra, a plain north-west of Delhi. The Kauravas are commanded by Bhīshma, who falls transfixed with arrows by Arjuna.

7. *Droṇa-parvan.* In this the Kuru forces are commanded by Droṇa, and numerous battles take place. Droṇa falls in a fight with Dhṛishṭa-dyumna (son of Drupada).

8. *Karṇa-parvan.* In this the Kurus are led by Karṇa. Other battles are described. Arjuna kills Karṇa.

9. *Śalya-parvan.* In this S'alya is made general of the Kuru army.

The concluding battles take place, and only three of the Kuru warriors, with Duryodhana, are left alive. Bhīma and Duryodhana then fight with clubs. Duryodhana, chief and eldest of the Kurus, is struck down.

10. *Sauptika-parvan.* In this the three surviving Kurus make a night attack on the camp of the Pāṇḍavas and kill all their army, but not the five Pāṇḍavas.

11. *Strī-parvan* describes the lamentations of queen Gāndhārī and the other wives and women over the bodies of the slain heroes.

12. *Śānti-parvan.* In this Yudhi-shṭhira is crowned in Hastinā-pura. To calm his spirit, troubled with the slaughter of his kindred, Bhīshma, still alive, instructs him at great length in the duties of kings (*rāja-dharma* 1995–4778), rules for adversity (*āpad-dharma* 4779–6455), rules for attaining final emancipation (*moksha-dharma* 6456 to end).

13. *Anuśāsana-parvan.* In this the instruction is continued by Bhīshma, who gives precepts and wise axioms on all subjects, such as the duties of kings, liberality, fasting, eating, &c., mixed up with tales, moral and religious discourses, and metaphysical disquisitions. At the conclusion of his long sermon Bhīshma dies.

14. *Āśvamedhika-parvan.* In this Yudhi-shṭhira, having assumed the government, performs an Aśva-medha or 'horse-sacrifice' in token of his supremacy.

15. *Āśramavāsika-parvan* narrates how the old blind king Dhṛita-rāshṭra, with his queen Gāndhārī and with Kuntī, mother of the Pāṇ-ḍavas, retires to a hermitage in the woods. After two years a forest conflagration takes place, and they immolate themselves in the fire to secure heaven and felicity.

16. *Mausala-parvan* narrates the death of Kṛishṇa and Bala-rāma, their return to heaven, the submergence of Kṛishṇa's city Dvārakā by the sea, and the self-slaughter in a fight with clubs (*musala*) of Kṛishṇa's family—the Yādavas—through the curse of some Brāhmans.

17. *Mahāprasthānika-parvan* describes the renunciation of their kingdom by Yudhi-shṭhira and his four brothers, and their departure towards Indra's heaven in Mount Meru.

18. *Svargārohaṇika-parvan* narrates the ascent and admission to heaven of the five Pāṇḍavas, their wife Draupadī, and kindred.

Supplement or *Hari-vanśa-parvan*, a later addition, recounting the genealogy and birth of Kṛishṇa and the details of his early life.

The following is a more complete and continuous account of the story of the poem, which is supposed to be recited by Vaiśampāyana, the pupil of Vyāsa, to Janamejaya, great-grandson of Arjuna.

We have seen that the Rāmāyaṇa commences by recounting the genealogy of the Solar line of kings, of whom Rāmā was one. The heroes of the Mahā-bhārata are of the other great race, called Lunar. Here, however, as in the Solar race, the Brāhman compiler was careful to assign the origin of the second great dynasty of kings to a noted sage and Brāhman. I epitomize the genealogy as essential to the comprehension of the story :—

Soma, the Moon, the progenitor of the Lunar race, who reigned at Hastinā-pur, was the child of the Ṛishi *Atri*, and had a son named *Budha*, who married Iḷā or Iḍā, daughter of the Solar prince Ikshvāku, and had by her a son, *Aila* or *Purūravas*. The latter had a son by Urvaśī, named *Āyus*, from whom came *Nahusha*, the father of *Yayāti*. The latter had two sons, *Puru*[1] and *Yadu*, from whom proceeded the two branches of the Lunar line. In the line of *Yadu* we need only mention the last three princes, *Śūra*, *Vasu-deva*,[2] and *Kṛishṇa* with his brother *Bala-rāma*. Fifteenth in the other line—that of *Puru*—came *Dushyanta*, father of the great *Bharata*, from whom India is called Bhārata-varsha. Ninth from Bharata came *Kuru*, and fourteenth from him *Śāntanu*. This Śāntanu had by his wife Satyavatī, a son named *Vićitra-vīrya*. *Bhīshma* (also called Śāntanava, Deva-vrata, &c.), who renounced the right of succession and took the vow of a Brahmaćārī,[3] was the son of Śāntanu by a former wife, the goddess Gan-gā, whence one of his names is Gān-geya. *Satyavatī* also had, before her marriage with Śāntanu, borne *Vyāsa*, to the sage Parāśara; so that *Vićitra-vīrya*, *Bhīshma*, and *Vyāsa* were half-brothers;[4] and Vyāsa, although he

---

[1] This name *Puru* (nom. case *Purus*) is probably the original of Porus, whose country in the Pañjāḇ, between the Hydaspes and Acesines, was conquered by Alexander the Great.

[2] Pṛithā or Kuntī, wife of Pāṇḍu, and mother of three of the Pāṇḍu princes, was a sister of Vasu-deva, and therefore aunt of Kṛishṇa.

[3] *I.e.*, perpetual celibacy. *Adya-prabhṛiti me brahmaćaryam bhavishyati ; Aputrasyāpi me lokā bhavishyanty akshayā divi* (I. 4060).

[4] Parāśara met with Satyavatī when quite a girl, as he was crossing the river Yamunā (Jumnā) in a boat. The result of their intercourse was a child, Vyāsa, who was called Kṛishṇa, from his swarthy complexion, and Dvaipāyana, because he was brought forth by Satyavatī on an island (*dvīpa*) in the Jumnā. (See Mahā-bhārata I. 2416, 2417, and 4235.)

retired into the wilderness, to live a life of contemplation, promised his mother that he would place himself at her disposal whenever she required his services. Satyavatī had recourse to him when her son Vićitra-vīrya died childless, and requested him to pay his addresses to Vićitra-vīrya's two widows, named Ambikā and Ambālikā. He consented, and had by them respectively two children, *Dhṛita-rāshṭra*, who was born blind, and *Pāṇḍu*, who was born with a pale complexion.[1] When Satyavatī begged Vyāsa to become the father of a third son (who should be without any defect), the elder wife, terrified by Vyāsa's austere appearance, sent him one of her slave-girls, dressed in her own clothes; and this girl became the mother of *Vidura* (whence he is sometimes called Kshattṛi).[2]

Dhṛita-rāshṭra, *Pāṇḍu*, and *Vidura* were thus brothers, sons of Vyāsa, the supposed author or compiler of the Mahā-bhārata. Vyāsa after this retired again to the woods; but, gifted with divine prescience, appeared both to his sons and grandsons whenever they were in difficulties, and needed his advice and assistance.

---

[1] The mother of Pāṇḍu was also called Kauśalyā; and this name (which was that of the mother of Rāma-ćandra) seems also to be applied to the mother of Dhṛita-rāshṭra. Paleness of complexion, in the eyes of a Hindū, would be regarded as a kind of leprosy, and was therefore almost as great a defect as blindness. The reason given for these defects is very curious. Ambikā was so terrified by the swarthy complexion and shaggy aspect of the sage Vyāsa (not to speak of the *gandha* emitted by his body), that when he visited her she closed her eyes, and did not venture to open them while he was with her. In consequence of this assumed blindness her child was born blind. Ambālikā, on the other hand, though she kept her eyes open, became so colourless with fright, that her son was born with a pale complexion (I. 4275–4290). Pāṇḍu seems to have been in other respects good-looking—*Sā devī kumāram ajījanat pāṇḍu-lakshaṇa-sampannaṃ dīpyamānaṃ vara-śriyā.*

[2] Vyāsa was so much pleased with this slave-girl that he pronounced her free, and declared that her child, Vidura, should be *sarva-buddhimatāṃ varaḥ*, 'the most excellent of all wise men.' Kshattṛi, although described in Manu as the child of a S'ūdra father and Brāhman mother, signifies here the child of a Brāhman father and S'ūdra mother. Vidura is one of the best characters in the Mahā-bhārata, always ready with useful advice (*hitopadeśa*) both for the Pāṇḍavas and for his brother Dhṛita-rāshṭra. His disposition leads him to side with the Pāṇḍu princes and warn them of the evil designs of their cousins.

The two brothers, Dhṛita-rāshṭra and Pāṇḍu, were brought up by their uncle Bhīshma,[1] who, until they were of age, conducted the government of Hastinā-pur.[2] Dhṛita-rāshṭra was the first-born, but renounced the throne, in consequence of his blindness. The other brother, Vidura, being the son of a Śūdra woman, could not succeed, and Pāṇḍu therefore, when of age, became king (I. 4361). Meanwhile Dhṛita-rāshṭra married Gāndhārī, also called Saubaleyī or Saubalī, daughter of Subala, king of Gāndhāra. When she first heard that her future husband was blind, she from that moment showed her respect for him, by binding her own eyes with a handkerchief, and always remaining blindfolded in his presence.[3] Soon afterwards a Svayaṃvara was held by king Kuntibhoja, and his adopted daughter, Pṛithā or Kuntī, then chose Pāṇḍu for her husband. She was really the child of a Yādava prince, Śūra, who gave her to his childless cousin Kuntibhoja; under whose care she was brought up:—

One day, before her marriage, she paid such respect and attention to a powerful sage named Durvāsas, a guest in her father's house, that he gave her a charm and taught her an incantation, by virtue of which she might have a child by any god she liked to call into her presence. Out of curiosity, she invoked the Sun, by whom she had a child, who was born clothed in armour.[4] But Pṛithā (Kuntī), fearing the censure of her relatives, deserted her offspring, after exposing it in the river. It was found by Adhiratha, a charioteer (*sūta*), and nurtured by his wife Rādhā; whence the child was afterwards called Rādheya, though

---

[1] They were all three thoroughly educated by Bhīshma. Dhṛita-rāshṭra is described as excelling all others in strength (I. 4356), Pāṇḍu as excelling in the use of the bow, and Vidura as pre-eminent for virtue and wisdom (4358).

[2] Hastinā-pur is also called Gajasāhvaya and Nāgasāhvaya.

[3] *Sā paṭam ādāya kṛitvā bahu-guṇaṃ tadā Babandha netre sve rājan pativrata-parāyaṇā* (I. 4376). She is described as so devoted to her husband that *Vāćā'pi purushān anyān suvratā nānvakīrtayat.*

[4] The Sun afterwards restored her *kanyātva* (I. 4400).

named by his foster-parents Vasu-sheṇa. When he was grown up, the god Indra conferred upon him enormous strength, and changed his name to Karṇa.[1]

After Pāṇḍu's marriage to Pṛithā, his uncle Bhīshma wishing him to take a second wife, made an expedition to visit Śalya, king of Madra, and prevailed upon him to bestow his sister Mādrī upon Pāṇḍu, in exchange for vast sums of money and jewels. Soon after this second marriage Pāṇḍu undertook a great campaign, in which he subjugated so many countries, that the kingdom of Hastinā-pur became under him as glorious and extensive as formerly under his ancestor Bharata (I. 4461). Having acquired enormous wealth, he distributed it to Bhīshma, Dhṛita-rāshṭra, and Vidura, and then retired to the woods to indulge his passion for hunting, living with his two wives as a forester on the southern slope of the Himālayas. The blind Dhṛita-rāshṭra, who had a very useful charioteer named Sañjaya, was then obliged, with the assistance of Bhīshma as his regent, to assume the reins of government.

We have next an account of the supernatural birth of Dhṛita-rāshṭra's sons :—

One day the sage Vyāsa was hospitably entertained by queen Gāndhārī, and in return granted her a boon. She chose to be the mother of a hundred sons. After two years she produced a mass of flesh, which was divided by Vyāsa into a hundred and one pieces, as big as the joint of a thumb. From these in due time the eldest, Duryodhana, 'difficult to be subdued' (sometimes called Su-yodhana, see p. 382, note 2), was born. At his birth, however, various evil omens took place; jackals yelled, asses brayed, whirlwinds blew, and the sky seemed on fire. Dhṛita-rāshṭra, alarmed, called his ministers together,

---

[1] He is also called Vaikartana, as son of Vikartana or the Sun, and sometimes Vṛisha. Karṇa is described (4405) as worshipping the Sun till his back became warm (*ā-prishṭha-tāpāt*, *i.e.*, 'till after midday,' when the sun began to shine behind him). Compare Hitop., Book II. v. 32.

who recommended him to abandon the child, but could not persuade him to take their advice. The miraculous birth of the remaining ninety-nine sons then occurred in due course.[1] There was also one daughter, called Duḥśalā (afterwards married to Jayad-ratha).

Next follows the description of the supernatural birth of the five reputed sons of Pāṇḍu :—

One day, on a hunting expedition, Pāṇḍu transfixed with five arrows a male and female deer. These turned out to be a certain sage and his wife, who had assumed the form of these animals. The sage cursed Pāṇḍu, and predicted that he would die in the embraces of one of his wives. In consequence of this curse, Pāṇḍu took the vow of a Brahmaćārī,[2] gave all his property to the Brāhmans, and became a hermit.

Thereupon his wife Pṛithā (also called Kuntī), with his approval, made use of the charm and incantation formerly given to her by Durvāsas, and had three sons, Yudhi-shṭhira, Bhīma, and Arjuna, by the three deities, Dharma, Vāyu, and Indra respectively :—

Yudhi-shṭhira was born first, and at the moment of his birth a heavenly voice was heard to utter these words, 'This is the most virtuous of men.' Bhīma, the son of Pṛithā and Vāyu, was born on the same day as Duryodhana. Soon after his birth, his mother accidentally let him fall, when a great prodigy—indicative of the vast strength which was to distinguish him—occurred; for the body of the child falling on a rock shivered it to atoms. On the birth of Arjuna auspicious omens were manifested; showers of flowers fell,[3] celestial minstrels filled the air with harmony, and a heavenly voice sounded his praises and future glory.

Mādrī, the other wife of Pāṇḍu, was now anxious to have children, and was told by Pṛithā (Kuntī) to think on any god she pleased. She chose the two Aśvins (see p. 11), who appeared to her, and were the fathers of her

---

[1] Their names are all detailed at I. 4540.

[2] The *brahmaćarya-vrata*, or vow of continence.

[3] Showers of flowers are as common in Indian poetry as showers of blood; the one indicating good, the other portending evil.

twin sons Nakula and Sahadeva. While the five princes were still children, Pāṇḍu, forgetting the curse of the sage whom he had killed in the form of a deer, ventured one day to embrace his wife Mādrī, and died in her arms. She and Pṛithā (Kuntī) then had a dispute for the honour of becoming a Satī (see p. 312), which ended in Mādrī burning herself with her husband's corpse (I. 4896). Pṛithā and the five Pāṇḍu princes were then taken by certain Ṛishis, or holy men—companions of Pāṇḍu—to Hastinā-pur, where they were presented to Dhṛita-rāshṭra, and all the circumstances of their birth and of the death of Pāṇḍu narrated. The news of the death of his brother was received by Dhṛita-rāshṭra with much apparent sorrow; he gave orders for the due performance of the funeral rites, and allowed the five young princes and their mother to live with his own family. The cousins were in the habit of playing together:—

In their boyish sports the Pāṇḍu princes excelled the sons of Dhṛita-rāshṭra, which excited much ill-feeling; and Duryodhana, spiteful even when a boy, tried to destroy Bhīma by mixing poison in his food, and then throwing him into the water when stupefied by its effects (I. 5008). Bhīma, however, was not drowned, but descended to the abode of the Nāgas (or serpent-demons), who freed him from the poison (5052), and gave him a liquid to drink which endued him with the strength of ten thousand Nāgas. From that moment he became a kind of Hercules.

Then Duryodhana, Karṇa, and Śakuni[1] devised schemes for destroying the Pāṇḍu princes, but without success.

The characters of the five Pāṇḍavas are drawn with much artistic delicacy of touch, and maintained with general consistency throughout the poem.[2] The eldest,

---

[1] S'akuni was the brother of Gāndhārī, and therefore maternal uncle (*mātula*) of the Kaurava princes. He was the counsellor of Duryodhana. He is often called Saubala, as Gāndhārī is called Saubalī.

[2] Complete consistency must not be expected in such a poem as

Yudhi-shṭhira, is the Hindū ideal of excellence—a pattern of justice, integrity, calm passionless composure, chivalrous honour, and cold heroism.[1] Bhīma is a type of brute courage and strength: he is of gigantic stature, impetuous, irascible, somewhat vindictive, and cruel even to the verge of ferocity, making him, as his name implies, 'terrible.' It would appear that his great strength had to be maintained by plentiful supplies of food; as his name Vṛikodara, 'wolf-stomached,' indicated a voracious appetite; and we are told that at the daily meals of the five brothers, half of the whole dish had to be given to Bhīma (I. 7161). But he has the capacity for warm unselfish love, and is ardent in his affection for his mother and brothers. Arjuna rises more to the European standard of perfection. He may be regarded as the real hero of the Mahā-bhārata,[2] of undaunted bravery, generous,[3] with refined and delicate sensibilities, tender-hearted, forgiving, and affectionate as a woman, yet of superhuman strength, and matchless in arms and athletic exercises. Nakula and Sahadeva are both amiable, noble-minded, and spirited.[4] All five are as unlike as possible to the

---

the Mahā-bhārata, which was the growth of several centuries. The act of the five Pāṇḍavas, described p. 385, cannot be reconciled with their usual probity and generosity, though committed under great provocation. Bhīma appears to have been most in fault, which is so far consistent.

[1] Yudhi-shṭhira, 'firm in battle,' was probably of commanding stature and imposing presence. He is described as *Mahā-siṉha-gati*, 'having a majestic lion-like gait,' with a Wellington-like profile (*Pralambojjvala-ćāru-ghoṇa*) and long lotus-eyes (*kamalāyatāksha*).

[2] Strictly, as in the Iliad, there is no real hero kept always in view.

[3] Perhaps it may be objected that some of Arjuna's acts were inconsistent with this character. Thus he carried off Subhadrā, the sister of Kṛishṇa, by force. It must be borne in mind, however, that Kṛishṇa himself encourages him to this act, and says, *Prasahya haranaṃ Kshatri-yāṇām praśasyate* (I. 7927). Compare p. 391.

[4] The five Pāṇḍu princes are known by various other names in the

hundred sons of Dhṛita-rāshṭra, commonly called the *Kuru* princes, or *Kauravas*,[1] who are represented as mean, spiteful, dishonourable, and vicious.

So bad indeed are these hundred brothers, and so uniformly without redeeming points, that their characters present few distinctive features. The most conspicuous is the eldest, Duryodhana,[2] who, as the representative of the others, is painted in the darkest colours, and embodies all their bad qualities. When the Mahā-bhārata (like the Rāmāyaṇa) is regarded as an allegory, then Duryodhana (like Rāvaṇa) is a visible type of the evil principle in human nature[3] for ever doing battle with the good and divine principle, symbolized by the five sons of Pāṇḍu.

The cousins, though so uncongenial in character, were educated together at Hastinā-pur, the city of Dhṛita-

---

Mahā-bhārata, some of which it may be useful here to note. Yudhi-shṭhira is also called Dharma-rāja, Dharma-putra, and sometimes simply Rājan. His charioteer was called Indrasena. Bhīma's other names are Bhīmasena, Vṛikodara, Bāhuśālin. Arjuna is also called Kirīṭin, Phālguna, Jishṇu, Dhanañjaya, Bībhatsu, Savyasāćin, Pāka-śāsani, Guḍā-keśa, S'veta-vāhana, Nara, Vijaya, Kṛishṇa, and some-times *par excellence* Pārtha, though Bhīma and Yudhi-shṭhira, as sons of Pṛithā, had also this title. Nakula and Sahadeva are called Mādreyau (as sons of Mādrī), and sometimes Yamau (the twins).

[1] This name, however, is occasionally applied to the Pāṇḍavas, as they and the sons of Dhṛita-rāshṭra were equally descendants of Kuru.

[2] 'Difficult to conquer,' cf. p. 408. The names of all are given in Ādi-Parvan 4541. Duḥśāsana is one of the most conspicuous.

[3] There are certainly many points in his character, as well as in that of Rāvaṇa, which may be compared to Milton's conception of Satan. Perhaps his intimacy with the Asura Ćārvāka may be in-tended to mark him out as a type of heresy and infidelity, as well as of every other bad quality. In the case of Rāvaṇa it is remarkable that he gained his power by penance, and that he is described as well read in the Veda (Rām. VI. xciii. 58). Some Rākshasas, such as Vibhīshaṇa, Atikāya, are described as religious (Rām. VI. lxxi. 31). Cf. Manu VII. 38.

rāshṭra, by a Brāhman named Droṇa,[1] who found in the Pāṇḍu princes apt pupils. From him the five sons of Pāṇḍu acquired 'intelligence and learning, lofty aims, religious earnestness, and love of truth.' All the cousins were equally instructed in war and arms; but Arjuna, by the help of Droṇa, who gave him magical weapons, excelled all, distinguishing himself in every exercise, 'submissive ever to his teacher's will, contented, modest, affable, and mild,' and both Bhīma and Duryodhana learnt the use of the club from their cousin Bala-rāma (I. 5520).

Their education finished, a tournament was held, at which all the youthful cousins displayed their skill in archery, in the management of chariots (*ratha-ćaryā*), horses, and elephants, in sword, spear, and club exercises, and wrestling. The scene is graphically described (I. 5324):—

An immense concourse of spectators cheered the combatants. The agitation of the crowd was like the roar of a mighty ocean. Arjuna, after exhibiting prodigies of strength, shot five separate arrows simultaneously into the jaws of a revolving iron boar, and twenty-one arrows into the hollow of a cow's horn suspended by a string. Suddenly there was a pause. The crowd turned as one man towards a point in the arena, where the sound of a warrior striking his arms in defiance[2] rent the sky like a thunder-clap, and announced the entrance of another combatant. This proved to be a warrior named *Karṇa*, who entered the lists in full armour, and after accomplishing the same feats in archery, challenged Arjuna to single combat. But each champion was required to tell his name and pedigree; and Karṇa's parentage being doubtful (see p. 377), he was obliged to retire, 'hanging his head with shame like a drooping lily.'

---

[1] Droṇa appears to have kept a kind of school, to which all the young princes of the neighbouring countries resorted (I. 5220). He married Kṛipī, sister of Kṛipa, and had by her a son, Aśvatthāman.

[2] So in Vishṇu-purāṇa, p. 513: 'Kṛishṇa having dived into the pool struck his arms in defiance, and the snake-king, hearing the sound, came quickly forth.'

Karṇa, thus publicly humiliated, became afterwards a conspicuous and valuable ally of the Kurus against his own half-brothers. His character is well imagined. Feeling keenly the stain on his birth, his nature was chastened by the trial. He exhibited in a high degree fortitude, chivalrous honour, self-sacrifice, and devotion. Especially remarkable for a liberal and generous disposition,[1] he never stooped to ignoble practices like his friends the Kurus, who were intrinsically bad men.

The tutor's fee (*Gurv-arthra*, see pp. 195, 242, Manu II. 245, Raghu-vaṉśa V. 17) which Droṇa required of his pupils for their instruction was, that they should capture Drupada, king of Pańćāla, who was his old schoolfellow, but had insulted him by repudiating his friendship (I. 5446) :—

They therefore invaded Drupada's territory and took him prisoner; but Droṇa generously spared his life, and gave him back half his kingdom. Drupada, however, burning with resentment, endeavoured to procure the birth of a son, to avenge his defeat, and bring about the destruction of Droṇa. Two Brāhmans undertook a sacrifice for him, and two children were born from the midst of the altar, out of the sacrificial fire, a son, Dhṛishṭa-dyumna, and a daughter, Kṛishṇā or Draupadī, afterwards the wife of the Pāndavas (see p. 387).

After this, Yudhi-shṭhira was installed by Dhṛita-rāshṭra as Yuva-rāja or heir-apparent, and by his exploits soon eclipsed the glory of his father Pāṇḍu's reign.

The great renown gained by the Pāṇḍu princes excited the jealousy and ill-will of Dhṛita-rāshṭra, but won the affections of the citizens. The latter met together, and after consultation declared that, as Dhṛita-rāshṭra was blind, he ought not to conduct the government, and that as Bhīshma had formerly declined the throne, he ought not to be allowed to act as regent. They therefore pro-

[1] He is often to this day cited as a model of liberality. Hence his name, Vasu-sheṇa.

posed to crown Yudhi-shṭhira at once. When Duryodhana heard of this, he consulted with Karṇa, Śakuni, and Duḥśāsana, how he might remove Yudhi-shṭhira out of the way, and secure the throne for himself:—

Urged by Duryodhana, Dhṛita-rāshṭra was induced to send the Pāṇḍava princes on an excursion to the city of Vāraṇāvata, pretending that he wished them to see the beauties of that town, and to be present at a festival there. Meanwhile Duryodhana instigated his friend Puroćana to precede them, and to prepare a house for their reception, which he was to fill secretly with hemp, resin, and other combustible substances, plastering the walls with mortar composed of oil, fat, and lac (*lākshā*, *jatu*). When the princes were asleep in this house, and unsuspicious of danger, he was to set it on fire. The five Pāṇḍavas and their mother left Hastinā-pur amid the tears and regrets of the citizens, and in eight days arrived at Vāraṇāvata, where, after great demonstrations of respect from the inhabitants, they were conducted by Puroćana to the house of lac. Having been warned by Vidura, they soon discovered the dangerous character of the structure, and with the assistance of a miner (*khanaka*) sent by Vidura, dug an underground passage, by which to escape from the interior (I. 5813). Then they devised a counterplot, and agreed together that a degraded outcaste woman (*nishādī*) with her five sons should be invited to a feast, and stupefied with wine. Bhīma was then to set fire to the lac-house in which they were all assembled (see note 2, p. 380). This was done. Puroćana was burnt, as well as the woman with her five sons, but they themselves escaped by the secret passage (*surun-gā*). The charred bodies of the woman and her sons being afterwards found, it was supposed that the Pāṇḍava princes had perished in the conflagration, and their funeral ceremonies were actually performed by Dhṛita-rāshṭra. Meanwhile they hurried off to the woods; Bhīma, the strong one, carrying his mother and the twins, and leading his other brothers by the hands when through fatigue they could not move on. Whilst his mother and brothers were asleep under a fig-tree, Bhīma had an encounter with a hideous giant named Hiḍimba, whom he slew.[1] Afterwards he married Hiḍimbā, the sister of this monster, and had a son by her named Ghaṭotkaća.

By the advice of their grandfather Vyāsa, the Pāṇḍava princes next took up their abode in the house of a

---

[1] This forms the subject of a celebrated episode, edited by Bopp.

Brāhman at a city called Ekaćakrā. There they lived for a long time in the guise of mendicant Brāhmans, safe from the persecution of Duryodhana. Every day they went out to beg for food as alms (*bhikshā, bhaiksha*), which their mother Kuntī divided at night, giving half of the whole to Bhīma as his share (cf. p. 381). While resident in the house of the Brāhman, Bhīma delivered his family and the city of Ekaćakrā from a fierce giant (or Rākshasa) named Baka (or Vaka), who forced the citizens to send him every day a dish of food by a man, whom he always devoured as his daintiest morsel at the end of the repast.[1]

The turn had come to a poor Brāhman to provide the Rākshasa with his meal. He determined to go himself, but lamented bitterly the hardness of his fate. Upon this, his wife and daughter addressed him in language full of the deepest pathos, each in turn insisting on sacrificing herself for the good of the family. Lastly, the little son, too young to speak distinctly, ran with beaming eyes and smiling face to his parents, and in prattling accents said, 'Weep not, father; sigh not, mother.' Then breaking off and brandishing a pointed spike of grass, he exclaimed, 'With this spike will I kill the fierce man-eating giant.' His parents, hearing this innocent prattle of their child, in the midst of their heartrending anguish felt a thrill of exquisite delight. In the end Bhīma, who overheard the whole conversation, undertook to convey the meal to the monster, and, of course, speedily despatched him (I. 6202).

After this Vyāsa appeared to his grandsons, and informed them that Draupadī, the daughter of Drupada, king of Pańćāla, was destined to be their common wife:[2]—

---

[1] This story forms a touching episode, which has been printed by Bopp, and translated by Milman.

[2] Polyandry is still practised among some hill-tribes in the Himālaya range near Simla, and in other barren mountainous regions, such as Bhotan, where a large population could not be supported. It prevails also among the Nair (Nāyar) tribe in Malabar. Our forefathers, or at least the ancient Britons, according to Cæsar, were given to the same

In real fact she had been in a former life the daughter of a sage, and had performed a most severe penance, in order that a husband might fall to her lot. S'iva, pleased with her penance, had appeared to her, and had promised her, instead of one, five husbands. When the maiden replied that she wanted only one husband, the god answered, 'Five times you said to me, Grant me a husband; therefore in another body you will obtain five husbands' (I. 6433, 7322). This Ṛishi's daughter was thereupon born in the family of Drupada as a maiden of the most distinguished beauty, and was destined to be the wife of the Pāṇḍavas.[1]

---

practice: 'Uxores habent deni duodenique inter se communes,' &c. De Bello Gallico, V. 14.

[1] Vyāsa, who is the type and representative of strict Brāhmanism, is made to explain at length the necessity for the marriage of Draupadī to five husbands (which is called a *sūkshma-dharma*, I. 7246). He also gifted Drupada with divine intuition (*ćakshur divyam*) to perceive the divinity of the Pāṇḍavas and penetrate the mystic meaning of what otherwise would have been a serious violation of the laws and institutions of the Brāhmans (7313). Hence Drupada became aware of his daughter's former birth, and that Arjuna was really a portion of the essence of Indra (*Śakrasyānśa*), and all his brothers portions of the same god. Draupadī herself, although nominally the daughter of Drupada, was really born, like her brother Dhṛishṭa-dyumna, out of the midst of the sacrificial fire (*vedī-madhyāt*, I. 6931; see p. 384), and was a form of Lakshmī. In no other way could her supernatural birth, and the divine perfume which exhaled from her person, and was perceived a league off (*krośa-mātrāt pravāti*), be accounted for. Vyāsa at the same time explained the mysterious birth of Kṛishṇa and Baladeva;—how the god Vishṇu pulled out two of his own hairs, one white and the other black, which entered into two women of the family of the Yādavas (Devakī and Rohiṇī), and became, the white one Baladeva, the black one Kṛishṇa (I. 7307; Vishṇu-purāṇa V. 1). The Mārkaṇḍeya-purāṇa (ch. 5) shows how the five Pāṇḍavas could be all portions of Indra, and yet four of them sons of other gods. When Indra killed the son of Tvashṭṛi (or Viśvakarman as Prajāpati, the Creator), his punishment for this *brahma-hatyā* was that all his *tejas*, 'manly vigour,' deserted him, and entered Dharma, the god of justice. The son of Tvashṭṛi was reproduced as the demon Vṛitra, and again slain by Indra; as a punishment for which his *bala*, 'strength,' left him, and entered *Māruta*, 'the Wind.' Lastly, when Indra violated Ahalyā, the wife of the sage Gautama, his *rūpa*, 'beauty,' abandoned him, and entered the Nāsatyau

In obedience to the directions of their grandfather, the five Pāṇḍavas quitted Ekaćakrā, and betook themselves to the court of king Drupada, where Draupadī was about to hold her Svayaṃvara :—

An immense concourse of princely suitors, with their retainers, came to the ceremony; and king Drupada eagerly looked for Arjuna among them, that, strengthened by that hero's alliance, he might defy Droṇa's anger. He therefore prepared an enormous bow, which he was persuaded none but Arjuna could bend, and proposed a trial of strength, promising to give his daughter to any one who could by means of the bow shoot five arrows simultaneously through a revolving ring into a target beyond. An amphitheatre was erected outside the town, surrounded by tiers of lofty seats and raised platforms, with variegated awnings. Magnificent palaces, crowded with eager spectators, overlooked the scene. Actors, conjurors, athletes, and dancers exhibited their skill before the multitude. Strains of exquisite music floated in the air. Drums and trumpets sounded. When expectation was at its height, Draupadī in gorgeous apparel entered the arena, and the bow was brought. The hundred sons of Dhṛita-rāshṭra strained every nerve to bend the ponderous weapon, but without effect. Its recoil dashed them breathless to the ground, and made them the laughing-stock of the crowd.

Arjuna now advanced, disguised as a Brāhman. I here translate a portion metrically (I. 7049, &c.) :—

A moment motionless he stood and scanned
The bow, collecting all his energy.
Next walking round in homage, breathed a prayer
To the Supreme Bestower of good gifts;
Then fixing all his mind on Draupadī
He grasped the ponderous weapon in his hand,
And with one vigorous effort braced the string.

---

or Aśvins. When Dharma gave back the *tejas* of Indra, Yudhi-shṭhira was born; when the Wind gave up Indra's *bala*, Bhīma was born; and when the Aśvins restored the *rūpa* of Indra, Nakula and Sahadeva were born. Arjuna was born as half the essence of Indra. Hence, as they were all portions of one deity, there could be no harm in Draupadī becoming the wife of all five.

Quickly the shafts were aimed; they flew;
The mark fell pierced; a shout of victory
Rang through the vast arena; from the sky
Garlands of flowers crowned the hero's head,
Ten thousand fluttering scarfs waved in the air,
And drum and trumpet sounded forth his triumph.

I need not suggest the parallel which will at once be drawn by the classical scholar between this trial of archery and a similar scene in the Odyssey.

When the suitors found themselves outdone by a mere stripling in the coarse dress of a mendicant Brāhman, their rage knew no bounds. A real battle ensued:—

The Pāṇḍu princes protected Drupada, and enacted prodigies. Bhīma tore up a tree, and used it as a club. Karṇa at last met Arjuna in single combat, rushing on him like a young elephant. They overwhelmed each other with showers of arrows, which darkened the air. But not even Karṇa could withstand the irresistible onset of the godlike Arjuna, and he and the other suitors retired vanquished from the field, leaving Draupadī as the bride of Arjuna.

Arjuna having been chosen by Draupadī, the five brothers returned with her to their mother, who being inside the house, and fancying that they had brought alms, called out to them, 'Share it between you' (*bhuṅkteti sametya sarve*, I. 7132). The words of a parent, thus spoken, could not be set aside without evil consequences; and Drupada, at the persuasion of Vyāsa, who acquainted him with the divinely ordained destination of his daughter,[1] consented to her becoming the common wife of the five brothers. She was first married by the family-priest Dhaumya to Yudhi-shṭhira (I. 7340), and then, according to priority of birth, to the other four.[2]

---

[1] See note 1, p. 387. Drupada at first objected. Yudhi-shṭhira's excuse for himself and his brothers is remarkable; *Pūrveshām ānupūrvyeṇa yātaṃ vartmānuyāmahe* (I. 7246).

[2] She had a son by each of the five brothers—Prativindhya by

The Pāṇḍavas, being now strengthened by their alliance with the powerful king of Pañćāla, threw off their disguises; and king Dhṛita-rāshṭra thought it more politic to settle all differences by dividing his kingdom between them and his own sons. He gave up Hastinā-pur to the latter, presided over by Duryodhana, and permitted the five Pāṇḍavas to occupy a district near the Yamunā (Jumnā), called Khāṇḍava-prastha, where they built Indraprastha (the modern Delhi), and, under Yudhi-shṭhira as their leader, subjugated much of the adjacent territory by predatory incursions (I. 6573).

One day, when Arjuna was bathing in the Ganges, he was carried off by the serpent-nymph Ulūpī, daughter of the king of the Nāgas, whom he married (I. 7809). Afterwards he married Ćitrān-gadā, daughter of the king of Maṇipura, and had a child by her named Babhru-vāhana (I. 7883).

Wandering for twelve years in the forests, to fulfil a vow, Arjuna came to Prabhāsa, a place of pilgrimage in the west of India, where he met Kṛishṇa,[1] the details of

---

Yudhi-shṭhira; Sutasoma by Bhīma; S'rutakarman by Arjuna; S'atānīka by Nakula; S'rutasena by Sahadeva (I. 8039). Arjuna had also another wife, Subhadrā, the sister of Kṛishṇa, with whom he eloped when on a visit to Kṛishṇa at Dvārakā. By her he had a son, Abhimanyu. He had also a son named Irāvat by the serpent-nymph Ulūpī. Bhīma had also a son, Ghaṭotkaća, by the Rākshasī Hiḍimbā (see p. 385); and the others had children by different wives (Vishṇu-purāṇa, p. 459). Arjuna's son Abhimanyu had a son Parīkshit, who was father of Janamejaya. Parīkshit died of the bite of a snake; and the Bhāgavata-purāṇa was narrated to him between the bite and his death.

[1] See note 1, p. 387. I enumerate some of the other names by which Kṛishṇa is known in the Mahā-bhārata, as follows:—Vāsudeva, Keśava, Govinda, Janārdana, Dāmodara, Dāśārha, Nārāyaṇa, Hṛishīkeśa, Purushottama, Mādhava, Madhu-sūdana, Aćyuta. (See V. 2560). In the Draupadī-haraṇa (75) Kṛishṇa and Arjuna are called *Kṛishṇau*.

whose early life have already been given (p. 332), and who here first formed a friendship with Arjuna, and took him to his city Dvārakā, where he received him as a visitor into his own house (I. 7905). Soon afterwards, some of the relatives of Kṛishṇa celebrated a festival in the mountain Raivataka, to which both Arjuna and Kṛishṇa went. There they saw Bala-rāma, elder brother of Kṛishṇa (p. 332), in a state of intoxication (*kshīva*)[1] with his wife Revatī; and there they saw Subhadrā, Kṛishṇa's sister. Her beauty excited the love of Arjuna, who, after obtaining Kṛishṇa's leave, carried her off (see note 2, p. 389) and married her (I. 7937). In the twelfth year of his absence he returned with her to Indra-prastha.

The Pāṇḍavas and all the people of Indra-prastha then lived happily for some time under the rule of Yudhishṭhira, who, elated with his conquests, undertook, assisted by Kṛishṇa, to celebrate the Rājasūya, a great sacrifice, at which his own inauguration as paramount sovereign was to be performed.

A great assembly (*sabhā*) was accordingly held:—

Various princes attended, and brought either rich presents or tribute (II. 1264). Among those who came were Bhīshma, Dhṛitarāshṭra and his hundred sons, Subala (king of Gandhāra), S'akuni, Drupada, S'alya, Droṇa, Kṛipa, Jayad-ratha, Kuntibhoja, S'iśu-pāla, and others from the extreme south and north (Drāviḍa, Ceylon, and Kāśmīr, II. 1271).[2] On the day of the inauguration (*abhisheka*) Bhīshma, at the suggestion of the sage Nārada, proposed that a respectful oblation (*argha*) should be prepared and offered in token of worship to the best and strongest person present, whom he declared to

[1] Compare Megha-dūta, verse 51, where Bala-rāma's fondness for wine is alluded to. See also Vishṇu-purāṇa V. 25.

[2] The details in this part of the poem are interesting and curious. As shown by Professor H. H. Wilson, they throw light on the geographical divisions and political condition of India at an early epoch.

be Kṛishṇa. To this the Pāṇḍavas readily agreed; and Sahadeva was commissioned to present the offering. Śiśu-pāla (also called Sunītha), however, opposed the worship of Kṛishṇa; and, after denouncing him as a contemptible and ill-instructed person (II. 1340), challenged him to fight;[1] but Kṛishṇa instantly struck off his head with his discus called Su-darśana.[2]

After this, Dhṛita-rāshṭra was persuaded to hold another assembly (*sabhā*) at Hastinā-pur; and Vidura was sent to the Pāṇḍavas, to invite them to be present (II. 1993). They consented to attend; and Yudhi-shṭhira was easily prevailed on by Duryodhana to play with Śakuni. By degrees Yudhi-shṭhira staked everything—his territory, his possessions, and last of all Draupadī. All were successively lost; and Draupadī, then regarded as a slave, was treated with great indignity by Duḥśāsana. He dragged her by the hair of the head into the assembly; upon which Bhīma, who witnessed this insult, swore that he would one day dash Duḥśāsana to pieces and drink his blood[3] (II. 2302). In the end a compromise was agreed upon. The kingdom was given up to Duryodhana for twelve years; and the five Pāṇḍavas, with Draupadī, were required to live for that period in the woods, and

---

[1] Duryodhana also, in a subsequent part of the Mahā-bhārata, evinces scepticism in regard to the divine nature of Kṛishṇa (V. 4368).

[2] The story of Śiśu-pāla and his destruction by Kṛishṇa form the subject of the celebrated poem of Māgha. The particulars of the narrative as told in this book of the Mahā-bhārata are given by Dr. Muir in his Sanskrit Texts, vol. iv. The Vishṇu-purāṇa identifies Śiśu-pāla with the demons Hiraṇya-kaśipu and Rāvaṇa (Wilson, p. 437).

[3] This threat he fulfilled. The incident is noticeable as it is the subject of the well-known drama by Bhaṭṭa-nārāyaṇa called Veṇī-saṃbhāra, 'braid-binding,' which describes how the braided hair torn by Duḥśāsana was again bound together by Bhīma, who is made to say *Svayam ahaṃ saṃharāmi*, 'I myself will again bind the braid together.' See Sāhitya-darpaṇa, p. 169.

to pass the thirteenth concealed under assumed names in various disguises.

They accordingly retired to the Kāmyaka forest, and took up their abode on the banks of the Sarasvatī.

While they were resident in the forest, various episodes occurred, thus :—

Arjuna went to the Himālaya mountains to perform severe penance, and thereby obtain celestial arms. After some time S'iva, to reward him and prove his bravery, approached him as a Kirāta or wild mountaineer living by the chase, at the moment that a demon named Mūka, in the form of a boar, was making an attack upon him. S'iva and Arjuna both shot together at the boar, which fell dead, and both claimed to have hit him first. This served as a pretext for S'iva, as the Kirāta, to quarrel with Arjuna, and have a battle with him. Arjuna fought long with the Kirāta,[1] but could not conquer him. At last he recognized the god, and threw himself at his feet. S'iva, pleased with his bravery, gave him the celebrated weapon Pāśupata, to enable him to conquer Karṇa and the Kuru princes in war (III. 1650, 1664).

Many legends were also repeated to console and amuse the Pāṇḍu princes in their time of exile. For instance, we have here introduced (III. 12746–12804) the epic version of the tradition of the Deluge (the earliest account of which occurs in the Śatapatha-brāhmaṇa, see p. 29 of this volume), as follows :—

Manu, the Hindū Noah (not the grandson of Brahmā, and reputed author of the Code, but the seventh Manu, or Manu of the present period, called Vaivasvata, and regarded as one of the progenitors of the human race, Manu I. 61, 62), is represented as conciliating the favour of the Supreme Being by his austerities in an age of universal depravity. A fish, which was an incarnation of Brahmā (cf. p. 327), appeared to him whilst engaged in penance on the margin of a river, and accosting him, craved protection from the larger fish. Manu complied,

---

[1] This forms the subject of a celebrated poem by Bhāravi called the Kirātārjunīya. S'iva was regarded as the god of the Kirātas, who were evidently a race of aborigines much respected by the Hindūs for their bravery and skill in archery.

and placed him in a glass vessel. Having outgrown this, he requested to be taken to a more roomy receptacle. Manu then placed him in a lake. Still the fish grew, till the lake, though three leagues long, could not contain him. He next asked to be taken to the Ganges; but even the Ganges was soon too small, and the fish was finally transferred to the ocean. There he continued to expand, till at last, addressing Manu, he warned him of the coming Deluge.

Manu, however, was to be preserved by the help of the fish, who commanded him to build a ship and go on board, not with his own wife and children, but with the seven Ṛishis or patriarchs; and not with pairs of animals, but with the seeds of all existing things. The flood came; Manu went on board, and fastened the ship, as directed, to a horn in the fish's head. He was then drawn along[1]—(I translate nearly literally):—

Along the ocean in that stately ship was borne the lord of men, and through
Its dancing, tumbling billows, and its roaring waters; and the bark,
Tossed to and fro by violent winds, reeled on the surface of the deep,
Staggering and trembling like a drunken woman. Land was seen no more,
Nor far horizon, nor the space between; for everywhere around
Spread the wild waste of waters, reeking atmosphere, and boundless sky.
And now when all the world was deluged, nought appeared above the waves
But Manu and the seven sages, and the fish that drew the bark.
Unwearied thus for years on years the fish propelled the ship across
The heaped-up waters, till at length it bore the vessel to the peak
Of Himavān; then, softly smiling, thus the fish addressed the sage:
Haste now to bind thy ship to this high crag. Know me the lord of all,
The great creator Brahmā, mightier than all might—omnipotent.
By me in fish-like shape hast thou been saved in dire emergency.
From Manu all creation, gods, Asuras, men, must be produced;
By him the world must be created—that which moves and moveth not.

Another tale told in this section of the poem (III. 16619, &c.) may be cited for its true poetic feeling and pathos—qualities in which it is scarcely excelled by the

---

[1] There is still a later account of the Deluge in the Bhāgavata-purāṇa, where the fish is represented as an incarnation of Vishṇu. The god's object in descending as a fish seems to have been to steer the ship. In the Assyrian account (as interpreted by Mr. G. Smith) sailors and a helmsman are taken on board.

story of Admetus and Alcestis. I subjoin the briefest epitome :—

Sāvitrī, the beautiful daughter of a king Aśvapati, loved Satyavān, the son of an old hermit, but was warned by a seer to overcome her attachment, as Satyavān was a doomed man, having only one year to live. But Sāvitrī replies :[1]—

Whether his years be few or many, be he gifted with all grace
Or graceless, him my heart hath chosen, and it chooseth not again.

The king's daughter and the hermit's son were therefore married, and the bride strove to forget the ominous prophecy ; but as the last day of the year approached, her anxiety became irrepressible. She exhausted herself in prayers and penances, hoping to stay the hand of the destroyer ; yet all the while dared not reveal the fatal secret to her husband. At last the dreaded day arrived, and Satyavān set out to cut wood in the forest. His wife asked leave to accompany him, and walked behind her husband, smiling, but with a heavy heart. Satyavān soon made the wood resound with his hatchet, when suddenly a thrill of agony shot through his temples, and feeling himself falling, he called out to his wife to support him.

Then she received her fainting husband in her arms, and sat herself
On the cold ground, and gently laid his drooping head upon her lap ;
Sorrowing, she call'd to mind the sage's prophecy, and reckoned up
The days and hours. All in an instant she beheld an awful shape
Standing before her, dressed in blood-red garments, with a glittering crown
Upon his head : his form, though glowing like the sun, was yet obscure,
And eyes he had like flames, a noose depended from his hand ; and he
Was terrible to look upon, as by her husband's side he stood
And gazed upon him with a fiery glance. Shuddering she started up
And laid her dying Satyavān upon the ground, and with her hands
Joined reverently, she thus with beating heart addressed the Shape :
Surely thou art a god, such form as thine must more than mortal be !
Tell me, thou godlike being, who thou art, and wherefore art thou here ?

The figure replied that he was Yama, king of the dead ; that her husband's time was come, and that he must bind and take his spirit :—

---

[1] I translate as closely as I can to the original. This and other select specimens of Indian poetry have been more freely and poetically translated by Mr. R. Griffiths.

Then from her husband's body forced he out and firmly with his cord
Bound and detained the spirit, clothed in form no larger than a thumb.[1]
Forthwith the body, reft of vital being and deprived of breath,
Lost all its grace and beauty, and became ghastly and motionless.

After binding the spirit, Yama proceeds with it towards the quarter of which he is guardian—the south. The faithful wife follows him closely. Yama bids her go home and prepare her husband's funeral rites; but she persists in following, till Yama, pleased with her devotion, grants her any boon she pleases, *except* the life of her husband. She chooses that her husband's father, who is blind, may recover his sight. Yama consents, and bids her now return home. Still she persists in following. Two other boons are granted in the same way, and still Sāvitrī follows closely on the heels of the king of death. At last, overcome by her constancy, Yama grants a boon without exception. The delighted Sāvitrī exclaims—

Nought, mighty king, this time hast thou excepted: let my husband live;
Without him I desire not happiness, nor even heaven itself;
Without him I must die. 'So be it! faithful wife,' replied the king of death;
'Thus I release him;' and with that he loosed the cord that bound his soul.

During the residence of the five brothers in the forest, Jayad-ratha attempted to carry off Draupadī, while they were absent on a shooting excursion. This resembles in some respects the story of Sītā's forcible abduction by Rāvaṇa in the Rāmāyaṇa (III. 15572), which story, therefore, is here told (15945. See p. 366 of this volume).

In the thirteenth year of exile, the Pāṇḍavas journeyed to the court of king Virāṭa, and entered his service in different disguises:—

Yudhi-shṭhira called himself a Brāhman and took the name of Kan·ka (23); Arjuna named himself Vṛihan-nalā, and pretending to be a eunuch (*tritīyām prakṛitiṃ gataḥ*), adopted a sort of woman's dress, putting bracelets on his arms and ear-rings in his ears, in order, as he said, to hide the scars caused by his bow-string. He undertook in this capacity to teach dancing, music, and singing to the daughter of Virāṭa and

[1] Compare note 3, p. 198 of this volume.

the other women of the palace, and soon gained their good graces (IV. 310).

One day when Virāṭa and four of the Pāṇḍavas were absent, Duryodhana and his brothers made an expedition against Virāṭa's capital, Matsya, and carried off some cattle. Uttara the son of Virāṭa (in the absence of his father) determined to follow and attack the Kuru army, if any one could be found to act as his charioteer. Vṛihan-nalā (Arjuna) undertook this office, and promised to bring back fine clothes and ornaments for Uttarā and the other women of the palace (IV. 1226). When they arrived in sight of the Kuru army, the courage of Uttara, who was a mere youth, failed him. Vṛihan-nalā then made him act as charioteer, while he himself (Arjuna) undertook to fight the Kauravas. Upon that great prodigies occurred. Terror seized Bhīshma, Duryodhana, and their followers, who suspected that Vṛihan-nalā was Arjuna in disguise, and even the horses shed tears[1] (IV. 1290). Duryodhana, however, declared that if he turned out to be Arjuna, he would have to wander in exile for a second period of twelve years. Meanwhile Arjuna revealed himself to Uttara, and explained also the disguises of his brothers and Draupadī. Uttara, to test his veracity, inquired whether he could repeat Arjuna's ten names, and what each meant. Arjuna enumerated them (Arjuna, Phālguna, Jishṇu, Kirīṭin, S'vetavāhana, Bībhatsu, Vijaya, Kṛishṇa, Savyasāćin, Dhanañjaya), and explained their derivation[2] (IV. 1380). Uttara then declared that he was satisfied, and no longer afraid of the Kuru army (IV. 1393).

Arjuna next put off his bracelets and woman's attire, strung his bow Gāṇḍiva, and assumed all his other weapons, which had been concealed in a S'amī tree. They are described as addressing him suppliantly, and saying, 'We are your servants, ready to carry out your commands'[3] (IV. 1421). He also removed Uttara's standard and placed his own ape-emblazoned banner in front of the chariot. Then was fought a great battle between Arjuna and the Kauravas. In the end the whole Kuru army fled before him, and all the property and cattle of Virāṭa was recovered. Arjuna told Uttara to conceal the real circumstances of the battle, but to send messengers to his father's capital announcing his victory, which so delighted Virāṭa that he ordered the whole city to be decorated.

Not long afterwards Virāṭa held a great assembly, at

---

[1] Compare Homer, Iliad XVII. 426.

[2] See Arjuna's other names in note 4, p. 381.

[3] Compare note, p. 402.

which the five Pāṇḍavas attended, and took their seats with the other princes. Virāṭa, who did not yet know their real rank, was at first angry at this presumption (IV. 2266). Arjuna then revealed who they were. Virāṭa was delighted, embraced the Pāṇḍavas, offered them all his possessions, and to Arjuna his daughter Uttarā in marriage. Arjuna declined, but accepted her for his son Abhimanyu (IV. 2356).

A council of princes was then called by Virāṭa, at which the Pāṇḍavas, Kṛishṇa, and Bala-rāma were present, and a consultation was held as to what course the Pāṇḍavas were to take:—

Kṛishṇa, in a speech, advised that they should not go to war with their kinsmen until they had sent an ambassador to Duryodhana, summoning him to restore half the kingdom. Bala-rāma supported Kṛishṇa's opinion, and recommended conciliation (*sāman*), but Sātyaki, in an angry tone, counselled war (V. 40). Drupada supported him, and recommended that they should send messengers to all their allies, and collect forces from all parts. The upshot was that the family-priest of Drupada was despatched by the Pāṇḍavas as an ambassador to king Dhṛita-rāshṭra at Hastinā-pur, to try the effect of negotiation.

Meanwhile Kṛishṇa and Bala-rāma returned to Dvārakā. Soon afterwards Duryodhana visited Kṛishṇa there, hoping to prevail on him to fight on the side of the Kuru army.

On the same day Arjuna arrived there also, and it happened that they both reached the door of Kṛishṇa's apartment, where he was asleep, at the same moment. Duryodhana succeeded in entering first, and took up his station at Kṛishṇa's head. Arjuna followed behind, and stood reverently at Kṛishṇa's feet. On awaking, Kṛishṇa's eyes first fell on Arjuna. He then asked them both the object of their visit. Duryodhana thereupon requested his aid in battle, declaring that although Kṛishṇa was equally related to Arjuna, yet that, as he (Duryodhana) had entered the room first, he was entitled to the priority. Kṛishṇa answered that, as he had seen Arjuna first, he should give Arjuna the first choice of two things. On the one side, he placed himself, stipulating that he was to lay down his weapons and abstain from fighting.

On the other, he placed his army of a hundred million (*arbuda*) warriors, named Nārāyaṇas. Arjuna, without hesitation, chose Kṛishṇa; and Duryodhana, with glee, accepted the army, thinking that as Kṛishṇa was pledged not to fight, he would be unable to help the Pāṇḍavas in battle (V. 154).

Duryodhana next went to Bala-rāma and asked his aid; but Bala-rāma declared that both he and Kṛishṇa had determined to take no part in the strife.[1] Kṛishṇa, however, consented to act as Arjuna's charioteer, and soon afterwards joined Yudhi-shṭhira, who with his brothers was still living in the country of Virāṭa. Various attempts at negotiation followed, and before any actual declaration of war the Pāṇḍavas held a final consultation, at which Arjuna begged Kṛishṇa to undertake the office of a mediator. Kṛishṇa consented and departed for Hastinā-pura:—

Midway he was met by Paraśu-rāma and various Ṛishis, who informed him of their resolution to be present at the coming congress of Kuru princes. On reaching Hastinā-pura, Kṛishṇa retired to rest in the house of Vidura. In the morning he performed all the appointed religious ceremonies, dressed himself, put on the jewel Kaustubha (V. 3343), and set out for the assembly. Then followed the great congress. The Ṛishis, headed by Nārada, appeared in the sky, and were accommodated with seats. Kṛishṇa opened the proceedings by a speech, which commenced thus: 'Let there be peace (*śama*) between the Kurus and Pāṇḍavas.' Then, looking towards Dhṛita-rāshṭra, he said, 'It rests with you and me to effect a reconciliation.' When he had concluded a long harangue, all remained riveted and thrilled by his eloquence (V. 3448). None ventured for some time to reply, except Paraśu-rāma, the sage Kaṇva, and Nārada, who all advocated harmony and peace between the rival cousins. At length Duryodhana spoke, and flatly refused to give up any territory: 'It was not our fault,' he said, 'if the Pāṇḍavas were conquered at dice.' Upon that Kṛishṇa's wrath rose, and addressing Duryodhana, he said, 'You think that I am alone, but know that the Pāṇḍavas, Andhakas, Vṛishṇis, Ādityas, Rudras, Vasus, and Ṛishis are

---

[1] Compare Megha-dūta, verse 51, where Bala-rāma is described as *Bandhu-prītyā samara-vimukhaḥ*.

all present here in me.' Thereupon flames of fire, of the size of a thumb, settled on him. Brahmā appeared on his forehead, Rudra on his breast, the guardians of the world issued from his arms, Agni from his mouth. The Ādityas, Sādhyas, Vasus, Aśvins, Maruts with Indra, Viśvadevas, Yakshas, Gandharvas, and Rākshasas were also manifested out of his body; Arjuna was produced from his right arm; Bala-rāma from his left arm; Bhīma, Yudhi-shṭhira, and the sons of Mādrī from his back; flames of fire darted from his eyes, nose, and ears; and the sun's rays from the pores of his skin[1] (V. 4419–4430). At this awful sight, the assembled princes were compelled to close their eyes; but Droṇa, Bhīshma, Vidura, Sañjaya, the Ṛishis, and the blind Dhṛita-rāshṭra were gifted by Kṛishṇa with divine vision that they might behold the glorious spectacle of his identification with every form (cf. p. 135 of this volume). Then a great earthquake and other portents occurred, and the congress broke up. Kṛishṇa, having suppressed his divinity, reassumed his human form and set out on his return. He took Karṇa with him for some distance in his chariot, hoping to persuade him to take part with the Pāṇḍavas as a sixth brother. But, notwithstanding all Kṛishṇa's arguments, Karṇa would not be persuaded; and, leaving the chariot, returned to the sons of Dhṛita-rāshṭra (V. 4883).

Meanwhile Bhīshma consented to accept the generalship of the Kuru army (V. 5719). Though averse from fighting against his kinsmen, he could not as a Kshatriya abstain from joining in the war, when once commenced.[2]

Before the armies joined battle, Vyāsa appeared to his son Dhṛita-rāshṭra, who was greatly dejected at the prospect of the war, consoled him, and offered to confer sight upon him, that he might view the combat. Dhṛita-rāshṭra declined witnessing the slaughter of his kindred, and Vyāsa then said that he would endow Sañjaya (Dhṛita-rāshṭra's charioteer) with the faculty of knowing everything that took place, make him invulnerable, and enable him to transport himself by a thought at any time to any part of the field of battle (VI. 43–47).

---

[1] This remarkable passage, identifying Vishṇu with everything in the universe, is probably a later interpolation.

[2] Bhīshma, though really the grand-uncle of the Kuru and Pāṇḍu princes, is often styled their grandfather (*pitāmaha*); and though really the uncle of Dhṛita-rāshṭra and Pāṇḍu, is sometimes styled their father. He is a kind of Priam in caution and sagacity, but like a hardy old veteran, never consents to leave the fighting to others.

The armies now met on Kuru-kshetra, a vast plain north-west of the modern Delhi; the Kuru forces being commanded by Bhīshma, and the Pāṇḍavas by Dhṛishṭa-dyumna, son of Drupada (VI. 832). While the hosts stood drawn up in battle array, Kṛishṇa, acting as Arjuna's charioteer, addressed him in a long philosophical discourse, which forms the celebrated episode called Bhagavad-gītā (VI. 830–1532), an epitome of which is given at pp. 124–140 of this volume.

And now as the armies advanced a tumult filled the sky; the earth shook; 'Chafed by wild winds, the sands upcurled to heaven, and spread a veil before the sun.' Awful portents occurred; showers of blood fell;[1] asses were born from cows, calves from mares, jackals from dogs. Shrill kites, vultures, and howling jackals hung about the rear of the marching armies. Thunder roared in the cloudless sky. Then darkness supervened, lightnings flashed, and blazing meteors shot across the darkened firmament; yet,

> The mighty chiefs, with martial ardour fired,
> Scorning Heaven's portents, eager for the fray,
> Pressed on to mutual slaughter, and the peal
> Of shouting hosts commingling, shook the world.

There is to a European a ponderous and unwieldy character about Oriental warfare, which he finds it difficult to realize; yet the battle-scenes, though exaggerated, are vividly described, and carry the imagination into the midst of the conflict. Monstrous elephants career over the field, trampling on men and horses, and dealing destruction with their huge tusks; enormous clubs and iron maces clash together with the noise of thunder;

---

[1] So Jupiter rains blood twice in the Iliad, XI. 53 and XVI. 459. We have also the following in Hesiod, Scut. Herc. 384: Κὰδ δ' ἄῤ ἀπ' οὐρανόθεν ψιάδας βάλεν αἱματοέσσας.

rattling chariots dash against each other; thousands of arrows hurtle in the air, darkening the sky; trumpets, kettle-drums, and horns add to the uproar; confusion, carnage, and death are everywhere.

In all this, however, there is nothing absolutely extravagant; but when Arjuna is described as killing five hundred warriors simultaneously, or as covering the whole plain with dead and filling rivers with blood; Yudhishṭhira, as slaughtering a hundred men 'in a mere twinkle' (*nimesha-mātreṇa*); Bhīma, as annihilating a monstrous elephant, including all mounted upon it, and fourteen foot-soldiers besides, with one blow of his club; Nakula and Sahadeva, fighting from their chariots, as cutting off heads by the thousand, and sowing them like seed upon the ground; when, moreover, the principal heroes make use of mystical god-given weapons, possessed of supernatural powers, and supposed to be themselves celestial beings;[1]—we at once perceive that the utter unreality of such scenes mars the beauty of the description. Still it must be borne in mind that the poets

---

[1] About a hundred of these weapons are enumerated in the Rāmāyaṇa (I. xxix.), and constant allusion is made to them in battle-scenes, both in the Rāmāyaṇa and Mahā-bhārata. Arjuna underwent a long course of austerities to obtain celestial weapons from S'iva (see p. 393). It was by the terrific *brahmāstra* that Vaśishṭha conquered Viśvāmitra, and Rāma killed Rāvaṇa. Sometimes they appear to be mystical powers exercised by meditation, rather than weapons, and are supposed to assume animate forms, and possess names and faculties like the genii in the Arabian Nights, and to address their owners (see p. 397). Certain distinct spells, charms, or prayers had to be learnt for their due use (*prayoga*) and restraint (*saṃhāra*). See Rām. I. xxix., xxx., where they are personified; also Raghu-vaṇśa V. 57 (*Sammohanaṃ nāma astram ādhatsva prayoga-saṃhāra-vibhakta-mantram*). When once let loose, he only who knew the secret spell for recalling them, could bring them back; but the *brahmāstra* returned to its possessor's quiver of its own accord.

who brāhmanized the Indian Epics gifted the heroes with semi-divine natures, and that what would be incredible in a mere mortal is not only possible but appropriate when enacted by a demigod.[1] The individual deeds of prowess and single combats between the heroes are sometimes graphically narrated. Each chief has a conch-shell (*śankha*) for a trumpet, which, as well as his principal weapon, has a name, as if personified.[2] Thus we read :—

Arjuna blew his shell called Deva-datta, 'god-given,' and carried a bow named Gāṇḍīva. Kṛishṇa sounded a shell made of the bones of the demon Pañćajana and hence called Pāñćajanya, Bhīma blew a great trumpet named Pauṇḍra, and Yudhi-shṭhira sounded his, called Ananta-vijaya, 'eternal victory.'

The first great single combat was between Bhīshma and Arjuna. It ended in Arjuna transfixing Bhīshma with innumerable arrows, so that there was not a space of two fingers' breadth on his whole body unpierced.

Then Bhīshma fell from his chariot; but his body could not touch the ground, surrounded as it was by countless arrows (VI. 5658). There it remained, reclining as it were on an arrowy couch (*śara-talpe śayāna*). In that state consciousness returned, and the old warrior became divinely supported. He had received from his father the power of fixing the time of his own death,[3] and now declared that he intended retaining life till the sun entered the summer solstice (*uttarā-*

---

1 Aristotle says that the epic poet should prefer impossibilities which appear probable to such things as, though possible, appear improbable (Poetics III. 6). But previously, in comparing epic poetry with tragedy, he observes, 'the surprising is necessary in tragedy, but the epic poem goes further, and admits even the improbable and incredible, from which the highest degree of the surprising results' (III. 4).

2 Trumpets do not appear to have been used by Homer's heroes. Whence the value of a Stentorian voice. But there is express allusion in Il. XVIII. 219 to the use of trumpets at sieges.

3 Compare Kirātārjunīya III. 19.

yaṇa). All the warriors on both sides ceased fighting that they might view this wonderful sight, and do homage to their dying relative (VI. 5716). As he lay on his arrowy bed, his head hanging down, he begged for a pillow; whereupon the chiefs brought soft supports, which the hardy old soldier sternly rejected. Arjuna then made a rest for his head with three arrows, which Bhīshma quite approved, and soon afterwards asked Arjuna to bring him water. Whereupon Arjuna struck the ground with an arrow, and forthwith a pure spring burst forth, which so refreshed Bhīshma that he called for Duryodhana, and in a long speech begged him, before it was too late, to restore half the kingdom to the Pāṇḍavas (VI. 5813).

After the fall of Bhīshma, Karṇa advised Duryodhana to appoint his old tutor Droṇa—who was chiefly formidable from his stock of fiery arrows and magical weapons [1]—to the command of the army (VII. 150). Several single combats and general engagements (*sankula-yuddham, tumula-yuddham*), in which sometimes one party, sometimes the other had the advantage, took place. Here is an account of a single combat (VII. 544):—

High on a stately car
Swift borne by generous coursers to the fight,
The vaunting son of Puru proudly drove,
Secure of conquest o'er Subhadrā's son.
The youthful champion shrank not from the conflict.
Fierce on the boastful chief he sprang, as bounds
The lion's cub upon the ox; and now
The Puru chief had perished, but his dart
Shivered with timely aim the upraised bow
Of Abhimanyu.[2] From his tingling hand
The youthful warrior cast the fragments off,
And drew his sword, and grasped his iron-bound shield;
Upon the car of Paurava he leapt
And seized the chief—his charioteer he slew,
And dragged the monarch senseless o'er the plain.[3]

---

[1] These *āgneyāstra* were received by Droṇa from the son of Agni, who obtained them from Droṇa's father, Bharadvāja.

[2] The name of Arjuna's son by Subhadrā.

[3] The translation of this and the short passage at p. 401 is a

Amongst other battles a great fight was fought between Ghaṭotkaća and Karṇa, in which the former as a Rākshasa (son of the Rākshasī Hiḍimbā and Bhīma) assumed various forms, but was eventually slain (VII. 8104). This disaster filled the Pāṇḍavas with grief, but the fortunes of the day were retrieved by Dhrishṭa-dyumna (son of Drupada), who fought with Droṇa, and succeeded in decapitating his lifeless body,—not, however, till Droṇa had laid down his arms and saved Dhrishṭa-dyumna from the enormous crime of killing a Brāhman and an Āćāryá, by transporting himself to heaven in a glittering shape like the sun. His translation to Brahma-loka was only witnessed by five persons, and before leaving the earth he made over his divine weapons to his son Aśvatthāman. The loss of their general Droṇa caused the flight of the whole Kuru army (VII. 8879), but they appointed Karṇa general, in his place, and renewed the combat :—

In this engagement so terrible was the slaughter that the rivers flowed with blood, and the field became covered with mutilated corpses (VIII. 2550, 3899). Numbers of warriors bound themselves by oath (*saṃśap-taka*) to slay Arjuna, but were all destroyed, and an army of Mleććhas or barbarians with thirteen hundred elephants, sent by Duryodhana against Arjuna, were all routed by him (4133).

Then Bhīma and Duḥśāsana joined in deadly conflict. The latter was slain, and Bhīma, remembering the insult to Draupadī, and the vow he made in consequence (see p. 392), cut off his head, and drank his blood on the field of battle (4235).

Then occurred the battle between Karṇa and Arjuna :—

Arjuna was wounded and stunned by an arrow shot off by Karṇa, and seemed likely to be defeated had not the wheel of Karna's chariot come off. This obliged Karṇa to leap down, and his head was then shot off by one of Arjuna's arrows [1] (VIII. 4798). His death struck

---

slightly altered version of some spirited lines by Professor H. H. Wilson, given in vol. iii. of his collected works edited by Dr. R. Rost.

[1] This arrow is called in the text *Añjalika* (VIII. 4788). The

terror into the Kuru army, which fled in dismay, while Bhīma and the Pāṇḍu party raised a shout of triumph that shook heaven and earth.

On the death of Karṇa, Śalya, king of Madra, was appointed to the command of the Kuru army, then much reduced in numbers (IX. 327). Another general engagement followed, and a single combat between Śalya and Bhīma with clubs or maces, in which both were equally matched (IX. 594). Here is a version of the encounter:—

Soon as he saw his charioteer struck down,
Straightway the Madra monarch grasped his mace,
And like a mountain firm and motionless
Awaited the attack. The warrior's form
Was awful as the world-consuming fire,
Or as the noose-armed god of death, or as
The peaked Kailāsa, or the Thunderer
Himself, or as the trident-bearing god,
Or as a maddened forest elephant.
Him to defy did Bhīma hastily
Advance, wielding aloft his massive club.
A thousand conchs and trumpets and a shout,
Firing each champion's ardour, rent the air.
From either host, spectators of the fight,
Burst forth applauding cheers: 'The Madra king
Alone,' they cried, 'can bear the rush of Bhīma;
None but heroic Bhīma can sustain
The force of Śalya.' Now like two fierce bulls
Sprang they towards each other, mace in hand.
And first as cautiously they circled round,
Whirling their weapons as in sport, the pair
Seemed matched in equal combat. Śalya's club,
Set with red fillets, glittered as with flame,

---

arrows used in the Mahā-bhārata are of various kinds, some having crescent-shaped heads. It may be useful to subjoin a list of words for arrow, which occur constantly in the description of battles: *śara*, *vāṇa*, *ishu*, *śāyaka*, *patrin*, *kāṇḍa*, *viśikha*, *nārāća*, *vipāṭha*, *pṛishatka*, *bhalla*, *tomara* (a kind of lance), *śalya* (a dart), *ishīkā*, *śilīmukha*.

While that of Bhīma gleamed like flashing lightning.
Anon the clashing iron met, and scattered round
A fiery shower; then fierce as elephants
Or butting bulls they battered each the other.
Thick fell the blows, and soon each stalwart frame,
Spattered with gore, glowed like the Kinśuka,
Bedecked with scarlet blossoms; yet beneath
The rain of strokes, unshaken as a rock
Bhīma sustained the mace of S'alya, he
With equal firmness bore the other's blows.
Now like the roar of crashing thunder-clouds
Sounded the clashing iron; then, their clubs
Brandished aloft, eight paces they retired,
And swift again advancing to the fight,
Met in the midst like two huge mountain-crags
Hurled into contact. Nor could either bear
The other's shock; together down they rolled,
Mangled and crushed, like two tall standards fallen.

After this a great battle was fought between Yudhishṭhira and Śalya, who was at first aided and rescued by Aśvatthāman, but was eventually killed (IX. 919).

The Kauravas, after suffering continual reverses, rallied their scattered forces for a final charge, which led to a complete rout and general slaughter, Duryodhana, Aśvatthāman (son of Droṇa), Kṛita-varman (also called Bhoja), and Kṛipa (see note 1, p. 383) being the only chiefs of the Kuru army left alive.[1] Nothing remained of eleven whole armies (IX. 1581). Duryodhana, wounded, disheartened, and alarmed for his own safety, resolved on flight:—

On foot, with nothing but his mace, he took refuge in a lake, hiding himself under the water, and then, by his magical power, supporting it so as to form a chamber around his body.[2] The Pāṇḍavas, informed

---

[1] Sañjaya was taken by Dhṛishṭa-dyumna, and would have been killed had not Vyāsa suddenly appeared and demanded that he should be dismissed unharmed (compare p. 376).

[2] So I interpret *astambhayat toyam māyayā* (IX. 1621) and *vishṭabhya apaḥ sva-māyayā* (1680, 1739). Duryodhana is described as lying down and sleeping at the bottom of the lake (1705).

of his hiding-place, came to the lake, and Yudhi-shṭhira commenced taunting Duryodhana, 'Where is your manliness? where is your pride? where your valour? where your skill in arms, that you hide yourself at the bottom of a lake? Rise up and fight; perform your duty as a Kshatriya' (IX. 1774). Duryodhana answered, that it was not from fear, but fatigue, that he was lying under the water, and that he was ready to fight them all. He entreated them, however, to go and take the kingdom, as he had no longer any pleasure in life, his brothers being killed. Yudhi-shṭhira then continued his sarcasms, till at last, thoroughly roused by his goading words (*vāk-pratoda*), Duryodhana rose up out of the lake, his body streaming with blood and water (IX. 1865).

It was settled that a single combat with clubs should take place between Duryodhana and Bhīma; and when Bala-rāma heard that his two pupils (see p. 383) were about to engage in conflict, he determined to be present, that he might ensure fair play.[1]

Then followed the great club-fight (*gadā-yuddha*):—

The two combatants entered the lists and challenged each other, while Kṛishṇa, Bala-rāma, and all the other Pāṇḍavas sat round as spectators. The fight was tedious, the combatants being equally matched. At last Bhīma struck Duryodhana a blow on his thighs, broke them, and felled him to the ground. Then reminding him of the insult received by Draupadī, he kicked him on the head with his left foot (IX. 3313). Upon this Bala-rāma started up in anger, declaring that Bhīma had fought unfairly (it being a rule in club-fights that no blow should be given below the middle of the body), and that he should ever after be called *Jihma-yodhin* (unfair-fighter), while Duryodhana should always be celebrated as *Ṛiju-yodhin* (fair-fighter).

Bala-rāma thereupon returned to Dvārakā, and the five Pāṇḍavas with Kṛishṇa entered the camp of Duryodhana,

---

[1] An interesting episode about the *māhātmya* of Tīrthas, and especially of those on the sacred Sarasvatī (IX. 2006), is inserted in this part of the poem. The story of the Moon, who was afflicted with consumption, on account of the curse of Daksha, is also told (2030), as well as the celebrated legend of Vaśishṭha and Viśvāmitra (2296, see p. 361).

and took possession of it and its treasures as victors (IX. 3492).

The three surviving Kuru warriors (Aśvatthāman, Kṛipa, and Kṛita-varman), hearing of the fall of Duryodhana, hastened to the place where he was lying. There they found him weltering in his blood (IX. 3629), but still alive. He spoke to them, told them not to grieve for him, and assured them that he should die happy in having done his duty as a Kshatriya. Then leaving Duryodhana still lingering alive with broken thighs on the battle-field, they took refuge in a forest.

There, at night, they rested near a Nyagrodha-tree, where thousands of crows were roosting. Aśvatthāman, who could not sleep, saw an owl approach stealthily and destroy numbers of the sleeping crows (X. 41). This suggested the idea of entering the camp of the Pāṇḍavas by night and slaughtering them while asleep (*supta*).[1] Accordingly he set out for the Pāṇḍu camp, followed by Kṛipa and Kṛita-varman. At the gate of the camp his progress was arrested by an awful figure, described as gigantic, glowing like the sun, dressed in a tiger's skin, with long arms, and bracelets formed of serpents. This was the deity Śiva;[2] and after a tremendous conflict with him, Aśvatthāman recognized the god, worshipped and propitiated him (X. 251).

Aśvatthāman then directed Kṛipa and Kṛita-varman to stand at the camp-gate and kill any of the Pāṇḍu army that attempted to escape (X. 327). He himself made his way alone and stealthily to the tent of Dhṛishṭa-dyumna, who was lying there fast asleep. Him he killed by stamping on him, declaring that one who had murdered his father (Droṇa, see p. 405)—a Brāhman and an Ācārya—was not worthy to

[1] Hence the name *sauptika* applied to this section of the poem. Compare Homer's narrative of the night adventures of Diomed and Ulysses in the camp of the Trojans (Iliad X.).

[2] The description of Śiva in this passage is remarkable. Hundreds and thousands of Kṛishṇas are said to be manifested from the light issuing from his person. Many of Śiva's names also are enumerated as follows:—Ugra, Sthāṇu, Śiva, Rudra, Śarva, Īśāna, Īśvara, Giriśa, Varada, Deva, Bhava, Bhāvana, Śitikaṇṭha, Aja, Śukra, Daksha-kratu-hara, Hara, Viśvarūpa, Virūpāksha, Bahurūpa, Umāpati (X. 252).

die in any other way (X. 342). After killing every one in the camp and destroying the whole Pāṇḍu army (except the five Pāṇḍavas themselves with Sātyaki and Kṛishṇa, who happened to be stationed outside the camp), Aśvatthāman joined his comrades, and they all three proceeded to the spot where Duryodhana was lying. They found him just breathing (*kiṅćit-prāṇa*), but weltering in his blood and surrounded by beasts of prey. Aśvatthāman then announced that he was avenged, as only seven of the Pāṇḍu army were now left; all the rest were slaughtered like cattle (X. 531). Duryodhana hearing this, revived a little, and gathering strength to thank them and say farewell, expired; his spirit rising to heaven and his body entering the ground (X. 536).

Thus perished both armies of Kurus and Pāṇḍavas.

Dhṛita-rāshṭra was so overwhelmed with grief for the death of his sons, that his father Vyāsa appeared to him and consoled him by pointing out that their fate was predestined, and that they could not escape death. He also declared that the Pāṇḍavas were not to blame; that Duryodhana, though born from Gāndhārī, was really a partial incarnation of Kali[1] (*Kaler anśa*), and Śakuni of Dvāpara (see p. 330, note).

Vidura also comforted the king with his usual sensible advice, and recommended that the funeral ceremonies (*preta-kāryāṇi*) should be performed. Dhṛita-rāshṭra then ordered carriages to be prepared, and with the women proceeded to the field of battle (XI. 269).

There he met and became reconciled to the five Pāṇḍavas, but his wife Gāndhārī would have cursed them had not Vyāsa interfered. The five brothers next embraced and comforted their mother Pṛithā, who with the queen Gāndhārī, and the other wives and women, uttered lamentations over the bodies of the slain heroes, as one by one they came in sight on the field of battle (XI. 427–755).

---

[1] So also S'akuni is said to be an incarnation of Dvāpara (XVIII. 166).

Finally, the funeral obsequies (*śrāddha*) were performed at the command of Yudhi-shṭhira (XI. 779), after which he, with his brothers, entered Hastinā-pura in triumph.

All the streets were decorated; and Brāhmans offered him congratulations, which he acknowledged by distributing largesses among them (XII. 1410). Only one person stood aloof. This turned out to be an impostor, a friend of Duryodhana—a Rākshasa named Ćārvāka—who in the disguise of a mendicant reviled him and the Brāhmans. He was, however, soon detected; and the real Brāhmans, filled with fury and uttering imprecations, killed him on the spot (see p. 119).

After this incident, Yudhi-shṭhira, seated on a golden throne, was solemnly crowned (XII. 1443).

Nevertheless, restless and uneasy, and his mind filled with anguish at the slaughter of his kindred, he longed for consolation (*śānti*), and Kṛishṇa recommended him to apply to Bhīshma, who still remained alive on the field of battle, reclining on his soldier's bed (*vīra-śayana*), surrounded by Vyāsa, Nārada, and other holy sages. Accordingly, Yudhi-shṭhira and his brothers, accompaned by Kṛishṇa, set out for Kuru-kshetra, passing mutilated corpses, skulls, broken armour, and other evidences of the fearful nature of the war. This reminded Kṛishṇa of the slaughter caused by Paraśu-rāma, who cleared the earth thrice seven times of the Kshatriya caste (see p. 329). His story was accordingly narrated to Yudhi-shṭhira (XII. 1707–1805). They then approached Bhīshma lying on his couch of arrows (*śara-samstara-śāyinam*), and Kṛishṇa entreated him to instruct Yudhi-shṭhira, and calm his spirit.

Upon that Bhīshma, who had been lying for fifty-eight nights on his spiky bed (XIII. 7732), assisted by Kṛishṇa, Nārada, Vyāsa, and other Ṛishis, commenced a series of long and tedious didactic discourses (contained in the Śānti-parvan and Anuśāsana-parvan).[1]

---

[1] In XII. 1241 we have some curious rules for expiation (*prāyaś-ćitta*), and at 1393 rules for what to eat and what to avoid (*bhakshyābhakshya*). Some of the precepts are either taken from or founded on Manu. For instance, compare 6071 with Manu II. 238. Many of the moral verses in the Hitopadeśa will be found in the Śānti-parvan; and

Then having finished instructing his relatives, he bade them farewell, and asked Kṛishṇa's leave to depart. Suddenly the arrows left his body, his skull divided, and his spirit, bright as a meteor, ascended through the top of his head to the skies (XIII. 7765). They covered him with garlands and perfumes, carried him to the Ganges, and performed his last obsequies.

And here a European poet would have brought the story to an end. The Sanskṛit poet has a deeper knowledge of human nature, or at least of Hindū nature.

In the most popular of Indian dramas (the Śakuntalā) there occurs this sentiment: [1]—

'Tis a vain thought that to attain the end
And object of ambition is to rest.
Success doth only mitigate the fever
Of anxious expectation: soon the fear
Of losing what we have, the constant care
Of guarding it doth weary.

If then the great national Epic was to respond truly to the deeper emotions of the Hindū mind, it could not leave the Pāṇḍavas in the contented enjoyment of their kingdom. It had to instil a more sublime moral—a lesson which even the disciples of a divine philosophy are slow to learn—that all who desire rest must aim at union with the Infinite. Hence we are brought in the concluding chapters to a sublime description of the renunciation of their kingdom by the five brothers, and their journey towards Indra's heaven in the mountain Meru. Part of this (XVII. 24, &c.) I now translate:—

When the four brothers knew the high resolve of king Yudhi-shṭhira,
Forthwith with Draupadī they issued forth, and after them a dog
Followed: the king himself went out the seventh from the royal city,

---

the fable of the three fishes is founded on the story at 4889. For the contents of the Āśvamedhika, Āśramavāsika, and Mausala Parvans, see p. 374.

[1] See my translation of this play, 4th edition, p. 124 (recently published by W. H. Allen & Co., 13 Waterloo Place).

And all the citizens and women of the palace walked behind;
But none could find it in their heart to say unto the king, 'Return.'
And so at length the train of citizens went back, bidding adieu.
Then the high-minded sons of Pāṇḍu and the noble Draupadī
Roamed onwards, fasting, with their faces towards the east; their hearts
Yearning for union with the Infinite; bent on abandonment
Of worldly things. They wandered on to many countries, many a sea
And river. Yudhi-shṭhira walked in front, and next to him came Bhīma,
And Arjuna came after him, and then, in order, the twin brothers.
And last of all came Draupadī, with her dark skin and lotus-eyes—
The faithful Draupadī, loveliest of women, best of noble wives—
Behind them walked the only living thing that shared their pilgrimage—
The dog—and by degrees they reached the briny sea. There Arjuna
Cast in the waves his bow and quivers.[1] Then with souls well-disciplined
They reached the northern region, and beheld with heaven-aspiring hearts
The mighty mountain Himavat. Beyond its lofty peak they passed
Towards a sea of sand, and saw at last the rocky Meru, king
Of mountains. As with eager steps they hastened on, their souls intent
On union with the Eternal, Draupadī lost hold of her high hope,
And faltering fell upon the earth.

One by one the others also drop, till only Bhīma, Yudhi-shṭhira, and the dog are left. Still Yudhi-shṭhira walks steadily in front, calm and unmoved, looking neither to the right hand nor to the left, and gathering up his soul in inflexible resolution. Bhīma, shocked at the fall of his companions, and unable to understand how beings so apparently guileless should be struck down by fate, appeals to his brother, who, without looking back, explains that death is the consequence of sinful thoughts and too great attachment to worldly objects; and that Draupadī's fall was owing to her excessive affection for Arjuna; Sahadeva's (who is supposed to be the most humble-minded of the five brothers) to his pride in his own knowledge; Nakula's (who is very handsome) to feelings of

[1] Arjuna had two celebrated quivers, besides the bow named Gāṇḍīva, given to him by the god Agni. See Kirātārjunīya XI. 16.

personal vanity; and Arjuna's to a boastful confidence in his power to destroy his foes. Bhīma then feels himself falling, and is told that he suffers death for his selfishness, pride, and too great love of enjoyment. The sole survivor is now Yudhi-shṭhira, who still walks steadily forward, followed only by the dog:—

When with a sudden sound that rang through earth and heaven the mighty god
Came towards him in a chariot, and he cried, 'Ascend, O resolute prince.'
Then did the king look back upon his fallen brothers, and address'd
These words unto the Thousand-eyed in anguish—'Let my brothers here
Come with me. Without them, O god of gods, I would not wish to enter
E'en heaven; and yonder tender princess Draupadī, the faithful wife,
Worthy of endless bliss, let her too come. In mercy hear my prayer.'

Upon this, Indra informs him that the spirits of Draupadī and his brothers are already in heaven, and that he alone is permitted to ascend there in bodily form. Yudhi-shṭhira now stipulates that his dog shall be admitted with him. Indra says sternly, 'Heaven has no place for men accompanied by dogs' (*śvavatām*); but Yudhi-shṭhira is unshaken in his resolution, and declines abandoning the faithful animal. Indra remonstrates—'You have abandoned your brothers and Draupadī; why not forsake the dog?' To this Yudhi-shṭhira haughtily replies, 'I had no power to bring them back to life: how can there be abandonment of those who no longer live?'

The dog, it appears, is his own father Dharma in disguise (XVII. 88).[1] Reassuming now his proper form, he praises Yudhi-shṭhira for his constancy, and they enter heaven together. There, to his surprise, he finds Duryodhana and his cousins, but not his brothers or Draupadī. Hereupon he declines remaining in heaven without them.

---

[1] So I infer from the original, which, however, is somewhat obscure. The expression is *dharma-svarūpī bhagavān*. At any rate, the dog was a mere phantom created to try Yudhi-shṭhira, as it is evident that a real dog is not admitted with Yudhi-shṭhira to heaven.

An angel is then sent to conduct him to the lower regions and across the Indian Styx (*Vaitaraṇī*) to the hell where they are supposed to be. The scene which now follows may be compared to the Nekyomanteia in the eleventh book of the Odyssey, or to parts of Dante.

The particular hell to which Yudhi-shṭhira is taken is a dense wood, whose leaves are sharp swords, and its ground paved with razors (*asi-patra-vana*, see p. 55, note 2). The way to it is strewed with foul and mutilated corpses. Hideous shapes flit across the air and hover over him. Here there is an awful sensation of palpable darkness. There the wicked are burning in flames of blazing fire. Suddenly he hears the voices of his brothers and companions imploring him to assuage their torments, and not desert them. His resolution is taken. Deeply affected, he bids the angel leave him to share their miseries. This is his last trial. The whole scene now vanishes. It was a mere illusion, to test his constancy to the utmost. He is now directed to bathe in the heavenly Ganges; and having plunged into the sacred stream, he enters the real heaven, where at length, in company with Draupadī and his brothers, he finds that rest and happiness which were unattainable on earth.

CHAPTER XIV.

The Indian Epics compared with each other and with the Homeric Poems.

I PROCEED to note a few obvious points that force themselves on the attention in comparing the two great Indian Epics with each other, and with the Homeric poems. I have already stated that the episodes of the Mahā-bhārata occupy more than three-fourths of the whole poem.[1] It is, in fact, not one poem, but a combination of many poems; not a *Kāvya,* like the poem of Vālmīki, by one author, but an *Itihāsa* by many authors. This is one great distinctive feature in comparing it with the Rāmāyaṇa. In both Epics there is a leading story, about which are collected a multitude of other stories; but in the Mahā-bhārata the main narrative only acts as a slender thread to connect together a vast mass of independent legends, and religious, moral, and political precepts; while in the Rāmāyaṇa the episodes, though numerous, never break the solid chain of one principal and paramount subject, which is ever kept in view. Moreover, in the Rāmāyaṇa there are few didactic discourses and a remarkable paucity of sententious maxims.

It should be remembered that the two Epics belong to different periods and different localities. Not only was

---

[1] Although the Mahā-bhārata is so much longer than the Rāmāyaṇa as to preclude the idea of its being, like that poem, the work of one or even a few authors, yet it is the number of the episodes which, after all, causes the disparity. Separated from these, the main story of the Mahā-bhārata is not longer than the other Epic.

a large part of the Mahā-bhārata composed later than the Rāmāyaṇa, parts of it being comparatively modern, but the places which gave birth to the two poems are distinct (see p. 317). Moreover, in the Rāmāyaṇa the circle of territory represented as occupied by the Āryans is more restricted than that in the Mahā-bhārata. It reaches to Videha or Mithilā and An·ga in the East, to Su-rāshṭra in the South-west, to the Yamunā and great Daṇḍaka forest in the South. Whereas in the Mahā-bhārata (as pointed out by Professor Lassen) the Āryan settlers are described as having extended themselves to the mouths of the Ganges in the East, to the mouth of the Godāvarī on the Koromandel coast, and to the Malabar coast in the West; and even the inhabitants of Ceylon (Sinhala) bring tribute to the Northern kings. It is well known that in India different customs and opinions frequently prevail in districts almost adjacent; and it is certain that Brāhmanism never gained the ascendency in the more martial north which it acquired in the neighbourhood of Oude,[1] so that in the Mahā-bhārata we have far more allusions to Buddhistic scepticism than we have in the sister Epic. In fact, each poem, though often running parallel to the other, has yet a distinct point of departure; and the Mahā-bhārata, as it became current in various localities, diverged more into by-paths and cross-roads than its sister. Hence the Rāmāyaṇa is in some respects a more finished composition than the Mahā-bhārata, and depicts a more polished state of society, and a more advanced civilization.

---

1 Professor Weber (Ind. Stud. I. 220) remarks that the north-western tribes retained their ancient customs, which those who migrated to the east had at one time shared. The former (as represented in the Mahā-bhārata) kept themselves free from those influences of hierarchy and caste, which arose among the inhabitants of Ayodhyā (in the Rāmāyaṇa) as a consequence of their intermingling and coming more in contact with the aborigines.

In fact, the Mahā-bhārata presents a complete circle of post-Vedic mythology, including many myths which have their germ in the Veda, and continually enlarging its circumference to embrace the later phases of Hindūism, with its whole train of confused and conflicting legends.[1] From this storehouse are drawn much of the Purāṇas, and many of the more recent heroic poems and dramas. Here we have repeated many of the legends of the Rāmāyaṇa, and even the history of Rāma himself (see p. 366). Here also we have long discourses on religion, politics, morality, and philosophy, introduced without any particular connection with the plot. Here again are most of the narratives of the incarnation of Vishṇu, numberless stories connected with the worship of Śiva, and various details of the life of Kṛishṇa. Those which especially bear on the modern worship of Kṛishṇa are contained in the supplement called Hari-vanśa, which is itself a long poem—consisting of 16,374 stanzas[2]—longer than the Iliad and Odyssey combined.[3] Hence the religious system of the Mahā-bhārata is far more popular, liberal, and comprehensive than that of the Rāmāyaṇa. It is true that the god Vishṇu is connected with Kṛishṇa in the Mahā-bhārata, as he is with Rāma in the Rāmāyaṇa, but in the latter Rāma is every-

[1] It should be noted, that the germs of many of the legends of Hindū epic poetry are found in the Ṛig-veda. Also that the same legend is sometimes repeated in different parts of the Mahā-bhārata, with considerable variations; as, for example, the story of the combat of Indra—god of air and thunder—with the demon Vṛitra, who represents enveloping clouds and vapour. See Vana-parvan 8690, &c.; and compare with Śānti-parvan 10124, &c. Compare also the story of the 'Hawk and Pigeon,' Vana-parvan 10558, with Anuśāsana-parvan 2046.

[2] The Hari-vanśa bears to the Mahā-bhārata a relation very similar to that which the Uttara-kāṇḍa, or last Book of the Rāmāyaṇa, bears to the preceding Books of that poem.

[3] The Iliad and Odyssey together contain about 30,000 lines.

thing; whereas in the Mahā-bhārata, Krishṇa is by no means the centre of the system. His divinity is even occasionally disputed.[1] The five Pāṇḍavas have also partially divine natures, and by turns become prominent. Sometimes Arjuna, sometimes Yudhi-shṭhira, at others Bhīma, appears to be the principal orb round which the plot moves.[2] Moreover, in various passages Śiva is described as supreme, and receives worship from Kṛishṇa. In others, Kṛishṇa is exalted above all, and receives honour from Śiva.[3] In fact, while the Rāmāyaṇa generally represents one-sided and exclusive Brāhmanism,[4] the Mahā-bhārata reflects the multilateral character of Hindūism; its monotheism and polytheism, its spirituality and materialism, its strictness and laxity, its priestcraft and anti-priestcraft, its hierarchical intolerance and rationalistic philosophy, combined. Not that there was any intentional variety in the original design of the work, but that almost every shade of opinion found expression in a compilation formed by gradual accretion through a long period.

In unison with its more secular, popular, and *human*

---

1 As by Śiśu-pāla and others. See p. 392, with notes.

2 In this respect the Mahā-bhārata resembles the Iliad. Achilles is scarcely its hero. Other warriors too much divide the interest with him.

3 In the Bhagavad-gītā Kṛishṇa is not merely an incarnation of Vishṇu; he is identified with Brahma, the Supreme Spirit, and is so in numerous other places. It is well known that in Homer the supremacy of one god (Jove), and due subordination of the other deities, is maintained.

4 Some free thought, however, has found its way into the Rāmāyaṇa; see II. cviii. (Schl.); VI. lxii. 15 (Gorr., Bomb. lxxxiii. 14); VI. lxxxiii. 14 (Calc.). It is remarkable that in the Rāmāyaṇa the same gods are appealed to by Rāma and Rāvaṇa, just as by Greeks and Trojans in the Iliad; and Hanumat, when in Lan-kā, heard the Brahma-ghosha in the morning. Rāmāy. V. xvi. 41. This has been noticed by Weber.

character, the Mahā-bhārata has, as a rule, less of mere mythical allegory, and more of historical probability in its narratives than the Rāmāyaṇa. The reverse, however, sometimes holds good. For example, in Rāmāyaṇa IV. xl. we have a simple division of the world into four quarters or regions, whereas in Mahā-bhārata VI. 236, &c., we have the fanciful division (afterwards adopted by the Purāṇas) into seven circular Dvīpas or continents, viz., 1. Jambu-dvīpa or the Earth, 2. Plaksha-dvīpa, 3. Śālmali-dvīpa, 4. Kuśa-dvīpa, 5. Krauñca-dvīpa, 6. Śāka-dvīpa, 7. Push-kara-dvīpa; surrounded respectively by seven oceans in concentric belts, viz., 1. the sea of salt-water (*lavaṇa*), 2. of sugar-cane juice (*ikshu*), 3. of wine (*surā*), 4. of clarified butter (*sarpis*), 5. of curdled milk (*dadhi*), 6. of milk (*dugdha*), 7. of fresh water (*jala*); the mountain Meru, or abode of the gods, being in the centre of *Jambu-dvīpa*, which again is divided into nine Varshas or countries separated by eight ranges of mountains, the Varsha called *Bhārata* (India) lying south of the Himavat range.[1]

Notwithstanding these wild ideas and absurd figments, the Mahā-bhārata contains many more illustrations of real life and of domestic and social habits and manners than the sister Epic. Its diction, again, is more varied than that of the Rāmāyaṇa. The bulk of the latter poem (notwithstanding interpolations and additions) being by

[1] The eight ranges are Nishadha, Hema-kūṭa, Nishadha on the south of Meru; Nīla, S'veta, S'ṛiṅgin on the north; and Mālyavat and Gandha-mādana on the west and east. Beyond the sea of fresh water is a circle called 'the land of gold,' and beyond this the circle of the Lokāloka mountains, which form the limit of the sun's light, all the region on one side being illuminated, and all on the other side of them being in utter darkness. See Raghu-vaṇśa I. 68. Below the seven Dvīpas are the seven Pātālas, and below these are the twenty-one Hells (note 2, p. 55).

one author, is written with uniform simplicity of style and metre (see p. 335, note 2); and the antiquity of the greater part is proved by the absence of any studied elaboration of diction. The Mahā-bhārata, on the other hand, though generally simple and natural in its language, and free from the conceits and artificial constructions of later writers, comprehends a greater diversity of composition, rising sometimes (especially when the Indravajrā metre is employed) to the higher style, and using not only loose and irregular, but also studiously complex grammatical forms,[1] and from the mixture of ancient legends, occasional archaisms and Vedic formations.

In contrasting the two Indian poems with the Iliad and the Odyssey, we may observe many points of similarity. Some parallel passages have been already pointed out. We must expect to find the distinctive genius of two different people (though both of the Āryan race) in widely distant localities, colouring their epic poetry very differently, notwithstanding general features of resemblance. The Rāmāyaṇa and Mahā-bhārata are no less wonderful than the Homeric poems as monuments of the human mind, and no less interesting as pictures of human life and manners in ancient times, yet they bear in a remarkable degree the peculiar impress ever stamped on the productions of Asiatic nations, and separating them from European. On the side of art and harmony of proportion, they can no more compete with the Iliad and the Odyssey than the unnatural outline of the ten-headed and twenty-armed Rāvaṇa can bear comparison

1 Thus, *jīvase* (I. 732), *kurmi* (III. 10943, and Rāmāy. II. xii. 33), *dhita* for *hita* (Hari-vaṇśa 7799), *pariṇayāmāsa* for *pariṇāyayāmāsa*, *mā bhaiḥ* for *mā bhaishīḥ*, *vyavasishyāmi* for *vyavasāsyāmi*. The use of irregular grammatical forms is sometimes due to the exigency of the metre.

with the symmetry of a Grecian statue. While the simplicity of the one commends itself to the most refined classical taste, the exaggerations of the other only excite the wonder of Asiatic minds, or if attractive to European, can only please imaginations nursed in an Oriental school.

Thus, in the Iliad, time, space, and action are all restricted within the narrowest limits. In the Odyssey they are allowed a wider, though not too wide, a cycle; but in the Rāmāyaṇa and Mahā-bhārata their range is almost unbounded. The Rāmāyaṇa, as it traces the life of a single individual with tolerable continuity, is in this respect more like the Odyssey than the Iliad. In other points, especially in its plot, the greater simplicity of its style, and its comparative freedom from irrelevant episodes, it more resembles the Iliad. There are many graphic passages in both the Rāmāyaṇa and Mahā-bhārata which, for beauty of description, cannot be surpassed by anything in Homer. It should be observed, moreover, that the diction of the Indian Epics is more polished, regular, and cultivated, and the language altogether in a more advanced stage of development than that of Homer. This, of course, tells to the disadvantage of the style on the side of nervous force and vigour; and it must be admitted that in the Sanskrit poems there is a great redundance of epithets, too liberal a use of metaphor, simile, and hyperbole, and far too much repetition, amplification, and prolixity.

In fact, the European who wishes to estimate rightly the Indian Epics, must be prepared not to judge them exclusively from his own point of view. He should bear in mind that to satisfy the ordinary Oriental taste, poetry requires to be seasoned with exaggeration.

Again, an Occidental student's appreciation of many passages will depend upon his familiarity with Indian mythology, as well as with Oriental customs, scenery, and even the characteristic idiosyncrasies of the animal creation in the East. Most of the similes in Hindū epic poetry are taken from the habits and motions of Asiatic animals, such as elephants and tigers,[1] or from peculiarities in the aspect of Indian plants and natural objects. Then, as to the description of scenery, in which Hindū poets are certainly more graphic and picturesque than either Greek or Latin,[2] the whole appearance of external nature in the East, the exuberance of vegetation, the profusion of trees and fruits and flowers,[3] the glare of burning skies, the freshness of the rainy season, the fury of storms, the serenity of Indian moonlight,[4] and the gigantic mould in

---

[1] Thus any eminent or courageous person would be spoken of as 'a tiger of a man.' Other favourite animals in similes are the lion (*sin̲ha*), the ruddy goose (*ćakravāka* or *rathān·ga*), the buffalo (*mahisha*), the boar (*varāha*), the koïl or Indian cuckoo (*kokila*), the heron (*krauńća*), the ox (*gavaya*, i.e., *bos gavaeus*), &c. &c. A woman is sometimes said to have a rolling gait like that of an elephant. It should be noted, however, that similes in the Indian Epics, though far too frequent, are generally confined to a few words, and not, as in Homer, drawn out for three or four lines.

[2] The descriptions of scenery and natural objects in Homer are too short and general to be really picturesque. They want more colouring and minuteness of detail. Some account for this by supposing that a Greek poet was not accustomed to look upon nature with a painter's eye.

[3] The immense profusion of flowers of all kinds is indicated by the number of botanical terms in a Sanskṛit dictionary. Some of the most common flowers and trees alluded to in epic poetry are, the *ćūta* or mango; the *aśoka* (described by Sir William Jones); the *kin̲śuka* (butea frondosa, with beautiful red blossoms); the tamarind (*amlikā*); the jasmine (of which there are many varieties, such as *mālatī*, *jātī*, *yūthikā*, &c.); the *kuruvaka* (amaranth); the sandal (*ćandana*); the jujube (*karkandhu*); the pomegranate (*dāḍima*); the kadamba (*nīpa*); the tamarisk (*pićula*); the *vakula*, *karṇikāra*, *śringāṭa*, &c.

[4] See the beautiful description of night in Rāmāyaṇa (Gorr.) I. xxxvi. 15.

which natural objects are generally cast—these and many other features are difficult to be realized by a European. We must also make allowance for the difference in Eastern manners; though, after conceding a wide margin in this direction, it must be confessed that the disregard of all delicacy in laying bare the most revolting particulars of certain ancient legends which we now and then encounter in the Indian Epics (especially in the Mahā-bhārata) is a serious blot, and one which never disfigures the pages of Homer, notwithstanding his occasional freedom of expression. Yet there are not wanting indications in the Indian Epics of a higher degree of civilization than that represented in the Homeric poems. The battle-fields of the Rāmāyaṇa and Mahā-bhārata, though spoiled by childish exaggerations and the use of supernatural weapons, are not made barbarous by wanton cruelties;[1] and the descriptions of Ayodhyā and Lan·kā imply far greater luxury and refinement than those of Sparta and Troy.

The constant interruption of the principal story (as before described) by tedious episodes, in both Rāmāyaṇa and Mahā-bhārata, added to the rambling prolixity of the story itself, will always be regarded as the chief drawback in Hindū epic poetry, and constitutes one of its most marked features of distinction. Even in this respect, however, the Iliad has not escaped the censure of critics. Many believe that this poem is the result of the fusion of different songs on one subject, long current in various localities, intermixed with later interpolations, something after the manner of the Mahā-bhārata. But the artistic instincts of the Greeks required that all the parts and

---

[1] There is something savage in Achilles' treatment of Hector; and the cruelties permitted by Ulysses, in the 22nd Book of the Odyssey, are almost revolting. Compare with these Rāma's treatment of his fallen foe Rāvaṇa, in the Yuddha-kāṇḍa.

appendages and more recent additions should be blended into one compact, homogeneous, and symmetrical whole. Although we have certainly in Homer occasional digressions or parentheses, such as the description of the 'shield of Achilles,' the 'story of Venus and Mars,' these are not like the Indian episodes. If not absolutely essential to the completeness of the epic conception, they appear to arise naturally out of the business of the plot, and cause no violent disruption of its unity. On the contrary, with Eastern writers and narrators of stories, continuity is often designedly interrupted. They delight in stringing together a number of distinct stories—detached from each other, yet connected like the figures on a frieze. They even purposely break the sequence of each; so that before one is ended another is commenced, and ere this is completed, others are interwoven; the result being a curious intertwining of stories within stories, the slender thread of an original narrative running through them all. A familiar instance of this is afforded by the well-known collection of tales called 'Hitopadeśa,' and by the 'Arabian Nights.' The same tendency is observable in the composition of the epic poems—far more, however, in the Mahā-bhārata than in the Rāmāyaṇa.

Passing on to a comparison of the plot and the personages of the Rāmāyaṇa with those of the Iliad, without supposing, as some have done, that either poem has been imitated from the other, it is certainly true, and so far remarkable, that the subject of both is a war undertaken to recover the wife of one of the warriors, carried off by a hero on the other side; and that Rāma, in this respect, corresponds to Menelaus, while in others he may be compared to Achilles, Sītā answering to Helen, Sparta to Ayodhyā, Lan·kā to Troy. It may even be true that some sort of analogy may be traced between the parts played by Agamemnon and Sugrīva, Patroclus and Lakshmaṇa, Nestor and Jāmbavat.[1] Again, Ulysses,[2] in one respect, may be compared to Hanumat; and Hector, as the bravest warrior on the Trojan side, may in some points be likened to Indrajit, in others to the indignant Vibhīshaṇa,[3] or again in the Mahā-bhārata to Duryodhana, while Achilles has qualities in common with Arjuna. Other resemblances might be indicated; but these comparisons cannot be carried out to any extent without encountering difficulties at every step, so that any theory of an interchange of ideas between Hindū and Greek epic poets becomes untenable. Rāma's character has really nothing in common with that of Menelaus, and very little with that of Achilles; although, as the bravest and most powerful of the warriors, he is rather to be compared with the latter than the former hero. If in his anger he is occasionally Achillean, his whole nature is cast in a less human mould than that of the Grecian hero. He is the type of a perfect husband, son, and brother. Sītā also rises in character far above Helen, and even above Penelope,[4] both in her sublime devotion and loyalty to her husband, and her indomitable patience and endurance under suffering and temptation. As for Bharata and Lakshmaṇa, they are models of fraternal duty; Kauśalyā of maternal tenderness; Daśaratha of paternal love: and it may be affirmed generally that the whole moral tone of the Rāmāyaṇa is certainly above that of the Iliad. Again,

---

[1] Jāmbavat was the chief of the bears, who was always giving sage advice.

[2] When any work had to be done which required peculiar skill or stratagem, it was entrusted to πολύμητις Ὀδυσσεύς.

[3] Hector, like Vibhīshaṇa, was indignant with the ravisher, but he does not refuse to fight on his brother's side.

[4] One cannot help suspecting Penelope of giving way to a little womanly vanity in allowing herself to be surrounded by so many suitors, though she repudiated their advances.

in the Iliad the subject is really the anger of Achilles; and when that is satisfied the drama closes. The fall of Troy is not considered necessary to the completion of the plot. Whereas in the Rāmāyaṇa the whole action points to the capture of Lan·kā and destruction of the ravisher. No one too can read either the Rāmāyaṇa or Mahā-bhārata without feeling that they rise above the Homeric poems in this—that a deep religious meaning appears to underlie all the narrative, and that the wildest allegory may be intended to conceal a sublime moral, symbolizing the conflict between good and evil, and teaching the hopelessness of victory in so terrible a contest without purity of soul, self-abnegation, and subjugation of the passions.

In reality it is the religious element of the Indian Epics that constitutes one of the principal features of contrast in comparing them with the Homeric. We cannot of course do more than indicate here the bare outlines of so interesting a subject as a comparison between the gods of India, Rome, and Greece. Thus:—

Indra[1] and S'iva certainly offer points of analogy to Jupiter and Zeus; Durgā or Pārvatī to Juno; Kṛishṇa to Apollo; S'rī to Ceres; Pṛithivī to Cybele; Varuṇa to Neptune, and, in his earlier character, to Uranus; Sarasvatī, goddess of speech and the arts, to Minerva; Kārttikeya or Skanda, god of war, to Mars;[2] Yama to Pluto or Minos; Kuvera to Plutus; Viśvakarman to Vulcan; Kāma, god of

---

[1] Indra is, as we have already seen (p. 10), the Jupiter Pluvius who sends rain and wields the thunderbolt, and in the earlier mythology is the chief of the gods, like Zeus. Subsequently his worship was superseded by that of Kṛishṇa and S'iva.

[2] It is curious that Kārttikeya, the war-god, is represented in Hindū mythology as the god of thieves—I suppose from their habit of sapping and mining under houses. (See Mṛić-ćhakaṭikā, Act III.) Indian thieves, however, display such skill and ingenuity, that a god like Mercury would appear to be a more appropriate patron. Kārttikeya was the son of S'iva, just as Mars was the offspring of Jupiter.

love, to Cupid; Rati, his wife, to Venus;[1] Nārada to Mercury;[2] Hanumat to Pan; Ushas, and in the later mythology Aruṇa, to Eos (Ἠώς) and Aurora; Vāyu to Aeolus; Gaṇeśa, as presiding over the opening and beginning of all undertakings, to Janus; the Aśvinī-kumāras[3] to the Dioscuri (Διόσκουροι), Castor and Pollux.

But in Greece, mythology, which was in many respects fully systematized when the Homeric poems were composed,[4] never passed certain limits, or outgrew a certain symmetry of outline. In the Iliad and the Odyssey, a god is little more than idealized humanity. His form and his actions are seldom out of keeping with this character. Hindū mythology, on the other hand, springing from the same source as that of Europe, but spreading and ramifying with the rank luxuriance of an Indian forest, speedily outgrew all harmony of proportions, and surrounded itself with an intricate undergrowth of monstrous and confused allegory. Doubtless the gods of the Indian and Grecian Epics preserve some traces of their common origin, resembling each other in various ways; interfering in human concerns, exhibiting human infirmities, taking part in the battles of their favourite heroes, furnishing them with celestial arms, or interposing directly to protect them.

But in the Rāmāyaṇa and Mahā-bhārata, and in the Purāṇas to which they led, the shape and operations of

---

[1] In one or two points Lakshmī may be compared to Venus.

[2] As Mercury was the inventor of the lyre, so Nārada was the inventor of the Vīṇā or lute.

[3] These ever-youthful twin sons of the Sun, by his wife Sañjñā, transformed into a mare (*aśvinī*), resemble the classical Dioscuri, both by their exploits and the aid they render to their worshippers (see p. 11).

[4] Herodotus says (Euterpe, 53) that 'Homer and Hesiod *framed* the Greek Theogony, gave distinctive names to the gods, distributed honours and functions to them, and described their forms.' I conclude that by the verb ποιεῖν, Herodotus did not mean to imply that Homer *invented* the myths, but that he gave system to a mythology already current; see, however, Grote's History of Greece, I. 482, &c.

divine and semi-divine beings are generally suggestive of the monstrous, the frightful, and the incredible. The human form, however idealized, is seldom thought adequate to the expression of divine attributes. Brahmā is four-faced; Śiva, three-eyed and sometimes five-headed; Indra has a thousand eyes; Kārttikeya, six faces; Rāvaṇa, ten heads; Gaṇeśa has the head of an elephant. Nearly every god and goddess has at least four arms, with symbols of obscure import exhibited in every hand.[1] The deeds of heroes, who are themselves half gods, transport the imagination into the region of the wildest chimera; and a whole pantheon presents itself, teeming with grotesque fancies, with horrible creations, half animals, half gods, with man-eating ogres, many-headed giants and disgusting demons, to an extent which the refined and delicate sensibilities of the Greeks and Romans could not have tolerated.[2]

Moreover, in the Indian Epics, the boundaries between the natural and supernatural, between earth and heaven, between the divine, human, and even animal creations, are singularly vague and undefined; troops of deities and semi-divine personages appear on the stage on every occasion. Gods, men, and animals are ever changing places. A constant communication is kept up between the two worlds, and such is their mutual interdependence that each seems to need the other's help. If distressed mortals are assisted out of their difficulties by divine interposition, the tables are often turned, and perturbed gods, themselves reduced to pitiful straits, are forced to implore the aid of mortal warriors in their conflicts with

---

[1] The Roman god Janus (supposed to be for Dianus and connected with *dies*) was represented by two and sometimes four heads.

[2] It is true that Homer now and then indulges in monstrous creations; but even the description of Polyphemus does not outrage all probability, like the exaggerated horrors of the demon Kabandha, in the 3rd Book of the Rāmāyaṇa (see p. 356).

the demons.[1] They even look to mortals for their daily sustenance, and are represented as actually *living on the sacrifices* offered to them by human beings, and at every sacrificial ceremony assemble in troops, eager to feed upon their shares. In fact, sacrifice with the Hindūs is not merely expiatory or placatory; it is necessary for the *food* and *support* of the gods. If there were no sacrifices the gods would starve to death. This alone will account for the interest they take in the destruction of demons, whose great aim was to obstruct these sources of their sustenance. Much in the same way the spirits of dead men are supposed to depend for existence and happiness on the living, and to be fed with cakes of rice and libations of water at the Śrāddha ceremonies.

Again, not only are men aided by animals which usurp human functions, but the gods also are dependent on and associated with birds and beasts of all kinds, and even with plants. Most of the principal deities are described as using animals for their Vāhanas or vehicles. Brahmā is carried on a swan, and sometimes seated on a lotus; Vishṇu is borne on or attended by a being, half eagle, half man (called Garuḍa); Lakshmī is seated on a lotus or carries one in her hand; Śiva has a bull for his vehicle or companion; Kārttikeya, god of war, has a peacock;[2] Indra has an elephant; Yama, god of death, has a buffalo (*mahisha*);[3] Kāma-deva, a parrot and fish;[4] Gaṇeśa, a rat;[5] Agni, a ram; Varuṇa, a fish; Durgā, a tiger. The latter is some-

---

[1] Indra does so in the Śakuntalā and Vikramorvaśī.

[2] *Kārttikeya* is represented as a handsome young man (though with six faces). This may account for his being associated with a peacock.

[3] Perhaps from its great power.

[4] A parrot often figures in Indian love stories. He is also associated with a kind of crocodile as his symbol (whence his name *Makara-dhvaja*). Such an animal is kept in tanks near his temples.

[5] Supposod to possess great sagacity.

times represented with her husband on a bull, Śiva himself being also associated with a tiger and antelope as well as with countless serpents. Vishṇu (Hari, Nārāyaṇa) is also represented as the Supreme Being sleeping on a thousand-headed serpent called Śesha (or Ananta, 'the Infinite').

This Śesha is, moreover, held to be the chief of a race of Nāgas or semi-divine beings, sometimes stated to be one thousand in number, half serpents, half men, their heads being human and their bodies snake-like. They inhabit the seven Pātālas[1] or regions under the earth, which, with the seven superincumbent worlds, are supposed to rest on

---

[1] Pātāla, though often used as a gener. term for all the seven regions under the earth, is properly only one of the seven, called in order, *Atala*, *Vitala*, *Sutala*, *Rasātala*, *Talātala*, *Mahātala*, and *Pātāla*; above which are the seven worlds (Lokas), called *Bhū* (the earth), *Bhuvar*, *Svar*, *Mahar*, *Janar*, *Tapaḥ*, and *Brahma* or *Satya* (see note 2, p. 55); all fourteen resting on the heads of the great serpent. The serpent-race who inhabit these lower regions (which are not to be confounded with the Narakas or hells, note 2, p. 55) are sometimes regarded as belonging to only one of the seven, viz., Pātāla, or to a portion of it called Nāga-loka, of which the capital is Bhogavatī. They are fabled to have sprung from Kadrū, wife of Kaśyapa, and some of the females among them (Nāga-kanyās) are said to have married human heroes. In this way Ulūpī became the wife of Arjuna (p. 389, note 2), and, curiously enough, a tribe of the Rājputs claims descent from the Nāgas even in the present day. A particular day is held sacred to the Nāgas, and a festival called Nāga-pañćamī is kept in their honour about the end of July (S'rāvaṇa). Vāsuki and Takshaka are other leading Nāgas, to whom a separate dominion over part of the serpent-race in different parts of the lower regions is sometimes assigned. All the Nāgas are described as having jewels in their heads. Their chiefs, S'esha, Vāsuki, and Takshaka, are said to rule over snakes generally, while Garuḍa is called the enemy of Nāgas (*Nāgāri*); so that the term Nāga sometimes stands for an ordinary serpent. The habit which snakes have of hiding in holes may have given rise to the notion of peopling the lower regions with Nāgas. The Rev. K. M. Banerjea has a curious theory about them.

the thousand heads of the serpent Śesha, who typifies infinity—inasmuch as, according to a common myth, he supports the Supreme Being between the intervals of creation, as well as the worlds created at the commencement of each Kalpa (note 3, p. 330). Again, the earth is sometimes fabled to be supported by the vast heads and backs of eight male and eight female mythical elephants, who all have names,[1] and are the elephants of the eight quarters. When any one of these shakes his body the whole earth quakes (see Rāmāyaṇa I. xli.).

In fact, it is not merely in a confused, exaggerated, and overgrown mythology that the difference between the Indian and Grecian Epics lies. It is in the injudicious and excessive use of it. In the Rāmāyaṇa and Mahābhārata, the spiritual and the supernatural are everywhere so dominant and overpowering, that anything merely human seems altogether out of place.

In the Iliad and Odyssey, the religious and supernatural are perhaps scarcely less prevalent. The gods are continually interposing and superintending; but they do so as if they were themselves little removed from men, or at least without destroying the dramatic probability of the poem, or neutralizing its general air of plain matter-of-fact humanity. Again, granted that in Homer there is frequent mention of the future existence of the soul, and its condition of happiness or misery hereafter, and that the Homeric descriptions of disembodied spirits correspond in many points with the Hindū notions on the same

---

[1] The eight names of the male elephants are given in the Amarakosha, thus: Airāvata, Puṇḍarīka, Vāmana, Kumuda, Añjana, Pushpadanta, Sārva-bhauma, Supratīka. Four are named in Rāmāyaṇa (I. xli.), Virū-pāksha, Mahā-padma, Saumanas, and Bhadra. Sometimes these elephants appear to have locomotive habits, and roam about the sky in the neighbourhood of their respective quarters (see Megha-dūta 14).

subject[1]—yet even these doctrines do not stand out with such exaggerated reality in Homer as to make human concerns appear unreal. Nor is there in his poems the slightest allusion to the soul's pre-existence in a former body, and its liability to pass into other bodies hereafter—a theory which in Hindū poetry invests present actions with a mysterious meaning, and gives a deep distinctive colouring to Indian theology.

Above all, although priests are occasionally mentioned in the Iliad and the Odyssey, there is wholly wanting in the Homeric poems any recognition of a regular hierarchy, or the necessity for a mediatorial caste of sacrificers.[2] This, which may be called the sacerdotal element of the Indian Epics, is more or less woven into their very tissue. Brāhmanism has been at work in these productions almost as much as the imagination of the poet; and boldly claiming a monopoly of all knowledge, human and divine, has appropriated this, as it has every other department of literature, and warped it to its own purposes. Its policy having been to check the development of intellect, and keep the inferior castes in perpetual childhood, it encouraged an appetite for exaggeration more insatiable than would be tolerated in the most extravagant European

---

1 See the following passages, which bear on the existence of the ψυχή after death as an εἴδωλον in Hades: Il. XXIII. 72, 104: Od. XI. 213, 476; XX. 355; XXIV. 14. It is curious that the Hindū notion of the restless state of the soul until the S'rāddha is performed (see p. 247) agrees with the ancient classical superstition that the ghosts of the dead wandered about as long as their bodies remained unburied, and were not suffered to mingle with those of the other dead. See Odyss. XI. 54; Il. XXIII. 72; and cf. Aen. VI. 325: Lucan I. II.: Eur. Hec. 30.

2 A king, or any other individual, is allowed in Homer to perform a sacrifice without the help of priests. See Il. II. 411; III. 392. Nevertheless we read occasionally of a θυοσκοός, or 'sacrifice-viewer,' who prophesied from the appearance of the flame and the smoke at the sacrifice. See Il. XXIV. 221: Odyss. XXI. 144; XXII. 319.

fairy-tale. This has been done more in the Rāmāyaṇa than in the Mahā-bhārata; but even in the later Epic, full as it is of geographical, chronological, and historical details, few assertions can be trusted. Time is measured by millions of years, space by millions of miles; and if a battle has to be described, nothing is thought of it unless millions of soldiers, elephants, and horses are brought into the field.[1]

This difference in the religious systems of Europe and India becomes still more noteworthy, when it is borne in mind that the wildest fictions of the Rāmāyaṇa and Mahābhārata are *to this very day* intimately bound up with the religious creed of the Hindūs. It is certain that the more intelligent among them, like the more educated Greeks and Romans, regarded and still regard the fictions of mythology as allegorical. But both in Europe and Asia the mass of the people, not troubling themselves about the mystical significance of symbols, took emblem and allegory for reality. And this, doubtless, they are apt to do still, as much in the West as in the East. Among European nations, however, even the ductile faith of the masses is sufficiently controlled by common sense to prevent the fervour of religious men from imposing any great extravagance on their credulity; and much as the Homeric poems are still admired, no one in any part of the world now dreams of placing the slightest faith in their legends, so as to connect them with religious opinions and practices. In India a complete contrast in this respect may be observed. The myths of the Indian Epics are still closely interwoven with *present* faith. In fact, the capacity of an uneducated Hindū for accepting and admiring the most monstrous fictions is apparently unlimited. Hence the absence of all history in the literature of India. A plain

[1] Cf. extract from Aristotle's Poetics, p. 435, note 1, of this volume.

relation of facts has little charm for the ordinary Hindū mind.

Even in the delineation of heroic character, where Indian poets exhibit much skill, they cannot avoid ministering to the craving for the marvellous which appears to be almost inseparable from the mental constitution of Eastern peoples.

Homer's characters are like Shakespeare's. They are *true* heroes, if you will, but they are always *men;* never perfect, never free from human weaknesses, inconsistencies, and caprices of temper. If their deeds are sometimes praeterhuman, they do not commit improbabilities which are absolutely absurd. Moreover, he does not seem to delineate his characters; he allows them to delineate themselves. They stand out like photographs, in all the reality of nature. We are not so much told what they do or say.[1] They appear rather to speak and act for themselves. In the Hindū Epics the poet gives us too long and too tedious descriptions in his own person; and, as a rule, his characters are either too good or too bad. How far more natural is Achilles, with all his faults, than Rāma, with his almost painful correctness of conduct! Even the cruel vengeance that Achilles perpetrates on the dead Hector strikes us as more likely to be true than Rāma's magnanimous treatment of the fallen Rāvaṇa. True, even the heroes sometimes commit what a European would call crimes; and the Pāṇḍavas were certainly guilty of one inhuman act of treachery. In their anxiety to provide for their own escape from a horrible death, they

---

[1] Aristotle says that 'among the many just claims of Homer to our praise, this is one—that he is the only poet who seems to have understood what part in his poem it was proper for him to take himself. The poet, in his own person, should speak as little as possible. . . . Homer, after a few preparatory lines, immediately introduces a man, a woman, or some other character; for all have their character.' (Poetics III. 3.)

enticed an outcaste woman and her five sons into their inflammable lac-house, and then burnt her alive (see p. 385). But the guilt of this transaction is neutralized to a Hindū by the woman being an outcaste; and besides, it is the savage Bhīma who sets fire to the house. Rāma and Lakshmaṇa again were betrayed into a deed of cruelty in mutilating Śūrpa-ṇakhā. For this, however, the fiery Lakshmana was responsible. If the better heroes sin, they do not sin like men. We see in them no portraits of ourselves. The pictures are too much one colour. There are few gradations of light and shadow, and little artistic blending of opposite hues. On the one side we have all gods or demigods; on the other, all demons or fiends. We miss real human beings with mixed characters. There is no mirror held up to inconsistent humanity. Duryodhana and his ninety-nine brothers are too uniformly vicious to be types of real men. Lakshmaṇa has perhaps the most natural character among the heroes of the Rāmāyaṇa, and Bhīma among those of the Mahā-bhārata. In many respects the character of the latter is not unlike that of Achilles; but in drawing his most human heroes the Indian poet still displays a perpetual tendency to run into extravagance.

It must be admitted, however, that in exhibiting pictures of domestic life and manners the Sanskṛit Epics are even more true and real than the Greek and Roman. In the delineation of women the Hindū poet throws aside all exaggerated colouring, and draws from nature. Kaikeyī, Kauśalyā, Mandodarī (the favourite wife of Rāvaṇa),[1] and even the hump-backed Mantharā (Rāmāyaṇa II. viii.), are all drawn to the very life. Sītā, Draupadī, and

---

[1] What can be more natural than Mandodarī's lamentations over the dead body of Rāvaṇa, and her allusions to his fatal passion for Sītā in Rāmāyana VI. 95 (Gorresio's ed.)?

Damayantī engage our affections and our interest far more than Helen, or even than Penelope. Indeed, Hindū wives are generally perfect patterns of conjugal fidelity; nor can it be doubted that in these delightful portraits of the Pativratā or 'devoted wife' we have true representations of the purity and simplicity of Hindū domestic manners in early times.[1] We may also gather from the epic poems many interesting hints as to the social position occupied by Hindū women before the Muhammadan conquest. No one can read the Rāmāyaṇa and Mahā-bhārata without coming to the conclusion that the habit of secluding women, and of treating them as inferiors, is, to a certain extent, natural to all Eastern nations, and prevailed in the earliest times.[2] Yet various passages in both Epics clearly establish the fact, that women in India were subjected to

---

[1] No doubt the devotion of a Hindū wife implied greater inferiority than is compatible with modern European ideas of independence. The extent to which this devotion was carried, even in little matters, is curiously exemplified by the story of Gāndhārī, who out of sympathy for her blind husband never appeared in public without a veil over her face (see p. 377). Hence, during the grand sham-fight between the Kuru and Pāṇḍu princes, Vidura stood by Dhṛita-rāshṭra, and Kuntī by Gāndhārī, to describe the scene to them (see p. 383).

[2] It was equally natural to the Greeks and Romans. Chivalry and reverence for the fair sex belonged only to European nations of northern origin, who were the first to hold 'inesse foeminis sanctum aliquid' (Tac. Germ. 8). That Hindū women in ancient times secluded themselves, except on certain occasions, may be inferred from the word *asūryam-paśyā*, given by Pāṇini as an epithet of a king's wife ('one who never sees the sun')—a very strong expression, stronger even than the *parda-nishīn* of the Muhammadans. It is to be observed also that in the Rāmāyaṇa (VI. xcix. 33) there is clear allusion to some sort of seclusion being practised; and the term *avarodha*, 'fenced or guarded place,' is used long before the time of the Muhammadans for the women's apartments. In the Ratnāvalī, however, the minister of king Vatsa, and his chamberlain and the envoy from Ceylon, are admitted to an audience in the presence of the queen and her damsels; and although Rāma in Rāmāyaṇa VI. 99 thinks it necessary to excuse himself for

less social restraint in former days than they are at present, and even enjoyed considerable liberty.[1] True, the ancient lawgiver, Manu, speaks of women as having no will of their own, and unfit for independence (see p. 253 of this volume); but he probably described a state of society which it was the aim of the priesthood to establish, rather than that which really existed in his own time. At a later period the pride of Brāhmanism, and still more recently the influence of Muhammadanism, deprived women of even such freedom as they once enjoyed; so that at the present day no Hindū woman has, *in theory*, any independence. It is not merely that she is not her own mistress: she is not her own property, and never, under any circumstances, can be. She belongs to her father first, who gives her away to her husband, to whom she belongs *for ever*.[2] She is not considered capable of so

---

permitting his wife to expose herself to the gaze of the crowd, yet he expressly (99, 34) enumerates various occasions on which it was allowable for a woman to show herself unveiled. I here translate the passage, as it bears very remarkably on this interesting subject. Rāma says to Vibhīshaṇa—

'Neither houses nor vestments, nor enclosing walls, nor ceremony, nor regal insignia (*rāja-satkāra*), are the screen (*āvaraṇa*) of a woman. Her own virtue alone (protects her). In great calamities (*vyasaneshu*), at marriages, at the public choice of a husband by maidens (of the Kshatriya caste), at a sacrifice, at assemblies (*saṃsatsu*), it is allowable for all the world to look upon women (*strīṇāṃ darśanaṃ sārvalaukikam*).'

Hence S'akuntalā appears in the public court of king Dushyanta; Damayantī travels about by herself; and in the Uttara-rāma-ćarita, the mother of Rāma goes to the hermitage of Vālmīki. Again, women were present at dramatic representations, visited the temples of the gods, and performed their ablutions with little privacy; which last custom they still practise, though Muhammadan women do not.

[1] In Mahā-bh. I. 4719 we read:—*An-āvṛitāḥ kila purā striya āsan kāma-ćāra-vihāriṇyaḥ svatantrāḥ*, &c.

[2] Hence when her husband dies she cannot be remarried, as there is no one to give her away. In fact, the remarriage of Hindū widows, which is now permitted by law, is utterly opposed to all modern Hindū

high a form of religion as man,[1] and she does not mix freely in society. But in ancient times, when the epic songs were current in India, women were not confined to intercourse with their own families; they did very much as they pleased, travelled about, and showed themselves unreservedly in public,[2] and, if of the Kshatriya caste, were occasionally allowed to choose their own husbands from a number of assembled suitors.[3] It is clear, moreover, that, in many instances, there was considerable dignity and elevation about the female character, and that much mutual affection prevailed in families. Nothing can

---

ideas about women; and many persons think that the passing of this law was one cause of the mutiny of 1857. It is clear from the story of Damayantī, who appoints a second Svayaṃvara, that in early times remarriage was not necessarily improper; though, from her wonder that the new suitor should have failed to see through her artifice, and from her vexation at being supposed capable of a second marriage, it may be inferred that such a marriage was even then not reputable.

[1] See, however, the stories of Gārgī and Maitreyī (Bṛihad-āraṇyaka Upanishad, Röer's transl. pp. 198, 203, 242). No doubt the inferior capacity of a woman as regards religion was implied in the epic poems, as well as in later works. A husband was the wife's divinity, as well as her lord, and her best religion was to please him. See Sītā's speech, p. 364 of this volume; and the quotation from Mādhava Āćarya (who flourished in the fourteenth century), p. 372, note. Such verses as the following are common in Hindū literature: *Bhartā hi paramaṃ nāryā bhūshaṇam bhūshaṇair vinā*, 'a husband is a wife's chief ornament even without (other) ornaments.' Manu says (V. 151), *Yasmai dadyāt pitā tv enām bhrātā vānumate pituḥ, Taṃ śuśrūsheta jīvantaṃ saṃsthitaṃ ća na lan·ghayet.* See p. 284 of this volume. In IV. 198, Manu classes women with Śūdras.

[2] Especially married women. A wife was required to obey her husband implicitly, but in other respects she was to be independent (*svātantryam arhati*, Mahā-bhār. I. 4741).

[3] The Svayaṃvara, however, appears to have been something exceptional, and only to have been allowed in the case of the daughters of kings or Kshatriyas. See Draupadī-svayaṃvara 127; Mahā-bhār. I. 7926.

be more beautiful and touching than the pictures of domestic and social happiness in the Rāmāyaṇa and Mahābhārata. Children are dutiful to their parents [1] and submissive to their superiors; younger brothers are respectful to elder brothers; parents are fondly attached to their children, watchful over their interests and ready to sacrifice themselves for their welfare; wives are loyal, devoted, and obedient to their husbands, yet show much independence of character, and do not hesitate to express their own opinions; husbands are tenderly affectionate towards their wives, and treat them with respect and courtesy; daughters and women generally are virtuous and modest, yet spirited, and, when occasion requires, firm and courageous; love and harmony reign throughout the family circle. Indeed, in depicting scenes of domestic affection, and expressing those universal feelings and emotions which belong to human nature in all time and in all places, Sanskṛit epic poetry is unrivalled even by Greek Epos. It is not often that Homer takes us out of the battle-field; and if we except the lamentations over the bodies of Patroclus and Hector, the visit of Priam to the tent of Achilles, and the parting of Hector and Andromache, there are no such pathetic passages in the Iliad as the death of the hermit boy (p. 349), the pleadings of Sītā for permission to accompany her husband into exile (p. 364), and the whole ordeal

[1] Contrast with the respectful tone of Hindū children towards their parents, the harsh manner in which Telemachus generally speaks to his mother. Filial respect and affection is quite as noteworthy a feature in the Hindū character now as in ancient times. It is common for unmarried soldiers to stint themselves almost to starvation point, that they may send home money to their aged parents. In fact, in proportion to the weakness or rather total absence of the *national* is the strength of the *family* bond. In England and America, where national life is strongest, children are less respectful to their parents.

scene at the end of the Rāmāyaṇa. In the Indian Epics such passages abound, and, besides giving a very high idea of the purity and happiness of domestic life in ancient India, indicate a capacity in Hindū women for the discharge of the most sacred and important social duties.

We must guard against the supposition that the women of India at the present day have altogether fallen from their ancient character. Notwithstanding the corrupting example of Islāmism, and the degrading tendency of modern Hindūism, some remarkable instances may still be found of moral and even intellectual excellence.[1] These, however, are exceptions, and we may rest assured, that until Asiatic women, whether Hindū or Muslim, are elevated and educated, our efforts to raise Asiatic nations to the level of European will be fruitless.[2] Let us hope that when the Rāmāyaṇa and Mahā-bhārata shall no longer be held sacred as repositories of faith and storehouses of trustworthy tradition, the enlightened Hindū may still learn from these poems to honour the weaker sex; and that Indian women, restored to their ancient liberty and raised to a still higher position by becoming partakers of the 'fulness of the blessing' of Christianity, may do for our Eastern empire what they have done for Europe—soften, invigorate, and dignify the character of its people.

I close my present subject with examples of the religious and moral teaching of the two Indian Epics. A few sentiments and maxims, extracted from both poems, here follow:—

---

[1] In some parts of India, especially in the Marāṭhī districts, there is still considerable freedom of thought and action allowed to women.

[2] Manu gives expression to a great truth when he says (III. 145), *Sahasram tu pitṛīn mātā gauraveṇātiricyate*, 'a mother exceeds in value a thousand fathers.'

A heavy blow, inflicted by a foe,[1]
Is often easier to bear, than griefs,
However slight, that happen casually.
Rāmāyaṇa (ed. Bombay) II. lxii. 16.

To carry out an enterprise in words
Is easy, to accomplish it by acts
Is the sole test of man's capacity.
Rāmāyaṇa (ed. Gorresio) VI. lxvii. 10.

Truth, justice, and nobility of rank
Are centred in the King; he is a mother,
Father, and benefactor of his subjects.
Rāmāyaṇa (ed. Bombay) II. lxvii. 35.

In countries without monarchs, none can call
His property or family his own;
No one is master even of himself.
Rāmāyana (ed. Gorresio) II. lxix. 11.

Where'er we walk, Death marches at our side;
Where'er we sit, Death seats himself beside us;
However far we journey, Death continues
Our fellow-traveller and goes with us home.
Men take delight in each returning dawn,
And with admiring gaze, behold the glow
Of sunset. Every season, as it comes,
Fills them with gladness, yet they never reck
That each recurring season, every day
Fragment by fragment bears their life away.
As drifting logs of wood may haply meet
On Ocean's waters, surging to and fro,
And having met, drift once again apart;
So fleeting is a man's association

---

[1] Though some of these translations were made years ago from Böhtlingk's admirable collection of Indische Sprüche, I have since been assisted in my renderings of many examples by Dr. Muir's 'Religious and Moral Sentiments freely translated from Indian writers,' lately printed at Edinburgh, with an appendix and notes. I may not have succeeded so well as Dr. Muir, but rhymeless metre may have enabled me to keep somewhat closer to the original.

With wife and children, relatives and wealth,
So surely must a time of parting come.
Rāmāyaṇa (ed. Bombay) II. cv. 24–27.

Whate'er the work a man performs,
The most effective aid to its completion—
The most prolific source of true success—
Is energy without despondency.
Rāmāyaṇa (ed. Bombay) V. xii. 11.

Fate binds a man with adamantine cords,
And drags him upwards to the highest rank
Or downward to the depths of misery.
Rāmāyaṇa (ed. Bombay) V. xxxvii. 3.

He who has wealth has strength of intellect;
He who has wealth has depth of erudition;
He who has wealth has nobleness of birth;
He who has wealth has relatives and friends;
He who has wealth is thought a very hero;
He who has wealth is rich in every virtue.
Rāmāyaṇa (ed. Bombay) VI. lxxxiii. 35, 36.

Time is awake while mortals are asleep,
None can elude his grasp or curb his course,
He passes unrestrained o'er all alike.
Mahā-bh. I. 243.

Thou thinkest: I am single and alone—
Perceiving not the great eternal Sage
Who dwells within thy breast. Whatever wrong
Is done by thee, he sees and notes it all.
Mahā-bh. I. 3015.

Heaven, Earth, and Sea, Sun, Moon, and Wind, and Fire,
Day, Night, the Twilights, and the Judge of souls,
The god of justice and the Heart itself,
All see and note the conduct of a man.[1]
Mahā-bh. I. 3017.

A wife is half the man, his truest friend,
Source of his virtue, pleasure, wealth—the root
Whence springs the line of his posterity.
Mahā-bh. I. 3028.

---

[1] Compare Manu VIII. 86, p. 280 of this volume.

An evil-minded man is quick to see
His neighbour's faults, though small as mustard-seed;
But when he turns his eyes towards his own,
Though large as Bilva[1] fruit, he none descries.
Mahā-bh. I. 3069.

If Truth and thousands of Horse-sacrifices
Were weighed together, Truth would weigh the most.[2]
Mahā-bh. I. 3095.

Death follows life by an unerring law;
Why grieve for that which is inevitable?
Mahā-bh. I. 6144.

Conquer a man who never gives by gifts;
Subdue untruthful men by truthfulness;
Vanquish an angry man by gentleness;
And overcome the evil man by goodness.[3]
Mahā-bh. III. 13253.

Triple restraint of thought and word and deed,
Strict vow of silence, coil of matted hair,
Close shaven head, garments of skin or bark,
Keeping of fasts, ablutions, maintenance
Of sacrificial fires, a hermit's life,
Emaciation—these are all in vain,
Unless the inward soul be free from stain.
Mahā-bh. III. 13445.

To injure none by thought or word or deed,
To give to others, and be kind to all—
This is the constant duty of the good.
High-minded men delight in doing good,
Without a thought of their own interest;
When they confer a benefit on others,
They reckon not on favours in return.[4]
Mahā-bh. III. 16782, 16796.

---

[1] This is the Aegle Marmelos (*Bel*) or Bengal Quince, bearing a large fruit. It is esteemed sacred to Mahā-deva. Compare St. Matthew vii. 3, 4.

[2] Hitopadeśa IV. 135.

[3] See Rom. xii. 21. Compare the Pāli Rājovāda Jātaka (Fausböll's Ten Jātakas, p. 5), *Akkodhena jine kodham, Asādhum sādhunā jine, Jine kadariyam dānena, Saććena alika-vādinam.* See also Dhammapada 223.

[4] Compare St. Luke vi. 35.

An archer shoots an arrow which may kill
One man, or none ; but clever men discharge
The shaft of intellect, whose stroke has power
To overwhelm a king and all his kingdom.

Mahā-bh. V. 1013.

Two persons will hereafter be exalted
Above the heavens—the man with boundless power
Who yet forbears to use it indiscreetly,
And he who is not rich and yet can give.[1]

Mahā-bh. V. 1028.

Sufficient wealth, unbroken health, a friend,
A wife of gentle speech, a docile son,
And learning that subserves some useful end—
These are a living man's six greatest blessings.

Mahā-bh. V. 1057.

Good words, good deeds, and beautiful expressions
A wise man ever culls from every quarter,
E'en as a gleaner gathers ears of corn.

Mahā-bh. V. 1126.

The gods defend not with a club or shield
The man they wish to favour—but endow him
With wisdom ; and the man whom they intend
To ruin, they deprive of understanding ;[2]
So that to him all things appear distorted.
Then, when his mind is dulled and he is ripe
To meet his doom, evil appears to him
Like good, and even fortunate events
Turn to his harm and tend to his destruction.

Mahā-bh. V. 1122, 2679.

To curb the tongue and moderate the speech,
Is held to be the hardest of all tasks.[3]
The words of him who talks too volubly
Have neither substance nor variety.

Mahā-bh. V. 1170.

---

[1] Compare St. Mark xii. 41–44.

[2] *Quos Deus vult perdere prius dementat.*

[3] St. James iii. 8.

Darts, barbëd arrows, iron-headed spears,
However deep they penetrate the flesh,
May be extracted ; but a cutting speech,
That pierces, like a javelin, to the heart,
None can remove ; it lies and rankles there.
Mahā-bh. V. 1173.

Repeated sin destroys the understanding,
And he whose reason is impaired, repeats
His sins. The constant practising of virtue
Strengthens the mental faculties, and he
Whose judgment stronger grows, acts always right.
Mahā-bh. V. 1242.

Bear railing words with patience, never meet
An angry man with anger, nor return
Reviling for reviling, smite not him
Who smites thee ; let thy speech and acts be gentle.
Mahā-bh. V. 1270, 9972.

If thou art wise, seek ease and happiness
In deeds of virtue and of usefulness ;
And ever act in such a way by day
That in the night thy sleep may tranquil be ;
And so comport thyself when thou art young,
That when thou art grown old, thine age may pass
In calm serenity. So ply thy task
Throughout thy life, that when thy days are ended,
Thou may'st enjoy eternal bliss hereafter.
Mahā-bh. V. 1248.

Esteem that gain a loss which ends in harm ;
Account that loss a gain which brings advantage.
Mahā-bh. V. 1451.

Reflect that health is transient, death impends,
Ne'er in thy day of youthful strength do aught
To grieve thy conscience, lest when weakness comes,
And thou art on a bed of sickness laid,
Fear and remorse augment thy sufferings.
Mahā-bh. V. 1474.

Do naught to others which if done to thee
Would cause thee pain ; this is the sum of duty.
Mahā-bh. V. 1517.

How can a man love knowledge yet repose?
Would'st thou be learned, then abandon ease.
Either give up thy knowledge or thy rest.
Mahā-bh. V. 1537.

No sacred lore can save the hypocrite,
Though he employ it craftily, from hell;
When his end comes, his pious texts take wing,
Like fledglings eager to forsake their nest.
Mahā-bh. V, 1623.

When men are ripe for ruin, e'en a straw
Has power to crush them, like a thunderbolt.
Mahā-bh. VII. 429.

By anger, fear, and avarice deluded,
Men do not strive to understand themselves,
Nor ever gain self-knowledge. One is proud
Of rank, and plumes himself upon his birth,
Contemning those of low degree; another
Boasts of his riches, and disdains the poor;
Another vaunts his learning, and despising
Men of less wisdom, calls them fools; a fourth
Piquing himself upon his rectitude,
Is quick to censure other people's faults.
But when the high and low, the rich and poor,
The wise and foolish, worthy and unworthy,
Are borne to their last resting-place—the grave—
When all their troubles end in that last sleep,
And of their earthly bodies naught remains
But fleshless skeletons—can living men
Mark differences between them, or perceive
Distinctions in the dust of birth or form?
Since all are, therefore, levelled by the grave,
And all must sleep together in the earth—
Why, foolish mortals, do ye wrong each other?
Mahā-bh. XI. 116.

Some who are wealthy perish in their youth,
While others who are fortuneless and needy,
Attain a hundred years; the prosperous man
Who lives, oft lacks the power to enjoy his wealth.
Mahā-bh. XII. 859

A king must first subdue himself, and then
Vanquish his enemies. How can a prince
Who cannot rule himself, enthral his foes?
To curb the senses, is to conquer self.

Mahā-bh. XII. 2599.

Who in this world is able to distinguish
The virtuous from the wicked? both alike
The fruitful earth supports, on both alike
The sun pours down his beams, on both alike
Refreshing breezes blow, and both alike
The waters purify. Not so hereafter—
Then shall the good be severed from the bad;
Then in a region bright with golden lustre—
Centre of light and immortality—
The righteous after death shall dwell in bliss.[1]
Then a terrific hell awaits the wicked—
Profound abyss of utter misery—
Into the depths of which bad men shall fall
Headlong, and mourn their doom for countless years.

Mahā-bh. XII. 2798.

He who lets slip his opportunity,
And turns not the occasion to account,
Though he may strive to execute his work,
Finds not again the fitting time for action.

Mahā-bh. XII. 3814.

Enjoy thou the prosperity of others,
Although thyself unprosperous; noble men
Take pleasure in their neighbour's happiness.

Mahā-bh. XII. 3880.

Even to foes who visit us as guests
Due hospitality should be displayed;
The tree screens with its leaves, the man who fells it.[2]

Mahā-bh. XII. 5528.

---

[1] Compare St. Matthew xiii. 43, xxv. 46.

[2] This verse occurs in Hitopadeśa I. 60. Cf. Rom. xii. 20. Professor H. H. Wilson was induced to commence the study of Sanskṛit by reading somewhere that this sentiment was to be met with in Sanskṛit literature.

What need has he who subjugates himself
To live secluded in a hermit's cell?
Where'er resides the self-subduing sage,
That place to him is like a hermitage.

Mahā-bh. XII. 5961.

Do good to-day, time passes, Death is near.
Death falls upon a man all unawares,
Like a ferocious wolf upon a sheep.
Death comes when his approach is least expected.
Death sometimes seizes ere the work of life
Is finished, or its purposes accomplished.
Death carries off the weak and strong alike,
The brave and timorous, the wise and foolish,
And those whose objects are not yet achieved.
Therefore delay not; Death may come to-day.
Death will not wait to know if thou art ready,
Or if thy work be done. Be active now,
While thou art young, and time is still thy own.
This very day perform to-morrow's work,
This very morning do thy evening's task.
When duty is discharged, then if thou live,
Honour and happiness will be thy lot,
And if thou die, supreme beatitude.[1]

Mahā-bh. XII. 6534.

The building of a house is fraught with troubles,
And ne'er brings comfort; therefore, cunning serpents
Seek for a habitation made by others,
And creeping in, abide there at their ease.

Mahā-bh. XII. 6619.

Just as the track of birds that cleave the air
Is not discerned, nor yet the path of fish
That skim the water, so the course of those
Who do good actions, is not always seen.

Mahā-bh. XII. 6763, 12156.

Let none reject the meanest suppliant
Or send him empty-handed from his door.

---

1 The order of the text has been slightly changed in this translation, and a few liberties taken in the wording of it.

A gift bestowed on outcasts or on dogs
Is never thrown away or unrequited.

Mahā-bh. XIII. 3212.

Time passes, and the man who older grows
Finds hair and teeth and eyes grow ever older.
One thing alone within him ne'er grows old—
The thirst for riches and the love of gold.

Mahā-bh. XIII. 3676, 368a.

This is the sum of all true righteousness—
Treat others, as thou would'st thyself be treated.
Do nothing to thy neighbour, which hereafter
Thou would'st not have thy neighbour do to thee.
In causing pleasure, or in giving pain,
In doing good, or injury to others,
In granting, or refusing a request,
A man obtains a proper rule of action
By looking on his neighbour as himself.[1]

Mahā-bh. XIII. 5571.

No being perishes before his time,
Though by a hundred arrows pierced; but when
His destined moment comes, though barely pricked
By a sharp point of grass, he surely dies.[2]

Mahā-bh. XIII. 7607.

Before infirmities creep o'er thy flesh;
Before decay impairs thy strength and mars
The beauty of thy limbs; before the Ender,
Whose charioteer is sickness, hastes towards thee,
Breaks up thy fragile frame and ends thy life,[3]
Lay up the only treasure: do good deeds;
Practise sobriety and self-control;
Amass that wealth which thieves cannot abstract,
Nor tyrants seize, which follows thee at death,
Which never wastes away, nor is corrupted.[4]

Mahā-bh. XIII. 12084.

---

[1] Compare St. Matthew xxii. 39; St. Luke vi. 31.
[2] This occurs also in Hitopadeśa II. 15.
[3] Compare Eccles. xii. 1.
[4] Compare St. Matthew vi. 19; Job xxi. 23.

Heaven's gate is very narrow and minute,[1]
It cannot be perceived by foolish men,
Blinded by vain illusions of the world.
E'en the clear-sighted who discern the way,
And seek to enter, find the portal barred
And hard to be unlocked. Its massive bolts
Are pride and passion, avarice and lust.

Mahā-bh. XIV. 2784.

Just heaven is not so pleased with costly gifts,
Offered in hope of future recompense,
As with the merest trifle set apart
From honest gains, and sanctified by faith.[2]

Mahā-bh. XIV. 2788.

---

[1] Compare St. Matthew vii. 14.

[2] Compare St. Matthew vi. 1-4; St. Mark xii. 43, 44.

CHAPTER XV

The Artificial Poems. Dramas. Purāṇas. Tantras Nīti-śāstras.

I CAN only notice very briefly the remaining classes of Indian writings which follow on the Rāmāyaṇa and Mahābhārata. In their religious bearing, as constituting part of Smṛiti, and as chiefly drawn from the two great Epics, the eighteen Purāṇas possess the next claim on our attention. It will be convenient, however, to introduce here an enumeration of some of the more celebrated artificial poems and dramas, which are connected with the Epics, adding a few explanations and examples, but reserving the fuller consideration of these and other departments of Sanskṛit literature to a future opportunity.

The Artificial Poems.

Some of the best known of the artificial poems are :—

1. The *Raghu-vaṉśa* or 'history of Raghu's race,' in nineteen chapters, by Kālidāsa, on the same subject as the Rāmāyaṇa, viz., the history of Rāma-ćandra, but beginning with a longer account of his ancestors; 2. the *Kumāra-sambhava*, by Kālidāsa, on the 'birth of Kumāra' or Kārttikeya, god of war, son of S'iva and Pārvatī—originally in sixteen cantos, of which only seven are usually edited, though nine more have been printed in the *Pandit* at Benares; 3. the *Megha-dūta*, 'cloud-messenger,' also by Kālidāsa—a poem of 116 verses, in the Mandākrāntā metre (well edited by Professor Johnson), describing a message sent by a banished Yaksha to his wife in the Himālayas; a cloud being personified and converted into the messenger; 4. the *Kirātārjunīya*, 'battle of the Kirāta and Arjuna,' by Bhāravi, in eighteen cantos, on a subject taken from the fourth chapter of Mahā-bhārata III., viz., the penance performed by Arjuna, one of the Pāndava princes, and his

combat with S'iva disguised as a Kirāta or wild mountaineer (see p. 393); 5. the *Śiśupāla-badha* or 'destruction of S'iśu-pāla,' a poem in twenty cantos, by Māgha, on a subject taken from the seventh chapter of the Sabhā-parvan of the Mahā-bhārata, viz., the slaying of the impious S'iśu-pāla by Kṛishṇa at a Rājasūya sacrifice performed by Yudhi-shṭhira (see p. 392); 6. the *Naishadha* or *Naishadhīya*, by S'rī-harsha,[1] on a subject drawn from an episode in the sixth chapter of the Vana-parvan of the Mahā-bhārata, viz., the history and adventures of Nala, king of Nishadha.

The above six are sometimes called Mahā-kāvyas, 'great poems,' not with reference to their length (for they are generally short), but with reference to the subjects of which they treat. To these may be added :—

7. The *Ṛitu-saṃhāra* or 'collection of the seasons,' a short but celebrated poem by Kālidāsa, on the six seasons of the year (viz., *Grīshma*, the hot season; *Varshā*, the rains; *Śarad*, autumn; *Hemanta*, the cold season; *Śiśira*, the dewy season; *Vasanta*, the spring); 8. the *Nalodaya* or 'rise of Nala,' an artificial poem, also ascribed to one Kālidāsa, but probably not the composition of the celebrated poet of that name, on much the same subject as the Naishadha, and describing especially the restoration of the fallen Nala to prosperity and power; 9. the *Bhaṭṭi-kāvya*, 'poem of Bhaṭṭi,' according to some the work of Bhartṛi-hari or his son, on the same subject as the Rāmāyaṇa, written at Valabhī (Ballabhi) in the reign of S'rīdhara-sena (probably the king who reigned in Gujarāt from about A.D. 530–544); its aim being to illustrate the rules of Sanskṛit grammar, as well as the figures of poetry and rhetoric, by introducing examples of all possible forms and constructions, as well as of the Alaṅ-kāras (see p. 457); it is divided into two great divisions, viz., *Śabda-lakshaṇa*, 'illustration of grammar,' and *Kāvya-lakshaṇa*, 'illustration of poetry,' together comprising twenty-two chapters; 10. the *Rāghava-pāṇḍavīya*, an artificial poem by Kavi-rāja, giving a narrative of the acts of both the descendants of Raghu and Pāṇḍu, in

---

[1] He is supposed to have lived about the year 1000 (cf. note, p. 505). This S'rī-harsha was the greatest of all sceptical philosophers, and wrote a book called *Khaṇḍana-khaṇḍa-khādya* for the refutation of all other systems. It is alluded to in Naishadha VI. 113 (Premaćandra's commentary). The commentator Nārāyaṇa does not seem to have understood this. There are some philosophical chapters in the Naishadha.

such language that it may be interpreted as a history of either one or the other family; 11. the *Amaru-śataka* or *Amarū-śataka*, 'hundred verses of Amaru,' on erotic subjects, to which a mystical interpretation is given, especially as they are supposed to have been composed by the great philosopher S'an-karā-ćārya, when, according to a popular legend, he animated the dead body of king Amaru, his object being to become the husband of his widow, that he might argue on amatory subjects with the wife of a Brāhman, named Mandana; 12. the *Gīta-govinda* or 'Kṛishṇa in his character of Govinda (the Cow-finder or Herdsman) celebrated in song,' by Jaya-deva, a lyrical or erotic poem, thought to have been composed about the twelfth or thirteenth century of our era; it was written nominally to celebrate the loves of Kṛishṇa and the Gopīs, especially of Kṛishṇa and Rādhā; but as the latter is supposed to typify the human soul, the whole poem is regarded as susceptible of a mystical interpretation.

Some of these poems, especially the Raghu-vaṉśa, Kumāra-sambhava, Megha-dūta, and Ṛitu-saṃhāra of Kālidāsa (who, according to native authorities, lived a little before the commencement of the Christian era, but is now placed in the third century),[1] abound in truly poetical ideas, and display great fertility of imagination and power of description; but it cannot be denied that even in these works of the greatest of Indian poets there are occasional fanciful conceits, combined with a too studied and artificial elaboration of diction, and a constant tendency to what a European would consider an almost puerile love for alliteration and playing upon words (*wort-spiel*). Some of the other poems, such as the Kirātārjunīya, Śiśupāla-badha, Nalodaya, Naishadha, and Bhaṭṭi-kāvya, are not wanting in occasional passages containing poetical feeling, striking imagery, and noble sentiment; but they are artificial to a degree quite opposed to European canons of taste; the chief aim of the composers being to exhibit their artistic skill in bringing out the capabilities of the Sanskṛit language, its ductility, its adaptation to every kind of style

[1] Professor Weber places him either in the third or sixth century.

from the most diffuse to the most concise, its power of compounding words, its intricate grammatical structure, its complex system of metres, and the fertility of its resources in the employment of rhyme, rhythm, and alliteration. In fact, there is nothing in the whole range of Greek or Latin or any other literature that can be compared with these poems. Nearly every verse in them presents a separate puzzle—so that when one riddle is solved, little is gained towards the solution of the next—or exhibits rare words, unusual grammatical forms, and intricate compounds, as it were twisted together into complicated verbal knots, the unravelment of which can only be effected by the aid of a native commentary.

Of course, in such cases the sense, and even the strict grammatical construction, are sometimes sacrificed to the display of ingenuity in the bending and straining of words to suit a difficult metre or rhyme; and this art is studied as an end in itself, the ideas to be conveyed by the language employed being quite a secondary matter. To such an extreme is this carried, that whole verses are sometimes composed with the repetition of a single consonant,[1] while in other cases a string of epithets is employed, each of which will apply to two quite distinct words in a sentence, and thus be capable of yielding different senses, suited to

---

[1] English, I fear, would be quite unequal to such a task as the production of a verse like the following from the Kirātārjunīya (XV. 14)—

Na nonanunno nunnono nānā nānānanā nanu |
Nunno nunnonanunneno nānena nunnanunnanut ||

Or the following from Māgha (XIX. 114)—

Dādadoduddaduddādī dādādodūdadīdadoḥ |
Duddādaṃ dadade dudde dadādadadadodadaḥ ||

Though in Latin we have something similar in Ennius, *O Tite tute Tati tibi tanta tyranne tulisti.* It must be admitted, however, that the celebrated nursery stanza beginning *Peter Piper picked a peck of pepper* is an effort in the same direction.

either word, according to the will of the solver of the verbal puzzle.

Again, stanzas are sometimes composed so as to form fanciful shapes or figures, such as that of a lotus (*padma-bandha*); or so that the lines or parts of the lines composing the verses, whether read horizontally, diagonally, or perpendicularly, or in opposite directions, will yield significant and grammatical sentences of some kind, the sense being a matter of subordinate consideration. This is called the Fanciful-shape (*ćitra*) ornament.

The formation of the octopetalous *Lotus-stanza* is described in Sāhitya-darpaṇa X. p. 268. One of the commonest of these artificial stanzas, called *Sarvato-bhadra*, is a verse so contrived that the same syllables occur in each Pāda of the verse, whether read backwards or forwards, or from the centre to each extremity, while all the Pādas together read the same either downwards or upwards, whether the reader commence at the centre or each extremity. An example of this verse occurs in Kirātārjunīya XV. 25.

Still more complicated forms are occasionally found, as described by Dr. Yates in his edition of the Nalodaya.

Thus we have the *muraja-bandha*, a stanza shaped like a *drum;* the *khaḍga-bandha*, like a *sword;* the *dhanu-bandha*, like a *bow;* the *srag-bandha*, like a *garland;* the *vṛiksha-bandha*, like a *tree;* and the *go-mūtrikā*, like a *stream of cow's urine*, in uneven or undulating lines.

The art, too, of inventing and employing an almost endless variety of rhetorical figures called Alan·kāras, 'ornaments of speech,' for the sake of illustrating the various sentiments, feelings, and emotions depicted in dramatic and erotic poetry, is studied to a degree quite unknown in other languages, the most refined subtlety being shown in marking off minute gradations of simile, comparison, metaphor, &c. There are numerous works on this subject—which may be called a kind of *Ars poetica* or *rhetorica*—some of the best known of which are :—

1. The *Sāhitya-darpaṇa*, 'mirror of composition,' by Viśvanātha-kavi-rāja (said to have lived in Dacca about the fifteenth century), giving rules and canons for literary composition from simple sentences to epic poems and dramas, illustrated by examples from standard authors, especially dramatic (see p. 470, note 1). 2. The *Kāvyādarśa*, 'mirror of poetry,' by Daṇḍin. 3. The *Kāvya-prakāśa*, 'illumination of poetry,' by Mammaṭa (the commentary to which, by Govinda, is called Kāvya-pradīpa). 4. The *Daśa-rūpaka*, 'description of the ten kinds of dramatic composition called Rūpakas,' by Dhanañjaya (p. 469, note 2). 5. The *Kāvyālan·kāra-vṛitti*, 'explanation of the ornaments of poetry,' by Vāmana. 6. The *Sarasvatī-kaṇṭhābharaṇa*, 'necklace of the goddess of speech,' by Bhoja-deva. 7. The *Śṛin·gāra-tilaka*, 'mark of love,' a work by Rudra-bhaṭṭa, describing and illustrating by examples the various emotions, feelings, and affections of lovers, male and female (*nāyaka* and *nāyikā*), as exhibited in dramas, &c. 8. The *Rasa-mañjarī*, 'cluster of affections,' a work on the Rasas,[1] by Bhānu-datta, of much the same character as the last.

I add here a brief description of some of the commonest Alan·kāras. They are divided into two classes:—A. *Śabdālan·kāra*, those produced by the mere sound of words; B. *Arthālan·kāra*, those arising from the meaning. The tenth Books of the Sāhitya-darpaṇa and Bhaṭṭi-kāvya are devoted to the illustration of this subject.

Examples of A. are, 1. *Anuprāsa*, a kind of alliteration or repetition of the same consonants, although the vowels may be dissimilar, *e.g.*, *Samā-lin·gan an·gan*. 2. *Yamaka*, more perfect alliteration or repetition of vowels and consonants, *e.g.*, *Sakalaiḥ sakalaiḥ*. Various kinds of Yamaka will be found in Bhaṭṭi-kāvya X. 2–21; and in Kirātārjunīya XV. 52 there is a *Mahā-yamaka*.

Examples of B. are, 1. *Upamā*, comparison or simile (the subject of comparison is called *upameyam*, sometimes *prastuta*, *prakṛita*, *prakrānta*, *vastu*, *vishaya*; while the object to which it is compared is called *upamānam*, sometimes *a-prastuta*, *a-prakṛita*, &c.). It is essential to an *Upamā* that the *upameya*, the *upamāna*, and common attribute (*sāmānya-dharma*)

---

[1] There are ten Rasas or 'feelings,' enumerated as exemplified in dramatic composition. 1. *Śṛin·gāra*, love; 2. *Vīra*, heroism; 3. *Bībhatsa*, disgust; 4. *Raudra*, anger; 5. *Hāsya*, mirth; 6. *Bhayānaka*, terror; 7. *Karuṇa*, pity; 8. *Adbhuta*, wonder; 9. *Śānta*, calmness; 10. *Vātsalya*, parental fondness. Some authors only allow 1–8.

should be all expressed, and the complete subordination of the *upamana* to the *upameya* preserved; thus 'her face is like the moon in charmingness,' where 'her face' is the *upameya*; 'moon,' the *upamāna*; and 'charmingness,' the common quality. If the latter is omitted it is a *luptopamā* (see Bhaṭṭi-kāvya X. 30–35). 2. *Utprekshā*, a comparison in which the *upamāna* is beginning to encroach on the *upameya* and to assume equal prominence. It is thirty-two-fold, under two classes, one called *vāćya* when a word like *iva* is expressed, as 'her face shines as if it were a moon;' the other *pratīyamāna* when *iva* is understood (cf. Bhaṭṭi-k. X. 44). 3. *Rūpaka*, 'superimposition,' consisting in the superimposition (*āropa*) of a fancied form over the original subject, the *upameya* and *upamāna* being connected as if possessing equal prominence, and their resemblance implied rather than expressed; thus 'moon-face,' 'her face is the moon' (Bhaṭṭi-k. X. 28). 4. *Atiśayokti*, hyperbole, exaggeration, pleonasm (Bhaṭṭi-k. X. 42), in which the *upameya* is swallowed up in the *upamāna*, as when 'her moon' is used for 'her face,' or 'her slender stem' for 'her figure.' 5. *Tulya-yogitā*, in which the *upamāna* or *upameya* is connected with the common quality, as 'a snow-white flower' (Bhaṭṭi-k. X. 61; Kumāra-s. I. 2). 6. *Drishṭānta*, exemplification by comparing or contrasting similar attributes (Māgha II. 23). 7. *Dīpaka*, 'illuminator,' *i.e.*, using an illustrative expression, placed either in the beginning (*ādi*), middle (*madhya*), or end (*anta*) of a verse to throw light on a description (Bhaṭṭi-k. X. 22–24; Kumāra-s. II. 60). 8. *Vyāja-stuti*, artful or indirect eulogy in which praise is rather implied than directly expressed (Bhaṭṭi-k. X. 59). 9. *Ślesha* (*lit.* coalescence), paronomasia, using distinct words which have identity of sound, the meaning being different; thus *vidhau* may mean 'in fate' if it comes from *vidhi*, or 'in the moon' if from *vidhu*. 10. *Vibhāvanā*, description of an effect produced without a cause (Kumāra-sambhava I. 10). 11. *Viśeshokti*, description of a cause without its natural effect. 12. *Arthāntara-nyāsa*, transition to another matter, *i.e.*, the turning aside to state a general truth as an illustration of a particular case (Bhaṭṭi-k. X. 36; Kirātārjunīya VII. 15). 13. *Arthāpatti*, inference of one fact from another. 14. *Sāra*, climax. 15. *Kāraṇa-mālā*, series of causes. 16. *Vyatireka*, contrast or dissimilitude. 17. *Ākshepa*, hint. 18. *Sahokti*, a hyperbolical description of simultaneous action connected by the word *saha*. 19. *Parikara*, employment of a number of significant epithets. 20. *Saṃsṛishṭi*, conjunction, *i.e.*, the employment of more than one figure in the same verse independently of each other (Bhaṭṭi-k. X. 70). When there is a commixture or combination of more than one figure, it is called *San·kara*; especially when they are combined as principal and subordinates (*an·gān·gi-bhāva*).

To give examples from all the artificial poems enumerated (pp. 452, 453) would be wearisome. It will be sufficient to select a passage from Kālidāsa's Raghu-vaṉśa, and a few of the moral sentiments scattered through the Kirātārjunīya and the Sisupāla-badha. I first translate Raghu-vaṉśa X. 16–33. The inferior gods are supposed to be addressing Vishṇu as the Supreme Being (cf. a similar address in Kumāra-sambhava II.):—

Hail to thee, mighty lord, the world's creator,
Supporter and destroyer, three in one—
One in thy essence, tripartite in action![1]
E'en as heaven's water—one in savour—gains
From different receptacles on earth
Diversity of flavours, so dost thou,
Unchangeable in essence, manifest
Changes of state in diverse qualities.[2]
Unmeasured and immeasurable, yet
Thou measurest the world; desireless, yet
Fulfilling all desire; unconquered and
A conqueror; unmanifested, yet
A manifester; uniformly one,
Yet ever multiform from various motives.
Thy manifold conditions are compared
To those of clearest crystal, which reflects
Varieties of hue from diverse objects.
Though ever present in the heart, thou art
Held to be infinitely distant; free
From passion, yet austere in self-restraint;
Full of all pity, yet thyself untouched
By misery; the ever ancient one,
Yet never growing ancient; knowing all,
Yet never known; unborn, yet giving birth
To all; all-ruling, yet thyself unruled;
One in thyself, yet many in thy aspects.
Men hymn thy praises in seven songs; and say
Thou liest sleeping on the earth's seven seas;[3]
Thy face is seven-flamed fire, and thou thyself

[1] See p. 321. [2] See p. 321, note 2. [3] See p. 420.

The sole asylum of the world's seven spheres.[1]
From the four mouths of thee, pourtrayed as four-faced,
Proceeds the knowledge of life's fourfold objects,
Time's quadruple divisions through four ages,[2]
Man's fourfold distribution into castes.
On thee abiding in man's heart, the source
Of light, with minds and senses all subdued,
The pious meditate in hope of bliss.
Of thee the mystic nature who can fathom?
Unborn, yet taking birth; from action free,
Yet active to destroy thy demon-foes;
Seeming asleep, yet ever vigilant;
Possessing senses fitted for enjoyment,
Yet in all points restrained; protecting all
Thy creatures, yet apparently indifferent.
The ways which lead to everlasting bliss,
Though variously distinguished in the Veda,
Converge to thee alone; e'en as the streams
Of Gan·gā's waters to their ocean home.
Thou art the only way, the only refuge
Of all whose hearts are fixed on thee, whose acts
Are centred in thee, and whose worldly longings,
Checked and suppressed, have passed away for ever.
Thy greatness is displayed before our eyes
In this thy world and these thy mighty works;
Yet through the Veda and by inference
Alone can thy existence be established.[3]
How then can we, the finite, tell thy essence?
Since merely by the thought of thee thy creatures
Are purified, much more have other acts
Which have thee for their object, full reward.
As jewels lying deep in ocean's bed,
And fires deep hidden in the solar orb
Are far beyond the reach of mortals, so thy deeds
Exceed our praises. Naught is unattained
By thee, and naught is unattainable;
Yet love, and love alone, for these thy worlds

---

[1] See p. 431. [2] See p. 330, note 3.
[3] This is an allusion to the three Pramaṇas of the Sān·khya, viz., Pratyaksha, Anumāna, and Āpta-vaćana or S'abda; see p. 82.

Moves thee to act, leads to thy incarnations.[1]
That in the celebration of thy praises
Our voices are restrained, deign to ascribe
This to our limited capacities,
Not to the limitation of thy glory.

I next translate some moral sentiments and wise sayings from the Kirātārjunīya of Bhāravi:—

Those who wish well towards their friends disdain
To please them by fair words which are not true (I. 2).

Better to have a great man for one's foe
Than court association with the low (I. 8).

As drops of bitter medicine, though minute,
May have a salutary force, so words
Though few and painful, uttered seasonably,
May rouse the prostrate energies of those
Who meet misfortune with despondency (II. 4).

Do nothing rashly, want of circumspection
Is the chief cause of failure and disaster.
Fortune, wise lover of the wise, selects
Him for her lord who ere he acts, reflects (II. 30).

He who with patience and deliberation
Prepares the ground whence issue all his actions,
Obtains, like those who water seeds and roots,
An ample harvest of autumnal fruits (II. 31).

The body's truest ornament consists
In knowledge of the truth; of sacred knowledge
The best embellishment is self-control;
Of self-control the garniture is courage,
Courage is best embellished by success (II. 32).

In matters difficult and dark, concealed
By doubt and disagreement of opinion,
The Veda, handed down by holy men,
Explained with clearness, and well put in practice,
Like a bright lamp throws light upon the way,
Guiding the prudent lest they go astray (II. 33).

---

[1] See p. 320.

To those who travel on the rugged road
Trodden by virtuous and high-minded men,
A fall, if pre-ordained by destiny,
Becomes equivalent to exaltation;
Such falls cause neither evil nor distress,
The wise make failures equal to success (II. 34).

Would'st thou be eminent, all passion shun,
Drive wrath away by wisdom; e'en the sun
Ascends not to display his fullest light
Till he has chased away the mists of night (II. 36).

That lord of earth who, equable in mind,
Is on occasion lenient and kind,
Then acts in season with severity,
Rules like the sun by his own majesty (II. 38).

The man who every sacred science knows,
Yet has not strength to keep in check the foes
That rise within him, mars his Fortune's fame
And brings her by his feebleness to shame (II. 41).

Be patient if thou would'st thy ends accomplish,
For like to patience is there no appliance
Effective of success, producing surely
Abundant fruit of actions, never damped
By failure, conquering impediments (II. 43).

If the constituent members of a state
Be in disorder, then a trifling war
May cause a ruler's ruin, just as fire
Caused by the friction of the dried-up branches
Of one small tree, may devastate a mountain (II. 51).

Success is like a lovely woman, wooed
By many men, but folded in the arms
Of him alone who free from over-zeal
Firmly persists and calmly perseveres (III. 40).

The drops upon a lovely woman's face
Appear like pearls; no marks avail to mar,
But rather to her beauty add a grace (VII. 5).

The noble-minded dedicate themselves
To the promotion of the happiness
Of others—e'en of those who injure them.
True happiness consists in making happy (VII. 13, 28).

Let not a little fault in him who does
An act of kindness, minish aught its value (VII. 15).

If intercourse with noble-minded men,
Though short and accidental, leads to profit,
How great the benefit of constant friendship! (VII. 27).

As persons though fatigued forbear to seek
The shelter of the fragrant sandal-trees,
If deadly serpents lurk beneath their roots,
So must the intercourse of e'en the virtuous,
If vicious men surround them, be avoided (VII. 29).

A woman will not throw away a garland,
Though soiled and dirty, which her lover gave;
Not in the object lies a present's worth,
But in the love which it was meant to mark (VIII. 37).

To one who pines in solitude apart
From those he loves, even the moon's cool rays
Appear unbearable; for in affliction
Even a pleasant object heightens grief (IX. 30).

Wine is averse from secrecy; it has
A power to bring to light what is concealed—
The hidden qualities both good and bad (IX. 68).

True love is ever on the watch, and sees
Risks even in its loved one's happiness (IX. 70).

Youth's glories are as transient as the shadow
Of an autumnal cloud; and sensual joys,
Though pleasant at the moment, end in pain (XI. 12).

Soon as a man is born, an adversary
Confronts him, Death the Ender; ceaseless troubles
Begin; his place of birth—the world—
Must one day be abandoned; hence the wise
Seek the full bliss of freedom from existence (XI. 13).

Riches and pleasure are the root of evil;
Hold them not dear, encourage not their growth;
They are aggressors hard to be subdued,
Destroyers of all knowledge and of truth (XI. 20).

To one united with a much-loved object
The empty turns to fulness; evil fortune
Brings festive joys; and disappointment, gain;
But not to him who lives in separation—
He in the midst of friends feels solitary;
The pleasant causes grief; and life itself,
Before so dear, pains like a piercing shaft (XI. 27, 28).

The enemies which rise within the body,
Hard to be overcome—thy evil passions—
Should manfully be fought; who conquers these
Is equal to the conqueror of worlds (XI. 32).

Why give thyself to pleasure? this day's joys
Are thought upon to-morrow, then like dreams
They pass away and are for ever lost (XI. 34).

Who trusts the passions finds them base deceivers:
Acting like friends, they are his bitterest foes;
Causing delight, they do him great unkindness;
Hard to be shaken off, they yet desert him (XI. 35).

The clear and quiet minds of prudent men,
Though ruffled on the surface and disturbed
Like the deep waters of the ocean, fear
To pass the limits of self-mastery (XI. 54).

The friendship of the bad is like the shade
Of some precipitous bank with crumbling sides,
Which falling buries him who sits beneath (XI. 55).

The natural hostility of beasts
Is laid aside when flying from pursuers;
So also when calamities impend
The enmity of rivals has an end (XII. 46).

The following are from Book II. of the Śiśupāla-badha of Māgha (I translate nearly literally):—

Alliance should be formed with friendly foes,
Not with unfriendly friends; of friend and foe
The test is benefit and injury (37).[1]

[1] This verse occurs also in Hitopadeśa IV. 16.

He who excites the wrath of foes and then
Sits down inactively, is like a man
Who kindles withered grass and then lies near
While a strong wind is blowing from beyond (42).

He who by virtue of his rank, his actions,
And qualities, effects no useful purpose,
Is like a chance-invented word; his birth
Is useless, for he merely bears a name (47).

A man of feeble character resembles
A reed that bends with every gust of wind (50).

Soft words, intended to alleviate,
Often foment the wrath of one enraged,
Like drops of water poured on burning butter (55).

A rambling speech whose meaning is confused,
Though long, is spoken easily; not so
A clear, connected, logical discourse (73).

Two only sources of success are known—
Wisdom and effort; make them both thine own
If thou would'st rise and haply gain a throne (76).

Science is like a couch to sapient men;
Reclining there, they never feel fatigue (77).

A subtle-witted man is like an arrow,
Which rending little surface, enters deeply;
But they whose minds are dull, resemble stones,
Dashing with clumsy force, but never piercing (78).

The foolish undertake a trifling act
And soon desist, discouraged; wiser men
Engage in mighty works and persevere (79).

The undertaking of a careless man
Succeeds not, though he use the right expedients;
A clever hunter, though well placed in ambush,
Kills not his quarry if he fall asleep (80).

A monarch's weapon is his intellect;
His minister and servants are his limbs;
Close secrecy of counsel is his armour;
Spies are his eyes; ambassadors, his mouth (82).

That energy which veils itself in mildness
Is most effective of its object; so
The lamp that burns most brightly owes its force
To oil drawn upwards by a hidden wick (85).

Wise men rest not on destiny alone,
Nor yet on manly effort, but on both (86).

Weak persons gain their object when allied
With strong associates; the rivulet
Reaches the ocean by the river's aid (100).

A good man's intellect is piercing, yet
Inflicts no wound; his actions are deliberate,
Yet bold; his heart is warm, but never burns;
His speech is eloquent, yet ever true (109).

The Dramas.

If we bear in mind that the nations of modern Europe can scarcely be said to have possessed a dramatic literature before the fifteenth century of the present era, the antiquity of the extant Hindū plays, some of which may be traced back to about the first or second century of our era, will of itself appear a remarkable circumstance. But to the age of these dramas must be added their undoubted literary value as repositories of much true poetry, though of an Oriental type. They are also valuable as representing the early condition of Hindū society, and as serving to illustrate some of its present peculiarities; for notwithstanding the increasing intercourse with Europe, India, like other Eastern countries, is slow in delivering itself from subjection to the stereotyped laws of tradition which appear to be stamped on its manners and social practices.

In all likelihood the germ of the dramatic representations of the Hindūs, as of the Greeks, is to be sought for in public exhibitions of dancing, which consisted at first of simple movements of the body, executed in harmony with singing and music. Indeed, the root *naṭ* and the nouns *nāṭya* and *nāṭaka*, which are now applied to dramatic acting, are probably mere corruptions of *nṛit*, 'to dance,' *nṛitya*, 'dancing,' and *nartaka*, 'a dancer.' Of this dancing various styles were gradually invented, such as the *Lāsya* and *Tāṇḍava*,[1] to express different actions or various sentiments and emotions.

Very soon dancing was extended to include pantomimic gesticulations accompanied with more elaborate musical performances, and these gesticulations were aided by occasional exclamations between the intervals of singing. Finally, natural language took the place of music and singing, while gesticulation became merely subservient to emphasis in dramatic dialogue.

When we come to actual dramatic writing we are obliged to confess that its origin, like that of epic poetry, and of nearly every department of Sanskṛit composition, is lost in remote antiquity. There is evidence that plays were acted in India as early as the reign of Aśoka, in the third century B.C. At that period intercourse between India and Greece had certainly commenced, but it does not appear that the Hindūs borrowed either the matter or form of any of their dramas from the Greeks. (See Lassen's Ind. Alt. II. 507.)

Semitic nations have never inclined towards theatrical representations. The Book of Job is a kind of dramatic dialogue. The same may be said of parts of the Song of Solomon, and there is occasional dialogue in the Makāmāt of *al Harīrī* and Thousand and One Nights; but neither

---

[1] The *Tāṇḍava* is a boisterous dance regarded as the peculiar invention of S'iva; the *Lāsya* is said to have been invented by Pārvatī; the *Rāsamaṇḍala* is the circular dance of Kṛishṇa.

the Hebrews nor Arabs seem to have carried dramatic ideas beyond this point. Among the Āryans, on the other hand, as well as among the Chinese, the drama appears to have arisen naturally. At least, its independent origin in Greece and India—both which countries also gave birth independently to epic poetry, grammar, philosophy, and logic—can scarcely be called in question, however probable it may be that an interchange of ideas took place in later times. In fact, the Hindū drama, while it has certainly much in common with the representations of other nations, has quite a distinctive character of its own which invests it with great interest.

At the same time the English reader, when told that the author of the earliest Hindū drama which has come down to us—the *Mṛić-ćhakaṭikā* or 'Clay-cart'—probably lived in the first or second century of the Christian era, will be inclined to wonder at the analogies it offers to our own dramatic compositions of about fifteen centuries later. The dexterity with which the plot is arranged, the ingenuity with which the incidents are connected, the skill with which the characters are delineated and contrasted, the boldness and felicity of the diction are scarcely unworthy of our own great dramatists. Nor does the parallel fail in the management of the stage-business, in minute directions to the actors and various scenic artifices. The asides and aparts, the exits and the entrances, the manner, attitude, and gait of the speakers, their tones of voice, tears, smiles, and laughter are as regularly indicated as in a modern drama.

A great number of other ancient plays besides 'the Clay-cart' are extant, and many of the most celebrated have been printed. To classify these Hindū dramas according to European ideas, or even to arrange them under the general heads of tragedy and comedy, is impossible. Indeed, if a calamitous conclusion be necessary to constitute a tragedy, Hindū plays are never tragedies.[1] They are rather mixed representations, in which happiness and misery, good and evil, right and wrong, justice and injustice are allowed to blend in confusion until the end of the drama. In the last act harmony is restored, tranquillity succeeds to agitation, and the minds of the spectators, no longer perplexed by the ascendency of evil, are soothed and purified by the moral lesson deducible from the plot, or led to acquiesce in the inevitable results of Adṛishṭa (see p. 58). Such dramatic conceptions are, in truth, exactly what might be expected to prevail among a people who look upon no occurrence in human life as really tragic, but regard evil and suffering of all kinds as simply the unavoidable consequences of acts done by each soul, of its own free will, in former bodies.

Nevertheless, to invest the subject of dramatic composition with dignity, a great sage is, as usual (compare p. 371), supposed to be its inventor. He is called Bharata, and is regarded as the author of a system of music, as well as of an Alan·kāra-śāstra containing Sūtras or rules. His work is constantly quoted as the original authority for dramatic composition.[2] On Bharata's Sūtras followed various treatises which laid down minute precepts and regulations for the construction and conduct of plays, and subjected dramatic writing to the most refined and artificial rules of poetical and rhetorical style.

Besides the *Daśa-rūpaka*, *Kāvya-prakāśa*, *Kāvyādarśa*, and *Sāhitya-darpaṇa*, &c., mentioned at p. 457, others are named which treat of dramatic composition as well as of ornaments (*ālan·kāra*) and figures of rhetoric. For example: the *Kāvyālan·kāra-vṛitti*, by Vāmana; the

---

1 A rule states that the killing of a hero is not to be hinted at. This does not always hold good. No one, however, is killed on the stage.

2 Dr. Fitz-Edward Hall has a MS. of the work in 36 Books, of which 18, 19, 20, and 34 were printed at the end of his Daśa-rūpa. Dr. Heymann is now editing the whole work.

Alankāra-sarvasva, by Bhāma; the *Alan·kāra-kaustubha*, by Kavi Karṇapūraka; the *Kuvalayānanda*, by Apyaya [or Apya]-dīkshita; the *Ćandrāloka*, by Jaya-deva; and a work on music, singing, and dancing, called the *San·gīta-ratnākara*, by S'ārn·gadeva, thought by Wilson to have been written between the twelfth and thirteenth centuries.

These treatises classify Sanskṛit plays very elaborately under various subdivisions; and the Sāhitya-darpaṇa—a favourite authority[1]—divides them into two great classes, viz., 1. *Rūpaka*, 'principal dramas,' of which there are ten species; 2. *Upa-rūpaka*, 'minor or inferior dramas,' of which eighteen are enumerated. The trouble taken to invent titles for every variety of Hindū play, according to far more subtle shades of distinction than those denoted by our drama, melodrama, comedy, farce, and ballet, proves that dramatic composition has been more elaborately cultivated in India than in European countries. The ten species of *Rūpaka* are as follow:—

1. The *Nāṭaka*, or 'principal play,' should consist of from five to ten acts (*an·ka*), and should have a celebrated story (such as the history of Rāma) for its plot (*vastu*). It should represent heroic or godlike characters, and good deeds; should be written in an elaborate style, and be full of noble sentiments. Moreover, it should contain all the five 'joints' or 'junctures' (*sandhi*)[2] of the plot; the four kinds of action (*vṛitti*); the sixty-four members (*an·ga*) or peculiar properties; and the thirty-six distinctive marks (*lakshaṇa*). The hero or leading character (*nāyaka*) should be of the kind described as high-spirited but firm,[3]

---

[1] The Sāhitya-darpaṇa is in ten sections, treating of the nature and divisions of poetry, the various powers of a word, varieties of style, ornaments of style and blemishes (*dosha*). I have here consulted the late Dr. Ballantyne's translation of part of it, published at Benares.

[2] These five junctures are, 1. the *mukha* or 'opening'; 2. the *pratimukha* or 'first development of the germ (*vīja*) of the plot'; 3. the *garbha* or 'actual development and growth of the germ'; 4. the *vimarsha* or 'some hindrance to its progress'; 5. the *nirvahaṇa* or *upa-saṃhṛiti*, 'conclusion.'

[3] There are four kinds of heroes: 1. high-spirited but firm (*dhīrodātta*); 2. firm and haughty (*dhīroddhata*); 3. gay and firm (*dhīralalita*); 4. firm and mild (*dhīra-praśānta*).

being either a royal sage of high family (as Dushyanta in the S'akuntalā), or a god (as Kṛishṇa), or a demigod (*divyādivya*), who, though a god (like Rāma-ćandra) thinks himself a man (*narābhimānī*, see note 3, p. 358). The principal sentiment or flavour (*rasa*, see p. 457, note) should be either the erotic (*śṛin·gāra*) or heroic (*vīra*), and in the conclusion (*nirvahaṇa*) the marvellous (*adbhuta*). It should be composed like the end of a cow's tail (*go-puććhāgra*), *i.e.*, so that each of the acts is gradually made shorter. If it also contain the four *Patākā-sthānaka* or 'striking points,' and the number of its acts (*an·ka*) be ten, it is entitled to be called a *Mahā-nāṭaka*. An example of the *Nāṭaka* is the S'akuntalā, and of the *Mahā-nāṭaka* is the Bāla-rāmāyaṇa (see p. 508). 2. The *Prakaraṇa* should resemble the Nāṭaka in the number of its acts as well as in other respects; but the plot must be founded on some mundane or human story, invented by the poet, and have love for its principal sentiment, the hero or leading character being either a Brāhman (as in the Mṛić-ćhakaṭikā), or a minister (as in the Mālatī-mādhava), or a merchant (as in the Pushpa-bhūshita), of the description called firm and mild (*dhīra-praśānta*), while the heroine (*nāyikā*) is sometimes a woman of good family, sometimes a courtesan, or both. 3. The *Bhāṇa*, in one act, should consist of a variety of incidents, not progressively developed, the plot being invented by the poet. It should only have the opening and concluding juncture (see note 2, p. 470). An example is the *Līlā-madhu-kara*. 4. The *Vyāyoga*, in one act, should have a well-known story for its plot, and few females in its *dramatis personae*. Its hero should be some celebrated personage of the class called firm and haughty (*vīrod-dhata*). Its principal sentiments or flavours (*rasa*, see p. 457, note) should be the comic (*hāsya*), the erotic (*śṛin·gāra*), and the unimpassioned (*śānta*). 5. The *Samavakāra*, in four acts, in which a great variety of subjects are mixed together (*samavakīryante*); it dramatizes a well-known story, relating to gods and demons. An example is the *Samudra-mathana*, 'churning of the ocean' (described in Bharata's Sāstra IV.). 6. The *Dima*, in four acts, founded on some celebrated story; its principal sentiment should be the terrible (*raudra*); it should have sixteen heroes (a god, a Yaksha, a Rākshasa, a serpent, goblin, &c.). An example is the *Tripura-dāha*, 'conflagration of Tripura' (described in Bharata's S'āstra IV.). 7. The *Īhā-mṛiga*, in four acts, founded on a mixed story (*miśra-vṛitta*), partly popular, and partly invented; the hero and rival hero (*prati-nāyaka*) should be either a mortal or a god. According to some it should have six heroes. It derives its name from this, that the hero seeks (*īhate*) a divine female, who is as unattainable as a deer (*mṛiga*). 8. The *An·ka* or *Utsṛishṭikān·ka*, in one act, should have ordinary men (*prāk-*

ṛita-narāḥ) for its heroes; its principal sentiment should be the pathetic (*karuṇa*), and its form (*sṛishṭi*) should transgress (*utkrānta*) the usual rules. An example is the *Śarmishṭhā-yayāti*. 9. The *Vīthī*, in one act, is so called because it forms a kind of garland (*vīthī*) of various sentiments, and is supposed to contain thirteen members (*an·ga*) or peculiar properties. An example is the *Mālavikā*. 10. The *Prahasana*, properly in one act, is a sort of farce representing reprobate characters (*nindya*), and the story is invented by the poet, the principal sentiment being the comic (*hāsya*); it may be either pure (*śuddha*), of which the Kandarpa-keli, 'love-sports,' is an example; or mixed (*san·kīrṇa*), like the Dhūrta-ćarita, 'adventures of a rogue;' or it may represent characters transformed (*vikṛita*) by various disguises.

The eighteen Upa-rūpakas need not be so fully described. Their names are as follow:—

1. The *Nāṭikā*, which is of two kinds—*Nāṭikā* pure, and *Prakaraṇikā* differing little from the Nāṭaka and Prakaraṇa. The Ratnāvalī is an example of the Nāṭikā. 2. The *Troṭaka*, in five, seven, eight, or nine acts; the plot should be founded on the story of a demigod, and the Vidūshaka or 'jesting Brāhman' should be introduced into every act. An example is the Vikramorvaśī. 3. The *Goshṭhī*. 4. The *Saṭṭaka*. 5. The *Nāṭya-rāsaka*. 6. The *Prasthāna*. 7. The *Ullāpya*. 8. The *Kāvya*. 9. The *Prenkhana*. 10. The *Rāsaka*. 11. The *Saṃlāpaka*. 12. The *Śrī-gadita*, in one act, dedicated chiefly to the goddess Śrī. 13. The *Śilpaka*. 14. The *Vilāsikā*. 15. The *Durmallikā*. 16. The *Prakaraṇī*. 17. The *Hallīśa*, chiefly consisting in music and singing. 18. The *Bhāṇikā*.

As I have elsewhere stated (see Introduction to translation of the Śakuntalā), it is probable that in India, as in Greece, scenic entertainments took place at religious festivals, and especially at the Spring festival (*Vasantotsava*, corresponding to the present Holī) in the month Phālguna. Kālidāsa's Śakuntalā seems to have been acted at the commencement of the summer season—a period sacred to Kāma-deva, the Indian god of love. We are told that it was enacted before an audience 'consisting chiefly of men of education and discernment.' As the greater part of every play was written in Sanskrit, which was certainly not the vernacular of the country at the time when the dramas were performed, few spectators could have been present who were not of the learned classes. This circumstance is in accordance with the constitution of Hindū society, whereby the productions of literature, as well as the offices of state, were reserved for the privileged castes. The following is a brief account of the construction of an ordinary Hindū Nāṭaka :—

Every play opens with a prologue (*prastāvanā*), or, to speak more correctly, an introduction, designed to prepare the way for the entrance of the *dramatis personae.* The prologue commences with a benediction (*nāndī*) or prayer[1] (pronounced by a Brāhman, or if the stage-manager happens to be a Brāhman, by the manager himself), in which the poet invokes the favour of his favourite deity in behalf of the audience. The blessing is generally followed by a dialogue between the manager and one or two of the actors, in which an account is given of the author of the drama, a complimentary tribute is paid to the critical acumen of the spectators, and such a reference is made to past occurrences or present circumstances as may be necessary for the elucidation of the plot. At the conclusion of the prologue, the manager, by some abrupt exclamation, adroitly introduces one of the dramatic personages, and the real performance commences. The play being thus opened, is carried forward in scenes and acts; each scene being marked by the entrance of one character and the exit of another. The *dramatis personae* are divided into three classes — the inferior characters (*nīća*), who are said to speak Prākṛit in a monotonous unaccented tone (*anudāttoktyā*); the middling (*madhyama*); and the superior (*pradhāna*). These latter are to speak Sanskṛit with accent and expression (*udāttoktyā*). The commencement of a new act, like that of the whole piece, is often marked by an introductory monologue or dialogue spoken by one or more of the *dramatis personae*, and called *Vishkambha* or *Praveśaka.* In this scene allusion is made to events supposed to have occurred in the interval of the acts, and the audience is prepared to take up the thread of the story, which is then skilfully

[1] The fact that scarcely a single work in Sanskṛit literature is commenced without a prayer to some god, is, as Professor Banerjea has remarked, a testimony to the universal sentiment of piety animating the Hindū race.

carried on to the concluding scene. The piece closes, as it began, with a prayer for national prosperity, addressed to the favourite deity, and spoken by one of the principal personages of the drama.

Although in the conduct of the plot, and the delineation of character, Hindū dramatists show considerable skill, yet in the plot itself, or in the story on which it is founded, they rarely evince much fertility of invention. The narrative of Rāma's adventures and other well-known fictions of Hindū mythology are constantly repeated. Love, too, according to Hindū notions, is the subject of most of their dramas. The hero and heroine are generally smitten with attachment for each other at first sight, and that, too, in no very interesting manner. By way of relief, however, an element of life is introduced in the character of the *Vidūshaka* or 'jester,' who is the constant companion of the hero; and in the young maidens, who are the confidential friends of the heroine, and soon become possessed of her secret. By a curious regulation, the jester is always a Brāhman; yet his business is to excite mirth by being ridiculous in person, age, and attire. Strictly he should be represented as grey-haired, humpbacked, lame, and ugly. He is a species of buffoon, who is allowed full liberty of speech, being himself a universal butt. His attempts at wit, which are rarely very successful, and his allusions to the pleasures of the table, of which he is a confessed votary, are absurdly contrasted with the sententious solemnity of the despairing hero, crossed in the prosecution of his love-suit. On the other hand, the shrewdness of the heroine's confidantes never seem to fail them under the most trying circumstances; while their sly jokes and innuendoes, their love of fun, their girlish sympathy with the progress of the love-affair, their warm affection for their friend, heighten the interest of the plot, and contribute to vary its monotony.

Let me now introduce a few remarks on certain well-known plays, some of which have been already mentioned. And first with regard to the earliest extant Sanskṛit drama—the *Mṛiċ-ċhakaṭikā* or 'Clay-cart.'

This was attributed (probably out of mere flattery) to a royal author, king S'ūdraka, who is said to have reigned in the first or second century B.C. Its real author is unknown, and its exact date is, of course, uncertain. According to Professor Weber, so much at least may be affirmed, 'that it was composed at a time in which Buddhism was flourishing in full vigour.' Some, indeed, may be inclined to infer from the fact of its describing a *Śramaṇa* or Buddhist ascetic as appointed to the head of the Vihāras or monasteries, that one hundred years after Christ is too early an epoch to allow for the possibility of representing Buddhism as occupying such a position in India. At any rate, the date of this drama ought not to be placed before the first century of our era.[1] The play is in ten acts, and though too long and tedious to suit European theatrical ideas, has nevertheless considerable dramatic merit, the plot being ingeniously developed, and the interest well sustained by a rapid succession of stirring incidents and picturesquely diversified scenes of every-day life. In fact, its pictures of domestic manners and descriptions of the natural intercourse of ordinary men and women, followed by the usual train of social evils, make it more interesting than other Sanskṛit dramas, which, as a rule, introduce too much of the supernatural, and abound in overwrought poetical fancies unsuited to occidental minds.

I now give an epitome of this interesting drama, omitting the underplot, which is not essential to the unity of the play, though ingeniously interwoven with it.[2]

---

[1] Professor Lassen assigns it to about 150 after Christ.

[2] In composing this epitome from Professor Stenzler's edition of the text, I am bound to state that I have made free use of Professor H. H. Wilson's translation of the *Mṛiċ-ċhakaṭika*, to which, as well as to Professor Stenzler's edition, I am under the greatest obligations. Professor Wilson's translation is executed with a spirit and power which could only be displayed by a writer himself gifted with poetical and dramatic genius. Nevertheless, although I have made use of many of his expressions, I have not always ventured to depart so widely as he has done from the original text in giving my own translation.

The first scene represents a court in front of Ćāru-datta's house. His friend Maitreya, who, although a Brāhman, acts the part of a sort of jovial companion, and displays a disposition of mixed shrewdness and simplicity, laments Ćāru-datta's fallen fortunes, caused by his too great liberality. Ćāru-datta replies thus:—

Ćāru. Think not, my friend, I mourn departed wealth;
One thing alone torments me, that my guests
Desert my beggared house, like bees
That swarm around the elephant, when dews
Exhale from his broad front; but quickly leave
His dried-up temples when they yield no sweets.

Maitreya. The sons of slaves! These guests you speak of are always ready to make a morning meal off a man's property.

Ćāru. It is most true, but I bestow no thought
On my lost property; as fate decrees
Wealth comes and goes, but this is torture to me
That friendships I thought firm hang all relaxed
And loose, when poverty sticks closest to me.
From poverty, 'tis but a step to shame—
From shame, to loss of manly self-respect;
Then comes disdainful scorn, then dark despair
O'erwhelms the mind with melancholy thoughts,
Then reason goes, and last of all comes ruin.
Oh! poverty is source of every ill.

Mait. Ah well, cheer up! Let's have no more of these woebegone memories. What's lost can't be recovered.

Ćāru. Good! I will grieve no more. Go you, my friend,
And offer this oblation, just prepared,
Unto the gods, and mothers of us all.

Mait. Not I.

Ćāru. And why not, pray?

Mait. Why, what's the use, when the gods you have worshipped have done nothing for you?

Ćāru. Friend, speak not thus, for worship is the duty
Of every family; the gods are honoured
By offerings, and gratified by acts
Of penance and restraint in thought and word.
Therefore delay not to present the oblation.

Mait. I don't intend to go; send some one else.

Ćāru. Stay quiet then for a little, till I have finished
My religious meditation and prayer.

They are supposed here to retire, and a voice is heard behind the scenes—

Stop! Vasanta-senā, stop!

The heroine of the play now appears in front of Ćāru-datta's house pursued by the king's worthless but wealthy brother-in-law, called Saṃsthānaka,[1] who is an embodiment of everything vicious and mean, in exact contrast to Ćāru-datta.

Saṃsth. Stop! Vasanta-senā, stop! Why do you run away? Don't be alarmed! I am not going to kill you. My poor heart is on fire with love, like a piece of meat placed on a heap of burning coals.

Vas. Noble sir, I am only a weak woman.

Saṃsth. That is just why I don't intend murdering you.

Vas. Why, then, do you pursue me? Do you seek my jewels?

Saṃsth. No, I only seek to gain your affections.

At this point the frightened Vasanta-senā discovers that she is close to Ćāru-datta's house. He is not only loved by her, but greatly respected as a man of honour, and under cover of the evening darkness, now supposed to have supervened, she slips into the courtyard of his house by a side-door, and hides herself. A companion who is with the king's brother now counsels him to desist from following her by remarking—

An elephant is bound by a chain,
A horse is curbed by a bridle and rein;
But a woman is only held by her heart—
If you can't hold that, you had better depart.

Samsthānaka, however, forces his way into Ćāru-datta's house, and there finding Ćāru-datta's friend and companion, Maitreya, thus addresses him:—

Take this message to Ćāru.—Vasanta-senā loves you, and has taken refuge in your house. If you will deliver her up, you shall be rewarded by my everlasting friendship; if not, I shall remain your enemy till death. Give this message, so that I may hear you from the neighbouring terrace; refuse to say exactly what I have told you and I will crush your head as I would a wood-apple beneath a door.

He then leaves the stage.

Maitreya accordingly delivers the message. Soon afterwards

[1] We shall sometimes speak of him as the king's brother.

the heroine Vasanta-senā ventures into the presence of Ćāru-datta, asks pardon for intruding into his house, requests him to take charge of a golden casket containing her ornaments as a deposit left in trust, and solicits his friend's escort back to her own house.

Maitreya is too much alarmed to accompany her, so Ćāru-datta himself escorts Vasanta-senā home.

So far is an epitome of the first act.

At the commencement of the second act a gambler is introduced running away from the keeper of a gaming-house named Māthura, and another gambler, to whom the first gambler has lost money, who are both pursuing him.

1st Gambler. The master of the tables and the gamester are at my heels; how can I escape them? Here is an empty temple; I will enter it walking backwards, and pretend to be its idol.

Māthura. Ho! there! stop thief! A gambler has lost ten Suvarṇas, and is running off without paying. Stop him, stop him!

2nd Gambler. He has run as far as this point; but here the track is lost.

Māth. Ah! I see, the footsteps are reversed; the rogue has walked backwards into this temple which has no image in it.

They enter and make signs to each other on discovering the object of their search, who pretends to be an idol fixed on a pedestal.

2nd Gambler. Is this a wooden image, I wonder?

Māth. No, no, it must be made of stone, I think. (*So saying, they shake and pinch him.*) Never mind, sit we down here and play out our game. (*They commence playing.*)

1st Gambler. (*Still acting the image, but looking on and with difficulty restraining his wish to join in the game—Aside.*) The rattling of dice is as tantalizing to a penniless man as the sound of drums to a dethroned monarch; verily, it is sweet as the note of a nightingale.

2nd Gambler. The throw is mine, the throw is mine!

Māth. No, no, it is mine, I say.

1st Gambler. (*Forgetting himself and jumping off his pedestal.*) No, I tell you it is mine.

2nd Gambler. We've caught him!

Māth. Yes, rascal, you're caught at last; hand over the Suvarṇas.

1st Gambler. Worthy sir, I'll pay them in good time.

Māth. Hand them over this very minute, I say. (*They beat him.*)

1st Gambler. (*Aside to 2nd Gambler.*) I'll pay you half if you will forgive me the rest.

2nd Gambler. Agreed.

1st Gambler. (*Aside to Māth.*) I'll give you security for half if you will let me off the other half.

Māth. Agreed.

1st Gambler. Then good morning to you, sirs, I'm off.

Māth. Hullo! stop there, where are you going so fast; hand over the money.

1st Gambler. See here, my good sirs, one has taken security for half, and the other has let me off another half. Isn't it clear I have nothing to pay.

Māth. No, no, my fine fellow; my name is Māthura, and I'm not such a fool as you take me for. Don't suppose I'm going to be cheated out of my ten Suvarṇas in this way. Hand them over, you scoundrel.

Upon that they set to work beating the unfortunate gambler, whose cries for help bring another gamester who happens to be passing to his rescue. A general scuffle now takes place, and in the midst of the confusion the first gambler escapes. In his flight he comes to the house of Vasanta-senā, and finding the door open, rushes in. Vasanta-senā inquires who he is and what he wants. He then recites his story, and makes known to her that having been once in the service of Ćāru-datta, and having been discharged by him on account of his reduced circumstances, he has been driven to seek a livelihood by gambling. The mention of Ćāru-datta at once secures Vasanta-senā's aid, and the pursuers having now tracked their fugitive to the door of her house, she sends them out a jewelled bracelet which satisfies their demands, and they retire. The gambler expresses the deepest gratitude, hopes in return to be of use to Vasanta-senā at some future time, and announces his intention of abandoning his disreputable mode of life and becoming a Buddhist mendicant.

The third act opens with a scene inside Ćāru-datta's house. The time is supposed to be night. Ćāru-datta and Maitreya are absent at a concert. A servant is preparing their sleeping-couches, and commences talking to himself thus:—

A good master who is kind to his servants, even though he be poor, is their delight; while a harsh fellow who is always finding fault and has nothing but his money to be proud of, is a perpetual torment from morning to night. Well, well! one can't alter nature; an ox can't be kept out of a field of corn, and a man once addicted to gambling can't be induced to leave off. My good master has gone to a concert. I must await his return; so I may as well take a nap in the hall.

Meanwhile Ćāru-datta and Maitreya come back, and the servant delivers Vasanta-senā's golden casket, saying that it is his turn to take charge of it by night. They now lie down.

Mait. Are you sleepy?

Ćāru. Yes;

I feel inconstant sleep, with shadowy form
Viewless and wayward, creep across my brow
And weigh my eyelids down; her soft approach
Is like Decay's advance, which stronger grows.
Till it has mastered all our faculties,
And life is lost in blank unconsciousness.

The whole household is soon buried in slumber, when a thief named Śarvilaka is seen to approach.

His soliloquy, while he proceeds to accomplish his design of breaking into the house, is curious, as showing that an Indian burglar's mode of operation in ancient times differed very little from that now in fashion. Moreover, it appears that the whole practice of housebreaking was carried on by professional artists according to certain fixed rules and principles, which a master of the science, named Yogāćārya, had embodied in a kind of 'Thieves' Manual' for the better training of his disciples. It is evident, too, that the fraternity of thieves, burglars, and rogues had a special presiding Deity and Patron in India, much in the same way as in ancient Greece and Rome.

It may be noted also, as still more curious, that the particular burglar here introduced is represented as a Brāhman, that he is made to speak the learned language, Sanskṛit, and to display acquaintance with Sanskṛit literature, while all the subordinate characters in Indian dramas, including women of rank, are represented as speaking one or other of the provincial dialects called Prākṛit. Here is part of the burglar's soliloquy:—

I advance creeping stealthily along the ground, like a snake wriggling out of its worn-out skin, making a path for my operations by the sheer force of my scientific craft, and artfully constructing an opening just big enough to admit my body with ease.

This friendly night which covers all the stars
With a thick coat of darkness, acts the part
Of a kind mother, shrouding me, her son,
Whose valour is displayed in night assaults
Upon my neighbours, and whose only dread
Is to be pounced upon by royal watchmen.

Good! I have made a hole in the garden-wall, and am now in the midst of the premises. Now for an attack on the four walls of the house itself.

Men call this occupation mean, which thrives
By triumphing o'er sleeping enemies.
This, say they, is not chivalry but burglary;
But better far reproach with independence,
Than cringing service without liberty:
And did not Aswatthaman long ago
O'erpower in night-attack his slumbering foe?[1]

Then follows a little of the burglar's plain prose:—

Where shall I make my breach? Ah! here's a rat-hole—this is the very thing we disciples of the god Skanda hail as the best guide to our operations, and the best omen of success. Here, then, I must begin my excavation, that's clear; but how shall I proceed? The golden-speared god has taught four methods of making a breach, namely,—pulling out baked bricks, cutting through unbaked ones; soaking a mud wall with water, and boring through one made of wood. This wall is evidently of baked bricks, so they must be pulled out. Now for the shape of the hole. It must be carved according to some orthodox pattern—Shall it be like a lotus-blossom, the sun, a crescent, a lake, a triangle, or a jar? I must do it cleverly, so that to-morrow morning people may look at my handiwork with wonder, and say to each other, 'None but a skilled artist could have done this!' The jar-shape looks best in a wall of baked bricks. Be it so; now, then, to work! Reverence to the golden-speared god, Kārttikeya, the giver of all boons! Reverence to Yogāćārya, whose chief disciple I am, and

[1] This is an allusion to Kārttikeya or Skanda. The God of War was the patron of burglars, probably from the fact that excavations, mining operations, and the making of breaches in walls are often resorted to in Eastern warfare as in the present day. Professor H. H. Wilson states that modern thieves worship some of the forms of Durgā.

who was so pleased with his pupil that he gave me a magical pigment, which, when spread over my body, prevents any police-officer from catching sight of me and any weapons from harming my limbs. Ah! what a pity! I have forgotten my measuring-line. Never mind, I can use my Brāhmanical cord—a most serviceable implement to all Brāhmans, especially to men of my profession. It serves to measure a wall, or to throw round ornaments which have to be drawn from their places, or to lift the latch of a door, or to bind up one's finger when bitten by insects or snakes. And now to commence measuring. Good! the hole is exactly the right size; only one brick remains! Ah! botheration! I am bitten by a snake; I must bind up my finger and apply the antidote; that's the only cure. Now I am all right again. Let me first peep in. What! a light gleams somewhere! Never mind! the breach being perfect, I must creep in. Reverence to Kārttikeya! How now! two men asleep! Are they really asleep, or only shamming? If they are shamming, they won't bear the glimmer of this lamp when passed over their faces; they are fast asleep, I believe; their breathing is regular; their eyes are firmly closed, their joints are all relaxed, and their limbs protrude beyond the bed. What have we here? Here are tabours, a lute, flutes, and books; why, I must have broken into the house of a dancing-master; I took it for the mansion of a man of rank. I had better be off.

Maitreya here calls out in his sleep—

Master, I am afraid some thief is breaking into the house; take you charge of the golden casket.

Śarvil. What! does he see me? Shall I have to kill him? No, no, it's all right; he's only dreaming and talking in his sleep. But sure enough, he has hold of a casket of jewels wrapped up in an old bathing-dress. Very good! I will relieve him of his burden; but no, it's a shame to take the only thing the poor creature seems to possess; so I'll be off without more ado.

Mait. My good friend, if you *won't* take the casket, may you incur the curse of disappointing the wishes of a cow and of a Brāhman.

Śarvil. The wishes of a cow and a Brāhman! These are much too sacred to be opposed; so take the casket I must.

Accordingly he helps himself to the casket, and proceeds to make good his escape.

The noise he makes in going out rouses its inmates, and they discover that the house has been robbed. Cāru-datta is greatly shocked at the loss of Vasanta-senā's casket, which had been deposited with him in trust. He has only one valuable thing left

—a necklace or string of jewels forming part of the private property of his wife. This he sends by Maitreya to Vasanta-senā as a substitute for the casket.

The fourth act commences with a scene in Vasanta-senā's house. The burglar Śarvilaka is seen to approach, but this time with no burglarious designs. It appears that he is in love with Vasanta-senā's slave-girl, and hopes to purchase her freedom by offering as a ransom the stolen casket of jewels, being of course ignorant that he is offering it to its owner.

As he advances towards the house, he thus soliloquizes :—

I have brought blame and censure on the night,
I've triumphed over slumber, and defied
The vigilance of royal watchmen, now
I imitate the moon, who when the night
Is closing, quickly pales beneath the rays
Of the ascending sun, and hides himself.
I tremble, or I run, or stand aside,
Or seek deliverance by a hundred shifts,
If haply from behind some hurried step
Appears to track me, or a passer-by
Casts but a glance upon me ; every one
Is viewed by me suspiciously, for thus
A guilty conscience makes a man a coward,
Affrightening him with his unrighteous deeds.

On reaching the house, he sees the object of his affections—the female-slave of Vasanta-senā. He presents her with the casket, and begs her to take it to her mistress, and request in return freedom from further service. The servant-girl, on seeing the casket, recognizes the ornaments as belonging to her mistress. She then reproaches her lover, who is forced to confess how they came into his possession, and to explain that they were stolen entirely out of love for her. The altercation which ensues leads him to make some very disparaging remarks on the female sex generally. Here is a specimen of his asperities, which are somewhat softened down in the translation :—

A woman will for money smile or weep
According to your will ; she makes a man
Put trust in her, but trusts him not herself.
Women are as inconstant as the waves
Of ocean, their affection is as fugitive

As streak of sunset glow upon a cloud.
They cling with eager fondness to the man
Who yields them wealth, which they squeeze out like sap
Out of a juicy plant, and then they leave him.
Therefore are men thought foolish who confide
In women and in fortune, for their windings
Are like the coils of serpent nymphs, insidious.
Well is it said, you cannot alter nature;
The lotus grows not on the mountain-top,
Asses refuse to bear a horse's burden,
He who sows barley reaps not fields of rice;
Do what you will, a woman will be woman.

After other still more caustic aspersions, the thief Śarvilaka and his lover make up their differences, and it is agreed between them that the only way out of the difficulty is for him to take the casket to Vasanta-senā, as if he were a messenger from Ćāru-datta, sent to restore her property. This he does; and Vasanta-senā, who, unknown to the lovers, has overheard their conversation, astonishes Śarvilaka by setting her slave-girl free, and permitting her to become his wife; thus affording a practical refutation of his charge against women of selfishness and want of generosity.

Soon after the departure of the lovers an attendant announces the arrival of a Brāhman from Ćāru-datta. This turns out to be Maitreya, who is honoured by an introduction into the private garden attached to the inner apartments of Vasanta-senā's house. His passage through the courts of the mansion, no less than seven in number, is made an occasion for describing the interior of the splendid residence which a Hindū lady of wealth and fashion might be supposed, allowing for a little play of the imagination, to occupy.

The description affords a striking picture of Indian life and manners, which to this day are not greatly changed. The account of the courtyards will remind those who have seen Pompeii of some of the houses there, and will illustrate the now universally received opinion of the common origin of Hindūs, Greeks, and Romans. Of course the object of Maitreya's visit to Vasanta-senā is to confess the loss of the casket, and to request her acceptance of the string of jewels from Ćāru-datta as a compensation. The good man in his simplicity expects that she will politely decline the costly present tendered by Ćāru-datta as a substitute for her far less valuable casket of ornaments; but, to his surprise and disgust, she eagerly accepts the proffered compensation, and dismisses him with a few complimentary words, intending, however, as it afterwards appears, to make the acceptance of Ćāru-datta's compensation an excuse for going in person to his house, that she may see him once again and restore to him with her own hand both the necklace and casket.

The fifth act opens with a scene in Ćāru-datta's garden. A heavy thunderstorm is supposed to be gathering, when Maitreya enters, salutes Ćāru-datta, and informs him of the particulars of his interview with Vasanta-senā. The rain now begins to descend in torrents, when a servant arrives to announce that Vasanta-senā is waiting outside. On hearing this, Maitreya says:—

What can she have come for? Oh! I know what she wants. She considers the casket worth more than the necklace of jewels, and so she wants to get the balance out of you.

Ćāru-datta. Then she shall go away satisfied.

Meanwhile some delay occurs in admitting Vasanta-senā, which is made an occasion for introducing a dialogue between her and her attendant, in the course of which they are made to describe very poetically the grandeur of the approaching storm, the sudden accumulation of dense masses of threatening clouds, the increasing gloom followed by portentous darkness, the terrific rolling of thunder, the blaze of blinding lightning, the sudden outburst of rain, as if the very clouds themselves were falling, and the effect of all this upon the animals, some of which, such as the peacocks and storks, welcome the strife of elements with their shrillest cries. In her descriptions of the scene, Vasanta-senā speaks Sanskṛit, which is quite an unusual circumstance, and an evidence of her superior education—(no good sign, however, according to Eastern ideas)—the female characters in Indian dramas being supposed to be incapable of speaking anything but the ordinary provincial Prākṛit.[1] Vasanta-senā is ultimately admitted to the presence of

[1] There is a suitableness in this, however, when it is remembered that Prākṛit words are to Sanskṛit what Italian is to Latin. Harsh consonants are often softened off and compound ones are simplified. Piombo certainly comes more suitably from female lips than plumbum, and Sa-undalā than S'akuntalā.

Ćāru-datta, and before returning the necklace practises a little playful deception upon him as a set-off against that tried upon herself. She pretends that the string of pearls sent to her by Ćāru-datta has been accidentally lost by her; she therefore produces a casket which she begs him to accept in its place. This, of course, turns out to be the identical casket which the thief had carried off from Ćāru-datta's house. In the end, the whole matter is explained, and both casket and necklace are given over to Ćāru-datta, and the storm having now increased in violence, Vasanta-senā, to her great delight, is obliged to accept the shelter of his roof and is conducted to his private apartments. This brings five acts of the drama to a close.

At the commencement of the sixth act Vasanta-senā is supposed to be at Ćāru-datta's house waiting for a covered carriage which is to convey her away. While the vehicle is preparing, Ćāru-datta's child, a little boy, comes into the room with a toy-cart made of clay. He appears to be crying, and an attendant explains that his tears are caused by certain childish troubles connected with his clay-cart, which has ceased to please him since his happening to see one made of gold belonging to a neighbour's child. Upon this, Vasanta-senā takes off her jewelled ornaments, places them in the clay-cart, and tells the child to purchase a golden cart with the value of the jewels as a present from herself. While this is going on, the carriage which is to convey her away is brought up to the door, but is driven off again to fetch some cushions accidentally forgotten by the driver. Meanwhile an empty carriage belonging to Saṃsthānaka—the worthless brother-in-law of the king—which is on its way to meet him at an appointed place in a certain garden called Pushpa-karaṇḍaka, happens to stop for a moment, impeded by some obstruction in the road close to the door of Ćāru-datta's house. Vasanta-senā having been told that Ćāru-datta's carriage is ready and waiting for her, goes suddenly out and jumps by mistake into the carriage of the man who is most hateful to her, and the very man who is represented as persecuting her by his attentions in the first act. The driver of the empty vehicle, quite unaware of the passenger he has suddenly received, and finding the road now clear before him, drives on to meet his master. Soon afterwards the empty carriage of Ćāru-datta is brought to the door, and in connection with this incident an important part of the underplot of the drama is then introduced.

The seventh act continues this underplot, which, although ingeniously interwoven with the main action of the drama, is not sufficiently interesting to be worth following out in this epitome.

The eighth act commences with a scene in the Pushpa-karaṇḍaka garden. Our old friend the gambler of the second act, who has abjured his evil ways and is now converted into a Śramaṇa or Buddhist mendicant, appears with a wet garment in his hand. He begins his soliloquy with some verses, of which the following is a slightly amplified translation:—

Hear me, ye foolish, I implore—
Make sanctity your only store;
Be satisfied with meagre fare;
Of greed and gluttony beware;
Shun slumber, practise lucubration,
Sound the deep gong of meditation.
Restrain your appetites with zeal,
Let not these thieves your merit steal;
Be ever storing it anew,
And keep eternity in view.
Live ever thus, like me, austerely,
And be the home of Virtue merely.
Kill your five senses, murder then
Women and all immoral men.
Whoever has slain these evils seven
Has saved himself, and goes to heaven;
Nor think by shaven face and head
To prove your appetites are dead;
Who shears his head and not his heart
Is an ascetic, but in part;
But he whose heart is closely lopped
Has also head and visage cropped.

He then proceeds with his soliloquy thus:—

My tattered garment is now properly dyed of a reddish-yellow colour. I will just slip into this garden belonging to the king's brother-in-law, wash my clothes in the lake, and then make off as fast as I can.

(*A voice behind.*) Hollo! there! you wretch of a mendicant, stop, stop.

Mendicant. Woe's me! here is the king's brother himself coming. A poor mendicant once offended him, so now whenever he sees another like me, he slits his nose and drags him away like an ox. Where shall I take refuge? None but the venerated Buddha can be my protector.

Saṃsthānaka, the king's brother-in-law, now enters the garden, and laying hold of the luckless mendicant, commences beating him. A companion of Saṃsthānaka, however, here interposes, and begs that the mendicant may be released.

Saṃsthānaka then says :—

I will let him go on one condition, viz., that he removes all the mud from this pool without disturbing the water, or else collects all the clear water in a heap and then throws the mud away.

After some wrangling, and a good deal of nonsense of this sort, spoken by the king's brother, the mendicant is allowed to make off. Nevertheless, he still hangs about the precincts of the garden. In the meantime the carriage containing Vasanta-senā approaches.

Saṃsth. (*to his companion*). What o'clock is it? That driver of mine, Sthāvaraka, was ordered to be here sharp with the carriage, and has not yet arrived. I am dying with hunger; it is mid-day, and one cannot stir a step on foot; the sun is in mid-sky, and can no more be looked at than an angry ape; the ground is as parched as the face of Gāndhārī when her hundred sons were slain; the birds seek shelter among the branches; men panting with heat hide themselves from the sun's rays as well as they can in the recesses of their houses. Shall I give you a song to while away the time? My voice is in first-rate condition, for I keep it so with asafœtida, cumin-seed, cyperus, orris-root, treacle and ginger. (*Sings.*)

The driver Sthāvaraka now enters with the carriage containing Vasanta-senā.

Saṃsth. (*continues.*) Oh! here is the carriage at last.

On seeing it he is about to jump into the vehicle, but starts back in alarm, declaring that either a thief or a witch is inside. In the end he recognizes Vasanta-senā, and in his delight at having secured the object of his affection, kneels at her feet, in the attitude of a lover. She is at first terrified at the mistake she has made, then in her anger and scorn spurns him with her foot. This disdainful treatment so enrages the king's brother-in-law that he resolves to kill her on the spot. He tries first to induce his companion to put her to death, but he will not listen to so scandalous a proposal. Stopping his ears, he says :—

What! kill a woman, innocent and young,
Our city's ornament! were I to perpetrate

A deed so foul, who could transport my soul
Across the stream that bounds the other world?

Saṃsth. Never fear. I'll make you a raft to carry you across.

To this his companion replies, quoting with a little alteration from Manu:[1]—

The heaven and all ten quarters of the sky,
The moon, the light-creating sun, the winds,
This earth, the spirits of the dead, the god
Of Justice, and the inner soul itself,
Witness man's actions, be they good or bad.

Saṃsth. Conceal her under a cloth, then, and kill her under a cover.

His associate remaining firm in his indignant refusal to have any hand in the crime, Saṃsthānaka next tries first by bribes and then by threats to force the driver Sthāvaraka to do the deed for him.

Saṃsth. Sthāvaraka, my good fellow, I will give you golden bracelets; I will place you on a golden seat; you shall eat all the dainties from my table; you shall be chief of all my servants, only do as I bid you.

Sthāv. What are your commands?

Saṃsth. Kill Vasanta-senā.

Sthāv. Nay, sir; forgive her, sir; her coming hither was my fault; I brought her here in the carriage by mistake.

Saṃsth. Do as I command you. Am I not your master?

Sthāv. You are master of my body, but not of my morality. Pardon me, sir, I dare not commit such a crime.

Saṃsth. Why? What are you afraid of?

Sthāv. Of futurity.

Saṃsth. Futurity? Who is he?

Sthāv. The certain issue of our good and evil deeds.

Saṃsth. Then you won't murder her? (*Begins beating him.*)

Sthāv. Beat me or kill me, I will not commit such a crime.

Saṃsthānaka's companion now interferes and says:—

Sthāvaraka says well, he now a slave
Is poor and lowly in condition, but
Hopes for reward hereafter, not so those

---

[1] See page 280.

Who prosper in their wicked actions here,
Destruction waits them in another sphere.
Unequal fortune makes you here the lord,
And him the slave, but there 't may be inverted,
He to a lord and you to slave converted.

Saṃsth. What a pair of cowards! One of them is afraid of Injustice, and the other of Futurity. Well, I'm a king's brother-in-law, and fear no one. Be off out of my way, you son of a slave.

The slave Sthāvaraka then retreats. The king's brother, by pretending that the proposal to kill Vasanta-senā was only a joke, and by putting on a show of great affection for her, rids himself next of his companion, who would otherwise have defended her. He then strangles Vasanta-senā. Soon afterwards his companion and the driver of the carriage, unable to repress their fears for her safety, return and find her apparently dead. The king's brother-in-law horrifies them by confessing that he has murdered her. After much angry altercation they leave him. He then covers up the body with some leaves, and resolves to go before a judge and accuse Ćāru-datta of having murdered Vasanta-senā for the sake of her costly ornaments. Meanwhile the Buddhist mendicant, having washed his garments, returns into the garden and finds the body under a heap of leaves. He sprinkles water on the face, and Vasanta-senā revives. He is delighted to have the power of making some return to his benefactress, who formerly delivered him from the rapacity of the gaming-house keeper. He therefore does all he can to restore animation, and having at last succeeded, places her in a neighbouring convent to recover.

The ninth act opens with a scene in a court of justice. The judge before taking his seat soliloquizes thus:—

How difficult our task! to search the heart,
To sift false charges, and elicit truth!
A judge must be well read in books of law,
Well skilled in tracking crime, able to speak
With eloquence, not easily made angry,
Holding the scales impartially between
Friends, kindred and opponents; a protector
Of weak and feeble men, a punisher
Of knaves; not covetous, having a heart
Intent on truth and justice; not pronouncing

Judgment in any case until the facts
Are duly weighed, then shielding the condemned
From the king's wrath, and loving clemency.

Saṃsthānaka, the king's brother, now enters in a sumptuous dress and makes his accusation against Ćāru-datta of having murdered Vasanta-senā. It is proved that Vasanta-senā was last seen at Ćāru-datta's house. It is also discovered that some portions of her hair and the marks of her feet remain in the Pushpa-karaṇdaka garden, which leads to the conclusion that her body may have been carried off by beasts of prey. Ćāru-datta is therefore summoned, and as he enters the court says to himself:—

The court-house looks imposing; it is like
A sea whose waters are the advocates
Deep in sagacious thought, whose waves are messengers,
In constant movement hurrying to and fro,
Whose fish and screaming birds are vile informers,
Whose serpents are attornies'-clerks, whose banks
Are worn by constant course of legal action.

The king's brother now repeats his accusation, but the judge is not inclined to believe in the guilt of Ćāru-datta, who indeed makes his innocence clear to the whole court. Unhappily, however, just at this moment his friend Maitreya, who, by Ćāru-datta's request, is seeking for Vasanta-senā, that he may restore to her the jewels she had placed in his little son's clay-cart, hears on his road of the accusation brought against his friend, hurries into the court of justice, and is so enraged with the king's brother for accusing his friend that he strikes him, and in the struggle which ensues lets fall Vasanta-senā's jewels. It is admitted that these ornaments are being brought from Ćāru-datta's house, and this is thought to be conclusive evidence of his guilt. As a Brāhman he cannot legally be put to death;[1] but the king is a tyrant, and although the judge recommends banishment as the proper punishment under the circumstances, the king pronounces his sentence thus:—

Let Vasanta-senā's ornaments be hung round Ćāru-datta's neck; let him be led by the beat of drums to the southern cemetery, bearing his own stake, and there let him be put to death.

[1] Manu is very precise about this; but here is a proof that the laws of Manu were rather theoretical than ever strictly followed.

The tenth act introduces the road leading to the place of execution. Ćāru-datta enters bearing the stake,[1] and attended by two Ćāṇḍālas or low outcastes, who are sent to act as executioners.

One of the executioners calls out:—

Out of the way! out of the way! Make room for Ćāru-datta. Crowned with a garland of oleander flowers, and attended by executioners, he approaches his end like a lamp which has little oil left. Now then, halt! beat the drum! Hark ye, good people all! stop and listen to the proclamation of the sentence. 'This is Ćāru-datta, son of Sāgara-datta, who strangled Vasanta-senā in the Pushpa-karaṇḍaka garden for the sake of her ornaments, and was caught with the stolen property in his possession; we have orders to put him to death, that others may be deterred from committing a crime which both worlds forbid to be perpetrated.'

Ćāru. Alas! alas!

Even my friends and intimate compeers
Pass coldly by, their faces turned aside
Or hidden in their vestments; thus it is
That in prosperity, our enemies
Appear like friends, but in adversity
Those we thought friends behave like very foes.

The proclamation is repeated at intervals on the road to the place of execution, and some delay is thus occasioned. Meanwhile an affecting scene takes place. Ćāru-datta's little son is brought by Maitreya to bid his father farewell, and the executioner permits him to approach. The boy can only say, 'Father! Father!'

Ćāru-datta embraces him and says:—

What shall I give my son as a memento?
This sacred cord is all I can bestow;
It is an ornament of Brāhmans, better
Than pearls or gold—the instrument by which
Worship is paid to gods and ancestors.
This take, my son, and wear it for my sake.

The child then addressing the executioner says:—

Vile outcaste, where are you leading my father?

---

[1] The whole scene is very curious, and suggestive of a comparison with the Roman method of execution.

Ćāru. Crowned with a garland, bearing on my shoulder
The fatal stake, and deep within my heart,
Hiding my grief, I hasten to my grave
Like victim to the place of sacrifice.

Execu. Call us not outcastes. All wicked men, and all who harm the good, are the only outcastes.

Boy. If you are not outcastes, then why do you kill my father?

Execu. 'Tis the king's order; we are not to blame.

Boy. Kill me instead, and let my father go.

Execu. Rather for such a speech live long, my boy.

Ćāru. (*bursting into tears and embracing his child*).

This is true wealth—a child's devoted love—
A wealth which rich and poor enjoy alike—
A balm to soothe an agitated heart,
Better than cooling sandal or Uśīra.

The child is of course removed, but another delay is caused by Sthāvaraka, who drove Vasanta-senā to the garden, and who, as cognizant of the real facts, had been shut up by his guilty master, the king's brother-in-law. Sthāvaraka, on hearing the noise of the procession on its way to the place of execution, contrives to escape from his prison, and rushing towards the executioners, proclaims Ćāru-datta's innocence, and his master's guilt. Unhappily, however, just at this juncture his master appears on the scene, and declares that his servant Sthāvaraka, having been imprisoned for thieving, is unworthy of credit, and has made up this accusation out of spite and desire for revenge. Notwithstanding, therefore, the servant's repeated asseverations, his statements are disbelieved, and his efforts to save Ćāru-datta prove ineffectual. The procession and crowd now move on to the cemetery, and Ćāru-datta's condition seems altogether hopeless, when just as he is led to the stake, and the executioners are about to perform their office, the Buddhist mendicant is seen forcing his way through the crowd, leading a woman, who cries out, 'Hold! hold! I am the miserable creature for whose sake you are putting him to death.' This, to the astonishment of every one, proves to be Vasanta-senā herself, resuscitated and restored to health, through the instrumentality of the mendicant. The executioners immediately release Ćāru-datta, and as the king's brother-in-law in utter confusion and terror is observed to be making off, they attempt to seize him.

He appears likely to be torn to pieces by the infuriated crowd; but here Ćāru-datta gives a crowning evidence of the generosity of his character by protecting the villain who had come to feast his eyes on the dying agonies of his victim. He is actually, at Ćāru-datta's intercession, permitted to make his escape. The play ends in the elevation of Ćāru-datta to rank and honour, in the happiness of both hero and heroine, and in the promotion of the mendicant to the headship of all the Vihāras or Buddhist monasteries.

I pass on to the greatest of all Indian dramatists, *Kālidāsa.* He is represented by some native authorities (though on insufficient grounds) to have lived in the time of a celebrated king, Vikramāditya, whose reign forms the starting-point of the Hindū era called *Saṃvat,* beginning fifty-seven years B.C. This king had his capital in Ujjayinī (Oujein); he was a great patron of literature, and Kālidāsa is described as one of the nine illustrious men called the nine jewels of his court. It is, however, more probable that Kālidāsa lived and composed his works about the commencement of the third century.[1] His well-known poems have already been noticed at pp. 452–454.[2] He only wrote three plays — the *Śakuntalā*, the *Vikramorvaśī*, and the *Mālavikāgnimitra.* Of these, the Śakuntalā, in seven acts, is by far the most celebrated

---

[1] Professor Lassen places Kālidāsa about the year 250 after Christ. Dr. Bhāu Dājī assigns him to the reign of a Vikramāditya in the sixth century. Kālidāsa probably lived at Ujjayinī, as he describes it with much feeling in the Megha-dūta, and to this circumstance may probably be traced his supposed connection with the great Vikramāditya.

[2] Besides these, he is said to have written a poem called the *Setu-kāvya* or *Setu-bandha,* describing the building of Rāma's bridge, and written for Pravara-sena, king of Kaśmīr. A work on metres, called the Śruta-bodha, is also attributed to him. This last may be by another Kālidāsa. No doubt many works were ascribed to the greatest Indian poet, as to the greatest Indian philosopher, Śan-karāćārya, which they neither of them wrote.

and popular. I have endeavoured in my translation of this beautiful drama (sixth edition, published by W. H. Allen & Co.)[1] to give some idea of the merits of a work which drew unqualified praise from such a poet as Goethe in the following words (Mr. E. B. Eastwick's translation):—

Wouldst thou the young year's blossoms and the fruits of its decline,
  And all by which the soul is charmed, enraptured, feasted, fed?
Wouldst thou the earth and heaven itself in one sole name combine?
  I name thee, O S'akoontalā! and all at once is said.

I merely extract from my own translation of the *Śakuntalā* two passages. The following is the hero Dushyanta's description of a peculiar sensation to which he confesses himself subject, and to which perhaps the minds of sensitive persons, even in Western countries, are not altogether strangers (Act V., Translation, p. 121):—

Not seldom in our happy hours of ease,
When thought is still, the sight of some fair form,
Or mournful fall of music breathing low,

---

[1] As every Orientalist knows, Sir W. Jones was the first to translate the S'akuntalā, but he had only access to the Bengāl (Bengālī) recension. Two other recensions exist, one in the north-west (commonly called the Devanāgarī) and one in the South of India. The last is the shortest, and the Bengāl version is the longest. The Devanāgarī recension, translated by me into English, is generally considered the purest. Nevertheless Dr. R. Pischel in a learned dissertation maintains that the palm belongs to the Bengālī, and it must be admitted that in some cases the Bengāl version contains readings which appear more likely to represent the original. Professor Böhtlingk's edition of the Devanāgarī recension is well known. My edition of the same recension, with literal translations of the difficult passages and critical notes (published by Stephen Austin of Hertford), is now out of print. Dr. C. Burkhard has published a new edition of this recension with a useful vocabulary. A good edition of the Bengāl recension was prepared in Calcutta by Pandit Prem Chunder Tarkabāgish, and brought out in 1860 under the superintendence of Professor E. B. Cowell.

Will stir strange fancies, thrilling all the soul
With a mysterious sadness, and a sense
Of vague yet earnest longing. Can it be
That the dim memory of events long past,
Or friendships formed in other states of being,
Flits like a passing shadow o'er the spirit?

Here is a specimen of the poetical similes which occur constantly throughout the drama (Act V., Translation, p. 129):[1]—

The loftiest trees bend humbly to the ground
Beneath the teeming burden of their fruit;
High in the vernal sky the pregnant clouds
Suspend their stately course, and, hanging low,
Scatter their sparkling treasures o'er the earth:
And such is true benevolence; the good
Are never rendered arrogant by riches.

The two other dramas composed by Kālidāsa are the *Vikramorvaśī*, 'Urvaśī won by valour,' and the *Mālavikāgnimitra*, 'story of Mālavikā and Agnimitra,' the first of which is unequalled in poetical beauty by any other Indian drama except the Śakuntalā. The *Vikramorvaśī* is in only five acts, and its subject is easily told:[2]—

Urvaśī, a nymph of heaven—the heroine of the piece—is carried off by a demon, and is rescued by the hero, king Purūravas, who, of course, falls in love with her. The usual impediments arise, caused by the inconvenient fact that the king has a wife already; but in the end the nymph is permitted by the god Indra to marry the mortal hero. Subsequently, in consequence of a curse, Urvaśī becomes meta-

[1] This verse occurs also in Bhartṛi-hari II. 62. He was the author of 300 moral, political, and erotic verses called *Śṛin·gāra-śataka, Nīti-ś°*, and *Vairāgya-ś°*.

[2] Various editions of this play have been published; one by Lenz, another by myself. By far the best edition is by Dr. Bollensen. Professor H. H. Wilson's spirited verse translation is well known. A prose translation was made by Professor E. B. Cowell and published in 1851.

morphosed into a plant, and Purūravas goes mad. She is afterwards restored to her proper form through the efficacy of a magical gem, and her husband recovers his reason. They are happily reunited, but it is decreed that when Urvaśī's son is seen by his father Purūravas she is to be recalled to heaven. This induces her to conceal the birth of her son Āyus, and to intrust him for some years to the care of a female ascetic. Accidentally father and son meet, and Urvaśī prepares to leave her husband; but Indra compassionately revokes the decree, and the nymph is permitted to remain on earth as the hero's second wife.

As to the *Mālavikāgnimitra*, which is also rather a short play in five acts, the excellent German translation of it by Professor Weber of Berlin, published in 1856, and the scholarlike edition published in 1869 by Shankar P. Pandit of the Dekhan College,[1] have set at rest the vexed question of its authenticity, by enabling the student to compare it with Kālidāsa's acknowledged writings. So many analogies of thought, style, and diction in the Mālavikāgnimitra have been thus brought to light, that few can now have any doubt about the authorship of the extant drama. According to the statement in its own prologue, it is evidently the veritable production of the author of the Śakuntalā and Vikramorvaśī. Nevertheless, its inferiority to the two masterpieces of Kālidāsa—notwithstanding considerable poetical and dramatic merit, and great beauty and simplicity of style—must be admitted on all hands. Perhaps this may be accounted for by supposing the Mālavikāgnimitra to have been Kālidāsa's first theatrical composition. Or possibly the scenes in which the dramatic action is laid, afforded the poet no opportunity (as in the other two plays) of displaying his marvellous powers of describing the beauties of nature and the habits of animals in rural and sylvan retreats.

---

[1] A previous edition was published at Bonn in 1840 by Dr. Tullberg.

Its hero, king Agnimitra, is certainly a more ordinary and strictly human character than the semi-mythical Dushyanta and Purūravas, and the same may be said of its heroine Mālavikā, as compared with Śakuntalā and Urvaśī; but the plots of the three plays resemble each other in depending for their interest on the successful prosecution of love-intrigues under very similar difficulties and impediments.

In the Mālavikāgnimitra,[1] king Agnimitra (son of Pushpamitra, founder of the Śun-ga dynasty of Magadha kings) falls in love with a girl named Mālavikā—belonging to the train of his queen Dhāriṇī's attendants—from accidentally seeing her portrait. As usual, the Vidūshaka is employed as a go-between, and undertakes to procure the king a sight of the original. It happens that the principal queen, Dhāriṇī, has caused Mālavikā to be instructed in music, singing, and dancing. Hence in the second act a sort of concert (*San-gīta*), or trial of skill, is arranged, at which Mālavikā executes a very difficult part in a particular musical time—called the *Madhya-laya*—with wonderful brilliancy. This, of course, captivates the king, and destroys his peace of mind. In spite of the opposition of his two queens, Dhāriṇī and Irāvatī, and notwithstanding other hindrances, he contrives to carry on an intrigue with Mālavikā. Not that he attempts to marry her by unlawful means, nor even against the wishes of his other wives. Polygamy is, of course, held to be legitimate in the household of Oriental Rājas. The difficulty consists in conciliating his two queens. This, however, he contrives in the end to accomplish, and their assent to his union with Mālavikā is at last obtained. In the course of the plot a *Parivrājikā* or Buddhist female mendicant is introduced, which is regarded by Professor Weber as an argument for the antiquity of the drama. In the prologue Bhāsa and Saumilla are mentioned as two poets, predecessors of Kālidāsa.

I here give an example of a wise sentiment from the prelude. The stage-manager, addressing the audience, says:—

All that is old is not on that account
Worthy of praise, nor is a novelty
By reason of its newness to be censured.

---

[1] I have consulted Professor H. H. Wilson's epitome of the play in the appendix to his Hindū Theatre.

The wise decide not what is good or bad,
Till they have tested merit for themselves.
A foolish man trusts to another's judgment.

I come now to a more modern Indian dramatist named *Bhavabhūti* and surnamed *Śrī-kaṇṭha*, 'whose voice is eloquence.' His reputation is only second to that of Kālidāsa. In the prelude to two of his plays he is described as the son of a Brāhman named Nīlakaṇṭha (his mother being Jatūkarṇī), who was one of the descendants of Kaśyapa, living in a city called Padma-pura, and a follower of the Black Yajur-veda. He is said to have been born somewhere in the district Berar, and to have flourished at the court of Yaśovarman, who reigned at Kanouj (Kanyā-kubja) about A.D. 720.[1] Like Kālidāsa, he only wrote three plays. These are called the *Mālatī-mādhava, Mahā-vīra-ćarita*, and *Uttara-rāma-ćarita*.[2] Of these three the Mālatī-mādhava, in ten acts, is perhaps the best known to English Sanskrit scholars. The style is more laboured and artificial than that of Kālidāsa's plays, and some of the metres adopted in the versification are of that complex kind which later Hindū poets delight to employ for the exhibition of their skill.[3] In the prelude the poet is guilty of the bad taste of praising his own composition. Its plot, however, is more interesting than that of Kālidāsa's plays; its action is dramatic, and its pictures of domestic life and manners are most valuable, notwithstanding too free an introduction of the preternatural element, from which, as we have seen, the Mṛić-

---

1 According to Professor Lassen he lived about the year 710. Kanouj, now in ruins, ranks in antiquity next to Ayodhyā. It is situated in the North-west, on the Kālīnadī, a branch of the Ganges, in the district of Furruckabad.

2 *Ćarita* is sometimes written *ćaritra*.

3 Colebrooke especially mentions the Daṇḍaka metre, for an account of which see page 155 of this volume.

ćhakaṭikā is exceptionally free. The story of the *Mālatī-Mādhava* has been well epitomized by Colebrooke.[1] I give here but a bare outline :—

Two ministers of two neighbouring kings have agreed together privately that their children, Mādhava and Mālatī, shall in due time marry each other. Unhappily for the accomplishment of their project, one of the kings requires the father of Mālatī to make a match between his daughter and an ugly old court-favourite named Nandana. The minister, fearing to offend the monarch, consents to sacrifice his daughter. Meanwhile Mādhava is sent to finish his studies under an old Buddhist priestess named Kāmandakī, who had been Mālatī's nurse, and who contrives that she and Mādhava shall meet and fall in love, though they do not at that time make known their mutual attachment. Soon afterwards the king prepares to enforce the marriage of Mālatī with his favourite Nandana. The news, when brought to Mālatī, makes her desperate. Another meeting takes place in Kāmandakī's garden between her and her lover Mādhava, who is followed to the garden by a friend, Makaranda. During their interview a great tumult and terrific screams are heard. A tiger has escaped from an iron cage and spreads destruction everywhere. Madayantikā, sister of Nandana, happens to be passing and is attacked by the tiger. Mādhava and Makaranda both rush to the rescue. The latter kills the animal and thus saves Madayantikā, who is then brought in a half-fainting state into the garden. On recovering she naturally falls in love with her preserver Makaranda. The two couples are thus brought together, and Mālatī affiances herself there and then to Mādhava. At this very moment a messenger arrives to summon Madayantikā, Nandana's sister, to be present at Nandana's marriage with Mālatī, and another messenger summons Mālatī herself to the king's palace. Mādhava is mad with grief, and in despair makes the extraordinary resolution of purchasing the aid of evil demons by going to the cemetery and offering them living flesh, cut off from his own body, as food. The cemetery happens to be near the temple of the awful goddess Ćāmuṇḍā (a form of Durgā), presided over by a sorceress named Kapāla-kuṇḍalā and her preceptor, a terrible necromancer, Aghora-ghaṇṭa. They have determined on offering some beautiful maiden as a human victim to the goddess. With this object they carry off Mālatī, before her departure, while asleep on a terrace, and bringing her to the temple are about to kill her at Ćāmuṇḍā's shrine, when her cries attract the attention of Mādhava, who is at that moment in the

[1] See Professor E. B. Cowell's edition of his Essays, vol. ii. p. 123.

cemetery, offering his flesh to the demons. He rushes forward, encounters the sorcerer Aghora-ghaṇṭa, and after a terrific hand-to-hand fight kills him and rescues Mālatī, who is thus restored to her family. The remainder of the story, occupying the five concluding acts, is tediously protracted and scarcely worth following out. The preparations for Mālatī's marriage to Nandana go on, and the old priestess Kāmandakī, who favours the union of Mālatī with her lover Mādhava, contrives that, by the king's order, the bridal dress shall be put on at the very temple where her own ministrations are conducted. There she persuades Makaranda to substitute himself for the bride. He puts on the bridal dress, is taken in procession to the house of Nandana, and goes through the form of being married to him. Nandana, disgusted with the masculine appearance of his supposed bride, leaves Makaranda in the inner apartments, thus enabling him to effect an interview with Nandana's sister Madayantikā—the object of his own affections. Makaranda then makes himself known, and persuades her to run away with him to the place where Mālatī and Mādhava have concealed themselves. Their flight is discovered; the king's guards are sent in pursuit, a great fight follows, but Makaranda assisted by Mādhava defeats his opponents. The bravery and handsome appearance of the two youths avert the king's anger, and they are allowed to join their friends unpunished. In the midst of the confusion, however, Mālatī has been carried off by the sorceress Kapāla-kuṇḍalā in revenge for the death of her preceptor Aghora-ghaṇṭa. Mādhava is again in despair at this second obstacle to his union, but an old pupil of the priestess Kāmandakī, named Saudāminī, who has acquired extraordinary magical powers by her penances, opportunely appears on the scene, delivers Mālatī from the sorceress, and brings about the happy marriage of Mālatī with Mādhava and of Madayantikā with Makaranda.

The following description of Mādhava's first interview with Mālatī is from the first act :[1]—

One day by curiosity impelled
I sought the temple of the god of love.
There I roved to and fro, glancing around,
Till weary with my wandering I stood
Close to a pool that laved a Vakul tree

---

[1] Some expressions in my version have been suggested by Professor H. H. Wilson's, but I have endeavoured to make my own closer to the original.

In the court-yard and precincts of the temple.
The tree's sweet blossoms wooed a swarm of bees
To cull their nectar; and in idleness,
To while away the time, I laid me down
And gathered round me all the fallen flowers
To weave a garland, when there issued forth
From the interior fane a lovely maid.
Stately her gait, yet graceful as the banner
Waved by victorious Love o'er prostrate men;
Her garb with fitting ornaments embellished
Bespoke a youthful princess, her attendants
Moved proudly as became their noble rank;
She seemed a treasury of all the graces,
Or Beauty's store-house, where collected shone
A bright assemblage of all fairest things
To frame a perfect form; or rather was she
The very guardian goddess of love's shrine;
Or did the great Creator mould her charms
From some of Nature's loveliest materials—
The moon, the lotus-stalk, and sweetest nectar?
I looked and in an instant both my eyes
Seemed bathed with rapture and my inmost soul
Was drawn towards her unresistingly,
Like iron by the iron-loving magnet.

The other two plays of Bhava-bhūti, called *Mahā-vīra-ćarita* and *Uttara-rāma-ćarita,* form together a dramatic version of the story of the second Rāma or Rāma-ćandra, as narrated in Vālmīki's Rāmāyaṇa and Kālidāsa's Raghu-vaṉśa.

The *Mahā-vīra-ćarita,*[1] in seven acts (often quoted in the Sāhitya-darpaṇa under the title *Vīra-ćarita*), dramatizes the history of Rāma, the great hero (*mahā-vīra*), as told in the first six Books of the Rāmāyaṇa, but with some variations.

---

[1] Mr. John Pickford, one of my former Boden Scholars, some time Professor at Madras, has made a translation of this play from the Calcutta edition of 1857, and Professor H. H. Wilson has given an epitome of it in the appendix to his Hindū Theatre.

The author informs us in the prologue that his object in composing the play was 'to delineate the sentiment (*rasa*) of heroism (*vīra*, see note, p. 457) as exhibited in noble characters.' The marvellous (*adbhuta*) sentiment is also said to be depicted, and the style of the action is called *Bhāratī*.[1] The first five acts carry the story to the commencement of the conflict between Rāma and Rāvaṇa and between his army and the Rākshasas; but no fighting is allowed to take place on the stage, and no one is killed before the spectators. Indra and his attendant spirits are supposed to view the scene from the air, and they describe its progress to the audience; as, for example, the cutting off of Rāvaṇa's heads, the slaughter of the demons, the victory of Rāma and recovery of Sītā. The seventh and last act represents the aerial voyage of Rāma, Lakshmaṇa, Sītā, Vibhīshaṇa, and their companions in the celestial car Pushpaka (once the property of Rāvaṇa) from Lan-kā back to Ayodhyā. As they move through the air, they descry some of the scenes of their previous adventures, and many poetical descriptions are here introduced. The car at one time passes over the Daṇḍaka forest, and even approaches the sun. At length it descends at Ayodhyā. Rāma and Lakshmaṇa are re-united to Bharata and S'atrughna, and the four brothers once more embrace each other. Rāma is then consecrated king by Vasishṭha and Viśvāmitra.

The *Uttara-rāma-ćarita*,[2] in seven acts, continues the narrative and dramatizes the events described in the seventh Book or Uttara-kāṇḍa of the Rāmāyaṇa (see pp. 337–339). I give a brief epitome:[3]—

Rāma, when duly crowned at Ayodhyā, seemed likely to enter upon a life of quiet enjoyment with his wife. But this would not have satisfied the Hindū conception of the impossibility of finding rest in this world (compare p. 412), nor harmonized with the idea of the

[1] The word Bhāratī may perhaps mean simply 'language.' But we may note here that the Sāhitya-darpaṇa enumerates four kinds of style of dramatic action (*vṛitti*), viz., 1. the *Kaiśikī*, vivacious and graceful; 2. the *Sātvatī* or *Sāttvatī*, abounding in descriptions of brave deeds and characterized by the marvellous; 3. the *Ārabhaṭī*, supernatural and terrible; 4. the *Bhāratī*, in which the vocal action is mostly in Sanskṛit.

[2] The whole of this play is translated in Professor H. H. Wilson's Hindū Theatre.

[3] I have consulted the Rev. K. M. Banerjea's article in the 'Indian Antiquary' for May 1872.

pattern man Rāma, born to suffering and self-denial. We are first informed that the family-priest Vasishṭha, having to leave the capital for a time to assist at a sacrifice, utters a few words of parting advice to Rāma, thus: 'Remember that a king's real glory consists in his people's welfare.' Rāma replies: 'I am ready to give up everything, happiness, love, pity—even Sītā herself—if needful for my subjects' good.' In accordance with this promise he employs an emissary (named Durmukha) to ascertain the popular opinion as to his own treatment of his subjects, and is astonished to hear from Durmukha that they approve all his conduct but one thing. They find fault with him for having taken back his wife after her long residence in a stranger's house (*para-gṛiha-vāsa*). In short, he is told that they still gossip and talk scandal about her and Rāvaṇa. The scrupulously correct and over-sensitive Rāma, though convinced of his wife's fidelity after her submission to the fiery ordeal (p. 358), and though she is now likely to become a mother, feels himself quite unable to allow the slightest cause of offence to continue among the citizens. Torn by contending feelings, he steals away from his wife, while asleep, and directs Lakshmaṇa to seclude her somewhere in the woods. This is the first act. An interval of twelve years elapses before the second act, during which time Sītā is protected by divine agencies. In this interval, too, her twin sons, Kuśa and Lava, are born and entrusted to the care of Vālmīki, the author of the Rāmāyaṇa, who educates them in his hermitage. This leads to the introduction at the beginning of the second act of Vālmīki's stanza (drawn from him by his *śoka* or sorrow on beholding a bird, one of a pair, killed by a hunter), quoted from the Rāmāyaṇa (I. ii. 18), where it is said to be the first S'loka ever invented. An incident now occurs which leads Rāma to revisit the Daṇḍaka forest, the scene of his former exile. The child of a Brāhman dies suddenly and unaccountably. His body is laid at Rāma's door. Evidently some national sin is the cause of such a calamity, and an aërial voice informs him that an awful crime is being perpetrated; for a S'ūdra, named S'ambūka, is practising religious austerities instead of confining himself to his proper province of waiting on the twice-born (Manu I. 91). Rāma instantly starts for the forest, discovers S'ambūka in the sacrilegious act, and strikes off his head. But death by Rāma's hand confers immortality on the S'ūdra, who appears as a celestial spirit, and thanks Rāma for the glory and felicity thus obtained. Before returning to Ayodhyā, Rāma is induced to visit the hermitage of Agastya in the woods. Sītā now reappears on the scene. She is herself invisible to Rāma, but able to thrill him with emotions by her touch. Rāma's distraction is described with great feeling. 'What does this mean?' he says 'heavenly balm seems poured into my heart; a well-known touch changes my insensibility to life. Is it Sītā, or am I dreaming?' This leads on to the last act of the drama. In the end, husband and wife are re-united, but not without supernatural agencies being again employed, and not until Pṛithivī, the Earth, who, it appears, had taken charge of Sītā, restores her to the world. Vālmīki then introduces Kuśa and Lava to Rāma, who recognizes in them his two sons. Happiness is once more restored to the whole family, and the play closes.

We may note as remarkable that at the beginning of the fourth act a dialogue takes place between two young pupils of Vālmīki, who are delighted because some guests, having visited the hermitage, afford hopes of a feast at which flesh meat is to constitute one of the dishes. Manu's rule (V. 41; see p. 250 of this volume) is cited, whereby a *Madhu-parka* or offering of honey to a guest is directed to be accompanied with a dish of beef or veal; for on these occasions householders may kill calves, bulls, and goats (*vatsatarīm mahoksham vā mahājam va nirvapanti gṛiha-medhinaḥ*).

As a specimen of the poetry of the play, I here give Rāma's description of his love for his wife (translated by Professor H. H. Wilson):—

> Her presence is ambrosia to my sight;
> Her contact fragrant sandal; her fond arms,
> Twined round my neck, are a far richer clasp
> Than costliest gems, and in my house she reigns
> The guardian goddess of my fame and fortune.
> Oh! I could never bear again to lose her.

Two other well-known plays, the *Ratnāvalī* and the *Mudrā-rākshasa* (both translated by Professor H. H. Wilson), ought to be mentioned.

The *Ratnāvalī*, or 'jewel-necklace,' is a short play in four acts, attributed (like the Mṛić-ćhakaṭikā, see p. 475) to a royal author, king *Śrī Harsha-deva.*[1]

---

[1] This is probably a different Śrī Harsha from the author of the *Naishadha* or *Naishadhiya* (at p. 453). The *Nāgānanda* (see p. 508), a Hindū-Buddhist drama, is attributed to the same author. Hindū poets appear to have been in the habit of flattering kings and great men in this way. Professor E. B. Cowell is inclined to assign the

There is nothing of the supernatural about this drama. It may be called a comedy in which the characters are all mortal men and women, and the incidents quite domestic. The play is connected with what appears to have been a familiar story, viz., the loves and intrigues of a certain king *Udayana*, and *Vāsava-dattā*, a princess of Ujjayinī. This tale is told in the Kathā-sarit-sāgara. The king is there called Udayana (see the account in Wilson's Essays, Dr. Rost's edition, I. 191), and is said to have carried off Vāsava-dattā, who is there the daughter of Ćaṇḍa-mahāsena, while in the Ratnāvalī she is daughter of Pradyota, and is not said to be a princess of Ujjayinī. The same story (along with the stories of S'akuntalā and Urvaśī) is alluded to towards the end of the second act of the Mālatī-mādhava, and according to Professor Wilson is referred to by Kālidāsa in the Megha-dūta when he speaks of the *Udayana-kathā* as frequently recited in Ujjayinī (verse 32). Dr. Fitz-Edward Hall has shown in his Preface to Subandhu's *Vāsava-dattā* that this romance has scarcely any feature in common with the Ratnāvalī story except the name of its heroine. The plot of the Ratnāvalī resembles in its love-intrigues that of the Vikramorvaśī, Mālavikāgnimitra, &c., and in like manner presents us with a valuable picture of Hindū manners in medieval times. The poet seems to have had no scruple in borrowing ideas and expressions from Kālidāsa. The hero of the piece is generally spoken of as 'the King,' or else as *Vatsa-rājaḥ*, king of Vatsa—a country or people whose capital was *Kauśāmbhī*. He is, however, called *Udayana* at the end of the first act, and before the play commences he is supposed to be already married to *Vāsava-dattā*. His minister's name is *Yaugandharāyaṇa* or *Yogandharāyaṇa*, his Vidūshaka or jovial companion is called *Vasantaka*, and his general *Rumaṇvat*.

The first scene introduces a curious description of the sports and practical jokes practised at the Spring festival (now called Holī), when plays were generally acted, and still continue to be performed in some parts of India. *Sāgarikā* (otherwise called *Ratnāvalī*, from her jewel-necklace), a princess of Lan-kā (Ceylon), is accidentally brought to the king's court, falls in love with him, and paints his picture. The king is, of course, equally struck with her. His queen's jealousy is excited by the discovery of the picture. She even succeeds

---

Nāgānanda to a poet named *Dhāvaka*, mentioned in the Kāvya-prakāśa, while he conjectures that *Bāṇa*, the author of the Kādambarī, may have written the *Ratnāvalī*, which would place the date of this play (as shown by Dr. Fitz-Edward Hall) in the seventh century of our era. One native commentator on the Kāvya-prakāśa asserts that *Dhāvaka* wrote the *Ratnāvalī*.

in imprisoning *Sāgarikā* and putting fetters on her feet, and more than the ordinary impediments threaten to stop the progress of the love-affair. All difficulties, however, are eventually removed, and the play ends, as usual, by the king's conciliating his first wife and gaining a second.

I give one specimen of a sentiment uttered by the hero on hearing of the death of a brave enemy. He says: *Mṛityur api tasya ślāghyo yasya ripavaḥ purusha-kāraṃ varṇayanti;* that is,

> How glorious is the death of that brave man
> Whose very enemies applaud his prowess!

The *Mudrā-rākshasa*, or 'signet-ring Rākshasa,'[1] is by *Viśākha-datta*, and is a political drama in seven acts, attributed to the twelfth century.

This play is noteworthy as introducing the well-known Ćandra-gupta, king of Pāṭaliputra, who was happily conjectured by Sir W. Jones to be identical with the Sandrakottus described by Megasthenes in Strabo as the most powerful Rāja immediately succeeding Alexander's death, and whose date (about 315 B.C.) serves as the only definite starting-point in Hindū chronology. Another celebrated character is his crafty minister Ćāṇakya, the Indian *Macchiavelli*, and writer on Nīti or 'rules of government and polity,' and the reputed author of numerous moral and political precepts commonly current in India. He is represented as having slain king Nanda and assisted Ćandra-gupta to the throne. The principal design of the play is to describe how this wily Brāhman Ćāṇakya (also called Vishṇu-gupta) effects a reconciliation between a person named Rākshasa, the minister of the murdered Nanda, and the persons on whose behalf he was killed. At the beginning of Act VII. there is a curious scene in which a Ćaṇḍāla or executioner leads a criminal to the place of execution (*badhya-sthāna*). The latter bears a stake (*śūla*) on his shoulder, and is followed by his wife and child. The executioner calls out—

---

[1] If this title *Mudrā-rākshasa* is a compound similar to *Vikramorvaśī* and *Abhijñāna-śakuntalam*, where there is *madhyama-pada-lopa*, it might be translated, 'Rākshasa known by the signet-ring;' but it may possibly be one in which the terms are inverted. Some translate it as a *Dvandva*, 'Rākshasa and the signet-ring.' In the fifth act, Ćāṇakya's emissary Siddhārtha enters, bearing a letter marked with the signet-ring of the minister Rākshasa (*amātya rākshasasya mudrā-lāñćhito lekhaḥ*).

'Make way, make way, good people! let every one who wishes to preserve his life, his property, or his family, avoid transgressing against the king as he would poison.' (Cf. Mṛić-ćhakaṭikā, Act X.)

With regard to the interesting Hindū-Buddhist drama called *Nāgānanda* or 'joy of the snake-world,' I must refer those who wish for an account of its contents to Professor Cowell's Preface prefixed to Mr. Boyd's recent translation (see note, p. 505).

Some other well-known plays have been before noticed :—

Thus, for example, the student will find mentioned at p. 367 the *Hanuman-nāṭaka*, a *Mahā-nāṭaka* in fourteen acts;[1] the *Bāla-rāmāyaṇa*, a *Mahā-nāṭaka* in ten acts, by *Rāja-śekhara* (edited by Paṇḍit Govinda Deva S'āstri of Benares in 1869); the *Prasanna-rāghava* in seven acts (edited by the same in 1868); the *Anargha-rāghava;* and the *Veṇī-saṃhāra* at p. 392, note 3. The *Hāsyārṇava*, a comic and satirical piece in two acts, is described in the appendix to Professor Wilson's Hindū Theatre.

Before, however, taking leave of the Hindū Theatre I ought to note a curious allegorical and philosophical play by Krishṇa-miśra, who is supposed to have lived in the twelfth century of our era. The play is called *Prabodha ćandrodaya, i.e.*, 'rise of the moon of (true) intelligence or knowledge,' and its *dramatis personae* remind one of some of our old Moralities—acted in England about the time of Henry VIII.—in which the Virtues and Vices were introduced as persons for the purpose of inculcating moral and religious truth.

Thus in an old English Morality called *Every-man* some of the personifications are — God, Death, Every-man, Fellowship, Kindred, Good-deeds, Knowledge, Confession, Beauty, Strength, Discretion. In

[1] I possess an old and valuable MS. of this play, which I hope may one day be used in editing it. The edition published in Calcutta by Mahārāja Kālī-krishṇa Bahādur, in 1840, was not from the purest recension. It was lithographed at Bombay about ten years ago.

Hycke-scorner—Contemplation, Pity, Imagination, Free-will. In *Lusty Juventus*—Good Counsel, Knowledge, Satan, Hypocrisy, Fellowship, Abominable Living, God's Merciful Promises. Similarly in the Hindū Morality *Prabodha-ćandrodaya* we have Faith, Volition, Opinion, Imagination, Contemplation, Devotion, Quietude, Friendship, &c. &c., on one side; Error, Self-conceit, Hypocrisy, Love, Passion, Anger, Avarice, on the other. The two sets of characters are, of course, opposed to each other, the object of the play being to show how the former become victorious over the latter, the Buddhists and other heretical sects being represented as adherents of the losing side.

V. *The Purāṇas.*

I must now advert briefly to the eighteen Purāṇas. They constitute an important department of Sanskṛit literature in their connection with the later phases of Brāhmanism, as exhibited in the doctrines of emanation, incarnation, and triple manifestation (*tri-mūrti*, see pp. 321–324), and are, in real fact, the proper Veda of popular Hindūism, having been designed to convey the exoteric doctrines of the Veda to the lower castes and to women. On this account, indeed, they are sometimes called a fifth Veda (see note 2, p. 371). Their name *Purāṇa* signifies 'old traditional story,' and the eighteen ancient narratives to which this name is applied are said to have been compiled by the ancient sage *Vyāsa* (also called Kṛishṇa-dvaipāyana and Bādarāyaṇa), the arranger of the Vedas and Mahā-bhārata (p. 371, with note 2), and the supposed founder of the Vedānta philosophy (p. 101, note 2). They are composed chiefly in the simple Śloka metre (with occasional passages in prose), and are, like the Mahā-bhārata, very encyclopedical in their range of subjects. They must not, however, be confounded with the Itihāsas, which are properly the histories of heroic *men*, not *gods*, though these men were afterwards deified. The Purāṇas are properly the history of the gods themselves, interwoven with every variety of legendary tradition on other subjects. Viewing them as a whole, the theology they teach is anything but simple, consistent, or uniform. While nominally tritheistic—to suit the three developments of Hindūism explained at p. 324—the religion of the Purāṇas is practically polytheistic and yet essentially pantheistic. Underlying their whole teaching may be discerned the one grand doctrine which is generally found at the root of Hindū theology, whether Vedic or Purānic—pure uncompromising pantheism. But interwoven with the radically pantheistic and Vedāntic texture of these compositions, tinged as it is with other philosophical ideas (especially the Sān-khyan doctrine of Prakṛiti), and diversified as it is with endless fanciful mythologies, theogonies, cosmogonies, and mythical genealogies, we have a whole body of teaching on nearly every subject of knowledge. The Purāṇas pretend to give the history of the whole universe from the most remote ages, and claim to be the inspired revealers of scientific as well as theological truth. They dogmatize on physical science, geography, the form of the earth (see p. 420), astronomy, chronology; and even in the case of one or two Purāṇas, anatomy, medicine, grammar, and the use of military weapons. All this cycle of very questionable omniscience is conveyed in the form of leading dialogues (connecting numerous subordinate dialogues), in some of which a well-known and supposed divinely inspired sage, like Parāśara, is the principal speaker, and answers the inquiries put to him by his disciples; while in others, Loma-harshaṇa (or Roma-harshaṇa), the pupil of Vyāsa, is the narrator, being called Sūta, that is, 'Bard' or 'Encomiast,' as one of an order of men to whom the reciting of the Itihāsas and Purāṇas was especially intrusted.[1]

---

[1] A Sūta was properly the charioteer of a king, and was the son of a Kshatriya by a Brāhmaṇī. His business was to proclaim the heroic

Strictly, however, every Purāṇa is supposed to treat of only five topics :—1. The creation of the universe (*sarga*); 2. Its destruction and re-creation (*prati-sarga*); 3. The genealogy of gods and patriarchs (*vaṉśa*); 4. The reigns and periods of the Manus (*manv-antara*); 5. The history of the solar and lunar races of kings (*vaṉśānućarita*).[1]

---

actions of the king and his ancestors, as he drove his chariot to battle, or on state occasions. He had therefore to know by heart the epic poems and ancient ballads, in which the deeds of heroes were celebrated, and he had more to do with reciting portions of the Mahā-bhārata and Itihāsas than with the Purāṇas. In Mahā-bh. I. 1026 it is said that Sauti or Ugra-śravas (son of the Sūta Loma-harshaṇa) had learnt to recite a portion of the Mahā-bhārata from his father. Generally it is declared that Loma-harshaṇa learnt to recite it from Vaiśampāyana, a pupil of Vyāsa.

[1] Certainly the recounting of royal genealogies is an important part of the Purāṇas. It consists, however, of a dry chronicle of names. Similar chronicles were probably written by the early Greek historians, called λογογράφοι (Thuc. I. 21); but these developed into real histories, which the Indian never did. It was the duty of bards to commit their masters' genealogies to memory, and recite them at weddings or great festivals, and this is done by Bhāṭs in India to this day. In Rāmāyaṇa I. lxx. 19, however, it is the family-priest Vasishṭha who, before the marriage of the sons of Daśaratha with the daughters of Janaka, recites the genealogy of the solar line of kings reigning at Ayodhyā. This dry genealogy of a race of kings is sometimes called *Anuvaṉśa*. Several similar catalogues of the lunar race (Soma-vaṉśa or Aila-vaṉśa), who first reigned at Pratishṭhāna, and afterwards at Hastinā-pura, are found in the Mahā-bhārata (see especially one in prose, with occasional Ślokas called *Anuvaṉśa-śloka* interspersed, Mahā-bh. I. 3759, &c.). Professor Lassen gives valuable lists at the end of vol. i. of his Ind. Alt. It must be noted that both the *solar* and *lunar* races have collateral lines or branches. A principal branch of the *solar* consisted of the kings of *Mithilā* or *Videha*, commencing with the bad king *Nimi*, who perished for his wickedness (Manu VII. 41). His son was *Mithi* (who gave his name to the city), and his son was *Janaka* (so called as the real 'father of the race'); the great and good Janaka, learned in Brahmanical lore, being, it appears, a descendant of this first Janaka. The *lunar* race, to which the Pāṇḍavas belonged, had two principal branches, that of

On this account the oldest native lexicographer Amara-siṉha (see p. 161), whose date was placed by Professor H. H. Wilson at the end of the first century B.C., gives the word *Pańća-lakshaṇa*, 'characterized by five subjects,' as a synonym of Purāṇa. No doubt some kind of Purāṇas must have existed before his time, as we find the word mentioned in the Gṛihya-sūtras of Āśvalāyana (see p. 195 of this volume), and in Manu (see p. 207, note 1, and p. 249 of this volume). The fact that very few of the Purāṇas now extant, answer to the title Pańća-lakshaṇa, and that the abstract given in the Matsya-purāṇa of the contents of all the others, does not always agree with the extant works, either in the subjects described, or number of verses enumerated,[1] proves that, like the Rāmāyaṇa and Mahā-bhārata, they were preceded by more ancient works. In all probability there were *Mūla* or original Purāṇas, as there once existed also a *Mūla* Rāmāyaṇa and *Mūla* Mahā-bhārata. Indeed, in the Bhāgavata-purāṇa XII. vii. 7, six *Mūla-saṃhitāḥ* or original collections are specially declared to have been taught by Vyāsa to six sages, his pupils; and these six collections may have formed the bases of the present works, which, as we shall presently see, are arranged in three groups of six. At any rate, it appears certain that the Purāṇas had an ancient groundwork, which may have been in some cases

---

the *Yādavas* (commencing with *Yadu*, and comprising under it *Arjuna Kārtavīrya* and *Kṛishṇa*), and that of the kings of *Magadha*. The Yādavas had also a collateral line of kings of *Kāśī* or *Vārāṇasī*. For the solar and lunar genealogies see pp. 344 and 375 of this volume.

[1] Thus the *Bhavishya-purāṇa* ought to consist of a revelation of future events by Brahmā, but contains scarcely any prophecies. This work is rather a manual of religious observances; and the commencement, which treats of creation, is little else than a transcript of Manu. We may note, however, that Śan-kara Āćārya often quotes the extant Vishṇu-purāṇa.

reduced by omissions or curtailments, before serving as a basis for the later superstructures. This groundwork became more or less overlaid from time to time by accretions and incrustations; the epic poems, and especially the Mahā-bhārata, constituting the principal sources drawn upon for each successive augmentation of the original work. Nevertheless, it must always be borne in mind that the mythology of the Purāṇas is more developed than that of the Mahā-bhārata, in which (as properly an Itihāsa, and therefore only concerned with kings and heroic men) Vishṇu and Śiva are often little more than great heroes, and are not yet regarded as rival gods. In medieval times, when the present Purāṇas were compiled, the rivalry between the worshippers of Vishṇu and Śiva was in full force—the fervour of their worship having been stimulated by the Brāhmans as an aid to the expulsion of Buddhism—and the Purāṇas themselves were the expression and exponent of this phase of Hindūism. Hence the great antiquity ascribed to the present works by the Hindūs, although it may have had the effect of investing them with a more sacred character than they could otherwise have acquired, is not supported by either internal or external evidence. The oldest we possess can scarcely date from a period more remote than the sixth or seventh century of our era.

Of course the main object of most of the Purāṇas is, as I have already hinted, a sectarian one. They aim at exalting one of the three members of the Tri-mūrti, Brahmā, Vishṇu, or Śiva; those which relate to *Brahmā* being sometimes called *Rājasa* Purāṇas (from his own peculiar Guṇa *rajas*); those which exalt *Vishṇu* being designated *Śattvika* (from his Guṇa *sattva*); and those which prefer *Śiva* being styled *Tāmasa* (from his Guṇa *tamas*). The reason for connecting them with the three Guṇas will be understood by referring to p. 321.

I now give the names of the eighteen Purāṇas according to the above three divisions :—

A. The Rājasa Purāṇas, or those which relate to Brahmā, are, 1. *Brahma*, 2. *Brahmāṇḍa*, 3. *Brahma-vaivarta*, 4. *Mārkaṇḍeya*, 5. *Bhavishya*, 6. *Vāmana*.

B. The S'attvika Purāṇas, or those which exalt Vishṇu, are, 1. *Vishṇu*, 2. *Bhāgavata*, 3. *Nāradīya*, 4. *Garuḍa*, 5. *Padma*, 6. *Varāha*. These six are usually called Vaishṇava Purāṇas.

C. The Tāmasa, or those which glorify S'iva, are, 1. *Śiva*, 2. *Lin·ga*, 3. *Skanda*, 4. *Agni*, 5. *Matsya*, 6. *Kūrma*. These six are usually styled S'aiva Purāṇas. For the 'Agni,' an ancient Purāṇa called '*Vāyu*,' which is probably one of the oldest of the eighteen, is often substituted.

Although it is certainly convenient to group the eighteen Purāṇas in these three divisions in accordance with the theory of the Tri-mūrti or triple manifestation, it must not be supposed that the six Purāṇas in the first, or *Rājasa* group, are devoted to the exclusive exaltation of *Brahmā*, whose worship has never been either general or popular (see note 1, p. 325).

Though these six Purāṇas abound in legends connected with the first member of the Triad, they resemble the other two groups in encouraging the worship of either Vishṇu or S'iva, and especially of Vishṇu as the lover Krishṇa. According to Professor H. H. Wilson some of them are even favourites with the S'āktas (see p. 522 of this volume), as promoting the adoration of the goddess Durgā or Kālī, the personified energy of S'iva.

One of their number, the *Mārkaṇḍeya*, is (as Professor Banerjea has shown in the Preface to his excellent edition of this work) quite unsectarian in character.

This *Mārkaṇḍeya-purāṇa* is, therefore, probably one of the oldest—perhaps as old as the eighth century of our era. Part of it seems to be devoted to Brahmā, part to Vishṇu, and part consists of a *Devī-māhātmya* or exaltation of the female goddess. At the commencement *Jaimini*, the pupil of Vyāsa, addresses himself to certain sapient birds (who had been Brāhmans in a previous birth) and requests the solution of four theological and moral difficulties, viz., 1. Why did Vishṇu, himself being *nirguṇa* (see p. 86), take human form? 2. How could Draupadī become the common wife of the five Pāṇḍavas (see p. 386, with notes)? 3. Why had Bala-rāma to expiate the crime of Brahmanicide committed by him while intoxicated (see p. 391)? 4. Why did the five sons of Draupadī meet with untimely deaths, when Kṛishṇa and Arjuna were their protectors (see p. 389, note 2, and p. 410)?

Another of this group of Purāṇas, the *Brahma-vaivarta*, inculcates the worship of the young Kṛishṇa (*Bāla-kṛishṇa*) and his favourite Rādhā, now so popular in India; from which circumstance this work is justly regarded as the most modern of all the Purāṇas.

Of course it will be inferred from the statement at p. 326 that the second group of Purāṇas—the *Sāttvika* or *Vaishṇava*—is the most popular. Of these the *Bhāgavata* and *Vishṇu*, which are sometimes called *Mahā-purāṇas*, 'great Purāṇas,' are by far the best known and most generally esteemed.

The *Bhāgavata-purāṇa*,[1] in twelve Books, is perhaps the most popular of all the eighteen Purāṇas, since it is devoted to the exaltation of the favourite god Vishṇu or Kṛishṇa, one of whose names is Bhagavat.

It is related to the Ṛishis at Naimishāraṇya by the Sūta (see p. 510), but he only recites what was really narrated by the sage S'uka, son of Vyāsa, to Parīkshit, king of Hastinā-pura, and grandson of Arjuna, who in consequence of a curse was condemned to die by the bite of a snake in seven days, and who therefore goes to the banks of the Ganges to prepare for death. There he is visited by certain sages, among whom is S'uka, who answers his inquiry (how can a man best prepare to die?) by relating the Bhāgavata-purāṇa as he received it from Vyāsa.

Colebrooke believed it to be the work of the grammarian Vopadeva (p. 168 of this volume).

This Purāṇa has been well edited at Bombay with the commentary of Śrīdhara-svāmin.

---

1 A magnificent edition was commenced by Eugène Burnouf at Paris in the 'Collection Orientale,' but its completion was prevented by that great scholar's death.

Its most important Book is the tenth, which gives the early life of Krishṇa. This Book has its Hindī counterpart in the Prem Sāgar, and has been translated into nearly all the languages of India.

An epitome of this part of the work has already been given at p. 332. As an example of the style of the Purāṇas I here give the text of the story related at p. 334 of this volume. It is condensed in *Bhāgavata-purāṇa* X. lxxxix. 1, thus :—

Srī-Śuka uvāća | Sarasvatyās taṭe rājann Ṛishayaḥ satraṃ āsata | Vitarkaḥ samabhūt teshāṃ trishv adhīśeshu ko mahān || Tasya jijñāsayā te vai Bhṛigum Brahma-sutaṃ nṛipa | Taj jñaptyai preshayām-āsuḥ so 'bhyagād Brahmanaḥ sabhām || Na tasmai prahvaṇaṃ stotram ćakre sattva-parīkshayā | Tasmai ćukrodha Bhagavān prajvalan svena tejasā || Sa ātmany utthitam manyum ātma-jāyātmanā prabhuḥ | Aśiśamad yathā vahniṃ sva-yonyā vāriṇātmanaḥ || Tataḥ Kailāsam agamat sa taṃ devo maheśvaraḥ | Parirabdhuṃ samārebha utthāya bhrātaram mudā || Naićchat tvam asy utpathaga iti devaś ćukopa ha | Śūlam udyamya taṃ hantum ārebhe tigma-loćanaḥ || Patitvā pādayor Devī sāntvayāmāsa taṃ girā | Atho jagāma Vaikuṇṭhaṃ yatra devo Janārdanaḥ || Śayānaṃ Śriya utsan·ge padā vakshasy atāḍayat | Tata utthāya Bhagavān saha Lakshmyā satāṃ gatiḥ || Sva-talpād avaruhyātha nanāma śirasā munim | Āhate svāgatam Brahman nishīdātrāsane kshaṇam | Ajānatām āgatān vaḥ kshantum arhatha naḥ prabho || Atīva komalau tāta ćaraṇau te mahā-mune | Ity uktvā vipra-ćaraṇau mardayan svena pāṇinā || Punīhi sahalokam māṃ loka-pālāṅś-ća mad-gatān | Pādodakena bhavatas tīrthānāṃ tīrtha-kāriṇā || Adyāham Bhagaval lakshmyā āsam ekānta-bhājanam | Vatsyaty urasi me bhūtir bhavat-pāda-hatāṅhasaḥ ||

The above story affords a good example of the view taken by the Bhāgavata of the comparative excellence of the three members of the Tri-mūrti.

In VIII. vii. 44, the following sentiment occurs :—

> When other men are pained the good man grieves—
> Such care for others is the highest worship
> Of the Supreme Creator of mankind.

Perhaps the *Vishṇu-purāṇa* as conforming most nearly to the epithet *Pańća-lakshaṇa* (see p. 512), will give the best idea of this department of Sanskṛit literature.

It is in six Books, and is, of course, dedicated to the exaltation of Vishṇu, whom it identifies with the Supreme Being. Book I. treats of the creation of the universe; the peopling of the world and the descent of mankind from seven or nine patriarchs,[1] sons of Brahmā; the destruction of the universe at the end of a Kalpa (see p. 330, note) and its re-creation (*prati-sarga*); and the reigns of kings during the first Manvantara. Book II. describes the various worlds, heavens, hells, and planetary spheres; and gives the formation of the seven circular continents and concentric oceans as described at p. 420 of this volume. Book III. describes the arrangement of the Vedas, Itihāsas, and Purāṇas by Vyāsa, and the institution and rules of caste, in which it follows and resembles Manu. Book IV. gives lists of kings and dynasties. Book V. corresponds to Book X. of the Bhāgavata-purāṇa and is devoted to the life of Kṛishṇa. Book VI. describes the deterioration of mankind during the four ages, the destruction of the world by fire and water, and its dissolution at the end of a Kalpa.

The above is a bare outline of the contents of this Purāṇa. It is encyclopedical, like the others, and is rich in philosophical speculations and curious legends. A passage illustrating the Sān·khyan tone of its philosophy will be found quoted at p. 91 of this volume. The great sage Parāśara, father of Vyāsa (p. 375, note 4), is supposed to relate the whole Purāṇa to his disciple Maitreya. The narrative begins thus:[2]—

Having adored Vishṇu, the lord of all, and revered Brahmā and the rest, and done homage to the Guru, I will relate a Purāṇa, equal to the Vedas [*Praṇamya Vishṇuṃ viśveśam Brahmādīn praṇipatya ća* | *Gurum praṇamya vakshyāmi Purāṇam Veda-sammitam*, I. 3].

---

1 The seven patriarchs or sages (*saptarshayaḥ*, sometimes identified with the seven stars of the Great Bear) were created by Brahmā as progenitors of the human race, and are called his mind-born sons; they are, *Marīći*, *Atri*, *An·giras*, *Pulastya*, *Pulaha*, *Kratu*, and *Vasishṭha*. To these two others are added in Vishṇu-purāṇa I. vii., viz., *Daksha* and *Bhṛigu*. In Manu I. 35, *Nārada* is also added, making ten.

2 In my translations I have consulted Professor H. H. Wilson's great work, but I have had the text of the Bodleian MS. before me.

The metre is generally the simple Śloka, with occasional stanzas in the Indra-vajrā, Vaṇśa-sthavila, &c.

The following is a metrical version of the prayer of Parāśara, addressed to Vishṇu, at the beginning of Book I. 2, (with which compare similar descriptions of the Supreme Being in the Upanishads and Bhagavad-gītā, pp. 43, 131–135 of this volume):—

Hail to thee, mighty Lord, all-potent Vishṇu!
Soul of the Universe, unchangeable,
Holy, eternal, always one in nature,
Whether revealed as Brahmā, Hari, S'iva—
Creator or Preserver or Destroyer—
Thou art the cause of final liberation;
Whose form is one, yet manifold; whose essence
Is one, yet diverse; tenuous, yet vast;
Discernible, yet undiscernible;
Root of the world, yet of the world composed;
Prop of the universe,[1] yet more minute
Than earth's minutest particles; abiding
In every creature, yet without defilement;
Imperishable, one with perfect wisdom.

There is a curious story of the churning of the ocean for the production of the *Amṛita*, 'ambrosial food of immortality,' in Book I. 9, (compare p. 327 of this volume). It is noteworthy as differing considerably from that in Rāmāyaṇa I. xlv. The passage represents Indra and the gods as having lost all their strength—in consequence of a curse pronounced on them by the choleric sage Durvāsas—and so becoming subject to the demons. The gods apply to Vishṇu in their distress, and even Brahmā adores him in a long hymn. I give a portion of the story metrically, changing the order of the text in one or two places:—

---

[1] In the original these three attributes are, *Mūla-bhūto jagataḥ, jaganmayaḥ*, and *ādhāra-bhūto viśvasya*.

The gods addressed the mighty Vishṇu thus—
'Conquered in battle by the evil demons
We fly to thee for succour, Soul of all,
Pity and by thy might deliver us.'
Hari the lord, creator of the world,
Thus by the gods implored, all graciously
Replied—'Your strength shall be restored, ye gods;
Only accomplish what I now command;
Unite yourselves in peaceful combination
With these your foes; collect all plants and herbs
Of diverse kinds from every quarter; cast them
Into the sea of milk; take Mandara,
The mountain, for a churning-stick, and Vāsuki,
The serpent, for a rope; together churn
The ocean to produce the beverage—
Source of all strength and immortality—
Then reckon on my aid, I will take care
Your foes shall share your toil, but not partake
In its reward or drink th' immortal draught.'
Thus by the god of gods advised, the host
United in alliance with the demons.
Straightway they gathered various herbs and cast them
Into the waters, then they took the mountain
To serve as churning-staff, and next the snake
To serve as cord, and in the ocean's midst
Hari himself, present in tortoise-form,
Became a pivot for the churning-staff.
Then did they churn the sea of milk; and first
Out of the waters rose the sacred Cow,
God-worshipped Surabhi—eternal fountain
Of milk and offerings of butter; next,
While holy Siddhas wondered at the sight,
With eyes all rolling, Vāruṇī uprose—
Goddess of wine. Then from the whirlpool sprang
Fair Pārijāta, tree of Paradise, delight
Of heavenly maidens, with its fragrant blossoms
Perfuming the whole world. Th' Apsarasas
Troop of celestial nymphs, matchless in grace,
Perfect in loveliness, were next produced.
Then from the sea uprose the cool-rayed moon,
Which Mahā-deva seized; terrific poison
Next issued from the waters; this the snake-gods

Claimed as their own. Then seated on a lotus,
Beauty's bright goddess, peerless S'rī, arose
Out of the waves; and, with her, robed in white,
Came forth Dhanvantari, the gods' physician.
High in his hand he bore the cup of nectar—
Life-giving draught—longed for by gods and demons.
Then had the demons forcibly borne off
The cup, and drained the precious beverage,
Had not the mighty Vishṇu interposed.
Bewildering them, he gave it to the gods;
Whereat incensed the demon troops assailed
The host of heaven, but they with strength renewed
Quaffing the draught, struck down their foes, who fell
Headlong through space to lowest depths of hell.

The following is part of the prayer of Mućukunda, Book V. 23:—

Lord of the Universe, the only refuge
Of living beings, the alleviator
Of pain, the benefactor of mankind,
Show me thy favour and deliver me
From evil; O creator of the world,
Maker of all that has been and will be,
Of all that moves and is immovable,
Thyself composed of what possesses form,
And what is formless; limitless in bulk,
Yet infinitely subtle; lord of all,
Worthy of praise, I come to thee my refuge,
Renouncing all attachment to the world,
Longing for fulness of felicity—
Extinction of myself, absorption into thee.

The following account of the Kali or fourth age of the world—the age of universal degeneracy—is from Book VI. 1 (compare p. 330, note 3, of this volume):—

Hear what will happen in the Kali age.
The usages and institutes of caste,
Of order and of rank, will not prevail,
Nor yet the precepts of the triple Veda.
Religion will consist in wasting wealth,
In fasting and performing penances

At will; the man who owns most property
And lavishly distributes it, will gain
Dominion over others; noble rank
Will give no claim to lordship; self-willed women
Will seek their pleasure, and ambitious men
Fix all their hopes on riches gained by fraud.
Then women will be fickle and desert
Their beggared husbands, loving them alone
Who give them money. Kings instead of guarding
Will rob their subjects, and abstract the wealth
Of merchants, under plea of raising taxes.
Then in the world's last age the rights of men
Will be confused, no property be safe,
No joy and no prosperity be lasting.

There are eighteen *Upa-purāṇas* or 'secondary Purāṇas,' subordinate to the eighteen *Mahā* or principal Purāṇas, but as they are of less importance I shall do little more than simply give their names as follow:—

1. *Sanatkumāra*; 2. *Nara-siṉha* or Nṛi-siṉha; 3. *Nāradīya* or Vṛihan-nāradīya;[1] 4. *Śiva*; 5. *Durvāsasa*; 6. *Kāpila*; 7. *Mānava*; 8. *Auśanasa*; 9. *Vāruṇa*; 10. *Kālikā*; 11. *Śāmba*; 12. *Nandi*; 13. *Saura*; 14. *Pārāśara*; 15. *Āditya*; 16. *Māheśvara*; 17. *Bhāgavata* (thought to be a misreading for Bhārgava); 18. *Vāśishṭha*. Another list given by Professor H. H. Wilson varies a little, thus: 1. *Sanatkumāra*; 2. *Nara-siṉha*; 3. *Nandā*; 4. *Śiva-dharma*; 5. *Durvāsasa*; 6. *Bhavishya*; 7. *Kāpila*; 8. *Mānava*; 9. *Auśanasa*; 10. *Brahmāṇḍa*; 11. *Vāruṇa*; 12. *Kālikā*; 13. *Māheśvara*; 14. *Śāmba*; 15. *Saura*; 16. *Pārāśara*; 17. *Bhāgavata*; 18. *Kaurma*.

With regard to the second or *Nāra-siṉha Upa-purāṇa* we have an abstract of its contents by Rājendralāla Mitra in his Notices of MSS. (No. 1020), whence it appears that the general character of these works is very similar to that of the principal Purāṇas. For example, Chapters 1–5 give the origin of creation; 6. the story of Vaśishṭha; 18. the praises of Vishṇu; 22. the solar race; 23. the lunar race; 30. the terrestrial sphere. That this work was well known at least five hundred years ago is proved by the fact that Mādhavāćārya quotes from it.

[1] According to Rājendralāla Mitra this is called *Vṛihat* to distinguish it from the Nāradīya, one of the Mahā-purāṇas. He gives an abstract of it in No. 1021 of his valuable Notices of MSS.

The Tantras.

I have already alluded to the Tantras, which represent a phase of Hindūism generally later than that of the Purāṇas, although some of the Purāṇas and Upa-purāṇas, such as the Skanda, Brahma-vaivarta, and Kālikā, are said to teach Tāntrika doctrines, by promoting the worship of Prakṛiti and Durgā.

The Tantras are very numerous, but none have as yet been printed or translated in Europe. Practically they constitute a fifth Veda (in place of the Purāṇas) for the Śāktas or worshippers of the active energizing will (*śakti*) of a god—personified as his wife, or sometimes as the female half of his essence.[1]

It must here be remarked that the principal Hindū deities are sometimes supposed to possess a double nature, or, in other words, two characters, one quiescent, the other active. The active is called his *Śakti*.

Sometimes only eight S'aktis are enumerated and sometimes nine, viz., *Vaishṇavī*, *Brahmāṇī*, *Raudrī*, *Māheśvarī*, *Nārasinhī*, *Vārāhī*, *Indrāṇī*, *Kārttikī*, and *Pradhānā*. Others reckon fifty forms of the S'akti of Vishṇu, besides *Lakshmī*; and fifty of S'iva or Rudra, besides *Durgā* or *Gaurī*. *Sarasvatī* is named as a S'akti of Vishṇu and Rudra, as well as of Brahmā. According to the Vāyu-purāṇa, the female nature of Rudra (S'iva) became two-fold, one half *Asita* or white, and the other half *Sita* or black, each of these again becoming manifold. The white or mild nature includes the S'aktis *Umā*, *Gaurī*, *Lakshmī*, *Sarasvatī*, &c.; the black or fierce nature includes *Durgā*, *Kālī*, *Ćaṇḍī*, *Cāmuṇḍā*, &c.

This idea of personifying the will of a deity may have been originally suggested by the celebrated hymn (129) in

---

[1] It is remarkable, as noticed by Professor H. H. Wilson, that Kullūka-bhaṭṭa, in commenting on Manu II. 1, says, *Śrutiś-ća dvi-vidhā vaidikī tāntrikī ća*, 'revelation is two-fold, Vedic and Tāntric.'

the tenth Maṇḍala of the Ṛig-veda, which, describing the creation, says that Will or Desire (*Kāma*), the first germ (*prathamaṃ retaś*) of Mind, brought the universe into existence (see p. 20 of this volume).

But, in all probability, the Tāntrika doctrine owes its development to the popularizing of the Sāṅkhya theory of *Purusha* and *Prakṛiti* (as described at p. 86 and p. 91 of this volume). The active producing principle, whether displayed in creation, maintenance, or destruction—each of which necessarily implies the other—became in the later stages of Hindūism a living visible personification. Moreover, as destruction was more dreaded than creation or preservation, so the wife of the god Śiva, presiding over dissolution, and called *Kālī*, *Durgā*, *Pārvatī*, *Umā*, *Devī*, *Bhairavī*, &c., became the most important personage in the whole Pantheon to that great majority of worshippers whose religion was actuated by superstitious fears. Sometimes the god himself was regarded as consisting of two halves, representing the male principle on his right side, and the female on his left[1]—both intimately united, and both necessary to re-creation as following on dissolution. It may be easily imagined that a creed like this, which regarded the blending of the male and female principles, not only as the necessary cause

---

[1] This is the *Ardha-mārī* or half male half female form of S'iva. There are two divisions of the S'āktas: 1. the *Dakshiṇāćārins*, 'right-doers,' 'right-hand worshippers,' or *Bhaktas*, 'devoted ones,' who worship the goddess Pārvatī or Durgā openly, and without impure practices; 2. the *Vāmāćārins*, 'left-doers,' 'left-hand worshippers,' or *Kaulas*, 'ancestral ones,' who are said to perform all their rites in secret, a naked woman representing the goddess. The sacred books appealed to by 1. are called the *Nigamas*; by 2. the *Āgamas*. The forms of worship are said to require the use of some one of the five *Ma-kāras*, 'words beginning with the letter *m*,' viz., 1. *madya*, wine; 2. *māṉsa*, flesh; 3. *matsya*, fish; 4. *mudrā*, mystical gestures; 5. *maithuna*, intercourse of sexes.

of production and reproduction, but also as the source of strength, vigour, and successful enterprise, soon degenerated into corrupt and superstitious practices. And, as a matter of fact, the Tāntrika doctrines have in some cases lapsed into a degrading system of impurity and licentiousness.

Nevertheless the original Tantra books, which simply inculcate the worship of the active energizing principle of the deity—full as they are of doubtful symbolism, strange mysticism, and even directions for witchcraft and every kind of superstitious rite—are not necessarily in themselves impure. On the contrary, the best of them are believed to be free from gross allusions, however questionable may be the tendency of their teaching. The truth, I believe, is that they have never yet been thoroughly investigated by European scholars. When they become more so, their connection with a popular and distorted view of the Sāṅ-khyan theory of creation, and perhaps with some corrupt forms of Buddhism, will probably be made clear. It is certain that among the Northern Buddhists, especially in Nepāl, a kind of worship of the terrific forms of Śiva and Durgā appears to have become interwoven with the Buddhistic system.

In all probability, too, the mystical texts (*Mantras*) and magical formularies contained in the Tantras will be found to bring them into a closer relationship with the Atharva-veda than has been hitherto suspected.

As so little is known of these mystical writings, it is not possible to decide at present as to which are the most ancient, and still less as to the date to be assigned to any of them. It may, however, be taken for granted that the extant treatises are, like the extant Purāṇas, founded on older works; and if the oldest known Purāṇa is not older than the sixth or seventh century (see p. 513), an earlier date can scarcely be attributed to the oldest known

Tantra.[1] Perhaps the *Rudra-yāmala* is one of the most esteemed. Others are the *Kālikā*, *Mahā-nirvāṇa* (attributed to Śiva), *Kulārṇava* (or text-book of the Kaulas, see note, p. 523), *Śyāmā-rahasya*, *Śaradā-tilaka*, *Mantra-mahodadhi*, *Uḍḍīśa*, *Kāmada*, *Kāmākhyā*.

I now note some of the subjects of which they treat, merely premising that the Tantras are generally in the form of a dialogue between Śiva and his wife Durgā or Pārvatī, the latter inquiring as to the correct mode of performing certain secret ceremonies, or as to the mystical efficacy of various Mantras used as spells, charms, and magical formularies ; and the former instructing her.

Properly a *Tantra*, like a Purāṇa, ought to treat of five subjects, viz., 1. the creation ; 2. the destruction of the world ; 3. the worship of the gods ; 4. the attainment of all objects, especially of six superhuman faculties ; 5. the four modes of union with the Supreme Spirit. A great variety of other subjects, however, are introduced, and practically a great number of Tantras are merely handbooks or manuals of magic and witchcraft, and collections of Mantras for producing and averting evils. Such, at least, must be the conclusion arrived at, if we are to judge of them by the bare statement of their contents in the Catalogues published by Rājendralāla Mitra and others. I select the following as specimens of what they contain :—

Praise of the female energy ; spells for bringing people into subjection ; for making them enamoured ; for unsettling their minds ; for fattening ; for destroying sight ; for producing dumbness, deafness, fevers, &c. ; for bringing on miscarriage ; for destroying crops ; for preventing various kinds of evil ; modes of worshipping Kālī ; methods of breathing in certain rites ; language of birds, beasts, &c. ; worship of the female emblem, with the adjuncts of wine, flesh-meat, women, &c.

This last is said to be the subject of the Kāmākhyā-tantra.

---

[1] It has been noted that the oldest native lexicographer, Amara Siṉha, does not give the meaning 'sacred treatise' to the word *tantra*, as later writers do.

VI. *The Nīti-śāstras.*

This department of Sanskṛit literature may be regarded as including, in the first place, Nīti-śāstras proper, or works whose direct object is moral teaching; and, in the second, all the didactic portion of the epic poems and other works.

The aim of the *Nīti-śāstras proper* is to serve as guides to correct conduct (*nīti*) in all the relations of domestic, social, and political life. They are either, *A.* collections of choice maxims, striking thoughts, and wise sentiments, in the form of metrical stanzas; or, *B.* books of fables in prose, which string together stories about animals and amusing apologues for the sake of the moral they contain, or to serve as frameworks for the introduction of metrical precepts. These latter often represent wise sayings orally current, or are cited from the regular collections and from other sources.

But besides the Nīti-śāstras proper, almost every department of Sanskṛit literature contributes its share to moral teaching.

Any one who studies the best Hindū writings cannot but be struck by the moral tone which everywhere pervades them. Indian writers, although they do not trouble themselves much about the history of past generations, constantly represent the present condition of human life as the result of actions in previous existences. Hence a right course of present conduct becomes an all-important consideration as bearing on future happiness; and we need not be surprised if, to satisfy a constant longing for *Nīti* or guidance and instruction in practical wisdom, nearly all departments of Sanskṛit literature — Brāhmaṇas, Upanishads, Law-books, Epic poems, and Purāṇas—are more or less didactic, nearly all delight in moralizing and philosophizing, nearly all abound in wise sayings and prudential rules. Scarcely a book or writing of any kind begins without an invocation to the Supreme Being or to some god supposed to represent his overruling functions, and as each work proceeds the writers constantly suspend the main topic, or turn aside from their regular subject for the purpose of interposing moral and religious reflections, and even long discourses, on the duties of life. This is especially the case in the Mahā-bhārata.

Examples of the religious precepts, sentiments, and apophthegms, scattered everywhere throughout Sanskṛit literature, have already been given in this volume (see, for instance, pp. 278–291, 442–461).[1]

We now therefore turn, in conclusion, to the *two divisions of Nīti-śāstras proper.*

A. With regard to the regular collections of moral maxims, sentiments, &c., these are generally in metrical stanzas, and sometimes contain charming allusions to natural objects and domestic life, with occasional striking thoughts on the nature of God and the immortality of the soul, as well as sound ethical teaching in regard to the various relations and conditions of society. They are really mines of practical good sense. The knowledge of human nature displayed by the authors, the shrewd advice they give, and the censure they pass on human frailties—often in pointed, vigorous, and epigrammatic language—attest an amount of wisdom which, if it had been exhibited in practice, must have raised the Hindūs to a high position among the nations of the earth. Whether, however, any entire collection of such stanzas can be attributed to any

---

[1] I need scarcely mention here so well-known and valuable a work as Dr. Böhtlingk's *Indische Sprüche*, which contains a complete collection of maxims, &c., in three volumes, and gives the text of each apophthegm critically, with a German translation.

one particular author is doubtful. The Hindūs, for the reasons we have already stated, have always delighted in apophthegms. Numbers of wise sayings have, from time immemorial, been constantly quoted in conversation. Many thus orally current were of such antiquity that to settle their authorship was impossible. But occasional attempts were made to give permanence to the floating wisdom of the day, by stringing together in stanzas the most celebrated maxims and sayings like beads on a necklace; each necklace representing a separate topic, and the authorship of a whole series being naturally ascribed to men of known wisdom, like Bhartṛi-hari and Ćāṇaka (see p. 507), much in the same way as the authorship of the Purāṇas and Mahā-bhārata was referred to the sage Vyāsa (see p. 371). Among these collections it will be sufficient to note:—

1. The three hundred apophthegms, ascribed to *Bhartṛi-hari*[1] (see p. 533), of which the 1st S'ataka, or collection of a hundred verses, is on love (*śṛin·gāra*), and therefore more lyrical than didactic, the 2nd is on good conduct (*nīti*), and the 3rd on the renunciation of worldly desires (*vairāgya*). 2. The *Vṛiddha-ćāṇakya* or *Rājanīti-śāstra.* 3. The *Ćāṇakya-śataka* or hundred verses (109 in one collection translated by Weber) of *Ćāṇakya*, minister of Ćandra-gupta (see under Mudrā-rākshasa, p. 507). 4. The *Amaru-śataka* or one hundred erotic stanzas of Amaru (already described at p. 454). 5. The *Śārn·gadhara-paddhati*, 'S'ārn·gadhara's collection,' an anthology professing to collect sententious verses from various sources and to give the names of most of the authors, to the number of about 247.[2] Some verses, however, are anonymous.

There are numerous other collections of didactic and erotic stanzas, some of which are quite modern, *e.g.*, the *Subhāshitārṇava*, *Śānti-śataka*, *Nīti-san·kalana*, *Kavitāmṛita-kūpa*, *Kavitārṇava*, *Jnāna-sudhākara*, *Śloka-mālā*, the *Bhāminī-vilāsa* by Jagan-nātha, the *Ćaura-pańćāśika* by Vihlaṇa (edited with Bhartṛi-hari by Von Bohlen).

---

[1] Edited by Von Bohlen, with a Latin translation, in 1833.

[2] See Professor Aufrecht's article on this anthology in vol. xxvii. of the Zeitschrift der Deutschen Morgenländischen Gesellschaft.

B. As to the collections of fables and apologues, these form a class of composition in which the natives of India are wholly unsurpassed.

Sir W. Jones affirmed that the Hindūs claimed for themselves three inventions: 1. the game of chess (*ćaturanga*, see p. 258 of this volume); 2. the decimal figures (see p. 183); 3. the method of teaching by fables. To these might be added: 4. grammar (p. 163); 5. logic (p. 62).

It is thought that both the Greek fabulist Aesop and the Arabian Lokmān[1] (*Lukmān*) owed much to the Hindūs. Indeed, in all likelihood, some ancient book of Sanskṛit apologues, of which the present representative is the *Pańća-tantra*, and which has been translated or paraphrased into most of the dialects of India, as well as into Hebrew, Arabic, Syriac, Pahlavī, Persian, Turkish, Italian, French, German, English, and almost every known language of the literary world, is the original source of all the well-known fables current in Europe and Asia for more than two thousand years since the days of Herodotus (II. 134).[2]

---

[1] According to Herodotus and Plutarch, Aesop lived in the latter part of the sixth century B.C., and was once a slave at Samos. On being freed, he travelled about and visited Croesus, &c. As to Lokmān, probably such a person once lived, though thought by some to be an imaginary character. He is certainly more likely to have borrowed ideas from Indian fabulists than from Job, or Abraham, whose nephew he is said by some Arabic writers to have been. The 31st chap. of the Kurān is called after him, God being made to say, 'We have given him wisdom.'

[2] A Pahlavī version of the Pańća-tantra was the first real translation. It was made in the time of Nūshīrvān, about A.D. 570, and perished with much of the Pahlavī literature when the Arabs invaded Persia. Before its destruction it had been translated into Arabic, about A.D. 760, and was called *Kalīla wa Damna* (= Sanskṛit *Karataka* and *Damanaka*, the names of two jackals) or fables of the Brāhman Bīdpāi. The well-

This *Pańća-tantra*[1]—which is itself the original source of a still later work, the well-known class-book *Hitopadeśa*, 'friendly instruction'—derives its name from being divided into five chapters (*Tantras*); but it is also commonly called the *Pańćopākhyāna*, 'five collections of stories.' The date of the extant Pańća-tantra is usually placed about the end of the fifth century. But the fables of which it consists are many of them referable to a period long preceding the Christian era.

It has even been conjectured that the notion of instructing in domestic, social, and political duties by means of stories in which animals figure as the speakers, first suggested itself to Hindū moralists when the doctrine of metempsychosis had taken root in India. We have seen that a most elaborate theory of transmigration of souls through plants, animals, men, and gods was propounded by Manu at least 500 years B.C., to which date we have conjecturally assigned the existing Code of the Mānavas (see p. 56, note 1, and p. 275). Accordingly there is evidence that contemporaneously with the rise of

---

known Persian *Anvār-i-Suhaili*, 'lights of Canopus,' of Husain Vā'iz, written about the beginning of the fifteenth century, was also an amplification of the Pańća-tantra. Abū-l Fazl, Akbar's celebrated minister, also translated it into simpler Persian and called it *'Iyār-i-Dānish*, 'criterion of knowledge.' An Urdū version, called *Ḳhirad Afroz*, 'illuminator of the understanding,' was made in 1803 by Hāfizu'd dīn Ahmad. The Hebrew version is attributed to one Rabbi Joël. This was translated into Latin by John of Capua at the end of the fifteenth century; and from this various Italian, Spanish, and German translations were made. The English Pilpay's fables is said to have been taken from a French translation. The best of the Turkish versions, called *Humāyūn Nāmah*, was made, according to Mr. E. B. Eastwick, in the reign of the Emperor Sulaimān I., by 'Alī Chalabī bin Sālih.

[1] Edited by Kosegarten in 1848, and lately in India by Professors Bühler and Kielhorn. Translated into German, with an elaborate Introduction, by Professor Benfey in 1859.

Brāhmanism in Manu's time, and the consequent growth of antagonistic systems like Buddhism and the Sāṅkhya philosophy, fables were commonly used to illustrate the teaching of these systems. Thus :—

In the whole fourth Book of the *Sāṅkhya-pravaćana* (see p. 79, note 1) there are constant exemplifications of philosophical truth by allusions to the habits of animals, as recorded in popular stories and proverbs. (For example, *sarpa-vat*, 'like the serpent,' IV. 12; *bhekī-vat*, 'like the female frog,' IV. 16; *śuka-vat*, 'like the parrot,' IV. 25, &c.) Again, one of Kātyāyana's Vārttikas or supplements to a rule of the grammarian Pāṇini (IV. 2, 104; cf. IV. 3, 125) gives a name for the popular fable of the crows and owls (*Kākolūkikā*), the actual title of the fourth Tantra of the Pańća-tantra, *Kākolūkīya*, being formed according to another rule of Pāṇini (IV. 3, 88). This fable is also alluded to in the Sauptika-parvan of the Mahā-bhārata (see p. 409 of this volume). In that Epic, too, other well-known fables are related. For example, the story of the three fishes occurring in Hitopadeśa, Book IV., is found in Śānti-parvan 4889, &c., and that of Sunda and Upasunda in Ādi-parvan 7619.

The fables of the Pańća-tantra and Hitopadeśa are supposed to be narrated by a learned Brāhman named Vishṇu-śarman for the improvement of some young princes, whose royal father had expressed himself grieved by their idle, dissolute habits. Of course, the fables are merely a vehicle for the instruction conveyed. They are strung together one within another, so that before one is finished another is commenced, and moral verses from all sources are interwoven with the narratives.

A still larger collection of tales exists in Sanskṛit literature. It is called the *Kathā-sarit-sāgara*, 'ocean of rivers of stories,' and was compiled by *Soma-deva Bhaṭṭa* of Kaśmīr, towards the end of the eleventh or beginning of the twelfth century, from a still larger work named *Vṛihat-kathā* (ascribed to *Guṇāḍhya*) :—

The *Kathā-sarit-sāgara* [1] consists of eighteen Books (*Lambakas*), containing in all 124 chapters (*Taran·gas*). The second and third Books contain the celebrated story of Udayana (see p. 506). A contemporary of Soma-deva was *Kalhaṇa*, who is said to have written the *Rājataran·giṇī*, 'stream of kings'—a chronicle of the kings of Kaśmīr—about A.D. 1148. This is almost the only work in the whole range of Sanskrit literature which has any historical value. It is mostly composed in the common S'loka metre, and consists of eight chapters (*Taran·gas*).[2]

Other collections of tales and works of fiction—which are not, however, properly Nīti-śāstras—are the following:—

1. The *Daśa-kumāra-ćarita*, 'adventures of ten princes,' a series of tales in prose (but called by native authorities a *Kāvya* or poem) by *Daṇḍin*, who lived in the eleventh century. The style is studiously difficult, long compounds and rare grammatical forms being used. It was edited, with a long Introduction, by Professor H. H. Wilson in 1846. 2. The *Vetāla-pañća-vinśati*, 'twenty-five tales of a demon,' ascribed to an author named *Jambhala-datta*. It is the original of the well-known Hindī collection of stories called *Baitāl-paćīsī*. The stories are told by a Vetāla, or spirit, to king Vikramāditya, who tries to carry off a dead body occupied by the Vetāla. 3. The *Sinhāsana-dvātrinśat* (sometimes called *Vikrama-ćarita* or 'adventures of Vikramāditya'), stories related by the thirty-two images on king Vikramāditya's throne which was dug up near Dhārā, the capital of king *Bhoja*, to whom the tales are told, and who is supposed to have flourished in the tenth or eleventh century. It is the original of the Bengālī *Batriś Sinhāsan*. 4. The *Śuka-saptati* or 'seventy tales of a parrot,' translated into many modern dialects of India (*e.g.*, into Hindūstānī under the title *Totā-kahānī*; several Persian versions called *Tūtī-nāma* being also extant). 5. The *Kathārṇava*, 'ocean of stories,' a collection of about thirty-five comparatively modern stories, attributed to S'iva-dāsa. 6. The *Bhoja-prabandha*, a work by *Ballāla*,

---

[1] The whole work has been excellently edited by Dr. Hermann Brockhaus, all but the first five Lambakas being in the Roman character.

[2] The first six Books were edited and the whole work translated into French by M. Troyer in 1840, and analysed by Professor H. H. Wilson. See Dr. Rost's edition of his works.

celebrating the deeds of king Bhoja. 7. The *Kādambarī*, a kind of novel by *Vāṇa* or *Bāṇa*, who flourished in the seventh century at the court of Harsha-vardhana or S'īlāditya, king of Kanauj. An analysis of this work is given by Professor Weber (vol. i. p. 352 of his Indische Streifen). Good editions have been printed at Calcutta. 8. The *Vāsava-dattā*, a romance by *Subandhu*, written, according to Dr. Fitz-Edward Hall, not later than the early part of the seventh century (see the elaborate Preface to his excellent edition of the work in 1859). This and the previous story, although written in prose, are regarded (like 1) as Kāvyas or poems, and are supposed, like the Rāghava-pāṇḍavīya (p. 453), to contain numerous words and phrases which convey a double sense.

I conclude with examples from Bhartṛi-hari's apophthegms, from the Pañća-tantra, and from the Hitopadeśa.

The following are specimens from *Bhartṛi-hari*:—

Here in this world love's only fruit is won,
When two true hearts are blended into one;
But when by disagreement love is blighted,
'Twere better that two corpses were united (I. 29).

Blinded by self-conceit and knowing nothing,
Like elephant infatuate with passion,
I thought within myself, I all things knew;
But when by slow degrees I somewhat learnt,
By aid of wise preceptors, my conceit,
Like some disease, passed off; and now I live
In the plain sense of what a fool I am (II. 8).

The attribute most noble of the hand
Is readiness in giving; of the head,
Bending before a teacher; of the mouth,
Veracious speaking; of a victor's arms,
Undaunted valour; of the inner heart,
Pureness the most unsullied; of the ears,
Delight in hearing and receiving truth—
These are adornments of high-minded men
Better than all the majesty of Empire (II. 55).

Better be thrown from some high peak,
Or dashed to pieces, falling upon rocks;
Better insert the hand between the fangs

Of an envenomed serpent; better fall
Into a fiery furnace, than destroy
The character by stains of infamy (II. 77).

Now for a little while a child, and now
An amorous youth; then for a season turned
Into the wealthy householder; then stripped
Of all his riches, with decrepit limbs
And wrinkled frame, man creeps towards the end
Of life's erratic course; and, like an actor,
Passes behind Death's curtain out of view [1] (III. 51).

I now give, as an example of an Indian apologue, a nearly literal translation of a fable in the Pańća-tantra (Book V. 8th story):—

The Two-headed Weaver.[2]

Once upon a time there lived in a certain place a weaver (*kaulika*) named Manthara, all the wood-work of whose loom one day fell to pieces while he was weaving. Taking his axe (*kuṭhāra*), he set off to cut fresh timber to make a new loom, and finding a large Siṉśapā tree by the sea-side, and thinking to himself, 'This will furnish plenty of wood for my purpose,' began to fell it. In the tree resided a spirit (*vyantara*), who exclaimed on the first stroke of the axe, 'Hallo, there! what are you about? this tree is my dwelling, and I can't allow you to destroy it; for here I live very happily, inhaling the fresh breezes cooled by the ocean's spray.' The weaver replied, 'What am I to do? unless I get wood, my family must starve. Be quick, then, and look out for another house; for cut your present one down I must, and that too instantly.' The spirit replied, 'I am really quite pleased with your candour, and you shall have any boon you like to ask for; but you shall not injure this tree.' The weaver said he would go home and consult a friend and his wife; and would then come back and let the spirit know what gift he would be willing to take in compensation for the loss of the tree. To this the spirit assented. When the weaver returned home, he found there a particular friend of his—the village

---

[1] The parallel in Shakespeare need scarcely be suggested.

[2] I have omitted some verses in this story, and taken a few liberties. In my translations I have consulted Professor H. H. Wilson, and Professor Benfey's German translation.

barber (*nāpita*). To him he confided all that had occurred, telling him that he had forced the spirit to grant him a boon, and consulting his friend as to what he should demand. The barber said, 'My good fellow, ask to be made a king; then I'll be your prime minister, and we'll enjoy ourselves gloriously in this world and gain felicity in the next. Don't you know the saying?—

A king by gifts on earth achieves renown,
And, when he dies, in heaven obtains a crown.'

The weaver approved his friend's suggestion, but said he must first consult his wife. To this the barber strenuously objected, and reminded him of the proverb:—

'Give women food, dress, gems, and all that's nice,
But tell them not your plans, if you are wise.

Besides, the sagacious son of Bhṛigu has said as follows:—

If you have ought to do and want to do it,
Don't ask a woman's counsel, or you'll rue it.'

The weaver admitted the justice of his friend the barber's observations, but insisted that *his* wife was quite a model woman and wholly devoted to her husband's welfare, and that he felt compelled to ask her opinion. Accordingly he went to her, and told her of the promise he had extorted from the spirit of the tree, and how the barber had recommended his asking to be made a king. He then requested her advice as to what boon he should solicit. She replied, 'You should never listen, husband, to barbers. What can they possibly know about anything? Surely you have heard the saying:—

No man of sense should take as his adviser
A barber, dancer, mendicant, or miser.

Besides, all the world knows that royalty leads to a perpetual round of troubles. The cares of peace and war, marching and encamping, making allies and quarrelling with them afterwards, never allow a monarch a moment's enjoyment. Let me tell you then:—

If you are longing to be made a king,
You've set your heart upon a foolish thing;
The vase of unction at your coronation
Will sprinkle you with water and vexation.'

The weaver replied, 'What you say, wife, is very just, but pray tell me what I am to ask for.' His wife rejoined, 'I recommend you to seek the means of doing more work. Formed as you now are, you can never weave more than one piece of cloth at a time. Ask for an additional pair of hands and another head, with which you may keep a loom going both before and behind you. The profits of the first loom will be enough for all household expenses, and with the proceeds of the second you'll be able to gain consequence and credit with your tribe, and a respectable position in this world and the next.'

'Capital! capital!' exclaimed the husband, mightily pleased with his excellent wife's advice. Forthwith he repaired to the tree, and addressing the spirit, said, 'As you have promised to grant me anything I ask for, give me another pair of arms, and an additional head.' No sooner said than done. In an instant he became equipped with a couple of heads and four arms, and returned home, highly delighted with his new acquisitions. No sooner, however, did the villagers see him, than, greatly alarmed, they exclaimed, 'A goblin! a goblin!' and between striking him with sticks and pelting him with stones, speedilv put an end to his existence.

The following sentiments are also from the Pañća-tantra:—

Praise not the goodness of the grateful man
Who acts with kindness to his benefactors.
He who does good to those who do him wrong
Alone deserves the epithet of good (I. 277).

The misery a foolish man endures
In seeking riches, is a hundred-fold
More grievous than the sufferings of him
Who strives to gain eternal blessedness (II. 127).

Hear thou a summary of righteousness,
And ponder well the maxim: Never do
To other persons what would pain thyself (III. 104).

The little-minded ask: Belongs this man
To our own family? The noble-hearted
Regard the human race as all akin (V. 38).

As a conclusion, I subjoin some sentiments from the *Hitopadeśa* or book of 'friendly advice.' My translations are from the late Professor Johnson's excellent edition:—

HITOPADEŚA—INTRODUCTION.

A sapient man should think of storing up
Knowledge and wealth, as if old age and death
Could ne'er assail him, but should practise virtue
As if already in the grasp of death (3).

Of all possessions knowledge is the best,
For none can steal it, none can estimate
Its value, nor can any one destroy it (4).

Learning, the solver of perplexing doubts,
A sure revealer of the truths that lie
Beyond the sight—is like another eye
For all mankind—who has it not, is blind (10).

Fortune attends the lion-hearted man
Who acts with energy; weak-minded persons
Sit idly waiting for some gift of fate.
Banish all thought of destiny and act
With manly vigour, straining all thy nerve.
When thou hast put forth all thy energy
The blame of failure will not rest on thee (31).

The thought that destiny is ever working
Should not induce abandonment of effort;
Without exertion oil cannot be had
E'en from the seeds of unctuous Sesamum (30).

A chariot moves not with a single wheel,
So fortune acts not without human effort (32).

The fixed result of all one's acts committed
In former births, is called one's destiny;
Therefore let every man apply himself
Unweariedly to doing noble actions (33).

As from a lump of clay the potter moulds
Whate'er he pleases, so a man obtains
The destiny worked out by his own deeds (34).

Objects are best accomplished by exertion,
Not by mere wishes; not by any law
Enters the deer a sleeping lion's maw (36).

Even a blockhead may respect inspire
So long as he is dressed in gay attire;
A fool may cut a dash the wise among,
So long as he has sense to hold his tongue (40).

A piece of glass may like a jewel glow,
If but a lump of gold be placed below;
So even fools to eminence may rise
By close association with the wise (41).

By intercourse with men of lower grade
The mind is lowered; by companionship
With equals it preserves equality;
With higher men it reaches eminence (42).

HITOPADES'A—BOOK I.

Each morning, when thou risest, thus reflect:—
'Some great calamity to-day may happen,
Of sickness, sorrow, death, which will befall?' (3).

Never expect a prosperous result
In seeking profit from an evil quarter;
When there is taint of poison in the cup,
E'en the ambrosial draught which to the gods
Is source of life immortal, tends to death (5).

Subjection to the senses has been called
The road to ruin, and their subjugation
The path to fortune; go by which you please (29).

A combination of e'en feeble things
Is often potent to effect a purpose.
Even fragile straws when twisted into ropes
May serve to bind a furious elephant (35).

A man of truest wisdom will resign
His wealth and even life for good of others;[1]
Better abandon life in a good cause
When death in any case is sure to happen (45).

[1] 1 St. John iii. 16.

Even to foes who visit us as guests
Due hospitality should be displayed;
The tree screens with its shade the man who fells it [1] (60).

The good show pity even to the worthless,
The moon irradiates the meanest hovel (63).

Those who abstain from injury to all,
Who bear with all, and offer an asylum
To all mankind, are journeying to heaven (66).

The only friend that follows us at death
Is virtue; all besides dies with the body [2] (67).

Form neither friendship nor a slight acquaintance
With evil persons; does not charcoal burn
The hand, if hot, and blacken it, if cold? (82).

A good man's mind, even when moved to anger,
Suffers no lasting change; a torch of straw
Avails not to make ocean's waters hot (88).

A wicked man is like an earthen jar,
Broken with ease, repaired with difficulty;
A virtuous man is like a golden vessel,
Hard to be broken, quickly joined together (94).

One thing is in a bad man's heart, another
Is in his words, another in his deeds.
But oneness marks a man of noble mind
In heart, speech, conduct, all the three combined (103).

Wisdom is easy when displayed in giving
Advice to others, but one's self to follow
Good counsel, marks a man of high degree,
Such noble-minded men are rare to see (108).

---

1 Compare Rom. xii. 20: 'If thine enemy hunger, feed him; if he thirst, give him drink.' I have been informed on good authority that Professor H. H. Wilson was first induced to commence the study of Sanskṛit by reading casually in some book or newspaper that this sentiment was to be met with somewhere in Sanskṛit literature.

2 Compare Manu IV. 240, 242.

He has all wealth who has a mind contented.
To one whose foot is covered with a shoe
The earth appears all carpeted with leather (152).

'Tis right to sacrifice an individual
For a whole household, and a family
For a whole village, and a village even
For a whole country's good, but for one's self
And one's own soul, one should give up the world (159).

Accumulated wealth is best preserved
By liberal gifts; e'en as collected waters
Are best secured within a hollow tank,
When by an outlet they refresh the fields (165).

If men are rich with money they possess,
But give not nor enjoy, then are they rich
With money buried in the mines of earth (168).

What boots it to have wealth which is not given,
Nor yet enjoyed? What profits strength to one
Who ne'er assails his foes? Where is the use
Of sacred knowledge if it does not lead
To practice of religion? What avails
A soul to him whose senses are not conquered? (170).

Wealth joined with giving, liberality
Joined with kind words, knowledge without conceit,
Valour with mercy, these are four rare virtues (174).

The wise long not for the impossible,
And grieve not for the irretrievable,
Nor are they in calamity bewildered (181).

Some men, well-read in books, are blockheads still,
But he who puts in practice what he knows
Is truly wise; a medicine, though effective,
Effects no cure by knowledge of its name (182).

Make the best use of thy prosperity,
And then of thy reverses when they happen.
For good and evil fortune come and go
Revolving like a wheel in sure rotation (184).

Strive not too anxiously for a subsistence,
Thy Maker will provide thee sustenance;
No sooner is a human being born
Than milk for his support streams from the breast (190).

He by whose hand the swans were painted white,
And parrots green, and peacocks many-hued,
Will make provision for thy maintenance[1] (191).

How can true happiness proceed from wealth,
Which in its acquisition causes pain;
In loss, affliction; in abundance, folly (192).

A koïl's[2] only beauty is its note,
A woman's is devotion to her husband;
The beauty of the badly-formed is knowledge,
The beauty of ascetics is endurance (212).

Men place not such reliance in a mother,
Nor in a wife, nor in a son, nor brother,
As in a friend affectionate by nature (222).

Man's frame has ever death at hand, successes
Are followed by reverses, friendly meetings
Must end in partings, nothing here is lasting (224).

A friend the sight of whom is to the eyes
A balm, who is the heart's delight—who shares
Our joys and sorrows—is a treasure rare.
But other friendly persons who are ready
To share in our prosperity, abound—
Friendship's true touchstone is adversity (226).

Whoever, quitting certainties, pursues
Uncertain things, may lose his certainties.
What is uncertain is as good as lost (227).

---

[1] Compare St. Matthew vi.

[2] The kokila or koïl is the nightingale of India.

HITOPADEŚA—BOOK II.

The man who is accustomed to regard
With constant looks of sympathy the poor
Beneath him in position feels exalted ;
But he who with habitual envy views
Those higher than himself feels always poor[1] (2).

Let a man strive with earnestness to gain
Possessions unacquired ; when acquired
Let him with care preserve them ; when preserved
Let him increase them ; lawfully increased
Let them be used for acts of pious service (8).

By drops of water, falling one by one,
Little by little, may a jar be filled ;
Such is the law of all accumulations
Of money, knowledge, and religious merit (10).

What burden is too great for able men ?
What is too distant for the energetic ?
What is a foreign country to the wise ?
Who is a stranger to the kindly speaking ? (11).

Let prudent men engage in undertakings
Of diverse kinds, according to their will ;
Yet after all, the issue will be that
Which the Supreme Disposer shall determine (12).

No being perishes before his time,
Though by a hundred arrows pierced, but when
His destined hour comes, though barely pricked
By a sharp point of grass, he surely dies (15).

So long alone does every man fulfil
The true design of life, as long as he
Preserves his independence ; he is dead
Who lives in base subjection to another (20).

---

[1] This verse is amplified, but the sense of the original is, I think, fairly expressed.

How difficult the duty of a courtier!
If silent, he is thought a fool; if clever
In conversation, he is called a chatterer,
Or perhaps a magpie; if submissive, timid;
If now and then impatient under slights,
Then he is called ill-bred; if he should sit
Too close, he is decidedly intrusive;
If too far off, then diffident and sheepish;
The law of service is indeed abstruse,
E'en devotees would find it hard to master (25).

He lives to some good purpose in the world
Who lives for Brāhmans, relatives and friends.
Where is the man who lives not for himself? (34).

As by a toilsome effort some huge rock
Is forced uphill, but in an instant rolled
Down to the valley, so the soul of man
Is only by hard labour made upright,
But easily descends to depths of vice (44).

As one man digs a well, another builds
A lofty wall, so every human being
Sinks down or rises by his own exertions (45).

That man is sapient, who knows how to suit
His words to each occasion, his kind acts
To each man's worth, his anger to his power (48).

Is anything by nature beautiful,
Or the reverse? Whatever pleases each,
That only is by each thought beautiful (50).

Disinclination to begin a work
Through fear of failure, is a mark of weakness;
Is food renounced through fear of indigestion? (54).

That faculty which qualifies a man
To earn subsistence, and which wise men praise,
Should be preserved and carefully improved (63).

A jewel may be placed upon the foot,
And glass be raised to decorate the head,
But at the time of purchasing or selling,
Glass will be reckoned glass; a gem, a gem (66).

If glass be used to decorate a crown
While gems are taken to bedeck a foot,
'Tis not that any fault lies in the gems,[1]
But in the want of knowledge of the setter (72).

The wise have said that profitable lessons
May oftentimes be learnt e'en from a child;
When the sun sets a taper may give light (78).

A man may on affliction's touchstone learn
The worth of his own kindred, wife, dependants;
Also of his own mind and character.

'Reason indeed is stronger than brute force,'
Such is the truth the sounding drum proclaims,
Beaten by him who drives the elephant (85).

Kṛishna replied not to his cursing foe,
The lion answers not the jackal's yell,
But roars responsive to the thunder-cloud (86).

The hurricane uproots the lofty trees,
But injures not the grass that prostrate lies;
The mighty only fight against the mighty (87).

A minister is like a small-necked jar
Of wide capacity, but yielding little.
He who says 'What's a moment?' is a fool.
He who says 'What's a farthing?' will be poor (91).

An old domestic long employed in service
Is fearless though in fault; at other times
Acting unchecked he disregards his master (98).

He who is made the intimate associate
Of a king's sports, regards himself as king;
Contempt is sure to be displayed by one
Admitted to too close familiarity (100).

Ingenious men can make e'en falsehoods seem
Like truths, as skilful painters represent
Mountains and valleys on a level surface (112).

---

[1] Compare one of the meditations of Marcus Aurelius: 'Is such a thing as an emerald made worse than it was, if it is not praised?' Rev. F. W. Farrar's 'Seekers after God,' p. 306.

In case of some calamity impending,
In going a wrong road, or when a time
For action presses, brooking no delay,
Then only may a friend advise unasked (123).

He who is truly loved is still beloved,
Even when doing irritating acts;
Who does not feel the same respect for fire
Though it consume the treasures in his house? (132).

A man innately bad, though vigorous efforts
Be constantly applied for his improvement,
Will in the end revert to his old nature;
E'en as the curly tail of some young cur,
Though pressed and swathed with bandages for years,
Resumes its twist, when once again set free (136, 137).

Whate'er thou hast to take, that take thou quickly;
Give quickly what thou hast to give; do quickly
The work thou hast to do; if thou delay,
Time will drink up the spirit of thy act (145).

Bad men derive some beauty from the lustre
Of their connections, like the sooty powder
Laid on the eyelash of a lovely woman (157).

Just anger may be certainly appeased
By the removal of its cause, but how
Can any one allay the spite of him
Who cherishes unreasonable rancour? (159).

A hundred kindly acts are thrown away
Upon the bad; a hundred clever speeches
Are lost on him who cannot understand;
A hundred admonitions, on the man
Who will not put in practice what is said;
A hundred sapient precepts, on the senseless (161).

In sandal-trees are serpents, in the waters
Of pleasant pools are lovely lotus-flowers,
But also alligators; in enjoyments
Evils are present to destroy their zest;
No earthly pleasures are without alloy (162).

A bark displays its uses in the crossing
Of pathless waṭers; at th' approach of night
A lantern is of service; in a calm
A fan; and for an elephant's restraint
A hook; thus is there nothing upon earth
For which a remedy has not been planned
By the all-wise Creator, but, I think,
That Providence himself has failed to find
A fitting check to curb a wicked man (165).

A man, however strong, if destitute
Of zeal and fervour, is by all held cheap.
Who fears to trample upon burnt-out ashes? (173).

HITOPADES'A—BOOK III.

Advice tends only to exasperate,
Not to allay the anger of a fool;
Just as the drinking of nutritious milk
Only augments the venom of a serpent (4).

He who comparing well the strength and weakness
Of others, by himself, discovers not
The difference, is vanquished by his foes (8).

Seek not companionship with evil men,
But court association with the great;
The purest water in the hand of her
Who lives by selling drams, is called a dram (11).

Even kind words accompanied with smiles,
If spoken by bad men, excite suspicion,
Like scent of fragrant flowers out of season (25).

A husband is a wife's chief ornament;
She needs no other ornament but him;
Deprived of him, she shines not, though adorned (29).

A rock is not so easily upheaved
By a strong hand[1] as by a wooden lever;
This is the great advantage of good counsel,
That by an insignificant appliance
A great success may often be effected (45).

---

[1] I follow B.'s reading here.

When danger is far off, then cautiousness—
But when at hand, heroic fortitude—
Is the distinctive merit of a man
Of noble spirit; everywhere the great
Exhibit courage in adversity (47).

A feverish display of over-zeal
At the first outset, is an obstacle
To all success; water, however cold,
Will penetrate the ground by slow degrees (48).

A store of grain is of all stores the best;
A jewel in the mouth supports not life (58).

Whate'er the natural propensity
Of any one may be, that is most hard
To be subdued; thus, if a dog were raised
To a king's rank, would he not gnaw his shoe? (61).

That is no counsel where no elders are,
Those are no elders who declare no law,
That is not law which is not marked by truth,
That is not truth which is by fear affected (64).

Those who, neglecting accurate inquiries
Into the measure of a foe's resources,
Commence a fight, receive a cold embrace
By the sword's edge, and must be reckoned fools (70).

Advice, though good, and strictly in accordance
With books, is useless if it be not followed;
Mere knowledge of a medicine does not cure (71).

Man is a slave of money, not of man;
According to his wealth, his fellow-men
Hold him in honour or in disesteem (81).

The honours that a king confers, do more
To stimulate the courage of his subjects,
Than any hope of money recompense (91).

Even a foe, if he perform a kindness,
Should be esteemed a kinsman; e'en a kinsman,
If he do harm, should be esteemed a foe.

A malady, though bred within the body,
Does mischief; while a foreign drug that comes
From some far forest does a friendly work (101).

Speak kindly, without cringing; be heroic,
But not a boaster; be a generous giver,
But give your bounty to deserving persons;
Be ever bold, but always without harshness (106).

The king whose doctor, minister, and priest
Are flatterers, is speedily bereft
Of health, of treasure, and of piety.

The skilful man attains to wealth, the eater
Of wholesome food, to health—the healthy man
To ease; the diligent to utmost range
Of knowledge; the disciplined in heart
To true religion, riches, and renown (117).

A lofty station cannot be obtained
By one who acts with rashness, yielding solely
To impulse, nor by one whose energies
Of mind are paralysed by pondering
On ways and means of acting; great successes
Depend on hardihood combined with prudence (120).

What will books do for one who has no sense?
How can a mirror benefit the blind? (123).

The wisdom of a counsellor is shown
In healing breaches; of a wise physician
In complicated cases of disorder.
'Tis easy to be wise, when all is well (125).

Weak-minded men are easily bewildered
Even in trifling enterprises, those
Whose intellects are well-matured engage
In mighty undertakings and stand fast (126).

The goddess of good fortune ne'er deserts
That noble-minded monarch who withholds
The smallest piece of money, equally
With thousands, if it seem in danger
Of application to improper uses;
But readily bestows with open hand
E'en tens of millions on a fit occasion (127).

He is a fool who loses a possession
Through fear of some slight outlay; who would forfeit
A bale of goods rather than pay a toll (129).

A crocodile, however fierce, is powerless
Soon as he quits the water; even lions
Out of a forest might as well be jackals (139).

In this uncertain world, unstable as
The ocean stirred by winds, the sacrifice
Of one's own life to save the life of others
Is an exalted action, which results
From merit earned in former states of being (146).

HITOPADEŚA—BOOK IV.

An unwise man, when meeting with disaster,
Blames Destiny, and sees not that the fault
Lies in himself and in his own misdoings (3).

That man has wisdom who is wise enough
To remedy disaster when it happens (6).

Whatever fate decrees is not to be,
That will not happen; if it is to be,
'Tis sure to come to pass. Why drink not off
This anodyne—the antidote of care? (9).

Let not the labour of an honest servant,
Who strives to do his duty, seem in vain;
But cheer him with rewards, with heart, voice, look (12).

A low-born person should not be exalted
To any high position; once in office
He cannot easily be set aside.
Honour conferred upon a base-born man
Resembles an impression stamped on sand (13).

So long alone ought danger to be feared
As long as it is distant; when we see
The cause of apprehension close at hand,
We ought to fight against it fearlessly (17).

A monarch has a real ally in him
Who, faithful to his duty, disregarding
His royal master's likings and dislikings,
Tells him unwelcome salutary truths (21).

A man should ever strive to be at peace
Even with those who equal him in strength;
The victory in war is always doubtful.
Who but a silly person would commit
His friends, his army, realm, renown, and self
To the uncertain balance of a battle? (22, 23).

The monarch who distributes equitably
His riches, who conceals his spies from view,
Who keeps his counsel secret, and who says
No unkind words to those around him, he
May spread his kingdom even to the sea (54).

Whatever be the recompense obtained
By a Horse-sacrifice, accomplishing
All wishes; that will he achieve in full
Who gives protection to a fugitive (62).

External deference may be consistent
With malice in the heart,[1] for do not people
Bear wood upon their heads that they may burn it?
A running river may refresh a tree
While undermining by its stream the roots (64).

What cause have we to grieve for those who die?
Since when a child is born Mortality
Is the first loving nurse to fondle it
In close embrace, and not till thus caressed
May its own mother fold it to her breast (67).

Whither have gone the rulers of the earth
With all their armies, all their regal pomp,
And all their stately equipages? Earth,
That witnessed their departure, still abides (68).

---

[1] This amplification seems necessary to the sense.

All unobserved the body wastes away,
Moment by moment, like a crumbling jar
Of unbaked clay in water; when dissolved,
Then its decaying nature is perceived (69).

Nearer and ever nearer, day by day,
Doth death advance towards each living being,
E'en as an awful executioner
Draws nearer to a criminal condemned,
And drags him by slow degrees towards his doom (70).

Youth, beauty, life, a store of worldly goods,
Exalted rank, society of friends,
Are all unstable, let no man of sense
Be duped by trusting to their permanence (71).

As drifting logs of wood may haply meet
On ocean's waters surging to and fro,
And having met, drift once again apart,
So fleeting is the intercourse of men (72).

E'en as a traveller meeting with the shade
Of some o'erhanging tree, awhile reposes,
Then leaves its shelter to pursue his way,
So men meet friends, then part with them for ever (73).

This is no permanent companionship
Gained by residing with one's own frail body,
Much less by intercourse with other persons (76).

For union points to coming separation,
As birth to death's infallible approach (77).

As streams of rivers ever onward flow,
Never returning, so do day and night
Go on for ever, bearing off man's life (79).

As oft as men of thoughtful minds, reflect
On death's inexorable rod, impending
O'er their doomed heads, their energies relax
Like thongs of leather soaked by dropping rain (83).

'Tis ignorance that is the cause of sorrow
For those who die; if separation cause it,
Then with the lapse of time grief should increase;
As days pass on why does it rather cease? (85).

A panacea for the cure of blows
Dealt suddenly by unexpected strokes[1]
Of deep affliction, rending all the soul—
Is to control the will and stifle thought (86).

E'en in a forest vices may be practised
By those who foster there their evil passions;
While in a house, subjection of the senses
Is a true penance, and the home of one
Who, holding all his passions in restraint,
Engages in good actions, is a convent (87).

Cease not, whatever be thy mode of life,
Although distressed, to walk in righteous paths,
And act with justice towards every creature.
No outward badge is proof of piety (88).

Thou art thyself a stream whose sacred ford
Is self-restraint, whose water is veracity,
Whose bank is virtue, and whose waves are love;
Here practise thy ablutions, by mere water
The inner man can ne'er be purified (90).

That man attains to happiness who quits
This unsubstantial world—a world beset
With pains of birth and death, old age and sickness (91).

Pain and not pleasure has a real existence—
'Tis hence, the name of pleasure is applied
To that which gives relief from present pain (92).

A roaring noise, like that of autumn-cloud,
Should not be made in vain, one really great
Proclaims not his successes or reverses (95).

War not with many foes; by swarming insects
Even a mighty serpent is destroyed (96).

Lust, anger, love of money, overjoy,
Pride and conceit, this six-fold class of faults
Should be forsaken; then one may be happy (99).

---

[1] B.'s reading.

Good memory, activity in business,
Thoughtful deliberation, accuracy
Of information, firmness and concealment
Of counsel, are a minister's prime virtues (100).

Do nothing rashly, want of due reflection
Is the chief source of failure; Fortune, eager
To favour merit, of her own accord,
Chooses the man who acts deliberately (101).

The qualities and course of life of those [1]
Who live in distant places, out of sight,
Can only from their actions be inferred,
And actions must be judged of by results (105).

A swan that could not clearly see by night,[1]
Searching for food upon a lotus-pool,
Mistook the mirrored image of the stars
For tender shoots of lilies, then by day
The silly bird refused to peck the buds,
Thinking them stars; thus persons once deceived
Suspect deception even in the truth (106).

A mind which has been poisoned by the wicked
Confides not even in the good, a child
Once scalded by hot porridge will not drink
Even cold milk till he has blown upon it (107).

By gifts of money one may win a miser;
By gestures of respect, a stubborn man;
A simpleton by humouring his will;
A wise man, only by veracity (108).

Who would be guilty of unrighteous acts
For or against a body doomed to die
To-day or perhaps to-morrow by the pains
Of some disease, or some heartrending grief? (132).

Do rightly, knowing that thy life resembles
The moon's reflection on the quivering wave (133).

---

[1] B.'s reading.

In order to the increase of thy virtue
And of thy happiness, consort thou only
With righteous men, remembering that thy life
Is transient as the mirage of the desert (134).

If Truth and thousands of Horse-sacrifices
Were weighed together, Truth would be more weighty (135).

INDEX.

Observe—In the following Index the numbers indicate the pages. When more than one page is given, the numbers are separated by semicolons. A unit separated from a preceding number by a comma, indicates the number of a footnote.

Abhāva, 66.
Abhidhāna-ćintāmaṇi, 161.
Abhidhāna-ratnamālā, 161.
Abhijit, 341, 1.
Abhijñāna-śakuntala, 507, 1.
Abhimanyu, 389, 2; 398; 404.
Abhirāma-maṇi, 367.
Abhisheka, 391.
Abhyāsa, 93.
Ābhyudayika Śrāddha, 200.
Abū-l Fazl, 529, 2.
Āćāra, 208; 213; 261; 278; 292; 294.
Āćārya, 232; 240; 295; 409.
Accent, 153; 245, 2.
Acesines, river, 375, 1.
Achilles, 313, 1; 357, 1.
Action, 470.
Aćyuta, 390, 1.
Aćyuta-ćakravartin, 304.
Adbhuta, 457, 1.
Adhidaivikam, 217.
Adhikāra, 165.
Adhimāsa, 174.
Adhiratha, 377.
Adhishṭhāna, 198, 3.
Adhiyajñam, 217.
Adho-nivītāḥ, 196.
Adhvaryu (priests), 6; 216.
Adhyāpanam, 237.
Adhy-ātmam, 139.
Adhyātma-rāmāyaṇa, 368.
Ādhyātmika, 217; 278, 1.
Adhyāvāhanikam, 268.
Adhyayanam, 237.
Ādi Grantha, of Sikhs. 325, 1.
Ādi-parvan, 371, 1; 373.
Ādiśūra, 210, 1.
Ādīśvara, 210, 1.
A-diti, 9; 14.
Āditya, 521.
Ādityas, twelve, 10; 320; 399.
Āditya-vāra, 178, 1.
Admetus and Alcestis, 395.
Adṛishṭa, 3; 58; 71; 73; 74; 120; 282, 2; 469.
A-dvaita, 'non-dualism,' 102.
A-dvayam, 113, 4.
Aegle Marmelos, 444.
Aeneid, 58, 1.
Aesop, 529.
Āgama, 523, 1.
Agamemnon, 425.
Agastya, 234, 1; 353; 504.
Ages, four, 178, 2; 221.
Aghora-ghaṇṭa, 500; 501.
Āgneyāstra, 404, 1.
Agni, 11; 15; 16, 1; 189; 256; 321; 430; 514.
Agni, a prayer to, 27, 1.
Agni-hotra, 28, 1; 121; 148; 244; 254.
Agnihotra-homaḥ, 216.
Agnihotrin, 189, 1.
Agnimitra, 498.
Agni-purāṇa, 292; 368.
Agnishṭoma, 187; 231; 232, 1.
Agni-veśa, 369.
Agrahāyaṇa, 173, 3.
Agrāyaṇa, 158.
Ahalyā, wife of Gautama, 387, 1.
Ahan-kāra, 53, 3; 83; 84; 86; 117; 140; 221.
Āhavanīya fire, 188, 1; 189, 1; 196; 197.
Ahi, 14.
A-hiṉsā, 242, 2.
Ahura Mazda, 10.
Āhvaya, 261.
Aila, 375.
Aila-vaṉśa, 511, 1.
Airāvata, Indra's elephant, 353; 432, 1.
Aitareya Āraṇyaka, 245, 2.
Aitareya Upanishad, 35.
Aitareya-brāhmaṇa, 25; 28; 29; 32; 172; 245, 2; 330, 3.
Aitihāsikas, 158.
Aja, 344; 409, 2.
Ajīgarta, 26; 27.
Ājmīr, 325, 1.
Ākāśa, 53, 1; 67; 83; 83, 3.
Akbar, Emperor, 529, 2.
Ākhyāna, 207, 1; 249; 370, 1.
Ākhyāta, 151; 160.
Aksha-pāda, 65, 1; 79, 1
Akshapāda-darśana, 118.
Ākshepa, 458.
Alan-kāra-kaustubha, 470.
Alan-kāras, 456; 457.
Alan-kāra-sarvasva, 470.
Alan-kāra-śāstra, 469.
Albert, King Charles, 336, 1.
Alexander's death, 507.
Alexander's invasion, 252; 316.
Algebra, invention of, 174.
Algebra, Hindū, 180; 181.
Algebraists, Hindū, 181.
Allegory of two birds, 40; 222.
Allen, W. H. & Co., 495.
Alliteration, employment of, 455.
Almanacs, 178, 1.
Amara-kosha, 161; 432, 1.
Amara-siṉha, 512; 525, 1.
Amaru, 454.
Amarū-śataka, 454; 528.
Ambālikā, 376.
Ambarīsha, 27, 1; 344; 361, 1.
Ambashṭha, 210, 1; 225.
Ambikā, 376.
Amlikā, 423, 3.
Amṛita, 327; 518.
Amūlam mūlam, 81; 82.
Amūrta, 177.
Amyak, 159.
Analysis, 60; 161.
Ānanda-maya, 114.
Ānanda-tīrtha, 119

Ananta, 431.
Ananta-vijaya, 403.
Anargha-rāghava, 367; 508.
An-ārya, 310.
An-āryas, 308.
An-āśrita, 299.
Anasūyā, wife of Atri, 360, 1.
Anatomy, 184.
An-aupādhikaḥ sambandhaḥ, 63.
Anaximander, 52, 1.
Anaximenes, 52, 1.
Aṇḍa, 220.
Andhakas, 399.
Andromache, 313, 1; 440.
An·ga, kingdom of, 340; 417; 470; 472.
An·ga-rāga, 360, 1.
An·giras, 6; 203; 216; 235; 252, 2; 301; 517, 1.
An·gushṭha-mātra, 198, 3.
Anila (Wind), 256.
Animals, 55, 3; 276.
Añjalika, 405, 1.
Añjana, 432, 1.
An·ka, 183; 470; 471.
An·kuśa, 183.
Anna-maya, 114.
Anna-prāśana, 192; 232; 239.
Antaḥ-karaṇa, 53; 53, 3; 116.
Antaḥsañjñā, 56, 1.
Antarīksha, 197.
Antar-vedi, 196.
Anthropomorphism, 319.
Antiochus and Eumenes, 252, 1.
Antya, 243.
Anubandha, 163; 163, 3.
Anudāttoktyā, 473.
Anukramaṇī or 'Indices,' 184.
Anumāna, 61; 82; 117; 222.
Anumati, 158; 172.
An-upalabdhi, 117.
Anuprāsa, 457.
Aṇus or 'atoms,' 71.
Anuśāsana-parvan, 374; 411.
Anushṭubh metres, 155; 213, 1; 311; 335.
Ānuśravika, 48, 1.
Anuvaṇśa-śloka, 511. 1.
Anuvṛitti, 165.
Anvāhārya, 249.
Anvāhārya-paćana fire, 189, 1.
Anvār-i-Suhaili, 529, 2.
Anvashṭakya Śrāddha, 193.
Ānvīkshikī, 'logic,' 219.
Apad-dharma, 374.
Apara, 69.
Aparārka, 303.
Aparatva, 68.
Āpas, 'water,' 67; 84.
Āpasadaḥ, 244.
Āpastamba, 203; 203, 1; 236, 1; 302.
Āpastamba Gṛihya-sūtra, 187.
Āpastamba Śrauta-sūtra, 146; 187, 1.
Āpastambas, 187, 1.
Apavarga, 59; 63.
Aphorisms, 46.
Aphrodite, 327, 5.
Āpiśali, 161, 2.
Apologue, Indian, 534.
A-prakṛita, 457.
A-prastuta, 457.
Apsaras, 276; 519.
Āpta-vaćana, 82.
Apya-dīkshita, 470.
Āpyāya, 470.
Ārabhaṭī, 503, 1.
Arabs, 180, 2.
Araṇi, 15.
Araṇya-kāṇḍa, 337; 366.
Āraṇyakas, 34.
Arbuda, 399.
Archery, 184.
Architecture, 184.
Ardha-nārī (Śiva), 89; 322, 1; 523, 1.
Argha, 295; 295, 3; 391.
Ārhata-darśana, 118.
Aristotle, 51, 3; 57, 1; 61; 68, 1; 70; 85, 1; 103; 115; 116, 1; 403, 1.
Aritra, 227, 1.
Arjuna, 100; 126; 229, 1; 379; 387, 1; 403; 413; 419; 431, 1; 511, 1.
Āropa, 458.
Arrian, 252, 1.
Ārsha (revealed knowledge), 214.
Ārsha form of marriage, 190; 244.
Ars poetica, 456.
Artha, 63; 195.
Arthālan·kāra, 457.
Arthāntara-nyāsa, 458.
Arthāpatti, 117; 458.
Artha-vāda, 24.
Aruṇa, 428.
Arundhatī, 191.
Ārya, 'noble,' 310.
Ārya-bhaṭṭa, 175.
Aryaman, 16; 190.
Āryans, 6; 311.
Āryāshṭa-śata, 175.
Āryāvarta, 226, 1.
A-samavāyi-kāraṇa, 70.
Āsana, 'postures,' 93.
A-śauća, 6.
Āśaućam, 300.
Asceticism, 93; 94; 129.
Āshāḍha, 173, 3.
Ashāḍhā, 173, 3; 199.
Ashṭādhyāyī, 163.
Ashṭakā Śrāddha, 193; 199.
Ashṭakam Pāṇinīyam, 163.
Ashṭākshara, 154.
Ashṭa-mūrti, 323, 1.
Asiatic Researches, 96; 155, 2.
Asi-patra-vana, 415.
Asita, 520.
Aśoka, 371, 1; 423, 3; 467.
Aśoka inscriptions, 313.
Āśramas or 'Orders,' 215; 238.
Āśramavāsika, 411, 1.
Āśramavāsika-parvan, 374.
Assessors, 296.
Astrologer, 179.
Astrology, 174; 179.
Astronomy, 170; 172; 174.
A-śući, 216.
Āsura, 244.
Āsura form of marriage, 190.
Asura C'ārvāka, 382, 3.
Asuras, 159; 394.
Asūryam-paśyā, 437, 1.
Āśvalāyana Gṛihya-sūtra, 186; 186, 2; 188; 245, 2; 294, 3; 295, 2; 371, 1; 512.
Āśvalāyana Śrauta-sūtra, 146; 186, 2; 245, 2.
Āśvalāyana-brāhmaṇa, 25, 3.
Aśva-medha, 28, 1; 187; 340; 374.
Āśvamedhika-parvan, 374.
Asvāmi-vikraya, 261.
Aśva-pati, king of Kekaya, 341, 2.
Aśvattha, 'holy fig-tree,' 39, 3.
Aśvatthāman, 383, 1; 405; 407; 409; 481.
Aśvin, 365, 1.
Āśvina, 173, 3.
Aśvinī, 173, 3; 428, 3.
Aśvinī-kumāras, 428.
Aśvins, 11; 158; 379; 387, 1; 400.
Atala, 431, 1.
Atharvan, 216; 235.
Atharvān·giras, 195; 245, 2; 295.
Atharva-veda, 3; 5; 12; 22; 245, 2; 275.
Atharva-veda-prātiśākhya, 151.
Atheists, 249.
Athene, temple of, 133, 8.
Athenians, 224, 1.

Atikāya, 382, 3.
Ati-kṛiććhra penance, 273.
Atirātra, 341, 1.
Atiśayokti, 458.
Atithi, 250.
Atithi-bhojana, 188, 1.
Ātivāhika, 198, 3.
Ati-vyāpti, 63, 1.
Ātma-bodha, 110; 113.
Ātman, 63; 67; 74; 220; 222; 290, 3.
Ātmane-pada, 164; 165.
Ātma-tushṭi, 208.
Ātma-tyāginyaḥ, 299.
Ātma-vidyā, 219.
Atoms, 71.
Atri, 203; 301; 375; 517, 1.
Aufrecht, Professor, 528, 2.
Aulūkya-darśana, 118.
Aupamanyava, 159.
Aurangzīb, 325, 1.
Aurelius, Marcus, 45, 1; 142; 143; 544, 1.
Aurṇabhāva, 158.
Auśanasa, 521.
Austin, Stephen, 495, 1.
Authority of Veda, 215.
Auttami, Manu, 206, 1.
Avakā, 198, 3.
Āvaraṇa, 109.
Avarodha, 437, 2.
Avasathya fire, 189, 1.
Avayava, 'member of an argument,' 61; 64.
A-vidyā, 109.
A-vyakta, 82; 220.
Avyakta-gaṇita, 176, 3.
Avyayī-bhāva, 152.
Ayodhyā, 27, 1; 317; 335, 1; 351; 359; 499, 1.
Ayodhyā-kāṇḍa, 337; 366.
Āyogava, 225.
Āyur-veda, 184.
Āyus, 375.
Azalī, 'without beginning,' 51, 2.

Babhru-vāhana, 390.
Bādarāyaṇa, 101; 245, 2; 509.
Bāgdis, 210, 1.
Bahu-janma-bhāk, 18, 1.
Bahu-prajāḥ, 18, 1.
Bahurūpa, 409, 2.
Bāhuśālin, 381, 4.
Bahu-vrīhi, 152.
Bahv-ṛića, 216.
Baidya, 210, 1.
Bailee, 263.
Bailments, 263.
Baitāl-paćīsī, 532.
Baka, 386.
Bala, 'strength,' 387, 1.
Baladeva, 387, 1.
Bāla-kāṇḍa, 337; 366.
Bāla-kṛishṇa, 515.
Bālam-bhaṭṭa, 304.
Bala-rāma, 332; 374; 375; 383; 391; 398; 408; 515.
Bāla-rāmāyaṇa, 367; 508.
Bali, 188, 1; 194; 245; 259; 328.
Ballāla, 532.
Ballantyne, Dr., 60, 1; 70, 1; 74; 79, 1; 88, 1; 470, 1.
Bāṇa, 367; 533.
Bandyopādhyāya, 210, 1.
Banerjea, Professor K. M., 65; 73; 74, 2; 96; 210, 1; 365, 1.
Banerjea's Dialogues, 181.
Banians, 224, 2.
Banias, 224, 2.
Bāṇijya, 237, 2.
Baṇik, 224, 2.
Baniyās, 224, 2.
Bāpudeva Śāstrī, 175, 2.
Bard, 510.
Barth, M., Revue Critique, 255, 1.
Baṭn, 33.
Batrīś Siṇhāsan, 532.
Bauddha-darśana, 118.
Baudhāyana, 203; 203, 1; 302.
Baudhāyana Gṛihya Sūtras, 187.
Baudhāyana Śrauta Sūtras, 146.
Bear, Great, 517, 1.
Bediyās, 210, 1.
Behār, 302.
Benares, school of, 302; 304.
Benfey, Professor, 530, 1; 534, 2.
Bengal, 303.
Bengal, school of law, 302.
Bentinck, Lord William, 252, 2.
Berkeley, 53, 1; 82, 1; 84, 2; 89, 2.
Bhā (in algebra), 183.
Bhadra, 432, 1.
Bhādra, 173, 3.
Bhādrapada, 173, 3.
Bhadra-padā, 173, 3.
Bhāga, 178.
Bhagaṇa, 178.
Bhagavad-gītā, 39, 3; 47; 55, 3; 91; 91, 1; 93; 100; 122; 317; 324, 2; 401; 518.
Bhagavat, 515.
Bhāgavata-purāṇa, 126, 1; 327, 2; 331; 389, 2; 515; 516.
Bhāgavatas, 325, 1; 514; 521.
Bhagīratha, 344; 362; 363.
Bhāgīrathī, 363.
Bhāguri, 303.
Bhaiksha, 386.
Bhakshyābhakshya, 411, 1.
Bhaktas, 523, 1.
Bhakti (faith), 217; 326.
Bhakti, later theory of, 125.
Bhalla, 405, 1.
Bhāma, 470.
Bhāṇa, 471.
Bhāṇḍārkar, Professor, 167, 2; 187, 1; 236, 1; 245, 2
Bhāṇikā, 472.
Bhānu-datta, 457.
Bhāradvāja, 359; 404, 1.
Bhāradvāja (grammarian), 161, 2.
Bhāradvāja Gṛihya Sūtras, 187.
Bhāradvāja Śrauta Sūtras, 146.
Bharata, 345; 351; 359; 364; 420; 469.
Bharata (Sutras), 469.
Bhārata, 338, 1; 371, 1.
Bhāratam ākhyānam, 371, 2.
Bharata-mallika, 168.
Bharata-sena, 168.
Bhārata-varsha, 370; 375.
Bhāratī, 503, 1.
Bhāravi, 393, 1; 452.
Bhartṛi-hari, 167, 1; 453; 528; 533.
Bhāsa, 498.
Bhashā-pariććheda, 60, 1.
Bhāshya-pradīpa, 168.
Bhāshya-pradīpoddyota, 168.
Bhāskara, 176; 178; 180; 181.
Bhāskarāćārya, 97; 176.
Bhātiyās, 224, 2.
Bhaṭṭa, 232, 3.
Bhaṭṭa-divākara, 213, 2.
Bhaṭṭa-nārāyaṇa, 392, 3.
Bhaṭṭi-kāvya, 168; 367; 453; 454; 457.
Bhaṭṭoji-dīkshita, 168.
Bhāū Dājī, Dr., 494, 1.
Bhauma, 179.
Bhava, 409, 2.
Bhava-bhūti, 337; 359, 1; 367; 499.
Bhāvana, 409, 2.
Bhavishya, 514; 521.
Bhavishya-purāṇa, 512, 1.
Bhāvita, 183.
Bhayānaka, 457, 1.
Bhikshu, 211; 238; 254.

Bhikshuka, 245, 2.
Bhīls, 309, 1.
Bhīma, 379 ; 405 ; 414 ; 419.
Bhīmasena, 381, 4.
Bhīshma, 329, 2 ; 373 ; 375 ; 384 ; 391 ; 397 ; 401 ; 403 ; 411.
Bhīshma-parvan, 373.
Bhistīs (water-bearers), 224, 2.
Bhogavatī, 431, 1.
Bhoja, 367 ; 407 ; 532 ; 533.
Bhoja-deva, commentary of, 92, 2.
Bhoja-prabandha, 532.
Bhoja-rājā, commentary of, 92, 2.
Bhṛigu, 185 ; 203 ; 206 ; 221 ; 302 ; 335 ; 517, 1.
Bhu, 431, 1.
Bhūḥ, 159.
Bhukti, 297.
Bhūmi, 'earth,' 84.
Bhūr, 55, 2 ; 195.
Bhūta, 184.
Bhūta-yajña, 194 ; 245.
Bhuvaḥ or Bhuvar, 55, 2 ; 159 ; 195 ; 431, 1.
Bībhatsa, 457, 1.
Bībhatsu, 381, 4 ; 397.
Bible, 131, 2.
Bibliotheca Indica, 35, 1 ; 44, 2 ; 98, 1.
Binary compound, 71.
Bohlen, Von, 528, 1.
Bohn, 68, 1.
Böhtlingk, Professor, 168, 4 ; 169 ; 527, 1.
Bombay, school of law, 302.
Bopp, 385 ; 386.
Borrodaile, Mr. H., 305, 2.
Bose, 210, 1.
Bottomry, 264.
Brachmanes, 276, 1.
Brahma, 37 ; see Brahman.
Brahma (world), 431, 1.
Brahmā, 22, 1 ; 31 ; 40 ; 54 ; 83, 3 ; 91 ; 324 ; 325, 1 ; 343 ; 429 ; 514 ; 518.
Brahmā (son of), 79, 1.
Brāhma (form of marriage), 190.
Brahmaćārī, 375.
Brahma-ćārin, 192 ; 238 ; 241.
Brahmaćarya-vrata, 379, 2.
Brahma-ghosha, 419, 4,
Brahma-gupta, 175, 3 ; 176.
Brahma-hā, 270.
Brahmahatyā, 270 ; 387, 1.
Brahma-jijñāsā, 104.
Brahma-loka, 405.
Brahma-mīmāṉsā, 88.
Brahman (Supreme Spirit), 9 ; 83 ; 104 ; 105, 3 ; 189 ; 217.
Brahman (prayer, Veda), 214 ; 230, 1 ; 273.
Brāhmaṇa (portion of Veda), 5 ; 24 ; 25 ; 48 ; 56, 2.
Brāhmaṇa (prayer-offerer), 230, 1.
Brāhmaṇas (of each Veda), 25 ; 195.
Brahmāṇḍa, 514 ; 521.
Brahmāṇḍa-purāṇa, 368.
Brahmāṇī, 522.
Brāhmanicide, 315, 1.
Brāhmanism, 232 ; 233 ; 238.
Brāhmans, 223 ; 232, &c.
Brāhmans, Kshatriyas, and Vaiśyas, 232.
Brāhmans (of Konkan), 237, 1.
Brahma-pura, 116, 2.
Brahma-purāṇa, 252, 2 ; 514.
Brahma-siddhānta or Brahma-s°, 175 ; 176.
Brahmāstra, 402, 1.
Brahmāvarta, 209.
Brahma-vaivarta, 514 ; 515 ; 522.
Brahma-vidyā, 219.
Brahma-yajña, 194 ; 245 ; 245, 2 ; 271 ; 294, 3 ; 295, 2.
Brahmodyan, 295, 1.
Brahmojjhatā, 270.
Bṛihad - āraṇyaka Upanishad, 35 ; 36 ; 114 ; 133, 3 ; 345, 2.
Bṛihat-saṃhitā, 176 ; 179.
Brockhaus, Dr. Hermann, 532, 1.
Buddha, 47 ; 333.
Buddhi, 53, 3 ; 63 ; 83 ; 86 ; 109 ; 117 ; 140 ; 222.
Buddhīndriyāṇi, 84, 1.
Buddhism, 28, 1 ; 207, 1 ; 475 ; 513 ; 524.
Buddhist ascetics, 276, 1 ; 475.
Buddhistic scepticism, 314.
Budha, 179 ; 375.
Budha-vāra, 178, 1.
Bühler, Dr., 161, 2 ; 530, 1.
Bukka, court of King, 118.
Burgess, E., 176.
Burial in the ground, 299.
Burkhard, Dr. C., 495, 1.
Burmese language, 309, 1.
Burnell, Dr., 118 ; 245, 2.
C'a-hara, 183.
C'aitanya (intelligence), 120.
C'aitra, 173, 3 ; 365, 1.
C'aitya-yajña, 192.
C'akra, 183.
C'akravāka, 423, 1.
C'ākravarmaṇa, 161, 2.
C'akra-vartins, 204.
C'akra-vṛiddhi, 264.
C'akshur-divyam, 387, 1.
C'akshusha, Manu, 206, 1.
Calcutta Review, 335, 1 ; 338, 2 ; 340, 1 ; 356, 2.
Calcutta University, 302, 1.
Caldwell, Dr., 309, 1.
C'ampū, 369.
C'ampū-rāmāyaṇa, 367.
C'āmuṇḍā, 500 ; 522.
C'āṇakya, 507 ; 528.
C'aṇḍāla or C'āṇḍāla, 225 ; 229, 1 ; 270.
C'andana, 423, 3.
C'āndātas, 492.
C'aṇḍī, 522.
C'andra, 234, 2 ; 256 ; 330, 1 ; 360, 1.
C'āndra, 179.
C'andra-gupta, 224, 1 ; 313 ; 507.
C'andrāloka, 470.
C'āndrāyaṇa penance, 274.
C'āra, 257.
C'araka, 184.
C'araṇa or school, 187.
C'araṇa-vyūha, 187, 2.
Carey, 336, 1.
C'aru, 298.
C'āru-datta, 476.
C'ārvāka, 119 ; 120 ; 219 ; 411.
C'ārvāka-darśana, 118.
C'ārvākas, 119 ; 120.
C'ārvākas, doctrine of the, 352.
Caste, 210 ; 223.
Caste, loss of, 273.
Categories, Aristotelian, 66, 2.
Categories of Vaiśeshika, 66.
C'aṭṭopādhyāya, 218, 1.
C'atur-an·ga, 258 ; 351.
C'aturjea, 210, 1.
C'āturmāsya, 28, 1.
C'atushṭoma, 341, 1.
C'aula, 189 ; 192 ; 239.
Causation, theory of, 70.
Cebes, 58, 1.
Centauri, 310, 1.
Ceremonies, S'rāddha, 196 ; 266 ; 430.
Ceylon, 308.
C'hala, 64.
C'halita-rāma, 367.

Chambers's Encyclopaedia, 70, 1 ; 166, 1.
Chambhārs, leather-cutters, 224, 2.
C'handaḥ-śāstra, 153.
C'handas, 145 ; 153 ; 154 ; 214.
C'hando-ga, 216.
C'handogya Upanishad, 35 ; 37 ; 38 ; 49 ; 102.
Chess, 529.
China, 173, 2.
Chinese drama, 468.
Chinese language, 309, 1.
Chitpāvan, 224, 1.
Christ, 131, 2.
Christ and other Masters, 28, 1 ; 59, 1.
Christianity, 2 ; 131, 2.
Christians, Syrian, 122, 3.
Chronicle, 511, 1.
Chuteerkote, 356, 2.
Cicero, 72, 1 ; 73, 4 ; 77, 2 ; 83, 3.
Cicero, Tusc. Disp., 58, 1 ; 75, 2 ; 252, 1.
C'īnas, 229, 1.
C'itrā, 173, 3 ; 456.
C'itrakūṭ, C'itra-kūṭa, 244, 1 ; 356, 2.
C'itrān-gadā, 390.
C'itra-ratha, 354.
C'itta, 53, 3 ; 93 ; 117
Civil code, 261.
Clay-cart, 475.
Codes, eighteen, after Yājñavalkya, 300.
Colebrooke, 43, 1 ; 171, 1 ; 291, 1 ; 296, 1 ; 300 ; 500.
Colebrooke's Indian Algebra, 176.
Colebrooke's Bhāskara, 180.
Comedy, 468.
Compound interest, 264.
Confidantes, heroine's, 474.
Confucius, 47.
Consumptive persons, 270, 1.
Contract, 262 ; 263.
Copernicus, 32.
Cosmogony (Vaiśeshika), 77.
Cow (sacred), 519.
Cowell, Professor E. B., 35 1 ; 44, 2 ; 60, 1 ; 71, 1 ; 77 ; 296, 1 ; 300, 1 ; 495, 1.
Cowell, Mr. Herbert, 267, 1.
Cowell's Tagore Law Lectures, 302, 1.
Creator, 518.
Crimes (great), 269.
Crimes (secondary), 270.
Criminal code, Manu's, 268.
C'ūḍā-karman, 189 ; 192 ; 239.
Curzon, Mr., 340, 1.
Cust, Mr. R. N., 335, 1 ; 338, 2 ; 340, 1.
C'ūta, 423, 3.
Cyclopes, 310, 1.

Dadhi, 420.
Dāḍima, 423, 3.
Daiva, 244 ; 282, 2.
Daiva form of marriage, 190.
Daiva, S'rāddha, 200.
Daivata, 157 ; 158.
Daksha, 172, 1 ; 203 ; 234, 2 ; 302 ; 517, 1.
Daksha-kratu-hara, 409, 2.
Dāksheya, 162.
Dākshī, 162.
Dakshiṇā, 197 ; 236, 1.
Dakshiṇa (fee), 187, 1 ; 236.
Dakshiṇa (fire), 189, 1.
Dakshiṇa (hearth), 188, 1.
Dakshiṇāćārins, 523, 1.
Damanaka, 529, 2.
Ḍamaru, 183.
Damayantī-kathā, 367.
Dām-dupaṭ, 264, 2.
Dāmodara, 184 ; 390, 1.
Dānam, 237.
Dāna-saṃvananā, 352.
Dancing, 184 ; 467.
Daṇḍa, 177 ; 290, 1.
Daṇḍaka forest, 348, 1 ; 417 ; 503.
Daṇḍaka metre, 155.
Daṇḍī, 255.
Daṇḍin, 367 ; 532.
Daniel, 136, 4.
Dante, 415.
Darśa, 246.
Darśanas, 46 ; 56, 2.
Darśa-pūrṇamāsa, 28, 1.
Darwinians, 79.
Dāsa, 210, 1.
Daśa-gītikā, 175.
Daśa-hara, 365, 1.
Daśa-kumāra-ćarita, 257, 2 ; 532.
Daśama-grantha (Sikh), 325, 1.
Dāsa-pati, 256, 1.
Daśaratha, 330 ; 335, 1 ; 337 ; 344 ; 347 ; 426.
Daśaratha-jātaka, 316, 1.
Daśaratha's ministers, 339.
Dāśārha, 390, 1.
Daśa - rūpa, Daśa - rūpaka, 367 ; 457.
Dasras, 11.
Dasyus, 310.
Datta, 210, 1.
Dattaka-ćandrikā, 305.
Dattaka-mīmāṅsā, 304.
Dattasyānapakarma, 261.
Dattātreya, 324, 2.
Dawn, 16 ; 17.
Dāya, 262 ; 265.
Dāya-bhāga, 267, 1 ; 303.
Dāya-krama-saṅ-graha, 304.
Dāya-tattva, 304.
De, 210, 1.
Death, 18 ; 31 ; 32 ; 36 ; 37 ; 41 ; 209, 1.
Debt, 261.
Debts, three, 254, 1.
Decimal figures, 529.
Defendant, 297.
Degeneracy, 520.
Delhi, 205 ; 370 ; 390.
Deluge, tradition of the, 393.
Deposits, law of, 263.
Deśasth, 224, 2.
Desire, 20 ; 52, 1.
Destroyer, 518.
Deva, 409, 2.
Deva-bodha, 303.
Deva-datta, 403.
Devāḥ, 276.
Devakī, 126 ; 331 ; 332 ; 387, 1.
Devala, 162.
Devalaka, 218, 1.
Devaraḥ 197.
Devas, 244.
Devatā, Devatāḥ, 241 ; 276.
Deva-vrata, 375.
Deva-yajña, 194 ; 245.
Devī, 523.
Devī-māhātmya, 514.
Devrukh, 224, 2.
Dhamma-pada, 207, 1.
Dhana, 183.
Dhanañjaya, 367 ; 381, 4 ; 397 ; 457.
Dhanishṭhā, 171.
Dhanu-bandha, 456.
Dhanur-veda, 184.
Dhanvantari, 520.
Dhārā, 532.
Dhārāṇa, 93.
Dharaṇa, 293.
Dharaṇi (glossary), 161.
Dharaṇī-dhara, 303.
Dharma, 65 ; 234, 2 ; 387, 1.
Dharmādharma, 271, 1.
Dharma-jijñāsā, 99.
Dharma-mūlam, root of law, 293.
Dharma-putra, 381, 4.
Dharma-rāja, 381, 4.
Dharma-ratna, 303, 2.
Dharma-śāstra, 202 ; 203 ; 207, 1 ; 213.
Dharma-sūtras, 202.
Dharnā, 264, 3.

Dhātu, 163.
Dhātu-pāṭha, 163, 1.
Dhaumya, 302; 389.
Dhī, 283, 2.
Dhigvaṇa, 225.
Dhīralalita, 470, 3.
Dhīra-praśānta, 470, 3.
Dhīrodātta, 470, 3.
Dhṛishṭa - dyumna, 373; 384; 387, 1; 401; 405; 407, 1; 409.
Dhṛita-rāshṭra, 373; 374; 376; 377.
Dhūrjaṭi, 323.
Dhūrta-ćarita, 472.
Dhyāna, 93.
Dialogue, dramatic, 467.
Dianus, 429, 1.
Didhishu, 197.
Diet, rules of, 250.
Dig-ambara, 323.
Dilīpa, 344.
Dima, 471.
Diodorus, 224, 1; 318.
Diodorus Siculus, 252, 1; 332, 2.
Diogenes, 52, 1.
Dion Chrisostomos, 313; 313, 1.
Dionysos, 276, 1.
Diophantus, 181.
Dīpaka, 458.
Dīpakalikā, 303.
Dīpālī, 325, 1.
Diś, 67.
Dīvālī, 325, 1.
Divā-svapna, 193.
Divya, ordeal, 271.
Divyādivya, 471.
Dola-yātrā, 325, 1.
Domestic manners (Hindū), 436.
Ḍoms, 210, 1.
Ḍosha, 63; 470, 1.
Dower, 268.
Draco, laws of, 268, 1.
Drāhyāyaṇa S'rauta Sūtras, 146.
Dramas, 466; 470.
Dramas of Greeks. 467.
Draupadī, 366; 373; 384; 405; 408; 514.
Dravatva, 69.
Drāviḍa, 210, 1; 229, 1; 302.
Drāviḍian races and languages, 309, 1.
Drāviḍian school of law, 305.
Dravya, 53, 1; 66; 76.
Dṛikāṇa, 173, 2.
Dṛishadvatī, 205; 209.
Dṛishi, 144, 1.
Dṛishṭa, 82.
Dṛishṭānta, 64; 458.
Droṇa, 373; 383; 388; 391; 404.
Droṇa-parvan, 366; 373.
Drupada, 384; 391; 398.
Dugdha, 420.
Duḥkha, 63; 68.
Duḥśalā, 379.
Duḥśāsana, 385; 392; 405.
Durgā, 158; 217; 322, 2; 325, 1; 427; 431; 514; 522; 523.
Durgā, images of, 365, 1.
Durgā-pūjā, 365, 1.
Durmallikā, 472.
Durvāsas, 377; 518.
Durvāsasa Upa-purāṇa, 521.
Dur-vipāka, 55, 1.
Duryodhana, 374; 378; 380; 385; 397; 404.
Dushyanta, 375; 495.
Dūtān-gada, 367.
Dvaidha, 298.
Dvaipāyana, 375, 4.
Dvaita-vādin, 79.
Dvandva, 152, 255.
Dvāpara, 178, 2; 221; 301; 302; 329, 2; 410, 1.
Dvārakā, 332; 408.
Dvesha, 68.
Dvi-ja, 'twice-born,' 192; 223; 232; 294.
Dvi-jāti, 223.
Dvikaṃ śatam, 264.
Dvīpa, 375, 4; 420.
Dvy-aṇuka, 71.
Dyaus, 9; 12.
Dyaush-pitar, 9; 9, 1.

Earth, 189.
Earth and Heaven (union of), 90.
Eastwick, Mr. E. B., 495; 529, 2.
Eclectic School, 91, 1; 118; 122.
Eggeling, Professor J., 170.
Ego, 84.
Ego-ism, 83.
Egyptians, ancient, 268, 1.
Ekaćakrā, city of, 386.
Eka-jāti, 223.
Ekākshara. 93, 1.
Ekam evādvitīyam, 38.
Ekapadī, 191.
Ekoddishṭa S'rāddha, 200; 247.
Eleatics, 52, 1.
Elphinstone, Mr., 207, 1.
Elphinstone's India, 89, 1; 229, 2; 256, 1.
Emūsha, 328, 1.
Empedocles, 52, 1; 73, 2.
Encomiast, 510.
Entity, 20.
Epic poetry, 306.
Epic poetry, principal characteristics of, 307.
Epics, Indian, compared together and with Homer, 416.
Epictetus, 142; 143.
Epicurus, doctrines of, 72, 1.
Epos, 307.
Ether, 53, 1; 67; 83; 83, 3.
Ethnology of India, 309, 1.
Etymologist, 160.
Etymology, 156.
Every-man (morality), 508.
Evidence, law of, 271.
Expiation, 273; 274; 287.

Fables, 526; 529.
Fakīr or Faqīr, 94, 1.
False evidence, 270.
Farrar, Dr., 45, 1; 142; 544, 1.
Female mendicant, Buddhist, 498.
Ficus religiosa, 15, 1.
Finnish language, 309, 1.
Fish, eating of, 250.
Five per cent., 265.
Flesh, eating of, 250; 505.
Flood, tradition of, 29.
Frederic the Great, 257, 2.
Funeral ceremonies, 196; 247; 299.
Furruckabad, 499, 1.
Future life, belief in a, 31.

Gadā-yuddha, 408.
Gadya (prose), 369.
Gajasāhvaya, 377, 2.
Gālava, 161, 2.
Gambler, 478.
Gaṇaka, 174.
Gaṇapati, 127, 1.
Gāṇapatyas, 127, 1; 325, 1.
Gandha, 68; 376, 1.
Gandhamādana, 420, 1.
Gandhāra country, 162.
Gāndhārī, 377; 378.
Gandharva, 276.
Gāndharva (marriage), 190.
Gandharvas, 159; 400.
Gandharva-veda, 184.
Gāṇḍiva, 127; 397; 403; 413, 1.
Gaṇeśa, 127, 1; 293; 325, 1; 429; 430.
Gaṇeśa-gītā, 127, 1.
Gaṇeśa-purāṇa, 127, 1.
Gan-gā, 361; 362; 375.
Ganges, 276, 1; 412.

Ganges, story of, 361.
Gāngeya, 375.
Gānguli, 210, 1.
Gaṇita, 176.
Garbha, 470, 2.
Garbha Upanishad, 58, 1.
Garbhādhāna, 239.
Garbha-lambhana, 192; 239.
Gārbhikam enas, 238.
Garga, 180.
Garga-siddhānta, 175.
Gārgī, 439, 1.
Gārgya, 160; 161, 2; 302.
Gārhapatya fire, 187; 188, 1; 189, 1; 196; 197.
Garmanes, 276, 1.
Gāros or Garrows, 309, 1.
Garuḍa, 430; 431, 1; 514.
Gāthā, 195; 299.
Gāthā Ahunavaiti, 131, 2.
Gāthikāḥ, 295.
Gauḍa, 210, 1; 336, 1.
Gauḍa-pāda, 83, 1; 88.
Gaur, 210, 1.
Gaurī, 522.
Gautama, 49; 65, 1; 76; 301; 302.
Gavaya, 423, 1.
Gāyatrī text, 3; 17; 134, 2; 154; 195; 214; 231; 274.
Gāyatrī metre, 155.
Genealogies, 511, 1.
Gesticulations, pantomimic, 467.
Ghana arrangement of text, 152, 1; 245, 2.
Ghaṭī, 177.
Ghaṭikā, 177.
Ghaṭotkaća, 385; 389, 2; 405.
Ghosha, 210, 1.
Ghrāṇa, 73.
Giriśa, 409, 2.
Gīta-govinda, 367; 369; 454.
Glossaries, 161.
Gnostics, 57, 1.
Go-badhaḥ, 271.
Gobhila's Gṛihya Sūtras, 186; 186, 2.
Go-dāna, 189.
Godāvarī, river, 339, 1; 417.
Goethe, 495.
Gogra, river, 339, 2.
Gokarṇa, 354.
Gokula, 332.
Goldstücker, Professor, 147, 2; 150, 1.
Gomūtrikā, 456.
Gonarda, 167.
Gonḍ, 309, 1.
Goṇikā, 167.
Gopa, 210, 1.
Go-patha Brāhmaṇa, 25.
Gopīs, 325, 1; 332; 454.
Go-puććhāgra, 471.
Goraksha, 237, 2.
Gorresio, 336, 1; 338; 354, 1; 364, 1; 442.
Gos, 210, 1.
Goshāla, 210, 1.
Goshṭhī, 472.
Gotama (of Nyāya), 60, 74.
Gotama (law-book), 203.
Gotra or family, 248.
Gough, Professor A. E., 60, 1; 62; 63, 2; 67; 167, 1.
Govardhana, 356, 1; 367.
Govind, 325, 1.
Govinda, 390, 1; 454, 457.
Govinda Deva Śāstrī, 508.
Govinda-rāja, 203; 303.
Graha-rajña, 293.
Grāma, village, 258.
Grammar, 161; 529.
Grantha, 232, 3.
Granthīs, 232, 3.
Grāsāććhādana, 267.
Gravitation, 181.
Greeks, 173, 2; 361; 467.
Greeks and Romans, 33.
Griffith, Professor R., 125, 2; 336, 1; 362; 395, 1.
Gṛiha-prapadana, 193.
Gṛiha-stha, 196; 238; 241; 243; 245, 2.
Gṛihya (domestic rites), 186.
Gṛihya Sūtras, 145; 186; 300; 308.
Grīshma, 453.
Guḍākeśa, 381, 4.
Guhyaka, 276.
Gujarāt, 236, 1; 332.
Guṇa (of the Vaiśeshika), 66; 68.
Guṇa (three), 56, 1; 85; 275; 513.
Guṇāḍhya, 532.
Gun-gu, 173.
Gurjara, 210, 1.
Guru, 56, 1; 232; 232, 3; 238; 240; 241; 242.
Guru Nānak, 325, 1.
Gurutva, 69.
Guru-vāra, 178, 1.
Gurv-artha, 384.

Häberlin, 110.
Hadīs, 24.
Hāḍis, 210, 1.
Haituka, 219.
Haj, 244, 1.
Hājjī, 244, 1.
Hāla, 367.
Halāyudha, 161; 332, 2.
Hall, Dr. F., 79, 1; 175, 2; 252, 2; 533.
Hallīśa, 472.
Haṉsa, 243.
Hanuman-nāṭaka, 367; 508.
Hanumat, 356; 359; 367; 419, 4; 426; 428.
Hara, 217; 320; 409, 2.
Hārāvalī, 161.
Hardwick, Mr., 28, 1; 59, 1.
Hari, 134, 2; 518.
Hari-dāsa's comment, 77.
Haridvār, 244, 1.
Hari Nārāyaṇa, 431.
Hari-nātha, 368.
Hariśćandra, 26.
Hārīta, 203; 301.
Hari-vaṉśa, 317; 331; 366; 374; 418; 418, 2.
Harriot, 182, 1.
Harsha-vardhana, 533.
Hastināpur, 370; 390.
Hastinā-pura, 126; 373; 374; 411; 511, 1.
Hāsya, 457, 1.
Hāsyārṇava, 508.
Haug, Professor, 25.
Heads of law (eighteen), 261.
Heaven, 189.
Heavens (seven), 218; 431, 1.
Hector, 313, 1; 426.
Hecuba, 313, 1.
Hells, 217; 420, 1.
Hema-ćandra, 161.
Hemādri, 168.
Hema-kūṭa, 420, 1.
Hemanta, 453.
Heracleitus, 52, 1.
Herakles, 276, 1.
Hercules, 332, 2; 357, 2.
Hero, 474.
Herodotus, 224, 1.
Heroes (four kinds), 470, 3.
Heroine, 474.
Hesiod, 52, 1; 428, 4.
Hetu (reason), 61.
Hetu-śāstra, 218.
Hetv-ābhāsa (fallacy), 64.
Hiḍimbā, 385; 389, 2; 405.
Hill-tribes, 309, 1.
Himavat, 361; 394; 413.
Hiraṇya-garbha, 89; 114.
Hiraṇya-kaśipu, 328; 392, 2.
Hiraṇyāksha, demon, 327.
History of kings of Kaśmīr, 532.
Hitopadeśa, 376, 2; 411, 1; 425; 530; 531; 533; 537.
Holī, 472; 506.
Homa (oblation), 194; 245; 245, 1.
Homer, 310, 1; 313; 428, 4.
Horā, 173. 2.
Horace, 156.

Horoscope, 178, 1; (of Rāma's birth), 344, 2.
Hospitality, 250.
Hotṛi, 216.
Hṛishikeśa, 390, 1.
Hūlī or Holī, 325, 1.
Hūm, 274.
Humāyūn Nāmah, 529, 2.
Hunter, Dr. (Orissa), 210, 1; 244, 1.
Hycke-scorner, 509.
Hydaspes, river, 375, 1.
Hydra, 357, 2.

Iććhā, 68.
Iḍā, 375.
Idolatry, 218, 1.
Idols, 12; 218.
Īhā-mṛiga, 471.
Ikshu, 420.
Ikshvāku, 344; 375.
Ilā, 375.
Iliads, 306; 313; 357, 1; 401, 1; 421.
Incarnation, doctrine of, 317; 318.
Incarnations of Vishṇu, 327.
Indian Antiquary, 224, 2; 236, 1: 503, 3.
Indian Vedāntists, 52, 1.
Indices to Veda, 184.
Indische Alterthumskunde, 371, 1.
Indische Sprüche, Böhtlingk's, 527, 1.
Indische Streifen (Weber), 367; 533.
Indo-Āryans, 47.
Indra, 10; 13; 14; 16, 1; 189; 256; 308; 321; 429; 430.
Indra and Vishṇu, hymns to, 27, 1.
Indra, poetical sketch of, 13; 14.
Indrajit, 426.
Indrāṇī, 522.
Indra-prastha, 390; 391.
Indrasena, 381, 4.
Indra-vajrā, 156; 335, 2.
Indriya, 63; 73.
Indu, 10.
Inference, 61.
Inheritance, law of, 265.
Intercalary month, 174.
Interest on money, 264.
Irāvat, 389, 2.
Irāvatī, 498.
Īśa Upanishad, 35.
Īśāna, 409, 2.
Īśāvāsya Upanishad, 35.
Ishīkā, 405, 1.
Ishṭi (preference), 326.
Ishṭis (desiderata), 167, 1.
Ishu, 405, 1.
Īśvara, 74; 77; 88; 409, 2,
Īśvara-ćandra Vidyāsāgara. 120.
Īśvara-praṇidhāna, 93.
Itihāsa, 37; 195; 207, 1; 249; 295; 299; 306; 371, 1; 416; 509; 513.

Jagad-ambā, 91.
Jagan-nāth, 210, 1; 244, 1.
Jagatī, 154; 335, 2.
Jāhnavī, 363.
Jahnu, 363.
Jaimimi, 98; 98, 1.
Jaimini (Mīmāṇsā), 98; 118; 245, 2.
Jaiminīya-nyāya-mālā-vistara, 98, 1.
Jainas or Jains, 118.
Jala, 420.
Jāliyās, 'fishermen,' 210, 1.
Jalpa, 'mere wrangling,' 64.
Jamad-agni, 329, 2.
Jāmbavat, 426.
Jambhala-datta, 532.
Jambu-dvīpa, 420.
Jamshīd, 224, 1.
Jana (people), 285, 1.
Janaka, 335, 1; 341, 2; 345; 511, 1.
Janamejaya, 371, 1; 374; 389, 2.
Janar, 55, 2; 431, 1.
Janārdana, 390, 1.
Jane-o, 240, 1.
Janitva, 197.
Janma-patra, 178, 1.
Janmāshṭamī, 332, 1.
Janus, 429, 1.
Japa-yajña, 245; 246; 294, 3.
Japyam, 241.
Jarbharī, 122, 1.
Jāt, 210, 1.
Jaṭā, arrangement of text, 152, 1; 245, 2.
Jāta-karman, 192; 239.
Jāti (birth), 210, 1.
Jāti (futile replies). 64.
Jātī (flower), 423, 3.
Jatu, 385.
Jatūkarṇī, 499.
Jāvāli, 49; 120, 2; 312, 3; 315; 351; 364.
Jaya-deva, 367; 454; 470.
Jayad-ratha, 366; 379; 391; 396.
Jester, 474.
Jews, 56, 2.
Jhalla (club-fighter), 276.
Jihma-yodhin, 408.
Jīmūta-vāhana, 303; 304.
Jishṇu, 381, 4; 397.
Jīvātman, 40; 51; 74; 109; 110; 222.
Jñāna, 59; 323; 326.
Jñāna-kāṇḍa, 33.
Job, 19; 467.
Johaentgen, Dr., 213, 2; 290, 2; 290, 3.
John of Capua, 529, 2.
Johnson, Professor F., 452; 536.
Jones, Sir W., 35, 3; 44, 2; 82, 1; 245, 2; 507.
Jovian cycle of sixty years, 179.
Junctures (Sandhi), 470.
Jupiter (planet), 179.
Jupiter Pluvius, 10; 276, 1.
Justice, administration of, 260.
Jvālā-mukhī, 244, 1,
Jyaishṭha, 173, 3.
Jyeshṭhā, 173, 3.
Jyotis (fire, light), 84.
Jyotisha (astronomy) 145; 170.
Jyotishṭoma, 187; 232, 1; 240; 341, 1.

Kabandha, 356; 366; 429, 2.
Kādambarī, 367; 533.
Kadrū, 431, 1.
Kaikeyī, 341; 348; 352.
Kailāsa, 406.
Kaiśikī (style), 503, 1.
Kaiyaṭa or Kaiyyaṭa, 168.
Kākolūkikā, 531.
Kākolūkīya, 531.
Kakutstha, 344.
Kāla, 3; 67.
Kalā, 177; 178.
Kāla-nirṇāya, 118.
Kalāpa (grammar), 170.
Kaler anśa, 410.
Kalhaṇa, 532.
Kali, 28, 1; 178, 2; 221; 301; 330, 3; 410; 520.
Kālī, 514; 522; 523.
Kālidāsa, 359, 1; 366; 452; 454; 494.
Kālidāsa's dramas, 366.
Kālikā, 521; 522; 525.
Kalīlah Damnah, 529, 2.
Kālīnadī, 499, 1.
Kāliya (serpent), 332.
Kali-yuga, 300; 330, 3.
Kalki, 333; 333, 1.
Kalpa (period of time), 178; 206, 1; 322; 330, 3; 432; 517.
Kalpa (ceremonial), 145; 146; 195; 232.

Kalpa-sūtra, 146.
Kalyāṇa, 252, 1.
Kāma, 324, 1.
Kāmada, 525.
Kāmadeva, 430.
Kāma-dhenu, 361.
Kāma-gā, 299.
Kāmākhyā, 525.
Kamalāyatāksha, 381, 1.
Kāmandakā, 500.
Kambojas, 229, 1 ; 361.
Kāmya Śrāddha, 199.
Kāmyaka forest, 373 ; 393.
Kaṇāda, 65 ; 79, 1.
Kaṇāda's Sūtra, 71 ; 74 ; 245, 2.
Kanarese, 309, 1.
Kanauj, 499 ; 499, 1 ; 533.
Kāṇḍa (arrow), 405, 1.
Kandahar, 162.
Kandarpa-keli, 472.
Kañjalāla, 210, 1.
Kan·ka, 396.
Kanoj, 361.
Kanouj Brāhmans, 210, 1 ; 224, 2.
Kaṇsa, 126, 1 ; 328 ; 331 ; 332.
Kaṇsāris (braziers), 210, 1.
Kanyākubja, 210, 1 ; 499.
Kanyātva, 377, 4.
Kapāla-kuṇḍalā, 500 ; 501.
Kapila, 79, 1 ; 81 ; 85 ; 362.
Kāpila, 521.
Kapila's Aphorisms, 88.
Karaṇa, 70 ; 225.
Kāraṇa-mālā, 458.
Kāraṇa-śarīra, 53, 2.
Karaṇas, eleven, 178, 1.
Karaṇī, 149, 2.
Karataka, 529, 2.
Kārikā (verses), 167, 1.
Karkandhu, 423, 3.
Karkaṭa, 344, 2.
Karma-dosha, 56, 1.
Karma-kāṇḍa, 33.
Karmakāra, 210, 1.
Karma-mīmāṇsā, 98.
Karman, 66 ; 69 ; 326.
Karma - phala, 208 ; 209 ; 212 ; 213 ; 275 ; 278 ; 288.
Karma-vipāka, 55 ; 55, 1.
Karmendriyāṇi, 84, 1.
Karṇa, 373 ; 383 ; 384 ; 385.
Karṇa-parvan, 473.
Karṇāṭa, 210, 1 ; 224, 2.
Karṇa-vedha, 239.
Karṇikāra, 423, 3.
Kārtavīrya, 511, 1.
Kārttika, 173, 3.
Kārttikeya, 324, 1 ; 427, 2 ; 430, 2 ; 452 ; 481.
Kārttikī, 522.
Karuṇa, 457, 1.
Kārya, 70.
Kārya-darśana, 260.
Kashāya-vāsas, 293.
Kāshṭhā, 177.
Kāśī, 511, 1.
Kāśī-nātha, 325, 1.
Kaśyapa, 161, 2 ; 234, 2 ; 302 ; 344 ; 347 ; 431, 1.
Kātantra (grammar), 170.
Kaṭa-pūtana, 276.
Kaṭha, 39, 3 ; 40.
Kaṭha Śrauta Sūtras, 146.
Kaṭha Upanishad, 21, 2 ; 35.
Kathaei, 252, 1.
Kāṭhaka Gṛihya Sūtras, 187.
Kathārṇava, 532.
Kathā-sarit-sāgara, 532.
Kātthakya, 159.
Kātyāyana, 151 ; 166 ; 531.
Kātyāyana's law - treatise, 203 ; 302.
Kātyāyana's Śrauta Sūtra, 146 ; 148 ; 341, 1.
Kaulas, 523, 1.
Kaulika (weaver), 534.
Kaunakhya, 270.
Kauravas, 373 ; 382 ; 397 ; 407.
Kaurma, 521.
Kauśalyā, 341 ; 348 ; 364 ; 376, 1.
Kauśāmbhī, 506.
Kaushītaki-brāhmaṇa, 25.
Kaushītaki-brāhmaṇa Upanishad, 35 ; 106, 1.
Kaustubha, 399.
Kautsa, 159.
Kavi Karṇa-pūraka, 470.
Kavirāja, 368.
Kāvya, 306, 2 ; 315 ; 316 ; 370, 1 ; 416 ; 472.
Kāvyādarśa, 367 ; 457.
Kāvya-lakshaṇa, 453.
Kāvyālan·kāra-vṛitti, 457 ; 469.
Kāvya-pradīpa, 457.
Kāvya-prakāśa, 457.
Kāyastha, 210, 1 ; 224, 2 ; 225 ; 296, 1.
Kearns, Rev. I. F., 110, 2.
Kena Upanishad, 35.
Kendra, 173, 2.
Kern, Professor, 175.
Keśānta, 239.
Keśava, 390, 1.
Ketu, 180, 1 ; 252, 1.
Kevalātman, 322.
Khaḍga-bandha, 456.
Khanaka, 385.
Khaṇḍana - khaṇḍa - khādya, 453, 1.
Khāṇḍava-prastha, 390.
Khāsias, 309, 1.
Khatrī, 224, 2 ; 252, 1.
Khila, 207, 1.
Khīrad Afroz, 529, 2.
Khonds or Kus, 309, 1.
Kielhorn, Professor, F., 161, 2 ; 168, 1 ; 530, 1.
Kiṅćit-prāṇa, 410.
Kiṇśuka, 407 ; 423, 3.
Kirāta, 393 ; 452 ; 453.
Kirāta (mountaineer), 229, 1 ; 393, 1.
Kirātārjunīya, 229, 1 ; 373 ; 393, 1 ; 403, 3 ; 452 ; 461.
Kirīṭin, 381, 4 ; 397.
Kishkindhyā-kāṇḍa, 337.
Kokila, 423, 1 ; 541, 2.
Kolīs, 224, 2.
Kols, 309, 1.
Konkanasth, 224, 2.
Korawars, 309, 1.
Kośa, 113 ; 271, 1 ; 297.
Kośala, 317 ; 335, 1.
Kosegarten, 530, 1.
Koshṭīs, 224, 2.
Koṭa, 309, 1.
Krama, arrangement of text, 245, 2.
Krama text, 152, 1.
Krānti pāta, 181.
Kratu, 517, 1.
Krauṅća, 423, 1.
Krauṅća-dvīpa, 420.
Kraya-vikrayānuśaya, 261.
Kṛipa, 383, 1.
Kṛipī, 383, 1 ; 391 ; 407 ; 409.
Kṛishi, 227, 1 ; 237, 2.
Kṛishṇa, 90, 2 ; 122 ; 126 ; 217 ; 330 ; 358, 3 ; 381, 4 ; 397 ; 511, 1 ; 515.
Kṛishṇa (life of), 331 ; 517.
Kṛishṇa (names of), 390, 1.
Kṛishṇa (wives of), 312.
Kṛishṇā (Draupadī), 384.
Kṛishṇa-dvaipāyana, 509.
Kṛishṇa-miśra, 508.
Kṛishṇa-tarkālan·kāra, 304.
Kṛishṇau, 390, 1.
Kṛit affixes, 152 ; 170.
Kṛita age, 178, 2 ; 221 ; 301 ; 330, 3.
Kṛitavarman, 407 ; 409.
Kṛittikā, 170 ; 173, 3.
Kshaṇa, 177.
Kshatra, 228, 1.
Kshatriya, 17, 1 ; 22, 2 ; 49 ; 212 ; 223 ; 224, 2.
Kshattṛi, 376.
Kshetra, 140.
Kshīva, 391.

Kuhū (new moon), 158; 172.
Kula, 296, 1.
Kulāla, 210, 1.
Kulārṇava, 525.
Kulīna, 'noble,' 210, 1.
Kullūka, 4, 1; 6; 13, 3; 22, 1; 188, 1; 203; 207, 1; 210, 1; 213, 2; 301; 302; 303; 522, 1.
Kumāra, 452.
Kumāra-sambhava, 321, 1; 324, 1; 452.
Kumārila, 98, 1; 232, 3.
Kumbha-kāra or potters, 224, 2.
Kumbha-karṇa, 354, 1.
Kumbhārs or potters, 224, 2.
Kumuda, 432, 1.
Ku-nakhin, 270, 1.
Kuntī, 373; 374; 375, 2; 377; 386; 437, 1.
Kuntibhoja, 377; 391.
Kurān, 4; 24; 33; 102, 1.
Kūrma, 327; 327, 3; 514.
Kuru-kshetra, 373; 401.
Kurus, 308; 384.
Kuruvaka, 423, 3.
Kus or Khoṇḍs, 309, 1.
Kuśa, 335, 1; 504.
Kuśa-dvīpa, 420.
Kuśa grass, 195; 196; 273.
Kusīda-vṛiddhi, 264.
Kuśika Śrauta Sūtras, 146.
Kuśī-lavau, 335, 1.
Kusumāñjali, 60, 1; 71, 1; 77.
Kūṭa-sthaḥ, 130, 2.
Kuthumi or Kuṭhumi, 302.
Kuṭṭaka, 176; 176, 2.
Kuvalayānanda, 470.
Kuvera, god of wealth, 256; 354; 427.
Kymar range of mountains, 356, 1.

Laestrygones, 310, 1.
Laghu-kaumudī, 168.
Lakhimā-devī, 305.
Laksha, 183.
Lākshā, 385.
Lakshaṇa, 243; 470.
Lakshmaṇa, 345; 348; 356; 364; 425; 426; 503.
Lakshmī, 325, 1; 327; 358; 368; 387, 1; 430; 522.
Lāmbādies, 309, 1.
Lambaka, 532.
Lan-kā, 337; 339, 1; 344, 1; 356; 419, 4; 503.
Lassen, Professor, 126, 1; 294, 1; 313; 339, 1; 371, 1; 499, 1; 511, 1.
Lāsya, dance, 467.
Lāṭyāyana Śrauta Sūtras, 146.
Laugākshi Śrauta Sūtras, 146.
Laukika (secular), 278, 1.
Laukikāgni, 299.
Lava, 335, 1; 504.
Lavana, 420.
Law, schools of, 302.
Laya, 92.
Left-hand worshippers, 523, 1.
Lekhya, 293.
Lethe, 58, 1.
Lexicographers, 161.
Lex talionis, 268.
Liddon, Canon, 59, 1.
Lidhu, 169, 1,
Likhita (lawyer), 203; 301; 302.
Likhita (written document), 297.
Līlā-madhukara, 471.
Līlāvatī, 176; 176, 3; 183.
Lin-ga, 169, 1; 198, 3; 322; 514.
Lin-ga-śarīra, 53, 2; 109.
Liptā, 173, 2.
Loans, law of, 262.
Locke, 80, 2.
Logic, Hindū, 61; 529.
Logician, Hindū, 62.
Loha-kāra (smiths), 224, 2.
Lohārs (smiths), 224, 2.
Lokākshi, 302.
Lokāloka, 420, 1.
Lokas, 431, 1.
Lokāyatas, 120.
Lokāyatikas, 120.
Lokmān, 529.
Loma-harshaṇa, 510.
Lomapāda, 340.
Loṇārīs, 224, 2.
Lorinser, Dr., 126, 1; 131 2; 135, 2; 137, 1.
Lotus-stanza, 456.
Lucretius, 52, 1; 54, 1; 72, 1; 76, 1; 80, 1; 83, 3; 105, 4.
Lunar line of kings, 375; 511, 1.
Luptopamā, 458.
Lusty Juventus, 509.

Macchiavelli, 507.
Madayantikā, 500.
Mādhava, 118; 390, 1; 500.
Mādhavāćārya, 98, 1; 119; 302; 305; 371, 2; 439, 1; 521.
Madhu-parka, 250; 505.
Madhusūdana, 390, 1.
Madhusūdana Gupta, 184.
Madhya-deśa, 226, 1.
Madhya-laya, 498.
Madhyama, 473.
Madhya-mandira, 119.
Mādhyandina S'ākhā, 150; 245, 2.
Mādhyandinas, 245, 2.
Madras, 302.
Mādreyau, 381, 4.
Mādrī, 252, 1; 312; 373.
Madya, 250.
Magadha, 361.
Magadha, kings of, 313.
Maghā, 173, 3.
Māgha, 13, 2; 173, 3; 453.
Māgha, month of, 171.
Māgha, poem of, 392, 2.
Mahā-bhārata, 31; 205; 245, 2; 306; 361, 2; 366; 370; 405, 1.
Mahā-bhāshya, 92, 2; 167.
Mahā-bhūta, 83; 221.
Mahā-deva, 323; 519.
Mahājan, 264, 2.
Mahā-kāvyas, 453.
Mahā-nāṭaka, 367; 471.
Mahā-nirvāṇa, 525.
Mahā-padma, 432, 1.
Mahā-pātakas, 269.
Mahā-prasthānika-parvan, 374.
Mahā-purāṇas, 515.
Mahar, 55, 2; 431, 1.
Mahā-rāshṭra, 210, 1; 302.
Maharshis, 136, 2; 206, 1; 301.
Mahāsinha-gati, 381, 1.
Mahat, 83; 91; 220; 221; 222.
Mahātala, 431, 1.
Māhātmya, 408, 1.
Mahāvīra-ćarita or °ćaritra, 337; 359, 1; 360, 1; 367; 499; 502.
Mahā-yajña, 188; 188, 1; 194; 244; 267; 288, 3.
Mahā-yamaka, 457.
Mahā-yuga, 178; 221; 330, 3.
Maheśvara, 119; 161; 304; 521.
Māheśvarī, 522.
Mahisha, 423, 1; 430.
Māhishya, 149, 2; 225.
Maithila, 210, 1.
Maithila school, 304.
Maitra S'rauta Sūtras, 146.
Maitrāksha-jyotika, 276.
Maitrāyaṇa, 44, 2.
Maitrāyaṇī Upanishad, 44; 44, 2.
Maitrāyaṇīya Upanishad, 44.

Maitrāyaṇīya Gṛihya Sūtras, 187.
Maitreyī, 439, 1.
Maitrī Upanishad, 44, 2.
Makāmāt of Harīrī, 467.
Makaranda, 500.
Ma-kāras, 523, 1.
Malabar coast, 329, 2.
Mala-māsa, 174.
Mālatī, 423, 3; 500.
Mālatī-mādhava, 155, 499.
Mālavikā, 472; 498.
Mālavikāgnimitra, 494; 497.
Malayālam, 309, 1.
Malcolm's Persia, 224, 1.
Male-arasars, 'hill-kings,' 309, 1.
Mālī, 210, 1.
Malimluća, 174.
Mallāh (prize-fighters), 276.
Mālyavat, 420, 1.
Mammaṭa, 457.
Mānāpamāna, 255, 2.
Manas, 53; 53, 3; 63; 67; 76; 83; 109; 117; 220; 221.
Māna-sāra, 185.
Mānava Gṛihya Sūtras, 187.
Mānava S'rauta Sūtras, 146.
Mānava-kalpa-sūtra, 187; 205, 2.
Mānavas, 205; 207, 1.
Mānavas, Code of, 213; 291.
Mandākinī, 351, 1.
Mandākrāntā, 452.
Mandala, 18; 18, 1.
Maṇḍala of the Ṛik, ninth, 6.
Mandanis, 290, 1.
Mandara, 357, 3; 519.
Mandoćća, 179.
Mandodari, 436.
Māṇḍūkī-śikshā, 149, 3.
Māṇḍukya Upanishad, 35.
Man-gala, 179.
Man-gala-vāra, 178, 1.
Mankind, deterioration of, 517.
Mano-maya, 114.
Māṃsa-bhakshaṇa, 250.
Mansel, Dean, 115.
Manthara, 534.
Mantra-mahodadhi, 525.
Mantra portion of the Veda, 5; 11; 245, 2.
Mantra-jārgaras, 245, 2.
Mantras (texts), 3; 4, 1; 22; 524; 525.
Manu, 4; 4, 1; 5; 6; 30; 56, 2; 202; 203; 220; 303; 491, 1; 512, 1.
Manu's Code, 203
Manushya-loka, 197.
Manushya-yajña, 194; 246.
Manv-antara, 206, 1; 221; 330, 3; 511.
Manv-artha-muktāvalī, 303.
Marāthī country, 236, 1.
Marāṭhī empire, 256, 3.
Mārgaśīrsha, 173, 3.
Mārīća, 354; 517, 1.
Mārīći, 206; 276; 302; 344.
Mārkaṇḍeya, 366.
Mārkaṇḍeya-purāṇa, 387, 1; 514.
Marriage, forms of, 244.
Marriage portion, 267.
Marriage rite, 190; 244.
Mars, 179.
Marshman, 336, 1.
Māruta (the Wind), 387, 1.
Maruts, 10; 14; 400.
Marvāḍī (merchants), 224, 2.
Maśaka S'rauta Sūtras, 146.
Mātali, 357.
Materialists, 120, 2; 352.
Māṭhavya, 259, 1.
Mathematical science, 172.
Mathurā, 330, 2; 332.
Matsya, 327; 397; 514.
Matsya purāṇa, 512.
Mātula, 380, 1.
Mauna-vrata, 254.
Mauñji-bandhana, 240; 294.
Mausala-parvan, 374; 411, 1.
Māyā, 83; 108; 140.
Mechanical arts, 185.
Medhātithi (lawyer), 203; 303.
Medicine, 184.
Medinī, 161.
Megasthenes, 207, 1; 224, 1; 238, 1; 257, 2; 276, 1; 312; 318; 507.
Megasthenes, caste-divisions of, 224, 1; 237, 2.
Megha-dūta, 359, 1; 367; 390, 1; 452; 494, 1.
Mekhalā, 240.
Menakā, 361.
Mercury, 179.
Meru (mount), 357, 3; 412; 413; 420.
Metaphor, 456.
Metaphysics, Hindū, 61.
Metempsychosis, 11; 18; 56, 1; 56, 2; 530.
Metre, 153; 155, 1.
Mill, J. S., 66, 2.
Mill's India, 95; 224, 1; 256, 1.
Millar, 224, 1.
Milman, Dean, 129, 1; 386, 1.
Milton's Satan, 354, 1.
Mīmāṃsā, 46; 98; 206, 1; 219; 232, 3.
Mīmāṃsaka, 3; 100; 220.
Mīmāṃsā-sūtra, 98, 1; 100, 1.
Mind-born sons, 517, 1.
Minerva, 355, 1.
Misals of Sikhs, 325, 1.
Misarū-miśra, 305.
Miśra, 305, 1.
Miśra-dāmodara, 367.
Miśra-vṛitta, 471.
Mitāksharā, 291; 303; 304.
Mithi, 511, 1.
Mithilā, 345; 345, 2; 511, 1.
Mithilā (school of law), 291; 302; 304.
Mithyā-jñāna, 104.
Mitra, 10; 16; 210, 1.
Mlećcha, 229, 1; 243; 276; 405.
Mlećcha-deśa, 229, 1.
Mlećchas, 405.
M'Mahon, Rev. J. H., 68, 1; 115, 1.
Modaka, 210, 1.
Mohammed, *see* Muhammad.
Moksha, 59.
Moksha-dharma, 374.
Monasteries, 475.
Money-lender, 264.
Mongol language, 309, 1.
Months, names of, 173, 3.
Montriou, W. A., 292, 1.
Morality, 508.
Mṛććhakaṭikā, 93, 2; 296, 1; 313; 324, 1; 330, 3; 366; 468; 475.
Mṛiga-śiras, 173, 3.
Mućukunda, 520.
Mudrā-rākshasa, 505; 507.
Mugdha-bodha, 168.
Mugdha-bodhinī, 168.
Muhammad, 3; 244, 1.
Muhūrta, 177.
Muhūrtas, 170.
Muir, Dr. John, 12, 1, 2; and passim.
Mūka, 393.
Mukha, opening, 470, 2.
Mukhopādhyāya, 210, 1.
Mukhurjea, 210, 1.
Mukti, 59.
Mūla Mahā-bhārata, 512.
Mūla-prakṛiti, 82.
Mūla-rāmāyaṇa, 311; 338, 1; 512.
Mūla-saṃhitāḥ, 512.
Mullen's Essay, 88, 1.
Müller, Professor Max, 9, 1; 12, 2; and passim.
Muṇḍa, 293.
Muṇḍaka Upanishad, 35; 39; 39, 2; 110, 1.
Muni, 254; 255.

Muraja-bandha, 456.
Murāri, 359, 1 ; 367.
Mūrdhāvasikta, 225.
Mūrta, 177.
Mūrtti, 53, 1.
Musala, 374.
Musalin (club-armed), 332, 2.
Musalmāns, 244, 1.
Mushrooms, eating of, 250.
Music, 184.
Muslims, 4 ; 251, 1.
Muttra, 356, 1.
Mythology, Grecian, 319 ; 427 ; 428.
Mythology, Post-vedic, 321 ; 418 ; 428–434.

Naćiketas, 40 ; 41.
Nāḍī, 177.
Nāḍikā, 177.
Nāga (serpent-demons), 332, 2 ; 380 ; 431 ; 431, 1.
Nāga-kanyās, 431, 1.
Nāga-loka, 431, 1.
Nāgānanda, 505, 1 ; 508.
Nāga-pañćamī, 431, 1.
Nāgasāhvaya, 377, 2.
Nāgoji-bhaṭṭa, 92, 2 ; 168.
Nahusha, 375.
Naigama, 157 ; 158.
Naighaṇṭuka, 156 ; 158.
Naimittika Śrāddha, 200.
Nair tribe, 386, 2.
Nairuktas (etymologists), 158.
Nairuktikas, 156, 1.
Naishadha, 453, 1 ; 454.
Naishṭhika, 238.
Naivedya, 218.
Naiyāyikas, 62 ; 65 ; 66 ; 73, 1 ; 87.
Nakshatra, 172 ; 172, 1 ; 178, 1 ; 179 ; 199.
Nakshatra-darsa, 174.
Nakula, 380 ; 387, 1 ; 402 ; 413.
Nakulīśa, 118.
Nala (story of), 13, 2 ; 251, 2 ; 330, 3.
Nala (king), 344.
Nala (monkey-general), 356.
Nalodaya, 453 ; 454.
Nāma-karaṇa, 239.
Nāma-karman, 239.
Namāz, 244, 1.
Nāṇaka (coin), 264 ; 293.
Nānak Shah, 325, 1.
Nāna Sāhib, 224, 2.
Nanda, 332.
Nandā, 521.
Nandana, 500.
Nanda-paṇḍita, 304 ; 305.
Nāndī, 324, 1 ; 473 ; 501.
Nandi-grāma, 352.
Nāpita, 210, 1 ; 535.
Nara, 381, 4.
Narābhimānī, 471.
Nārāća, 405, 1.
Nārada, 26 ; 37 ; 203 ; 301 ; 302 ; 411 ; 428 ; 517, 1.
Nārada-siddhānta, 175.
Nāradīya, 514 ; 521.
Narakas, 55, 2 ; 431, 1.
Narāśaṉsa, 159.
Nārāśaṉsī, 195 ; 295.
Nara-siṉha, 328 ; 521 ; 522.
Nara - siṉha Upa - purāṇa, 521.
Nārāyaṇa, 217 ; 358 ; 390, 1 ; 399.
Narmadā, 339, 2.
Nartaka, 467 ; 470.
Nāsatyau, 11 ; 158 ; 387, 1.
Nāsik (from *nāsikā*), 353, 3.
Nāstika, 219.
Nāstikyam, 271.
Nāthāćārya-ćūḍāmaṇi, 304.
Nāṭikā, 472.
Nāṭya, 467.
Nāṭyarāsaka, 472.
Nava S'āk (nine divisions), 210, 1.
Nāyaka, 470.
Nāyar, 386, 2.
Nāyikā, 471.
Nectar, 520.
Nekyomanteia, 415.
Nepāl, 524.
Nestor, 426.
New Testament, 131, 2.
Nić, 164, 1.
Nīća, 473.
Nicholson, John, 318, 1.
Nidāna-sūtra, 153.
Nidarśana (example), 61.
Nigama, 157 ; 523, 1.
Nigamana (conclusion), 61.
Nighaṇṭu, 156 ; 159 ; 245, 2.
Night, 16 ; 22 ; 423, 4.
Nigraha-sthāna, 64.
Nihilism, 115.
Niḥśreyasa, 59.
Nikshepa, 261.
Nīla, 420, 1.
Nīla-kaṇṭha (S'iva), 323.
Nīlakaṇṭha-bhaṭṭa, 305.
Nīl-giri hills, 309, 1.
Nimb tree, leaves of, 299.
Nimesha, 177 ; 402.
Nimi, 344 ; 511, 1.
Nimitta-kāraṇa, 70.
Nindā, 25.
Nīpa, 423, 3.
Nipāta, 151 ; 160.
Nir-guṇa, 86 ; 106 ; 112, 2 ; 514.
Nirṇaya, 64.
Nirṇaya-sindhu, 200.
Nirukta, 122, 1 ; 145 ; 156 ; 157 ; 158 ; 217.
Nirukta - pariśishṭa, 159 ; 161.
Nirvahaṇa, 470, 2 ; 471
Nirvāṇa, 59.
Nir-vikalpa, 112, 3.
Nishādas, 159 ; 310, 1.
Nishadha, 420, 1.
Nīshādī, 385.
Nishka, 293.
Nish-kramaṇa, 239.
Nishphala, 144, 2.
Nīti, 507 ; 526.
Nīti-śāstras, 146 ; 526.
Nīti-śāstras proper, 526.
Nitya (S'rāddha), 188, 1 ; 199 ; 247.
Nivṛitti, 165.
Niyama, 93.
Non-Āryan races, 311.
Northern Buddhists, 524.
Notation (in algebra), 181.
Nṛi-siṉha Upa-purāṇa, 521.
Nṛitya, 467.
Nullity, 20.
Numeration, system of, 183.
Nūshīrvān, 529, 2.
Nyagrodha tree, 409.
Nyāsa-dhārin, 263.
Nyāya, 46 ; 60 ; 65 ; 86, 1 ; 219.
Nyāya (Sūtras), 60, 1.
Nyāya-mālā-vistara, 118.
Nyāya-sūtra-vṛitti, 60, 1.

Oḍras, 229, 1.
Odyssey, 306 ; 355, 1 ; 389 ; 415 ; 421 ; 422.
Om, 93 ; 159 ; 195 ; 214, 1.
Omens, 184.
Ordeal, ten forms of, 271, 1.
Ordeal, trial by, 271 ; 297.
Orissa, 210, 1 ; 244, 1.
Ormazd, 10.
Orphic hymns, 106, 2.
Ovid's Metamorphoses, 330, 3.
Oxus, 7.

Pada (traditional art), 77.
Pada text, 150 ; 152 ; 245, 2.
Padārtha, 53, 1 ; 66 ; 80, 2.
Padma, 368 ; 514.
Padma-bandha, 456.
Padma-pura, 499.
Padma-purāṇa, 302.
Padya (verse), 369.

Pahlavas, 361.
Pahlavī, 529, 2.
Paiśāća (marriage), 190; 244.
Paitāmaham astram, 357; 3.
Paitāmaha siddhānta, 175.
Paithīnasi, 302.
Pakaśāsani, 381, 4.
Pāka-yajña, 188; 188, 1; 232; 245; 246.
Pala, 177; 293.
Palibothra, 313; 332, 2.
Pālita, 210, 1.
Pańćagavya penance, 273.
Pańćāgni, 189, 1.
Pańća-janāḥ, 159; 403.
Pāńćajanya, 403.
Pańća-kośa, 113.
Pańćāla, 49; 390.
Pańća-lakshaṇa, 512; 516.
Pańćānana, 323, 1.
Pańćān-ga, 178, 1.
Pańća-rātraka, 338, 1.
Pańća-siddhāntikā, 175.
Pańća-tantra, 54, 2; 294, 2; 529, 2; 530; 531; 533; 536.
Pańća-tapās, 95; 254.
Pańćavatī, 353, 3.
Pańća-vinśa Brāhmaṇa, 25.
Pańća-yajna, 188.
Pańćī-karaṇa, 111, 1.
Pańćī-krita, 111, 1.
Panćopākhyāna, 530.
Pāṇḍavas, 346, 2; 373; 401; 408; 515.
Pāṇḍu, 373; 376; 377.
Pāṇi-grahana, 191.
Pāṇigrahaṇikā mantrāḥ, 263.
Paṇin, 162.
Pāṇini, 118; 149; 150; 156, 2; 162; 531.
Pāṇini-darśana, 118.
Pāṇini's grammar, 152; 161.
Pańjāb, 232, 3; 252, 1.
Pantheism, 34; 102; 110; 115; 510.
Para, 69.
Pāradas, 229, 1.
Parāka (penance), 273.
Paramāṇu, 177.
Pāramārthika (existence), 108.
Paramātman, 40; 51; 74; 222; 324.
Parāśara, 203; 302; 375; 510; 518; 521.
Parāśara's Code, 118; 301; 302; 305.
Parāśara-siddhānta, 175.
Parāśara - smṛiti - vyākhyā, 305.
Pāraskara's Gṛihya - sūtra, 187; 203, 1; 295, 3.
Parasmai-pada, 164.
Paraśu-rāma, 329; 329, 2; 346; 347; 399; 411.
Paratva, 68.
Parda-nishīn, 437, 2.
Paribhāshā, 163, 2.
Paribhāshendu-śekhara, 168, 1.
Pārijāta, 519.
Parikara, 458.
Parīkshit, 389, 2; 515.
Parimāṇāni, 68.
Parishad, 217; 219.
Pariśishṭa (supplements), 184.
Parīts (washermen), 224, 2.
Parivrājaka, 238; 254; 498.
Parmenides, 52, 1.
Pārtha, 381, 4.
Partnership, 262.
Pārushye, 261.
Pārvaṇa Śrāddḥa, 199; 247.
Pārvatī, 322; 322, 2; 324, 1; 325, 1; 427; 523, 1.
Paryan-ka-bandha, 93, 2; 324, 1.
Pāśa, 183.
Pāshaṇḍin (heretic), 219; 299.
Paśu-kalpa, 192.
Pāśupata (weapon), 393.
Pāśupatas, 119
Paśu-pati, 119.
Paśu-yajña, 28, 1.
Pāta, 179.
Patākā-sthānaka, 471.
Pātāla, 55, 2; 363; 420, 1; 431, 1.
Pātaliputra, 167, 2; 224, 1; 507.
Pātańjala-darśana, 118.
Patańjali, 92; 166; 294, 1.
Pāṭī-gaṇita, 176, 3.
Pativratā, 437.
Patriarchs, 517.
Patrin, 405, 1.
Patroclus, 425.
Paulastya, 354, 1.
Pauliśa-siddhānta, 175.
Pauloma, 371, 1.
Pauṇḍra (trumpet), 403.
Pauṇḍrakas, 229, 1.
Paurava, 404.
Paurṇamāsa, 246.
Pausha, 173, 3.
Paushya, 371, 1.
Pavitra, 240, 1.
Penance, 273; 274; 287.
Penelope, 355, 1.
Persians, 361.
Pervasion in logic, 62.
Peshwa, 256, 3.
Phaedo of Plato, 58, 1.
Phaedrus, 42, 1,
Phala, 63.
Phālguna, 173, 3; 325, 1; 381, 4; 397; 472.
Phalgunī, 173, 3.
Phallus, 322, 1.
Philosophy, common creed, 50.
Philosophy, six systems of, 46.
Pickford, Mr. John, 502, 1.
Pićula, 423, 3.
Pilpay's fables, 529, 2.
Piṇḍa, 200; 247; 248; 266.
Pin-gala, 153.
Pin-gala-nāga, 153.
Pippala, 39, 3.
Piśāća, 276.
Pischel, Dr. R., 495, 1.
Pisistratus, 371.
Piśunī, 351, 1.
Pitāmaha, 400, 2.
Pitṛis, 6; 18; 159; 241; 247; 276.
Pitri-yajña, 194; 245.
Plaintiff, 297.
Plaksha-dvīpa, 420.
Planets, nine, 180.
Plato, 42, 1; 50, 3; 53, 2; 56, 2; 73, 2; 75, 2; 81, 1; 83, 2; 104, 2; 106, 3; 109, 1; 131, 2; 224, 1.
Plato (Republic), 224, 1.
Plato (Timaeus), 224, 1.
Platonic idealism, 103.
Platonic realism, 70.
Platonists, 53, 2.
Plays, Hindū, 466.
Poems, artificial, 452; 454.
Poems, Homeric, 416.
Poison, 519.
Poitā, 240, 1.
Polyandry, 386, 2.
Polygamy, 243.
Polyphemus, 429, 2.
Porus, 375, 1.
Post-vedic literature, 204.
Prabhā-kara, 232, 3.
Prabhāsa, 390.
Prabhūs, 224, 2.
Prabodha-ćandrodaya, 508; 509.
Praćaṇḍa-pāṇḍava, 367.
Pradhāna, 53, 1; 82; 90, 2; 91; 105, 3; 473.
Pradhānā, 522.
Prāḍ-vivāka, 296, 1.
Prahasana, 472.
Prahlāda, 328.

Prajāpati, 154 ; 206 ; 217 ; 234, 2 ; 273 ; 327, 3.
Prajāpatis, 206, 1 ; 244 ; 301.
Prājāpatya (marriage), 190 ; 244.
Prājāpatya penance, 273.
Prakaraṇa, 471.
Prakaraṇī, 472.
Prakaraṇikā, 472.
Prakrānta, 457.
Prākṛit, 313 ; 473 ; 480 ; 485, 1.
Prakṛita, 457.
Prakṛiti, 80 ; 84 ; 86 ; 139 ; 140 ; 522 ; 523.
Pramā, 59 ; 61 ; 63 ; 82.
Pramāṇa (philosophical), 60 ; 82 ; 93 ; 117 ; 222.
Pramāṇam, 233 ; 297.
Prameya, 63.
Prāṇa, 38 ; 177.
Prāṇa-maya, 114.
Prāṇātman, 114.
Praṇava, 93.
Prāṇāyāma, 93.
Praṇidhi, 257 ; 263.
Prasanna Kumār Ṭhākur, 304 ; 305, 1.
Prasanna-raghava, 367 ; 508.
Praśna Upanishad, 35.
Prastāvanā (prologue), 473.
Prasthāna, 472.
Prastuta, 457.
Prathamam retas, 523.
Prātibhāsika (existence), 108.
Pratigraha, 237 ; 262.
Pratijñā (proposition), 61.
Pratimā, 218, 1 ; 241.
Pratimā-parićāraka, 218, 1.
Pratimukha, 470, 2.
Prati-nāyaka, 471.
Prātipadika, 163.
Prātiśākhyas, Vedic, 149 ; 150.
Prati-sarga (re-creation), 511 ; 517.
Pratishṭhāna, 511, 1.
Pratītākshara, 304.
Prativādin (defendant), 297.
Prativindhya, 389, 2.
Pratīyamāna, 458.
Pratyabhijñā, 119.
Pratyabhijñā-darśana, 118.
Pratyāhāra (grammatical), 163, 3 ; 169, 1.
Pratyāhāra (restraint), 93.
Pratyaksha, 61 ; 117 ; 222 ; 352.
Prauḍha Brāhmaṇa, 25.
Pravaćana, 145.
Pravaha, 179.
Pravāhaṇa, 49.
Pravara-sena, 494, 2.
Pravargya, 341, 1.
Praveśaka, 473.
Pravṛitti, 63.
Prayāga, 359.
Prāyaś-ćitta, 55, 1 ; 208 ; 209 ; 212 ; 213 ; 273 ; 278 ; 287 ; 292 ; 299 ; 411, 1.
Prayatna, 68.
Prayer, 473.
Prayoga, 402, 1.
Prayojana (motive), 64.
Precepts (moral), 278 ; 441 ; 442 ; 461 ; 533 ; 536.
Prem Chunder Tarkabāgish, 495, 1.
Premiss in logic, 61.
Prem Sāgar, 126, 1 ; 516.
Pren-khana, 472.
Preserver, 518.
Preta-kāryāṇi (funeral rites), 410.
Pretya-bhāva, 63.
Priam, 313, 1 ; 400, 2.
Prinsep's tables, 344, 1.
Pṛishatka, 405, 1.
Pṛithā, 373 ; 375, 2 ; 377 ; 410.
Pṛithaktva, 68.
Pṛithivī, 12 ; 67 ; 84 ; 427 ; 505.
Privileges, six (of Brahmans), 237, 1.
Problems (from Līlāvatī), 183.
Pronunciation, 149.
Properties (an-ga), 470.
Propertius, 252, 1.
Property, law of, 262.
Proposition in logic, 61.
Protagoras, 104, 1 ; 131, 2.
Pūga, 296, 1.
Pukkasa, 225.
Pulaha, 517, 1.
Pulastya, sage, 302 ; 354, 1 ; 517, 1.
Pulastya-siddhānta, 175.
Puṇḍarīka, 432, 1.
Puṇsavana, 192 ; 239.
Purāṇa, 37 ; 91 ; 195 ; 207, 1 ; 249 ; 295 ; 368 ; 509 ; 510 ; 514 ; 521.
Purī, 210, 1 ; 244, 1.
Pūrṇa-prajña, 118 ; 119.
Purоćana, 385.
Purohita, 257, 2 ; 276.
Puru, 332 ; 375.
Purusha, 21, 1 ; 21, 2 ; 22 ; 82 ; 87 ; 90, 2 ; 140 ; 523.
Purusha-paśu, 85.
Purusha-sūkta, 3 ; 9 ; 11 ; 21 ; 44, 1 ; 207, 1 ; 214 ; 219.
Purushottama, 91, 3 ; 135, 1 ; 390, 1.
Pūrvā, 199.
Pūrva-mīmāṇsā, 98.
Pūrva-paksha, 99.
Pūshan, 16.
Pushkara, 325, 1 ; 420.
Pushpa-danta, 432, 1.
Pushpaka, 354 ; 359 ; 503.
Pushpamitra, 167, 2.
Pushya, 173, 3.
Put, 249.
Put-tra, 249, 1.
Pythagoras, 47 ; 56, 2 ; 82, 1 ; 142 ; 181.

Qualities, three, 56, 1 ; 85 ; 275 ; 513.
Qualities of the Vaiśeshika, 68.
Quality, 66.

Races (solar and lunar), 511, 1.
Rādhā, 325, 1 ; 332 ; 377.
Rāḍha or Rāṛh, 210, 1 ; 454 ; 515.
Rādheya, 377.
Rāga (musical), 184.
Rāghava, 344.
Rāghavābhyudaya, 367.
Rāghavapāṇḍavīya, 368 ; 453 ; 533.
Rāghava-vilāsa, 368
Raghu, 344.
Raghu-nandana, 252, 2 ; 304.
Raghu-nāthābhyudaya, 369.
Raghu-vaṇśa, 181 ; 228, 1 ; 344, 1 ; 359, 1 ; 367 ; 452 ; 459.
Rāgiṇī (musical), 184.
Rahasya, 32 ; 275.
Rāhu, 180, 1.
Raivata, Manu, 206, 1
Raivataka (mountain), 391.
Rājadharma, 374.
Rajaks (washermen), 210, 1.
Rājanya, 22, 2 ; 149, 1 ; 228.
Rājarshis, 134, 1.
Rajas (guṇa), 85 ; 140 ; 222 ; 275 ; 321.
Rājasa Purāṇas, 513 ; 514.
Rāja-śekhara, 367 ; 508.
Rājasūya, 391 ; 453.
Raja-taran-giṇī, 368 ; 532.
Rāja-yakshma, 234, 2.
Rājendralāla, Mitra, 87, 1 ; 525.
Rājput, 210, 1 ; 224, 2 ; 335, 1.
Rājputāna, 325, 1.
Rākā, 158 ; 172.
Rākshasa (demon), 276 ; 310 ; 348, 1 ; 400.

Rākshasa (marriage), 190.
Rākshasī, 355.
Rāma, 244, 1; 343; 344; 502; 503; 504.
Rāma's banishment, 348.
Rāma's birth, 344.
Rāma (second), 330.
Rāma and Lakshmaṇa, 345; 351, 1.
Rāma and Rāvaṇa, 357.
Rāma-ćandra, 315, 1; 329, 2; 330; 346, 1; 360, 1.
Rāmaćandra - ćaritra - sāra, 369.
Rāma-ćaraṇa, 368.
Ramage's 'Beautiful Thoughts,' 142.
Rāma-gītā, 368.
Rāma-hṛidaya, 368.
Rāma-līlā, 365.
Rāma-navamī, 365, 1.
Rāmānuja, 118; 325, 1.
Rāma-setu, 356, 1.
Rāma-vilāsa, 368.
Rāmāyaṇa, 306; 315; 335; 366; 367; 368.
Rāmāyaṇa (epitome of), 335.
Rāmāyaṇa (recension of), 336.
Rāmāyaṇa-māhātmya, 368.
Ramdoolal Dey, 249, 3.
Ramesurum, 356, 2.
Rāmopākhyāna, 366; 366, 1.
Ramūsies, 309, 1.
Rangārīs (dyers), 224, 2.
Rasa, 68; 457; 471.
Rāsaka, 472.
Rasa-mañjarī, 457.
Rasana, 73.
Rasātala, 431, 1.
Raseśvara, 118.
Rāśi, 178; 182.
Ratha-ćaryā, 383.
Ratha-kāra, 149; 149, 2; 224, 2.
Rathān-ga, 423, 1.
Rationalism, 218.
Rationalistic Brāhmanism, 50.
Ratnāvalī, 437, 2; 505; 506.
Raudra, 457, 1; 471.
Raudrī, 522.
Rāvaṇa, 309, 1; 328; 330; 337; 339; 353; 392, 2; 503.
Rāvaṇa, description of, 342; 421; 429.
Realism, 70.
Reasoning, 61.
Reciters of the Rāmāyaṇa, 336.
Recorde, Robert, 182, 1.
Regions, seven, 431, 1.
Regnier, M. Adolphe, 150, 2.
Retaliation, 269.
Revatī, 391.
Revenue, 258.
Rhetoric (figures of), 469.
Rhyme (employment of), 455.
Ṛibhus, 14; 14, 2; 149, 2.
Ṛićīka, 27, 1.
Right-hand worshippers, 523, 1.
Ṛig-veda, 5; 19; 21; 23; 101; 245, 2.
Ṛig-veda-prātiśākhya, 149; 150; 151.
Ṛigvedī Brāhmans, 224, 2; 245, 2.
Ṛiju-yodhin, 408.
Ṛik, 5; 6.
Ṛiṇa, 183.
Ṛiṇādāna, 261.
Ṛishi, 3; 29; 191; 241; 244; 375; 399.
Ṛishyaśṛin-ga, 340.
Ṛitu-saṃhāra, 453.
Ṛitv-ij, 231, 1; 232.
Rivalry between sects, 513.
Röer, Dr., 35, 3; 39, 1; 60, 1; 203, 1; 291, 2; 292, 1.
Rohiṇī, 234, 2; 332; 387, 1.
Rohita, 26.
Roma-harshaṇa, 510.
Romaka-siddhānta, 175.
Rost, Dr., 252, 1; 506; 532, 2.
Roth, Professor, 38, 1; 158, 1.
Royal Asiatic Society, 158; 179.
Rū (in algebra), 182.
Rudra, 322; 322, 1; 399; 409, 2.
Rudra-bhaṭṭa, 457.
Rudrāksha berries, 324, 1.
Rudra-yāmala Tantra, 525.
Runjit Siṇh, 325, 1.
Rūpa, 68; 182; 387, 1.
Rūpaka, 458.
Ryot (cultivator), 227, 3; 258, 2.

Śabara-svāmin, 98, 1.
Śabda (sound), 4.
Śabda (verbal authority), 61; 117; 222.
Śabda-kalpadruma, 55, 1.
Śabda-lakshaṇa, 453.
Śabdālan-kāra, 457.
Sabhā, 260; 391; 392.
Sabhā-parvan, 373.
Sabhya (fire), 189, 1.
Sać-ćid-ānanda, 106; 111, 5; 113, 3.
Sacrifice, 28, 1; 430.
Sad-āćāra, 209; 293.
Sādhyas, 136, 2; 276; 400.
Sagara, 79, 1; 344; 361; 362.
Sāgara, 363.
Sāgarikā, 506.
Sahadeva, 380; 387, 1; 402.
Sāhasa, 261.
Sāhitya-darpaṇa, 367; 456; 457.
Sahokti, 458.
Ṣaiqal-gar, 224, 2.
Śaiva-darśana, 118.
Śaiva Purāṇas, 514.
Śaiva sect, 94; 325, 1.
Śāka-dvīpa, 420.
Śākala-śākhā, 150.
Śākalya, 161, 2.
Śākapūṇi, 159.
Śakas, 229, 1; 361.
Śākaṭāyana, 160; 161; 161, 2.
Śākhā, 150; 187.
Śākhānta-ga, 216.
Śakrasyāṇśa, 387, 1.
Sākshiṇaḥ (witnesses), 297.
Śāktas, 322, 1; 322, 2; 325, 1; 514; 522.
Śakti, 91; 217; 322, 2; 522.
Śakuni, 373; 380; 385; 391; 392; 410, 1.
Śakuntalā, 58, 1; 95; 128, 1; 256, 2; 259, 1; 361; 437, 2; 494.
Śalātura, Śālāturīya, 162.
Śālīs (weavers), 224, 2.
Śālmali-dvīpa, 420.
Śalya (king), 184; 378; 391; 405, 1; 406.
Śalya-parvan, 373.
Śama, 399.
Samādhi, 93; 323.
Samāhāra, 169, 1.
Sāman, 5; 398.
Samānodaka-bhāva, 248.
Sāmānya, 66; 69.
Sāmānya-dharma, 457.
Samavakāra, 471.
Samāvartana, 195; 239; 242.
Samavāya, 66; 69.
Samavāyi-kāraṇa, 51, 3; 53, 1; 70.
Sāma-veda, 3; 6; 25; 245, 2.
Sāma-veda priest, 216.
Sāma-veda Upanishads, 35.
Samayāćāra, 145; 186.
Sāmayāćārika Sūtras, 145; 186; 202; 203; 208; 213.
Śāmba, 521.
Śambhu, 183.
Sambhūya samutthāna, 261.
Śambūka, 504.
Saṃhāra (restraint), 402, 1.
Saṃhitā text, 152.

Saṃhitās of the Veda, 245, 2; 275.
Śamī tree, 196.
Saṃlāpaka, 472.
Samoyedic language, 309, 1.
Saṃśaptaka, 405.
Saṃśaya, 64.
Saṃsṛishṭi, 458.
Samudra-mathana, 471.
Saṃvarta's Code, 203; 302.
Saṃvat, 494.
Saṃvido vyatikrama, 261.
Sāmyāvasthā, 85.
Saṃyoga, 68.
San (in grammar), 164, 1.
Sanat-kumāra, 37; 521.
Saṅćayana (of ashes), 199.
Sandhi (juncture in drama), 470; 470, 2.
Sandhi (rules of), 152; 245, 2.
Sandhyās, 241; 280, 1.
Sandhyā-vandana, 245, 2.
Śāṇḍilya, Aphorisms of, 125. 2.
Sandrokottos or Sandrakottus, 224, 1; 507.
San·gīta, 498.
San·gīta-dāmodara, 185.
San·gīta-darpaṇa, 184.
San·gīta-ratnākara, 184; 470.
San·graha-parvan, 370, 1.
Śani (Saturn), 179.
Śani-vāra, 178, 1.
Sañjaya, 378; 400; 407, 1.
Sañjñā, 163, 2; 428, 3.
Śan·kara Āćārya or Śan·karāćārya, 39, 3; 46; 73; 101, 2; 104; 107; 110; 122; 303, 1; 325, 1; 454; 494, 2.
San·kara (of figures), 458.
San·kara-jātīyāḥ, 224.
Śan·kara-miśra, 62; 68.
Śan·kha, 183; 203; 301; 302; 403.
Śān·khāyana, 146.
Śan·khāyana-brāhmaṇa, 25.
Śān·khāyana Gṛihya Sūtras, 186.
Sān·khya philosophy, 39; 46; 73; 79; 86, 1; 118; 219; 531.
Sān·khya Guṇas, 51, 3; 85, 1.
Sān·khya Sūtras, 79, 1.
San·khyā (synthesis), 60.
San·khyāḥ (numbers), 68.
Sān·khya-kārikā, 48, 1; 51, 1; 55, 3; 73, 2; 79, 1; 80, 2; 83, 1.
Sān·khya-pravaćana, 79, 1; 221; 290, 2; 531.
Sān·khya-pravaćana-bhāshya, 79, 1; 85.
San·kīrṇa, 472.
Sannyāsin, 238; 254; 303, 1.
Sanskāra (ceremonies), 188; 192; 232; 238; 239; 243.
Sanskāra (quality), 69; 138.
Sanskaraṇa, 161.
Sanskṛit, 485.
Sanskṛita, 161.
Śānta (rasa), 457, 1.
Śāntā, Daśaratha's daughter, 340.
Śāntanava, 375.
Śāntanava's Phiṭ-sūtras, 161, 2.
Śāntanu, 375.
Sāntapana (penance), 273.
Santhāls, 309, 1.
Śānti, 411.
Śānti-parvan, 366; 374; 411.
Sapiṇḍatā (sapiṇḍaship), 248; 266.
Saptapadībhava, 191.
Saptarshayaḥ (seven patriarchs), 517, 1.
Sapta-śataka, 367.
Sapta-śatī, 367.
Śara, 405, 1; 458.
Śarabhan·ga (an ascetic), 252, 1.
Śarad, 453.
Śaradā-tilaka, 525.
Saramā, sons of, 198.
Sārasvata, 210, 1.
Sarasvatī, 205; 209; 298; 393; 408, 1; 427; 522.
Sarasvatī-kaṇṭhābharaṇa, 457.
Sarayū, river, 339, 2.
Śārdūla-vikrīḍita, metre, 213, 2.
Sarga (creation), 511.
Śarīra, 63; 73.
Śarmishṭhā-yayāti, 472.
Śārn·ga-deva, 184; 470.
Śārn·gadhara-paddhati, 368.
Sarpāri, 431, 1.
Sarpis, 420.
Śarva, 409, 2.
Sarva-darśana-san·graha, 80, 2; 118; 119; 120; 338, 1.
Sarva-nāman, 169, 1.
Sarvato-bhadra, 456.
Sārva-bhauma, 431, 2.
Śāstra, 46; 261; 283, 2; 371, 2.
Śatānīka, 389, 2.
Śatapatha-brāhmaṇa, 3; 25; 29; 31; 35; 56, 2; 148; 294, 3; 320; 327, 2; 328, 1; 341, 1.
Śātātapa's Code, 203; 302.
Satī, 196, 1; 201; 207, 1; 244, 1; 251; 252, 2; 312.
Śatru-ghna, 345; 503.
Śatruñjaya-māhātmya, 367.
Saṭṭaka, 472.
Sattva, 85; 140; 222; 275; 321.
Sāttvatī or Sātvatī (style), 503, 1.
Sāttvika Purāṇas, 513–515.
Saturn, 179.
Satya (age), 55, 2; 328; 333; 431, 1.
Sātyaki, 398; 410.
Satyāshāḍha Śrauta Sūtras, 146.
Satyavān, 395.
Satyavatī, 371, 1; 375.
Saubala, 380, 1.
Saubaleyī, 377.
Saubalī, 377; 380, 1.
Saudhanvana, 149, 2.
Saumanas, 432, 1.
Saumitri, 345.
Saumilla, 498.
Śaunaka, 150.
Śaunaka Śrauta Sūtras, 146.
Śaunakīyā C'aturādhyāyikā, 151.
Sauptika-parvan, 374; 409, 1.
Saura, 177; 179; 521.
Saura-siddhānta, 175.
Sauryas or Sauras, 325, 1.
Sauti, 510, 1.
Sautrāmaṇī, 301, 2.
Śavalā, 361.
Sāvana (month), 177; 179.
Savanas (three), 241; 254.
Sāvitṛī, 16; 17; 191; 346, 1.
Sāvitrī (Gāyatrī), 17; 195; 214; 214, 1; 274.
Savya-sāćin, 381, 4; 397.
Śayaka (arrow), 405, 1.
Sāyaṇa, 39; 118; 153; 156.
Scepticism, 49; 120; 351; 417.
Schlegel, Augustus William, 336, 1.
Schools of Hindū law, 302.
Scythians, 361.
Seclusion of Hindū women, 437, 2.
Sects, Hindū, 325; 325, 1; 326.
Seekers after God (Farrar's), 142.
Sena (tribe), 210, 1.
Senaka (grammarian), 161, 2.
Seneca, 142.

Sentiments, moral, 278; 441; 461; 533.
Sesamum seed, 200.
Śesha, serpent, 235, 1; 332, 2; 431; 431, 1.
Śeshādri, Rev. Nārāyan, 235, 1.
Seton-Karr, Mr., 252, 2.
Setu, 356, 1.
Setu-bandha, 367; 494, 2.
Setu-kāvya, 494, 2.
Shaḍ-vinśa Brāhmaṇa, 25.
Shahādat, 244, 1.
Shakespeare, 110, 3; 435.
Shankar P. Pandit, 497.
Shaṭ-karmāṇi, 237.
Siamese language, 309, 1.
Siddha (divine being), 136, 2; 519.
Siddhānta (astronomical), 175.
Siddhānta (in logic), 64.
Siddhānta-kaumudī, 168.
Siddhānta-muktāvalī, 60, 1.
Siddhānta-śiromaṇi, 176.
Siddhārtha, 507, 1.
Śīghroćća, 179.
Sikalgars, 224, 2.
Sikh chief, 325, 1.
Sikhs of the Pañjāb, 325, 1.
Śikshā, 145; 149.
Śīla (morality), 208.
Śīlāditya, 367; 533.
Silāra (king), 303.
Śilīmukha, 405, 1.
Śilpa (mechanical arts), 185.
Śilpaka, 472.
Śilpa-śāstra, 184.
Sīmantonnayana, 192; 239.
Sīmā-vivāda-dharma, 261.
Simla, 386, 2.
Simpīs (tailors), 224, 2.
Sinclair, Mr. W. F., 224, 2; 227, 1.
Singing, 184; 467.
Sinha, 423, 1.
Sinhala, 344, 2.
Sinhāsana-dvātrinśat, 532.
Sinīvālī, 158; 173.
Sinśapā, 534.
Sipāhīs, 224, 2.
Śīpāla, 198, 3.
Śiśira, 453.
Śiśu-pāla, 391; 419, 1.
Śiśupāla-badha, 453; 464.
Sita (black), 522.
Sītā, 335, 1; 353; 426; 503; 504.
Sītā, rape of, 337.
Sītā-phal, 351, 1.
Śitikaṇtha, 409, 2.
Śiva, 9; 50; 276, 1; 321; 322; 409, 2; 429, 430; 513; 514; 518; 521.
Śiva-dharma, 521.
Śiva-rātri, 325, 1.
Śiva Sūtras, 163, 1.
Śivājī, 256, 3.
Śivikā, 358.
Six privileges of Brāhmans, 237.
Skanda, 368; 427; 481; 481, 1; 514; 522.
Ślesha, 458.
Śloka, 155; 213.
Śloka (invention of), 311, 1; 504.
Smārta-bhaṭṭāćārya, 304, 2.
Smārta Sūtras, 145; 186.
Śmaśāna (burning-ground), 196; 299.
Smith, Mr. G., 394, 1.
Smṛiti, 4; 101; 144; 145; 208; 213; 220; 293; 301; 452.
Smṛiti-ćandrikā, 305.
Smṛiti-tattva, 304.
Snāna, 195; 242.
Snātaka, 196; 295.
Sneha, 69.
Socrates, 58, 1.
Śoka, 504.
Solar line of kings, 343; 344.
Solomon, Song of, 467.
Soma (ceremonies and sacrifice), 6; 28, 1; 274.
Soma (juice), 274.
Soma (god), 189.
Soma (moon), 234, 2; 375.
Soma (plant), 6; 14.
Soma-deva, 531; 532.
Soma-deva, Bhaṭṭa, 531.
Somā-rudrā, 275.
Soma-siddhānta, 175.
Soma-vanśa, 375; 511, 1.
Soma-vāra, 178, 1.
Somnath, 322, 1.
Sonārs, 224, 2.
Soul (universal), 9; 21; 22; 34.
South Indian school, 305.
Sparśa, 68.
Sphoṭāyana, 161, 2.
Spirit (universal), 8; 9; 21; 22; 34; 103.
Spirituous liquor (drinking), 250.
Śrāddha, 26, 1; 121, 4; 196; 199; 200; 247; 266; 270, 1; 300; 411; 430; 433, 1.
Śraddhā, 346, 1.
Srag-bandha, 456.
Śramaṇa, 276, 1; 312, 3; 475; 487.
Śrauta-sūtra, 145; 146; 184; 186.
Śravaṇa (nakshatra), 173, 3.
Śrāvaṇa (month), 171; 173, 3; 431, 1.
Śravishṭhā, 171.
Śreṇī, 296, 1; 297.
Śreshṭhin, 296, 1.
Śrī, 427; 520.
Śrīdhara-sena, 367.
Śrīdhara-svāmin, 515.
Śrī-gadita, 472.
Śrī-harsha, 453; 453, 1; 505.
Śrī-kaṇṭha, 499.
Śṛin·gāra, 457, 1; 471; 528.
Śrin·gāra-tilaka, 457.
Śṛingāṭa, 423, 3.
Śṛin·gin, 420, 1.
Śrī-vatsa, 332.
Śruta, 3; 144.
Śruta-bodha, 153; 494, 2.
Śrutakarman, 389, 2.
Śrutasena, 389, 2.
Śruti, 24; 25, 2; 33; 48, 1; 144; 214; 220; 293.
Śruti-dvaidham, 216.
Stage-manager, 473.
Stanzas, fanciful shapes of, 456.
Stenzler, Prof., 186, 2; 188; 201, 1; 203, 1; 292, 1; 295, 3; 301, 3; 475, 2.
Steya, 261; 270.
Sthālīpāka, 191.
Sthāṇu, 323; 409, 2.
Sthapati (architect), 185.
Sthāpatya-veda, 184.
Sthāvara, 56, 1.
Sthūla-śarīra, 53, 2.
Strabo, 221; 224, 1; 252, 1; 257, 2; 259, 1; 268, 1; 276, 1; 278, 2; 308, 1; 318; 507.
Strī-dhana, 267; 267, 1.
Strī-parvan, 374.
Strī-pun-dharma, 261.
Strī-san·grahaṇa, 261.
Subala (king), 377; 391.
Subandhu, 367; 533.
Subhadrā, 381, 3; 389, 2; 391.
Śubhan·kara, 185.
Su-bhaṭa, 367.
Subodhinī, 304.
Śūdra, 212; 223; 439, 1.
Śūdraka, 475.
Sūfī-ism, 33; 102, 1.
Sugrīva, 337; 356; 359; 425.
Suicide, 299.
Śuka, 515.
Śuka-saptati, 532.

Ṣukha, 68.
Śukra, 179; 301; 409, 2.
Śukra-vāra, 178, 1.
Sūkshma-dharma, 387, 1.
Sūkshma-śarīra, 53, 2; 198, 3.
Śukti, 110, 4.
Sulaimān I., 529, 2.
Śūla-pāṇi, 303.
Śulka, 267.
Sumantu, 302.
Sumitrā, 341.
Sun, 16; 17.
Śunaḥśepha, 25; 27.
Sundara-kāṇḍa, 337; 367.
Sundara-miśra, 367.
Śun-ga dynasty, 498.
Sunītha, 392.
Sunnah or Sunna, 24.
Śūnya, 83, 3; 105, 4; 183.
Suparna, 276.
Supplements to Veda, 184.
Suppressions of breath, three, 240.
Supratīka, 432, 1.
Supreme Being, epithets of, 43.
Śūra (Yādava king), 377.
Surabhi, 519.
Surā-pāna, 270; 420.
Surāshṭra, 417.
Surgery, 184.
Surīs (spirit sellers), 210, 1.
Śūrpa-ṇakhā, 353; 366.
Surun-gā, 385.
Sūrya, 11; 16; 256; 321; 344.
Sūrya-siddhānta, 175; 176; 178.
Sūryā, 346, 1.
Sūryā-sūkta, 191, 1.
Su-shupti, 111, 4.
Su-śruta, 184.
Sūta (charioteer, bard), 377; 510; 515.
Sutala, 431, 1.
Sūtars (carpenters), 224, 2.
Sutasoma, 389, 2.
Sūtra, 60.
Sūtra-dhāra or carpenter, 224, 2.
Sūtras of Pāṇini, 162; 163; 164.
Sūtras (aphorisms), 25; 46.
Sūtras (Buddhist), 147, 3.
Sūtrātman, 114.
Suttee (Satī), 196, 1.
Śuvarna, 293.
Su-yodhana, 378.
Sva (in algebra), 183.
Sva-dharma, 297.
Svādhyāya, 194; 245; 245, 2.
Svar, 55, 2; 159; 195; 431, 1.
Svargārohaṇika-parvan, 374.
Svāroćisha (Manu), 206, 1.
Svayam-bhū, 206, 1; 217; 220.
Svāyambhuva (Manu), 206; 221; 330, 3.
Svayaṃvara, 251; 377; 388; 438, 2; 439, 3.
Śveta, 122, 3.
Śveta (mountains), 420, 1.
Śveta-dvīpa, 126, 1.
Śvetaketu, 49.
Śveta-lohita, 122, 3.
Śveta-śikha, 122, 3.
Śvetāśva, 122, 3.
Śvetāśvatara Upanishad, 43; 44, 1; 122.
Śveta-vāhana, 381, 4; 397.
Swinging festival, 325, 1.
Śyāmā-rahasya, 525.
Śyan (in grammar), 164, 1.
Syllogism, 62.
Synthesis, 60; 82.
Tāḍakā, 354.
Taddhita affixes, 152, 169.
Tagore Law Lectures, 267, 1.
Tailī (oilman), 210, 1; 224, 2.
Taittirīya (Yajur-veda), 5; 6; 35; 234, 2.
Taittirīyas or Taittirīyakas, 205; 245, 2; 335, 1.
Taittirīya - brāhmaṇa, 25; 328, 1.
Taittirīyāraṇyaka, 149.
Taittirīya Upanishad, 35.
Taj-jalān, 102, 1.
Takshaka, 354; 431, 1.
Talātala, 431, 1.
Talava-kāra Upanishad, 35, 2.
Talmud, 24.
Tamas, 67; 85; 140; 222; 275; 321.
Tāmasa (Manu), 206, 1; 513; 514.
Tamil, 309, 1.
Tāmisra (hell), 335.
Tāmraparṇī, 344, 2.
Tāṇḍava, 467.
Taṇḍula, 271, 1.
Tāṇḍya Brāhmaṇa, 25.
Tan-mātras, 83; 221.
Tāntīs (weavers), 210, 1.
Tantra, 91; 322, 1; 522–525; 530.
Tantrī, 210, 1.
Tāntrika doctrines, 322, 2; 524.
Tapaḥ or tapar (heavenly sphere), 55, 2; 431, 1.
Tapas (austerity), 323.
Tapas (theory of), 342, 1.
Tapta-kṛiććhra (penance), 273.
Tapta-māsha, 271, 1.
Tāraka (a Daitya), 324, 1.
Taran-ga, 532.
Tarka, 64; 220.
Tarka-san-graha, 60, 1; 70; 72; 74.
Tarka-vidyā, 219.
Tarkin, 220.
Tarpaṇa, 241.
Tartar tribes, 309, 1.
Tatpara (measure of time), 177.
Tatpurusha, 152.
Tattva, 80; 80, 2.
Tattva-jñānam, 104.
Tattva-samāsa, 21, 1; 79, 1; 290, 3.
Tattvas, twenty-five, 80, 2; 82; 219.
Tawhīd, 244, 1.
Taxation, six heads of, 259.
Taxes, 258; 259.
Te Deum, 136, 2.
Tejas, 67; 84; 387, 1.
Telemachus, 440, 1.
Telingī, 224, 2.
Telīs or oilmen, 224, 2.
Telugu, 309, 1.
Telugu country, 245, 2.
Terms in arithmetic and algebra, 182.
Tertiary compound, 71.
Testamentary power, 265.
Thales, 52, 1; 112, 1.
Thirty-three gods, 321, 2.
Thomson, Mr., 124, 1; 138.
Thracians, 252, 1.
Thunderer, 14.
Tibetan language, 309, 1.
Tila, 200.
Timaeus, 50, 3; 51, 3; 53, 2; 56, 2; 81, 1; 103, 1.
Time, hymn in praise of, 22.
Tirhut, 302.
Tīrtha, 244, 1; 408, 1.
Tithi, 177.
Tithi-tattva, 304.
Tomara, 405, 1.
Topics of the Nyāya, 60; 64.
Toraṇa, 185.
Tota kahānī, 532.
Townships, 258.
Toxicology, 184.
Tradition (smṛiti), 144.
Tragedy, 468; 469.

Trailokya, 218.
Trajan, Emperor, 313.
Transfiguration, 135, 2.
Transmigration, 11; 31; 56; 56, 2; 217; 222; 334; 530.
Trasa-reṇu, 71.
Trayam brahma, 214.
Trayī vidyā, 214.
Treasure-trove, 259.
Tretā (age), 178, 2; 221; 301; 302; 328; 330, 3.
Tretā (three fires), 188; 189, 1.
Triad, 11; 217; 321.
Tri-daṇḍa, 121, 2.
Tri-daṇḍin, 131, 2.
Tri-kāṇḍa, 161.
Tri-lin·ga, 224, 2.
Trimūrti, 11; 217; 321; 509; 514; 516.
Tri-ṇāćiketa, 214, 1.
Tri-padā, 155.
Tripura-dāha, 471.
Trishṭubh metre, 154; 335, 2.
Triśūla, 183.
Tri-suparṇa, 214, 1.
Tri-vikrama, 329, 1; 367.
Tri-vṛit, 154; 240.
Troṭaka, 472.
Troyer, M., 532, 2.
Truṭi, 177.
Try-ambaka, 323, 1.
Tuḍa, 309, 1.
Tulā, 271, 1; 297.
Tulasī, 271, 1.
Tulasī-dāsa or Tulsī-dās, 368.
Tullberg, Dr., 497, 1.
Tulya-yogitā, 458.
Tungusic (Mantchu) language, 309, 1.
Turanian languages, 309, 1.
Turanian races, 229.
Turkish language, 309, 1.
Turpharī, 122, 1.
Tūti-nāma, 532.
Tvashṭṛi, 14; 387, 1.

Ućća, 179.
Udāharaṇa, 61.
Udaka-dāna, 247; 248.
Udātta-rāghava, 367.
Udāttokti, 473.
Udayana (king), 506.
Udayana Āćārya, 77.
Uddhāra, 267.
Uḍḍiśa, 525.
Udgātṛi, 6; 216.
Udyoga-parvan, 373.
Ugra, 409, 2.
Ugra-śravas, 510, 1.
Ujjayinī (Oujein), 176; 330, 3; 494; 494, 1.
Ujjvala-datta, 161, 2.
Ulkā-mukha, 237; 276.
Ullāpya, 472.
Ulūka, 65, 1.
Ulūpī, 389, 2; 431, 1.
Ulysses, 426.
Uma, 361; 522; 523.
Umāpati, 409, 2.
Uṇādi-sūtras, 161, 2.
Unmarried girls, 268.
Upādāna-kāraṇa, 53, 1.
Upa-dharma, 246.
Upādhi, 63, 1; 113, 2.
Upādhyāya, 232.
Upamā, 457.
Upamāna, 61; 117; 457; 458.
Upameya, 457; 458.
Upanaya, 61.
Upanayana, 189; 192; 239.
Upanishads, 4; 21, 2; 32; 32, 1; 34; 35; 56, 2; 122; 216.
Upāṉśu, 246.
Upapātaka, 270.
Upa-purāṇa, 146; 521.
Upa-rūpaka, 470; 472.
Upasad, 341, 1.
Upa-saṃhṛiti, 470, 2.
Upasarga, 151, 160.
Upavāsa (fast), 325, 1.
Upa-veda, 184.
Upendra-vajrā, 156.
Uposhita (fasting), 253.
Urvaśī, 375.
Uśanas, 203; 301.
Ushas, 11; 17; 428.
Usury, 263; 264.
Utkala, 210, 1.
Utprekshā, 458.
Utsava, 325, 1.
Utsṛishṭikān·ka, 471.
Uttarā, 199.
Uttara-kāṇḍa, 337; 359; 365, 1.
Uttara-mīmāṉsā, 98.
Uttara-paksha, 99.
Uttara-rāma-ćarita, 337; 365, 1; 367; 499; 502; 503.
Uttarāyaṇa, 403.

Vāć (word), 214.
Vāćaspati Miśra, 92, 2; 305.
Vāćya, 458.
Vāda (controversy), 64.
Vādhūna Śrauta Sūtras, 146.
Vādin (plaintiff), 297.
Vāg-daṇḍayoḥ pārushye, 272.
Vāhana, 430.
Vaidika, 278, 1.
Vaidika (repeaters of Veda), 245, 2.
Vaidya, 210, 1; 225.
Vaijayantī, 304; 305.
Vaikartana, 378, 1.
Vaikhānasa Śrauta Sūtras, 146.
Vaikuṇṭha, 334.
Vaimānika, 276.
Vairāgya, 93; 528.
Vaiśākha, 173, 3.
Vaiśampāyana, 371, 1; 374; 510, 1.
Vaiśeshika philosophy, 46; 53, 1; 60; 65; 71; 77; 85; 219.
Vaiśeshika Sūtras, 60, 1; 62; 64, 1.
Vaishṇavas, 325, 1; 515.
Vaishṇavi, 522.
Vaiśravaṇa, 354.
Vaiśvadeva-homa, 188, 1.
Vaiśya, 22, 2; 212; 223; 224, 2; 349, 1.
Vaitānika oblations, 188; 254.
Vaitaraṇī, 415.
Vaivasvata (seventh Manu), 30, 1; 206, 1; 330, 3; 344.
Vājasaneyins, 5; 150.
Vājasaneyi-prātiśākhya, 151; 152.
Vājasaneyi-saṃhitā, 25.
Vaka, 386.
Vākovākyam, 295; 295, 1.
Vakula, 423, 3.
Valabhi, 367.
Valabhī, 453.
Valabhi-pura, 367.
Vallabhāćārya, 325, 1.
Vallī (Kaṭha Upanishad), 42.
Vālmīki, 311, 1; 314; 315; 366; 367; 368; 416; 504.
Vāmāćārins, 523, 1.
Vāmadeva, 339.
Vāmana (dwarf), 320; 328; 432, 1; 469; 514.
Vāmana's Kāśikā Vṛitti, 168.
Vāṇa, 405; 533.
Vana-parvan, 361, 2; 366; 373.
Vānaprastha, 211; 238; 241; 254; 301.
Vāṇīs, 224, 2.
Vaṉśa (genealogy), 511.
Vaṉśa brāhmaṇa, 118.
Vaṉśānućarita, 511.
Vaṉśa-sthavila, 518.
Vāra, 178, 1.
Varada, 409, 2.
Varāha (boar), 327; 423, 1.
Varāha-mihira, 175; 176; 179; 367.

Vārāha Śrauta Sūtras, 146.
Vārāhī, 522.
Varajī (betel-grower), 210, 1.
Vārāṇasī, 511, 1.
Vāraṇāvata (city), 385.
Vārdhushika, 264.
Vārdhushya, 271.
Vārendra, 210, 1.
Vārhaspatya Sūtras, 120.
Varṇa (caste), 210, 1 ; 223.
Varṇa-san·karaḥ, 224.
Varsha, 420 ; 453.
Vārtā-karma, 237.
Vārttika-kāra, 166.
Vārttikas, 151 ; 166 ; 167, 1 ; 531.
Varuṇa, 10 ; 12 ; 13 ; 16 ; 26 ; 189 ; 191 ; 197 ; 256 ; 431 ; 521.
Vāruṇī, 519.
Vasanta (spring), 453.
Vasantaka, 506.
Vasanta-senā, 477 ; 479.
Vasantotsava, 472.
Vāsava - dattā, 367 ; 506 ; 533.
Vaśishṭha, 203 ; 302 ; 315, 1 ; 339 ; 347 ; 361 ; 402, 1 ; 408, 1 ; 504 ; 511, 1 ; 517, 1 ; 521.
Vāsishṭha, 368.
Vāsishṭha-rāmāyaṇa, 368.
Vāsishṭha-siddhanta, 175.
Vastu, 53, 1 ; 103 ; 104 ; 457 ; 470.
Vastu-parīkshā, 193.
Vāstu-purusha, 185.
Vasu (king), 210, 1 ; 371, 1.
Vasu-deva, 312 ; 331.
Vāsudeva, 331 ; 332 ; 375 ; 390, 1.
Vāsuki (serpent), 327 ; 354 ; 431, 1 ; 519.
Vasus, 399 ; 400.
Vasu-sheṇa, 378 ; 384, 1.
Vaṭa or Banyan (Ficus Indica), 39, 3.
Vatsa, 437, 2.
Vātsalya, 457, 1.
Vatsa-rāja, 506.
Vātsyāyana, 65.
Vatup (in grammar), 163, 3.
Vāyu, 10 ; 67 ; 83 ; 428.
Vāyu-purāṇa, 514.
Veda, 2 ; 208 ; 509 ; 522.
Veda (repetition of), 194 ; 195 ; 236 ; 245 ; 245, 2 ; 274.
Vedābhyāsa, 237.
Vedān·gas (six), 145 ; 146 ; 161.
Vedānta, 46 ; 73, 3 ; 98 ; 101 ; 208.
Vedānta-paribhāshā, 109, 2.
Vedānta-sāra, 101, 2 ; 113, 6.
Vedānta-sūtra, 47 ; 245, 2.
Vedāntist formula, 38.
Vedāntists, 39.
Vedārs, 309, 1.
Vedārtha-prakāśa, 371, 2.
Veda-vāhya, 144, 2.
Vedic Nakshatras (twenty-seven), 172, 1.
Vedic prosody, 155.
Veṇī-saṃhāra, 392, 1 ; 508.
Venus (planet), 179.
Vetāla, 532.
Vetāla-pańća-vinśati, 532.
Vibhāga, 68 ; 261.
Vibhāṇḍaka, 340.
Vibhīshaṇa, 309, 1 ; 354, 1 ; 356 ; 359 ; 382, 3 ; 503.
Vićitra-vīrya, 375 ; 376.
Vidarbha-rāja, 367.
Videha, 335, 1 ; 417 ; 511, 1.
Vidhi, 24.
Vidhi-yajña, 246.
Vidura, 376 ; 385 ; 392 ; 399 ; 410 ; 437, 1.
Vidūshaka or jester, 474 ; 498.
Vidyā, 283, 3 ; 295.
Vighaṭikā, 177.
Vihāras, 475 ; 494.
Vīja, 220 ; 470, 2.
Vīja-gaṇita, 174, 2 ; 176 ; 182.
Vijaya, 381, 4 ; 397.
Vijaya-nagara, 118.
Vijñāna-bhikshu, 79, 1 ; 92, 2.
Vijñāna-maya-kośa, 113.
Vijñāneśvara, 291.
Vikalā, 178.
Vikāra (production), 83 ; 140.
Vikaraṇa, 164.
Vikartana, 378, 1.
Vikramāditya, 494 ; 494, 1 ; 532.
Vikramorvaśī, 494 ; 496.
Vikṛita, 472.
Vikshepa, 109 ; 112, 4.
Vikukshi, 344.
Vilāsikā, 472.
Village government, 258.
Vimarsha or hindrance, 470, 2.
Vināḍī, 177.
Vindhya, 308.
Vipātha, 405, 1.
Vīra, 457, 1 ; 471.
Vīra-ćarita, 502.
Virādha, 310, 1.
Virāj, 22 ; 22, 1 ; 206, 1 ; 220.
Vīra-mitrodaya, 304.
Vīraṇa, 193.
Vīra-śayana, 411.
Virāṭa (king), 373.
Virāṭa-parvan, 373.
Virgil, 53, 2 ; 56, 2 ; 58, 1 ; 106, 2.
Virūpa, 101.
Virūpāksha, 409, 2 ; 432, 1.
Viśākhā, 173, 3.
Viśesha, 66 ; 69 ; 71.
Viśeshokti, 458.
Visha (poison), 184 ; 271, 1.
Vishaya, 53, 1 ; 73 ; 84 ; 457.
Vishkambha, 473.
Vishṇu, 9 ; 50 ; 79, 1 ; 203 ; 217 ; 276, 1 ; 301 ; 320 ; 430 ; 431 ; 513 ; 520.
Vishṇu (of the Ṛig-veda), 320 ; 321.
Vishṇu-gupta, 507.
Vishṇu-purāṇa, 91 ; 368 ; 387, 1 ; 389, 2 ; 514 ; 516.
Vishṇu-śarman, 531.
Vishṇu-yaśas, 336, 1.
Vishuvat, 181.
Viśikha, 405, 1.
Vision of the Universal Form, 135 ; 400.
Viśravas, 354, 1.
Viśvadevas, 400.
Viśvakarman, 387, 1.
Viśvāmitra, 17, 1 ; 27, 1 ; 185 ; 302 ; 315, 1 ; 345 ; 361 ; 402, 1 ; 408, 1.
Viśva-nātha Kavirāja, 368 ; 457.
Viśva-prakāśa, 161.
Viśva-rūpa, 303 ; 409, 2.
Viśve Devāḥ, 189 ; 200.
Vitala, 431, 1.
Vitāna (hearths), 188 ; 188, 1.
Vitaṇḍa (cavilling), 64.
Vīthī, 472.
Vivāda-ćandra, 305.
Vivāda ćintāmaṇi, 305.
Vivādaḥ svāmipālayoḥ, 261.
Vivāda-ratnākara, 305.
Vivāda-tāṇḍava, 304.
Vivāha (marriage), 190 ; 239 ; 243 ; 244.
Vivasat, 344.
Vopadeva, 168 ; 515.
Vow of continence, 379, 2.
Vraja, 332.
Vrata, 253 ; 325, 1.
Vrātyatā, 271.
Vṛiddha Yājñavalkya, 204 ; 292.
Vṛiddhi, 264.
Vṛiddhi-pūrta, 200.
Vṛihaj-jātaka, 176.
Vṛihan-nalā, 396 ; 397.
Vṛihannāradīya, 521.

Vṛihaspati, 179 ; 203 ; 302.
Vṛihaspati (aphorisms of), 120 ; 121.
Vṛihaspati-siddhānta, 175.
Vṛihat, 204.
Vṛihat-kathā, 531.
Vṛikodara, 381.
Vṛiksha-bandha, 456.
Vṛindāvana, 332.
Vṛisha, 378, 1.
Vṛishṇis, 399.
Vṛitra, 10 ; 14 ; 387, 1 ; 418, 1.
Vṛitti, 209 ; 470.
Vyāhṛitis (three), 195 ; 214, 1.
Vyāja-stuti, 458.
Vyākaraṇa (grammar), 145 ; 150 ; 161.
Vyakta-gaṇita, 176, 3.
Vyāpaka, 'pervader,' 62.
Vyāpti, 62 ; 63, 1.
Vyāpya, 62.
Vyāsa, 46 ; 101 ; 203 ; 252, 2 ; 302 ; 316 ; 368 ; 371, 2 ; 375 ; 378 ; 385 ; 407, 1 ; 410 ; 411 ; 509 ; 510, 1 ; 515.
Vyatireka, 458.
Vyavahāra, 209 ; 255 ; 278 ; 285 ; 292 ; 296.
Vyavahāra-ćintāmaṇi, 305.
Vyavahāra-mayūkha, 305.
Vyavahāra-padam, 297.
Vyavahāra-tattva, 304.
Vyāvahārika (existence), 108.
Vyāyoga, 471.

Weaver, two-headed, 534.
Weber, 25, 1 ; 29 ; 56, 2 ; 171, 1 ; 313, 1 ; 332, 1 ; 367 ; 497 ; 533.
Weber's Indische Streifen, 31, 1.
Weber's Indische Studien, 43, 1 ; 330, 3.
Western school, 305.
Wheeler, Mr. Talboys, 213, 2 ; 249, 3 ; 316, 1 ; 369, 1.
Whitney, Prof. W. D., 7, 1 ; 38, 1 ; 151 ; 151, 2 ; 171, 1 ; 173, 2 ; 175, 2.
Whitney's Oriental Studies, 330, 3.
Widows, marriage of, 253 ; 438, 2.
Wife (directions for choosing), 243.
Wilkins, Sir C., 124, 1.
Wills Act (Hindū), 265, 2.
Wilson, Professor H. H., 25, 3 ; 73, 2 ; and passim.
Wilson's Glossary, 264, 3.
Wilson's Hindū Theatre, 257, 2.
Winking of eyes, 13, 2.
Witnesses, 13, 3 ; 272 ; 297.
Wives (four or three), 243 ; 293.
Wives, character of, 436 ; 437.
Women and wives, duties of, 284.
Women, position of, 134, 1 ; 441.
World, destruction of, 517.
Wort-spiel, 454.
Written evidence, 245, 2 ; 293 ; 297.

Yā (in algebra), 183.
Yādavas, 332 ; 374 ; 511, 1.
Yadu, 332 ; 375.
Yajanam, 237.
Yājanam, 237.
Yajña, 320.
Yajña-pātra, 196.
Yājñavalkya, 190 ; 203 ; 232, 3 ; 245, 2 ; 285, 1 ; 303.
Yājñavalkya, Code of, 391.
Yājñavalkya, commentary on, 303.
Yājñavalkya Vṛihad, 292.
Yājñika-deva, 148.
Yājñika (ritualist), 158 ; 245 2.
Yajñopavīta, 192 ; 195 ; 232, 3 ; 239.
Yajur-veda, 6 ; 25 ; 43, 1.
Yajur-veda, Black, 6 ; 44 ; 245, 2.
Yajur-veda, White, 6 ; 245, 2.
Yajurvedī, 224, 2.
Yajus, 6.
Yajvan (sacrificer), 276.
Yak (in grammar), 164, 1.
Yaksha, 276 ; 400.
Yama, 11 ; 18 ; 41 ; 189 ; 197 ; 198 ; 203 ; 256 ; 280, 2 ; 301 ; 427 ; 430.
Yama (abode of), 56, 1.
Yama (forbearance), 93.
Yama (hymn to), 19 ; 299.
Yamaka, 457.
Yamau (twins), 381, 4.
Yamī, 18.
Yamunā (river), 375, 4 ; 417.
Yaṇ (in grammar), 164, 1.
Yāska, 16, 1 ; 156 ; 156, 1 ; 156, 2.
Yaśodā, 332.
Yaśovarman, 499.
Yates, Dr., 155 ; 456.
Yati, 255.
Yātudhānas, 310.
Yaugandharāyaṇa, 506.
Yavanas, 229, 1 ; 316 ; 361.
Yāvat-tāvat, 182.
Yayāti, 331 ; 375.
Yellow garments, 293.
Yoga, 46 ; 82, 1 ; 92 ; 130, 4 ; 153 ; 219 ; 294 ; 323.
Yoga (Sūtras of), 92, 2.
Yogāćārya, 480.
Yoga-kshema, 260.
Yogas (twenty-seven), 178, 1.
Yoga-vāsishṭha, 368.
Yogeśa, 324, 1.
Yogin, 94 ; 113, 1 ; 324, 1.
Yojana (measure), 178, 180.
Yoni (female symbol), 322, 1.
Yuddha-kāṇḍa, 337.
Yudhi-shthira, 366 ; 373 ; 374 ; 379 ; 384 ; 385 ; 387, 1 ; 389, 1 ; 396 ; 399, 402 ; 403 ; 407 ; 408 ; 411 ; 419.
Yugas (four), 178 ; 178, 2 ; 179 ; 221.
Yukti, 111, 3.
Yūpa, 29 ; 341, 1.
Yūthikā, 423, 3.
Yuva-rāja (heir-apparent), 384.

Zahr, 33.
Zakāt, 244, 1.
Zamīndār, 258, 2.
Zand-Avastā, 131, 2.
Zeno, 82, 1.
Zeus, 9 ; 106, 2 ; 133, 8.
Zodiac (divisions of), 170.
Zoroaster, 47.

THE INDO-ROMANIC ALPHABET

WITH THE

EQUIVALENT SANSKṚIT LETTERS AND RULES FOR PRONUNCIATION.

VOWELS.

A, a, for अ, pronounced as in rur*a*l; Ā, *ā*, for आ, ा, as in t*a*r, f*a*ther; *I, i,* for इ, ि, as in f*i*ll; Ī, *ī*, for ई, ी, as in pol*i*ce; *U, u,* for उ, ु, as in f*u*ll; *Ū, ū,* for ऊ, ू, as in r*u*de; *Ṛi, ṛi,* for ऋ, ृ, as in mer*ri*ly; *Ṛī, ṛī,* for ॠ, ॄ, as in ma*ri*ne; *E, e,* for ए, े, as in pr*ey*; *Ai, ai,* for ऐ, ै, as in *ai*sle; *O, o,* for ओ, ो, as in g*o*; *Au, au,* for औ, ौ, as in H*au*s (German); *ṉ* or *ṃ*, for ं, i.e. the Anusvāra, sounded like *n* in French mo*n*, or like any nasal; *ḥ*, for ः, i.e. the Visarga or a distinctly audible aspirate.

CONSONANTS.

K, k, for क्, pronounced as in *k*ill, see*k*; *Kh, kh,* for ख्, as in in*kh*orn; *G, g,* for ग्, as in *g*un, do*g*; *Gh, gh,* for घ्, as in lo*gh*ut; N·, n·, for ङ्, as in si*ng* (sin·).

C', ć for च्, as in dolce (in music),=English *ch* in *ch*ur*ch*, lur*ch* (lurć); *C'h, ćh,* for छ्, as in chur*chh*ill (ćurćhill); *J, j,* for ज्, as in *j*et; *Jh, jh,* for झ्, as in he*dge-h*og (he*jh*og); *Ñ, ñ,* for ञ्, as in si*n*ge (si*ñ*j).

Ṭ, ṭ, for ट्, as in *t*rue (*ṭ*ru), *Ṭh, ṭh,* for ठ्, as in an*th*ill (an*ṭh*ill); *Ḍ, ḍ,* for ड्, as in *d*rum (*ḍ*rum); *Ḍh, ḍh,* for ढ्, as in re*dh*aired (re*ḍh*aired); *Ṇ, ṇ,* for ण्, as in *n*o*n*e (*ṇ*u*ṇ*).

T, t, for त्, as in wa*t*er (as pronounced in Ireland); *Th, th,* for थ्, as in nu*t-h*ook (but more dental); *D, d,* for द्, as in *d*ice (more like *th* in *th*is); *Dh, dh,* for ध्, as in a*dh*ere (more dental); *N, n,* for न्, as in *n*ot, i*n*.

P, p, for प्, as in *p*ut, si*p*; *Ph, ph,* for फ्, as in u*ph*ill: *B, b,* for ब्, as in *b*ear, ru*b*; *Bh, bh,* for भ्, as in a*bh*or; *M, m,* for म्, as in *m*ap, ja*m*.

Y, y, for य्, as in *y*et; *R, r,* for र्, as in *r*ed, yea*r*; *L, l,* for ल्, as in *l*ie; *V, v,* for व्, as in *v*ie (but like *w* after consonants, as in t*w*ice).

S', ś, for श्, as in *s*ure, se*ss*ion; *Sh, sh,* for ष्, as in *sh*un, hu*sh*; *S, s,* for स्, as in *s*ir, hi*ss*; *H, h,* for ह्, as in *h*it.

Fuller directions for pronunciation will be found in a 'Practical Grammar of the Sanskṛit Language,' by Monier Williams, third edition, published by the Delegates of the Clarendon Press, Oxford, and sold by Macmillan and Co., and by W. H. Allen & Co., 13, Waterloo Place. Also in a Sanskṛit-English Dictionary, published by the same.